MANAGEMENT
Analysis, Concepts and Cases

MANAGEMENT
Analysis, Concepts and Cases

W. WARREN HAYNES
JOSEPH L. MASSIE
University of Kentucky

PRENTICE-HALL, INC., *Englewood Cliffs, N. J.*
1961

Library of Congress Catalog Card No.: 61-12977

PRINTED IN THE UNITED STATES OF AMERICA

54840—C

Preface

THIS book is an introduction to management. Its main aim is to relate traditional treatments of management and modern quantitative and behavioral research. It places a greater than usual stress on theory, without neglecting the skills required to relate the theory to practice. It focuses attention on new research developments, without abandonment of the knowledge that has been built up in the past. It tries to substitute concepts and analysis for detailed descriptions and formulas; it aims at the development of a critical attitude toward all administrative thought, with the hope that the reader will reach a synthesis of his own. Thus the book avoids indoctrination in established positions and encourages an exploratory attitude.

The authors take the view that a study of management must be based on the fundamental disciplines on which management of necessity rests. Therefore a considerable portion of the book stresses economics, sociology, statistics, organization theory, the theory of decision making, and mathematics as they apply to management. The treatment of mathematics comes late in the book and is elementary in character; the other disciplines play an integral part throughout the volume. A background in introductory economics, in college algebra, and in accounting should suffice, although additional work in statistics and in the behavioral sciences would be helpful.

The book presents each subject on three levels. First, in the odd numbered chapters, there is an introduction to the fundamental concepts in that area of management—in organization, in control, in statistical methods, or whatever the subject may be. Next, in the even numbered chapters, is presented a series of extracts on the same subject. We have found that some students are confused by these extracts, which present a variety of views, rather than one consistent pattern of thought. The choice of extracts aims deliberately at presentation of such a diversity of views. We hope that most readers, instead of seeking dogmatic conclusions and settled views, will accept the challenge of weighing the diversity of opinion against current research and their own experience.

The extracts are followed by a series of cases. Each case (with a few obvious exceptions) is the description of an actual situation requiring analysis and a search for a solution. The authors believe that a study of the cases will contribute to a deeper understanding of management, and will indicate the relevance and the limitations of the theories that have been presented. No manager can operate mechanically from a rule book; only actual practice in identifying problems faced by management and simulation of this practice through the study of cases can build the skills required to relate theory to practice.

While it is true that the chapters are not organized along the usual lines of industrial management books, all of the subjects are treated here except those that are heavily descriptive in character. The authors have deliberately excluded discussions of plant location and the different types of buildings, heating systems, air conditioning, lighting, and similar subjects that add little to the reader's analytical tool kit. The subject of plant layout is given a subordinate position. But this book does cover the central topics of production control, quality control, wage incentives, inventory control, organization, and time and motion study. The treatment of these subjects differs from the usual discussions in that each topic has been placed in the setting of the fundamental analysis that is relevant. The authors believe, for example, that an understanding of the fundamentals of control will make the study of quality control more meaningful. The topic of wage incentives is best treated in a setting dealing with human organization and motivation. The result is that some topics usually treated in a single chapter are distributed over several chapters. This is true of production control, some phases of which appear in the general chapters on control, others in chapters on schematic analysis in management, others in chapters on the economic aspects, and others in chapters on mathematical models.

The authors are indebted to a large number of writers and publishers, particularly those who have granted permission to include extracts from their works. Individual acknowledgments are made in footnotes accompanying these extracts. The authors are also grateful for permission to include a few cases written by others (most of the cases are the work of the authors). We wish to express gratitude to Jacob J. Blair of the University of Pittsburgh, Carl L. Moore of Lehigh University, John E. Dykstra of the University of North Carolina, Paul E. Holden and Frank K. Shallenberger of Stanford University, and to the University of Western Ontario and the Institut pour l'Etude des Methodes de Direction de l'Entreprise (Lausanne, Switzerland).

The authors are in debt to those colleagues who contributed to improvements of the manuscript. Thanks are especially due Martin Solomon, Jr., who is largely responsible for the pages on statistical quality control.

W. W. H.
J. L. M.

Contents

1

Introduction: Modern Management Thought

EVERY institution requires methods for making decisions, ways of co-ordinating activities of the undertaking, ways of communicating information and ideas, and ways for evaluating the success of an enterprise in meeting its objectives. Every institution requires management. Some managers are effective, others weak; but management, good or bad, is universal and of great importance.

Management pertains to that most unpredictable phenomenon, the human being. It is concerned with his contacts with fellow human beings, and his behavior under a wide range of pressures and influences, some not easily subject to measurement. The study of management as a separate discipline is relatively undeveloped. Books on management do not reflect the level of attainment or maturity found in works on the natural sciences or even in much of the social sciences. Management theories and generalizations are basically not well developed and have not been fully tested against the facts.

Frequently, generalizations in one book written by an experienced manager are diametrically opposed to those in another. (Illustrations of this sort will appear in later chapters.) The present state of knowledge of management calls for great humility and offers a real challenge.

However, small advances have been made in the past, and today new research techniques are developing, new theories are being tested, and new experiments are pointing the way to a more profound understanding of the ways in which our institutions are managed and the ways in which this management can improve. Accordingly, this book aims at much more than a simple review of the present knowledge of management. It seeks to stimulate a critical attitude toward what is already known, rather than to indoctrinate the reader with a set of dogmas. It seeks to provoke interest in new developments—to point to the future rather than to the past. Some readers may be disappointed not to find the "truth" spelled out clearly and concisely and without reservations; but it is hoped that most will find that the task of reaching their own conclusions and of discovering new ideas will be an adventurous and exciting occupation.

The Development of Management Thought

It is far more important to concentrate upon recent developments and current lines of research than to review the historical growth of the subject. Certain principles of management can be traced back many centuries—some authors, for example, cite Moses on the "span of control"—but there has not been a continuous historical development of management theory over the years. Instead, there has been the sporadic recurrence of certain ideas, formulated independently by different writers, at different times, and in different circumstances.

Therefore, it is misleading to give primary credit for the development of management thought to one group. The "scientific management" movement in the United States has had an enormous influence, mostly to the good, but is only one strand of ideas important to the managers of the future. There are a number of idea sources that deserve comment. This chapter will emphasize some of those that have made important contributions to management thought; but even this is an oversimplification, for it leaves out relatively new theoretical developments (such as cybernetics and information theory) which may prove to be of great importance in the future.

Figure 1-1 is a diagrammatic presentation of the most important contributions to modern management thought. The streams of thought summarized in the diagram are:

1. The "scientific management" movement, including F. W. Taylor and his followers.
2. The advocates of the traditional "principles of management." This category overlaps the first, since Taylor himself developed some of the best known principles, but the emphasis here is somewhat different.
3. The human relations movement, defined broadly to cover several divergent approaches to the sociology and psychology of organization.
4. Managerial economics which involves an application of economic theory to specific management problems.
5. Recent applications of the behaviorial sciences to management problems.
6. Management accounting, particularly those aspects of accounting important in decision-making and control.
7. Modern quantitative approaches, including the development of mathematical models, applications of probability theory, linear programming, and the various contributions of operations research.

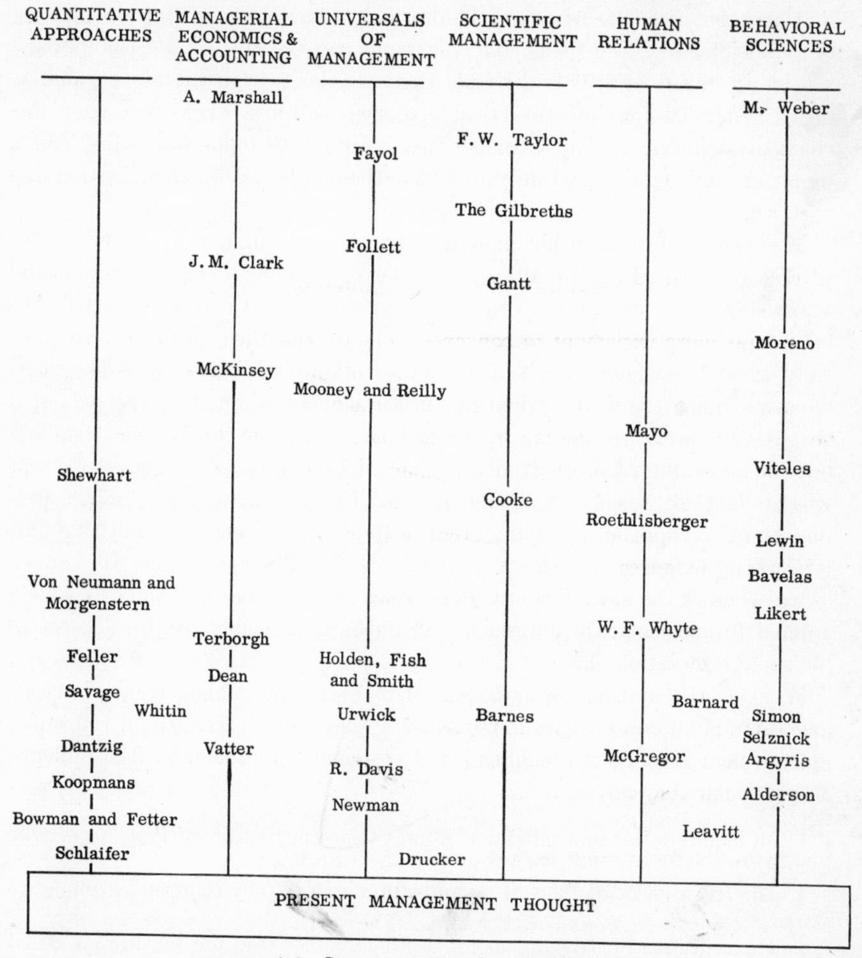

FIGURE 1-1 Streams of Thought on Management

Management is faced with the task of selecting concepts from all of these areas, and integrating them in the process of making decisions about both major policies and day-to-day operations.

The "Scientific Management" Movement

Any discussion of the history of management thought starts with the "scientific management" movement, because it encompasses the first group of writers to win wide attention. F. W. Taylor, the leader of the school, remains the most famous author on management subjects, having had a world-wide influence for the last half century. Taylor himself disclaimed credit for founding the movement—he was aware that most of the ideas he advocated had been practiced by managers before him. Taylor's contribution was one of publicizing existing ideas, but the same can be said of most important writers in any field. This does not deny Taylor's originality in converting broad generalizations into practical management tools. His work as a mechanical engineer, a plant manager, a consultant to industrial firms, and a writer gave him the opportunity to bridge the gap between generalization and practice.

The expression "scientific management" belongs in quotation marks for several reasons. First of all, there is no agreement (even among natural scientists) on the definition of the term "*scientific*." If it refers to a particular method by which hypotheses are developed and then checked systematically against the facts, much of Taylor's work would fall short. The great danger in using the word "scientific" in the manner adopted by this school is that it calls for a prejudging of conclusions. In other words, the term has become an emotional propagandistic device, based on the willingness to accept what is labeled "science" as sound without further examination. Since it is important to adopt an inquiring attitude to all approaches, it is felt that this type of prejudgment should be avoided. (In the same manner, it can be asked whether the more modern term "*management science*," which is widely applied to mathematical approaches to business decisions, is also subject to the same reservations.)

What Taylor and his followers meant by "scientific management" is clear, and there is no doubt of its importance. They were interested in reforming management through a thoughtful and systematic approach to its problems. In particular they advocated:

1. An inquiring frame of mind that refuses to accept past practices as necessarily correct.
2. The replacement of rules of thumb with more carefully thought out guides to action.
3. The collection of data to support decisions rather than the reliance on casual judgments.

Whether or not these ideas on management can be called scientific, they are likely to produce better approaches to many management problems. In the hands of Taylor they led to the following specific applications:

1. The elimination of waste effort.
2. More emphasis on fitting workers to particular tasks.
3. Greater care in training workers to the specific requirements of their jobs.
4. Greater specialization of activities—for example, the drawing of more definite lines between management activities and detailed operations.
5. The establishment of standards for performance.

At the time these views were published, there were great benefits to be derived from their application, for most management was extremely haphazard. Even today, managers can improve many operations by a simple reflection on the way in which the work is being done; observation indicates that there is still room for improvement. However, these five principles have limitations and are more suited to intensive application in some activities than in others. In fact, the blind application of current generalizations was precisely what Taylor originally attacked. It would be unfortunate for "scientific managers" to fall into this same trap.

It is unnecessary to develop Taylor's contributions in detail here. Basic elements of his philosophy will be explained in several later chapters, which will also include his own words describing his famous pig iron handling experiment, in motion and time study, and his *On the Art of Cutting Metals*, which demonstrates that Taylor was an early practitioner of quantitative approaches to management. At various points, mention will be made of his other contributions, such as the "Exception Principle," illustrating his ideas on organization.

Later chapters will also reflect the influence of Taylor's leading colleagues. The influence of Frank Gilbreth on modern management remains strong, especially in the area of motion study. References will be made to H. L. Gantt's contribution to the scheduling of production, recognizing that modern scheduling techniques are based on his work in developing Gantt charts.

Critics of the Scientific Management Movement

Critics of Taylor and his followers have argued for several decades that his analysis was weak in his attention to human factors. They have stated that "scientific management" has neglected organizational and motivational considerations. It would be unfair to state that Taylor and Gilbreth ignored these considerations completely. In fact, a considerable part of Taylor's writings was devoted to questions of how to introduce changes and win cooperation. Also, Frank Gilbreth's wife, Lillian, who worked closely with him, was a trained psychologist. Nevertheless, it is true that in practice, Taylor had difficulty in persuading his followers to understand his ideas or carry them on, largely because of labor or management resistance. In the 1920's and 1930's, "efficiency experts," trained in the methods of Taylor, Gilbreth, and other "scientific" managers, were often held in contempt because of their alleged treatment of human beings as automatons without attention to their needs or attitudes.

Two recent writers on organization, March and Simon, have described the scientific management movement as "physiological organization theory."[1] This title emphasizes that scientific managers were concerned with repetitive tasks on the production floor, for which the muscular capacities are the most important limitations. Such a theory neglects the areas of problem-solving and decision-making which are of key importance on other managerial levels, and underestimates their importance even at the routine production level.

[1] James G. March and Herbert A. Simon, *Organizations* (New York: John Wiley & Sons, 1958), pp. 12–22.

March and Simon are also critical of the simple theories of motivation followed by the scientific management school; this school placed most of its emphasis on wage incentives to the neglect of the other aspects of motivation.

Universal Principles of Management

Throughout the twentieth century, and to a lesser extent in the nineteenth and even earlier periods, there have been attempts to establish universal generalizations about management. These principles have been expressed in prescriptive form: "no man should have two bosses," or "no more than eight men should report to one superior." Taylor himself was an important contributor to the development of these principles, though Henri Fayol,[2] a French contemporary of Taylor, is more representative of the school. Fayol was a successful industrialist, a director of a steel and coal combine. Colonel Lyndall Urwick, a British management expert, is a well-known exponent of this viewpoint. Most of the authors of this type of literature were active businessmen or public administrators, anxious to share their experience with the rest of the world; the "ivory tower" expert on management is a more recent development. Most of the traditional textbooks on management have stressed the principles of management formulated by this school of thought.

The best known principles of management have come under attack in recent years. Critics have pointed to contradictions among the principles. They have noted that little attention to motivational considerations has been given; and hasty pronouncements on what should be done have been made, without examining the assumptions underlying such pronouncements. There is a growing view that these principles no longer represent the heart of our knowledge of management, but instead are a small part of the total body of administrative thought.

The Human Relations Movement

Taylor and his followers overemphasized the mechanical and physiological character of management; it was inevitable that there would be a reaction. In the 1930's there was a growing stress on human relations, largely under the leadership of Elton Mayo and F. J. Roethlisberger, whose work in the famous Hawthorne studies has been a major influence on management thought. It is an oversimplification to let one or two authors represent this movement, for research and theory concerning human relations or small groups began to appear in many places. However, the books on the Hawthorne studies were the most widely read.

[2] The key works of the authors mentioned in this book will be listed in the annotated bibliography at the end of each odd numbered chapter.

These studies took place in the Hawthorne plant of the Western Electric Company in the late 1920's and early 1930's. The original intent of the research workers was to find relationships between "improved" working conditions and productivity. For example, there were attempts to measure the effects of improved lighting and the introduction of rest periods. Special groups of workers were organized into "test" and "control" rooms and careful records were kept of their performance. Results revealed little consistent relationship between the changes in physical working conditions and productivity. In fact, when the "improvements" were removed, productivity remained above the initial levels. Rather than give up because of the negative character of the research findings, Mayo, Roethlisberger, and their associates attempted to attach new meanings to the findings. They stressed the changes in human relationships that had been introduced along with the changes in physical working conditions. For example, the fact that these workers had been selected for special attention and were under observation may have been more important than the physical changes themselves. Thus, as the research in the Hawthorne plant continued, greater attention was paid to the ways in which sociological changes affected the attitudes and production of the workers. Interviews with thousands of workers were used to extend knowledge of workers' attitudes and responses.

There were substantial differences among the research workers on how far they should go in interpreting the findings. Elton Mayo, who served as the social philosopher of the group, was able to draw extremely broad conclusions about the whole trend of Western civilization. He argued that industrialization, with its specialization and removal of face to face contact between management and the workers, was a source of frustration and psychological deterioration. He regretted the reduced importance of the small, spontaneous group in large-scale industry. He took the view that it was the managers' responsibility to repair the damage that had been done by specialization and mechanization of work. For example, he felt that management should plan the organization, either to permit the spontaneous formation of voluntary small groups, or to organize small groups deliberately to provide the kind of face to face association that was needed.

Throughout the human relations movement, there was considerable emphasis on "participation," or the deliberate attempt by management to permit subordinates to take active roles in the decision-making process. The old "Army sergeant" methods of supervision were to be replaced by a gentler, more permissive type of control, under which the subordinates were to be encouraged to express themselves freely, to make suggestions, and to take part on committees in determining important decisions. Workers would no longer be cogs in the machine, or automatons merely following orders from above. They were to be active participants in the productive process, with feelings and sentiments to be taken into account any time changes were to be introduced. Junior boards of directors, suggestions systems, and increased face to face discussions with lower management levels were means by which participation was to be increased.

Some members of the human relations school of thought remained cautious about stating definite conclusions. Roethlisberger, for example, was especially reluctant to find simple generalizations in his research work. He and some of his associates were impressed with the complexity of human behavior and so convinced of the "uniqueness" of each situation, that they preferred to treat each case as one that should be examined on its own merits. Thus the "case method" became an important feature of human relations work. Roethlisberger preferred to train managers by having them consider and analyze particular cases actually experienced in industry, rather than have them learn from theoretical generalizations. Thus, for a period, there was a division between case method advocates and those who were seeking to develop theory. In more recent years, this division has lessened with a more active participation of the case method supporters in the development of the underlying theory.

The human relations approach developed rapidly into a popular view of "how to deal with people." Strong criticism has been directed at those proponents of the approach who stated clichés on ways to make employees happy. Perhaps too much time was spent on techniques of *manipulating* people, in place of seeking a greater understanding of the basic reasons for their actions. The attempt of many "human relation experts" to practice human relations on employees has caused the original leaders of the school to criticize the superficial direction taken by the popularizers in the field.

Applications of the Behavioral Sciences to Management Problems

The Mayo-Roethlisberger school of thought is difficult to separate from other research work in sociology and psychology. If there is a distinction, it is related to the fact that some other researchers, trained in the social sciences, were more interested in working from theory to the detailed facts in particular situations, rather than in the opposite direction. One of the most important of such researchers was Kurt Lewin, who founded a field of theory and research known as "group dynamics." To develop Lewin's theories here would go beyond the scope of this introductory chapter. It is enough to cite his work on "democratic" and "authoritarian" groups to indicate the nature of his findings. Lewin and his associates generally concluded that "democratic" groups, in which there was active member participation in decisions, were more productive both of human satisfaction and of achievement of the group objective. Thus, they also came to stress group participation.

Since World War II, there has been such an expansion of work on the behavioral sciences in management, that a short summary would be too sketchy to be of great interest. A significant portion of this book will go more deeply into the findings and into criticisms of the findings. There is a wide range of literature on the subject, including Herbert Simon's fundamental work on organization theory, and various books on motivation and managerial psychology.

Chester Barnard

One writer is particularly difficult to classify, but because he is considered by many to be the outstanding writer on management, he deserves special attention in this introductory review. Chester Barnard combines elements of all of the developments discussed so far. As a practical business man and government administrator, he has been willing to generalize about what he has learned from experience. In this respect, he differs from most of the other writers on the "principles" of management in the greater profundity of his thought—the greater willingness to state underlying assumptions, to examine the motivational implications of his theories, and to criticize earlier ideas. Barnard's works, particularly his *Functions of the Executive,* had an important influence on the human relations movement. He, like they, placed considerable stress on informal organization. He also emphasized the complexity of human motivation, with strong views on the limitations of financial incentives.

Barnard has had a deep influence on the development of modern organization theory. Herbert Simon's outstanding work, *Administrative Behavior,* reflects this influence, for example, in the treatment of authority. In fact, most of the subjects in recent theoretical works, whether concerned with communication, status, or ethical influences, are to be found in Barnard's pioneer works.

Managerial Economics and Managerial Accounting

It might be expected that economics had always had a significant influence on management thought and practice. By definition, economics is concerned with choice—with decision-making when resources can be devoted to alternative ends. However, it has been only in recent decades that economics and management have become significantly joined. First of all, economics was not developed with the primary objective of helping business men. Instead it was aimed at the analysis of broader social problems—questions of government controls, international trade, business cycles, and taxation. Furthermore, economic theory was developed on a level of abstraction remote from business practice—or at least was expressed in a form that business men found difficult to use.

More recently, however, it has become clear that economics has much to contribute to management. Economics, like management, is concerned with optimization; it is concerned with the future rather than the past. The economist's viewpoint on costs and revenues is one that some business men reach almost intuitively, but which others might well study as a means of avoiding error. For example, the economist likes to emphasize that in the short run, fixed costs are irrelevant to decision-making; they are "sunk" and should be treated as bygones. No doubt some management decisions are too much concerned with sunk costs and too little concerned with maximizing future profits. In recent years, there has been a close relationship between developments in managerial economics and in mathematical approaches to decision-making, for both are concerned with the systematic treatment of certain decisions in which quantities are involved.

In a sense, accounting has always been "managerial accounting," for it has aimed at assisting managers in the interpretation of their situation. Since accounting goes back to the Italian Renaissance, it can be considered one of the oldest streams that compose modern management thought. Emphasis, however, has always been on "financial accounting," on balance sheets and income statements. Attention has been paid to the accurate (and conservative) reporting of past events, which is different from the gathering of data in a form that will permit control and will assist in making decisions about future events.

In the late nineteenth century, there was a beginning of cost accounting, which has continued to develop ever since. Cost accounting has been more directly aimed at application by management—particularly in the control of costs—than has financial accounting. Until recently, however, cost accounting has also frequently failed to express data in a form most useful for decision-making. A growing body of accountants felt the need for a special attention to accounting for management purposes, and the expression "managerial accounting" has become common recently. "Managerial accounting" starts with the recognition of the need to treat costs in different ways for different decisions. A cost figure, appropriate in one situation, may be misleading in another. Thus, there has been a stress on "tailor-making" costs to particular needs.

There has been a close parallel between the development of managerial economics and managerial accounting. It is clear that each has been influenced by the other, and that in modern management practice they are becoming inseparable.

Modern Quantitative Approaches

One of the most significant trends in management is the increased use of quantitative methods of analysis. Management has long made use of numerical data, but in recent years there has been a great increase in the application of mathematics and statistics to these data. The developments in this direction, "management science" or "operations research," have their roots in the same mathematical and statistical developments that led to other quantitative fields, such as econometrics, psychometrics, sociometrics, and biometrics.

These quantitative approaches vary widely in character. Two varieties will be discussed here. The first is linear programming, the best known of the recent developments in mathematical decision-making. If one has a clear-cut objective, and if he has a definite idea of the constraints under which he is operating, linear programming will find the optimum solution to his problem, provided that he can fit mathematical equations to the key relationships. By constraints, it is meant certain minimum conditions that must be met. In production, for example, an important limitation is the capacity of a department. Each department may set its own specific objectives and face varied constraints in its search for its own optimum solution. Solutions to these departmental problems provide definite and useful information in tackling the problems for the firm as a whole. It is true that an optimum solution from the viewpoint of one department may not be consistent with the optimum solution from the viewpoint of another. Nevertheless, the definite answers given by use of linear programming enable top management to identify the areas of conflict, and thus to help them discover exactly what needs attention.

Statistical methods, a second variety of quantitative analysis, are undoubtedly more pervasive in management than is linear programming, partly because they are older in application and partly because of their versatility. The best known uses of statistical methods involve sampling theory. It is often inferred from the characteristics appearing in a sample what the larger universe, from which this sample is taken, resembles. Moreover, probability theory is finding new applications to problems that are not strictly of a sampling character, that is, problems in using past experience in determining optimum policies for the future.

Current developments in management point to a greater use of these and other quantitative approaches. The electronic computer is making it possible to apply mathematical and statistical models that a few years ago would have been unmanageable. However, quantitative approaches will not displace managerial judgment and qualitative evaluations. They are only part of the conceptual tools available to modern management.

The Functions of Management

What does a manager do? What distinguishes him from a person who is not a manager? A detailed answer to this question is the subject of this book; it will help if the reader will relate his own past experiences to serve as framework for his thought.

Lists of functions are arbitrary but usually include such words as decision-making, organizing, planning, directing, controlling, staffing, co-ordinating, communicating, motivating, and evaluating. Each of these words will have some immediate meaning to the reader. The rest of the chapters in this book, however, should clarify and supplement these first impressions.

Management is necessarily a broad subject. It involves doing the job *through people.* Some writers consider this so important that they make it a definition of management itself. In any case, it is clear that the human or personnel side of management is extremely important; many otherwise sound ideas have failed because of the inability to win the co-operation or, at least, the acceptance of those who must put the ideas into practice.

Management must *set objectives.* Without objectives, management would be difficult, if not impossible. Clear-cut objectives can give a sense of direction to the organization that should improve co-ordination and heighten motivation.

Managers must *make decisions.* In the last few years, research workers have concentrated on the decision-making process itself; this book supplies an introduction to this new area of subject matter.

Some books stress *leadership* as a major management characteristic. This is true, but there is the need to identify the concepts and analysis implied in this generalization. More important is to supply content to these abstract ideas.

The Structure of this Book

The structure of this book is quite simple:

1. Four chapters discuss the concept of *organization* as a structure of communication and authority to fit the needs of the situation.
2. Two chapters consider the relation of *motivation* to managerial duties.
3. Two chapters summarize the meaning of *policies, decision-making,* and *planning* in management.
4. After two chapters introduce the general concept of *control,* the last half of the book develops a variety of approaches involved in decision-making and control.

This book is composed of two types of chapters. The odd numbered ones supply the fundamental analysis. These chapters attempt to cover management thought as it exists today, along with the controversial issues that persist. The chapters try to do more than survey their respective subjects. They aim at stimulating real thought about the behavioral or quantitative analysis that may be applicable. The reader is encouraged to reflect on the relevance of new developments in management. Whether the discussion is one of traditional principle or modern theories, the tone is critical. The authors wish to discourage a blind acceptance of ideas and instead to stimulate original thought on the part of the reader. They wish also to stimulate interest in new developments, so that the reader will maintain a continued interest in the growing body of research and theory on management.

The even numbered chapters contain two kinds of material. First, they include extracts from the vast literature on management. Most of these are taken from works that are becoming classics; others highlight key issues that deserve attention. Some of the extracts will help the reader review the key ideas in the odd numbered chapters, by providing statements on these subjects by outstanding writers. Other extracts go beyond this by supplying extensions of the subjects previously discussed. Frequently, there are conflicts in the views expressed in the extracts; these conflicts make it clear that there is no unanimity on many of the major topics in management; they should also help the reader formulate his own views.

The second type of material in the even numbered chapters consists of cases. Most of these are actual business situations that require analysis. A few of the cases are based on situations familiar to most students, thus bringing the subject matter closer to situations with which they are acquainted. In either case, the objective is the development of skills in the application of theory and common sense to realistic management problems.

The authors hope to encourage the *education* of managers for the future, not the mere *training* in present procedures. An educated manager is a person who recognizes what he does not know, possesses a curiosity about his own experiences, and can receive communication of new knowledge from others.

The authors hope to help the manager develop a better *way of thinking* and a broader *point of view.* Throughout the book, the emphasis is on concepts, analysis, and theory, rather than on description and lists of advantages and disadvantages. Throughout, the aim is the stimulation of thought processes rather than the memorization of pat answers, and throughout there is an emphasis on ideas that hold promise for the future development of management rather than on the clichés that have been accepted in the past.

Bibliographical Note

The concentrated study of management began with the writings of Frederick W. Taylor and Frank and Lillian Gilbreth. These writings have been collected and are available in two volumes: Frederick Winslow Taylor, *Scientific Management* (1947), and W. R. Spriegel and C. E. Myers, eds., *The Writings of the Gilbreths* (1953). Extracts from these writings appear in Chapter 2 of our book, but all serious management students should read at least Taylor's short and interesting statement of *The Principles of Scientific Management* included in the above reprint. If the reader is interested in the evolution of the thinking of other scientific managers, George Filipetti's *Industrial Management in Transition* (1949) provides a concise summary.

Many articles have appeared over the years in management journals. A number of these are now available in books of readings including F. A. Shull's *Selected Readings in Management;* Koontz and O'Donnell's *Readings in Management;* and Richards and Nielander's *Readings in Management.*

Textbooks on industrial management are numerous and will not be mentioned by name here. Several handbooks which provide convenient reference for step by step procedures, illustrative charts and other details are Alford and Bangs, *Production Handbook;* H. B. Maynard, *Industrial Engineering Handbook;* and Ireson and Grant, *Handbook of Industrial Engineering and Management.* Many subjects introduced in the following chapters will be found in greater detail in these handbooks.

Those interested in the evaluation of education for business and management should read the report financed by the Carnegie Foundation by Frank Pierson, *The Education of American Businessmen,* and the study financed by the Ford Foundation by R. A. Gordon and J. E. Howell, *Higher Education for Business.*

Questions and Problems

Some clues to answers may appear in the even numbered chapters following each set of questions.

1. From this chapter and your past experiences, develop a definition of management which you can use as a guide as you study this book.

2. The words *art* and *science* are often discussed at length as they relate to management. Determine what these words mean and offer your own first guess as to their application in management thinking.

3. Scientific management, as developed by Taylor and Gilbreth in the early twentieth century, was the beginning of a concentrated study of management as a separate field of study.

(a) Why did this study develop at so late a date?

(b) Why has its importance increased so rapidly?

(c) What importance would you give to: the use of the corporate forms of organization, size of industrial enterprise, the Industrial Revolution, the importance of research in other areas of knowledge?

4. Some observers include management as a "profession." What would be the criteria that you would use in your appraisal of the professional characteristics of management?

5. The study of management is not restricted to business organization. Universal principles of management should be so stated as to remain valid in many different applications.

(a) From your study in other disciplines point out the nature of "principles."

(b) Do you think there can be universal principles of management?

6. Why do you think that the Hawthorne study is considered a classic in the development of management thinking?

7. Why are the behavioral (social) sciences important in management?

8. Is a concentrated study of economics and accounting sufficient for the development of managers?

9. The study of liberal arts is generally considered helpful in the education of managers. What elements of a liberal education should improve the thinking and actions of managers?

10. What are the advantages of quantitative approaches in the development of a subject such as management?

11. State in your own words what you consider to be the essential functions performed by a manager as compared with the functions performed by other employees of a firm.

2

Extracts on the Place of Management in Modern Society

THIS chapter includes excerpts on the role of management in an industrial society, followed by several outstanding statements on education for management. The first author is the "father of scientific management," F. W. Taylor. His ideas may be taken as typical of a whole school of thought, including Frank and Lillian Gilbreth, Henry L. Gantt, and others.

Taylor wrote at a time when the Industrial Revolution and the growth of large financial combinations were accomplished facts. A contemporary of Taylor, Thorstein Veblen, illustrates a different perspective on the "machine age" and "efficiency experts." Extracts from Veblen's writings raise fundamental questions concerning the place of management in society. Similar extracts from the work of a more recent writer, James Burnham, also ask where management fits into our modern industrial environment. Elton Mayo emphasizes that the problems of modern society are interrelated with the problems of management.

If management is a separate field for concentration, an educational approach should be developed to improve the understanding of basic concepts and the performance in actual business situations. The extract from R. A. Gordon summarizes conclusions based upon a Ford Foundation study of the place of business education in society. The "Gordon Report" has served as a catalyst and has stimulated business schools to examine their programs and to seek new directions.

Research in management and in the education for management in the future promises to advance on a much broader front than in the past. Not only economists and management specialists, but also social (behavioral) scientists and other "liberally" educated persons are showing increased interest in management. The extract from Harbison and Myers provides a framework for this broader perspective. The quotations from *Social Science Research on Business* point up the place of psychologists, sociologists, and political scientists in management research. The principles supporting recent experiments in developing liberally trained executives are summarized in the extract by Siegle.

The last extract, taken from an entertaining book called *Parkinson's Law,* serves a number of purposes. It may be read as a satire on modern management thought; it contains enough truth to warrant serious consideration as a contribution to the body of management thought itself. At the same time this extract warns us to be duly skeptical of broad generalization, it stimulates us to look for still new generalizations.

Extract A

Principles of Scientific Management (F. W. Taylor)

It will doubtless be claimed that in all that has been said no new fact has been brought to light that was not known to some one in the past. Very likely this is true. Scientific management does not necessarily involve any great invention, nor the discovery of new or startling facts. It does, however, involve a certain *combination* of elements which have not existed in the past, namely, old knowledge so collected, analyzed, grouped, and classified into laws and rules that it constitutes a science; accompanied by a complete change in the mental attitude of the working men as well as of those on the side of management, toward each other, and toward their respective duties and responsibilities. Also, a new division of the duties between the two sides and intimate, friendly cooperation to an extent that is impossible under the philosophy of the old management. And even all of this in many cases could not exist without the help of mechanisms which have been gradually developed.

It is no single element, but rather this whole combination, that constitutes scientific management, which may be summarized as:

Science, not rule of thumb.
Harmony, not discord.
Cooperation, not individualism.
Maximum output, in place of restricted output.
The development of each man to his greatest efficiency and prosperity.

The writer wishes to again state that: "The time is fast going by for the great personal or individual achievement of any one man standing alone and without the help of those around him. And the time is coming when all great things will be done by that type of cooperation in which each man performs the function for which he is best suited, each man preserves his own individuality and is supreme in his particular function, and each man at the same time loses none of his originality and proper personal initiative, and yet is controlled by and must work harmoniously with many other men. . . ."

The first illustration is that of handling pig iron, and this work is chosen because it is typical of perhaps the crudest and most elementary form of labor which is performed by man. This work is done by men with no other implements than their hands. The pig-iron handler stoops down, picks up a pig weighing about 92 pounds, walks for a few feet or yards and then drops it on to the ground or upon a pile. This work is so crude and elementary in its nature that the writer firmly believes that it would be possible to train an intelligent gorilla so as to become a more efficient pig-iron handler than any man can be. Yet it will be shown that the science of handling pig iron is so great and amounts to so much that it is impossible for the man who is best suited to this type of work to understand the principles of this science, or even to work in accordance with these principles without the aid of a man better educated than he is. . . .

We found that this gang were loading on the average about 12½ long tons per man per day. We were surprised to find, after studying the matter, that a first-class pig-iron handler ought to handle between 47 and 48 long tons per day, instead of 12½ tons. This task seemed to us so very large that we were obliged to go over our work several times before we were absolutely sure that we were right. Once we were sure, however, that 47 tons was a proper day's work for a first-class pig-iron handler, the task which faced us as managers under the modern scientific plan was clearly before us. . . .

Finally we selected one from among the four as the most likely man to start with. He was a little Pennsylvania Dutchman who had been observed to trot back home for a mile or so after his work in the evening, about as fresh as he was when he came trotting down to work in the morning. . . . This man we will call Schmidt. . . .

Schmidt started to work, and all day long, and at regular intervals was told by the man who stood over him with a watch, "Now pick up a pig and walk. Now sit down and rest. Now walk—now rest," etc. He worked when he was told to work, and rested when he was told to rest, and at half-past five in the afternoon had his 47½ tons loaded on the car. And he practically never failed to work at this pace and do the task that was set him during the three years that the writer was at Bethlehem. And throughout this time he averaged a little more than $1.85 per day, whereas before he had never received over $1.15 per day, which was the ruling rate of wages at that time in Bethlehem. That is, he received 60 per cent higher wages than were paid to other men who were not working on task work. One man after another was picked out and trained to handle pig iron at the rate of 47½ tons per day until all of the pig iron was handled at this rate, and the men were receiving 60 per cent more wages than other workmen around them.

The writer has given above a brief description of three of the four elements which constitute the essence of scientific management: first, the careful selection of the workman, and, second and third, the method of first inducing and then training and helping the workman to work according to the scientific method. Nothing has as yet been said about the science of handling the pig iron. The writer trusts, however, that before leaving this illustration the reader will be thoroughly convinced that there is a science of handling pig iron, and further that this science amounts to so much that the man who is suited to handle pig iron cannot possibly understand it, nor even work in accordance with the laws of this science, without the help of those who are over him.[1]

Extract B

The Instinct of Workmanship (Thorstein Veblen)

Within the effective bounds of modern Christendom no one can wholly escape or in any sensible degree deflect the sweep of the machine's routine.

Modern life goes by clockwork. So much that no modern household can dispense with a mechanical time-piece; which may be more or less accurate, it is true, but which commonly marks the passage of time with a degree of exactness that would have seemed divertingly supererogatory to the common man of the high tide of handicraft. . . .

Both in its incidence on the workman and on the members of the community at large, therefore, the training given by this current state of the industrial arts is a training in the impersonal, quantitative apprehension and appreciation of things, and it tends strongly to inhibit and discredit all imputation of spiritual traits to the facts of observation. It is a training in matter-of-fact; more specifically it is a training in the logic of the machine process. Its outcome should obviously be an unqualified materialistic and mechanical animus in all orders of society, most pronounced in the working classes, since they are most immediately and consistently exposed to the discipline of the machine process. But such an animus as best comports with the logic of the machine process does not, it appears, for good or ill, best comport with the native strain of human nature in those peoples that are subject to its discipline. . . .

The businessmen in control of large industrial enterprises are beginning to appreciate something of their own unfitness to direct or oversee, or even to control, technological matters, and so they have, in a tentative way, taken

[1] F. W. Taylor, *Principles of Scientific Management,* as reprinted in *Scientific Management* (New York: Harper & Brothers, 1947), pp. 139–41, 40–48.

to employing experts to do the work for them. Such experts are known colloquially as "efficiency engineers" and are presumed to combine the qualifications of technologist and accountant. . . .

It would doubtless appear that a trained inability to apprehend any other than the immediate pecuniary bearing of their manoeuvres accounts for a larger share in the conduct of the businessmen who control industrial affairs than it does in that of their workmen, since the habitual employment of the former holds them more rigorously and consistently to the pecuniary valuation of whatever passes under their hands; and the like should be true only in a higher degree of those who have to do exclusively with the financial side of business. The state of the industrial arts requires that these several factors should cooperate intelligently and without reservation, with an eye single to the exigencies of this modern wide-sweeping technological system; but their habitual addiction to pecuniary rather than technological standards and considerations leaves them working at cross purposes. So also their (pecuniary) interests are at cross purposes; and since these interests necessarily rule in any pecuniary culture, they must decide the line of conduct for each of the several factors engaged. . . .

Efficiency conduces to the common good, and is also a meritorious and commendable trait in the person who exercises it. But under the canons of self-help and pecuniary valuation the test of efficiency in economic matters has come to be, not technological mastery and productive effect, but proficiency in pecuniary management and the acquisition of wealth.[2]

Extract C

The Managerial Revolution (James Burnham)

In simplest terms, the theory of the managerial revolution asserts merely the following: Modern society has been organized through a certain set of major economic, social, and political institutions which we call capitalist, and has exhibited certain major social beliefs or ideologies. Within this social structure we find that a particular group or class of persons—the capitalists or *bourgeoisie*—is the dominant or ruling class in the sense which has been defined. At the present time, these institutions and beliefs are undergoing a process of rapid transformation. The conclusion of this period of transformation, to be expected in the comparatively near future, will find society organized through a quite different set of major economic, social, a[n]d political institutions and exhibiting quite different major social beliefs or ideologies. Within the new social structure a different social group or class—the managers—will be the dominant or ruling class. . . .

[2] From *The Instinct of Workmanship* by Thorstein Veblen, Copyright 1914 by The Macmillan Company, 1941 by Ann B. Sims, reprinted by permission of The Viking Press, Inc., pp. 311, 318, 345, 347–348, 349.

It should be noted, and it will be seen in some detail, that the theory of the managerial revolution is not merely predicting what may happen in a hypothetical future. The theory is, to begin with, an interpretation of what *already* has happened and is now happening. Its prediction is simply that the process which has started and which has already gone a very great distance will continue and reach completion. . . .

It would seem obvious that in capitalist society it would be the capitalists who, in decisive respects at least, do the managing. If they do not manage the instruments of production, how could they maintain their position as ruling class, which depends upon control over the instruments of production? This is obvious, and the answer to this question is that they could not. It is the fact that during the past several decades the *de facto* management of the instruments of production has to a constantly increasing extent got out of the hands of the capitalists that so plainly proves society to be shifting away from capitalism and the capitalists losing their status as the ruling class. In ever-widening sectors of world economy, the actual managers are not the capitalists, the *bourgeoisie;* or, at the very least, the managerial prerogatives of the capitalists are being progressively whittled down. The completion of this process means the elimination of the capitalists from control over the economy; that is, their disappearance as a ruling class. . . .

The third type [of task] consists of the tasks of the technical direction and co-ordination of the process of production. All the necessary workers, skilled and unskilled, and all the industrial scientists will not turn out automobiles. The diverse tasks must be organized, co-ordinated, so that the different materials, tools, machines, plants, workers are all available at the proper place and moment and in the proper numbers. This task of direction and co-ordination is itself a highly specialized function. Often it, also, requires acquaintance with the physical sciences (or the psychological and social sciences, since human beings are not the least among the instruments of production) and with engineering. But it is a mistake (which was made by Veblen, among others) to confuse this directing and co-ordinating function with the scientific and engineering work which I have listed under the second type of task. After all, the engineers and scientists of the second type are merely highly skilled workers, no different in kind from the worker whose developed skill enables him to make a precision tool or operate an ingenious lathe. They have no functions of guiding, administering, managing, organizing the process of production, which tasks are the distinctive mark of the third type. For these tasks, engineering and scientific knowledge may be, though it is not always, or necessarily, a qualification, but the tasks themselves are not engineering or science in the usual sense.

It is this third type of function which, in the fullest and clearest meaning, I call "managing;" and those who carry out this type of function are they whom I call the "managers." Many different names are given them. We may often recognize them as "production managers," operating executives, superintendents, administrative engineers, supervisory technicians; or, in government (for they are to be found in governmental enterprise just as in private enterprise) as administrators, commissioners, bureau heads, and so on. I mean by managers, in short, those who already for the most part in contemporary society are actually managing, on its technical side, the actual process of production, no matter what the legal and financial form—individual, corporate, governmental—of the process. . . .

These changes have meant that to an ever-growing extent the managers are no longer, either as individuals or legally or historically, the same as the capitalists. There is a combined shift: through changes in the technique of production, the functions of management become more distinctive, more complex, more specialized, and more crucial to the whole process of production, thus serving to set off those who perform these functions as a separate group or class in society; and at the same time those who formerly carried out what functions there were of management, the *bourgeoisie,* themselves withdraw from management, so that the difference in function becomes also a difference in the individuals who carry out the function. . . .

The general basis of the managerial ideologies is clear enough from an understanding of the general character of managerial society. In place of capitalist concepts, there are concepts suited to the structure of managerial society and the rule of the managers. In place of the "individual" the stress turns to the "state," the people, the folk, the race. In place of gold, labor and work. In place of private enterprise, "socialism" or "collectivism." In place of "freedom" and "free initiative," planning. Less talk about "rights" and "natural rights;" more about "duties" and "order" and "discipline." Less about "opportunity" and more about "jobs." In addition, in these early decades of managerial society, more of the positive elements that were once part of capitalist ideology in its rising youth, but have left it in old age: destiny, the future, sacrifice, power. . . . Of course, some of the words of the capitalist ideologies are taken over: such words as "freedom" are found in many ideologies since they are popular and, as we have seen, can be interpreted in any manner whatever.[3]

Extract D

The Human Problems of an Industrial Civilization (Elton Mayo)

The industrial inquiry nevertheless makes clear that the problems of human equilibrium and effort are not completely contained within the area controlled by factory organization and executive policy. Certain of the

[3] Copyright © 1941 by James Burnham, reprinted from *The Managerial Revolution* by James Burnham by permission of The John Day Company, Inc., publisher, pp. 74–75, 78, 79–80, 82, 190–191.

sources of personal disequilibrium, and especially the low resistance to adverse happenings in the ordinary workroom, must be attributed to the developing social disorganization and consequent *anomie* which is in these days typical of living conditions in or near any great industrial centre. This developing *anomie* has changed the essential nature of every administrative problem—whether governmental or industrial. It is no longer possible for an administrator to concern himself narrowly with his special function and to assume that the controls established by a vigorous social code will continue to operate in other areas of human life and action. All social controls of this type have weakened or disappeared—this being symptomatic of the diminished integrity of the social organism. The existing situation, both within the national boundaries and as between nations, demands therefore that special attention be given to restatement of the problem of administration as the most urgent issue of the present. . . .

We are faced with the fact, then, that in the important domain of human understanding and control we are ignorant of the facts and their nature; our opportunism in administration and social inquiry has left us incapable of anything but impotent inspection of a cumulative disaster. We do not lack an able administrative *élite,* but the *élite* of the several civilized powers is at present insufficiently posted in the biological and social facts involved in social organization and control. So we are compelled to wait for the social organism to recover or perish without adequate medical aid. . . .

A century of scientific development, the emergence of a considerable degree of social disorganization—these and certain effects of education have led us to forget how necessary this type of non-logical social action is to achievement and satisfaction in living. Before the present era, changes in method of living tended to come gradually, usually there was no sudden disruption of slowly evolved methods of working together. Even now one can witness in Europe the successful accomplishment of a necessary economic duty as a purely social function, comparable with the ritual performances of a primitive tribe. The vintage activities and ceremonies of the French peasantry, for example, in the Burgundy district, present features essentially similar to the activities of the primitive, although at a higher level of understanding and skill. In the United States we have travelled rapidly and carelessly from this type of simple social and economic organization to a form of industrial organization which assumes that every participant will be a devotee of systematic economics and a rigid logic. This unthinking assumption does not "work" with us, it does not "work" in Russia; it has never "worked" in the whole course of human history. The industrial worker, whether capable of it or no, does not want to develop a blackboard logic which shall guide his method of life and work. What he wants is more nearly described as, first, a method of living in social relationship with other people and, second, as part of this an economic function for and value to the group. The whole of this most important aspect of human nature

we have recklessly disregarded in our "triumphant" industrial progress. . . .
. . . The chief difficulty of our time is the breakdown of the social codes that formerly disciplined us to effective working together. For the non-logic of a social code the logic of understanding—biological and social—has not been substituted. The situation is as if Pareto's circulation of the *élite* had been fatally interrupted—the consequence, social disequilibrium. We have too few administrators alert to the fact that it is a human social and not an economic problem which they face. The universities of the world are admirably equipped for the discovery and training of the specialist in science; but they have not begun to think about the discovery and training of the new administrator.[4]

Extract E

Higher Education for Business (R. A. Gordon and J. E. Howell)

It seems to us that there are at least four different aspects of the field of "administration and organization" that need to be distinguished. Failure to make these (or similar) distinctions, we suspect, is one important reason why many schools have had so much difficulty in deciding what should be taught in this field. The four aspects that need to be distinguished are: (1) methods of managerial problem-solving, an area which for brevity we shall call management analysis, (2) organization theory, (3) management principles, and (4) human relations.

By *management analysis* we mean an explicitly rational approach to the making of decisions about the allocation of resources within the firm. What is involved is a study of the methods available for the analysis and solution of the substantive problems which are the concern of economic management. The scientific approach to managerial decision-making has had its greatest development within the area of production management, beginning with Frederick Taylor and his disciples and extending up to the latest developments in operation analysis. Since the Second World War, quantitative and, more broadly, scientific methods of analysis have been applied to a steadily widening area of management problems.

The methods available for a scientific or rational approach to managerial decision-making can be viewed broadly or narrowly. Broadly considered, they include any techniques that help the decision-maker to discover and evaluate alternatives and to make that choice which seems, in the light of given objectives, to be most rational. In this broad sense, management analysis includes all analytical and informational tools that contribute to a scientific approach to any management problem. The methods used may be quite

[4] Elton Mayo, *The Human Problems of an Industrial Civilization* (New York: The Macmillan Co., 1933). Copyright assigned to The President and Fellows of Harvard College, 1946, pp. 173, 177, 180–181, 188.

crude, and little in the way of rigorous quantitative analysis may be involved. In this broad sense, a considerable part of the business curriculum may be concerned with management analysis. . . .

Organization theory, or "theory of administration," is concerned with the scientific study of human behavior in organizations. It deals with how human beings function in organizations, with what conditions are necessary to secure effective action within organizations, and with the problems that arise in connection with making and implementing decisions in an organizational context. It might also be described as dealing with the internal organizational "environment" of the business firm (and other types of organizations). . . .

In contrast to the first two, that part of the field of management which we would label *principles of management* is concerned with describing and distilling the best of current management practices into a set of generalizations which workers in this area call principles. It differs from organization theory, also, in terms of methodology (more pragmatic), level of abstraction (less theoretical), the viewpoint from which problems are considered (more the viewpoint of higher management officials), and emphasis placed on individual attitudes and motivation (less emphasis on the individual as a variable). On the other hand, the more scientifically based portion of management principles can be derived from organization theory, just as some of the hypotheses the organizational theorist might wish to test might originate as "principles" of management. The two fields overlap and supplement each other. . . .

A Suggested Requirement

Our own recommendation is that schools include in their degree requirements a specification of three to six semester hours in the general area of organization theory and management principles, possibly including human relations. Schools will need to experiment to determine how instruction in these areas should be organized. . . .

On the side of organization theory, there is not inconsiderable literature by sociologists, psychologists, political scientists, and economists. The material on management principles is more widely known and, unlike that on organization theory, has already been synthesized in some widely used texts. We suspect that, for the time being, the wisest procedure at the undergraduate level is to plan a course that will combine in some proportions not only organization theory and management principles but also some human relations, particularly since the significant generalizations in the last named area are really a part of the broader area of organization theory.[5]

[5] Robert Aaron Gordon and James Edwin Howell, *Higher Education for Business* (New York: Columbia University Press, 1959), pp. 179, 180, 181, 185–186.

Extract F

Management in the Industrial World (F. Harbison and C. A. Myers)

We propose to look at management from three different perspectives and thus to build a threefold concept of its development in industrial society.

From one perspective, management is an *economic resource,* or a factor of production. In this respect, it is similar to capital, labor, or natural resources and is combined with them in varying factor proportions in productive processes. Managerial resources, like capital, for example, must be accumulated and effectively employed or invested in productive activity. In important respects, the problem of the generation and accumulation of managerial resources is similar to that of capital formation. And, as we shall show in subsequent chapters, capital-intensive industrial development is almost always intensive in its requirements for high-talent manpower, i.e., for managerial resources. A country's economic development may be limited by a relative shortage of this critical factor, or that development may be accelerated significantly by a high capacity to accumulate it. In many instances, moreover, management is an even more critical factor in industrialization than capital, and it is almost always more vital to development than either labor or natural resources.

From a second perspective, management is a *system of authority*. In industrial society there are the managers and the managed. Within the managerial hierarchy itself, there are lines of command and patterns of authority in all levels of decision-making. In a very real sense, management is a rule-making and rule-enforcing body, and within itself it is bound together by a web of relationships between superiors and subordinates. The exercise of authority by management is indispensable to industrial development, and the nature of that development will be critically influenced by the manner in which such authority is applied. Indeed, management is ineffective as a resource unless it can operate effectively as a system of authority in industrial society. In viewing management from this perspective, we shall be interested in how authority is acquired, maintained, and exercised and also in the philosophies and policies which are developed to make its use legitimate.

From the third perspective, management is a *class* or *an elite*. In any industrial society, the members of management are a small, but usually aggressive minority. In varying degrees in different countries, they enjoy a measure of prestige, privilege, and power as an elite. Entry into the management class is of necessity restricted, and thus it is important to map the avenues of access to its ranks and to identify those who are its gatekeepers. The matter of access, of course, has an important bearing upon the capacity of a country to accumulate the management it requires, and it also has a bearing on the operation of management as a system of authority. And, as we have already indicated, the origins of a country's organization builders are important determinants of the initial direction and pace of the march toward industrialism. . . .

It follows from our threefold analysis that, in the age of modern technology, no country can expect to industrialize unless it can finance and build on a sizable scale the particular kinds of educational institutions which an industrial society demands. In this "century of science," the outlays for scientific and technical education have become enormous in all advanced countries, and in most, great stress has been laid as well on management-training institutions to develop the administrative skills which a modern society demands. The advanced industrial economy requires an investment in a fully developed system of general education, and at the same time, it demands that its basic educational institutions become more functionally oriented to the training of skilled technicians, engineers, scientists, and administrators. But it also requires the lowering of arbitrary noneducational barriers to entry into the managerial hierarchy as well as some vertical and horizontal mobility within the managerial class itself. In some societies, the processes of generation of managerial manpower have been spearheaded by the state; in others, by private initiative. As industrialization advances and even as it is being started in the presently underdeveloped countries, however, the means of generating and accumulating managerial resources is increasingly a matter for careful planning, judicious investment, and conscious effort. In the logic of industrialization with modern technology, high-talent manpower is not just naturally born. It does not grow wild; on the contrary, it requires very careful seeding and most meticulous cultivation. The generation of needed high-talent manpower, therefore, is perhaps the most difficult task facing the underdeveloped countries in their drive to industrialize. . . .

There is little reason to fear that the working masses in modern industrial states will be exploited by the emerging professional managerial class. Industrialism makes possible a higher material standard of living. But at the same time, management is generally forced to share its rule-making prerogatives with agencies which directly or indirectly represent the workers' interest. Thus the odds are in favor of greater recognition of the rights and dignity of the individual worker as industrialization advances.[6]

Extract G

Social Science Research on Business: Product and Potential (Robert A. Dahl, Mason Haire, and Paul Lazarsfeld)

There is, of course, a close logical relationship between the study of business and the behavioral sciences. Indeed, the study of business *is* a behavioral science, studying a sample of behavior in a particular context. How-

[6] Frederick Harbison and Charles A. Myers, *Management in the Industrial World* (New York: McGraw-Hill Book Company, Inc., 1959), pp. 19–20, 121, 122.

ever, the flow of ideas and facts between the areas has not been as full and detailed as one might hope. . . .

The student of business tends to see problems in terms of the goals of the operation and within the confines of the industrial organization. He sees problems of production, control, evaluation, and management. The psychologist, not surprisingly, has tended to see psychological problems. Many of them have immediate and pressing relevance for the student of business, but their detail and relevance have not always been clear. The psychologist sees problems related to production—the nature of the productive performance, of the people who do it, and of the motivation to do it well or quickly. He sees the problems of management and control in the fields of communication, leadership, group effects, and the like. However, he sees them—and states them —as psychological problems, and, as such, they are not maximally available to students of business. . . .

Certain areas of business administration seem to rest specifically on psychological concepts. For example, pay plans are partly built on notions about motivation—both about kinds of motives and their gradients of growth. Similarly, the treatment of seniority rests on a base of assumption about the use of reward and its effect on behavior. The problem of satisfaction and the general area of human relations dealt with here, would be in this class.

Some problems seem to depend on simple technological contribution from well developed areas of psychology. Selection and classification, or the design of equipment are good examples of this type.

A large group of problems remain where joint effort seems most appropriate. In the area of social perception, for example, we have barely opened the field of role perceptions in hierarchial structures. Some work has been done on the perception of one level by another, and it looks promising. Some exists in self-perceptions characteristic of different levels, and, likewise, it should develop. We have virtually nothing of what has been called "psychological job descriptions." That is, descriptions of the aspects of the job which, besides simple duties, make demands on the person—the fact, for example, that a waitress is caught between the customer's demands and the kitchen's inflexibility. Such phenomena, at different levels, have all sorts of costs to the organization, from higher pay scales, turnover and absenteeism, to ulcers and coronary pathology in executives.

In the labor-management field, the problem of dual allegiances seems to have important cognitive and motivational implications for practice. Role perceptions (and misperceptions) of one another in bargaining relationships have been studied. In one case, in a rare example, a careful study of the behavioral effects of arbitration has been done. This is an unusually good case in which the policies and practices from business can be investigated in the tradition of behavioral sciences. . . . Similar studies seem appropriate on the Law of Effect. Presumably disciplinary punishments are handed out on the assumption that the behavior will be modified. In general societal behavior, the determinants and the criteria are too complex to make study easy.

Here, the criteria of good behavior are explicit and available, the population is relatively stable, and the opportunity to test hypotheses seems endless.

In the area of management behavior, also, there seems to be a rich field. We need simple studies of what happens like Sune Carlson's study of Swedish executives. The studies of decision go beyond these. The motivation of management has been very little investigated—though some attention has been given to compensation plans under high tax rates. Job descriptions of management are inadequate, but our knowledge of the perceptions of members of management of their jobs is even more so.

In general, the time seems ripe for a joint effort of students of business administration and the ancillary behavioral disciplines, bringing concepts and methods from a variety of fields to bear on a set of common problems.[7]

Extract H

Liberal Education for Executives (P. E. Siegle)

Much has been written and discussed about the ever increasing number of programs in the liberal arts for business and industrial executives. No matter what the program—be it the experimental series developed by the Bell System of A. T. & T., the Pomona College summer program, the Vassar Institute for Women in Business, the Clark University Institute of Liberal Studies for Executives, Southwestern University's Institute for Executive Leadership, the Wabash College Personal Development Program, or the policy-level discussions of the Humanities Center for the Liberal Arts in an Industrial Society—they are all rooted in common principles.

First, they represent industry's increasing awareness that merely technically trained personnel are not adequate to meet industry's changing needs. Industry demands not only specialists and "broad gauged" persons but also those who are both specialists *and* broad gauged.

Second, they demonstrate a growing concern on the part of both industry and academia for developing persons who, for the good of the society, must have their horizons broadened and their lives enriched for the new leisure and for changing, growing responsibilities as citizens.

Third, they indicate some validity to the idea that liberal education can, for many people, more profitably, come *after* specialized training and years of experience on the specialized job rather than *before*.

Fourth, they give credence to the assumption that a special kind of program must be developed for the person who has had a broad living experience which must be taken into account as an important dimension in adult education.

[7] Robert A. Dahl, Mason Haire, and Paul Lazarsfeld, *Social Science Research on Business: Product and Potential* (New York: Columbia University Press, 1959), pp. preface, 47, 91–92.

Fifth, they make clear the growing tendency to look upon *liberal education* as the way to achieve a much-needed base for personal growth.[8]

EXTRACT I

Parkinson's Law (C. N. Parkinson)

Work expands so as to fill the time available for its completion. . . .

Granted that work (and especially paperwork) is thus elastic in its demands on time, it is manifest that there need be little or no relationship between the work to be done and the size of the staff to which it may be assigned. A lack of real activity does not, of necessity, result in leisure. A lack of occupation is not necessarily revealed by a manifest idleness. The thing to be done swells in importance and complexity in a direct ratio with the time to be spent. This fact is widely recognized, but less attention has been paid to its wider implications, more especially in the field of public administration. . . .

The validity of this recently discovered law must rest mainly on statistical proofs, which will follow. Of more interest to the general reader is the explanation of the factors underlying the general tendency to which this law gives definition. Omitting technicalities (which are numerous) we may distinguish at the outset two motive forces. They can be represented for the present purpose by two almost axiomatic statements, thus: (1) "An official wants to multiply subordinates, not rivals" and (2) "Officials make work for each other."

To comprehend Factor 1, we must picture a civil servant, called A, who finds himself overworked. Whether this overwork is real or imaginary is immaterial, but we should observe, in passing, that A's sensation (or illusion) might easily result from his own decreasing energy: a normal symptom of middle age. For this real or imagined overwork there are, broadly speaking, three possible remedies. He may resign; he may ask to halve the work with a colleague called B; he may demand the assistance of two subordinates, to be called C and D. There is probably no instance in history, however, of A choosing any but the third alternative. By resignation he would lose his pension rights. By having B appointed, on his own level in the hierarchy, he would merely bring in a rival for promotion to W's vacancy when W (at long last) retires. So A would rather have C and D, junior men, below him. They will add to his consequence and, by dividing the work into two categories, as between C and D, he will have the merit of being the only man who comprehends them both. It is essential to realize at this point that C and D are, as it were, inseparable. To appoint C alone would have been impossible. Why? Because C, if by himself, would divide the work with A and so assume almost the equal status that has been refused in the first instance to B; a status the more emphasized if C is A's only possible successor. Subordi-

[8] Peter E. Siegle, *New Directions in Liberal Education for Executives* (Chicago: Center for Study of Liberal Education for Adults, 1958), p. 1.

nates must thus number two or more, each being thus kept in order by fear of the other's promotion. When C complains in turn of being overworked (as he certainly will) A will, with the concurrence of C, advise the appointment of two assistants to help C. But he can then avert internal friction only by advising the appointment of two more assistants to help D, whose position is much the same. With this recruitment of E, F, G, and H the promotion of A is now practically certain.

Seven officials are now doing what one did before. This is where Factor 2 comes into operation. For these seven make so much work for each other that all are fully occupied and A is actually working harder than ever. An incoming document may well come before each of them in turn. Official E decides that it falls within the province of F, who places a draft reply before C, who amends it drastically before consulting D, who asks G to deal with it. But G goes on leave at this point, handing the file over to H, who drafts a minute that is signed by D and returned to C, who revises his draft accordingly and lays the new version before A.

What does A do? He would have every excuse for signing the thing unread, for he has many other matters on his mind. Knowing now that he is to succeed W next year, he has to decide whether C or D should succeed to his own office. He had to agree to G's going on leave even if not yet strictly entitled to it. He is worried whether H should not have gone instead, for reasons of health. He has looked pale recently—partly but not solely because of his domestic troubles. Then there is the business of F's special increment of salary for the period of the conference and E's application for transfer to the Ministry of Pensions. A has heard that D is in love with a married typist and that G and F are no longer on speaking terms—no one seems to know why. So A might be tempted to sign C's draft and have done with it. But A is a conscientious man. Beset as he is with problems created by his colleagues for themselves and for him—created by the mere fact of these officials' existence—he is not the man to shirk his duty. He reads through the draft with care, deletes the fussy paragraphs added by C and H, and restores the thing back to the form preferred in the first instance by the able (if quarrelsome) F. He corrects the English—none of these young men can write grammatically—and finally produces the same reply he would have written if officials C and H had never been born. Far more people have taken far longer to produce the same result. No one has been idle. All have done their best. And it is late in the evening before A finally quits his office and begins the return journey to Ealing. The last of the office lights are being turned off in the gathering dusk that marks the end of another day's administrative toil. Among the last to leave, A reflects with bowed shoulders and a wry smile that late hours, like gray hairs, are among the penalties of success.[9]

[9] C. Northcote Parkinson, *Parkinson's Law* (Boston: Houghton Mifflin Company, 1957), pp. 2–7.

3

Traditional Principles of Organization and a Modern Synthesis

ANY study of management must devote a large part of its attention to organization. In spite of its importance and in spite of the attention it has received in the past, even the simplest questions on the subject of organization still cannot be answered with a high degree of certainty. For example, suppose three students have decided to study together for an exam. In all probability they will give little thought to the organization of this activity. However, if they are interested in achieving economical use of their time, they might consider the following questions, all matters of organization:

1. Would it be a good idea to appoint a leader to direct the discussion? To do so might insure a more logical flow of ideas but might reduce the interest of the followers.
2. Should there be rules limiting the extent to which one member of the group may interrupt the other? Or rules limiting the time one member may take up?
3. How should the group decide on which subjects will be reviewed? By vote? By unanimous agreement? By permitting a leader to dictate the outline of the discussion?
4. What penalties or sanctions should be applied to a member who chooses to waste time? Who is to decide when time is actually being wasted?

Even questions on the simplest kind of organization are open to great uncertainty. A short rule book answering these questions would be reassuring, but at our present state of knowledge, such a book is of doubtful value. The character and intelligence of the organization members are factors to be considered. If one member knows more than the others about the subject, the organization might well take this into account; if one member has a greater ability to organize materials or to direct discussion, this might also be significant. Furthermore, it might be useful to ascertain whether the members know each other well and understand each other's point of view.

The illustration of a three man study group points out the main elements that compose an organization. Organization is concerned with channels of communication, with patterns of influence, and with lines of authority and loyalty. The best definition of organization runs in terms of those elements: communication, influence, authority, and loyalty. Some writers emphasize that organization is concerned with the allocation of the tasks among the members of the undertaking. Others emphasize what would seem to be the opposite—the integration of the activities of the members. The first implies the second, that is, if activities are allocated, they must be co-ordinated. While organization can be defined in terms of such allocation and co-ordination, these are some of its aims rather than its essential defining characteristics. Traditionally, discussions of organization emphasize three primary types: line organization, line-and-staff organization, and functional organization.

Types of Organization

Line organization

The simplest type of organization, the line organization, is illustrated in Figure 3-1. Lines of authority are direct, with no advisory or auxiliary activities attached. Such an organization is common in small firms, but is relatively unknown in medium or large undertakings. This form is simple and clear-cut, but provides no room for staff specialists.

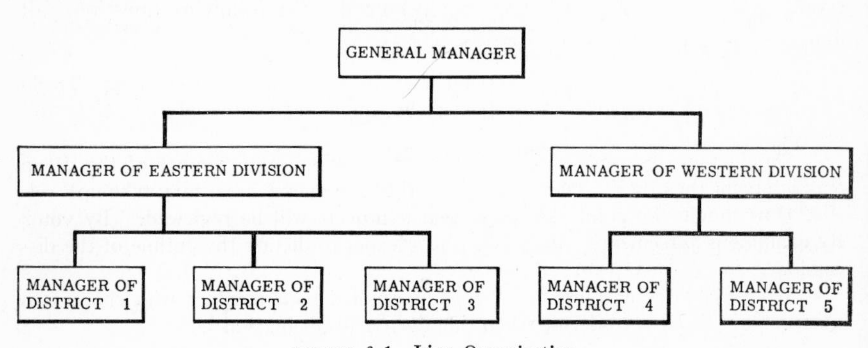

FIGURE 3-1 Line Organization

Line-and-staff organization

Most organizations are more complex than the simple line organization. The line-and-staff organization provides for advisory staff positions, as indicated in Figure 3-2.

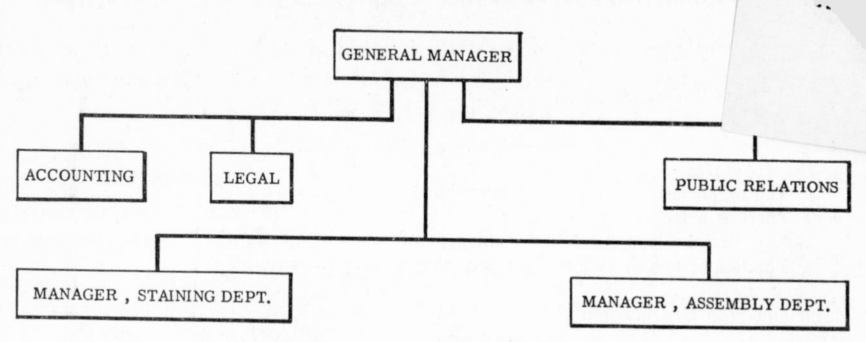

FIGURE 3-2 Line-and-Staff Organization

The difficulty in describing a line-and-staff organization is that the term *staff* does not have a single, unambiguous meaning. The term usually refers to those positions and departments that are of a purely advisory nature. They have the power to recommend, but have no authority to enforce their preferences on other departments. Some writers argue that the line officials are "doers" and the staff members are "thinkers," a distinction subject to obvious limitations. Others suggest that the staff members are concerned with planning rather than carrying out plans. Another way of stating the distinction is that the line gives formal orders to the next lower level, while the staff exerts its influence indirectly, through the line official superior to the particular staff official, not directly to the lower levels.

In actual practice it is often difficult to determine which departments are line or staff. The production and sales departments are normally classified as line. However, what about a small sales department in a company mainly concerned with producing on government contract? Is the accounting department a line or staff department? Is a production control department, which makes out schedules which the production department is expected to follow, a line or staff department? Where does a maintenance department fit into such a classification?

Table 3-1 presents the advantages and disadvantages of line and line-and-staff organizations. The reader should ask himself how useful such a list is likely to be in practice. Is the question of organization normally one of selecting between these two forms? To what extent are the considerations in these lists the important ones in organizational planning?

TABLE 3-1

A TYPICAL LIST OF THE ADVANTAGES AND DISADVANTAGES OF ALTERNATIVE FORMS OF ORGANIZATION

Line Organization

Advantages
1. It is simple.
2. There is a clear-cut division of authority and responsibility.
3. It is stable.

TABLE 3-1 (Continued)

4. It makes for quick action.
5. Discipline is easily maintained.

Disadvantages
1. The organization is rigid and inflexible.
2. There is a lack of expert advice.
3. Key men are loaded to the breaking point.
4. The loss of one or two capable men may cripple the enterprise.

Line-and-Staff Organization

Advantages
1. It is based on planned specialization.
2. It brings expert knowledge to bear upon management.
3. It provides more opportunity for advancement for able workers, in that a greater variety of responsible jobs are available.

Disadvantages
1. There may be confusion about the relation of staff members to line positions.
2. The staff may be ineffective for lack of authority to carry out its recommendations.
3. Line supervisors may resent the activities of staff members, feeling that the prestige and influence of line men suffer from the presence of the specialists.

Functional organization

A survey of operating organizations reveals that few of the so-called "staff" departments are restricted to advisory or planning capacities. Within the area of their specialty, most such departments do, in fact, have some authority over lower line departments. Some staff officers are more influential than some line department heads. The cases of organizations following the strict theory of line-and-staff are rare.

Because of the conflict between theory and actual practice, another term is needed to describe the more usual type of organization; it may be called *functional organization.* This form recognizes that the specialists have authority over line officials at lower levels. Some writers would argue that this authority should be restricted to the area of the specialty, although in actual practice, even this rule would fail to describe what always occurs; it is difficult to confine influence to definite channels.

However, even a "typical" functional organization is complex. It consists of a number of branches or divisions, each of which has staff specialists with counterparts in the central office. The organization becomes functional when these specialists are, in part, responsible to their counterparts in higher headquarters. For example, if the branch personnel officer is partly responsible to the over-all company personnel department (or industrial relations department), the organization is stressing functional lines of influence. In many organizations there is a tendency for marketing people to communicate with marketing people at other levels, production people with production people, and so on.

A central line organization almost always exists along with functional channels; usually a branch specialist will think of himself as reporting primarily to the top line official in that branch. Thus, there is no clear point at which an organization becomes "functional"; it is a matter of degree depending upon the amount of communication and influence conducted through the functional channels.

Unfortunately, the term *functional organization* can be used in other ways. F. W. Taylor applied the expression to a special kind of supervision at the shop level. Taylor believed that the task of the foreman should be split into a number of specialized tasks. The worker, instead of reporting to one boss, would be responsible to eight: a gang boss, a speed boss, a repair boss, an inspector, a time and cost clerk, an instruction card clerk, an order of work clerk, and a disciplinarian. Taylor's aim was to use specialists in supervising the worker. Figure 3-3 illustrates his functional organization. This form is seldom found or approximated in modern practice, because of the confusion created by the large number of bosses. Functional organization of the type first discussed is extremely common, and undoubtedly the most pervasive form, in spite of the fact that it also creates difficulties in defining exactly "who is boss."

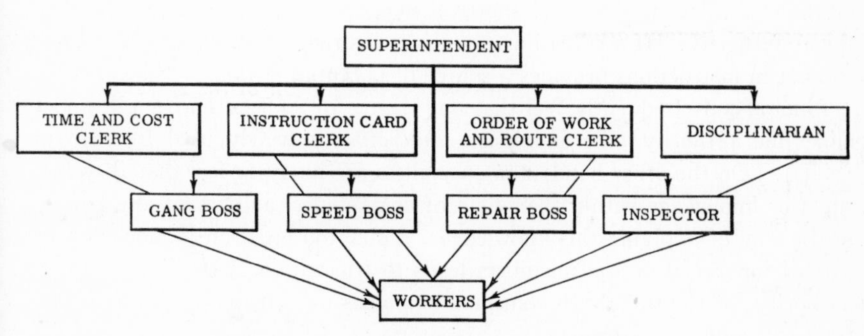

FIGURE 3-3 Taylor's Functional Organization

A Choice Among These Forms

The choice among the three forms of organization discussed is not a matter of selecting one package, but determining the right balance among the three. At one extreme is the line organization with no staff specialists at all; it is rare except in small undertakings. At the other extreme is a form of functional organization that deemphasizes the position of the line organization. Since there may be a tendency for the vertical functional channels to pull apart, this extreme can present special difficulties of co-ordination. Consequently, some stress on the line principle is almost universal. The pure line-and-staff organization falls in between, but as has already been stated, the purely advisory character of the staff positions is seldom maintained in actual practice.

Thus the typical organization is best described as a line-and-staff organization with some measure of functional authority for certain specialists, or as a functional organization with some limitations on functional authority. A management that attempts to follow a strict line-and-staff theory may try to suppress functional channels, but usually fails to destroy them completely. Management cannot permit the line to be undermined by such channels. The problem is one of balance between the line and functional principles. Staff departments almost always manage to acquire a degree of functional authority. Management frequently faces the need to keep this authority within bounds.

The Human Aspects of Line and Staff

The relations between the line and staff elements (or the line and functional elements) of an organization are a constant source of friction. Study after study has revealed tension between line and staff officials. Some writers would argue that the tension arises from the violation of the principle of unity of command (to be discussed shortly) whenever staff officials assume functional authority. If a subordinate receives instructions from several sources, conflict in instructions provides a source of potential strife.

Line officials frequently feel that any degree of staff authority will undermine line authority (the expression *undermine* is widely used by such officials). On the other hand, staff specialists are likely to feel that they have superior knowledge within their field of competence, and resent any barriers in the way of applying this knowledge. Thus, too great an influence on the part of functional or staff members leads to frustration in the line; too little authority for the staff, with continual emphasis on "channels," leads to frustration among the specialists.

There are several ways to handle the problem. One is to restrict the staff to a purely advisory role. A well-known writer on organization even suggests that the staff offices be abolished whenever possible. The development of specialization in management, however, is a natural and inevitable outcome of the growing complexity of business, and line officials are continually more dependent on those with special skills and special knowledge. It is reasonable to accept the need for specialists and to recognize that these officials are likely to influence their subordinates. That this may lead to conflict is one of the "facts of life" that management must face. The answer is to improve the communication between line and staff—to train the staff to be aware of line attitudes and sensitivities and to train the line to respect the value of special skills. Avoidance of conflict is only one objective of organizational planning, and in some cases may be compromised to permit attainment of other objectives.

The Uses and Abuses of Charts and Manuals

Figure 3-4 presents a chart of an actual company organization. Study of the chart will give insight into organization in practice.

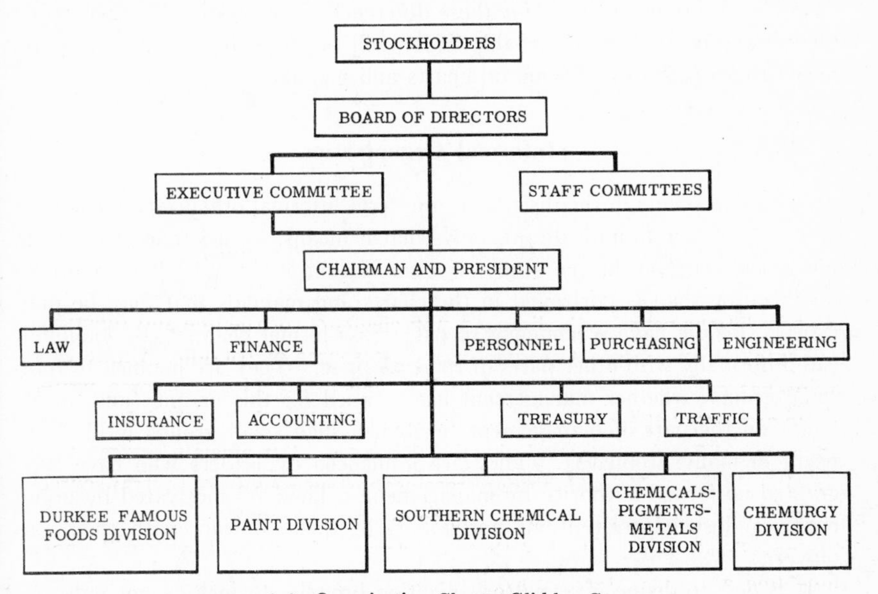

FIGURE 3-4 Organization Chart—Glidden Company

A great deal is not shown on such charts. For example, informal lines of communication undoubtedly exist throughout the organization; officials on the same level have varying degrees of influence over other parts of the organization. Vertical lines drawn from box to box provide little insight into the superior-subordinate relationships involved; some superiors may maintain a close control over their subordinates; others may encourage subordinates to make important decisions on their own; some departments may be highly decentralized, and others an integral part of the main undertaking.

However, organization charts are not useless. They are a form of communication. When there is doubt about who reports to whom, they help resolve such doubt. They help new employees learn how they fit into the over-all undertaking. They give a quick view to outsiders of the component departments of the enterprise. They may assist in resolving organizational disputes. Charts are only a beginning to the understanding of organization; but overuse of charts, the constant need to refer to them to settle jurisdictional disputes, may be symptomatic of a poor organization rather than an effective one.

Large undertakings frequently go beyond the simple drawing of charts. They design organization manuals, which define in words the relations among departments and officials and which help clarify jurisdictions; they present lists of responsibilities and duties of company officials, with indication of departments or officials higher and lower in the hierarchy. Opinions differ on the extent to which stress should be placed on such manuals, and the degree of refinement desirable in the definition of duties. Later sections of this chapter will present reasons for these differences in viewpoint. Organization planning is not yet, and probably never will be, something that can be reduced to a routine of drawing up charts and manuals.

Informal Organization

At several points in the discussion, the term informal organization has been used. It is time to indicate precisely what it means, for it is one of the most important concepts in the study of organization. There is much more to organization than is portrayed in the charts and manuals that may be published. People have a tendency to cut across formal channels to communicate informally with other parts of the enterprise. They are inclined to form small groups, whether management has planned for this or not (and an attempt on the part of management to abolish such small groups is likely to result in many problems). They are influenced by leaders who have been granted no formal authority by management. They are motivated by group norms and social conventions not a part of their contract with their employers.

It is best to define informal organization broadly, to include not only unplanned communication and group formation, but also the customs, social norms, mores, and ideals that are an important feature of such communication and such groups. So defined, it is clear that informal organization is a pervasive feature of all undertakings. The cliques of workers or managers that form at all levels are important illustrations, as are the restrictive devices which discourage employees from producing more than informally determined group quotas. Also included are patterns of influence that some members of the organization develop, even though these go far beyond the organization plan.

It is a mistake to conclude that informal organization is essentially destructive. It is true that it does at times make the higher manager's job more difficult. Nevertheless, it is clear that informal organization is necessary to the functioning of formal organization. It helps tie the structure together. It gives the members a feeling of belonging. Membership in small groups contributes to a sense of security as well as to individual satisfaction; even the "grapevine," which disturbs some observers, plays a constructive role in filling in gaps in the formal communication system.

Later chapters will contain material on small groups which will broaden the discussion of informal organization. The point made here is that informal organization is an inevitable attribute of any undertaking. An understanding of it will contribute to the knowledge of employee morale, motivation, and productivity.

Some Traditional Principles of Organization

Traditional discussions of organization have concentrated on "universal principles." Unfortunately, there has never been a consensus on what these principles are. A complete listing of such principles would run into the hundreds. There are, however, a few widely known ones that have become part of the language of management. Four of them will be discussed here.

1. Unity of Command
2. Span of Control
3. The Exception Principle
4. The Scalar Principle

Unity of command

Henri Fayol, a French management theorist, deserves credit for publicizing the principle of unity of command, but no doubt the idea had occurred to many managers long before his time. The principle is well known in this form: no man can serve two bosses. In management texts, it usually reads: no member of an organization should report to more than one superior.

In such simple form this principle is controversial, for as a description of actual organizational practice, it meets many exceptions. A survey of large organizations reveals numerous cases in which people are reporting to more than one superior. However, the proponents of the principle are not interested in describing actual practice, but *prescribing* correct practice. There are many cases in which reporting to two or more superiors has resulted in confusion and loss of productivity. Such situations are conducive to conflict and poor morale. Nevertheless, the cure should not be a rigid rule prohibiting everything but a unified command.

The trouble with the unity of command idea is that if pushed to its extreme, it requires that all instructions—indeed all influence of any kind—must flow through one superior to his subordinates. Many managers feel that it is desirable for some influence to flow more directly from those who have specialized knowledge to those who will put such knowledge into action. Previously discussed was the "functional authority" that certain specialized departments may have over people lower down the line. It is common for a company with several branches to permit a staff officer in the central offices to have some influence over subordinates in a branch. For example, a central marketing department or a central purchasing department may contact its counterpart at lower levels, the branch marketing department or the branch purchasing department, without contacting the branch manager. Certainly it is important to keep the branch manager informed on important decisions, but it is not imperative that he must be checked on all matters that arise. To require the central purchasing department to go through line channels in all cases, along with all the other business that must be conducted, could cause congestion in those channels. Such a situation could lead to confusion and conflict, but the cost of slow, indirect communication must be weighed against the cost of potential conflict.

A specific example may make this point clear. In manufacturing concerns, production control departments are frequently responsible for scheduling work. The line production foreman generally accepts the schedules as authoritative, even though the organization chart shows no line of authority from production control to the foreman. The foreman considers his supervisor to be his boss, but he is willing to accept instructions from other directions. If a conflict arises, he will no doubt appeal to his line superior, but this does not deny that the production control department normally exerts a direct influence.

In the light of such exceptions to the unity of command idea, some writers suggest a different wording of the principle. For example, it could be stated: no member of an organization should report to more than one superior on any single function. In other words, a foreman may report to his line superior on output and efficiency, at the same time accepting the authority of production control on scheduling. This way of stating the principle is more realistic.

One last illustration will summarize this discussion of the principle of unity of command. It is common for the president of a corporation to report, not to one superior, but to a board of directors. In some cases the president may look upon the chairman as his superior, but more commonly he thinks of himself as reporting to the entire board. The principle of unity of command, as usually stated, would imply that this arrangement is unsound; yet the widespread use of this organizational pattern suggests that it is workable.

The whole question of unity of command needs a restatement in a more flexible form: each undertaking should periodically investigate the possibility that some members are unduly confused by the lack of clarity in or multiplicity of channels of authority. Such an investigation may suggest that a simplification or clarification of lines of authority is in order.

Span of control

Like unity of command, the famous principle of span of control arouses doubt when expressed in an extreme form. The principle states that there is a limit to the number of subordinates that should report to one superior. Some writers (V. A. Graicunas in "Relationship in Organization," in L. Gulick and L. Urwick, eds., *Papers on the Science of Administration,* pp. 181–187) state precisely that five or eight people are the maximum number one man can supervise.

Supervision of too many people can lead to trouble. The superior will not have the time to devote to any one subordinate to do an adequate job of supervision. He may be distracted by the large number of contacts required in his position so that he neglects important questions of policy. Some theorists have pointed out that as the number of people reporting to a superior increases arithmetically, the number of possible interrelationships among them and with the superior increases geometrically, rapidly reaching a point at which the structure becomes too complex for management by a single individual.

The critics of the principle have shown that to reduce the number of subordinates reporting to each official may require an increase in the number of tiers in the organization. This, in turn, will increase the distance from top management to the bottom of the hierarchy and may mean less effective upward and downward communication. Some companies have deliberately increased the span of control to numbers that advocates of the principle would pronounce dangerous. Sears-Roebuck, for example, has widened the span with the objective of reducing the amount of supervision from above. This policy is claimed to contribute to decentralization, and thus to greater morale and greater initiative on the part of subordinate managers.

The appropriate span depends upon a number of considerations. It is easy to supervise a large number of subordinates doing routine jobs and located in a single room; but it is difficult to supervise highly diverse and specialized personnel scattered widely geographically. The ability of the employees, their willingness to assume responsibility, and the general attitude of management towards delegation and decentralization should influence the decisions on span of control.

A restatement of the principle converts it into an obvious suggestion: organizational planners should consider whether too many or too few subordinates are reporting to superiors. Some may object that this restatement weakens the point, but this is no doubt better than the encouragement of mechanical applications which might result from stronger versions.

The exception principle

Frederick W. Taylor advocated another widely accepted generalization, the exception principle. According to this concept, decisions which recur frequently should be reduced to a routine and delegated to subordinates, leaving more important issues and exceptional matters to superiors. Thus, the president of a company should not be concerned with breakdowns in the plumbing which can be corrected by maintenance personnel. The president may see to it that proper accounting procedures are adopted. Once they are installed, however, he should not have to waste his time in ascertaining that the debits and credits are posted in the proper ledgers. Relieving higher executives from details allows them more time to devote to top policy and to crises that arise.

The exception principle is sound under analysis. Unlike the principles already discussed, it is invariably stated in a form that makes its application a matter of degree. It does not provide a simple rule for determining what should be reduced to a routine and delegated, and what should not, but it does suggest that managers will profit by investigating possibilities of greater delegation. Many managers have given little thought to the possibility of delegating a large proportion of their less important decisions, or even to the possibility that a systematic approach to such decisions may reduce them to a routine. Such managers are frequently so involved in the decision-making process that they neglect important issues.

In a sense a great deal of mechanization consists of replacing human decisions with automatic machine responses. Automation (which will be discussed in a later chapter) applies the exception principle; through automation we delegate to a machine or a group of machines the power to correct their own variations from predetermined standards. Humans determine what those standards are to be, but servomechanisms built into the equipment determine whether the standards are being met and, if not, what corrective action is necessary. The exception principle is one principle of organization that stands up to close examination without requiring a restatement in a different form.

The scalar principle

The scalar principle is more difficult to specify. If it means simply that every undertaking should have some kind of hierarchy involving superior-subordinate relationships, it may be widely applicable. The need for such a hierarchy is apparently pervasive; even democracy cannot be defined in terms of its complete absence, for democratic groups find it necessary to develop means (whether by election or other devices) to set up hierarchies to make decisions. Perhaps only small groups of people who meet for recreation or conversation manage to avoid some kind of vertical structure.

Some of the advocates of the scalar principle mean much more when they write on the subject. They imply that most organizations could place greater stress on hierarchy, and greater stress on definition of responsibilities up and down the line. When applied this way, the scalar principle becomes controversial. The extent to which supervision from above is desirable, and the extent to which definition of responsibilities is productive, are matters of degree on which this principle is unclear. In planning an organization it may be appropriate to begin with the vertical structure of authority, but this provides little guidance in determining what the character and extent of that authority should be.

Other Principles

A full discussion of only a few of the most famous principles has been presented. The principles of organization are innumerable, but not all are on the same level of abstraction. For example, Fayol favored a principle of *appropriateness,* that seeks to fit the human and material organization to the "objects, resources, and needs of the undertaking." This is a broad principle that could apply to engineering and medicine as well as to organization. Some so-called principles are simply definitions, such as that of *co-ordination,* which means "to unite and correlate all activities." Others are expressions of ethical views.

Even those writers who believe that the principles of organization are universal cannot agree on what the principles are. It is true that Colonel Urwick has been able to fit the principles from the works of six different writers into what he calls a "coherent and logical pattern,"[1] but not all of his readers are able to see the order that is apparent to him. Table 3-2 contains a list of some of the best known principles, with brief statements of each. The reader should evaluate their strengths and weaknesses.

TABLE 3-2

SOME WELL-KNOWN PRINCIPLES OF ORGANIZATION *

Principle of the Objective: Each part and subdivision of the organization should be the expression of a definite purpose in harmony with the objective of the undertaking.

Principle of Authority and Responsibility: Responsibility for the execution of work must be accompanied by the authority to control and direct the means of doing the work.

Principle of Ultimate Authority: The responsibility of a higher authority for the acts of its subordinates is absolute.

Principle of Assignment of Duties: The duties of every person in an organization should be confined as far as possible to the performance of a single leading function.

Principle of Definition: The duties, authority, responsibility, and relations of everyone in the organizational structure should be clearly and completely prescribed in writing.

Principle of Homogeneity: An organization, to be efficient and to operate without friction, should be so designed that only duties and activities that are similar or are directly related are combined for execution by a particular individual or a particular group.

Principle of Organization Effectiveness: The final test of an industrial organization is smooth and frictionless operation.

Organization should determine the selection of personnel rather than personnel determine the nature of organization.

A member does not, by delegation, divest himself of responsibility.

Two members should not delegate responsibility to the same member.

[1] Urwick, *Elements of Administration* (London, Sir Isaac Pitman, Second Edition, 1947) p. 118.

TABLE 3-2 (Continued)

The number of stages of delegation of responsibilty should be as few as practicable.

Responsibilities should be defined by identifying and then grouping the elements of administration.

Responsibilities delegated and reserved must be mutually exclusive.

A particular responsibility is better performed by one member than by two or more.

Whereas organizational principle is a science, the practice of organization is an art.

* Adapted from L. P. Alford and H. Russell Beatty, *Principles of Industrial Management* (New York: The Ronald Press Company, 1951), pp. 159–160; and Alvin Brown, *Organization of Industry* (Englewood Cliffs, N. J.: Prentice-Hall, Inc., 1947), pp. 2–8.

Alternative Approaches to Organization

It is apparent that there is a conflict in views on organization. There are a number of schools of thought on the subject, some stressing the need for direction from above, others the need for freedom below; some advocating greater clarification of functions, and others warning against too exact a confinement of personnel in neat boxes. It will be informative to examine these alternative approaches to organization, for there is a great deal of truth in each.

Most of the remainder of this chapter will be devoted to reviewing seven approaches to organization. The number seven is arbitrary—it would be possible to combine or split them. Few writers have adhered strictly to one approach. Each approach is in a sense an "ideal type," which some writers approximate, but which few hold in a pure form. The advantage of constructing such ideal types is to clarify the elements that go into making a more balanced synthesis. The seven approaches are:

1. Formalism
2. The Spontaneity Approach
3. The Participation Approach
4. Challenge and Response
5. Specialization
6. The Directive Approach
7. Checks and Balances

Formalism

The central theme of formalism is that each member of an undertaking must know precisely what his position is, to whom he is responsible, and what his relation to other job-holders is to be. The emphasis is on the delineation of functions and responsibilities. This line of thought leads to the following specific recommendations:

1. Organization charts should be carefully drawn, prominently displayed, and strictly followed.

2. Detailed job descriptions should be drawn up for all important positions.
3. Definite channels of command should be planned. Rules should prohibit the skipping of ranks or cutting across channels.
4. Unity of command should be maintained.
5. The planning of positions and departments should precede the consideration of particular individuals who might fill those positions.

The proponents of formalism claim a number of advantages for the approach. Definite boundaries should reduce conflict. "Empire-building" is restrained. The overlapping of responsibilities is avoided. Gaps in responsibilities are filled. "Passing the buck" becomes more difficult. More exact standards of performance are established and these act as a motivating force. A sense of security arises from clarification of the task. Opportunities for favoritism and "politics" are reduced because evaluation and placement can be based on more objective specifications.

How can these conclusions be supported? It is desirable to investigate the assumptions on which they rest. The following views are the most probable bases for formalistic organization theory:

1. Members of an organization are unable to work out relations among their positions without thorough guidance and planning.
2. Some members are aggressive and will trespass on the domain of others unless clear boundaries are drawn. This arouses hostility which may reduce the effectiveness of the undertaking.
3. Some members are reluctant to assume responsibilities unless assigned a definite task.
4. Members generally prefer the security of a definite task to the freedom of a vaguely defined one.
5. Delineation of clear-cut responsibilities offers an incentive by providing a more exact basis for evaluation.
6. It is possible to predict in advance the responsibilities that will be required in the future.
7. Members are prone to conflict and if this conflict is permitted to arise it takes a toll in personal energy and productivity.
8. Justice is more certain if the enterprise is organized on an objective, impersonal basis.

These assumptions have validity. However, they are not completely correct for all individuals and all undertakings. Furthermore, there are strong critics of formalism who attack it as mechanistic—emphasizing orderly structures rather than people. The critics are less worried about duplication and overlapping than the rigidity that formalism may encourage. Some managers favor the skipping of ranks. There is a fear that too much stress on a neat structure may impede informal communication and may cause congestion in the formal channels.

There has been a trend away from formalism in some firms. In a recent reorganization of General Electric, only loose job descriptions have been written, providing a short list of things a member could not do rather than a long list of what he could do. General Motors has been moving in the same direction. Paradoxically, these companies are extremely large ones in which the advantages of formalism would appear to be particularly strong.

Formalism is thus a controversial issue. It is probably best to look upon it as a matter of degree that can be extended more advantageously in some situations than in others. The task of management is to decide how far this tendency should be carried, and this involves a comparison of its benefits and costs. Before this is possible, the advantages of other approaches to organization require attention.

The spontaneity approach

In recent years there has been a growing body of thought at the opposite extreme from formalism—one which advocates scope for the spontaneous formation of groups and communication systems with a minimum of direction from above. The famous Hawthorne studies have been a strong influence in this direction, especially in their heavy stress on the importance of informal organization. Informal organization may be the most effective co-ordinating force, providing human satisfaction and stimulating co-operation and productivity. Changes in formal organization should take into account the possible impact on informal organization. Some theorists argue that formal organization should be built around the "natural" informal groups that develop spontaneously.

The assumptions underlying this approach are obviously different from those of formalism:

1. All the required relationships cannot be planned in advance because requirements change unpredictably.
2. Spontaneous relationships are direct and economical and adjust to changing conditions.
3. Spontaneous relations are more satisfying and lead to co-operation and high morale.
4. High morale is essential to high productivity.

Formalists would attack the tendency toward overlapping, gaps, insecurity, vagueness, and injustice which might arise without prior planning. Many studies demonstrate that informal groups can be restrictive rather than constructive. Too much can be made of "getting along" when some people need to be told what to do. Perhaps the effect of this approach, which is part of the recent emphasis on "human relations," is to create complacent "organization men," highly cooperative, but not effective individualists.

The participation approach

The emphasis on participation is another recent trend in organization theory. Along with the spontaneity approach, it underlies what is called "human relations" in management. Advocates of this view stress the need for a flow of ideas from the bottom of the organization as well as the top. Participation involves face to face relationships which lead, it is claimed, to fuller understanding, to a pooling of diverse talents, and to a greater willingness to carry through with decisions once they are made. The result is more satisfaction and productivity and the development of individuals for positions of higher responsibility. Participation helps make members more amenable to change. It is also consistent with the democratic values of Western society.

There are a number of ways in which participation can occur. Committees, conferences, suggestion systems, and joint consultative schemes are media of group effort. Many argue, however, that participation depends mainly upon the training and attitudes of the members—on the willingness of managers to take an interest in the ideas of subordinates and to consult with them on impending decisions. Thus, participation can assume either a formal or informal character.

Some assumptions underlying the participation approach are:

1. Joint effort makes decisions more acceptable—presumably even when the ideas of some participants are not incorporated in the final outcome.
2. Members understand best what they have helped create.
3. Familiarity breeds respect.
4. Human beings enjoy regular association with each other.
5. People want to take part in decisions and all of them are capable of doing so.

Study of these assumptions will raise doubts. It is not clear that group endeavor is superior to individual endeavor in all cases; the dramatic results achieved by forceful individualists cannot be ignored. Joint decisions may be muddy compromises. Joint action may result in fuzzy responsibility. Again there is the "organization man" argument; participation may be a disguise for manipulation, providing another device for assuring compliance.

Despite these limitations, the participation movement remains one of the strongest trends in management circles. The complete absence of participation is inconceivable, even in a totalitarian society; the other extreme, which would amount to democratic voting on all policies, is unworkable. A mean position, rather than an extreme, on the use of this view is no doubt appropriate.

Challenge and response

The next approach stresses the need for enthusiasm and initiative throughout the organization. It asserts that this will be forthcoming when the members, particularly those on managerial levels, are granted sufficient autonomy and wide enough scope to make their job interesting and challenging. The advocates of this view favor the "light touch" in supervision, and the use of indirect measurements and standards as opposed to direct controls. "Decentralization" and "delegation" are the bywords of this school of thought. It is called the challenge-and-response approach.

Peter Drucker, the leading spokesman of this view, argues that departments should be organized around products rather than skills and processes. Such product departments are more conducive to autonomy, while functional departments are almost necessarily parts of a larger whole. Drucker prefers "flat" or "horizontal" structures, and thus opposes limitation of the span of control. He feels that specialists must remain in their place to assure that they do not interfere with the freedom of the line managers.

Such a view rests on the following implicit assumptions:

1. People want to work and work best when not watched closely.
2. The errors that might be avoided by close supervision are less costly than the harm done to morale and initiative.
3. A constant flow of innovation is imperative and autonomy is conducive to such innovation.
4. There is a tremendous pent-up supply of managerial talent waiting to be released if challenges are applied.

This approach may be overly optimistic about the readiness of men to act responsibly when giving autonomy, and overly pessimistic about their tendency to mediocrity when under control. It might be wise to recognize that some people are incompetent, others lazy, and still others disloyal or dishonest. Decentralization has its limits—in some activities, the economies of scale are too great to warrant their dispersion over the various departments or branches. Centralized policies enforcing a degree of uniformity may be important to the maintenance of a sense of "corporate integrity." Initiative and originality in the branches are more important in some industries than in others.

Thus, provision for challenge and response is not an absolute ideal which can be reached by formula. The approach fills an important need, however, by stressing that organization planning is more than the construction of neat patterns; it is concerned with people who have potentialities that must be tapped if the enterprise is to survive.

The specialization approach

Writers on management have long maintained that a central objective of organization is the allocation of functions and responsibilities among departments and individuals. In fact, some theorists define organization in these terms. All organization involves some specialization of this sort. However, what is called here the "specialization approach" goes further. It advocates that the division of labor be carried to a high degree of refinement, so that each job is restricted to a "single, simple task." The approach also favors organization around skills, processes, or subpurposes to achieve the full benefits of specialized skills and knowledge. In this respect, the specialization approach is opposed to Drucker's view, reviewed above, that organization should be based on end products. Those who stress specialization believe that experts should be introduced at various levels of the organization, and that they must be given sufficient authority to see to it that their superior knowledge is applied. F. W. Taylor advocated such views in some of his works, and this led him to favor "functional organization."

This approach, like the others, is based upon certain assumptions, not always explicitly expressed in the literature:

1. Simple tasks are easier to learn and lead to higher productivity by concentrating attention on a narrow area.
2. Supervision is more competent and successful when departments are organized around special skills or processes.
3. The problem of co-ordinating functional departments is less important than the benefits of specialization they produce.
4. The problem of maintaining interest in a narrow task is not serious.
5. Line officials will not be seriously "undermined" by the authority or influence of functional specialists.
6. There are economies of scale in the centralized management of particular specialized functions.

Many research studies suggest that specialization at the work place can be overdone. Narrow tasks may dull interest, induce monotony, increase fatigue, and remove the stimulus that comes from seeing the job as a larger whole. Specialization creates problems of co-ordination—the conflict between staff specialists and line officials is too common to be ignored. Functional organization may become an obstacle to decentralization.

The retreat from the stress on specialization is one indication of its weakness. Nevertheless, specialization must be one of the major concerns of organization planning. It may become more important as technological change makes enterprise more dependent upon the skills of experts.

The directive approach

There are trends in organization theory. One approach that is outmoded in Western democracies is the emphasis on direction from top management. However, one of the major stresses in organization planning is that on hierarchy—on the authority of superiors over subordinates. Extreme advocates of "directivitis" emphasize the need for tight control from above. The stress would be on supervision, reports, penalties, and other controls.

Although there is little literature supporting a directive approach, it has some advantages worth stressing.

1. Planning and direction from above may assure co-operation.
2. If superior knowledge exists at the center, it may be well to assure that this knowledge is not wasted through noncompliance with directions.

3. It would appear that many organization members do not perform effectively, either because of inertia or ignorance, without guidance from above.

The discussion of other alternatives, particularly the need for challenge and response and spontaneity, indicates the limits of too much emphasis on central direction. In addition, there are ideological objections to methods that are, or appear to be, in conflict with the democratic philosophy of Western society.

Checks and balances

The last of the approaches has its most familiar applications in the political sphere. The Constitution of the United States, for example, is based, in part, on the view that power in one department or branch must be offset by countervailing power elsewhere. It is widely recognized that too great a concentration of power in one place may lead to irresponsible action (or inaction).

The notion of checks and balances has its applications in industry as well as in government. The view that inspection departments must be separate from the activities to be inspected is one illustration. The widely accepted opinion that auditing departments must be independent is another. The systems by which boards of directors represent a diversity of interests, with "outside" as well as "inside" directors, are attempts to check the power of top executives.

The assumptions underlying this approach are:

1. Power corrupts and thus must be restrained.
2. Some members of organizations place personal goals ahead of enterprise needs.

There may be doubts that effective leadership can develop where checks predominate. Instead of fostering co-operation, checks and balances place one department against the other. If teamwork is the goal, it may be desirable to keep obstacles to such teamwork at a minimum. Each undertaking must consider what price it is willing to pay to check irresponsibility—the chief price being the reduction in interest, vigor, and co-operation that dispersion of authority may entail.

Toward a Modern Synthesis

Seven approaches to organization are six too many. Yet all of the approaches contain important truths. Each is based on assumptions that are sometimes relevant. Each suggests structural arrangements worthy of consideration. The manager will do well to consider all of the approaches and fit them to his needs; this is preferable to concluding that a one-sided attack on any problem is adequate.

A modern synthesis is needed to pull together ideas from all of the approaches. Such a synthesis would start with the recognition that each approach is a matter of degree. There are degrees of formalism, from the planning of each minor activity to the complete absence of formal planning. There are degrees of direction, from extreme absolution to the complete dispersion of authority. There are degrees in the application of line, staff, and functional organization. Different principles of organization have different degrees of importance.

Each existing organization contains elements of all of the approaches. The problem of planning an organization is one of finding the balance appropriate to the circumstances—a balance to fit the objective and make an optimum use of the available resources. Thus, the organization appropriate for a firm doing routine business with little technological change will differ from that suited to a firm in electronics or atomic energy. The organization keyed to highly educated, highly motivated personnel will not bring the best results in one dependent on migratory labor.

More attention must be paid to the problems of diagnosis and prescription in planning organizations. The organizer might well approach his client in the same way the physician approaches his patient. Is there something wrong? What are the symptoms? What fundamental difficulties do these symptoms suggest? What kinds of treatment will best fit this diagnosis? The analogy with medicine is particularly apt. Like the doctor, the organizer may frequently have difficulty with his diagnosis. However, he should never apply the cure until he has some views on the disease. Bleeding as a universal treatment for every ailment in medicine has long been outmoded.

Two tendencies have hindered progress in the field of organization. One is the adherence to dogmas based on hidden assumptions and casual observation. The other is the inclination on the part of the critics of these dogmas to disregard all existing hypotheses. The main task of this chapter has been to move toward a synthesis of approaches, drawing on the wisdom of the past to gain a fuller and more flexible attack on the problem of organization in the future.

Bibliographical Note

The works cited here are products of the twentieth century. One of the earliest works on organization is Henri Fayol's *General and Industrial Management* (first published in French in 1916; in English in 1949). Fayol's book has an uncertain status in the field of management: some authorities consider it a profound pioneering work, while others note its superficiality as compared with scientific endeavors in other fields. Most of Fayol's principles ran in the direction of formalism, as did many other leading works on management. Among these are Lyndall Urwick, *Elements of Administration* (1943); Paul E. Holden, Lounsbury S. Fish, and Hubert L. Smith, *Top-Management Organization and Control* (1949); E. Peterson and E. G.

Plowman, *Business Organization and Management* (3rd edition, 1953); and Ralph C. Davis, *The Fundamentals of Top Management* (1952).

Some early writers broke away from formalism, placing more stress on the sociological character of organization. Mary Parker Follett was a pioneer in this direction. Some of her articles have been edited by H. C. Metcalf and L. Urwick in *Dynamic Administration* (1941). The "human relations" movement of the 1930's and 1940's led the reaction against formalism. Elton Mayo's *The Human Problems of an Industrial Civilization* (1933) and *The Social Problems of an Industrial Civilization* (1945) are broad philosophical statements of this development. Much more empirical are the volumes on the Hawthorne studies, partly influenced by Mayo. The outstanding discussion of the Hawthorne studies is F. J. Roethlisberger and W. J. Dickson, *Management and the Worker* (1939). The flow of "human relations" literature since that time is too voluminous to list here.

Peter Drucker's *The Practice of Management* (1954) is the leading expression of what we have called the challenge and response approach to organization. Drucker's effective writing style has gained him wide attention in business circles; some of his views are controversial but highly provocative. Drucker's works (including earlier volumes) have done more than any other to publicize the decentralization movement in large American firms.

Ernest Dale's *Planning and Developing the Company Organization Structure* (1952) takes a less dogmatic position than is usual. Dale's volume covers empirical studies of business firms and shows considerable judgment in relating traditional prescriptions to the circumstances of individual undertakings.

Citations of a different type of literature on organization will appear at the end of Chapter 5.

Questions and Problems

1. Consider an organization (business, social, or governmental) with which you are familiar.
   (a) Draw an organization chart.
   (b) What patterns of communication, influence, authority and loyalty are most crucial?
   (c) Is it a line, line-and-staff, or functional organization?
   (d) How much influence do the staff or functional officers have? Are they purely advisory or do they exert functional authority?
   (e) Is there any evidence of conflict between line and staff officials?
   (f) Does the organization chart reveal the true character of the organization?
   (g) Is there any evidence of informal organization?
2. Which of the following departments or positions is line, staff, or functional?
   (a) The plant manager
   (b) The accounting department
   (c) The treasurer
   (d) The foreman
   (e) The board of directors
   (f) The executive vice-president
   (g) The personnel director
   (h) The maintenance department
3. Compare the extent of participation in several classes you attend. Does participation in this context mean the same thing that it means in industry?
4. Does classroom organization violate the principle of span of control?

5. What is the relation between the exception principle and delegation of authority?

6. Are all managers equally successful in applying the exception principle? Explain. Do you consider this principle important?

7. Do all organizations familiar to you comply with the scalar principle? Are all organizations hierarchical?

8. Is there a conflict between the following approaches to organization?
   (a) The directive approach and the participation approach
   (b) Formalism and the directive approach
   (c) Formalism and participation
   (d) Specialization and challenge-and-response
   (e) Other pairs

9. The text has presented seven approaches to organization. Can you think of other ways to classify them, involving a smaller or larger number?

10. The authors express the view that organization planning requires achievement of a *balance* among the approaches to organization. The appropriate balance will vary from one undertaking to another.
   (a) Why has military organization stressed formalism and direction from above?
   (b) What balance among the approaches would work best for a charitable fund raising drive?
   (c) Industrial organization has become more participative and less directive in recent decades. What is the reason for this?
   (d) There has been a trend towards decentralization of management in many large American firms. What is the reason for this? Does this trend have limitations?

11. How could the concepts of diagnosis and prescription be fitted into the problem of organization?

12. Some critics of committees would like to reduce them to a minimum or abolish them. Do you agree? Discuss.

13. Even as early as Adam Smith's *Wealth of Nations* (1776) there was recognition of the advantages of specialization. Why has any question been raised about this trend in recent years?

14. Why did the authors of the Constitution of the United States stress checks and balances? Should industry imitate this emphasis?

15. In recent years there have been strong criticisms of the traditional principles of organization. What are the reasons for these criticisms? What kind of knowledge could take their place?

16. Is informal organization essential to industrial operations? Discuss.

4

Extracts and Cases on Organization

THE preceding chapter has presented several views of organization. This chapter will start by quoting a number of the outstanding writers on the subject. No doubt, each author makes the most convincing argument for his respective position. The reader, however, should approach each extract critically, asking himself whether there is consistency from one writer to the next. The reader may also find it useful to fit these extracts into the seven approach framework of the preceding chapter.[1]

The cases that follow present an opportunity to apply the principles learned so far to problems of organization. Again the approach should be critical. Do the principles tell more about the cases than does ordinary common sense? Is the synthesis of the seven approaches helpful in diagnosing the situations in these cases? Or are the skills achieved by studying the cases themselves more useful than any listing of principles or attempts at theory.

Extracts

EXTRACT A

Elements of Administration (L. Urwick)

. . . in good engineering practice design must come first. Similarly, in good social practice design should come first. Logically it is inconceivable

[1] The authors have deliberately avoided passages explaining the significance of each extract. The reader should consider where each extract fits into the general framework.

that any individual should be appointed to a position carrying a large salary, without a clear idea of the part which that position is meant to play in the general social pattern of which it is a component, the responsibilities and relationships attached to it, and the standard of performance which is expected in return for the expenditure. It is as stupid as to attempt to order an expensive piece of machinery without a specification.

It is cruel because the main sufferers from a lack of design in organization are the individuals who work in the undertaking. If an employer buys a man without any clear idea in his own mind of the exact duties for which he requires him and the kind of qualifications needed to discharge those duties, the chances are that he will blame the man if the results do not correspond with his vague notion of what he wanted him for.

It is wasteful because unless jobs are clearly put together along lines of functional specialization it is impossile to train new men to succeed to positions as the incumbents are promoted, resign, or retire. A man cannot be trained to take over another's special personal experience: and yet if jobs are fitted to men rather than men to jobs that is precisely what the employer must try to do. Consequently, every change in personnel becomes a crisis, an experiment in personalities . . .

It is inefficient, because if an organization is not founded on principles, then those directing it have nothing to fall back on but personalities . . . the administrator who tries to substitute amiability for definite planning in questions of organization will find sooner rather than later that "the personal touch" issues in an epidemic of personal touchiness. Unless there are principles on which he can fall back and which are understood by everyone in the undertaking, it is inevitable that in matters of promotion and similar issues men will start "playing politics." . . .

In short, a very large proportion of the friction and confusion in current society, with its manifest consequences in human suffering, may be traced directly to faulty organization in the structural sense. A machine will not run smoothly when fundamental engineering principles have been ignored in its construction. Attempts to run it will inevitably impose quite unnecessary and unbearable strain on its components.[2]

Extract B

Top-Management Organization and Control (Paul E. Holden, Lounsbury S. Fish, and Hubert L. Smith)

A good organization chart for the company as a whole, with auxiliary charts for each major division, is an essential first step in the analysis, clarification, and understanding of any organization plan. The process of chart-

[2] L. Urwick, *Elements of Administration,* 2nd edition (London: Pitman, 1947), pp. 38–39.

ing the organization is one good test of its soundness, as any organization relationship which cannot be readily charted is likely to be illogical and therefore confusing to those working under it.

Organization planning in many companies ends with the preparation of a set of organization charts. These give a good general idea of the primary divisions of the company but do not stipulate how each unit of the organization should function.

Organization charts should therefore be supplemented by written specifications defining the essential requirements of each level of management, each department, each committee, and each key job or group of similar jobs. Only by a thorough understanding of their respective parts in the whole management picture are individual executives and agencies able to devote their full energies to effective discharge of their proper functions, avoiding duplication of effort, friction, and working at cross purposes which result from lack of organization clarification. Such written specifications should cover functions, jurisdiction, responsibilities, relationships, limits of authority, objectives, and the means for measuring performance.[3]

Extract C

Management and the Worker (F. J. Roethlisberger and William J. Dickson)

All of the experimental studies pointed to the fact that there is something more to the social organization than what has been formally recognized. Many of the actually existing patterns of human interaction have no representation in the formal organization at all, and others are inadequately represented by the formal organization. This fact is frequently forgotten when talking or thinking about industrial situations in general. *Too often it is assumed that the organization of a company corresponds to a blueprint plan or organization chart.* Actually, it never does. In the formal organization of most companies little explicit recognition is given to many social distinctions residing in the social organization. The blueprint plans of a company show the functional relations between working units, but they do not express the distinctions of social distance, movement, or equilibrium previously described. The hierarchy of prestige values which tends to make the work of men more important than the work of women, the work of clerks more important than the work at the bench, has little representation in the formal organization; nor does a blueprint plan ordinarily show the primary groups, that is, those groups enjoying daily face-to-face relations. Logical lines of horizontal and vertical co-ordination of functions replace the actually existing patterns of interaction between people in different social places. The formal

[3] Paul S. Holden, Lounsbury S. Fish, and Hubert L. Smith, *Top-Management Organization and Control* (New York: McGraw-Hill Book Co., Inc., 1948), pp. 5–6.

organization cannot take account of the sentiments and values residing in the social organization by means of which individuals or groups of individuals are informally differentiated, ordered, and integrated. Individuals in their associations with one another in a factory build up personal relationships. They form into informal groups, in terms of which each person achieves a certain position or status. . . .

It is well to recognize that informal organizations are not "bad," as they are sometimes assumed to be. Informal social organization exists in every plant, and can be said to be a necessary prerequisite for effective collaboration.[4]

Extract D

Executive Action (Edmund P. Learned, David N. Ulrich, and Donald R. Booz)

Some of the hazards of imposing too logical and rigid an organization structure upon a company should by now be apparent. In a company where operations have become confused, and the initiative and ingenuity of individual operating personnel cannot get matters straightened out again, formal planning may enter as a substitute. The overdevelopment of formal operating procedures will, then, in turn act as a damper on whatever spirit of initiative still remains. Some individuals, seeking the comfort of form and order in a fast-changing environment, will seize avidly upon regulations and try to crystallize them once and for all. Others may derive a more aggressive satisfaction from the imposition and observance of authority for its own sake, regardless of the need. Still other individuals make the existing framework more rigid as a defense against the encroachments of their own subordinates. . . .

Thus we see that organization planning can be best understood as part of a complex administrative process. The organization chart itself does not present a complete or accurate picture of operations. The actual working practices of a company do not conform to the ideal requirements of organization theory, and they cannot be made to fulfill those requirements through the further elaboration of theory itself. Certain social forces tend also to shape the application of theory in ways that may either help or hinder the enterprise. The problem therefore falls to the executive of administering the working practices and human needs of a company to get the results that are considered ideal by the organization theorist. . . .

. . . all the evidence gathered in this study suggested that there is no substitute for face-to-face contact as a means of insuring adequate communication in an organization. In a great many companies communication breaks

[4] F. J. Roethlisberger and William J. Dickson, *Management and the Worker* (Cambridge, Mass.: Harvard University Press, 1947), p. 559.

down because words are assumed to have a more common meaning than they have. The context in which they are transmitted and received is not given adequate weight. Frequent personal contact among executives, staff men, and supervisors appears to be necessary to guarantee that orders, instructions, information, and expressions of attitude and opinion will in fact be understood.

We therefore offer the hypothesis that any administrative unit should be small enough to permit the executive or supervisor in charge of it to engage in frequent face-to-face contact with its members.[5]

Extract E

The Organization Man (William H. Whyte, Jr.)

Whatever we call human relations, they are central to the problem of The Organization and the individual, and the more we find out about the effect of the one on the other, the better we can find more living room for the individual. But it's not going to be done if many of those who propagate the doctrine cling to self-proving assumptions about the overriding importance of equilibrium, integration, and adjustment. The side of the coin they have been staring at so intently is a perfectly good one, but there is another side and it should not be too heretical at least to have a peek at it. Thousands of studies and case histories have dwelled on fitting the individual to the group, but what about fitting the group to the person? What about *individual* dynamics? The tyranny of the happy team? The adverse effects of high morale? . . .

Another fruitful approach would be a drastic re-examination of the now orthodox view that the individual should be given less of the complete task, the team more of it. For a century we have been breaking down tasks into the components and sub-components, each to be performed by a different cell member, and this assembly-line mentality has affected almost everything that men do for a living, including the arts. . . .

If we truly believe the individual is more creative than the group, just in day-to-day routine there is something eminently practical we can do about it. Cut down the amount of time the individual has to spend in conferences and meetings and team play. This would be a somewhat mechanical approach to what is ultimately a philosophical problem, but if organization people would take a hard look at the different kinds of meetings inertia has accumulated for The Organization, they might find that the ostensibly negative act of cutting out many of them would lead to some very positive benefits over and above the time saved. Thrown more on their own resources, those who have nothing to offer but the skills of compromising other people's

[5] Edmund P. Learned, David N. Ulrich, and Donald R. Booz, *Executive Action* (Boston: Harvard Business School, 1951), pp. 147, 153, and 210.

efforts might feel bereft, but for the others the climate might be envigorating. Of itself such a surface change in working conditions would not give them more freedom, but it would halt a bad momentum. It would force organization to distinguish between what are legitimate functions of the group and what are not. . . .

The organization man is not in the grip of vast social forces about which it is impossible for him to do anything: the options are there, and with wisdom and foresight he can turn the future away from the dehumanized collective that so haunts our thoughts. He may not. But he can.

He must *fight* The Organization. Not stupidly, or selfishly, for the defects of individual self-regard are no more to be venerated than the defects of co-operation. But fight he must, for the demands for his surrender are constant and powerful, and the more he has come to like the life of the organization the more difficult does he find it to resist those demands, or even to recognize them. . . .[6]

Extract F

The Practice of Management (Peter Drucker)

. . . organization structure must apply one or both of two principles:

It must whenever possible integrate activities on the principle of *federal decentralization,* which organizes activities into autonomous product businesses, each with its own market and product and with its own profit and loss responsibility. Where this is not possible it must use *functional decentralization* which sets up integrated units with maximum responsibility for a major and distinct stage in the business process.

Federal decentralization and functional decentralization are complementary rather than competitive. Both have to be used in almost all businesses. Federal decentralization is the more effective and more productive of the two. But the genuinely small business does not need it, since it is in its entirety an "autonomous product business." Nor can federalism be applied to the internal organization of every large business; in a railroad, for example, the nature of the business and its process rule it out. . . .

In the last ten years it [federal decentralization] has been adopted or fully developed by Ford and Chrysler (General Motors has had it since 1923 or so), General Electric and Westinghouse, all the major chemical companies (except duPont who had developed it by 1920), most of the large oil companies, the largest insurance companies, and so forth. And the principle is being expounded in articles and speeches, in management magazines and management meetings so that by now the phrase at least must be familiar to every American manager.

[6] From *The Organization Man* by William H. Whyte, Jr. Copyright © 1956 by William H. Whyte, Jr. By permission of Simon and Schuster, Inc.

These are the main reasons for its emergence as the dominant structural principle of modern large business enterprise:

1. It focuses the vision and efforts of managers directly on business performance and business results.

2. Because of this, the danger of self-deception, of concentrating on the old and easy rather than on the new and coming, or of allowing unprofitable lines to be carried on the backs of the profitable ones, is much lessened. The facts do not stay hidden under the rug of "overhead" or of "total sales figures."

3. The advantages are fully as great in respect to management organization. Management by objectives becomes fully effective. The manager of the unit knows better than anyone else how he is doing, and needs no one to tell him. Hence the number of people or units under one manager no longer is limited by the span of control; it is limited only by the much wider span of managerial responsibility . . .

4. A Sears experiment showed dramatically the impact of decentralization on the development of tomorrow's managers.

> Right after the war Sears hired a large number of young men. They were divided arbitrarily. About one-third were put into the large stores, one-third into the small stores, one-third into the mail-order business. Five years later the best of the young men in the large stores were getting to be section managers; and the best of the young men in the small stores were getting ready to be managers of small stores themselves. In the mail-order houses there were actually more openings during these years. But mail-order has always been organized by functional specialization. The best of the young men placed there had left the company; the others were five years later, still clerks punching a time clock. . . .

5. Finally, federal decentralization tests men in independent command early and at a reasonably low level.[7]

Extract G

Scientific Management (Frederick W. Taylor)

Under the ordinary or military type [of organization] the workmen are divided into groups. The men in each group receive their orders from one man only, the foreman or gang boss of that group. This man is the single agent through which the various functions of the management are brought into contact with the men. Certainly the most marked outward characteristic of functional management lies in the fact that each workman, instead of coming in direct contact with the management at one point only, namely, through his gang boss, receives his daily orders and help directly from eight different bosses, each of whom performs his own particular function. Four

[7] Peter F. Drucker, *The Practice of Management* (New York: Harper & Brothers, 1954), pp. 205–210.

of these bosses are in the planning room and of these three send their orders to and receive their returns from the men, usually in writing. Four others are in the shop and personally help the men in their work, each boss helping in his own particular line or function only. . . . Thus the grouping of the men in the shop is entirely changed, each workman belonging to eight different groups according to the particular functional boss whom he happens to be working under at the moment. . . .

The greatest good resulting from this change is that it becomes possible in a comparatively short time to train bosses who can really and fully perform the functions demanded of them, while under the old system it took years to train men who were after all able to . . . perform only a portion of their duties. . . .[8]

EXTRACT H
General and Industrial Management (Henri Fayol)

For any action whatsoever, an employee should receive orders from one superior only. Such is the rule of unity of command, arising from general and ever-present necessity and wielding an influence on the conduct of affairs, which to my way of thinking, is at least equal to any other principle whatsoever. Should it be violated, authority is undermined, discipline is in jeopardy, order disturbed and stability threatened. This rule seems fundamental to me and so I have given it the rank of principle. As soon as two superiors wield their authority over the same person or department, uneasiness makes itself felt and should the cause persist, the disorder increases, the malady takes on the appearance of an animal organism troubled by a foreign body, and the following consequences are to be observed: either the dual command ends in disappearance or elimination of one of the superiors and organic well-being is restored, or else the organism continues to wither away. In no case is there adaptation of the social organism to dual command.[9]

Cases

Case A:
Organization of a Commerce College

The College of Commerce of the University of Kentucky has always been organized as one unit coming directly under the dean. No change in this

[8] Frederick Winslow Taylor, *Scientific Management* (New York: Harper & Brothers, 1947), pp. 99–104. This extract originally appeared in Taylor's *Shop Management,* first published in 1903.

[9] Henri Fayol, *General and Industrial Management* (London: Sir Isaac Pitman & Son, 1949), p. 24.

arrangement has taken place since the foundation of the College in 1925, despite the growth in the student body to over 1,000 students in the 1940's and 1950's. This means that the entire faculty of over 30 reports directly to the dean. Sometimes reference was made to the "Economics Department" but it was in fact an integral part of the College; there was no departmental chairman. Teachers of a wide variety of subjects reported to one head: economics, accounting, marketing, management, secretarial studies, personnel management, finance, business law, statistics, and so forth. The only separate organization within the College was the Bureau of Business Research which was headed by a director reporting to the dean.

Thus a large number of people reported to the dean: over 30 faculty members, the director of the Bureau of Business Research, two secretaries, and a janitor. In addition, the student body of the College reported to the dean on administrative and disciplinary matters, so that every day the dean could expect to be in session with at least several students. The dean also had a number of committee responsibilities. In addition, he managed the student loan fund for the entire university, a function entailing additional meetings with students.

The dean had from time to time considered the possibility of departmentalization of the College, but had never considered this to be a pressing issue. The faculty members had differing views on the subject. One member expressed the view that he would favor establishment of an assistant deanship rather than the setting up of separate departments.

Case B:

The Zorach Printing Company

For thirteen years, from 1939 to 1952, Miss Zorach had acted as president of the Zorach Printing Company. She and her sisters had inherited the majority of the common stock in the company from their father, and Miss Zorach felt it was her responsibility to manage the company on behalf of the family. The company was not particularly profitable; in fact, profits in some years were offset by losses in others. Only one dividend payment had been made in the entire period. In addition, Miss Zorach sacrificed part of her salary to keep the company solvent. At one point it was necessary to borrow a large sum of money to finance the outlays of the company, and the debt was still large.

Over the years Miss Zorach had sought a manager to whom she could delegate responsibility for running the company. She had little success with the selection of such managers, however, and found it necessary to continue in control. Finally, in 1952, she turned over the presidency to a Mr. Abner, whom she had known for several years because of his interests in the printing business. Before his appointment, Miss Zorach had several discussions with Mr. Abner on the policies of the company. She was to become vice president and was to remain active in the company, with responsibility for managing the office, for part of the estimating work, for some selling and contact with customers, and other miscellaneous functions. Miss Zorach informed Mr. Abner of several long term policies of the company: *equal pay for women, no printing business for the liquor industry, and high quality work.*

The board of directors, which included representatives of the owners of the company debt, approved the appointment of Mr. Abner as president, and no doubt some directors were happy to see the change in central management. Within a few months after his appointment, Mr. Abner's relations with Miss Zorach had deteriorated. She felt that she was not given the responsibilities on which they had agreed; for example, she had little control over the office. Later, a new plant superintendent, appointed by Mr. Abner, was rude to Miss Zorach and requested in strong terms that she stop interfering in the plant. At times Miss Zorach felt that orders for which she was responsible were delayed in the plant and she was not always satisfied with the quality of the work. One time she insisted on refunding money to one customer on whose order there was a serious error, even though the customer had missed the error in proofreading and even though the president was opposed to the refund. The crisis came, however, when the president granted pay increases to the men without providing equal increases for the women. There were even negotiations for liquor printing business—several directors supported the view of the president that this business should be sought if it added to the profits of the business.

In the meantime, there were indications of deteriorating morale. The employees were beginning to form *cliques,* some loyal to Miss Zorach and others to Mr. Abner. Several employees left the company.

Case C:

Standard Oil Company of California [10]

The Standard Oil Company of California has been a leader in organization planning for several decades. Early in the depression of the 1930's the company established the first Department on Organization in any concern. Ever since, this Department has had as its objective the development, maintenance and improvement of organization structures throughout the company. The Department has also had the responsibility for systematizing the administration of salaries and wages, a function frequently handled by personnel departments in other companies. The influence of the Department on Organization and of the top management's philosophy of organization is felt throughout the Standard Oil Company of California in its operations around the world.

[10] This case was prepared by Professor W. W. Haynes for the University of California at Berkeley as a basis for class discussion. It is not designed to present either a correct or incorrect illustration of the handling of administrative problems.

The Management Guides

The Department on Organization has published a booklet on its approach called *The Management Guide.* This booklet is widely known in business circles; it has run through two editions, in 1948 and 1956. Its main purpose is to describe the construction of what the company calls management guides for particular positions. These guides, in the words of the booklet, "define the functions, responsibilities, authorities, and principal relationships of management positions at all levels." The guides are a means of formally setting forth usage, corporate practice, and tradition governing a position. They are also a way of assuming the careful planning of the allocation of functions and providing a clear understanding of how each position relates to others in the organization.

The philosophy of organization underlying the management guide approach is expressed in the following quotation from the booklet:

"Organization planning requires that the organization structure and the allocation of functions to specific positions be clear-cut, not only to achieve the objectives of the enterprise, but to have a reference point from which to proceed in marking out other co-ordinate and subordinate positions and their functions."

"The Guide serves the . . . purposes of indicating overlapping responsibilities, so that the situation may be altered or clarified as necessary, and of highlighting matters requiring special attention and co-ordination."

"Conflicts between individuals over jurisdiction are immediately disposed of by reference to the Management Guide."

"Management needs to know to what position specific enterprise's activities have been delegated, and, as a corollary, whom to hold accountable for its accomplishment."

In summary, the guides have as their main purpose "the demarcation of the size, weight, and character of each position, its function, responsibilities and authority, and relationships, and its place in and relation to the entire organization structure of the enterprise." The guides help determine the channels to be used in seeking approval for proposals on important matters. They are used as training devices by providing the new occupant of a position with knowledge of his function, responsibility, authority and relationships. The guides provide a means of evaluating the performance of subordinates by stating objectives against which that performance can be measured. The guides also are useful in the selection of candidates for a position.

Evolution of Management Guides

The development of the management guides is related to the spread of job descriptions in American industry. The Standard Oil Company of California has felt, however, that the usual job descriptions are too much oriented toward wage administration and too little concerned with the definition of the less tangible features of positions on managerial levels, such as limitations on authority and the relationships with other positions.

The first step taken in the development of management guides was the construction of lists of principal functions, relationships, and the extent of authority of each management position. Later a section on objectives and responsibilities was added; it contained instructions on the necessary attitude of mind of the occupant of the position and even explained the manner in which the function was to be fulfilled. Since 1942, however, the guides have not contained instructions on how to do the job. The trend has been away from enumerating details, such as the normal relationships with subordinates. It was recognized that one of the responsibilities of a manager was discretion in determining just how he was to carry out his responsibilities; therefore, the guides now cover only the broad features of each position. By 1947 the general form of the guides was standardized, though it should be noted that the guides undergo revision from time to time. Table 4-1 presents a guide for a particular position; this illustration is taken from *The Management Guide* and is not necessarily descriptive of any presently existing position in the corporation. Table 4-2 presents a similar guide for the manager of an Organization Department. Though again this guide is not exactly descriptive of the situation in Standard Oil's present Department on Organization, Table 4-2 does provide further insight into the company's thinking on organization and is worthy of detailed study.

Reorganization of the Company in 1954

In 1954 a substantial reorganization of the Standard Oil Company of California was instituted. This reorganization did not reduce the emphasis on management guides; in fact the revision of these guides was a central instrument of the reorganization itself. The main objective of the reorganization was to relieve the top management of the company of the details of operations in particular areas so that it could concentrate on over-all policy and give greater emphasis to its foreign subsidiaries. The central corporation had for decades a number of subsidiary corporations controlled through 100% stock ownership, but until that time its most important operations, along the West Coast, were managed directly. It was felt that the rapid expansion of the company in the post-war period and particularly the expansion of its foreign operations made this organization unmanageable. The tendency was to give the immediate detailed problems of management on the West Coast priority over the longer range issues. Therefore, the company established a new corporation, called the Standard Oil Company of California, Western Operations, Inc., to take over exploration, production, refining, transportation, wholesaling, retailing, and other functions on the West Coast.

Thus, the Standard Oil Company itself became a holding company, with Western Operations its largest subsidiary.

Figures 4-1 and 4-2 present partial organization charts for the Corporation and for Western Operations respectively. The charts include illustrations of each kind of operating company or department but are incomplete for purposes of simplicity.

Several special features not immediately apparent from these charts deserve emphasis. The top executives of the company, including most of the functional officers, carried additional responsibilities as contact officers for particular operating companies. A contact officer was to serve as representative of the interests of such operating companies and was also to counsel the heads of operating companies on matters involving more than one functional activity. For example, the President, Mr. T. S. Petersen, acted as contact officer for Western Operations, Inc., The California Company and the Standard Oil Company of Texas. The Vice President for Exploration, Mr. Crandall, acted as contact officer for the Chevron Oil Company, which was responsible for geophysical surveys. The functional officers (as functional officers rather than as contact officers) were to provide counsel and advice in their fields of special competence. They were responsible for the "functional co-ordination" of activities within such fields whether in the corporation or in operating companies. Operating companies were expected to seek the services of such functional officers but the officers would provide assistance and "functional guidance" whether requested or not. The functional officers were of course responsible for making recommendations concerning over-all policies affecting their functional area.

The Communications Guide

At the time of the reorganization of the company in 1954, another publication called the Communications Guide, was distributed to assist in the clarification of the relations among positions. This Guide provided that when dealing with "policy, operating, and administrative" matters the corporation officers and staff could communicate directly with each other, as appropriate; that heads of corporation staff departments could communicate directly with operating companies over their names (though they must bring matters of importance to the attention of the functional officers to whom they reported); that the head of an operating company could delegate to a member of his management the authority to carry on certain communications, provided that these did not propose changes in policy; that heads of operating companies could communicate directly with functional officers provided the matter was not within the province of a staff department; and that heads of operating companies could communicate directly with each other. Similar rules were provided for communications among other positions.

The Communications Guide was not as restrictive of communications as it might at first appear. The Guide made it clear that it did not contain a strict set of rules which must always be followed. In an emergency direct communication with any executive was permitted. The individual could in any case use discretion in the use of channels, keeping in mind the necessity of informing the appropriate executives. The Guide did not rule against informal communications (oral or written) cutting across channels on a personal basis but instead stated that such communication was desirable. Matters of a routine administrative or operating nature which were within established policies could be handled across lines, provided again that the responsible executive was fully informed.

Other Functions of the Department on Organization: Pay Administration

The Department on Organization was concerned with much more than the spread of the management guide approach. In fact, it should be made clear that the actual construction of the guides was delegated to particular departments under the functional guidance of the Department on Organization and similar departments within the operating companies. The Department on Organization spent a great deal of its time on two other major functions: the evaluation of jobs and positions for the purpose of salary and wage administration; and the review of organizations procedures and manpower requirements in various parts of the enterprise.

The Department started co-ordinating wage and salary administration for the company in 1936 and since then has been continually concerned with this problem. In 1957 it published a pamphlet entitled *People and Pay Checks* explaining company procedures on salaries and wages. This pamphlet was widely known and apparently well received throughout the company. The principles described by the pamphlet covered most of the nearly 40,000 employees of the company. One of the basic ideas in the plan was that analysis of the job should be separated from evaluation of the particular individual holding the job. The steps involved in paying the job were the preparation of job descriptions; the classification of jobs involving similar levels of job requirements; the determination of what other companies pay for like jobs; and the relating of the pay structure to the job values. The management guides served as job descriptions for managerial positions; and executive guides did the same for the top positions in the company. The Standard Oil Company used a method involving ranking according to factor comparison rather than a point system. Benchmark jobs, called Standards of Value, were the basis of factor comparison. Not everyone on a similar job received the same pay; although most jobs subject to overtime provisions of Fair Labor Standards Act are paid fixed rates, provision was made for time progression increases in pay on some jobs and for merit increases on others.

The Company decentralized responsibility for pay administration. Line supervisors at lower levels signed job descriptions, approved job evaluations, and at appropriate levels helped set pay policies. But specialized staff employees, such as those in the Department on Organization and in similar departments in the operating companies, were responsible for assisting line supervisors in preparing job descriptions, in job evaluation and in the interpretation of pay policy. The Department on Organization acted as a consulting service on pay problems throughout the enterprise. A continuing interchange of personnel between the Department on Organization and other departments helped assure dissemination of the over-all perspective on pay administration to other departments.

An interesting exception to the usual job evaluating procedures applied to professional or technical employees. It had been found that some of these employees would reach a maximum level of pay in their technical positions and would then transfer to administrative positions where there still remained a promotion ladder. This had the unfortunate result in some cases of reducing the number of highly qualified technical men by transfer to positions in which administrative duties precluded maximum development and utilization of their technical talents. As a result the company has extended the ladder for promotion of professional specialists and has recognized that it may be desirable to pay the man in the job rather than the job itself. In other words, for certain positions, the particular incumbent made the job what it was and the pay system must take this into account. This was, of course, an exception to the usual evaluation procedures. The Department on Organization did not feel that the administration of salaries for professional specialists departed basically from the over-all job evaluation program.

Survey Teams and Manpower Controls

On the whole the pay administration system applied by the Standard Oil Company of California appears similar to that of many other companies; again the Company had led in a systematic approach to this problem. An unusual feature is the central staff agency involved should be a Department on Organization rather than the Personnel Department. More unusual, and perhaps more controversial within the company, has been the Department's responsibility for conducting surveys in various parts of the enterprise to determine where organizational procedures or the use of manpower have been defective.

The Department on Organization's initial establishment was based on the desire to trim manpower in the depression of the 1930's. The Department made surveys which led to manpower cuts, for example in the reorganization of the use of motor cars. In more recent years the Company has avoided cutting the work force in periods of recession; in fact it has taken pride in its avoidance of layoffs that have been experienced in some other oil companies. Standard Oil has, however, frozen the work force at times and permitted attrition through retirement and resignations. Despite this change in practice as compared with the depression, the Department on Organization's role in the depression layoff has not been forgotten in all parts of the organization; this may help account for the impression that the Department is viewed with awe by some other departments.

In recent years the role of the Department on Organization in the survey of manpower usage has varied from problem to problem. The Department has encouraged operating companies to make their own surveys and to make the necessary corrections. But in some cases the Department has established survey teams, including on such teams personnel from the department being surveyed. A recent case has been a survey of the Producing Department of the Western Division (now Western Operations) in which over 500 employees were interviewed. This survey disclosed that the increased size of overhead staff was due to detailed, highly centralized controls and a close check on work at a number of management levels. The survey recommended greater delegation of responsibilities, a simplification of controls, and the elimination of considerable paperwork. The Producing Department carried out many of the recommendations prior to completion of the report, with the result of a substantial reduction in supervisory and staff work. This experience was an impetus to a company-wide program of decentralization, to be discussed below.

Several other illustrations will indicate the kind of work done by the Department on Organization in recent years:

1. A study of the problem of controlling maintenance and minor construction work. The Department felt that there was a particular lack of control of manpower in this kind of work largely because of the difficulty of measurement and standardization. The Department recommended procedures for surveying such work, in particular departments, and for improving planning and the control of costs.

2. A study of geophysical surveys, all of which were formerly contracted to outside firms. The question was whether at least some geophysical work should be done by company crews. The Department assisted the Vice President-Exploration in this study.

3. A study of the operations of the Atlantic and Pacific fleets of the company; it was found that the two fleets were not as well co-ordinated as they might be. The reorganization of the fleets has led to the more efficient use of tankers.

The Department on Organization has succeeded in getting its recommendations across in a number of ways. As much as possible it has tried to work with the surveyed department, so that such a department will, as a participant, be more interested in bringing about the improvements desired. As has been stated, the Department has encouraged the individual departments to make their own surveys, using the Department on Organization as a consulting agency if necessary. In a few cases the Department has worked with the President of the corporation to stimulate necessary reorganizations.

The Department on Organization has not originated all of its studies; many suggestions have come from the field and have been referred to the Department because of its experience with surveys and with organizational problems.

Decentralization of the Company

Like many other large-scale firms in the post-war era, the Standard Oil Company of California has taken great interest in decentralization of its operations. Members of the Department on Organization have claimed that the management guides have themselves been instruments of decentralization; by clarifying the responsibilities of positions at lower levels the guides have reduced the uncertainty about the locus of authority to make decisions and have thus reduced the number of reference of such decisions to higher headquarters. Officials in line departments have agreed that more decisions are made in the field in Standard Oil of California than appears to be the case in most competing companies.

Since 1954 top management has increased the pressure to decentralize. The separation of "the Corporation" from Western Operations was one step in that direction. The study of the Producing Department already mentioned also stimulated interest in decentralization. In 1957, the company prepared a brochure called *Our New Way of Doing Business* which had as its objective the encouragement of further decentralization. The phrase "our new way of doing business" has become well known in the management of the company and has no doubt stimulated interest in greater delegation than had previously existed. A high official in one operating company, however, expressed the view that this new program had not affected his operations to any significant degree since his organization was already of necessity highly decentralized; the geographical spread of his business had long before required substantial delegation.

The company hoped to achieve many improvements through its decentralization program. It hoped to speed up decisions, to increase the sense of responsibility at lower levels, to stimulate initiative, to increase interest in work, to reduce staff work, to divert attention from non-essentials to key issues, and to improve the development of managers and supervisors. The general principles involved in this program are listed in Table 4-3.

Some Management Viewpoints

There appeared to be widespread acceptance of the management guide approach to organization at the higher levels of management. In fact, most executives interviewed expressed considerable enthusiasm for the guides and were unable to see how the business could operate without them. The large size of the company was cited as a major factor making the guides necessary; but several officials expressed the view that smaller companies could profit from such an approach. Some managers admitted that the guides were not something to which they referred frequently but they were grateful that the guides were available in case of need. Quite generally the officials looked upon the guides as a means of preventing overlaps and for settling jurisdictional problems.

There was little feeling that the guides interfered with informal communication; in fact, the usual view was that the definition of positions involved in the guides provided a basis from which informal communications could flow more freely. The officials were inclined to believe that a less well planned structure would result in chaos, with no one knowing where he stood. One official made it quite clear that the formal organizational planning did not interfere with his informal communication by enumerating the telephone calls he received during an hour-and-a-half of interview time. The calls came from other departments and from Western Operations with no regard for formal channels. They involved requests for information and advice.

Officials believed that the guides did not reduce the flexibility of the organization. The guides were subject to revision. Furthermore the guides were quite general in character, leaving considerable scope for interpretation; this was especially true for the guides for high level positions. Some officials admitted that some particular jobs were extremely difficult to describe in a guide, especially when the work in such jobs varied greatly as the situation required; the guides had less meaning in such cases.

Generally the officials felt that the guides stimulated initative. The guides specified just what the position objective was and clarified the limits of authority. Within those limits the manager could go ahead full speed without fear that he would get in some one else's way. One official asserted that he had never seen a case in which managers failed to fill in a gap not covered by the guides. He noted that in some competing companies which gave less attention to organizational planning the officials were frequently confused about their authority and had to check constantly with higher headquarters.

Several officials pointed out that the construction of the guides was of great value in itself. It was beneficial to put the scope of a new position on paper, for this forced management to think through just where that position fitted in and how it affected already existing positions. A change in one position might well require the revision of the guides for other positions and it was a good idea to work this out in advance.

The guides did in practice leave some gaps in responsibilities and did permit some overlaps of authority. But the general view was that these problems were more serious in less organization-conscious companies. The process of drawing up the guides exposed most gaps and overlaps.

One official expressed the interesting view that the company was not really decentralized. He doubted that any company that insisted on as much uniformity in procedures as existed in Standard Oil of California was really decentralized. He argued that the structure appeared decentralized to those within the company because the trend was away from the greater centralization that had existed in the past. This official was perhaps the least enthusiastic for the management guides, though even he favored their retention. He felt that the guides meant little in practice, particularly in higher level positions. He and several other officials seemed to believe that the chief value of the guides was in providing a basis for salary administration.

Another official was highly favorable to the salary aspects of the management guides in that they gave an objective basis for comparing job requirements within the company and with other companies. But he, contrary to the general view, wondered whether formal organizational planning had not been pushed too far and whether there was not too much emphasis on preplanned channels of communication. He felt, however, that the problems arising from the system were infrequent.

Much more controversial than the management guides themselves was the status of the Department on Organization, particularly in its authority to conduct surveys and make recommendations concerning other parts of the enterprise. A substantial minority of the officials interviewed expressed some opposition to the surveys. One felt that there were too many surveys and that they were disruptive of morale. Members of the Department on Organization themselves recognized that there was some resentment of their surveys in parts of the company. Some departments not only opposed the surveys but did not even care to seek the advice of the Department. On the other hand, one line official expressed gratitude for recommendations made by a survey team which enabled him to reorganize operations for which he was the new head without taking the full blame for the shake-up. Another corporation official claimed that he still observed excess personnel in some departments, which indicated that there was still survey work to be done.

Though the status of the Department on Organization remained controversial in some parts of the company, there was general agreement that its relations with other departments had improved. The Department took more trouble to consult with other sections of the company. It made certain that survey teams included personnel from the surveyed department. It attempted to suggest changes rather than impose them. And the greater interchange of personnel between the Department and the rest of the company had increased understanding of its work.

TABLE 4-1

MANAGEMENT GUIDE
GENERAL MANAGER, MANUFACTURING DIVISION *

I. *Function*

Conducts the manufacturing, packaging, plant facilities and equipment operation, engineering, maintenance, plant and process design, technical service, plant and warehouse construction activities of the company, and warehousing.

II. *Responsibilities and authority*

The responsibilities and authority stated below are subject to established policies.

TABLE 4-1 (Continued)

A. Operations and Activities

1. Formulates, or receives and recommends for approval, proposals for policies on manufacturing, packaging, plant facilities and equipment operation, engineering, maintenance, plant and process design, technical service, and plant and warehouse construction activities; administers such policies when approved; and conducts such activities for the company.

2. Establishes and administers procedures pertaining to manufacturing, packaging, plant facilities and equipment operation, engineering, maintenance, plant and process design, technical service, and plant and warehouse construction.

3. Recommends new or altered products and the discontinuance of products.

4. Operates such warehouses as are necessary to the accomplishment of his function.

5. Conducts necessary buying activities, calling upon the services of the Supply and Transportation Department when necessary.

B. Organization of His Division

1. Recommends changes in the basic structure and complement of his Division.

2. Recommends placement of positions not subject to the provisions of the Fair Labor Standards Act in the salary structure.

3. Arranges for preparation of new and revised Management Guides and position and job description.

C. Personnel of His Division

1. Having ascertained the availability of qualified talent from within the company, hires personnel for, or appoints employees to, positions other than in management within the limits of his approved basic organization.

2. Approves salary changes for personnel not subject to the provisions of the Fair Labor Standards Act who receive not over $........ per month, and recommends salary changes for such personnel receiving in excess of that amount.

3. Approves wage changes for personnel subject to the provisions of the Fair Labor Standards Act.

4. Recommends promotion, demotion, and release of personnel not subject to the provisions of the Fair Labor Standards Act.

5. Approves promotion, demotion, and release of personnel subject to the provisions of the Fair Labor Standards Act.

6. Approves vacations and personal leaves, except his own.

7. Prepares necessary job and position descriptions.

D. Finances of His Division

1. Prepares the annual budget.

2. Administers funds allotted under the approved annual budget, or any approved extraordinary or capital expenditure program, or any appropriation.

3. Approves payment from allotted funds of operating expenses and capital expenditures not in excess of $........, which are not covered by the approved budget, any approved expenditure program, or an appropriation.

4. Recommends extraordinary or capital expenditures.

5. Administers fiscal procedures.

6. Receives for review and recommendation the items of the annual budgets of the staff departments and the field divisions coming within his province.

III. *Relationships*

A. President

Reports to the President

B. General Manager, Marketing Division

Co-ordinates his activities and co-operates with the General Manager of the Marketing Division on matters of mutual concern.

C. Department Managers

Co-ordinates his efforts and co-operates with the Department Managers and seeks

TABLE 4-1 (Continued)

and accepts functional guidance from them on matters within their respective provinces.

D. Government, Labor, and Vendors

Conducts such relationships with representatives of government and labor and with vendors as are necessary to the accomplishment of his function.

E. Others

Establishes and maintains those contacts necessary to the fulfillment of his function.

* Source: *The Management Guide.*

Note: This guide does not describe a presently existing position in the company, but illustrates the materials included in the guides.

TABLE 4-2

MANAGEMENT GUIDE

MANAGER, ORGANIZATION DEPARTMENT *

I. *Function*

Furnishes functional guidance to the heads of the organizational components of the company by advising and assisting in the development, maintenance, and improvement of plans of management embracing: organization structures and complements; functions, responsibilities and authority, and relationships; control over wages, salaries, operating expenses, and manpower; and company, department, and division policies on these matters.

II. *Responsibilities and Authority*

The responsibilities and authority stated below are subject to established policies.

A. Activities

1. Develops plans to the end that each organizational component of the company is a logical, separable, integral part of the whole organization, having commensurate responsibility, authority, and accountability for results within clearly defined limits.

2. Defines and clarifies the function, responsibilities and authority, and relationships of each new or altered management position in collaboration with the company management, and maintains in a current state Management Guides covering management positions, making such Guides available to all concerned.

3. Fosters the centralization of control and the decentralization of responsibility for details and commensurate authority for their accomplishment, ensuring that decisions are made at the lowest practicable level of management at which they can be made intelligently.

4. As requested or as he deems advisable, conducts studies to determine the soundness and adequacy of the company's organization plan, and formulates, or receives and recommends for approval, proposals for changes in that plan.

5. As requested or as he deems advisable, reviews the conduct of affairs of organizational components to ensure that manpower shall be consistent with requirements and results, and encourages and assists in the preparation of operating and performance standards to serve as guides in the control of manpower.

6. Initiates periodic appraisals of the functions of the company to determine their necessity and adequacy in the light of the company objective. Formulates, or receives and recommends for approval, proposals for the elimination of nonessential or nonproductive functions, methods and procedures, and for the establishment of new ones, to ensure that manpower shall be utilized economically.

7. Reviews, edits, and approves job and position descriptions prepared by other members of management, and conducts the necessary job and position evaluations to formulate proposals for equitable salary and wage structures. Prepares and disseminates company, departmental, and divisional salary and wage guides based upon the approved company structures, and advises and assists members of management in the administration of salaries and wages within their respective organizational components.

8. Formulates, or receives and recommends for approval, proposals for policies, and

TABLE 4-2 (Continued)

maintains in a current state in a Policy Manual all policies formally adopted, furnishing copies of all policies, as approved, to the Secretary-Treasurer for dissemination.

9. Formulates, or receives and recommends for approval, proposals for changes in the Management Guides, and maintains in a current state all approved changes in such Guides for dissemination to holders thereof.

10. As requested, advises members of management in the preparation of the annual budget and requests for extraordinary or capital expenditures, making recommendations on the appropriateness of items to be included.

11. Formulates, or receives and recommends for approval, proposals for the establishment or modification of controls over expenditures.

B. Organization of His Department

1. Recommends changes in the basic structure and complement.

2. Recommends placement of positions not subject to the provisions of the Fair Labor Standards Act in the salary structure.

3. Arranges for preparation of new and revised Management Guides and position and job descriptions.

C. Personnel of His Department

1. Having ascertained the availability of qualified talent from within the company, hires personnel for, or appoints employees to, positions other than in management within limits of his approved basic organization.

2. Approves salary changes for personnel not subject to the provisions of the Fair Labor Standards Act who receive not over $........ per month, and recommends salary changes for such personnel receiving in excess of that amount.

3. Approves wage changes for personnel subject to the provisions of the Fair Labor Standards Act.

4. Recommends promotion, demotion, and release of personnel not subject to the provisions of the Fair Labor Standards Act.

5. Approves promotion, demotion, and release of personnel subject to the provision of the Fair Labor Standards Act.

6. Approves vacations and personal leaves, except his own.

7. Prepares necessary job and position descriptions.

D. Finances of His Department

1. Prepares the annual budget.

2. Administers funds allotted under the approved annual budget, or any approved extraordinary or capital expenditure program, or any appropriation.

3. Approves payment from allotted funds of operating expenses and capital expenditures not in excess of $........, which are not covered by the approved budget, any approved expenditure program, or an appropriation.

4. Recommends extraordinary or capital expenditures.

5. Administers fiscal procedures.

6. Receives for review and recommendation the items of the annual budget of other staff departments and the field divisions coming within his province.

III. *Relationships*

A. President

Reports to the President.

B. Other Department Managers and Division General Managers.

Advises and assists other Department Managers and Division General Managers in the fulfillment of their respective functions in matters within his province, and co-ordinates his activities and co-operates with them in matters of mutual concern.

C. Others

Establishes and maintains those contacts necessary to the fulfillment of his function.

* Source: *The Management Guide.*

Note: This guide does not describe a presently existing position in the company, but illustrates the materials included in the guides.

STANDARD OIL COMPANY OF CALIFORNIA
STOCKHOLDERS

BOARD OF DIRECTORS
EXECUTIVE COMMITTEE

CHAIRMAN OF THE BOARD

PRESIDENT

VICE PRESIDENT FINANCE	TREASURER	VICE PRESIDENT LEGAL	SECRETARY	VICE PRESIDENT MFG. & RESEARCH	VICE PRESIDENT MARKETING	VICE PRESIDENT EXPLORATION & PROD.	VICE PRESIDENT FOREIGN CRUDE SALES	FUNCTIONAL OFFICERS (PARTIAL LIST)
ECONOMICS	ENGINEERING	CREDIT	LABOR RELATIONS	ORGANIZATION	PERSONNEL	PRODUCT ENGINEERING	PUBLIC RELATIONS	CORPORATION STAFF (PARTIAL LIST)
WESTERN OPERATIONS INC.	CALIFORNIA CHEMICAL CO.	CALIFORNIA RESEARCH CORP.	SALT LAKE REFINING CO.	IRAN CALIFORNIA OIL CO.	STANDARD OIL COMPANY OF BRITISH COLUMBIA LIMITED	STANDARD OIL COMPANY OF TEXAS	THE CALIFORNIA COMPANY	OPERATING COMPANIES (PARTIAL LIST)

FIGURE 4-1 Corporate Organization

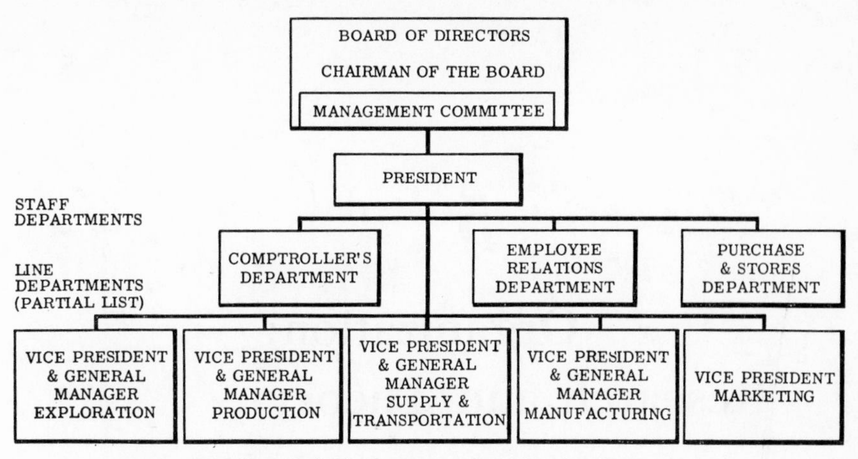

FIGURE 4-2 Standard Oil Company of California, Western Operations, Inc.

TABLE 4-3

WAYS OF ACHIEVING GREATER DECENTRALIZATION *

1. Delegate authority for decision to the lowest practicable level of management.
2. Delegate authority to field management for planning and conducting operations.
3. Delegate authority to field management for co-ordination of departmental, inter-departmental and inter-company matters at field points.
4. Disseminate adequate policy information to field management.
5. Discontinue excessively close supervision, re-checking, and re-analysis at many levels.
6. Discontinue the requirement for transmitting voluminous detail upward through successive levels of management so that answers to anticipated questions will be immediately available.
7. Prepare reports, economic analyses, budget estimates and forecasts only to the degree of precision compatible with the basic data available.
8. Delegate responsibility to field management for technical studies which can be carried out in the field as well or better than at headquarters.
9. Substitute thorough but informal checks of plans and proposals during field visits by headquarters management in place of re-analysis of field reports and recommendations at headquarters.
10. Concentrate management effort on developing policy and long range plans, providing counsel, guidance and co-ordination, and checking field performance.
11. Reduce the number, frequency, and detail of reports.
12. Simplify budget, appropriations, and forecasting procedures.
13. Simplify presentations for the purpose of securing approval of budget and major projects and curtail the supporting data including charts, maps and similar materials.

* Source: *Our New Way of Doing Business.*

5

Organization: Research and Theory

THE preceding discussion of organization has advanced two propositions: the traditional views of organization are worthy of consideration if placed in the right perspective; and our knowledge of organization is still extremely limited. Much work is currently being done on organization theory to overcome the limitations of previous generalizations. The aim of this chapter is to provide insight into research and theoretical developments in this area.

In approaching the subject of the "modern theory of organization," two obstacles present themselves. One is the difficulty of separating the modern from the traditional. The famous Hawthorne studies, for example, took place in the 1920's and 1930's, yet are closely related to current thought on organization and small groups. Chester Barnard's book, *The Functions of the Executive,* appeared in 1938, but remains one of the two or three most influential books on modern management thought. Organization theory, like most other studies, has developed gradually, not in revolutionary leaps. The other obstacle to defining modern organization theory is that so much is being written, it is impossible to locate "the" modern organization theory. Sometimes the literature gives the impression that there is one main strand of thought and research on organization, but a closer look at the subject reveals that this is far from the case. Dozens of articles are published every year, but little progress has been made in integrating the views of the scattered research workers.

Because of the variety of the current work on organization, only the most promising ideas can be discussed here. This chapter focuses on two main developments: first, the research on small groups (sometimes known as "group dynamics"), and second, the theories of Herbert A. Simon and his followers (most recently published in James G. March and Herbert A. Simon, *Organizations*). This choice is somewhat arbitrary; there is a great deal of interesting work being done on the subject that fits into neither category.

Modern organization theory and research differ from traditional approaches in several respects:

1. Current theories attempt to be "descriptive" rather than "prescriptive." That is, they try to generalize about organizations as they actually operate, rather than to jump to conclusions about what is "good" organization. The "descriptive" theorists believe that a more adequate understanding of existing organizations must precede attempts to tell managers what they "ought" to do.
2. Current theories are more explicit about underlying assumptions than traditional works. The early writers on organization were hortatory; they hoped to convince their readers of certain principles that they had found useful in their own experience; but they were weak on the examination of the assumptions and the logical reasoning leading to their generalizations and prescriptions.
3. Current theorists attempt to be "operational." That is, they try (not always successfully) to express their generalizations in a form that can be tested against observations. This does not mean that these generalizations have, in fact, been supported by systematic empirical studies—most of them have not. However, it is desirable to express views in a form in which some kind of test is possible at a future date.

One other feature of modern organization theories deserves a place in this list: the attempt to express theories in a mathematical form. To date, most of the literature on organization is nonmathematical, and the desire of some writers to describe an important aspect of human behavior in a mathematical form remains controversial. A discussion of mathematical "models" will be postponed to a later chapter.

Small Group Research

It is presumptuous for nonspecialists to summarize the conclusions of the many experiments that have been conducted on small groups. Fortunately, several professional social psychologists have reviewed the findings; the following discussion will depend heavily on these summaries.[1]

The emphasis on small groups in a book on management requires justification. Most firms and government institutions are much larger than the groups of three to twenty people that are the object of small group research. However, large organizations are composed of small groups, some of which are established formally while others develop spontaneously. A study of these parts should clarify the larger whole. Furthermore, some undertakings,

[1] The four summaries most directly influencing this discussion are: (1) George C. Homans, *The Human Group* (New York: Harcourt, Brace and World, Inc., 1950); (2) Josephine Klein, *The Study of Groups* (London: Routledge & Kegan Paul, 1956); (3) Hubert Bonner, *Group Dynamics: Principles and Applications* (New York: Ronald Press, 1959); and (4) Harold J. Leavitt, *Managerial Psychology* (Chicago: The University of Chicago Press, 1958).

for good or for bad, are placing greater reliance on committees and problem-solving groups.

The following summary of small group research is necessarily incomplete and oversimplified. It will serve, however, as an introduction to some of the central findings and hypotheses.

Groups Versus Independent Individuals

Why form groups in the first place? Do they contribute or detract from productivity? The answer depends on two considerations: the nature of the problem to be solved and the characteristics of the members of the groups. Let us consider several illustrations:

1. If the group consists of members with equal skill performing a simple task, group interaction will slow production. In this case, group interaction has little to contribute to performance of the task.
2. If one member is more skilled, the group may be more productive than independent individuals because of the guidance of the skilled operator.
3. If, however, the task is so complex that the members do not recognize that some solutions are more expert than others, confusion may result. If the skilled operators can demonstrate the correctness of expert solutions, productivity will increase; if not, there may be conflict.
4. If the task is one of reaching a decision or solving a problem, rather than direct production, group effort has advantages and limitations. The pooling of ideas of members will bring in points that might have been neglected. The members will have a sense of participation and may be more willing to carry out the decision. Nevertheless, groups consume time and tend to stress conformity rather than originality.

There are no simple generalizations on the superiority of group endeavor. This research does not provide exact formulas by which managers can decide when groups are needed and when they should be avoided.

Group Networks [2]

Suppose it has been decided to form a group. It is then necessary to determine its internal structure, including the communications network. Considerable work has been done measuring the effects of alternative networks. Let us consider a five man group. It may be organized in many ways, two of which are diagrammed in Figure 5-1. The first network (the star) indicates that members A, B, D, and E may communicate freely with member C (two-way communication is assumed), but not with each other. The second network, in Figure 5-1 (the circle), indicates that each member can communicate freely with two others but not with the rest of the group. Experiments with these two networks support the following conclusions:

[2] This section is based on Leavitt, *op. cit.*, pp. 193–199.

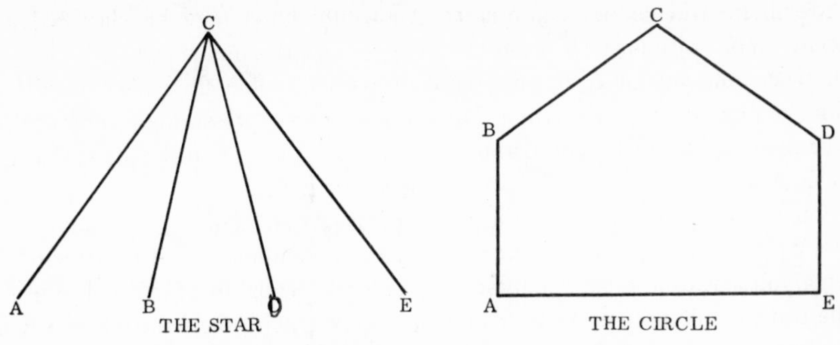

FIGURE 5-1 Two Communication Networks

1. Output will be faster for the star.
2. Morale of members A, B, D, and E will be higher in the circle. Member C, however, will be more enthusiastic about the star because of his central position in that network.
3. Member C will probably be leader in the star network. Any member can become leader in the circle; leadership may rotate in this case.
4. The members may accept change more readily in the circle. If change is important, this advantage may offset the lower speed of the circle.

The circle is a more participative or equalitarian organization, providing greater membership control over the outcome. It also provides more information to members on how well they are doing, thus contributing to job satisfaction. However, it may also create so much communication that output suffers. Thus, this line of research supports the view of earlier chapters, that greater participation is not universally "better" or "more effective."

Group Norms and Cohesiveness

Small groups are more than mechanical collections of individuals. To use a favorite expression of sociologists, group members "interact" on each other. Different patterns of interaction will influence the behavior of the group. One of the clearest illustrations of this point, one supported by one research study after another, is that groups tend to establish norms (goals, rules of behavior, concepts of right and wrong) which have an impact on individual attitudes and output. Whether we like it or not, most members frame their actions and decisions in terms of the views of others in the group. There is a considerable tendency to conform to an estimate of the group average, though this may be offset by a desire to demonstrate skill or to impress supervisors. Individuals may strive for success, but determination of what is success is heavily influenced by group attitudes. If fraternity brothers frown on intellectual activity, the individual fraternity member is less likely to extend himself in this direction—or more likely to cover up his reading of Kafka and his admiration for Picasso.

Members who do not conform to group standards may be classified as eccentrics or "rate busters." No doubt some societies and some small groups are more tolerant of eccentrics than others (on some university faculties oddness may even contribute to success), but the pressure to conform is difficult to resist. The group thus helps set the pace of work; it influences the level of aspiration toward which the individual aims.

Some studies, particularly the work of Homans, suggest that increased interaction among group members increases "friendliness." Unfortunately, casual observation raises doubts; this question calls for further research. The converse is more certain: if individuals like each other, their group will be more cohesive and the group norms more powerful. It is true that interaction helps clarify misunderstandings that arise from ignorance—many people suspect the worst until fully informed of the actions of the others. In a disturbing situation, in which the work is unpleasant or unrewarding, a person may turn on those closest at hand. Furthermore friendly communication can frequently impair the effectivness of the group in reaching its goals: an all-day "coffee break" is not usually productive of anything other than interaction.

In spite of the uncertainties about the findings, there can be little doubt that group interaction and group norms are of primary importance in determining the outcome of most kinds of activities. Managers may find it valuable to examine the impact that groups have on morale and productivity, provided that they are willing to avoid snap judgments or dogmatic generalizations in evaluating group processes.

Group Leadership [3]

A great deal of the small group research has been concerned with "democratic," "authoritarian," and "laissez-faire" leadership patterns. The research of Lewin, the founder of a whole school of thought on "group dynamics," seemed to demonstrate that "democratic" groups, in which members were permitted to work out their own problems with opportunities to consult with the leader, were the most effective. An authoritarian atmosphere tended to reduce initiative, and to promote hostility or apathy. In this case, research results supported the emphasis on group participation. For example, during World War II Lewin conducted experiments in changing people's food habits. The objective was to encourage more consumption of meats that are usually rejected—kidneys and beef hearts. For some groups, the appeal was in the form of lectures, demonstrations, and patriotic statements. For others, the lectures were followed by free group discussion. Only three per cent of the women who merely listened to the lectures changed to the recommended foods, while 32 per cent of those who discussed the problem made the change.

[3] This section is based on Bonner, *op. cit.*, pp. 23–25.

In more recent work on small groups, there is a growing recognition that group participation is not the only means of doing the job. Creative individuals may perform more adequately outside of group pressures. Some recent studies even suggest that there are occasions when direction from above will lead the group more effectively to the solution, with less individual frustration. It would have been best to avoid the terms *democratic* and *authoritarian* in this type of research; they may carry connotations that bias the results. No doubt the emphasis on participation, and the de-emphasis of one-way communication from above, has had a healthy effect on American industry in the last few decades, as far as the dignity of the employee is concerned. However, the group is not always superior to individuals nor must every decision be discussed by a committee. The pervasive existence of hierarchies is strong evidence that they perform a necessary function. There is little research to support the view that "leaderless groups" are the most effective way of accomplishing a task.

Breakdowns of Communication

Restrictions or breakdowns of communication can have strong effects on group and individual behavior. Without communication people develop a distorted view of what others are doing, and these views are likely to result in hostility. When people are organized in groups and communication breaks down among these groups, the tendency toward hostility may be reinforced. If members of the group imagine a "threat" from the outside—and it is easy for human beings to fall into this pattern—they join the other members in a defensive compact against the outsiders. Most readers of this discussion have undoubtedly participated in such a process. Such defensiveness may lead to open conflict or to its opposite, the repression of ill feeling; in either case, the effects on total productivity and on individual satisfaction may be negative.

There is a two-way interaction between communication and hostility. Breakdowns in communication may foster hostility; but hostility clearly interferes with communication. The total effect of this self-reinforcing pattern can be highly destructive. While these conclusions appeal to common sense, there are objections to conclusions that everyone must be in full communication with everyone else all of the time. It is not even certain that a little bit of conflict now and then is a bad thing; the formation of "one big happy family" may look like the ideal, but on closer examination may prove to be a happy but stagnant party of inactive yes-men.

Limitations of Small Group Research

The reader will naturally want to approach the findings of small group research with the same critical attitude he applies to other developments in management. Several questions are particularly troublesome:

1. Are the findings of research on experimental groups applicable to more complex industrial situations? Most of the research in this area has been conducted in the laboratory, frequently with students as the participants. It is true that there are also many studies (such as the Hawthorne studies) of small groups in actual industrial situations, but the bridge between the experimental studies and the industry studies needs further development.

2. Are there implicit value judgments involved in some of the small group studies? While it is clear that the intent of most students of small groups is to be "descriptive" before they make recommendations, it is not clear that they have entirely avoided considerations of what is "good" and "bad" in their observations. The early emphasis on "democratic" leadership suggests that there may have been some inclination to demonstrate that group participation and democratic leadership is inherently more effective. Much of this research began in a period in which "permissive" and "nondirective" approaches were fashionable—in bringing up children, in education, and in industrial leadership. In recent years, small group research workers have shown greater care in avoiding prejudgment of such issues—and there are studies that suggest that some degree of direction from superiors may be effective in getting the job done.

3. The extreme enthusiasts for "group dynamics" have neglected the tyranny of the group. Group pressures can be as effective in suppressing and intimidating the individual as the autocratic leader. "Group-belongingness" may involve the sacrifice of the individual to group norms. Co-operation is not always the ultimate goal that some of the extremists make it out to be: co-operation may amount to conformity.

4. Some writers have neglected the creativity of the individual outside of the group. Whyte, in *The Organization Man,* asks whether people really *think* in groups. If they merely talk and exchange information, it is unlikely that they are creating new ideas and new ways of doing the job. Groups frequently work toward a compromise, which may involve the sacrifice of individual imagination. The authors of this book are appalled at the rapid expansion of committee work in universities; the trend toward group decision-making is growing so rapidly that only an active attack on "group-think" and "belongingness" can free faculty people to give them time for teaching and research.

Significance of Small Group Research for Business

In spite of these criticisms, the progress in the study of small groups remains one of the most impressive developments in the study of human behavior so far as its application to management is concerned. The signs are strong that this field will progress more rapidly in the future, carrying important implications not only for small groups but also for larger organizations.

If this evaluation of small group research is correct, management has two reasons for being interested. One is to keep up with research developments as they occur. The other is to be aware of the importance of small groups in current business decisions. Uncertainty about some of the present hypotheses should not blind managers to the value of a viewpoint that takes groups into account. Human beings are conditioned by group norms and pressures; the manager who recognizes this fact is more likely to take probable group and individual reactions into account in his decisions. Such a manager will not be surprised to encounter group resistance to a policy that appears to benefit its members: he will realize that the policy may conflict with group norms in a subtle way. He will not attack the resistance as irrational, but will recognize it as a "natural" kind of human behavior; and consequently he will be able to maintain a perspective that can prevent unnecessary tension and hostility.

There is little doubt that attention to group norms, to patterns of group leadership, to informal as well as formal organization, to the impact to communication networks, to the strengths and weaknesses of committee decisions, can contribute to the effectiveness of management. Managers will have to use judgment in separating the relevant generalizations from the irrelevant, the tested from the untested; but they must be concerned with groups, for groups are pervasive. Managers must answer for themselves questions of when planning group activities becomes "manipulation." There is a line between constructive "influence" and dignity-destroying "manipulation." Managers of the future will be faced with the problem of drawing that line.

Simon's Organization Theory

The most influential contemporary writer on organization is Herbert A. Simon. He himself has been influenced by the views of Chester Barnard, and has collaborated with other research workers, to the extent that it is difficult to identify his personal contribution; his most recent book on organization was written in collaboration with James G. March.[4] Thus, it may be unjust to label this theory "Simon's Organization Theory." However, it is difficult to see what other title is appropriate.

Simon has incorporated some of the findings of small group research in his theory. His approach differs from small group theory in several respects: he has incorporated material from all of the behavioral and social sciences, including sociology, political science, economics, psychology, and business and public administration, and has at times expressed his ideas in mathematical form. Simon also differs from small group research and from "human relations" research in attempting to emphasize the rational features of decision-making, as opposed to the stress on emotions that has won interest in the past. Thus, Simon's theory falls into an intermediate position between economics, in which a high degree of rationality is usually assumed, and Freudian psychology, in which the stress is on the subconscious. Simon recognizes important limits to rationality, but believes that organization theory should stress the consequences of *intended* rationality within those limits.

[4] James G. March and Herbert A. Simon, *Organizations* (New York: John Wiley & Sons, 1958).

The framework of Simon's theory

The framework of Simon's organization theory is found in his earlier work, *Administrative Behavior;*[5] his recent articles and books are concerned with parts rather than the whole. In *Administrative Behavior,* Simon views an organization as a structure of decision-makers; his theory is one of decision-making as well as one of organization. Decisions must be made at all levels of the undertaking—some of them high level decisions affecting many members, others relatively unimportant decisions about detail. Each decision is based on a number of premises, and Simon's attention is focused on how these premises are determined. Some of the premises pertain to the decision-maker's personal references, some to his social conditioning, and some to the communications he receives from other parts of the organization. Top management cannot dictate to each organization member what each decision must be, but it can influence some (perhaps the most important) premises on which the decisions are based. It can create a structure which will permit and stimulate the transmission of appropriate messages and influences.

The three terms Simon uses most frequently are: *communication, authority,* and *identification.* The organizer must build a *communication* network which will supply the *information* necessary for the decision. Without such information, the decision-maker cannot fit his decisions to the requirements of the situation. Some communications carry *authority;* they are accepted as premises for decision without deliberation as to their convenience or expediency. In his treatment of authority, Simon is influenced by Barnard; the Barnard-Simon theory has been controversial, but has led to a clarification of the problem. Special attention to the Barnard-Simon definition of authority will appear below.

Like authority, organizational *loyalties* (or *identifications*) simplify the decision-making process. Each member cannot take time to review all of the values involved in every decision; he will accept some premises on a faith based on attachment to the enterprise goals or to the leaders. Thus, in most cases loyalties help co-ordinate decisions by assuring that the members are taking the goals of the leaders into account. Narrow loyalties, for example loyalties to departmental goals, may have the opposite effect of pulling the organization in several directions. The failure of marketing and production departments to work together is a frequent illustration of this point. The marketing department may seek to meet the delivery requirements of the customers; the production department may aim at the smooth flow of orders through the plant; but these two goals can conflict, in that rush orders disrupt production schedules and lower productivity within the plant. Thus loyalties can also become confusing and disruptive in their effects. Group feeling, teamwork, or a sense of joint participation do not always contribute

[5] Herbert A. Simon, *Administrative Behavior* (New York: The Macmillan Co., 1957).

to over-all goals; they may instead support subgoals which are difficult to reconcile with the main objectives.

The consequence of this kind of reasoning (to translate Simon's descriptive analysis into rules for action) is that managers, especially higher managers, must be concerned with the *manipulation of the flow or influences to the individual decision maker.*

Simon insists that the flow of communications must be kept simple. Excess communication is frustrating; there must be ways of separating relevant influences from those that do not matter. This thought is a corrective to the position that some "group dynamics" research workers take—the more communication the better. The division of work permits specialization in the communication flow. In addition, the individual can ignore many messages as irrelevant; habit helps us focus attention on the important influences. The organization should encourage the formation of the required habits, but not to the extent that nonroutine issues are handled in a routine way.

The Barnard-Simon Position on Authority

The Barnard-Simon theory of authority is called an "acceptance" theory. A communication carries authority if it is accepted by the recipient as authoritative. This view has startled those who think of authority as belonging only to higher management—a right based on "natural law" or at least on the sanction of legislation. Our laws recognize that boards of directors have certain rights and obligations with regard to corporations. Such boards may delegate part of their authority to chief executives, who in turn may delegate to lower officials, and so on. Critics of the Barnard-Simon position insist that authority must be based on legal sanction, flowing from the top down through the organization. Thus, conflict exists between a legalistic, or formal, theory of authority and the acceptance theory.[6]

Actually the acceptance theory permits attention to the legal and social basis for authority. One reason people accept instructions from above as authoritative is that they recognize the legal support of top management. They realize that the Constitution of the United States, for example, guarantees certain rights of private property. In general, the customs and mores of society lend support to the enforcement of these rights. None of these considerations is contradictory to the acceptance view.

The value of the acceptance theory lies in its recognition of the individual's decision on whether he will act on a communication he receives. The question then becomes one of examining when acceptance does and does not

[6] Among the supporters of the formal theory, which is the traditional theory, are Harold Koontz and Cyril O'Donnell, in their *Principles of Management,* 2nd edition (New York: McGraw-Hill Book Co., Inc., 1959), pp. 48–53. If the reader feels that this discussion is too favorable to the acceptance view, he may want to read Koontz and O'Donnell as an antidote.

occur. There are different kinds of sanctions and penalties that management can apply to win acceptance. Hitler won acceptance of his authority through parades, patriotic appeals, and the threat of concentration camps. The knowledge that pay increases can depend on one's acceptance of authority helps keep people in line. In Western societies today, there is more emphasis on positive rewards than on negative sanctions, but in either case the aim is to win acceptance. The question of leadership is one of determining what patterns of management will be more effective in winning the consent of the followers. To assume, as the formal theorists do, that authority is authority because it flows from above, discourages attention to what managers can and should do to win support. A manager who has never thought about whether his orders will be followed or not, and who has never considered ways of increasing understanding and acceptance of these orders, is not likely to be effective. Barnard and Simon have performed a service in emphasizing that the acceptance of authority is a subject worthy of thought and analysis.

Administrative Man and Organization Planning

In the study of organization, Simon believes that it is essential to displace the concept of the "economic man" with that of the "administrative man." In dealing with the internal operations of a firm, it is not appropriate to assume, as economists do for larger scale problems, that the decision-maker has omniscient knowledge, that he is capable of weighing all the alternatives or considering all of the variables involved in those alternatives. The administrator cannot hope to reach the "best" solution. He must be content with solutions that "satisfy" rather than "maximize."

An understanding of the limitations of the individual decision-maker is basic to organization planning. If all members were omniscient, organizations would be unnecessary. While it is impossible to create a structure which will bring the results that omniscience would provide, it is possible to design a structure which will direct attention to the more important variables, which will simplify the communication flow, which will encourage patterns of loyalty that will contribute to the enterprise goals, and which will foster habitual responses to certain routine stimuli. The organization must be stable enough to permit expectations of the behavior of others. There must be plans and policies and a communication of these to the members concerned.

Programs: The Reduction of Decision-Making to Routines

The difficulty with the discussion of Simon's theory up to this point is that it is extremely general. It supplies a framework, but does not fill in that framework with details to guide organization planners. However, Simon's more recent work, particularly March and Simon's *Organizations,* suffers from an opposite fault—a long flow of generalizations about detail with few strands to pull them together. *Organizations* is consequently impossible to summarize. It will be necessary to select a few major points for special attention.

An interesting section of the March and Simon volume pertains to *programs;* that is, procedures for reducing to a routine the processes required for certain decisions. The fact that organizations frequently use such routines substantiates Simon's point that people do not always seek the "best" or "optimal" decisions, but must often be content with selection from satisfactory alternatives. Routine or programmed approaches to decisions cannot provide the best solution, for they are bound to simplify and generalize. What they do accomplish is a reduction in decision time and in the amount of management time taken up in relatively unimportant decisions.

March and Simon do not mention Taylor's "exception principle," but it is clear that their discussion of programs is related to that concept. Taylor advocated the delegation and routinization of repetitive decisions; March and Simon are concerned with the circumstances in which this will be desirable and the extent of routine that is possible. They point out that programs are not necessarily completely rigid; there are degrees of routinization.

March and Simon list a number of generalizations concerning programming. These generalizations are representative of their procedure throughout their book. The following is a selected list: [7]

1. The greater the programming of individual activities in an organization, the greater the *predictability* of those activities.
2. The greater the *repetitiveness* of activities, the greater the programming. This point was recognized by Taylor. Thus programming will be more extensive for clerical and factory jobs. More and more computers are being used to handle routine decisions.
3. Programming assists in the *co-ordination* of an organization by giving other segments a better basis for predicting responses.
4. Programming will concern itself primarily with those operations that are most easily observed. It will govern quality and quantity if these magnitudes are easily measured.

A systematic study of programming, along the lines suggested by March and Simon, would result in greater skills in determining what aspects of management can and cannot be reduced to routine. This is an important area in which modern organization theory is most likely to make a significant contribution to practical management.

Group Identification

One additional line of analysis will be taken from March and Simon's work to illustrate their way of looking at organizations. The issue is the extent to which individuals identify with the group to which they belong. As indi-

[7] March and Simon, *Organizations,* pp. 142–150.

cated earlier in this chapter, small group researchers are interested in this subject. The contribution of March and Simon is the construction of a framework for integrating previously unrelated research findings. They start with a series of hypotheses: [8]

1. The stronger the employee's identification with a group, the more likely his goals will conform to group norms. This conclusion is consistent with the discussion of small groups earlier in this chapter.
2. The greater the perceived prestige of the group, the stronger the tendency of the individual to identify with it. That is, a group with a high reputation for getting things done is likely to win a greater loyalty from its members.
3. The greater the extent to which members share goals, the stronger the identification with the group.
4. The more frequent the interaction among the members of the group, the greater the identification with the group.
5. The greater the satisfaction of personal needs in the group, the stronger the identification with the group.
6. The less the interpersonal competition within the group, the greater the identification with the group.

Having listed these hypotheses, March and Simon proceed to construct a diagram that pulls them together. Figure 5-2 presents this diagram, which is typical of other diagrams throughout the book.

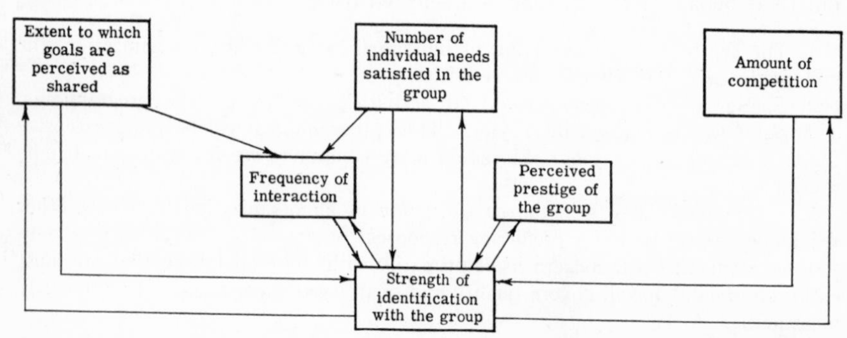

FIGURE 5-2 Factors Affecting Group Identification *

* Based on diagram on p. 66 of March and Simon, *Organizations.*

The diagram clarifies the interdependence of the variables involved. For example, the sharing of goals not only contributes to identification; identification strengthens the sharing of goals. Frequent interaction supports identification and identification increases interaction. Such a diagram simplifies relationships that otherwise may appear extremely complex.

March and Simon discuss other factors influencing the variables shown in Figure 5-2. For example, what factors contribute to the prestige of the group? The authors suggest that this depends on both the position of the group in society and on individual standards. If the group is highly success-

[8] *Ibid.,* pp. 65–66.

ful in achieving its goals, its social status is increased. If the group is composed of individuals with high social status, the group itself will tend to have a high status. Furthermore, the higher the *visibility* of the group, the higher its status. The higher the distinctiveness of the group the higher its visibility. And so on.

Similarly, there are a number of considerations affecting the frequency of interaction among the members of the group: exposure to each other, the cultural pressure to participate in the group, and similarities in background. The authors go on to analyze factors influencing the sharing of goals and the extent of competition.

Conclusions

March and Simon would be the first to admit that most of their generalizations have not been tested systematically. Their objective is to state hypotheses as clearly as possible (with diagrams) and then show the interrelationship of these hypotheses. Before tests can be made, however, March and Simon's statements must be precisely understood, and attention must be focused on the interdependence of hypotheses.

A reading of current work on organization may lead either to optimism or pessimism about the future of organization theory: optimism, because at last research workers are putting their ideas in order; pessimism, because much empirical work remains to be done before these ideas can be confidently accepted.

There is a great deal of other research and theorizing that cannot be summarized within the bounds of this chapter; more effort is being devoted to the study of organization than ever before. The casual observations and careless generalizations of earlier decades are being replaced by more cautious and more systematic attacks on the problem. It is likely that the careful methods followed by modern research workers will produce theories in which greater confidence will be possible.

While this research activity is taking place, the manager is left in a difficult position. He cannot wait until a clearly formulated and carefully tested set of theories is available. He must make organizational decisions now; even the failure to act involves a choice. Perhaps the best advice is as follows:

1. Do not be impressed by simple generalizations, even if they are sold as "universal principles."
2. Approach the problem of organization as one involving diagnosis and prescription similar to that in medicine. In other words, do not hold a rule book in one hand and an organization chart in the other to see how they check. Instead, determine just what the trouble is. Where are there difficulties that arise from the organization structure? What seem to be the most likely reasons for these difficulties? What changes in organization will remedy the situation?
3. Avoid the search for perfection. No organization can handle every issue

without friction. A little conflict among organization members may be a sign of life. Do not assume that a reorganization that will diminish this conflict is necessarily superior; placing everyone in a definite box or flattering everyone into cooperation may reduce initiative and imagination.

4. Recognize that each undertaking is unique, requiring organizational features fitting the particular circumstances at hand: the environment, the social and cultural attitudes of the members, the needs arising from technology, the type of leadership available, and the goals that are to be met.

5. Make use of both the traditional views on organization and the hypotheses of "modern" organization theory as suggestions that may be useful in making the diagnosis or proposing a solution. Recognize that there are conflicts in these generalizations; some may be more relevant than others to the situation at hand.

There is no way in which the judgment of the managers can be bypassed in organization planning. The manager who has read and reflected on published literature will have more ideas at his disposal and therefore should be more effective (if he uses these ideas flexibly). In the future, the reliance on subjective judgment may be diminished, but the need for management decisions on organizations based on personal evaluations will never be completely replaced by a science of human behavior.

Bibliographical Note

The primacy of place in modern organization theory belongs to Chester I. Barnard's *The Functions of the Executive* (1938). Barnard's dissatisfaction with traditional views led him to formulate a more systematic theory, based on attention to sociological and psychological forces. He became concerned with the fundamentals of leadership, authority, communication, and motivation. His book is difficult reading but is rich in insights. Barnard had a direct influence on Herbert A. Simon's *Administrative Behavior* (1st edition, 1947), which also promises to become a classic. Simon pays particular attention to decision-making, a subject that ever since has been a central concern of administrative theory. James G. March and Herbert A. Simon, *Organizations* (1958), summarizes and integrates more recent developments in the theory of organization.

There are many works about small groups, which has become a leading subject for research in sociology and social psychology. Among the outstanding works are George C. Homans, *The Human Group* (1950) and Josephine Klein, *The Study of Groups* (1956). Herbert Bonner's *Group Dynamics: Principles and Applications* (1959) is a useful overview of the subject.

Closely related are books on managerial psychology. Among these are Mason Haire's *Psychology in Management* (1956) and Harold Leavitt's *Managerial Psychology* (1958).

Several books of readings provide a useful introduction to theory and research on organization. Among these are Robert Dubin, *Human Relations in Administration: The Sociology of Organization* (2nd edition, 1961), and Albert H. Rubenstein and Chadwick J. Haberstroh, *Some Theories of Organization* (1960). Mason Haire has edited an excellent collection of essays on current research in organization entitled *Modern Organization Theory* (1959).

Questions and Problems

1. Do the natural sciences emphasize description or prescription? Is the same true of engineering and medicine? What should be the practice of the study of management in this respect?

2. Can you think of cases in which formation of a group may interfere with individual performance? Of cases in which it furthers such performance? What are the differences in the two situations?

3. Would you rather be a member of the star or the circle in Figure 5-1? Explain. In which would your productivity be higher?

4. What use could a manager make of small group research? Some firms send their managers to schools in group dynamics. What benefits could they expect to receive from such training?

5. Does small group research help explain such employee practices as "featherbedding," restrictions on output, and slowdowns?

6. Discuss the relationship between "democratic" and "authoritarian" leadership and the participation and directive approaches discussed in Chapter 3.

7. In the United States, classroom procedure is more participative and spontaneous than in Europe. Which pattern is preferable? How is this related to research on leadership?

8. Cite an illustration from your own experience of a breakdown in communication. What were its consequences?

9. What are your views on the subject of "manipulation" of subordinates that has received so much attention in recent critiques of management?

10. State in a few words the framework of Simon's theory of organization. In what ways is it different from traditional approaches? How does it relate to small group research?

11. Relate the distinction between programmed and non-programmed decisions to Taylor's "exception principle."

12. Apply the March-Simon generalizations on programming to the question of whether letters and reports should be filed in a routine manner.

13. The United States Marines are claimed to exhibit high group identification. Does the March-Simon analysis of identification help explain why such might be the case?

14. Think of a case familiar to you of an administrator who has authority. Is his authority based on acceptance or is it better understood from a legalistic point of view? Discuss.

15. Give illustrations of managerial activities that are usually programmed. Is there a trend toward more programming of managerial activities? Why?

16. What kinds of questions are left unanswered by the type of theory developed by Simon? What kinds of research does it call for?

6

Research Studies in Organization

THIS chapter will review a number of empirical studies, including both laboratory experiments in organization and analyses of actual organizations in operation. The student should approach these studies somewhat differently from most of the cases in this volume. Most of the cases are descriptions of actual problem situations; the student is asked to determine what the problem is, to explain why the problem exists, and to attempt to reach a solution. In this chapter, however, the case analysis has already been completed by the research worker. The objective is to learn as much as possible from the conclusions of the research worker. The student should also ask himself whether he agrees with the analysis and whether the conclusions are relevant in other kinds of situations.

Study A

Managerial Psychology: An Experiment in One-Way and Two-Way Communication (Harold Leavitt)

Leavitt describes an experiment in which a pattern of rectangles is drawn on a sheet of paper, but only one person is permitted to see the paper. It is his task to communicate the pattern by describing it in words to other people in the room. One possible pattern is shown here:

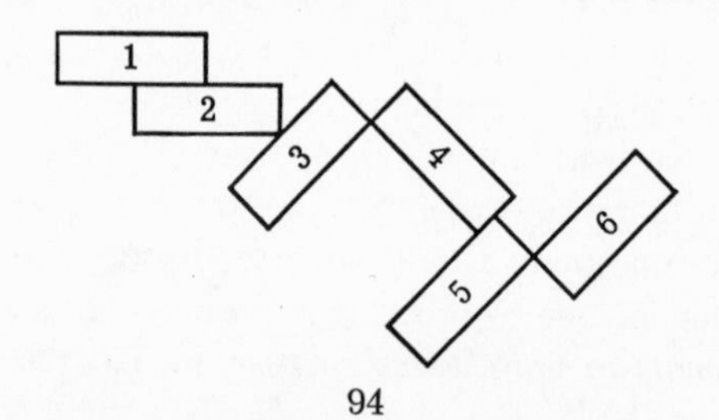

Several restrictions govern the placement of the rectangles. They must touch each other either at corners or midpoints along the line. All the angles must be either 90° or 45°. A large variety of such patterns is possible.

The task of the communicator is to supply enough instructions to his audience so that each listener can draw the pattern on a sheet of paper. He asks the listeners to draw an accurate picture of the pattern. He tries to supply instructions in words as rapidly as possible. The experiment is conducted in two ways:

1. First, the communicator turns his back on the audience and calls out the instructions. The listeners are not permitted to communicate back in any way. The communication is one-way.
2. Then two-way communication is tried. The communicator faces the listeners and permits them to ask questions freely. This time a different pattern is used.

Two measurements of the effectiveness of the communication are applied: the accuracy of the listeners' diagrams and the time the communication takes.

Leavitt summarizes his findings from this type of experiment as follows:

"Under experimental conditions these findings have emerged from this game: (1) One-way communication is considerably *faster* than two-way communication. (2) Two-way communication is *more accurate* than one-way, i.e., more people in the audience correctly reproduce the drawing under two-way conditions. (3) The receivers are more sure of themselves and make more correct judgments of how right or wrong they are in the two-way system. (4) The sender finds himself feeling psychologically under attack in the two-way system, because his receivers pick up his mistakes and oversights and *let him know about them.* The receivers may make snide remarks about the sender's intelligence and skill, and, if the receivers are trying very hard and taking the task seriously, they may actually get angry at the sender, and he at them. (5) The two-way method is relatively noisy and disorderly—with people interrupting the sender and one another, with the slowest man holding up the rest, and so on. The one-way method, on the other hand, appears neat and efficient to an outside observer, but the communication is less accurate.

"Such a demonstration points out both the advantages and the costs of one-way and of two-way communication. If *speed* alone is what is important, then one-way communication has the edge. If *appearance* is of prime importance, if one wishes to look orderly and business-like, then the one-way method again is preferable. If *one doesn't want one's mistakes to be recognized,* then again one-way communication is preferable. Then the sender will not have to hear people implying or saying that he is stupid or that there is an easier way to say what he is trying to say. Of course, such comments may be made about him whether he uses one-way or two-way communication, but under one-way conditions he will not have to listen to what is said, and it will be harder for anyone to prove that mistakes were made by A rather than B. If *one wants to protect one's power,* so that the sender can blame the receiver instead of taking blame himself, then one-way communication is again preferable. The sender can say: 'I told you what to do; you just weren't bright enough to get the word.' If he uses two-way communication, the sender will have to accept much of what blame there is, and it will be apparent to all that he deserves some of it; *but he will also get his message across.*"[1]

Study B

Management and Morale: Experiments in Illumination (F. J. Roethlisberger)

The best known studies in human relations are those conducted in the Hawthorne plant of the Western Electric Company. They are called "the Hawthorne studies." Since the studies covered a number of years and thousands of workers, it is impossible to summarize them in entirety. Therefore, attention is focused on one study: the experiments in illumination. The original intention of these experiments was the determination of the relation of the quality and quantity of illumination to productivity. The workers concerned were divided into two groups. The "test group" worked under different illumination intensities. The "control group" worked under constant illumination intensity. When the intensity for the first group was increased from 24 to 46, and then to 70 foot candles, production increased. However, it increased in both rooms, and by about the same amount in the room in which the illumination was not changed.

In another experiment, no change in illumination took place, but the workers were led to believe it was increased. The workers favored the improved lighting, but there was little effect on output. Similarly, when they believed lighting intensity was reduced, they complained, but output remained the same.

In still another experiment, the intensity was reduced to .06 of a foot candle, approximately equal to moonlight. Not until this low level was reached was there a significant effect on output.

F. J. Roethlisberger summarizes the findings:

"What did the experimenters learn? Obviously, as Stuart Chase said, there was something 'screwy,' but the experimenters were not quite sure who or what was screwy—they themselves, the subjects, or the results. One thing was clear: the results were negative. Nothing of a positive nature had been learned about the relation of illumination to industrial efficiency. If the results were to be taken at their face value, it would appear that there was no relation between illumination and industrial efficiency. However, the investigators were not yet quite willing to draw this conclusion. They re-

[1] Reprinted from *Managerial Psychology* by Harold J. Leavitt by permission of The University of Chicago Press, pp. 121–124. © 1958 by University of Chicago.

alized the difficulty of testing for the effect of a single variable in a situation where there were many uncontrolled variables. It was thought, therefore, that another experiment should be devised in which other variables affecting the output of workers could be better controlled.

"A few of the tough-minded experimenters already were beginning to suspect their basic ideas and assumptions with regard to human motivation. It occurred to them that the trouble was not so much with the results or with the subjects as it was with their notion regarding the way their subjects were supposed to behave—the notion of a simple cause-and-effect, direct relationship between certain physical changes in the workers' environment and the responses of the workers to these changes. Such a notion completely ignored the human meaning of these changes to the people who were subjected to them." [2]

In evaluating the illumination experiment and other studies Roethlisberger goes on to say:

"It was clear that the responses of workers to what was happening about them were dependent upon the significance these events had for them. In most work situations the meaning of a change is likely to be as important, if not more so, than the change itself. This was the *éclaircissement,* the new illumination, that came from the research. It was an illumination quite different from what they had expected from the illumination studies. Curiously enough, this discovery is nothing very new or startling. It is something which anyone who has had some concrete experience in handling other people intuitively recognizes and practices. Whether or not a person is going to give his services wholeheartedly to a group depends, in good part, on the way he feels about his job, his fellow workers, and supervisors—the meaning for him of what is happening about him." [3]

Study C

The Social Structure of the Restaurant (William F. Whyte)

William F. Whyte and his associates engaged in a fourteen-month study of restaurants, with emphasis on the human problems involved. Restaurants differ from factories in a number of ways. The product is perishable, so that there is a problem of co-ordinating production with demand. The employee comes in direct contact with the customer, complicating the human relationships. The most difficult problems arise in larger restaurants where there is considerable division of labor. There may be a manager, several supervisors, waitresses, bartenders, pantry workers, kitchen workers, runners, dishwashers, and other specialists.

[2] F. J. Roethlisberger, *Management and Morale* (Cambridge, Mass.: Harvard University Press, 1941), pp. 10–11.

[3] *Ibid.,* p. 15.

The position of the waitresses was especially difficult. They received instructions from fifty to one hundred customers a day. They also received orders from the supervisors and had to communicate with pantry workers, bartenders, and checkers. In their position they were prone to considerable emotional tension. Some waitresses reduced this tension by initiating communication with the customer, thus originating part of the action. Waitresses who seldom originated action were particularly tense and subject to breakdowns. Supervisors who avoided giving too many orders to the waitresses, and who instead relieved the load by receiving orders from customers, were more successful in holding down tension.

Whyte and his associates directed their attention to the relations among higher status and lower status employees. Cooks, for example, had higher status than supply men. They were older, had greater seniority, were more skilled, and were paid much more. When the lower status supply men originated orders to the cooks, there was tension. One supply man avoided calling orders to the cooks, asking the cooks to inform him when items were ready. He received better co-operation from the cooks. On the basis of this type of observation, Whyte proposes the general hypothesis that relations will be smoother when higher status individuals initiate action.

Another illustration supporting this hypothesis pertained to relations between female waitresses and male countermen. When the waitresses called orders to the countermen, there was conflict. When a barrier was built between the waitresses and the countermen, by requiring the waitresses to fill out order slips so that face to face interaction was less important or even blocked off, the operation ran more smoothly. Whyte suggests that the lower status of female workers in such operations accounts for these differences; men become irriated if they must take instructions from women.

The study suggests that attention should be given to the relation of the line of authority and the flow of work. In other industries it would be worthwhile to determine whether disagreement between the status system and the pattern of origination of instructions is responsible for conflict. If such is the case, it may be possible, as in the restaurant industry, to introduce simple changes to reduce unnecessary tension.[4]

Study D

Conflicts Between Line and Staff Officers (Melville Dalton)

Many studies have indicated that the relation between line and staff officers in an organization is a critical one. One study, conducted in three factories

[4] This section is based on William Foote Whyte, "Social Structure of the Restaurant," *American Journal of Sociology* (Jan. 1949), pp. 302–308, republished in Robert Dubin, *Human Relations in Administration* (Englewood Cliffs, N. J.: Prentice-Hall, Inc., 1951), pp. 60–67.

by sociologist Melville Dalton, points out that the theory of line-and-staff organization, which assumes that the staff people are purely advisory and that their advice and assistance will be welcomed by line officers is not realistic. In fact, conflict between line and staff officers was frequently so great it interfered with attainment of the company's goals. The failure to recognize that this situation is a predictable outcome of line and staff relationships aggravated the problem.

Moreover, Dalton found that the character of the staff officials contributed to the problem. Staff officers were unusually ambitious and individualistic. They sought status and recognition and became dissatisfied when they did not achieve these goals. Younger than the line officers, they were restless and driving. The older line officials were irritated by what they thought to be instructions from the younger staff officers. In addition, some of the staff people were inexperienced in human relationships, and failed to understand why their ideas were considered impracticable by the line officers. The staff personnel had attained a higher level of formal education, which may have given them a sense of superiority, but which did not increase their popularity with the line. The staff officers had different attitudes on dress and appearance and used better English. All of these factors created a barrier between the line and staff.

Power struggles between the line and staff were common. The line officers were skeptical of the value of the staff personnel and resented their intrusion in spheres which were essentially line. The staff officers, on the other hand, considered themselves expert on matters on which the line people were ignorant. The line officers did not always understand why higher management had inflicted these interfering specialists upon their departments, and suspected that this was another way of bringing them under control. They feared staff innovations which might break up existing informal arrangements and which might reveal inadequacies in past departmental efficiency.

Dalton is cautious in concluding that these patterns are pervasive in industry, although other studies support his conclusions. There can be little doubt that the kind of conflict he describes is widespread, taking special forms in particular firms. Dalton's recommendations are not reproduced here, because they present only one possible approach to the problem and are, in fact, somewhat controversial. More important for management is to become aware of the problem; only then will it be possible to work out a solution (or a partial solution since the complete absence of friction is unattainable) appropriate in the circumstances.[5]

[5] Melville Dalton, "Conflicts Between Staff and Line Managerial Officers," *American Sociological Review,* June 1950, most of which is reprinted in Robert Dubin, *Human Relations in Administration* (Englewood Cliffs, N. J.: Prentice-Hall, Inc., 1951), pp. 128–138.

Study E

The Effects of Co-operation and Competition (A. Mintz)

Mintz conducted a simple experiment illustrating one type of research on small groups. Two persons were instructed to pull a wedge, attached to a line and rod, out of a narrow-necked bottle. The two wedges were of such a size that if both were pulled at once, a jam would occur. Usually the subjects avoided a jam by making an arrangement for priorities. When Mintz introduced stress and competition into the situation by allowing water to enter the bottle, and by rewarding the one who extracted his wedge before it got wet, the wedges were jammed. The subjects did not take time to arrange the operation to avoid jams.

Of course, such an experiment covers only a small part of co-operation and competition. Management can use competition to spur employees on to greater effort; but this experiment suggests that there are cases in which such attempts will create more confusion than production.[6]

Study F

An Accounting Organization (Herbert A. Simon)

While most of Simon's work has been in the description of organizations and in the formulation of descriptive theories, he has also assisted in giving advice on actual organizations. It is clear that his theories, described in Chapter 5, have played an important part in suggesting recommendations. For example, Simon and several colleagues made a study of the accounting organization of a large firm. The central issue was the appropriate extent of centralization or decentralization in accounting. Simon rejected traditional approaches to this question and insisted that the issues were ones concerning human behavior. He expressed the view that "the reshuffling of departments, or what not—if it has any point at all, makes that point through its effects on the behaviors of individual executives and groups of executives. That is to say, it works through . . . identifications and loyalties, authority, communications."[7] The problem is one of predicting the consequences of reorganization in terms of human behavior, and this calls for attention to the particular situation rather than to rule books.

The question in this study was what organization of the accounting department would contribute most to supplying useful information at the needed points. Accounting data are used in making decisions. The objective should

[6] The experiment by Mintz, originally written up in his article, "Nonadaptive Group Behavior" in the *Journal of Abnormal Psychology* (1951), is summarized in Josephine Klein, *The Study of Groups* (London: Routledge and Kegan Paul, 1956), pp. 35–36.

[7] Herbert A. Simon, *Administrative Behavior,* 2nd edition (New York: The Macmillan Co., 1957), p. xix.

be to direct the flow of data to the decision-making unit. Analysis was necessary to determine what kinds of data were needed by the vice president, the factory manager, and so on. Only when this analysis was complete was it possible to recommend changes in the organization structure.

The recommendations based on this analysis were as follows: (1) A small group of analysts should be formed to assist top management. These analysts would be concerned with special studies rather than with periodic reports. They would study the profitability of possible changes in operating methods and equipment. (2) At the factory department level there should be one or more accounting analysts, familiar with local operations, who could interpret the periodic financial and cost statements for the department heads. Thus, the whole organization was to take a form which would bring the information to bear on decisions in which that information was needed.[8]

[8] The original publication of this study (which develops many points not summarized here) is Herbert A. Simon, Harold Guetzkow, George Kozmetsky, and Gordon Tyndall, *Centralization Versus Decentralization in Organizing the Controller's Department* (New York: Controllership Foundation, 1954). A brief summary appears in Simon, *Administrative Behavior,* 1957, pp. xix–xx.

7

Motivation, Incentives, and Morale

WHY do people work? Why do some strive for the highest attainments while others are content with mediocrity? Such questions are central to management, but like most big questions, they evoke complicated and uncertain answers. There are no simple rules for stimulating employees to greater effort.

The subject of motivation is closely related to that of organization. In organizing, interest lies in creating a structure (or permitting one to grow) that will encourage personnel to make full use of their skills and talents. If there is a line between organization and motivation, organization is concerned with relations among individuals (or positions), while motivation pays more attention to the attitudes and efforts of each individual separately. However, there is no need to draw a line; this chapter will simply extend the discussion of motivation beyond the analysis of the preceding chapters.

Motivation is thought of in two ways. It is said that managers "motivate" their employees, or fail to do so. Used this way, it implies that the concern is with how superiors influence subordinates. The dictionary, however, defines a "motive" as something within the individual which incites him to action. Basic needs of the individual result in his striving. Looking at the subject this way, the problem for management is discovering these needs.

Theories of Motivation

A monistic theory of motivation

One theory is that people work for one goal—more money. Such a theory is monistic; it seeks a single cause of behavior. A critical study of this theory will lead to its rejection and to a more complete, pluralistic explanation.

The monistic theory accepts the notion of "economic man"—the man who acts only to increase his monetary rewards. Such a theory states that the higher the pay, the greater the effort. If pay is made to depend on effort, the effort will increase. The rewarding of "correct behavior" should lead to the "reinforcement" of that behavior. The theory under discussion is illustrated in Figure 7-1, in which greater effort not only leads to greater pay, but also the reward of greater pay stimulates greater effort.

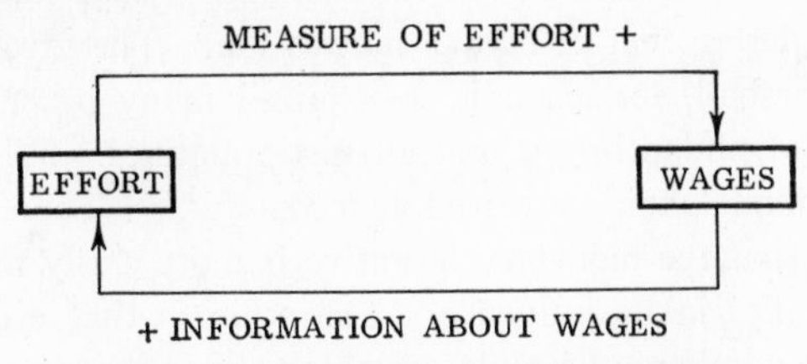

FIGURE 7-1 Effort-Reward-Effort Model

This theory carries the following implications, frequently stated as "principles" in management textbooks:

1. An individual incentive is more effective than a group incentive. Thus, according to this view, individual piece rates, which pay a set amount for every unit a man turns out, should provide a high incentive. If an individual receives pay according to his own effort, he knows he can influence his own pay packet and will work harder. In a group incentive system, the whole group shares the rewards for his efforts, so that the individual incentive is diluted. If some members of the group work harder and others relax, there may be strains and resentments resulting from the "unfairness" of spreading the reward over the entire group.
2. The incentive is more effective the more rapidly the wage payment reflects the added production. Bonuses at the end of the year are less effective than those at the end of the week, for the individual loses sight of rewards far off in the future.
3. The greater the reward for added output, the greater will be the stimulus. According to this line of reasoning, the Taylor differential piece-rate system, which pays a higher piece rate for total output to workers surpassing "standard" output, will provide an extremely high reward for reaching standard. A straight piece-rate will be more effective than a 50% bonus system, which shares the savings in wage cost resulting from higher productivity between the workers and management. The 50% bonus will be more effective than straight hourly pay.

Even a supporter of this monistic theory (if there is any) would agree that management must weigh the benefits of an incentive system against its costs. Thus, the Taylor differential piece rate might pay such large rewards as to increase wage costs faster than it raises output. Whether this is the defect that has led to the system's disappearance is not clear—the Taylor system is defective also as an incentive in placing too much pressure on the worker and creating too many tensions.

In any case, there is much evidence to raise doubts about the universality of the three principles just stated. Some group bonus systems have produced remarkable results. The most widely publicized successes in incentives have been profit-sharing or savings-sharing plans, involving large groups (in which, according to the monistic theory, the incentive should be low) and considerable delay in payment. However, a number of profit-sharing plans have failed. Apparently the problem of incentives is more complex than a simple, one-motive theory will admit. The solution is to revise or scrap the theory.

Evaluation of the Monistic Theory. The assumption of "economic man" is an old one in economic theory; but the economists have never claimed that it is an accurate description of human motivation. The great English economist, Alfred Marshall, for example, recognized many other human aspirations, and wrote of philanthropic and altruistic motives. Why then has the concept of "economic man" survived in economics? There are two main reasons. One is that the monetary incentive is more easily measured, partly because it is steadier in its influence. The other is that economics is concerned with large numbers of people, in which the influence of other motives may cancel out. The test of the usefulness of the "economic man" assumption is whether it leads to verifiable predictions—and economists believe that in taking large numbers of individuals, it does. This is an oversimplified discussion of a central issue in the methodology of economics; the main point is that an assumption, partially true for the single unit, may be highly relevant for large aggregates of such units.

The subject of management, however, is concerned with individual motivation. Every study on the subject of motivation and morale presents evidence of the complicated character of human willingness to work. The "economic man" hypothesis is no longer adequate. It is true that older books on management restricted their attention chiefly to monetary incentive schemes, but recently there has been a broadening of perspective.

Nevertheless, monetary incentives should not be neglected. They *are* important and will receive considerable attention in this chapter and the next. The position that money never acts as an incentive is as narrow-minded as its antithesis. It will receive the ridicule it deserves from those students who are working themselves to the point of exhaustion to earn money to stay in school. They know that monetary rewards have something to do with their willingness to spend hours working rather than sleeping late. The fact is that the relative importance of monetary and nonmonetary incentives is not known; the best assumption is that they are all worthy of management's attention.

A pluralistic theory

A more complete theory of motivation recognizes that individuals work to fulfill a variety of needs, not one kind. The psychologists and sociologists working on this subject break these needs into the following categories:

1. Subsistence needs—the basic need for food, clothing and housing common to the whole human race.
2. Social needs—the need to relate one's self to his fellow human beings.
3. Status needs—the desire to win a satisfactory position in the status ladder.
4. The need for self-esteem—the need to find a position in the world that will permit the individual to have respect for himself.
5. The need for self-fulfillment—the need to find an occupation that will permit one to apply his skills, and allow him to realize his potential.

Some writers combine the last four into two categories: social needs and ego needs. Regardless of the classification, however, the stress is on the individual's need for approval by his contemporaries and for recognition of his attainments. Equally important is the stress on self-respect; an employee who does not believe in what he is doing will lose interest in his task.

One mistake management can make is to assume that all employees are alike in motivation. The pluralistic approach should be taken as a flexible guide. No doubt those close to starvation are more concerned with subsistence needs. Thus, some writers refer to a *hierarchy of needs*, with the subsistence or physiological needs coming first. *When these are satisfied*, they will no longer motivate. Differences in individual needs then become important to motivation.

Where do monetary incentives fit into this framework? Monetary rewards help us meet subsistence needs, but money is also a symbol of status and permits us to purchase items that carry status. In a wealthy country like the United States, money acts as an incentive primarily because it fulfills social and status objectives. We could subsist on much lower levels of income but we could not clothe and house ourselves (and especially transport ourselves) in a style that would impress our fellow-beings or at least avoid their scorn.

In this connection, many studies point out that employees are less concerned with the *absolute level* of their wages than in their relation to the wages of other workers. If workers feel that pay relationships are unfair, they become discontented even though their pay may be high from the subsistence point of view. Even subsistence is a relative matter and is partly socially determined. Most Americans would suffer on incomes that less fortunate Asians find bearable. What the American today considers necessary for existence consists of many items his great grandparents never knew, such as electric lights and refrigeration. Thus, there is a complicated interrelationship among the needs outlined in our theory. The main point is to recognize that there are many different needs and that these vary in character from individual to individual.

Aspiration Levels, Productivity and Morale

James March and Herbert Simon have constructed a model consistent with the preceding discussion. They place emphasis on a psychological concept—

"level of aspiration." It will be useful to contrast this model with the simple effort-reward-effort model shown at the beginning of this chapter. Figure 7-2 presents a diagram illustrating the aspiration level model.[1]

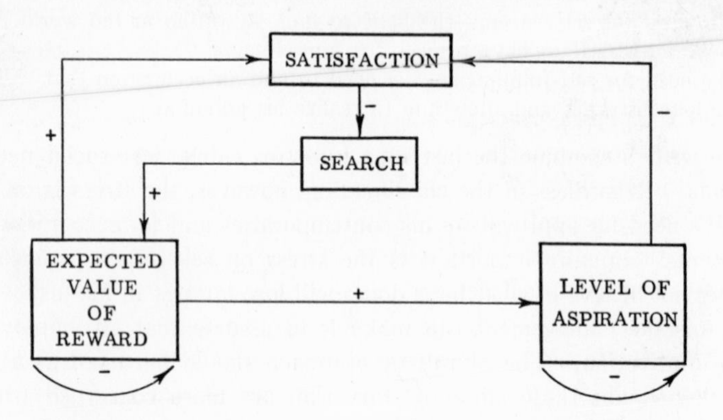

FIGURE 7-2 General Model of Adoptive Motivated Behavior

The following list gives the main generalizations incorporated in this diagram:

1. The lower the individual's satisfaction, the greater the search for alternative ways or better ways of doing the job.
2. The greater the search, the greater the expected reward. That is, the more one searches for better ways of doing the job the higher his expectation of achieving higher rewards.
3. The greater the expected reward, the higher the satisfaction.
4. The higher the expected reward, the higher the level of aspiration.
5. The higher the level of aspiration, the lower the satisfaction.

Suppose an individual is dissatisfied with his present lot. He then searches for alternatives to improve the situation. One of these may be to increase production, in the expectation that this will increase the rewards, especially, let us say, monetary rewards. The higher rewards lead to higher satisfaction. At the same time, there may be an increase in the level of aspiration—the individual, having reached this higher level, wishes to go on to greater heights. The increase in aspiration level lowers satisfaction. Whether the net effect is greater satisfaction depends on which is rising faster: the rewards or the level of aspiration. If the level of aspiration rises about the same rate as the expected reward, the individual will continue to be motivated by his mild dissatisfaction. If the level of aspiration does not rise while the rewards rise, the individual becomes complacent and his search activity declines. If, on the other hand, the level of aspiration jumps beyond the possible reach of the individual, the result may be frustration or even neurotic behavior.

March and Simon conclude from this kind of analysis that high satisfac-

[1] James G. March and Herbert A. Simon, *op. cit.*, p. 49.

tion does not necessarily stimulate productivity. They state that motivation to produce "stems from a present or anticipated state of discontent and a perception of a direct connection between individual production and a new state of satisfaction." [2] It is not necessary to comment that March and Simon do not restrict their discussion to monetary rewards; the same reasoning can be applied to nonmonetary satisfactions.

At first it appears that the March-Simon model is contradictory to the effort-reward-effort model, even when that model is broadened to include nonmonetary incentives. The earlier model seems to imply that higher wages, by leading to higher satisfaction, stimulate greater effort; but in March and Simon it is dissatisfaction that stimulates effort. The contradiction is only apparent. The individual certainly *expects* higher satisfaction from the rewards of greater effort; this expectation may lead to dissatisfaction with present wage levels and may thus stimulate effort. Whether actual increased satisfaction is achieved depends on what happens to aspiration levels.

The most important result of this discussion is doubt that higher morale or satisfaction necessarily leads to greater output. Recent empirical studies support this doubt. A good situation for productivity is one in which employees have enough confidence in management that they will not continually seek other positions; they are slightly restless with their present status (monetary or otherwise) and thus are seeking ways of improving it; but they can see ways of improving that status through their own efforts. Such employees will not become complacent yes-men; but they also will not become frustrated retreaters from the world.

Workers' Attitudes Toward Jobs

In investigating the subject of motivation, research workers have studied what employees want from their jobs. Over 150 interview studies of workers' attitudes on the jobs show variation in conclusions. Most of the studies rank *security,* or steadiness of employment, as the job attribute most important to the worker. The second highest rating is given *recognition* or *interest.* Wages rank lower on the list.

These studies are of interest because they tend to confirm that monetary rewards are not all-important; but the findings are limited in significance. The interviewer does not always communicate fully with the employee. The terms, such as "security," are ambiguous. The employee himself may not really know what motivates his effort; some important motives may be unconscious. There are individual differences in attitudes toward wages or security. Thus, it is unreasonable to conclude from these studies that wages are unimportant in motivation. At best, they indicate diversity in worker

[2] *Ibid.,* p. 51.

opinions about job characteristics important to them. Managers should be aware of this diversity of opinion, and avoid the tendency to assume that motives important to higher management (who work in a different environment with different kinds of opportunities and rewards) are those that govern all employees. It may well be that motives for the same person change in different stages of life.

Wage Incentives

A classification of wage incentive systems

Historically, wages have received primary attention as a motivating force. Writers have traced wage incentive plans back to biblical times. Piecework systems of pay were known by the thirteenth and fourteenth centuries, but it was not until the time of F. W. Taylor and Frank Gilbreth that wage incentives were based on carefully determined standards. Since their time, there has been continuous experimentation with a wide variety of systems, but there is little evidence of how successful these systems have been in practice. This chapter will deal with broad categories, not with any individual system. The reader should first understand the distinctions among the following classifications:

A. *Day wages verus incentive wages.* The expression "day wage" is used to refer to payment by time, whether the actual time period used is the hour, the week, or the month. Such wages are still the most common, despite all of the experimentation with incentive systems. No added payment is made for added effort, at least not directly. The worker may recognize that future promotions and wage increases will be influenced by his present performance, and thus be indirectly motivated.

Incentive plans offer a direct reward for greater effort, although this reward may take a number of different forms. It is assumed that the worker will respond to this reward and produce more than he would on payment by time.

B. *Individual versus group incentives.* Individual wage incentive systems reward each employee according to his performance. If he works above standard, he receives more than standard pay. Group plans are based on the performance of a number of individuals taken together; if a member of the group is slower than standard, while the group as a whole is above standard, he will still receive extra pay. Individual systems are more common than group plans. Group plans frequently receive a great deal of publicity because of spectacular results sometimes achieved in increased output.

C. *Weekly incentive systems versus long-term collective systems.* Both individual and group incentives may be paid at short intervals, weekly or some other such period. Individual incentives are almost always paid this way. Some group plans, especially those plans that take the company or plant as the unit, pay less frequently, four times a year, or even once a year. Profit-sharing and savings-sharing plans fall in the latter classification.

D. *Piecework versus other incentive plans.* Piecework, that is, payment according to the number of pieces completed, remains the most common incentive system, largely because of its simplicity. Sometimes it is placed in a separate category from all other incentive plans, although it is clear that it differs from them only in degree. Piecework may be on either an individual or group basis; but individual piece rates are more common.

E. *Profit-sharing versus savings-sharing plans.* The long-term collective systems fall into two main categories. Profit-sharing pays some share of the company profits to the employees at quarterly or annual intervals. There has been a considerable history of experimentation with profit-sharing plans. More recently (since World War II), company-wide or plant-wide savings-sharing plans have received wide publicity even though only a small number of companies operate on such plans. In general, they reward the employees for cutting company-wide wage costs below some predetermined ratio. One of the best known of these, the Scanlon Plan, will be discussed in the next chapter.

F. *Plans based on production versus plans based on other measures.* Emphasis of the plans discussed so far is on comparisons of production with some standard (though this is not true of profit-sharing or savings-sharing, which will reward the employees for any kind of contribution made to profits). Some plans base the rewards on other measures. Some companies, for example, adjust the pay according to the employee's merit rating. This merit rating will emphasize considerations in addition to output: quality of product, dependability, initiative, attendance, reduction of waste. Special bonuses for quality are sometimes paid.

An evaluation of incentive plans in general

At our present state of knowledge, a categorical report on the effectiveness of incentive systems is not possible. Results have been contradictory, with successes and failures of plans that are similar. Those who have studied wage incentives have not succeeded in separating the effects of the bonuses from the effects of other changes made at the same time. For example, in the introduction of piece rates, a company will frequently review its methods and its time standards to insure that the standards used for wage payments are appropriate; but if there is an increase in output, it may well be due to the improvement in management rather than greater employee effort.

There are many positions for which time standards are difficult to establish and for which, therefore, direct wage incentives are uncommon. Company presidents or college professors do not perform in a manner that is easily measurable; the former may be paid a profit-sharing bonus for which direct measurement of output is unnecessary; the latter could receive bonuses according to some merit-rating system (perhaps even a rating by students). Too much stress on quantity of output may undermine quality standards. It is not surprising, in view of the long list of disadvantages in Table 7-1, that incentive systems cover only about 30% of the employees in the United States and Great Britain. The Soviet Union places greater stress on wage incentive plans than do Western nations.

Many people have attempted to study the effectiveness of incentive plans, through statistical studies, questionnaires, individual case studies, and controlled experiments. Marriott's survey of these studies suggests that still little is known about the subject.[3] Wage incentives are part of a total situation, and research workers have not had success in separating the influence of wages from other factors. Marriott and other observers argue that incentive systems have their main effect, not on employee effort, but upon organization and supervision. On the whole, incentive systems, if properly managed, are useful. The point is that they must be properly managed, and this involves more than the mere introduction of a formula for computing bonuses.

TABLE 7-1

ADVANTAGES AND DISADVANTAGES OF WAGE INCENTIVE SYSTEMS

Advantages

When well designed and properly applied, payment by results can generally be relied upon to yield increased output, lower costs of production, and higher earnings for the workers.

Work study associated with payment by results is a direct stimulus to improve the organization of work and to eliminate lost time and other waste.

Labor and total costs per unit of output can be estimated more accurately in advance.

Less direct supervision is needed to keep output up to a reasonable level.

Disadvantages

There is a tendency for quality to deteriorate unless there is a stricter system of checking and inspection.

Payment by results may lead to opposition or restriction of output when new machines and methods are proposed or introduced. This is because of the fear that the job may be restudied and earnings reduced.

When paid by results, workers tend to regard their highest earnings as normal and therefore to press for a considerably higher minimum wage.

The amount and cost of clerical work is increased.

There is danger of disregarding safety regulations and thereby increasing accidents.

Some workers tend to overwork and to undermine their health.

Jealousies may arise among workers because some are able to earn more than others or because fast workers are dissatisfied with slower or older workers in the group.

It is difficult to set piece or bonus rates accurately. If they are too low, workers may be under pressure to work too hard and become dissatisfied; if too high, they may slacken their efforts to avoid a revision of rates.

Source: R. Marriott, *Incentive Payments Systems: A Review of Research and Opinion* (London: Staples Press), pp. 46–47.

[3] R. Marriott, *Incentive Payment Systems: A Review of Research and Opinion* (London: Staples Press), pp. 131–132 and *passim.*

The failures of incentive systems

A history of applications of incentive systems would reveal many failures—cases in which the results were unnoticeable or even negative. Mismanagement has been largely responsible, though union or informal group resistances have contributed to the failures. Before 1930, many plans were introduced with insufficient care. Frequently jobs were not standardized and time standards were inaccurately determined. This created discrepancies among jobs, some paying bonuses with little effort ("loose standards"), and some with such tight standards that no bonuses were possible. Tension was the result.

A notorious practice in early years was "rate-cutting." If the workers were successful in producing above standard and earning large bonuses, managers often tightened the standard. This can destroy worker confidence in management or cause general antipathy, especially among unionized workers.

Studies have revealed that workers may restrict output even when on an incentive system. Sometimes union leaders encourage restrictionism, but non-union workers have also resorted to the practice. It would be wrong to conclude that these restrictions are always a deliberate plot to sabotage management. Frequently they are a part of what has been called "informal organization" in an earlier chapter. By custom and tradition, workers build up attitudes about what levels of output are "right" and "wrong." Where management has not taken labor into its confidence, there may be suspicion of standards that management may set. The fear of unemployment accounts for restrictions; workers do not want to work themselves out of a job.

The best managements can have problems in setting standards. While "rate-cutting" is discredited today in management circles, it is sometimes difficult to draw the line between what is and is not "rate-cutting." Often workers themselves are able to find short-cuts in doing the job; as a result their bonuses become higher, giving the appearance that standards are "loose." Opportunities for this method of increasing bonuses vary from one job to the next, leading to discrepancies in pay. A new form of rate-cutting has come into practice—introduction of a new method along with a new time standard. It is unreasonable to request that management refrain from introducing new methods when they will cut costs; but it is understandable that employees may resent this as a new way of avoiding high bonuses.

If incentives are to work, management must work closely with labor to win its confidence. Along with improved organization and communications, management must combine nonfinancial incentives with wage incentives. However, there are no simple guides, and, as previous chapters on organization have demonstrated, there is plenty of disagreement, even on the general direction management should take. Managers must consider the alternatives, and work out the answers, not by reference to neat formulas, but by hard thought about the needs of the particular situation.

Sound management of wage incentives

This chapter has been devoted to a general view of incentives, not the technicalities of particular systems. This is done in the belief that the particular characteristics of a system are much less important than the way it is introduced and maintained. A simple set of rules governing wage incentives has not been provided, but the following list, summarizing the key points of this chapter, may be useful:

1. Management should recognize that the effectiveness of incentives depends on the total situation, which includes worker-management confidence, relations with the union, the quality of communication and of supervision, and the traditions of the industry.
2. Management should not introduce an incentive system until it has taken action to provide a full understanding of what is involved. This may require procedures for the participation of employees and negotiations with the union.
3. Management should avoid actions that could be interpreted as "unfair." There must be machinery for handling grievances. Management must avoid actions that resemble "rate-cutting," not an easy task in view of the need to change methods and rates from time to time.
4. It is essential that management pay in proportion to output, once output has risen above that required for the guaranteed pay. Some of the older plans paid employees only one-half or three-fourths of the savings from extra output, but this is no longer acceptable to the unions or the employees. Management will still find increased productivity profitable, even if it does not reduce wage costs per unit, for the overhead costs will be spread over a greater output.
5. Management should train supervisors all the way down the line to understand the incentive system, so that the foremen and department managers will be able to deal with problems within their own departments.
6. Great care should be taken in setting the standards to avoid rates that are too loose or too tight. Chapter 13 will deal with setting standards. Without sound standards it is impossible to have fair incentive rates.

Many other specific requirements could be listed. Today it is accepted that there must be a guaranteed hourly minimum wage. If low output persists, it may be desirable to transfer the employee to another department. If the quantity bonus undermines quality standards, it will be necessary to specify rules on the quality that is required. This may involve an increase in inspection costs. In all systems there must be a provision for paying the employee a fair hourly wage for down-time over which he has no control.

General Conclusions on Morale

Morale is a consideration throughout this book, but it requires some special attention. High morale is generally assumed to contribute to high performance, but there are exceptions. It is unlikely that the fully satisfied individual will be the one to strive hardest toward a higher goal. The authors suggest that what seems to be conducive to immediately improved morale may, in some cases, be destructive. For example, application of a "soft" discipline to a rule-breaker may at first contribute to his "growth," but in the long run may confuse him because of the lack of clarity in the standards of enforcement. Not only must one look at the morale of the particular individual, but also at that of the entire work force, which may resent the inconsistent way in which discipline is negotiated with a single individual for the sake of his morale.

What if morale and productivity come into conflict as sometimes occurs? This is a question that books on human relations do not usually face; and perhaps there is no answer, for management itself must weigh the goals it hopes to achieve. Nevertheless, to deny that the issue ever exists is a disservice to management, which must be prepared to face such issues when they arise.

Assuming that morale is always conducive to productivity (and probably it usually is), this does not mean that it is all to the good. Recently, critics of the human relations literature have suggested that complacent, conformist "organization men" are the result of the effort to make everyone feel at home at his workplace. There is still room, even on management levels, for the irritable, irritating, rude, imaginative, driving individualist who does not care what people think.

In spite of criticism, the human relations movement has contributed significantly to the improvement of management. Factories and offices are more human places of work. The dignity of the individual is enhanced by present methods of supervision. He now has a voice in actions that under former "army sergeant" methods of supervision were precluded. Business is more democratic than ever before, and in a democratic society this is a healthy development. But democracy can be distorted to cover subtle forms of autocracy; and "participation" can develop into a futile cycle of committee meetings to recommend the appointment of still more committees.

Morale is thus a complicated subject. The educated manager will be aware of the variety of views, and flexible enough to apply the methods appropriate under the circumstances; he will avoid fads; he will be able to distinguish the charlatan in applied psychology from the honest seeker after truth; he will study new research findings and new theoretical developments, and revise his views as knowledge of the subject of human behavior develops. In dealing with morale, it will be the manager's job to sift the theories, to examine the facts, and in the end to apply his personal judgment.

Bibliographical Note

Barnard's *Functions of the Executive* (1938) is again an excellent starting point in a bibliography on motivation. Books on wage incentives were common in earlier years, but Barnard was a pioneer in the recognition of the deeper sociological and psychological foundations of incentives. Some readers will find his views extreme (an extract is presented in the next chapter), but none can deny the importance of going beyond a simple assumption that greater pay motivates more work. A. H. Maslow's *Motivation and Personality* (1954) is a readable discussion of the subject by a professional psychologist. Maslow emphasizes the hierarchy of needs and its relation to motivation. William F. Whyte's *Money and Motivation* (1955) presents a sociological approach, with direct references to the problem of motivation in industry. A. Zalesnik, C. R. Christensen, and F. J. Roethlisberger, *The Motivation, Productivity, and Satisfaction of Workers* (1958) is of special interest, since it relates the Mayo-Roethlisberger views on human relations to modern research. Douglas McGregor's *The Human Side of Management* (1960) is a brief textbook emphasizing the participation and challenge and response approaches to motivation.

There are many books on the techniques of wage administration, but most of them lack the psychological depth and empirical basis desired. Charles W. Lytle's *Wage Incentive Methods* (1942) is an outstanding presentation of earlier thinking. J. Keith Louden and J. Wayne Deegan, *Wage Incentives* (2nd edition, 1959) presents a standard contemporary view. James F. Lincoln's *Incentive Management* is a provocative (if somewhat repetitive) discussion of group incentives and profit-sharing by a manager who has had immense success in actual practice.

R. Marriott's *Incentive Payments Systems: A Review of Research and Opinion* (1958) is not only an excellent review of the whole subject of wage incentives; it is also an outstanding critique of the present state of knowledge.

Questions and Problems

1. To what extent do you think you will be motivated by monetary and non-monetary rewards in the following decisions?
   (a) Selection of a position upon graduation.
   (b) Deciding whether or not to take courses or continue your education in other ways after graduation.
   (c) Deciding to transfer to another firm later in your career.
   (d) Deciding how much effort you will put into your job.
   (e) Deciding whether you will work extra time in the evenings or on weekends.
   (f) Deciding whether or not you will accept a transfer to an entirely new location.
   (g) Deciding when you will retire.
2. Do you think your acquaintances would answer the question in (1) the same way? Are there individual differences in the importance of monetary and non-monetary rewards? Do you think that your answers to the first question will be different twenty years from now?
3. Would you work more effectively on a piece-rate or on straight day wages? Would the answer depend on the job in question?
4. Why are some group bonus systems restricted to management levels?
5. According to the discussion of the hierarchy of needs one might expect that the most primitive savages would place the greatest stress on subsistence needs, while Americans would be more motivated by ego needs. Is this true? Do the Buddhist lamas in Tibet fit into this frame of thought?
6. What experiences might raise your level of aspirations? Is it true that slight satisfaction would stimulate your search for better ways of doing a job?
7. Evaluate the following: "Profit-sharing violates the principles of sound wage management in two ways. It does not restrict the reward to the individual re-

sponsible for the added profit. It pays a reward long after the effort that led to the profit. Therefore profit-sharing should be abandoned."

8. Evaluate the following: "Profit-sharing promises to revolutionize labor-management relations, by bringing employee goals in line with those of management. It recognizes the social interdependence of members of a firm, increases feelings of responsibility and contributes to a sense of teamwork. In time all firms will go over to profit-sharing or some other collective bonus plan."

9. Why are some unions opposed to incentive pay systems? Why do other unions accept or even encourage incentive payments?

10. Piecework systems of pay often create tensions about time standards. Explain.

11. In some cases union-management committees have tried to set time standards jointly. Is this a sound idea?

12. In spite of the fact that people usually produce more under an incentive wage system, many managements do not use them because of the problems that they induce. What kinds of problems do you think incentive systems will create?

13. Specialists in human relations stress the improvement of morale of employees. What is meant by morale? How would you measure morale?

8

Extracts and Cases on Motivation

WHILE the previous chapter discussed important factors in a theory of motivation and incentives, this chapter will provide extracts from some of the leading thinkers on the subject. The first group of quotations are selected from writings by Chester I. Barnard. His personal experience as a chief executive of a telephone company and as a member of numerous policy making groups enabled him to write one of the classics in managerial literature. The second extract is a report of the results of research by leading sociologists directing their attention to problems of human relations in a business firm. The third selection, by Rensis Likert, represents the result of research by a psychologist concentrating on the relation of motivation to productivity. The reader will be able to develop his views on motivation more completely by interrelating the views in these extracts with the theory developed in Chapter 7.

The cases in this chapter offer specific applications in operating situations of the ideas previously explained. The nature of research creates unique problems illustrated in the first case. The second case summarizes the human relations program of International Business Machines Corporation—a classic illustration of using "fringe benefits" to provide an atmosphere within which workers are motivated. The two plans explained in the Ashland Oil case have been adopted widely in industry in recent years. The Lincoln Electric Company's "incentive management" has been discussed widely. The Scanlon Plan represents a system used in many firms to provide motivation for employees on a company-wide basis. In each of these cases, the student should appraise the alternatives for motivating workers.

EXTRACT A

Functions of the Executive (Chester Barnard)

. . . Under a money economy and the highly specialized production of material goods, the range and profusion of material inducements are very great. The complexity of schedules of money compensation, the difficulty of securing the monetary means of compensation, and the power of exchange which money gives in organized markets, have served to exaggerate the importance of money in particular and material inducements in general as incentives to personal contributions to organized effort. It goes without elaboration that where a large part of the time of an indivdual is devoted to one organization, the physiological necessities—food, shelter, clothing—require that material inducements should be present in most cases; but these requirements are so limited that they are satisfied with small quantities. The unaided power of material incentives, when the minimum necessities are satisfied, in my opinion is exceedingly limited as to most men, depending almost entirely for its development upon persuasion. . . .

. . . it seems to me to be a matter of common experience that material rewards are ineffective beyond the subsistence level excepting to a very limited proportion of men; that most men neither work harder for more material things, nor can be induced thereby to devote more than a fraction of their possible contribution to organized effort. It is likewise a matter of both present experience and past history that many of the most effective and powerful organizations are built up on incentives in which the materialistic elements, above bare subsistence, are either relatively lacking or absolutely absent. Military organizations have been relatively lacking in material incentives. The greater part of the work of political organizations is without material incentive. Religious organizations are characterized on the whole by material sacrifice. It seems to me to be definitely a general fact that even in purely commercial organizations material incentives are so weak as to be almost negligible except when reinforced by other incentives. . . .

Inducements of a personal, non-materialistic character are of great importance to secure cooperative effort about the minimum material rewards essential to subsistence. The opportunities for distinction, prestige, personal power, and the attainment of dominating position are much more important than material rewards in the development of all sorts of organizations, including commercial organizations. . . . Even in strictly commercial organizations, where it is least supposed to be true, money without distinction, prestige, position, is so utterly ineffective that it is rare that greater income can be made to serve even temporarily as an inducement if accompanied by suppression of prestige. . . .

Ideal benefactions as inducements to cooperation are among the most powerful and the most neglected. By ideal benefaction I mean the capacity of organizations to satisfy personal ideals usually relating to non-material, future, or altruistic relations. They include pride of workmanship, sense of adequacy, altruistic service for family or others, loyalty to organization in patriotism, etc., aesthetic and religious feeling. They also include the opportunities for the satisfaction of the motives of hate and revenge, often the controlling factor in adherence to and intensity of effort in some organizations. . . .

Men often will not work at all, and will rarely work well, under other incentives if the social situation *from their point of view* is unsatisfactory. Thus often men of inferior education cannot work well with those of superior education, and vice versa. Differences not merely of race, nation, religion, but of customs, morals, social status, education, ambition, are frequently controlling. Hence, a powerful incentive to the effort of almost all men is favorable associational conditions from their viewpoint. . . .

Another incentive . . . is that of customary working conditions and conformity to habitual practices and attitudes. . . . It is taken for granted that men will not or cannot do well by strange methods or under strange conditions. . . .

Another indirect incentive . . . often of controlling importance is the opportunity for the feeling of enlarged participation in the course of events. It affects all classes of men under some conditions. It is sometimes, though not necessarily, related to love of personal distinction and prestige. Its realization is the feeling of importance of result of effort because of the importance of the cooperative effort as a whole. . . .

The most intangible and subtle of incentives is that which I have called the condition of communion. . . . It is the feeling of personal comfort in social relations that is sometimes called solidarity, social integration, the gregarious instinct. . . . It is the opportunity for comradeship, for mutual support in personal attitudes.[1]

Extract B

The Motivation Productivity, and Satisfaction of Workers (A. Zaleznik, C. R. Christensen, and F. J. Roethlisberger)

According to this theory, then, the conditions under which the traditional rewards of management no longer motivate are:

1. When the workers' subsistence needs are no longer paramount and when their needs for membership, status, and self-development become activated.
2. When workers start trying to satisfy these needs on the job.
3. When the way work is traditionally organized allows little or no opportunity for the satisfaction of these new needs and thus they become thwarted.

[1] Chester I. Barnard, *The Functions of the Executive* (Cambridge, Mass.: Harvard University Press, 1938), pp. 142–148. Copyright, 1938 by the President and Fellows of Harvard College.

In conclusion it should be noted that this theory not only accounts for why the traditional rewards no longer motivate. It also accounts for the frozen state that management has got its workers and itself into. Given its traditional conception of its task and given the motivational situation to be as we have described it, the frozen state must be a consequence. . . .

. . . the frozen state seems to emerge under the following conditions or set of assumptions about the inherent nature of workers, of organizations, and of managements' relation between them.

1. Man (the worker) is just incapable of directing himself to the goals of the organization of which he is a member. In this respect there is no life in him; he can be only pushed from behind, there is no pull from ahead.

2. Between his own needs and goals and the goals of the organization there is no relation except through his need for a steady job in order to satisfy his subsistence needs, which are the main (almost exclusive) part of his inherent nature at work.

3. With respect to the management of people, therefore, management's major task on the one hand is to divide jobs into their most elementary steps (methods work), time them to see what should be done in seconds (time study), rate them against a scale of an increasingly more difficult job to find complexity and worth (job evaluation), and cost them by each individual operation (cost control).

4. And on the other hand—this is the more so-called human relations or getting-things-done-through-people part of the job—to lead each separate person fairly but firmly in the direction where it is not part of his inherent nature to go.

5. And insofar as it is possible, to let each individual worker satisfy his other needs away from the job as a consumer and in organizations specialized to take care of each one neatly but separately.

6. And when this does not quite work and some of man's social needs rear their ugly heads at work, and small groups form that control the productivity of their members, (1) ignore them—say it isn't so, or (2) "let's break them up—you can't let social groups run the factory," or (3) retime the job—"you can't let them get away with it," or (4) let the foreman deal with them—"he's in the middle," or (5) get a human relations expert to tell the foreman how to "handle" them, or (6) send middle management to school to tell the foremen how to "handle" them, or (7) send top management to school to tell middle management how to tell foremen how to "handle" them, and so on.

7. And when the magic of the "black magicians" (i.e., the techniques of the methods people, time and motion study people, job evaluators, and merit raters) and the magic of the "white magicians" (i.e., the techniques of the "charm school" people, the "getting-things-done-through-people" people in business and business schools) fail and workers still remain apathetic and indolent and put forth only minimum effort, what then? Well (1) "I told you so in the first place" and (2) "let's get some more black and white magicians—there's no end to the new tricks that they have up their sleeves."

8. And when, in spite of all this direction, manipulation, and control, which it is management's *inherent nature* to exercise, a few stray egos still raise their heads, what then? "Well, let's let those 'soreheads' go to the union. This organization specializes in workers with such ego needs. We'll bargain with these needs once or so a year and have real big 'white magicians' to help us do it. They are experts in dealing with persons whose social and ego needs have been thwarted. . . ."

. . . [The manager] could get out of his difficulty (at least the theoretical part of it) by just making another set of assumptions—exactly the opposite from those he customarily makes—about what his task is supposed to be. . . . For example:

1. Instead of assuming that the worker is incapable of directing himself to the goals of the organization, let management assume that he can, and that although it is not part of his inherent nature to do this, it is one of the ways of satisfying many of his needs, if he so chooses and has a chance to do so.

2. Instead of assuming that it has to put into the worker certain capacities (e.g., capacities for growth and assuming responsibility) with which his inherent nature has not endowed him, let management assume that these capacities are there (by all available research evidence) in the first place but that as a result of experience they have become invisible in the second place and that management cannot put them there in any case.

3. Instead of assuming that motivating is something that it does (its job), let management assume that motivating is something that the workers do (their job).

4. So, instead of setting up and administering its organization for workers whose inherent capacities are to be led, directed, and motivated, let management assume a new leadership role of creating the conditions (technological, sociological, psychological, and through its own behavior) whereby workers can realize their "own goals best by directing their own efforts toward organizational objectives."

Before taking issue too quickly with these suggestions, let us just add:

1. There is nothing in the facts of research that prevents management from making these assumptions; to the contrary it might be said that the facts are begging for someone to make them, because,

2. These assumption[s] make intelligible many things that are now unintelligible.

3. They are big time savers. By assuming certain capacities to be prepotent and which under certain conditions will tend to develop, it cuts down the time that one has to spend in trying to develop something out of nothing, which is a difficult feat and consumes time. Preoccupation time (a kind of time which the time and motion study experts are not too concerned with) is decreased substantially. . . .

In the past thirty years a number of things have been tried. To mention only some, there have been (1) *counseling programs* for workers and supervisors directed at improving the channels of communication; (2) *participative management programs* aimed at getting all parts of the organization involved in the setting and implementation of organizational goals; (3) *multiple management programs, consultative management programs, grass roots programs, Junior Boards of Directors, Work Councils,* and the more abundant use of *committees*—all with similar aims; (4) *profit-sharing programs;* (5) *suggestion box systems* to utilize the imaginative resources of workers; (6) the *Scanlon Plan* to involve the Union more realistically in organizational objectives; (7) *decentralization programs* aimed at giving more managers more responsibility but also more people to supervise so that they cannot be directed and supervised so closely; (8) *job enlargement programs* aimed at allowing workers to fulfill better their social and ego needs; (9) *supervisory training programs* aimed to help supervisors to implement more behavioristically management's new conceptions of its task; (10) *executive development programs* aimed to acquaint managers with the increasing fund of knowledge about the social aspects of administration; (11) *executive educational programs* aimed to acquaint managers with the traditions and values of Western European culture, and so forth. . . .

What about designing a program for worker education involving the same concepts, methods, materials, and "cultural islands" with which educators and responsible management training officers are now conducting educational, developmental, and training programs for their first, second, third, and so on, levels of management? It would involve participant-centered, student-worker-centered discussions, cases, problems, and some lectures perhaps, all conducted under permissive conditions which would allow workers to express their own points of view and feelings without fear of censure of ridicule.[2]

Extract C

Motivation and Increased Productivity (Rensis Likert)

Two conditions appear to be necessary for a subordinate to react favorably to his superior's attempts to influence his behavior. First the influence attempts should be ones which he has reacted favorably to in the past—that is, they need to be familiar. Second, the influence attempts, as seen by the subordinate, should be supportive rather than threatening. And he will see them this way when they contribute to his sense of importance and personal worth; he will see them as threatening when they decrease his sense of personal worth.

From these conditions it is possible to derive a modified theory of management and the day-to-day operating procedures required to implement it.

Thus, for example, it is possible to state the following principles based on this theory: Any attempt to produce a change in an organization will work best when the people whose behavior needs changing want themselves to change. An attempted change, therefore, will work better when management creates a situation in which people can see the possibility and desirability of change and even initiate the change, rather than merely being ordered to change.

Research findings show that supervisors improve in their handling of human relations much more when provided with objective measurements about their operation and then stimulated to discuss these measurements with their subordinates as a group, than when they are merely given a supervisory training program. A supervisory training program is, after all, just another way of ordering a foreman to change his behavior.

[2] A. Zaleznik, C. R. Christensen, and F. J. Roethlisberger, *The Motivation, Productivity, and Satisfaction of Workers* (Boston: Division of Research, Harvard Business School, 1958), pp. 403–427.

Another operating principle based on this modified theory is also related to the best way to bring about changes and improvements. This principle indicates that an organization will perform more effectively when it functions as a network of integrated and coordinated teams, each of which has a high team spirit, high performance goals related to its part of the total job, favorable attitudes toward its supervision and management, and confidence and trust in them. These teams are knit into an integrated and coordinated organization by supervisors, managers and staff, who hold overlapping memberships in two or more teams or groups. . . .[3]

EXTRACT D

Managerial Psychology (Harold J. Leavitt)

Consider the profit-sharing plan as an extreme contrast to bare individual incentives. Consider, for example, a small company of, say, three hundred employees which chooses, instead of individual incentives, one of the many varieties of such plans. Assume it chooses the Scanlon plan, which is itself an extreme within the profit-sharing group. In a sense such a plan does not properly belong in a chapter on money incentives, for though it begins with money incentives and though money incentives derive from it, it can be better thought of as a plan for the psychological reorganization of a company.

The elements of the plan are these: (1) A monthly bonus for *everyone* in the plant based on an index of the over-all productivity of the plant—an index that is a satisfactory measure of improvement in the organization's efficiency. (2) The introduction of production committees. If every man's take-home pay is tied not to his individual productivity but to the productive efficiency of the company as a whole, then the production committee becomes the mechanism for tying everyone's efforts to the goal of productivity.

Notice that this plan includes the same assumptions made in individual plans. But profit-sharing plans also add two others: interdependency and social and egoistic needs.

These two additions are surprisingly important. The underlying proposition of individual incentives reads something like this: Individuals will work harder if they are individually rewarded with money for harder individual work. The profit-sharing modification is of this order: Organizations will work harder if they are organizationally rewarded for harder organizational work.

The two propositions do not even contradict one another. The second is

[3] Rensis Likert, "Motivation and Increased Productivity," *Management Record,* Vol. XVIII, No. 4 (April, 1956), pp. 128–131, as reprinted M. D. Richards and W. A. Nielander, *Readings in Management* (Cincinnati: Southwestern Publishing Co., 1958), p. 398.

an extension of the first. We do not have to prove one right and the other wrong; we have only to decide whether we are dealing with *independent* or *interdependent* individuals and with simply motivated or multiply motivated ones.

The second proposition assumes that individuals in industrial organizations are both socially and economically interdependent. It therefore defines an individual's job differently than the first. His job is no longer to punch his press as productively as possible; it is to punch his press in a social environment, to think about ways of improving the operation of his press and the company, to help whenever helping other people in the plant will contribute to the over-all efficiency of the organization, and finally, when faced with unusual decisions, to try to make those decisions which will contribute to total efficiency.

One result of such a plan is an increase in feelings of responsibility for the total operation on the part of all members of the organization. For now it is harder to make management the scapegoat for all problems. If production, and therefore the bonus share, drops, there is no tight rate to blame it on. If some people work too slowly or stupidly, it costs everyone something. What should everyone, not just management, do about it?

This increase in employees' "ownership attitude," however, is not an unmixed blessing. Even though most managers insist they want their people to develop one, an ownership attitude in each employee means that each employee may take a serious interest in things management considers its private property. It may mean, for example, that the machine operator now expresses interest in the sales manager's decisions. He may question such decisions. He may want an accounting for the sales department's failure to bring in a large order. At this level secondary and tertiary changes in atmosphere and organizational structure are likely to occur. Notions about secrecy, about prerogatives of one group or another, are likely to be battered down.

If profit-sharing plans succeed in developing what they set out to develop, a strongly active desire on the part of everyone in the plant to improve the plant, what then? Where individual incentives so often sharpen the line between management and employees, these profit-sharing plans tend to obviate it. They tend to push the whole organization in the direction of oneness, in which everything is everybody's business. The new control problem may not be how to get people to work on time but how to keep them from henpecking management. . . .

Several of these plans have by now been tested in many small companies, generally with good success. They have not been put through the harder test of a depressed economy, however, nor have they yet been applied to very large firms. Psychologically they make sense in that they open channels of communication and create a situation in which at least one goal, the goal of greater productive efficiency, is spread more widely through all levels of the organization.[4]

Case A:

Supervision and Motivation of a Group of Research Workers

One of the authors of this book is in charge of a small group conducting research on management. The objective is to obtain a series of case studies on important decisions made by firms in a number of different industries. Four graduate assistants are employed to assist in the project. All of them are part-time graduate students working towards doctorates in economics and business. Two of the assistants have taken over one year of graduate work and have previously been engaged in teaching or research. Another has completed most of his work for the doctorate and has had some years of experience in business and farming. The third is new as a graduate student, but has been engaged in business for almost ten years before returning to university work.

The leader of the research project is a full-time teacher with a number of administrative and committee responsibilities. He has limited time to devote to the project and to supervision of the assistants. His office is located at some distance from the offices of the assistants; because of limited space it is impossible to bring the whole research group together. The schedules of the leader and of the assistants are different, and at times the assistants are in the field. The question is the determination of methods for supervising and motivating the assistants to accomplish as much high quality work as possible.

Each assistant is required to put in nineteen hours of work per week on the research project. Each has been assigned a particular part of the project for special attention, but it is difficult to separate the research into compartments. One research worker is bound to run into research findings that will be of value to the others.

Several methods for supervising the group have occurred to the project leader:

1. Setting up definite office hours in which each assistant must be at work on the project.
2. Continual checks on progress made; for example, on material that has been written up.
3. A series of meetings at which group members can report progress in research.
4. Time cards on which the assistants will keep records of the time devoted to the project.
5. Working up subprojects which the assistants can use as material for doctoral

[4] Harold J. Leavitt, *Managerial Psychology* (Chicago: The University of Chicago Press, 1958), pp. 180–184.

dissertations or master's theses, so that in addition to the pay earned they will make progress toward completing their graduate work.

Case B:

Statement of IBM on Human Relations

Since the very inception of IBM, recognition of the need for good human relations has been a fundamental fact in the conduct of all company business. A practical program has been established by recognizing the applicability of the "Golden Rule" and its effectiveness in a business operation, and by encouraging on a day-to-day basis, as well as through formal programs, the best possible development of each job to accommodate the needs and ambitions of the individual.

IBM's human relations programs, both formal and informal, are designed to accomplish a number of objectives. Every effort is made to maintain full employment so that an employee is not plagued with fear of job insecurity. Our salary policies are geared so that an employee can earn—and is encouraged to earn—the maximum amount his ability permits. Many educational opportunities are made available to an employee so that he can continuously expand his ability and opportunity to advance. And, it is our objective to provide the employee with some economic protection in case of illness or accident as well as upon retirement.

Here are some of the specific employee benefit plans made available by IBM. All are entirely company paid.

First, there are three programs covering sickness, accident and medical expense for which all regular employees are eligible from the first day of employment, regardless of any personal insurance an employee may have.

The Sickness and Accident Plan provides a benefit equal to an employee's regular salary when he is absent from work because of illness or accident for a period of six months. After this period, further absence is given individual consideration.

Family Hospitalization benefits, covering an employee and his eligible family members, provide payment of 75% of the charges for hospital room and board up to $20 a day plus hospital charges for other services, supplies and treatments up to $300. Coverage is for 70 days of each period of hospitalization.

To assist an employee in the event he or a member of his family incurs medical expenses not covered under the Family Hospitalization Plan, IBM provides a Family Major Medical Plan. Payment is made for 75% of each individual's covered expenses, in excess of $200 each year; the maximum allowance is $10,000 and may be renewed. The Plan helps to minimize the possibility of an employee's savings being wiped out by heavy medical expenses.

If, after ten or more years of continuous service, an employee should become totally and permanently disabled, full pay for two years followed by a monthly income for life is provided by the Total and Permanent Disability Pay Plan. This is in addition to benefits received under the Sickness and Accident Plan. Such an employee is also provided with continued coverage under the Family Hospitalization, Major Medical, and Life Insurance Plans. The Group Life Insurance Plan provides protection for each employee from the first day of employment.

An employee retiring at age 65 after five or more years of continuous service with the company receives a regular monthly income. The lifetime income provided by the Retirement Plan is based on length of service, or length of service and earnings, whichever provides the greater amount. The Group Life Insurance Plan for Retired Employees replaces the plan for regular employees, and coverage under the Family Hospitalization and Major Medical Plans is provided.

Annually, each employee receives eight holidays as well as a vacation based on length of service, as follows:

Length of Service	*Vacation*
Less than 1 year	Varies, according to service
1–8 years	Two weeks
8–20 years	Three weeks
20 or more years	Four weeks

At the twenty-fifth year and at five-year intervals thereafter, each employee receives an additional Service Anniversary Vacation in that year. In the twenty-fifth year it is one extra week; in the thirtieth year, two weeks; in the thirty-fifth year, four weeks; in the fortieth year, six weeks.

A company-sponsored Suggestion Plan was set up by IBM in 1928 and has continued to date. Awards made under the plan are based on a percentage of first-year savings to the company resulting from adoption of a suggestion, and can range as high as $25,000. Employees received more than $600,000 for 14,084 suggestions adopted by IBM in 1959.

An employee is strongly encouraged to improve himself and to advance within IBM by educational training offered him through unique company programs as well as grants for attending outside educational institutions. Instruction ranges from job-related training and management seminars to graduate-level study at universities near IBM locations. Both technical and liberal arts subjects are included.

The company currently has twenty-five educational centers to carry out its programs, and instruction is also offered at plant, laboratory, and branch office locations. During 1959, over 137,000 courses in company-conducted classes were completed by IBM participants.

The scope of IBM education programs was enlarged in September, 1960, when the company opened its Systems Research Institute, offering graduate-level courses in data processing system design, programming and operation. It is the only school of its kind in the United States.

In 1959, IBM introduced a Tuition Refund Plan, which now provides refunds for 75% of an employee's educational expenses up to $250 a year upon satisfactory completion of approved courses taken outside scheduled working hours. During the same year, the company announced that it would match contributions made by employees to accredited educational institutions up to $1,000 for each institution per calendar year.

In 1959, as a memorial to its founder, the company inaugurated the Thomas J. Watson Memorial Scholarship Plan which awards 50 four-year college scholarships annually on a competitive basis. Twenty-five of these scholarships go to students who are children of IBM employees, the remainder to other high school students in private, parochial, and public schools throughout the nation.

Through an Employee Stock Purchase Plan, approved by IBM stockholders in 1958, any employee with one or more years of continuous service, may purchase IBM stock through payroll deductions to a maximum of 10% of his salary at a price 15% below the average market price on the date of purchase. This plan is subject to annual renewal.

Finally, it should be emphasized that all employees at IBM are salaried. The recent removal of plant employees from the status of "hourly workers" represents a new landmark in employee relations because it reflects the company's appreciation of the dignity of all its people.

IBM's employee turnover rate is substantially lower than the national average and an increasing number of employees annually join the IBM Quarter-Century Club.

IBM's growth is the result of a number of reasons, but the most important of all are respect for the individual, a vivid awareness that good employee relations are fundamental to success, and implementation of this awareness by sound and progressive policies and programs.[5]

Case C:

The Ashland Oil & Refining Company (A)

The kind of financial incentives used in the Ashland Oil & Refining Company has been fundamentally affected by the nature of the growth of the company, the personal characteristics and ideas of its executives, and by the environmental setting. After the firm started to grow rapidly, the management initiated what it called the employee dividend and encouraged stock ownership. Both approaches met with success but certain problems have caused management to restudy their place in the company.

[5] International Business Machines, "Human Relations in IBM," Company Release, 1960.

Early Personnel Practices

Swiss Oil Corporation, a small predecessor of Ashland Oil, employed mountain labor in drilling oil wells.

Prior to 1924 it used simple employment procedures and simple wage plans. "Fringe benefits" were of the paternalistic type; that is, maintaining a company town with school, church, recreation centers, and so forth. Wage policies were typewritten in 1920:

> Each rate card must have the O.K. of the Superintendent under whom the employee is to work. Each time a rate is changed the new rate must have the O.K. of the Superintendent. These rate cards are to be used in making up the payrolls.
>
> A board or Mess record book is to be kept and each man eating a meal must have had that meal checked against his name during meal time. The amount of board to be deducted from each man's pay will be made up from this board record book and the meals charged at 50 cents each.
>
> Daily Time Distribution Sheets must show the distribution of the work as relates to the location and amount of time put in on each operation.
>
> There are two classes of wages for employees: those getting straight time per day and those getting time and board.

The chief executive of the refining subsidiary emphasized the idea of a "company family" from its beginning in 1924. The aim was to stress the personal aspects of management-employee relations with a closely knit group or team working together as a part of a family. This approach was easier for the company to employ during the 1930's when it was small. Since its primary location was in a small town, direct contacts among personnel after working hours were possible. The company built up morale by consciously picking new employees that "would fit in" with the social structure of the firm. All of these policies continued with little change even though the company grew rapidly. However, problems arose which made the approach more difficult as size increased.

Several techniques were used by the company to further the feeling of belonging. For 30 years or more annual Christmas parties including professional entertainment, gifts for children of employees, and refreshments, have been held. These parties became an institution in those communities in which a number of employees and friends of the company lived.

The operating employee in a refinery serves as an attendant to keep a watchful eye on gauges, pipes, and so forth, while capital equipment turns out the product. The ratio of the total number of workers to total capital invested is low. Refinery workers are of three general types: operational, maintenance, and custodial. The operational workers are organized into shifts and then into working groups of four men each. The maintenance workers clean and repair the refining equipment at frequent intervals. Custodial employees are chiefly plant guards and janitors.

Current Personnel Practices

Ashland Oil places little stress on formal systems of job evaluation, merit rating and wage surveys. Individual incentive wage systems are not used: an hourly wage payment is typical in the petroleum industry. Some of the fringe benefits provided by the company are summarized in an annual report:

"Ashland Oil has endeavored to be in the forefront in the development of employee benefit plans. Our Company is now contributing more than $3,000,000 per year to the cost of a comprehensive welfare and benefit program for employees. The cost to the Company of these and other special benefits is equal to 20% of the base salary of employees.

"The Company pays the entire cost of sickness and disability benefits under which normal earnings of employees are continued for various periods of time depending upon length of service.

"Employees and the company contribute jointly to the cost of hospitalization and surgical insurance for employees and their families and to group life insurance. Death benefits are equal, on the average, to the equivalent of two years' base compensation with double indemnity in the case of accidental death.

"Ashland's pension and retirement plans are comprehensive and are intended to give better than average protection to its employees."

One of the compensation techniques used by the company was described in a prospectus:

"On April 24, 1948, the Board of Directors authorized a profit-sharing plan, commencing as of October 1, 1947, for the benefit of all employees, including officers, of the company and its subsidiaries. . . . Pursuant to the plan, the Board of Directors has approved the payment to employees of an employee-dividend for each quarter-fiscal year commencing with the quarter-fiscal year ended December 31, 1947."

Details of the plan were explained to the employees in a letter which stated, in part, as follows:

"The total dividend of $107,340.28 as approved by the Board for the first payment to our employees under this plan is arrived at by taking 7.5% of the adjusted consolidated net earnings of the company for the last three months of 1947, to the extent that such earnings exceeded 25¢ per share on the 1,006,880 shares of common stock of the company outstanding on December 31, 1947. The earnings of the company on which the employee-dividend is based have been adjusted to eliminate nonrecurring losses or profits, including inventory abnormalities, and are intended to reflect accurately the profits resulting from current operations. . . . Your proportionate share of this employee-dividend is determined by the total wages earned by all employees. The total employee-dividend being paid at this time is equal to approximately 9.4% of the company's payroll of $1,141,145 earned during the period, and thus your accompanying payment, before deduction for social security and income taxes as required by law, should equal 9.4% of your salary of wage earnings for the three months ended December 31, 1947. . . . There are no secrets concerning the profits of the Company and any employee should feel free to request further information concerning our employee-dividend plan."

After the dividend plan had been in effect for one year, the chief executive expressed his opinion in the company magazine:

"After having tried out the employee-dividend plan for a full year, it is the opinion of the management of the company that it has worked successfully. We believe all of you appreciate this additional compensation, and because of your sharing in the profits of the company, there is a greater interest and effort on the part of everyone toward the success of our company and its day-to-day operations. With the continued co-operation and best efforts of the more than 2,000 men and women who now comprise our organization, we hope to so increase the efficiency of our operations and to add to the earnings of the company and thus to the size of each of your employee-dividend payments."

The employee-dividend originated in 1941 as a bonus in lieu of wage increases which at that time were governmentally controlled. From that date until 1947, the bonus was paid at the end of the year with no set pattern for its computation or distribution. On March 2, 1948, the Chairman explained more of the philosophy of the employee dividend in a letter to the employees:

"Employee-dividend payments will be in addition to and entirely separate from the regular salaries and wages. . . . In the same manner that heretofore the directors of the Company have met every three months and decided whether the profits of the Company are such to justify the payment of a dividend to the stockholders, they will now decide whether the profits remaining after provision for dividends to the stockholders are sufficient to justify the payment of a dividend—to our employees. Employee-dividends will be affected principally by the earnings of the company, but may be influenced by other factors as determined by the Board of Directors. . . . We believe that all employees recognize the direct connection between their individual efforts and the success of the company. The purpose of this employee-dividend plan is to emphasize that, also, there is a direct connection between profits of the company and the funds that can be made available for earnings of our employees. Every company has to be financially successful in order to pay adequate salaries and wages. It must be even more successful in order to justify the payment of employee-dividends, as we now propose."

In a comment to the Board of Directors, the Chairman said:

> I believe the employee-dividend plan will instill considerable interest in our stock and in our earnings. It gives us a vehicle to encourage that interest by the sending of a letter each quarter, along with employee-dividends, giving such information concerning current operations and earnings as we believe will be interesting to our employees.

The management of the company also encourages the purchase of shares of stock in the company. The chief executive expressed his opinion in a speech:

> Application of seniority is one of the growing practices being forced on industry, that tends to weaken the operation of our present economic system, a system which, theoretically, is based on competition, individual initiative, and personal incentive. When no advantage accrues to the individual in return for extra effort, as is true today for millions of employees, not only are the problems of management increased, but there results a tremendous loss of productive capacity which, I am sure, is significant in the overall economy of our country. If employees prefer seniority to opportunity, and thereby lose incentive for personal effort, then the management of business must find other incentives for efficient production. The most promising approach, in my opinion, is through stock ownership by employees and the sharing of corporate profits. Although such plans do not afford an opportunity for individual recognition among the rank and file, they give the employees, as a group, a stake in the success of the enterprise and make them conscious of their collective achievements. The members of the team play a better game when they are encouraged to know the final score and are permitted to share in the awards to the victors.

On March 20, 1950 the company offered 50,000 shares of $1.20 Cumulative Convertible Preferred Stock to the employees:

> . . . at a price of $20 per share—the number of shares an employee may subscribe for may not exceed a number obtained by multiplying by 15% his estimated average monthly salary or wages before income tax—Payments for subscriptions will be in twenty installments of $1 per share per month. Each employee's subscription will be a direction to deduct the amount of each installment from his salary or wages each month until the subscription is paid. . . . He shall not have the right to receive a certificate for such shares or to sell such shares until the expiration of said nineteen-month period. . . . Each subscriber shall have the right to cancel his subscription and withdraw from this plan at the end of any month by giving the company 10 days' notice. The company shall thereupon refund to such subscriber all payments made by him under his subscription with interest on his monthly balances in his stock purchase account at the rate of 3% per annum.

By 1960 almost 2,000 employees owned stock in their company. This group had continued to grow gradually through the encouragement of the company in stock purchase plans in 1953, 1956 and 1960. Employees through these offerings owned a substantial number of the nearly 7,000,000 (common and preferred) shares outstanding. The stockholders had increased to more than 42,000 by 1960.

During the 1950's, the management continued its emphasis on its employee dividend plan and on the stock purchase plan. It was confronted with problems, however, which caused it to make changes and to rethink its approach to motivation.

During times of low profits, the employee dividend, was small and so the company changed to an annual payment basis. Employee ownership of stock increased the workers' interest in the financial condition of the company. There were different views as to whether the two plans, employee dividend and stock purchase plan, were desirable. Both plans were continued.

Case D:

The Lincoln Electric Company

The most famous incentive plan of modern times is that of the Lincoln Electric Company of Cleveland, Ohio, a concern with under 2,000 employees. The Lincoln Electric Company has a profit-sharing plan under which approximately 80 per cent of the company profits are distributed to the employees. The profit-sharing bonuses are extremely large, amounting to approximately the equivalent of the basic wages and salaries. As a result, the total earnings of the employees are at least double the average earnings in comparable concerns. The interesting question about this plan is why it works so successfully when profit-sharing has failed in other companies.

The Lincoln Electric Company is the largest producer of electrodes and arc welding equipment in the United States. The company was founded in 1896. Mr. James F. Lincoln took over as president in 1913 and it was under his management that the incentive system developed. One of his first acts, in 1914, was to establish an Advisory Board, with one elected worker from each department, to advise him on management problems. This committee meets with top management every other Monday. It discusses grievances and suggestions for improving working conditions. New committee members are elected each month, so that memberships continually rotate. There is no union.

The Advisory Board has assisted in introducing changes in the Lincoln Electric Company. For example, the Board helped originate a shorter work week. The Board assisted in introducing the profit-sharing plan itself in 1934. In fact, Mr. Lincoln was not enthusiastic about the idea at first. It was made clear to the employees that bonuses would have to be earned;

that they would arise from increased effort and productivity. Substantial bonuses were earned from the beginning.

The increased productivity under the incentive plan has not only permitted an enormous increase in wages and salaries, but also has enabled the company to cut prices, passing part of the savings in labor time to the consumer. It has also made possible an increase in dividends, though it is interesting that the dividends have increased much less than in most comparable companies. The dividend rate in 1934 was $2.50 per share; in 1943 it was $6.00 and has not changed much since that time.

The bonus paid to a particular worker depends on several considerations. First it varies with over-all company profits. The individual's portion of the part of profits set aside for bonuses depends, in part, on a merit rating done by his superior. A letter from Mr. Lincoln dated December 4, 1959 made this announcement:

> The Lincoln Electric Company paid its 1371 employees in Cleveland and its 38 district offices throughout the country $6,488,167 today in annual incentive pay. Each employee received a check representing payment for his or her extra contribution to the success of the company for the year. The amount of each check was determined by an individual merit rating of performance on the job for the year.
>
> Lincoln has paid this incentive every year since 1934, during which time the company has paid a total of $93,985,308 in addition to regular earnings and other benefits all of which are standard for the industry. This year the company also purchased $1,000,000 in retirement annuities covering each employee. The company also guarantees continuous employment to all employees with over two years service, thus securing them against lay-offs.

Mr. Lincoln's letter indicates that the average bonus per employee was about $4,730. This is more than the total wages of most non-supervisory employees in the United States.

Mr. Lincoln personally determines the bonuses of his immediate subordinates. All profit-sharing bonuses are paid at the end of the year. In addition, payments are made for cost-saving suggestions at the rate of one-half of expected savings during the first year. A Suggestion System Board reviews suggestions once a week. The Board is careful to explain to workers the impracticality of suggestions not adopted.

Great care is taken in the selection of new employees, with emphasis on intelligence quotients and extracurricular activities (such as athletics). The average age of foremen is kept down by promoting older supervisors to staff positions. The foremen are encouraged to discuss company-wide problems in weekly meetings. This gives the foremen a broader managerial viewpoint, prepares them for higher positions, and provides them with information to answer questions within their departments.

Mr. Lincoln has written at length about his ideas on incentives. He argues that too much emphasis is placed upon profits as the sole purpose of industry. This emphasis, he feels, distracts management from its main objective and tends to alienate the employees. The goal should instead be one of making a better product to be sold at a lower price, with profits a by-product of performing service. The aim in dealing with company personnel should be to develop latent abilities by stimulating the desire to develop. This can be done by providing challenging jobs, by building up a sense of teamwork and of individual responsibility to the team, by continually applying pressure for more and better work, and by promoting only on the basis of ability and performance. Mr. Lincoln argues that supervisors should be leaders rather than bosses; they should accept their subordinates as members of a team. He also emphasizes selection of employees with ability and initiative.

Mr. Lincoln stresses the importance of recognition. He states that the "worker must feel that he is recognized in accordance with his contribution to success. If he does not have that feeling of self-respect and the respect of others because of his skill, he will think he is being 'played for a sucker' if he increases his output so the owners can have more profit."

"It is not necessary that this reward be solely in money. As a matter of fact, the amateur athlete gets no money, yet he tries harder than the professional who is paid. This athlete, however, does get the respect and position resulting from his achievement. That is his reward." [6]

Mr. Lincoln also stresses competition as a driving force. While it is desirable to have a sense of team membership, he feels that it is also important to stress the drive to be outstanding in the group.

Mr. Lincoln's views on profit-sharing are of special interest. "Profit-sharing, in its many forms as generally applied, fails and for the same fundamental reasons. Profit-sharing does not distinguish the worker. He is likely to consider the share of the profit given him in the usual profit-sharing split somewhat in the nature of a tip to a Pullman porter. . . . The worker knows that manufacturing is necessary to the consumer. He is not so sure about profit. He thinks that the salary that the boss gets should satisfy him without any profit. Profit should be a by-product of service to the consumer, not an end in itself." [7]

Mr. Lincoln stresses that it is not enough to impose an incentive system from above. The problem is to get the employees to want the plan. For example, if the plan is tried out by a small group at first, the rest of the personnel may insist on being included. The workers must feel that the added effort they will put in under the plan will produce large rewards, both monetary and nonmonetary. Mr. Lincoln favors stock ownership plans, such as the one available to the employees of the Lincoln Electric Company, but he does not think that the company should put pressure on the employees to buy stock. Stock ownership creates a sense of responsibility for company success and acts as a powerful incentive in itself.

[6] James F. Lincoln, *Incentive Management* (Cleveland: Lincoln Electric Company, 1951), p. 81.

[7] *Ibid.*, pp. 106–107.

To the outside observer there are many possible explanations of the high motivation and the high productivity of the Lincoln Electric employees. Weighing the relative importance of these is a difficult task.[8]

Case E:

The Scanlon Plan at the Miami Tool Works, Inc.[9]

In the early summer of 1958, the top management of the Miami Tool Works was divided in its opinion concerning the operation of a "Scanlon Plan" wage incentive. This plan provided a bonus to all employees except the president, vice president, and four salaried salesmen according to savings reflected as a percentage of payroll costs to net dollar sales including additions to inventories. One group in top management, identified with factory operations, questioned whether the basic objectives of the plan were being achieved. This group also felt that bonus payments were draining the company of working capital, sorely needed for current operations as well as replacement of obsolete equipment. This drain on cash also impeded any plans for expansion.

The other group, comprising the top officers of the company identified with sales and finance, was less concerned about the operations of the Scanlon Plan. In fact, the president was quoted as stating that the plan was quite satisfactory since more dollars of net sales were being generated by fewer factory employees.

The Miami Tool Works had been founded in 1914 by William Johnson on the basis of his design of a high-precision, semiautomatic tool grinder. The business was built upon the manufacture of tools used to cut and thread steel, brass, and other metals. It also manufactured such inspection tools as gauges and micrometers. Under the founder, the business prospered largely because of the high-precision product achieved through the use of the machines which he had invented. These quality standards had been continued so that in 1958 the Miami name represented the finest of the jewelry grade cutting tools and gauges in the industry.

Most of the operations in manufacturing were machine-paced. Manual effort was required only in the insertion and removal of the work from the machine. The factory superintendent estimated this at about 2% to 3% of the total cycle time. The operator, however, influenced the total work done since he controlled the time between the removal of a finished piece and the

[8] This case is based on John D. Glover and Ralph M. Hower, *The Administrator: Cases on Human Relations in Business,* revised edition (Homewood, Ill.: Richard D. Irwin, 1952), pp. 533–584; and James F. Lincoln, *Incentive Management* (Cleveland: Lincoln Electric Company, 1951). For fuller discussions of the Lincoln system, readers are referred to those publications.

[9] Case prepared by Professor Jacob J. Blair of the University of Pittsburgh.

start of work on the next piece. Delays at this point could amount to 10% or more of the total cycle time.

In June, 1958, the company employed 115 persons in the office and 146 in the factory. In more normal times 262 persons were employed in the factory.

Labor Relations Background

In 1943, the company recognized the United Steel Workers of America as bargaining agent. Upon the suggestion of Mr. Damon, who was then works manager, the company proposed in the contract negotiations of 1948 the adoption of the Scanlon Plan, in lieu of a general wage increase. After its acceptance by the union, the plan remained in effect until the negotiations of 1950 when, upon a union request, it was withdrawn because it had failed to yield a bonus to the factory employees. In 1953, the Scanlon Plan was again proposed by Mr. Damon and accepted by the union in lieu of a general wage increase. At this time, the factor for computing the bonus was based upon the 1952 fiscal year which management now believes to be unfortunate due to the high ratio of payroll costs to total sales. Since this date, the plan has paid a good bonus to all employees covered by it, some monthly payments having reached a level of 17% to 25% of wages. (See excerpts from labor agreement in Table 8-1.)

The company followed the policy of paying at least the going rate of wages. According to the Chamber of Commerce and National Metal Trades Association, the earned rate paid by the company since 1953, including the bonus, exceeds the local labor rates by as much as 15 cents per hour. In this respect it is significant that all employees, including those in the bargaining unit, accepted a reduction of 12½% in working hours in February, 1958.

Labor turnover was low among the factory personnel. Fifty-four out of a total of 257 factory people had 20 years or more of service, 86 had from 19 to 10 years, and the remainder of 117 had less than 10 years of service, with the youngest in seniority having 6 years, 9 months of service as of December 31, 1957. A higher rate of turnover was found in the office staff. Out of a total of 115 employees, 33 had from 42 years to 20 years of service, 18 had from 19 to 10 years, with the balance of 64 having less than 10 years of service.

The Scanlon Plan in Theory and Practice

This wage payment plan was developed jointly by Clinton Golden, former international vice president, United Steel Workers of America, and Joseph Scanlon, then chairman of the wage incentive department of the same union. Golden was the idealist and theoretician (see his *Dynamics of In-*

dustrial Democracy). Scanlon was a practical realist, originally trained as a cost accountant, later becoming one of the most able negotiators representing his union, particuarly in bargaining incentive wage payment plans.

At its inception, the plan was largely a device by which marginal and submarginal companies in the steel industry could meet the union wage demands. Subsequently, as the plan developed, it won acceptance in even the more efficient companies as a wage incentive applicable to production, maintenance, supervisory, and clerical employees.

Basic to the operation of the plan was the value of the "bonus" factor. This factor was obtained by dividing total payrolls for all participating employees by total dollar value of sales plus inventories for a negotiated and agreed-upon base period—that is, a year, or an average of two or more years. Theoretically, this factor value, once established by negotiations, remains unchanged, except as wage increases or decreases may affect the numerator, or similar changes in selling prices, or product mix may affect the denominator. Realities, however, force departures from this standard. By the application of this factor to total sales and inventories for a given accounting period, an allowed or standard payroll figure was obtained. The difference between the allowed and the actual determines the amount of labor savings achieved during the accounting period. This was then reduced to a labor savings per hour (see Table 8-2). In the case of the Miami Tool Works, savings up to 25 cents per hour were split equally between the company and employees. Beyond this amount, employees received 75%, management 25%. In other plans, a fixed percentage of bonus earnings are placed into a pool from which management "makes up" the difference when actual payrolls exceed allowed payrolls.

It is expected that labor savings under the plan would be derived from two basic sources, the first increased effort and skill, the second suggestions for improvements arising out of the practical experience of those participating in the plan. In order to achieve these objectives, Scanlon and his associates developed an elaborate administrative structure of joint committees entirely independent and separate from the grievance procedure. At the Miami Tool Works 16 production committees were established. Meeting once each month, the production committees considered factory and office problems affecting payroll costs. Payroll costs would be influenced by the occupational groups included. The Scanlon Plan was flexible in this respect. Usually only the production and maintenance employees were included. At the Miami Works, all employees, except the president and vice president and salaried salesmen, were included. It was assumed that the practical knowledge of employees meeting at this level with representatives of management would develop many significant ideas for reducing payroll costs. Superimposed upon the production committee was a screening committee, representative of top management and local union officers. This was really an administrative group which received and approved the bonus determination for each accounting period, and also screened suggestions coming before it from the production committee.

Both the production and the screening committees had authority to inquire into any aspect of the administration of the plan. The production committee could question supervisors on any action which influenced payroll costs. The screening committee raised questions concerning pricing, product mix, inventories, and wage and salary matters. Management also had the responsibility of informing the employee representatives of all changes in salaries and prices which affected the value of the factor. Finally, the union was authorized to bring into the plant a representative of Mr. Scanlon to check any and all items of cost or income which entered into the determination of the factor.

Five Years of the Scanlon Plan, 1953–1958

In the five years since the reinstatement of the Scanlon Plan, certain results were observed. In the opinion of management, the plan served its purpose in meeting wage demands. In the first three of these five years, 1953 through 1955, hourly wage rates were raised by a total of 17½ cents per hour. Of this total, only 5½ cents had been granted as general wage increases, while 12 cents had been included in the factor.

The managers who supported the Scanlon Plan did so on the basis of the substantial reduction in labor costs achieved by it. They observed that the actual number of factory employees declined from 1954 through 1957, a period in which net sales had increased. Dollar sales per employee increased from $12,854 in 1954 to $18,746 in 1956. They then declined to $15,037 in 1957, but were still substantially above 1954.

An approximate determination of the savings in payroll was obtained by converting sales for 1955, 1956, and 1957 into estimated payrolls based upon 1954. In 1954, every dollar of payrolls generated $2.36 in sales. Had this same relationship continued, then the payrolls required to produce the reported sales in 1955, 1956, and 1957 would have been in round numbers, $1,598,000, $1,784,000, and $1,501,000 respectively, or a total of $4,883,000. Actual payrolls for the three years were $4,190,000. The gross payroll savings for the period was determined to have been $693,000. Bonus payments totaling $513,000 occurred during the same period. The net savings, largely attributed to the Scanlon Plan, amounted to $180,000 or 3.7% on estimated payrolls based on 1954.

The factory superintendent expressed dissatisfaction with the plan because it had not produced the process improvements expected of it. Only one suggestion had been received. This involved a new procedure for distributing engineering drawings in the plant. While it was accepted and put into effect, no reduction in cost resulted. The same official also said that productivity declined during slack periods, in spite of the bonus plan. Its advantages were therefore limited to periods of good business.

Some controversy arose between the union and management concerning layoffs in the plant at a time when the office force was not reduced. In recent layoffs the factory group was reduced by 110 employees, a reduction of 43%. Only six in an office force of 115 had been laid off. Consequently, the union claimed that a satisfactory bonus was not earned in 1957 because of the burden of the clerical and nonbargaining unit employees being carried by the bargaining unit group. Management replied by pointing out that while orders are smaller, the same number are being processed. Such claims, however, antagonized the office group so that a strained relationship developed. Some in the executive group feared that this might drive the clerical workers into the union.

The executive group expressed concern with the condition of the plan which required all information regarding salaries be made available to the screening committee. One executive stated that he felt some things should be sacred and among these were the salaries paid to management people. As a result of this condition, the union members on the screening committee constantly appraised the effectiveness of management and expressed their opinions concerning their appraisal in meetings. The results of the plan are shown in Table 8-3.

TABLE 8-1

EXCERPT FROM THE BASIC LABOR AGREEMENT WITH THE UNITED STEEL WORKERS OF AMERICA

The following provisions shall prevail with respect to the administration of the plant-wide incentive bonus plan (Scanlon Plan) which shall be effective for the duration of the Collective Bargaining Agreement.

In order to grant full participation in the benefits of increased productive efficiency which should result from the employee-management co-operative plan, a plant-wide efficiency bonus shall be applied. It shall remain in full force and effect during the term of this Agreement. Modifications or changes may be made in the ratio as provided in this Appendix.

The plant-wide incentive plan is designed to enable all employees of the Company to benefit from their increased co-operation and efforts, as reflected in increased productive efficiency.

The Basis of the Bonus Plan

The factor of labor costs to sales value which will include the sales in each specific accounting period plus or minus inventory change in finished goods and goods in process is the base used for the participating efficiency bonus. Records of 1952 were used in the development of a ratio of 48.5 cents in labor costs to each dollar of production value. Participation in any bonus earned as between the employees and the Company shall be on the basis spelled out in the Company Union agreement dated May 4, 1953.

Factors which may necessitate a change in the ratio of labor costs to production value: Substantial changes in the conditions which prevailed in establishing the present ratio may necessitate the changing of this ratio for the purpose of protecting the equity of either party in the benefits of the plan. The plan is designed to fairly compensate all employees for their

TABLE 8-1 (Continued)

ideas and efforts. Technological changes requiring capital expenditures may alter the ratio by reducing labor costs without any increase in productive efficiency on the part of the participants. Accounting practices and procedures may ascertain accurately the percentage of change herein affected.

An increase and/or decrease in selling price may alter the ratio either up or down. The presently applied ratio of product mix may experience an imbalance which may require change. An increase or decrease in rates of pay may alter the ratio either up or down. Changes of rates of pay to compensate for experience gained or for reclassification due to a change in the type of work performed are not changes in rates of pay which would properly affect the ratio. A substantial increase in the number of night shift employees receiving night shift premiums would require a change in ratio to that extent. Any other substantial influence not brought about by an increase or decrease in productive efficiency will furnish sufficient reason for an overall survey of the presently established ratio.

It is understood that in the event mechanical changes are suggested which eliminate a job or jobs, the Union and the Company will meet and make an earnest effort to place the employees affected on other jobs.

The productive efficiency bonus will be paid on the fourth pay day of each period, and will represent the bonus for the previous period. The Screening Committee will go over the facts and figures used in the calculation of the bonus before it is announced, in order to establish the greatest degree of faith and confidence in the calculated results. . . .

The calculation of the total bonus shall be made by the Company's Accounting Department. It shall then be audited, verified and approved by the accounting representative of Mr. Joseph Scanlon.

It shall then be presented (properly endorsed by Mr. Scanlon's representative) to the Screening Committee for examination and discusssion.

Immediately thereafter, copies of the calculation shall be posted on the several bulletin boards throughout the shop and office.

Each participant in the plan may figure his own bonus in the following manner:

On each bonus period calculation posted on the bulletin boards there will be a last line reading:

Employees' bonus percentage xx xxxx.

Each employee should multiply his total gross pay (received for the time worked) for the accounting period, by the above percentage. This is the amount of his Scanlon Plan bonus for the period.

To illustrate how this would be calculated for the seventh period, 1953:

The calculation posted shows the bonus percentage to each employee is *14.4*.

Let us assume that the employee in question received four weeks' pay (for time worked) during the period, totalling $240.00.

His bonus is then $240.00 × 14.4% which is $34.56.

TABLE 8-2

THE SCANLON PLAN AT THE MIAMI TOOL WORKS, INC.

Example Showing Bonus Computation under the Scanlon Plan

	Work in Process	Finished Goods		
Net Sales			$100,000	
Less—Products Bought Outside			1,000	$ 99,000
Inventories Balance				
Previous Month	$150,000	$175,000		
Current Month	175,000	165,000		
	$ 25,000	($ 10,000)		
Net Inv. Change			$ 15,000	
× Mark Up Factor			1.63	24,450
Sales Value of Production				$123,450
Sales Value of Production		$123,450		
× Labor Factor		.4540	$ 56,069	
Sales Value of Outside Purchase		$ 1,000		
× Labor Factor		.0850	85	
Allowed Payroll				$ 56,154
Bonus Cal. Payroll (Actual)				55,000
Gross Bonus Fund				$ 1,154
Total Hours Worked				27,450.6
Savings Per Hour				$ .0417
Bonus to Employees		$ 577		

Bonus to Employees

Management-Employee Share $\frac{\$.0417}{2} = \$.02085/\text{hour worked.}$

Per Cent Employee Bonus $\frac{.02085 \times 27,450.6}{55,000} = 1.04\%$

Bonus Over Accounting Period

160 Hours Worked at $\$2.25 \times .0104 = \$3.74$

TABLE 8-3

THE SCANLON PLAN AT THE MIAMI TOOL WORKS, INC.

SALES, PAYROLL AND BONUS, 1954 THROUGH 1957

Year	*Net Sales in $1,000*	*Partici-pating Payroll in $1,000*	*Sales per $ of Payrolls*	*Bonus in $1,000*	*Average Factory Employees*	*Sales per Factory Employee*	*Bonus as Per Cent Payroll*
1954	$3,008	$1,271	$2.36	$ 77	234	$12,854	11.0%
1955	3,773	1,386	2.72	203	259	14,555	13.5%
1956	3,982	1,409	2.82	212	263	18,746	15 %
1957	3,546	1,395	2.54	97	236	15,037	7 %

9

Policy Formulation, Planning, and Decision Making

EVERY undertaking involves a complicated pattern of decisions—from broad decisions about the objectives of the enterprise to specific decisions about day-to-day processes. Until recent years, little thought was given to the decision-making process in business; but since Barnard's pioneer volume, *The Functions of the Executive,* this subject has become a primary object of research. A discussion of policies, plans, and decisions, without reference to specific decisions, is abstract and philosophical; but an understanding of the decision-making process may be one of the most practical things we can learn. Like most abstract subjects, the study of decisions requires considerable attention to definition of the terms involved. Thus, this chapter is concerned with what is meant by expressions such as *a philosophy of management*, *objectives*, *policies*, *strategies*, *plans*, and *decisions*.

Policy Formulation

A *philosophy of management* covers those general concepts and integrated attitudes fundamental to the co-operation of a social group. Philosophies for firms may differ. One might be good for firm A but not useful for firm B. Often a firm's own members may not be conscious of a philosophy, yet it is effective. To understand the philosophy of a given firm, the *concept of the firm* must be understood. This will provide a picture of the "character" of the firm—how the firm got where it is, the place that it occupies in the industry, its strengths and weaknesses, an idea of the viewpoints of its managers, and its relationship to social and political institutions. Specifically, this concept can be determined from understanding:

(1) the existing personnel and their relationships,
(2) the history of the firm,
(3) the ethical framework of its managers, employees, customers, competitors, and suppliers,
(4) the industrial setting, which includes its operating processes and economic structure of the industry,
(5) the institutional setting, including the social forces and framework of government relationships.

Figure 9-1 illustrates the role that the philosophy of management plays in operations. Later sections of this chapter will develop how this philosophy is related to the other elements shown on the diagram—the basic objective, the policies, and the action itself.

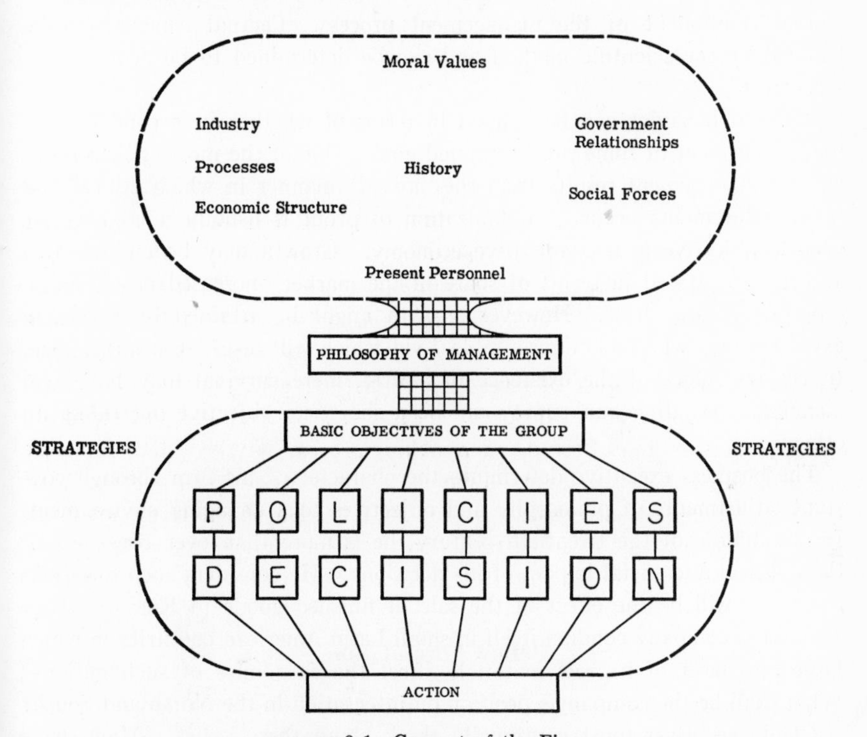

FIGURE 9-1 Concept of the Firm

Objectives. Human beings try to be purposive; that is, they are guided by general goals. A group of people in a co-operative effort retain their own personal goals, aims, and purposes, but in addition, their joint action must be guided by the *basic objectives of the group.* There is a hierarchy of objectives of the group (company, department, or other subdivision).

The objectives can be long range, or they may apply to the immediate future. One thing is certain; a group has many objectives.

Objectives tend to conflict with one another. Group objectives conflict with personal objectives of the individual members. In fact, group objectives or personal objectives may develop unconsciously. Some may be stated clearly and precisely and yet may be inconsistent with subtle and unconscious objectives. To analyze the development of a firm, it is important not to attribute all motivation to a single objective (e.g. maximization of profits). Understanding comes only from recognizing that objectives are extremely complex.

Objectives are value judgments and thus involve ethical questions—what ought to be. They may be considered to be "good" or "bad," but they cannot be proved to be "true" or "false." At this level, management cannot be a science. It is important to separate the ethical component from the factual component of the management process. Factual aspects can be handled by the scientific method and can be determined to be "correct" or "incorrect."

Rational behavior can be defined in terms of whether it is conducive to the achievement of some predetermined goal. One of the most critical problems in management results from the "mixed" manner in which ethical and factual statements occur. Maximization of profit is usually offered as the over-all objective in a competitive economy. Growth may be an objective and may be stated in terms of share of the market, increased power, or in absolute money terms. However, growth might be attained by accepting extra business which is "unprofitable," yet which will result in a larger firm. In certain stages of the existence of a firm, mere survival may have real meaning. Avoiding bankruptcy can be a short run objective overriding all others.

The business executive determines the character of his firm through constant adjustments of philosophy and objectives to a changing environment. In the middle of the twentieth century, he is more than ever conscious of the political and social impact of his decisions. He considers such questions as: What will be the effect of the sale of finished goods to Russia? How should the company conduct itself in small Latin American countries in which large purchases of its raw materials affect the economies of such nations? What shall be the company's position on integration in the North and South?

Chief executives must continually think about these issues. Many have written books explaining their views. Some believe that executives' responsibilities extend to an active participation in the improvement of the environment in which business operates; others believe that business should avoid assuming responsibility in political and social matters, but should adjust to conditions developed in the external environment.

In setting objectives, the executive must consider his obligations to a number of different groups. The difficulty is that conflicting obligations often occur.

1. According to the legal theory, a chief executive is to carry out actions within the framework given him by the board of directors and the stockholders. He must keep the interests of the *owners* (stockholders) in mind.

2. The obligation of the company to its *customers* is not only a legal matter, but also is good business. The emphasis on service and reliability is important to sales objectives. The executive may also feel that service in itself is a reason for the company's existence and morally necessary.

3. More and more executives are conscious of their obligations to *employees*. The healthy condition of the company is a prerequisite for the continued existence of jobs for its own people. In decisions to merge with another company, employees' interests are often a key issue. The labor union movement challenges management in its search for employee loyalty and identification.

4. The responsibility to *society* has received increased attention. Public relations and participation in community activities are areas in which company objectives are developed. Many executives place "promoting a given economic system" as an obligation to society. Others take the view that sound internal management is the only pertinent kind of public relations.

5. Obligations to the *government* carry different overtones. Some executives think that government regulation is a factor to be considered, but minimized if possible. Others feel an obligation to leave their positions in order to "serve their country" in executive positions. Still others believe that the company itself must help the government through close co-operation.

A manager develops the objectives of his company in the light of all of these obligations. In his decisions he must rationalize his own personal objectives with company objectives. Continued existence of the organization depends upon each member finding purposes in common with other members and with the organizational purposes.

Therefore, objectives of a company are fundamental, but difficult to state in words. When they are stated, they may sound fine, but too vague to be useful. Peter Drucker, however, observes that an essential of management is the establishment of useful objectives in every area of operation and at all levels, so that each member of the organization can see his own objectives. The combination of all of these subgroups of objectives results in joint objectives of the organization as a whole.

Policies. While objectives provide the goal toward which a manager aims, his policies provide the guides which will help him attain the goal. Policies are plans; policies are guides to action; more specifically, *policies include that body of understanding* (generally known by members of the group), *which makes the action of each member of the group in a given set of circumstances more predictable to other members.*

A manager must decide whether his decision will be considered as policy or merely as a one-shot decision. If it is a *precedent,* it takes on the character of a policy. Take, for example, the process of considering a grievance of a union member. Action in a specific case of John Jones may be agreed upon by both management and the union, but with the qualifying understanding that it will be "without prejudice." The intent of the qualifying agreement is that this specific case cannot be used in later cases as a precedent. In other words, the action in the case of John Jones would be a one-shot decision which does not establish policy. Of course, in spite of the intent at a given time, a decision can and often does have policy implications.

Many policies are formulated at the top, providing guides for lower echelons. Peterson and Plowman [1] call them *originated policies.* They serve as the rudder of the firm. Other policies are *imposed* from outside the firm. Some are institutionalized as law. Trade association rules and agreements of Trade Practices Conferences may act as imposed policies. Some policies are set only after a subordinate has *appealed* to his superior because of a specific problem not covered by previous policy statements.

Policies should provide for the exercise of judgment on the part of subordinates. Furthermore, the judgment and actions of members at lower levels can formulate policy. If the lower levels consistently perform in a given manner, and this performance is *known* without top management voicing a difference of judgment, subordinates may establish a precedent which carries the force of policy. Policy serves as a flexible guide; it is not synonymous with *rule* which states specifically what must or must not be done.

Generally, policies can be made clearer if put in writing. Many feel that written policies in manual form aid co-ordination. However, even when a manual is published, there are many implied policies, understood by the members of the organization, but not stated explicitly.

Policies serve several functions. As guides, they can make the actions of organization members more consistent. In addition, more decisions at lower levels of the hierarchy are possible. The proper use of policies allows a more flexible approach to specific problems. While they give direction and scope to specific decision-making, they should not be interpreted as ready-made decisions on detailed problems. Policies can speed decision-making since they provide a framework within which the decision can be made. They summarize past experience. They encourage planning by providing points of departure. Good policies should encourage initiative.

John Glover has summarized the characteristics required for a good business policy.[2]

1. It must delineate clearly the objective from which it is derived.
2. It must be in understandable writing.
3. It must prescribe criteria for current and future action.

[1] Elmore Peterson and E. Grosvenor Plowman, *Business Organization and Management* (Chicago: Richard D. Irwin, Inc., 1948), p. 313.

[2] John G. Glover, "Management Policy," *Advanced Management,* March, 1953, as reprinted in F. A. Shall, *Selected Readings in Management* (Homewood, Ill.: Richard D. Irwin, 1958), p. 123.

4. It must be stable but amenable to change, consistent with economic conditions and business requirements.
5. It must be a canon from which precepts of conduct can be derived.
6. Its edict must be capable of being accomplished.
7. It should prescribe method[s] of accomplishment in broad terms, but allow for the discretion of those responsible for preparing the precepts of conduct.
8. Its derivative rules of conduct must not be subject to the discretion of those who are governed by them.

Decisions. Within the framework of policies, the manager must make decisions (see Figure 9-1). In fact, much of management can be defined in terms of decision-making. A *decision* is a course of action which is consciously *chosen* for achieving a desired result. The manager must determine the choices available to him. He then must do more than choose among several predetermined alternatives; he must determine what possible actions are reasonable. He then should investigate the probable results of the alternative courses of action before he makes the decision. It is evident that he faces uncertainty. To find means of handling this uncertainty is one of the key subjects of later chapters in this book.

Strategies. In business, an important set of uncertainties results from the lack of information that a manager has concerning the actions of other human beings. A decision which might be optimum, assuming no reaction from others, could be a poor one when the counteractions of opponents are taken into account. Much of the process of thinking used in a game, like chess, is similar to that used by a manager. A manager is not sure what his competitor (opponent) will do. His action will depend on estimates of his competitor. *The planning for unpredictable contingencies about which fragmentary information is available, where the behavior of others is taken into account, can be called strategy.* It is an important concept in all cases in which the manager is confronted with those who are striving for goals which conflict with the goals of the manager: a supervisor faced with an unauthorized coffee break by his subordinates must consider a strategy accounting for the subordinates' reactions to any rules he may lay down; an industrial relations manager develops a complete strategy when faced with union demands in contract negotiations. Each executive possesses a conscious or unconscious strategy concerning the manner in which he builds his own department relative to other departments in the same firm. Strategy is important to any executive who is seeking advancement in the organization.

Strategy involves a time dimension. A policy decision today (even a decision on detail) limits the choices available tomorrow. Some decisions are irreversible, while others may be reversed when the appropriate opportunity occurs. For example, at one time the Jantzen Knitting Mills adopted a policy of simplification of lines, drastically restricting the number of designs.[3] This policy made possible a reduction of manufacturing costs (due

[3] See Franklin E. Folts, *Introduction to Industrial Management,* 4th edition (New York: McGraw-Hill Book Co., Inc., 1954), pp. 79–84.

to the reduction of set-up time) and a concentration of selling effort on the limited lines. Apparently the policy so strengthened the company that at a later stage it was possible to take advantage of the company reputation and move away from simplification. At later dates, the company diversified its product line, expanding into sweaters, sun-tan oil and other products.

A person's specific strategy will depend upon his own inclinations and his estimations of the strategies of others. Professor L. C. Sorrell, formerly of the University of Chicago, and William Newman of Columbia University have outlined and classified strategies that might be considered. The timing of action may involve any of a number of patterns:

1. Strike while the iron is hot.
2. Things must get worse before they get better.
3. Time is a great healer.
4. Keep one jump ahead.
5. Don't put off until tomorrow what can be done today.
6. Don't take action now, the problem may work itself out or not be a problem at all tomorrow.

Executives who decide to take the offensive can pick from many ideas:

1. Concentrate on offensive.
2. Avoid decisive engagement.
3. Get one's foot in the door.
4. Bore from within (the fifth column approach).

Managers who value group action seek strategies for joint action such as:

1. In union there is strength.
2. If you can't beat'em, join'em.
3. If someone opposes you, "butter him up" or give him definite responsibility.

Often an executive must find a defensive strategy, which might be:

1. Keep plugging regardless of lack of success.
2. Introduce a red herring to confuse the issues.
3. Counterattack.
4. Pass the buck.

These approaches are self-explanatory and should provide the reader with additional ideas which he could use himself, or give better understanding of the types of strategies which his opponent might use.

Action. The final outcome of the whole policy formulation and decision-making process discussed so far (and illustrated in Figure 9-1) is action itself. Somehow the objectives, plans, and decisions are converted into action—into the pounding of hammers or the pressing of buttons. The relationship between decisions and actions involves theoretical considerations which have not been clearly worked out, but further investigation at this point is beyond the scope of this chapter.

The Decision-Making Process

Figure 9-1 shows that the mental process by which a manager arrives at his objectives, policies, individual decisions, or strategies is an essential part of the study of management. Many of the recognized functions of management, such as planning, organizing, directing, and controlling, can be stated in decision-making terms. When we seek vicarious experience by solving business cases or we operate in an actual business firm, we are constantly solving problems. Many writers have dealt with decision-making methodologies: with the steps necessary for reaching a decision. Any outline of such steps would be an oversimplification, for the sequence is not rigidly fixed in actual practice; however, it may be useful to break down the process arbitrarily into the following five steps:

1. Consciousness of the problem-provoking situation.
2. Recognition of the problem and its definition.
3. Search for and analysis of available alternatives and their probable consequences.
4. Selection of the best solution.
5. Implementing the decision.

Consciousness of the problem-provoking situation

A decision is made within the circumstances of a given time and within the structure of past decisions and actions. A manager, at any given time, is not able to comprehend all of the facts impinging on the situation, for the situation is only partly under his control. His own past actions set the stage. Other factors must be taken as given; this actually simplifies the job for him. He makes decisions within organizationally predetermined objectives and policies.

The decision-making process in an organization involves a large number of individuals each of whom makes his contribution. Manager A may submit information which has only narrow meaning to him but is a missing link to B. B may not occupy the position which formally carries with it the authority to decide the matter, but he can offer a side opinion to C who is formally in the position. C may refer the matter to a group of specialists, D, E, and F, who report on the situation. Even the report from D, E, and F will affect the decision. C may mention it to G, one of his subordinates, and H, his superior. C may be influenced by the opinion of someone who is an outsider (e.g. a consultant). In such a situation it is difficult to determine how and by whom the decision-making process was started.

Consciousness of the situation by the manager will emerge gradually, raising doubts and confusion in his mind. At this stage, he might appreciate the wisdom in the saying—"If you can keep your head in all of this confusion, you don't understand the situation." One must face confusion with minimum frustrations, recognizing that confusion is inherent in the decision-making process.

Recognition of the problem and its definition

It takes understanding to recognize problems. Once the manager is aware that something needs attention, he can proceed to a recognition of a problem. It will probably be an obstruction to a previously determined goal. Since it is impossible for him to weigh all of the facts, he must develop a means of sifting out the relevant ones. In the classification of these facts, he can then define the problem in a definite manner. The more completely the problem can be stated, the easier the other steps will be; the more useful his framework of the statement of the problem at hand, the greater the chance that he can make a decision that is consistent with his goals. By this time he should have cleared his mind of his habitual or traditional responses to the situation. If the habitual had been sufficient, there would be no problem.

The key in defining the problem lies in the concept of the *strategic* or *limiting* factor. In World War II, a bridge over the Rhine was the limiting factor of the Allied advance; when it was taken intact, the entire situation changed. In a business organization, the factor might be a certain aspect of sales, the production capacity, additional working capital, or a disturbing human element. Many poor decisions result from the improper selection of the critical factor. The most damaging proof of a poor decision is to change the factor that has been considered critical, and then find the problem remains.

Search for and analysis of available alternatives and their probable consequences

Search for the available possibilities is critical to the entire decision-making process. The mind must be creative, for it must reshuffle the elements of the situation and create new, whole alternatives. In this process, the manager must relate the consequences of each alternative, which satisfy certain goals, with their effects on other goals. These other goals include other organizational goals, personal goals, and goals of others in the organization. Any decision is a matter of compromise. It is a matter of recognizing the relationship between the consequences of the decision on the goals in mind, and the future effect of the decision as a means toward other goals.

In his search one should feel free to consider what at first might be far-fetched alternatives. Too often, we feel that a good job in decision-making has been done if a second alternative is discovered and reasons are shown for the first one's superiority. Superficially, the advantages and disadvantages of each of two alternatives could be listed, and this list used in the evaluation. Furthermore, we might even fall into the trap of observing ten advantages of the first alternative against five advantages of the second, thus selecting the first.

Seeking alternatives and their consequences would be an extremely large task for even a simple problem if all variations of all alternatives were considered. It is possible for the human mind to be trained in the process of picking the most promising alternatives quickly. Past experience in similar decisions can help. Some people have an ability to organize factors rapidly so that it appears the decision was made intuitively. A great deal of interesting research remains to be done on how the human mind works and on how groups jointly reach a decision.

The premise is the key element in this aspect of decision-making. Each decision involves a large number of mental "If—then's"; "If we do this, then that result will occur." A general error in quick decisions is to consider the result without clearly recognizing the "if." It is necessary to train oneself and the group in searching for assumptions, many of which might be unconscious or at least concealed.

Premises may be value or factual. The distinction is important when testing their validity. A factual premise can be proved by observable and measurable means. A value premise can only be subjectively asserted to be valid. Many premises have both factual and value elements. In this connection, it is desirable to recognize one's biases. If we feel that we can eliminate our biases, we may be failing to consider the value premises to which we are attached.

Selection of the best solution

The selection of one alternative from among all of those considered is done by weighing the values and costs of each possibility. The technique can be a simple one, using no indexes, graphs, or quantitative weights. It may use an involved procedure. The best technique will depend upon the problem at hand, the situation, and the person making the decision. A simple technique could indicate superficial consideration of the factors or great skill on the part of the decision-maker. A complex technique could disclose new factors, but it might introduce so many side roads that the main problem is all but forgotten. Later chapters will discuss some of the available techniques of selection in different phases of management.

Evaluation of the solution depends upon the preceding process of thought. It will be based on the classifications, premises, and criteria used in the process.

The manager may generally seek a satisfactory solution without worrying whether it is the best. If the decision-making process becomes so involved and time consuming when the "best" is sought, he may settle for less. Some managers arrive at satisfactory solutions by short cuts; in fact all decision-making requires simplification.

Implementing the decision

Some action (or no action) is desired once the decision is made. In this final phase, the manager must consider the manner in which the organization will proceed as a result of the decision. The means of communicating the decision, the techniques of motivating the group to accept the decision, and effects of the decision on the co-ordination of others in the group are phases of implementing the decision covered in other parts of this book.

Planning

Nature of planning

Planning is that function of a manager in which he decides in advance what he will do. It is a decision-making process of a special kind; its essence is futurity. It is an intellectual process in which creative thinking and imagination are essential. A plan with broad scope includes setting objectives, policies, individual decisions, and strategies. Many plans are narrow in scope relating to a small set of interrelated decisions. They may be for a long period of time or for the immediate future.

All plans involve some *set of interrelated decisions.* The term *planning* has been used to mean decision-making, policy-making, and strategy-making, but it stresses the following aspects. First, planning may be an intellectual dry run or simulation. It may have an element of day dreaming. In an initial stage, it may involve what might be called vision.

Secondly, planning not only pertains to defining a problem which immediately confronts the manager, but often it mentally searches the future possibilities for problems that might appear. It does not mean that the manager should "cross the bridge before he comes to it," but it does mean that it will be helpful to look ahead to the river and consider the type of problems that might arise if he desires to cross.

Thirdly, like any type of decision-making, planning involves foreseeing future developments. It must be based on some type of forecast or prediction. The predictions then become the premises upon which the plans are based.

Fourthly, plans become premises for the decisions of the future. Detailed planning may include several plans which are mutually exclusive. It provides series and/or sets of decisions that can be made under various possible circumstances. Thus, planning aids in making specific decisions, since it includes all of the important alternatives which should be considered and the consequences of each.

Planning principles

Planning sets aside time for deliberate analysis. It helps prevent vacillation resulting from surprises in the turn of events. The linking of plans by various members of an organized group allows co-ordination of action at a given time. The adaptation of plans to the actions in the present requires continual redrafting. For example, if a firm maintains a long range plan for the next ten years, an intermediate plan for the next year, and a plan for the immediate future (the next month), it must continually recheck to make sure that the longer range plans remain consistent with the shorter range ones. Thus, a periodical revision of the longer range plans is necessary as the firm moves into the future. Koontz and O'Donnell have called this the *principle of navigational change.*[4] It does not mean that plans should be discarded as new facts develop, but that the firm should "tack" as does a sailing vessel—head for a given destination but shift actions back and forth to take advantage of immediate opportunities.

Planning is a prerequisite for other managerial functions such as organizing, directing, and control. This has been called the *principle of primacy of planning*. Objectives and policies are the result of planning, but in turn form the framework for further planning. Decision-making and determining strategies can be considered a part of planning. Planning is often considered a staff function, but this does not mean that it is unimportant for line executives.

The idea that planning is performed by managers of all types and at all levels has been called the principle of *pervasiveness of planning*. It is recognized that top level executives are concerned with broad plans (company wide) and plans reaching far into the future. Lower levels of managers make limited plans in the more immediate future. The implication might be that top executives should not be concerned with limited plans or plans in the immediate future. However, since top executives have problems of co-ordinating the various lengths of plans and the number of plans of narrow scope, they must keep in contact with the immediate details of actions; these components must remain consistent with the broad and long-range plans.

Planning requires that all members understand and utilize consistent planning premises. Koontz and O'Donnell call this the *principle of planning premises*. For example, if the sales manager makes his plans based on the premise of an increase of 10% in sales during the next year, the financial manager must understand this premise and plan current assets (specifically, cash, accounts receivable, and inventories) consistent with this increase in

[4] Koontz and O'Donnell have identified 14 principles of planning in *Principles of Management,* 2nd edition (McGraw-Hill Book Company, Inc., 1959), pp. 578–582. The discussion in this section is based in part on their analysis.

sales. Of course, the production manager, in scheduling production, must plan his output to care for this increase in sales. If any one part of the organization proceeds on the basis of a different premise, the result will be a lack of co-ordination.

The interchange of plans must provide complete information for each functional area involved. *Planning communication* then is a principle that should be recognized in the structure of plans. For this reason, each functional manager often circulates plans for his particular area to all others who might need the information as premises for their decisions. Committees serve a useful function at this stage, since each specialist can discuss his plans which then form a part of the plans of other specialists. With this tentative understanding, each can then circulate his understanding in writing. Later, further adjustments might be needed in the event that the written statements are still inconsistent.

The *commitment principle* refers to the question of how far into the future plans should be made. Since uncertainty will remain regardless of how much planning takes place, a manager should relate the degree of commitment of his resources to the need for definite plans. If raw materials have been purchased, men have been hired, and contracts have been negotiated, plans need to be "firmer" than if these commitments have not been made. Options in a contract, agreements to a range of delivery quantities rather than to a specific amount, short term leasing, purchasing rather than making certain parts, and other techniques can vary the commitment for specific action in the future. If commitments must be made in a fixed and exact manner, plans must be refined to a greater degree to insure fulfillment of obligations.

Plans can cause inflexibility in actions unless they provide for alternative ways in which the actions can be accomplished. The greater the use of alternative techniques, the greater is the cost. Therefore, the principle of *flexibility* of planning must be stated in terms of the relationship between the advantages of flexibility and its costs.

Conclusion

This chapter has provided a conceptual framework for understanding management. Policy formulation, decision making, and planning facilitate orderly development of a firm. These form the framework which eliminates "flying by the seat of one's pants." They offer means of avoiding "fighting fires" whenever they appear, and provide a means of optimizing the use of "fire fighting" equipment. A poor manager is often overworked because he takes care of problems only as they occur. Policies and plans will help him allocate his time.

In later chapters, the tools of planning and policy formulation will be studied. Budgeting is an illustration in the area of accounting. Mathematical models are a more precise means of stating premises and estimating the results of action. Charts draw a picture of plans. Forecasting assists in the establishment of some decision-making premises. Most of the remaining chapters discuss one phase or another of the decision-making process.

Bibliographical Note

The philosophy and theory of management has been the subject of a number of books in the last half century. Those oriented more specifically to organization theory have been mentioned in a previous note. Several cover all of the functions of management and attempt to develop a general theory. Ralph C. Davis's *The Fundamentals of Top Management* (1951) is one such book that has influenced a number of teachers of management. William H. Newman's *Administrative Action* (1951) collects much of the theory, which had developed by the middle of the century. More recently two other books discuss the principles of management: Harold Koontz and Cyril O'Donnell, *Principles of Management* (1959) and Dalton E. McFarland, *Management Principles and Practices* (1958). All of these books present a somewhat similar framework. All attempt to formulate prescriptive principles.

An entirely different approach to the study of top management has resulted in the policy cases developed at Harvard Business School, illustrated by the widely used book by George A. Smith and C. R. Christensen, *Policy Formulation and Administration* (1959). Other policy case books include William H. Newman and James P. Logan, *Business Policies and Management* (1959) and T. J. McNichols, *Policy Making and Executive Action* (1959). The case method is based on the view that an exposure to actual business situations contributes to administrative skills. Policy cases require consideration of the total company situation, with a search for key problem areas and an analysis of decision alternatives.

R. A. Gordon's *Business Leadership in the Large Corporation* (1945) presents a survey of administrative practices in large firms. Many business histories seek to determine the underlying philosophy of a single firm. John Jeuck's *Catalogues and Counters* (1950) and Joseph L. Massie's *Blazer and Ashland Oil* (1960) represent the historical case approach to management philosophy and policy.

Decision-making has rapidly become a primary area of research in management. H. A. Simon is a leader in this area. Logicians, psychologists, mathematicians and others have made interesting contributions. Manley Jones's *Executive Decision Making* (1957) and Peter F. Drucker's *The Practice of Management* (1954) summarize some of the general developments. Bibliographical notes to other chapters in this book refer to some of the work that has been done in special areas of decision-making.

In recent years a number of the practicing chief executives of large firms have written books or presented lectures on their reflections of their management philosophy. For a number of years *Fortune* Magazine has featured articles on the business policy and philosophy of particular firms.

The moral and ethical obligations of management are receiving increased attention in the literature. The *Harvard Business Review* publishes a number of provocative articles in this area. An interesting statement of management's responsibilities is in Benjamin M. Selekman's *A Moral Philosophy for Management* (1959). C. W. Churchman in *Prediction and Optimal Decision* (1961) raises the question of the development of a science of values.

Questions and Problems

1. Give an example of how the following affect the concept of a firm:
   (a) The structure of the industry
   (b) Technical processes
   (c) Social forces
   (d) Government relationships
   (e) History of the firm
   (f) Moral values
   (g) Characteristics of the present personnel

2. Is there any difference in the meaning of a company's "image" as considered by a public relations department, its "character," as observed by a business historian, and its "place in the economy" as seen by the operating personnel?

3. Some companies attempt to find "niches" in their industry different from the pattern of the majority of firms. What factors would cause one company to imitate others and a second company to attempt to do just the opposite?

4. A humorous sign is found on many walls:

REASON?

There's No Reason

It's Company Policy

Comment on this.

5. Consider any organization to which you belong and construct a hierarchy of objectives, including the over-all long-run objectives and the detailed short-run objectives of the organization.

6. It is said that strong, clear policies encourage members to make their own decisions. Comment.

7. How does a decision made by a group differ from a decision made by an individual?

8. The word "strategy" is used often by the military. Does the use of the term in this chapter differ from its military use?

9. Does the availability of a large amount of facts increase the difficulty of making a decision?

10. What is the difference between a value premise and a factual premise?

11. H. A. Simon explains that a manager often must "satisfice" rather than "maximize." What are some of the reasons that this may be true?

12. Give an example of the application of each of the principles of planning listed in this chapter.

10

Extracts and Cases in Policy and Decision Making

THE preceding chapter has offered a framework for thought about business policy. The purpose of the present chapter is to make these thoughts more concrete by considering specific illustrations of policies in well-known firms. As the reader considers each of these illustrations, he should ask himself whether the policy statements are meaningful and useful. Under what assumptions are the policies good ones?

Drucker's extract introduces his idea of "management by objectives," basic in a policy of decentralization (divisionalization), and used by more and more large companies. The statement by Westinghouse Electric Corporation explains the reasoning behind the decentralization trend.

Often the objectives of a company are unwritten. Ralph J. Cordiner of General Electric, however, states concisely one set of over-all objectives of one large company. Within these objectives can be seen the basis for a number of company-wide policies—decentralization, diversification, public relations, employee policies, and so forth.

The concept of diversification as a basic policy is illustrated by the extract about the Glidden Company. Du Pont's approach of top management is explained in the extract from the Wall Street Journal; and from the same publication, reasons are given for the U.S. Steel Corporation's use of a centralized form of organization.

The case on the Ashland Oil & Refining Company provides the basis for understanding a way of thinking at the level of the chief executive. This case enables the reader to analyze broad policies from the view of top management. A comparison of the thinking of the Ashland Oil management with that of the Standard Oil Company (California) described in Chapter 4 will be provocative and help the reader to understand some of the fundamental problems of organization.

EXTRACT A

The Practice of Management (Peter Drucker)

To manage a business is to balance a variety of needs and goals. This requires judgment. The search for the one objective is essentially a search for a magic formula that will make judgment unnecessary. But the attempt to replace judgment by formula is always irrational; all that can be done is to make judgment possible by narrowing its range and the available alternatives, giving it clear focus, a sound foundation in facts and reliable measurements of the effects and validity of actions and decisions. And this, by the very nature of business enterprise, requires multiple objectives.

What should these objectives be, then? There is only one answer: *Objectives are needed in every area where performance and results directly and vitally affect the survival and prosperity of the business.* These are the areas which are affected by every management decision and which therefore have to be considered in every management decision. They decide what it means concretely to manage the business. They spell out what results the business must aim at and what is needed to work effectively toward these targets.

Objectives in these key areas should enable us to do five things: to organize and explain the whole range of business phenomena in a small number of general statements; to test these statements in actual experience; to predict behavior; to appraise the soundness of decisions when they are still being made; and to enable practicing businessmen to analyze their own experience and, as a result, improve their performance. It is precisely because the traditional theorem of the maximization of profits cannot meet any of these tests—let alone all of them—that it has to be discarded.

At first sight it might seem that different businesses would have entirely different key areas—so different as to make impossible any general theory. It is indeed true that different key areas require different emphasis in different businesses—and different emphasis at different stages of the development of each business. But the areas are the same, whatever the business, whatever the economic conditions, whatever the business's size or stage of growth.

There are eight areas in which objectives of performance and results have to be set:

Market standing; innovation; productivity; physical and financial resources; profitability; manager performance and development; worker performance and attitude; public responsibility. . . .

The real difficulty lies indeed not in determining what objectives we need, but in deciding how to set them.

There is only one fruitful way to make this decision: by determining what shall be measured in each area and what the yardstick of measurement should be. For the measurement used determines what one pays attention to.[1]

Extract B

Basic Policy on Decentralization in Westinghouse

How are profits generated in a large and complex industrial enterprise like the Westinghouse Electric Corporation?

The answer lies in a basic management policy. It provides the individual manager with the tools and responsibility for profit from a product or product line. As a result, the large number and variety of products which otherwise might smother profit effort through their own weight are grouped selectively to become focal points in contributing to the Company's over-all profit. This policy is called decentralization.

Decentralization recognizes that the Westinghouse corporate entity is a number of different businesses . . . many of which are unrelated. It takes into account that the divisions of the Company, as well as departments within divisions, are characterized by individual combinations of markets, products, and manufacturing methods . . . and individual competitors specializing in their products.

To meet these circumstances, units are created at the first level in the organization at which the functions essential to the profit on a product line come together in that the heads of the major functions—basically sales, engineering and manufacturing—report to a manager who is responsible for the profit on each product line. Each decentralized unit becomes a "profit center."

As a consequence, the manufacturing divisions and departments are individually responsible for a share of the total Company profits based primarily on proportionate shares of total Company assets, although other economic facts and conditions may modify profit responsibility.

The Small Motor Division illustrates how operational decentralization works. It is divided into Aircraft Equipment and Industrial Motor Departments.

Each of these departments has its own manager and its own sales, engineering and manufacturing operations as well as allied activities. The managers of the departments report to the vice president in charge of the Small Motor Division. He is responsible for broad, comprehensive policy and direction.

The Transformer Division, with a big plant at Sharon, Pa., . . . is divided into a triad of profit units—Distribution Transformer & Instrument Transformer Department, Specialty Transformer Department and Power Transformer Department. . . .

[1] Peter F. Drucker, *The Practice of Management* (New York: Harper and Brothers, 1954), p. 62.

There are two fundamental reasons for decentralization. One is the fact that continuing growth of Westinghouse necessitates delegation of the over-all responsibility of division managers for profits. Thus profits become a direct concern of more individuals.

The other reason is that responsibility for profits stimulates personal efforts more effectively than any other type of responsibility.

For these reasons, decentralization became a way of life with Westinghouse management long before the current popularity of this effective method of profit generation, although what was quite complete decentralization a generation ago would not be so regarded now.

When Westinghouse started converting more than 20 years ago from a functional form of organization to decentralized profit and management responsibilities, it led the way in the electrical equipment industry and helped pioneer an industrial trend.

Prior to that time, Company-wide operations such as sales, engineering and manufacturing were directed by individuals at Westinghouse headquarters in East Pittsburgh, Pa. Typically, the engineering manager had primary responsibility for design of approximately 20 product lines then produced at all the Company's locations.

Progressive decentralization began with formation of 16 manufacturing divisions. Each division had its own management organization and each division manager was assigned the requisite plant facilities and sales, engineering and manufacturing personnel.

Each division similarly had its own balance sheet and profit-loss statement. In essence, the division managers operated like presidents of independent companies. . . .

As a rule, however, the managers of the individual profit units operate with optimum freedom within a framework of basic management policy with respect to profits and plans for the future.

Such a way of business life in Westinghouse assures judicious allocation of capital funds, of earnings retained for new or replacement machinery and buildings, and of new borrowed or equity money.

Additionally, this type of decentralization permits effective use of the resources and strengths existing in Westinghouse, contributes to greater strength of all the Company's individual operations, provides a central control over the amounts and velocities of dollars flowing between Company operations or from external sources, and enables economic utilization of inventories.

The existence of effective centralized controls in a few necessary areas actually increases the latitude of profit-unit managers, who are thus relieved of functions related only indirectly to their profit efforts.

As an example, Company-wide policies on labor relations are developed at headquarters. Other headquarters' functions for the benefit of individual profit units include matters involving tax requirements; sales and purchases involving several divisions; and long-range planning.

Still another benefit to Westinghouse of this concept of decentralized profit operations is the reservoir thus provided for skilled, experienced management personnel. Division managers guide each operating head of a profit unit in the acquisition of skills essential for greater responsibilities in the Company in the future. Training courses supplement this on-the-job education.

Hence decentralization in Westinghouse is the means toward greater over-all Company profits, both for dividends and for future growth. In addition, it helps assure the capable management manpower essential to the Company to meet its obligations to stockholders, employees, customers and the nation generally.[2]

Extract C

Diversification in The Glidden Company

Since The Glidden Company's founding in 1917, its record of growth has been rooted in a number of basic operational precepts—product diversification—decentralization—quality control—practical, applied research—personnel planning—affirmative labor relations—aggressive merchandising.

Today, Glidden is one of the four largest paint manufacturers in the world, and a major factor in such varied industries as food products, edible oils, soybean processing, pigments, metal powders, and naval stores.

Originally a producer of paints and varnishes, Glidden early recognized the value of diversification as a source of stability and growth. By 1919, the Company had acquired eleven paint plants throughout the country for easy and economical access to local markets. The next year Glidden began to produce refined vegetable oils and margarine.

During the early twenties, linseed oil facilities, zinc and barytes mines, three lithopone pigment plants and a new patent for making pure white lead were acquired. Shortly after, Glidden purchased a plant in Hammond, Indiana, as a source for lead pigments used in paint manufacturing. This operation provided the foundation for the Company's present role in the growing metal powders field.

By 1929, the Company was well established in the production of margarine and vegetable oil products. In that year E. R. Durkee & Company and six other concerns were purchased to broaden Glidden's line of food products. The present trade name, Durkee Famous Foods, was then adopted.

In 1934, Glidden obtained rights to an improved process of extracting soybean oil and proceeded with the construction of a soybean processing plant at Chicago, Illinois.

Since naval stores, chiefly rosin and turpentine, were principal constituents in the manufacture of paint, Glidden entered this field in 1935 through the

[2] Stockholder Relations Department, "Westinghouse Record," Westinghouse Electric Corporation, October, 1957.

acquisition of the Nelio Rosin Corporation. This was the beginning of the present Southern Chemical Division.

This twenty-year period (1917–1937), when sales increased from $2,000,000 to $45,000,000, was Glidden's "first phase of growth" and established the basic framework under which the Company operates. . . .

The "second phase of growth," from 1937 to 1954, witnessed an increase in annual sales volume to over $200,000,000. During this period, operations were consolidated, new products and markets were developed, and plant facilities were modernized and expanded. . . .

The Glidden Company is . . . embarking upon what might be termed a "third phase of growth." This program involves such projects as—titanium dioxide expansion—grain merchandising—terpene chemicals—paint distribution facilities—overseas operations—soybean derivatives—tall oil. In addition, the Company is continually exploring the acquisition of profitable going enterprises or products and the development of new products created by its own or outside research laboratories.

As a further impetus to growth, it is a basic policy of the Company to eliminate activities or products which are minor, fundamentally divergent, or incapable of producing a return proportionate to the financial and managerial investments required. Under this concept, Glidden has disposed of its metal-smelting, copra-crushing, formula feed and West Coast lithopone and flaxseed processing operations. These recent dispositions have freed over $8,500,000, making these funds available for use in more profitable ways.

By concentrating its managerial and financial resources upon those fields of activity that promise a high degree of success, The Glidden Company looks ahead confidently to the future.

In a company as diversified as Glidden, it is often difficult to view operations or products in their true light. Many times the value (or lack of value) of a particular product is magnified out of proportion to its real importance to the Company. It should be remembered that very few of the individual products in themselves are extremely-large profit producers. When consolidated, however, the resulting profit is substantial. This broad product diversification imparts an important element of stability to the business. . . .

Much of Glidden's success throughout the years can be attributed to a policy of management decentralization adopted shortly after the Company's inception. Partly the result of necessity and partly that of a philosophy, decentralization nonetheless is playing an important part in Glidden's development.

The over-all governing body is the Board of Directors composed of ten members, all of whom are full time working directors with managerial positions in the organization. A five man Executive Committee has authority to act for the Board between regular monthly meetings. Staff committees—Research, Patent, Bonus, Stock Option, Pension—are responsible for administration and planning within their respective fields. The Board and the

Executive Committee exercise the customary policy direction and long-range planning of the Company.

Glidden is organized into five operating divisions—Chemicals-Pigments-Metals, Southern Chemical, Chemurgy, Durkee Famous Foods, and the Paint Division. Each division has undivided responsibility for research, development, manufacture, and sales of its products. Since running a paint business obviously requires different techniques, from supervising grain merchandising or the production and sale of terpene chemicals, there is a minimum of interference at the operating level on the part of the Board and the President. They do, however, pass on basic operating policy and budgets, major capital expansion, and management compensation policy.[3]

Extract D

General Electric Company—Objectives

Briefly summarized, General Electric's objectives are as follows:

1. To carry on a diversified, growing, and profitable world wide manufacturing business in electrical apparatus, appliances, and supplies, and in related materials, products, systems, and services for industry, commerce, agriculture, government, the community, and the home.
2. To lead in research in all fields of science and all areas of work relating to the business in order to assure a constant flow of new knowledge that will make real the Company theme, "Progress Is Our Most Important Product."
3. To operate each decentralized business venture to achieve its own customer acceptance and profitable results by taking the appropriate business risks.
4. To design, make, and market all Company products and services with good quality and with inherent customer value, at fair, competitive prices.
5. To build public confidence and friendly feeling for products and services bearing the Company's name and brands.
6. To provide good jobs, wages, working conditions, work satisfactions, stability of employment, and opportunities for advancement for employees, in return for their loyalty, initiative, skill, care, effort, attendance, and teamwork.
7. To manage the human and material resources of the enterprise for continuity and flow of progress, growth, profit, and public service in accordance with the principles of decentralization, sound organization structure, and professional management.
8. To attract and retain investor capital through attractive returns as a continuing incentive for wide investor participation and support.
9. To cooperate with suppliers, distributors, retailers, contractors, and others who facilitate the production, distribution, installation, and servicing of Company products and systems.
10. To meet the Company's social, civic, and economic responsibilities with imagination and with voluntary action which will merit the understanding and support of all concerned among the public.

To the casual reader or listener, these broad objectives may sound vague and obvious, but thoughtful study will reveal that each of them represents a

[3] The Glidden Company, *A Report on Diversification,* May, 1956.

number of deliberate and important managerial decisions. They provide a direct expression of the Company's ethical standards, its managerial philosophy, and its continuing purposes—in a form which makes them understandable and acceptable, after study, to every member of the organization.[4]

Extract E

Du Pont's Rule by Committee

An unusual formula for decentralization in the management of a giant enterprise is that of E. I. du Pont de Nemours, of Wilmington, Delaware, the huge chemical company which is better known for such things as nylon than for the explosives which made its original fortune. Du Pont has dared the "unthinkable" and established for itself a rule by committee. . . .

Naturally Du Pont, like any other corporation, is governed in the final instance by a board of directors, which happens in this case to be heavily weighted with members of the Du Pont family. But in point of practice, the Company is run by a president, Crawford H. Greenewalt, and nine vice-presidents, each of whom has a single vote which could be the decisive one in the balloting that settles things in the executive sessions.

The "Ex Committee"—which, incidentally, constitutes one-third of the Du Pont Board of Directors—has no day-to-day functional responsibility. The members are paid to think and make policy decisions involving the general welfare and general activities of the Corporation. The only practical limitation on their power (aside from that implied in an occasional directive from the Board) is provided by the Du Pont committees on finance, audit and salary and bonus compensation. But since Du Pont committees are interlaced, the check-and-balance at the policy-making top does not appreciably inhibit action.

The heart of the "Ex Committee" system is the Wednesday meeting, to which the members bring the result of ruminative homework that covers the better part of the whole week including the weekend. . . .

The broad subjects which the Ex Committee considers run to such things as location of plants, the response to anti-trust suits, the continuance of old products and the development of new, appropriation requests from the ten Du Pont production departments and the fourteen staff or auxiliary organizations, the review of departmental projects, and the general consideration of "whither reports" (such as "whither nylon" or "whither titanium").

Every Friday afternoon Ex Committee members find on their desks a stack of documents which they are expected to digest by the following Wednesday. The manufacturing departments prepare monthly operating reports which go

[4] R. J. Cordiner, *New Frontiers for Professional Managers* (New York: McGraw-Hill Book Co., Inc., 1956), pp. 55–57, as reprinted in Harold Koontz and Cyril O'Donnell, *Readings in Management* (New York: McGraw-Hill Book Co., Inc., 1959), pp. 102, 103.

to the Ex Committee for consideration of the first and last Wednesday of the month. The Committee averages one meeting per month in a chart room, where sales and earnings of the departments are displayed. If slumps develop, the general managers involved are expected to be present with explanations. Five members of the Ex Committee constitute a quorum, and a minimum of four affirmative votes is required for the adoption of a resolution.

The Committee gives no orders, and it doesn't like to be put in the position of having to decide intracompany disputes between Du Pont production divisions. Moreover, the advice offered by the Committee members, either singly or as a group, can be rejected with impunity by men who think they have a better way. (However, as one Committee member puts it, "We sometimes resort to tactful persuasion.")

The ten Du Pont general managers who are entrusted with earning a profit on the Company's investment and working capital in the divisions devoted to electrochemicals, explosives, fabrics and finishes, film, Grasselli chemicals, organic chemicals, photo products, pigments, polychemicals, and textile fibers, hire their own personnel and have "substantially as much power as the average company president."

As for the Du Pont "service" departments—advertising, engineering, employee relations, public relations, traffic and so on—they are headed by directors appointed by the Ex Committee but do their own hiring and day-to-day planning. The heads of the secretary and treasury departments are elected by the Board; unlike other Du Pont officials, they are responsible to the president and the finance committee.

The theory which governs Du Pont is that "ten heads are better than one." While the Ex Committee arrangement lacks the hard-and-fast definition of a military organization, it might roughly be compared to a military General Staff sitting behind the front lines and concerning itself with problems of major strategy.

Though President Greenewalt naturally has the prestige that goes with being "primus inter pares," or first among equals, there seems to be no hidden power lurking behind the organization chart. The board of directors, a blend of former Du Pont officers, large stockholders and the members of the Ex Committee, meets once a month and maintains more direct control over the business than in most firms. But with the members of the Ex Committee contributing their say—and their very ponderable vote—in board sessions, the cooperation between board and top executive authority is smooth and unobtrusive.

The secret of the Du Pont success with the committee system would seem to reside in the recruitment and the balancing of its components. Every effort is made to avoid the development of a personal situation in which two evenly balanced factions might rise to fight for power.

Of the nine Ex Committee vice-presidents, two have a financial background, two are from research, two are primarily salesmen, two are from production, and one is from engineering. As things work out, this means that seven men almost invariably defer to two acknowledged authorities whenever a technical or financial subject is up for consideration. Where even splits occur, they are usually in relation to advertising or public relations, which do not entail any struggle for authority over the more tangible Du Pont assets or products.

Thus it is that a system which might rend a different type of organization works harmoniously for a huge concern which spends more than $120,000,000 a year on new construction, and $60,000,000 a year on research. One defect of the system is that it sometimes works slowly (it took 10 years to persuade some outlying industrial departments to move their headquarters into Wilmington). Committee members who have come up through division management sometimes complain that relegation to "thinking" and "advisory status" makes them feel "inhibited" and "frustrated." But on balance the committee members consider that if "seven men out of ten—all intellectually honest—can reach agreement, the chances are that it is sound." [5]

Extract F

The Managerial Art As Practiced by United States Steel Corporation

. . . Radical "divisionalization"—the sociologist's word for organizing a company into flexible units—may not be the best for all types of industry. It has not been used, for example, at United States Steel.

Here the nature of the product calls its own special turn. Since steel is a matter of putting several raw materials together and pushing them toward one final form (in this case the basic carbon "melt" which comes out as plate, strip bars, and structural shapes), a "chain of command" principle of organization, with authority centered at the top, seems best adapted to keep the ingredients flowing.

Thus the problem of getting cohesion in the U. S. Steel Corporation is simple enough in theory. In practice, however, U. S. Steel has been up against the facts of its own history.

Put together by the elder J. P. Morgan (a banker) and Judge Elbert Gary (a lawyer) out of a host of smaller companies, U. S. Steel seemed a triumph of "integration" in the early part of the century. Its dovetailed line began with ore, coal and limestone and ran upwards into the linked paraphernalia of blast furnaces, open hearths, blooming mills, soaking pits, rolling mills and the fabrication of basic shapes.

But the very hugeness of the U. S. Steel's "process unity" caught the baleful eyes of Teddy Roosevelt's trust-busters, and in the social climate of the

[5] John Chamberlain, "Rule by Committee," *Wall Street Journal,* December 27, 1956.

times Judge Gary's company soon discovered that to be too good was to be "bad."

The pragmatic problem facing Judge Gary was not to tighten up his organization but to decelerate the drive which had already given it control of two-thirds of the industry. With the Department of Justice hovering in the wings in a perpetually scowling posture, the wary Gary made no effort to streamline his subsidiaries. They maintained separate boards and engaged in costly duplicative effort, all of which gave Bethlehem Steel the opportunity to close the gap between the front-runner and the "place" horse in the great ingot tonnage race. . . .

Looked at on the map, U. S. Steel units in areas as far apart as Pittsburgh and Chicago would seem to require a "let alone" attitude from the top. But geography, here, is delusive, for basic steel problems remain essentially the same anywhere in the Middle West. Whether the coking coal goes to Chicago to meet the iron ore from Duluth, or whether the ore from Duluth journeys onward to Youngstown or Pittsburgh to meet the coal, is not a question to be adjudicated in U. S. Steel by "divisional" competition. The geographical apportionment of coal to ore must be in accordance with an overall plan.

Moreover, if a steel company's research staff can devise improvements for a continuous strip mill, the ideas are just as valid for use in the Chicago area as in the Irvin Works on a hill outside of Pittsburgh. Finally, a U. S. Steel sales organization in Indianapolis couldn't care less whether the bar steel it markets to a local manufacturer comes from Chicago or the Pittsburgh area. The origin of the product would merely be a matter of convenience and freight rates, not of competitive pride as between regions.

The nature of steel being what it is, one of the first jobs which faced the successors of Judge Gary was to put U. S. Steel's Chicago and Pittsburgh regions into one operational unit. In 1950, after a period of control by "management consultation," the concept of Central Operations was introduced.

Today Central Operations runs Chicago and Pittsburgh and the new Fairless Works on the Delaware in Eastern Pennsylvania as a single unit. This amounts to "chain of command" control of some two-thirds of U. S. Steel's 39 million ingot ton capacity.

Only the remaining third of the U. S. Steel empire is "decontrolled" through the new "divisional" device of "federal decentralization." An adaptive man, U. S. Steel's Chairman . . . , argues against the idea of putting the Oliver Mining unit (Minnesota) and the new Orinoco Mining (Venezuela) under the same divisional roof. Tropic and temperate zone mining problems obviously differ. Again the problem of Central Operations and those of the U. S. Steel West Coast subsidiary, Columbia-Geneva steel, are too far apart in space to be watched from a single conning tower.

Letting local conditions and special operational problems determine the kind of organization used, U. S. Steel today does have a sizable number of divisions besides the one big division of Central Operations. Its southern production is in the hands of Tennessee Coal and Iron. Practically all of the U. S. Steel wire business is done by American Steel and Wire. American Bridge is another specialty subsidiary. Other semi-autonomous divisions are National Tube, Oil Well Supply, U. S. Steel Homes, Michigan Limestone, and Universal Atlas Cement (which doesn't make steel at all).

But even the regional and specialty divisions report to Central Operations and they all make use of common "services" such as central research at Pittsburgh. Labor relations come within the purview of Pittsburgh, because the union is strong enough to force industry-wide bargaining on the Corporation.

It will be seen at a glance that where U. S. Steel moves outward from basic steel into fabrication, the need to service a specific type of customer promotes divisionalization. Such things as wire, bridge girders, tubular steel, prefabricated homes and oil drums are far closer to the retail trade than anything that may be found in Central Operations. This difference demands its own semi-autonomy within the Corporation make-up.

Thus the functional significance of differences which might otherwise seem schizophrenic in the U. S. Steel Corporation's organizational philosophy. The typical basic steel company, whether it is large or small, still resembles a military "line and staff" for the simple reason that its problems, even when huge, are best handled by Central authority. But where a steel company moves toward fabrication, or maintains a division on the far periphery of its geographical location, it tends toward a freer type of organization.

The problem is to localize decision-making at its point of impact—and it is the product and the market that must govern the issue of impact, not the loose modern habit of thinking of "centralization" as a naughty word and "decentralization" a good one.[6]

Case A:

Ashland Oil & Refining Company (B)

In 1957, a new era in the management of Ashland Oil & Refining Company began. The Company had been started and built by Paul G. Blazer, and in 1957 he was stepping down as Chairman of the Board of Directors. The new management had developed under the philosophy and policies of Blazer, and now was faced with basic decisions regarding the philosophy best suited to the characteristics of the new managers. Thus, the concepts used in the previous thirty years were being studied.

[6] John Chamberlain, "Autonomy vs. Central Control," *Wall Street Journal,* December 19, 1957.

Company History

The refining company was organized in 1924 as a subsidiary of Swiss Oil Corporation, a producer of Kentucky crude oil. Assets grew from $300,000 in 1924, when Blazer assumed management, to $8,000,000 by 1940; $24,-000,000 by 1947; $67,000,000 by 1949; and $200,000,000 by 1959. At no time during the entire history did the refining company end a year with a net loss. Its ratio of net income (after taxes) to owner's equity fluctuated between 6½ per cent (in 1934) and 40 per cent (in 1928 and 1948).

This growth was accomplished by accretion and by merger of approximately fifty companies. The most important acquisitions took place in 1930–1931 and 1948–1950. In the former period, the company acquired a refining company and a pipe-line; in the latter, Allied Oil Company, Aetna Oil Company, Freedom-Valvoline Oil Company, and Frontier Oil Refining Corporation merged with Ashland.

The fact that Ashland Oil was an "independent" in an industry dominated by large firms makes its success more interesting. Furthermore, a large portion of the profits throughout its history resulted from refining operations —a branch of the industry in which it is generally considered difficult to maintain stable earnings over a long period of time.

In 1957, operations included all the functions of an integrated oil company, except that the production and marketing phases were not balanced with the refining and transportation phases. The entire refining, transportation, and marketing phases were centered around the Ohio River and the Great Lakes. One of the important operating advantages that the company had maintained since its beginning had been its use of river barge transportation. After 1948 it also used the Great Lakes as a means of transportation. Its marketing territory was concentrated in Ohio, West Virginia, and Kentucky, with operations being expanded into Western Pennsylvania, Western New York, Southern Indiana, and Illinois. Several brand names were used and a high proportion of refined products was distributed through private brands. Production of crude oil centered in Eastern Kentucky until 1940. By 1957, production operations had been established in a number of oil fields.

Concepts of Chairman of the Board

An interesting fact in view of the company's growth is that the chief executive had been unacquainted with published management literature. He directed his attention to the operational problems of the company and read little of other ideas in the field of management. In the early history he gave little formal thought to concepts of direction, organization, and control. As the company grew, of course, his time increasingly was taken up with such problems. Comments in letters to the board began to offer more of his reasons and rationalizations on his executive process. This process was generally informal and often violated a number of the more generally discussed "principles of management," such as span of control, the exception principle, and certain aspects of the scalar principle. His concepts were the direct result of his personal abilities and preferences, the dynamics of the petroleum industry, and the place that his company occupied in that industry.

The techniques of the chief executive were especially adapted to smaller scale operations. Growth increased the difficulty of continued application of his methods. During his participation on the petroleum committees of the NRA, the chief executive was impressed by the disadvantages of a rigid and formal structure of organization and policies. He believed that the proper management of his small company should allow the informal organizations within the firm to express themselves. Formality was avoided to such an extent that a casual observer would conclude that there was little organization at all. Yet, it was felt by many that one of the major advantages the firm held over its competitors was in its superior co-ordination and co-operation.

Underlying the concepts of management that evolved, the idea of flexibility was pervasive and fundamental. Flexibility in this context refers to the adaptability to external changes, susceptibility to modification of actions, resiliency of policies, and responsiveness of the entire organization to meet new problems.

The chief executive's idea was that a small growing company in an expanding industry required adaptability. He believed that there were important advantages to be obtained for his firm through emphasis on smallness. Flexibility was one such important advantage. A major part of the concepts of management that proved useful can be classified under five types of flexibility:

1. technological,
2. marketing,
3. financial,
4. personnel, and
5. organizational.

1. Technological flexibility is the mechanical ability to change one's equipment to produce those products desired by consumers at the time and place at which they desire them. Two examples of this concept will clarify its meaning. In refining, it is possible to maintain specialized equipment so that the product mix from a barrel of crude oil can be varied. In 1949, at a time in which many refining companies were experiencing unusual pressure from the sudden drop in the price of residual fuel oil, this company was able to reduce its production of residual to almost zero and to increase the production of other products, prices of which had not declined. A second example of technological flexibility was in the transportation phase of the in-

dustry. While major oil companies depend, to a large extent, upon pipe lines for the economical land transportation of crude oil and refined products, this management built the company in its early years around the utilization of barge transportation on the inland waterways. This type of transportation enabled the company to purchase crude oil in fields that were not served by pipe lines, and to extend its marketing of finished products to areas in which the price was favorable even for only short periods of time. The emphasis on barges not only enabled the company to transport crude oil and oil products at a cost comparable with the efficient pipe lines, but also to maintain this economy on smaller shipments to and from temporary points which could not support the large fixed cost of a pipe line. By means of this type of flexibility, the company was able to adapt its refining and transportation operations to demand and supply conditions.

2. A second type of flexibility was in the marketing of finished products. Marketing flexibility exists when managerial techniques permit the distribution of refined products according to conditions on the spot. Four examples of the means by which Ashland Oil obtained a high degree of this flexibility will help clarify this concept. First, because of its flexible transportation system, the management was able to shift its marketing geographically. Whenever profitable prospects appeared in an unserved area, the company shifted into that area. Whenever demand or costs conditions were threatening profitable operations, it could move out quickly.

A second means of gaining marketing flexibility was through the use of independent jobbers, rather than through company-owned bulk plants. Under such arrangements the company was able to enter new marketing areas more quickly and to leave unprofitable ones. In other words, it could secure existing facilities for distribution in new areas, but was not chained by property ownership to unprofitable ones.

Thirdly, the company's pricing policies enhanced the marketing flexibility. The management found that it was necessary to adjust to the pricing policies of different reference marketers in six separate marketing territories. This situation required that the company develop administrative techniques to keep its prices responsive to the unique conditions of each territory.

A fourth means of increasing its marketing flexibility was through its use of different types of distribution channels in the same area. A large percentage of its gallonage was sold under private brands. In addition, the company sold under five different company brands. Such conditions complicated the co-ordination of marketing policies.

3. Ashland also achieved a high degree of financial flexibility by refraining from investing a large percentage of its funds in fixed assets. It often profitably used obsolete equipment long past the time when other companies had changed to newer methods. As a larger firm, in order to promote equity financing, Ashland paid special attention to its name in investment circles. The management sought additional funds at times in which it could obtain

them on a favorable basis, regardless of whether it saw a specific need for them.

4. Ashland also maintained a policy of personnel flexibility. Since the small company could afford only a limited number of specialists, all major executives were placed in jobs that developed "generalists." Although the company had no formal executive development program, an analysis of the past positions of the top seven executives showed that all but one had been in several departments of the company's operations. The positions were tailored to an individual man's abilities and needs in place of attempting to adapt the man to a rigid position description. Turnover of executive personnel had been low. The present managers, therefore, had been trained within the company.

Personnel policies were administered on an informal basis. Even after the company reached large size, it had few precisely stated personnel policies. Although the company recognized a union in 1933, it consistently was able to gain the support of a majority of its employees in times of crisis. A leader of the international union complained that often he had secured support for strikes only to find that the chief executive had appealed to the employees through direct and personal means and had succeeded in gaining their support. Company parties, the personal interest of the individual executives in an employee's family problems, and de-emphasis on status were some of the means by which the management secured employee loyalty and high morale. High morale, in turn, enabled the management to maintain these informal personal relationships among executives and employees.

5. Above all, the company stressed organizational flexibility. It stressed adjustment to changes in the administrative environment without serious losses of economy or effectiveness.

When the company was young and small, the chief was the only operating line executive. As the firm grew, he used executive assistants for a period prior to granting them line authority. Later, some of these "assistants to" became functional executives. Still later, sales divisions evolved.

Throughout the thirty-year period, the company had no organization chart. The chief executive believed that any attempt to formalize relationships contributed to a static concept of organization which would be inconsistent with his emphasis upon flexibility. There was no attempt to establish definite titles or clearly defined duties. Typical of the comments in interviews was this statement: "If you have really sharp departmental lines, you find people telling others that 'it is none of your business' and 'leave that to me.' . . . Nobody is going to take that attitude if they don't know themselves the limits of their responsibilities. . . . I have felt that you get more co-operation from people if your organization is so set up where they have to co-operate to get along."

No names or titles appeared on the doors of the executive offices. Each member of the executive team was thoroughly acquainted with the *modus operandi* and could quickly explain who took care of the various duties within the company. Even at the time of sudden and rapid growth through merger, there was no attempt at the top to formalize organizational planning.

Little use was made of the development of a formal status system. The dynamics of the oil industry argues against stressing status. The chief executive looked upon any definite position title as a potential strait jacket. He felt that if an executive were allowed to become identified with some segment of the organization through clear delegation, he would be outlining a bailiwick in which that executive would feel a vested interest. He might oppose a change that would tend to destroy his delegated departmental "empire," even though it would increase the effectiveness of the organization as a whole.

Throughout the history of the company, the emphasis was placed upon keeping the number of levels at a minimum. This preference for the "flat" organization resulted in numerous executives reporting to the top. By 1957, there were approximately fifteen line executives who reported directly to the chief. An additional fifteen staff and/or functional executives expanded the level of subordinates with whom the chief executive maintained contact.

In Ashland, direct vertical communications were encouraged. In order to avoid the inaccuracies that tend to be added to information as it flows through a number of levels, the chief executive often gave orders to and sought information from the lowest level. The success of this jumping of ranks depended upon the chief executive's interest in details, the company's low executive turnover, high morale on the lower levels, and a size of operations that permitted maximum use of informal and personal relationships. The chief executive observed that "it is everybody's responsibility to not only do their job but to make sure that others who are affected by their work are informed of something that they might not otherwise know."

When the firm was small, most of the co-ordination was the result of strong direction and control by the chief executive. Numerous quantitative reports were required by him for his decisions. After the firm became large, each department head sought to receive these reports, as a result of his inability to obtain all of his information about the plans of the other departments. In the event that the plans of one department appeared to be inconsistent with those of another, a telephone call was used to maintain co-ordination bilaterally and informally. This system resulted in a large flow of reports among the departments and a tremendous dependence on telephone communications.

Written memoranda and formal committees were foreign to this system, because the chief executive believed that both injected rigidity into executive action. He thought that a written memorandum would remain in the files long after it had been superseded. Committee meetings were considered to be time consuming and not efficient in a firm that depended on its quick action as a major administrative advantage.

Operational Policies

After 1930, the company was vertically integrated; that is, it combined production with refining, marketing, and transportation. Throughout its history, the chief executive considered the refining branch as the firm's chief source of profits; he considered that the company engaged in the other operations only to maintain efficient refining throughput.

By 1954, the company owned wells that produced only 7.31% of its refining requirements. This percentage was much lower than that of any refining company of equal or larger size. After the proration legislation in the middle of the 1930's, managements of other oil companies placed their largest amounts of capital expenditures in the search for additional supplies of crude oil. Ashland's management intermittently stressed its production branch, but did so only at times in which the excess profits tax provided especially strong incentive.

The management of Ashland used the refining branch as the reference for all its policies and decisions. The instability of refining margins required that the management maintain the ability to change decisions rapidly. The importance of fixed costs in the refining process and the resulting low incremental cost of the extra barrels of throughput caused Ashland's management to seek to stabilize and maximize its refining margins by means of a high degree of the various ideas of flexibility. While the company was small and its refining equipment was simple, the management achieved unusual success in shifting its product mix to those fractions that were currently selling at the most profitable prices. It retained this ability to shift even after reaching large size; however, it was evident that size had decreased the ease by which these changes could be made.

Transportation costs in the petroleum industry are especially important in a firm's ability to operate profitably. Both the supply of crude oil for a refinery and the refined products for customers must be transported economically. The economics of pipe line operations offered advantages in land transportation to those companies that could afford to build and operate them. Large inch lines are particularly efficient.

The management of Ashland met its transportation problem by maximizing its use of the Ohio River, which flowed through its territory. By the means of river barges and towboats, the company was able, with small capital outlay, to maintain a transportation advantage to certain markets until large inch pipe lines were built. The use of such a method of transportation obviated the company's dependence on common carriers.

The reluctance of the management to set any fixed integration pattern had an important impact on the nature of its growth. All branches were forced to balance their operations with refining at capacity. In times of decreased demand for oil products, the sales branch became a potential limiting factor to economical refining operations. It was desirable to seek new independent jobbers. If sufficient outlets were not available or if other companies purchased Ashland's jobber outlets, the management became especially receptive to offers of merger from small independent companies. During these times of decreased demand, most independents were experiencing financial problems. As a result, both parties looked favorably on a merger.

In most of the mergers that were accomplished, marketing facilities were the chief interest of the Ashland management. The two periods in which most mergers took place were periods of difficulty in the oil industry (1930–1931 and 1949–1950). Purchase of these marketing properties facilitated adjustment in the integration pattern necessary to keep refining throughput at capacity. This policy of giving primary importance to refining thus led to growth in marketing at times in which properties could be obtained on a most favorable basis.

Although the majority of the mergers were with independent companies that possessed good marketing outlets, the fact that each company also owned a refinery provided the foundation for still further growth. In every case, the refining equipment was small, obsolete, and not valued highly in the negotiations. Yet after the mergers, the Ashland management continued to operate the acquired refineries at a throughput that exceeded the level attained by the former companies. In this way, the initial attempt to seek marketing outlets resulted in still greater increase in throughput, and in turn, new pressures for more sales outlets.

In general, the operating policies in the four branches looked to the "interstices" or niches in the industry which had been neglected by the major companies. The chief executive often commented that he was not as interested in the conventional approaches to operations as he was in the unconventional. He felt that the greatest advantage that an independent could gain over the large companies was in the avoidance of any rigid pattern of operations.

As a small company, this specialization in the niches of the industry proved to be an important reason for success. As the firm grew, it became increasingly difficult to find niches sufficiently large to accommodate the company's complete operations.

TABLE 10-1

ANNUAL EARNINGS IN RELATION TO CAPITAL STOCK AND SURPLUS
ASHLAND OIL & REFINING COMPANY

	Average Capital Stock and Surplus	*Net Earnings after Taxes*	*Per Cent of Earnings to Capital and Surplus after Taxes*
1924 *	$ 266,445	$ 32,890	12.34%
1925	316,909	68,040	21.47%
1926	500,561	160,843	32.13%
1927	696,242	201,357	28.92%
1928	876,197	383,570	43.78%
1929	1,185,135	204,429	17.25%

TABLE 10-1 (Continued)

1930	1,500,324	174,940	11.66%
1931	1,652,709	125,964	7.62%
1932	1,795,152	304,051	16.94%
1933	2,097,597	416,205	19.84%
1934	2,250,833	142,747	6.34%
1935	2,316,697	327,233	14.12%
1936	3,783,295	677,583	17.91%
1937	3,994,365	694,228	17.38%
1938	4,343,809	566,242	13.04%
1939	4,887,521	746,890	15.28%
1940	5,577,174	696,938	12.50%
1941 **	5,991,854	632,779	10.56%
1942	6,454,680	1,103,605	17.10%
1943	6,938,730	733,866	10.58%
1944	7,256,251	771,939	10.64%
1945	9,122,204	980,087 ***	10.74%
1946	11,157,068	1,325,139 ***	11.88%
1947	12,495,705	2,898,034	23.19%
1948	19,608,248	7,856,992	40.07%
1949	40,718,825	9,324,781	22.90%
1950	56,504,508	10,004,484	17.71%
1951	67,492,198	12,137,972	17.98%
1952	82,363,617	5,700,273	6.92%
1953	94,135,003	8,407,616	8.93%
1954	94,819,881	6,628,076	6.99%
1955	96,371,722	10,106,032	10.49%
1956	104,070,716	13,503,942	12.98%
Avg. 33 Yrs.	23,008,921	2,993,581	13.01%

* Figures shown are for Ashland Refining Company from its organization until 1936 when that company and Swiss Oil Corporation were merged to form Ashland Oil & Refining Company.

** Nine months period due to change in fiscal year.

*** Earnings reflect abnormal amount of exploratory drilling and recovery of excess profits taxes paid in 1942, 1943 and 1944.

11

Control

CONTROL is so pervasive in management that no single chapter could contain all of its features. Most of the remaining subjects in this book involve control either directly or indirectly; this is the case with inventory control, production control, time standards, quality control, and so on. This chapter will discuss the essence of control—the basic features that run through all of its applications. This emphasis should help the reader keep sight of the fundamentals of control, sometimes submerged in the details of special applications.

Control is universal to nature. Human activities have always made use of control, consciously or not. In driving an automobile, for example, we must continually compare the actual direction of the vehicle with its planned direction; if the actual performance falls short of plans, we are in danger of hitting a pedestrian or a fireplug. Fortunately, a complicated network of signals, receptors, transmitters, and muscles prevents such mishaps; control is at work, even though in this case we may not be fully aware of all of the mechanisms that have contributed to the corrective action. This chapter is concerned, however, with the conscious application of the principles of control in management.

Definition and Fundamentals of Control

Advancements in human activities have been achieved largely by developing better techniques of control. Control is an essential feature of scientific management. In fact, much of the precision of a managerial education is focused on the improvement of control techniques. Double entry bookkeeping made accounting an early tool of financial control. Statistical methods have contributed to many types of control. Instrumentation using electronic devices is central to the concept of automatic control.

Fundamentally, control is any process that guides activity toward some predetermined goal. The essence of the concept is in determining whether the activity is achieving the desired results. Notice that the "desired results" are assumed to be known. In other words, the concept of control cannot exist without planning. The essentials of a control system involve:

1. A predetermined goal, a plan, a policy, a standard, a norm, a decision rule, a criterion, or a yardstick;
2. A means of measuring activity;
3. A means of comparing activity with a criterion, and
4. Some mechanism which will correct the current activity so as to achieve the desired results.

The manager must understand how to apply this fundamental concept in many specialized areas. He applies the concept in such activities as budgetary control, quality control, inventory control, production control, personnel control.

A predetermined criterion

The most important single idea in control is to determine to some degree what *should* be the results, or at least what is *expected* from a given action. In the last two chapters, the processes of planning and policy were discussed; they are prerequisites for control. Planning can yield some benefits without control, but control cannot exist without some element of planning for the future. Sometimes our shortcut terminology fails to reflect this fact. For example, to economize on words, we speak of production control instead of production planning and control.

Many different names can be given to the predetermined criterion. Sometimes it is a general qualitative plan—such as improvement of morale, doing a good job, or adjustment to society. The difficulty with the use of such qualitative statements is the lack of precision in what is meant. For this reason, the evolution of managerial techniques in the twentieth century has involved greater use of quantitative approaches. In any science, a quantitative means of expression contributes to precision.

Standards provide a way of stating what should be accomplished. The foundations of scientific management are techniques that yield good standards. These standards can be in terms of time, money, physical units, or some index. Time study is a technique by which management determines the standard time that a normal man should take in doing a given job. Cost standards furnish norms that are helpful in analyzing expenditures. Physical units may be used as the denominator for quotas by which salesmen can be evaluated. Physical units, such as ton-miles of freight, units per machine hour, or pounds of scrappage per unit of output, provide a basic, simple, and direct yardstick for operations. The choice of the unit of measurement will influence the control procedure.

Measurement of actual performance

A performance cannot be checked unless there is a means of determining what the performance has been in a *past* period. This may appear to be a simple matter; but unless the basis of measurement is defined, confusion can develop. The effectiveness of a control system depends upon the prompt reporting of past results to the persons who have power to produce changes. The unit of measurement should be consistent with the predetermined criterion, and reported in a form that facilitates easy comparison. For example, if we are interested in knowing our past monetary cost of production, a report in physical units will not give the type of information that can be readily interpreted; we will need to express the units in money terms.

The degree of accuracy to which measurement will be carried will depend upon the needs of the specific application. All measurement is accurate only to some limited degree. In many instances in management, it is desirable to round a number so as to emphasize important magnitudes. Concern over some small error might overshadow major elements and confuse the decision maker rather than contribute to greater precision.

Comparison of actual performance with predetermined criteria

Much of management thinking involves a study of variations. Since all activity yields some variation, it is important to determine the limits within which this variation can be held and still be considered to be "in control." A manager must be able to distinguish between unimportant variation and variation indicating need for correctives. If he continues to look for trouble in all cases, he will be occupied with trivial matters and not have time for variations requiring his attention. He must concentrate on the exceptions or bottlenecks. To concentrate on these important variations, he must have techniques that show him the problems quickly. Simple methods of comparing actual results with the predetermined goal will often provide new insights into the problems confronting him.

The accountant and the statistician frequently speak of variances. The accountant watches variances of actual costs from budgeted amounts. The statistician applies a useful technique called "analysis of variance." It enables him to estimate whether results from samples are due to chance or to some assignable cause.

The purpose of comparing past performance with planned performance is not only to determine when a mistake has been made, but to enable the manager to *predict* future results. A good control system will provide quick comparisons so that he can attend to possible trouble while the operation is "in control." Comparison of actual performance through time will often show a significant trend which might indicate a danger signal. The manager cannot change the past, but he can use his understanding of it to help him operate in the present to make future operations better.

Control charts are pictorial means of presenting a mass of actual data so that their significance can be understood. Ratios, indexes, and averages are techniques available to the manager to highlight significant relationships. A study of these relationships is frequently more fruitful than the collection of confusing masses of data.

Decision for corrective action

The purpose of comparison of the planned with the actual is, of course, to make needed corrections. The required action can be determined from the quantitative data generated by the previous three steps. The decision that must be made at this point is the culmination of the control process. The decision to take no corrective action at that time might be warranted. Chester Barnard has explained that "the fine art of executive decision consists in not deciding questions that are not now pertinent, in not deciding prematurely, in not making decisions that cannot be made effective, and in not making decisions that others should make." [1]

The manager is usually so busy that he must use techniques to aid him in deciding when to make a decision. His observations are mere samples of the total activity, and as such he must weigh the probabilities in an attempt to avoid two types of errors: he may take corrective action when no action is needed; and secondly, he may fail to take action when some correction is needed.

Assuming that the manager has determined that there is need for some corrective action, he then must decide what type of action is warranted. Even when he finds out the "best" action to be taken, he is faced with a number of problems. He must fit this action into his organizational relationships with other managers. He must decide upon the mean between over-controlling and letting the operation run itself.

Take, for example, a manufacturing process involving heating materials. The process calls for the material to remain between 270° and 300° F (the predetermined criterion). Looking at the thermometer, the operator observes that the temperature is 280° F (the measure of actual performance). His duty is to turn on the source of heat soon enough to keep the actual heat within the prescribed limits (comparison of actual with the desired heat). If he turns the source on (corrective action) too soon, he may cause the material to become too hot; if he fails to turn the heat on soon enough, the material may become too cold. The proper corrective action will depend upon his knowledge of the lag between the time he acts and the time the

[1] Chester I. Barnard, *The Function of the Executive* (Cambridge, Mass.: Harvard University Press, 1938), p. 194.

material will start to get hotter, the amount of heat available, the quantity of material involved, and other conditions of the process. If he is uncertain of some conditions, he may take corrective action too soon or fail to act soon enough. If he is untrained, he may hesitate in his decision to take action at all. Regardless of the precision of the predetermined criterion and the accuracy of the thermometer, the control of the process will be poor unless the operator takes corrective action in the proper manner at the right time.

Useful Generalizations on Control

Strategic point control

Optimum control can be achieved only if critical, key, or limiting points can be identified, and close attention directed to adjustments at those points. Greater control does not necessarily result from a greater number of control points. It is usually possible to find certain limiting factors or bottlenecks which can be adjusted so that changes are forced at other points not being watched. For example, a state can control the weight of trucks on its highways by carefully locating weighing stations on sections of its highways over which most of the trucks must travel. The addition of a number of weighing stations on secondary roads probably will not increase this control significantly. Close and concentrated attention to the strategic points will tighten up the system.

An auditor of a set of financial books does not attempt to look at every entry. He has developed, through experience, key spots that show most of the essential information. His intensive attention to these strategic spots will give him a good picture of the total situation. It will also give him evidence on whether to look deeper into the matter.

Good control of a situation does not mean maximum control. Control is often expensive. Moreover, increased control may create other problems. One secret of good control is to establish strategic points where corrective action will be easiest and most effective.

Organizational suitability

The line between the control function and other functions of management is not clearcut. Planning is a prerequisite. Organizing provides the structure and process within which control can take place. *Controls should be tailored to fit the organization.* The organizational concept of authority and responsibility relates directly to the problem of maintaining a system of checks on the managerial activity of subordinates.

Drucker [2] states this in another way. He stresses the establishment of

[2] Peter Drucker, *The Practice of Management* (New York: Harper and Brothers, 1954).

objectives for each member of an organization, the distribution of all necessary information to each member so that he can make his own changes in order to meet his objectives, and the *self-control* of each unit in the organization. In his opinion, control as domination of a superior over a subordinate is inappropriate in modern management.

A later chapter on managerial accounting will show that successful decentralization of authority depends upon careful identification of controllable factors and noncontrollable ones. If cost and revenue records can be shaped to focus attention on those factors which can be adjusted by a definite manager, there will be less possibility of "buckpassing." If a manager is not reprimanded for a situation out of his control, he will be less frustrated and more able to "hoe his own row."

Control in direct manner

One of the greatest disadvantages of extensive control systems is the multiplication of written reports, added electrical circuits, or oral passing of information between units of an organization. The designer of an optimum system will weigh the advantages of extra channels against the costs in time and money of the extra contacts. Control becomes synonymous with "red tape" when the costs exceed the advantages. Therefore, any control system should be designed to maintain direct contact between the controller and the controlled.

In modern management, one of the best means of controlling an operation is through the supervisor. In spite of the myriad of functional control specialists, e.g. the comptroller, the inspector, the expediter, the function of control remains essentially with the line managers. The loss in time and decrease in accuracy accompanying a complex network of control channels are chief enemies of large scale operations. Direct lines of control will usually be faster and more economical. Personal observation, furthermore, provides a "feel" for the total situation. It makes it easier to discriminate between important facts and trivial ones.

Flexible control

Even the best plans and other predetermined criteria need to be changed from time to time. The measurement of performance, comparison with the criteria, and corrective action must provide a flexible system which will adjust to changes. For example, the variable budget has proved to be valuable to financial control of a dynamic operation by providing information at various rates of operation. Mechanical controls are supplemented by hand controls. If there is a probability that emergencies may arise that cannot be handled by the automatic device, mechanical controls are supplemented by hand controls. The pilot of an airplane, for example, might place the plane "on automatic pilot" during the stable part of the flight, but substitute the human control system during critical stages. Production scheduling at capacity should include, in the basic design of the system, means by which it can accommodate emergency orders.

Judgment meets its critical test in control when it appears that standards or plans require revision. In order to maintain control, standards cannot be changed continually. However, some replanning may be needed. A control system should provide for some resiliency, but should retain its basic structure.

Feedback—an essential of control

Recently, a concept fundamental to all control has received renewed attention. Feedback is as old as the controls on windmills, the fly-ball governor of Watt's steam engine, and the steering of steamships. However, the trend toward automation since World War II has made feedback more important in modern instrumentation.

Feedback is the process of adjusting future actions based upon information about past performance. There are many applications of the idea in various disciplines. The conditioned reflex in human beings is one simple example. A teacher who has lectured and carefully explained an idea asks questions of his students in order to determine his future classroom actions; he needs to know how well his illustrations are understood by the student before he can tell whether to proceed to another point. The most important modern applications of the feedback principle have involved the use of electronic circuitry in relating the input of a machine to its output.

Thus, the feedback concept is common to ordinary control as well as to automatic control. The difference is that it has been discussed more thoroughly and precisely in its applications in electronic circuits. The electrical engineer directs his attention to a "closed loop" system (one in which the information of actual performance is fed back to the source of energy by electrical or mechanical means in an endless chain); the social psychologist directs his attention to an "open loop" system (one in which the human being performs some action based on information of actual performance to adjust the supply of energy to the operations).

Feedback involves interdependence of one part of a system with another. The classical illustration of a thermostat brings out its essentials. The thermostat is a control device of the closed loop variety which measures actual temperature in a room, compares it with the planned temperature, feeds this information back to the source of heat (the furnace), and opens or closes a valve to make any necessary corrections.

It is helpful to make a diagram of the essential aspects of a system in order to point out specifically what is being controlled, what is providing the energy, and so forth. A simple diagram (see Figure 11-1) describes a closed loop system. Notice that in closed loop feedback no preset pattern of performance need be determined; the furnace is turned on only when the temperature declines by a significant amount. In other words, a periodic cycle of turning the furnace on for five minutes every fifteen minutes may be considered a type of "automatic" system, but it does not employ feedback (neither open loop or closed loop). The difference is that the periodic cycle is set, based upon *expected* need for heat, whereas, both types of feedback are based on the *actual* performance of the furnace.

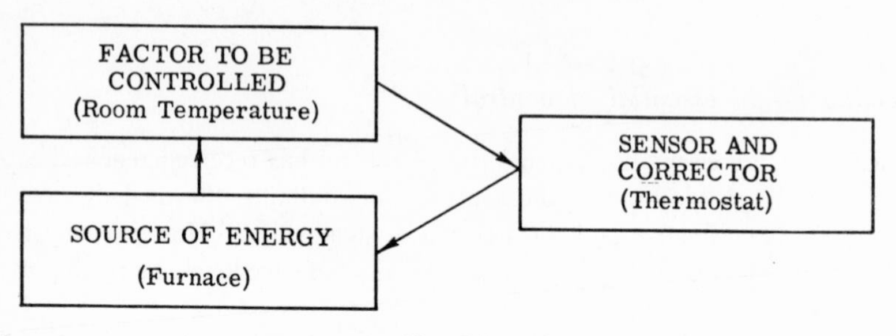

FIGURE 11-1 Closed Loop Feedback

Similarly, does the ordinary home automatic clothes washing machine involve feedback? Can it be said that hand washing of clothes uses open loop feedback whereas the "automatic" machine does not involve any feedback? Could you imagine a way in which the automatic machine could be made to operate with closed loop feedback? (Automatic electric toasters differ in types depending upon whether a periodic cycle or feedback is basic to the design.)

Some of the greatest difficulties of developing a good feedback system result from the fact that:

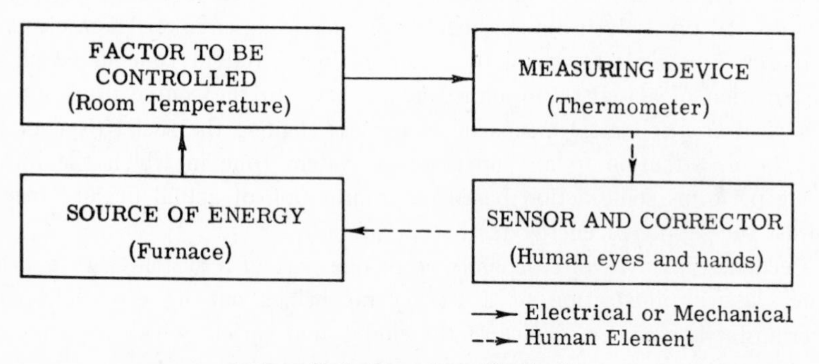

FIGURE 11-2 Open Loop Feedback

1. There must be some error (decline in the heat of the room) before action is taken.
2. There may be a lag between the time action is indicated and the actual correction.

To minimize the error, the sensor could operate within tight limits, e.g. between 70.5 degrees and 69.5 with desired temperature at 70 degrees. Notice that there are at least two types of lags:

1. The time between the measurement of the need for action and the time the control device notifies the source of energy, and
2. The time between the receipt of notice and the effected results.

The problem resulting from these lags is that of overcorrection which causes the system to oscillate. If this oscillation is stable (the same frequency and the same amplitude), error will remain, but it will follow a pattern around the standard. If there is a tendency for constant overcorrection, then an increasing error can be expected.

The feedback concept is a useful one in understanding management controls. It is fundamental to the engineering of instrumentation and mechanical controls. It is a helpful idea in understanding human control systems. It has become part of the language of management.

Human Factors of Control

So far in this chapter the fundamentals of control and some of the useful generalizations that form the theory for managerial control have been studied. In application, these fundamentals and generalizations are affected by the actual conditions under which they are applied. The manager should seek to comprehend special features of control which in the final analysis will determine his effectiveness. He must recognize the importance of human beings in control systems.

Learned, Ulrich, and Booz have developed the human aspects of control concisely.[3] "The effectiveness of a control system is in a large measure determined by the extent to which it has been incorporated into the daily routines and expectations of the personnel affected by it. Information on past operations merely describes what is already beyond change. The control system becomes effective only when it enters the thinking of all participants, showing them what is expected of them and allowing them to show their capacity in performance. To approach this idea, a long period of discussion, argument, and adjustment is usually necessary. Over time, differences of interpretation can be thrashed out and mutual understandings can develop. The meaning which people give a control system in terms of their own outlook is as critical as the technical design of the system."

The fact that a control system is well designed may cause it to be opposed by lower levels of management. Controls tend to fence in the manager. An efficient and reasonable system of control may be ineffective if the people

[3] Edmund Learned, David Ulrich, and Donald Booz, *Executive Action* (Boston: Division of Research, Harvard Business School, 1951), p. 122.

involved feel that it collects irrelevant data and its standards are unreasonable. No matter how technically sound the standards are shown to be, the people controlled will not be convinced unless the standards fit their expectations and group habits.

In an effective control system, reports must fit the needs of the upper levels of management and must also yield meaningful information to the lower levels. If subordinates believe that superiors are using reported information to cause additional troubles for the subordinates, there will be an incentive to disguise the facts or to obstruct the free flow of information. It is natural for a person to report favorable information (which is relatively unimportant to superiors since no corrections are needed) and to withhold unfavorable information (which is the type a control system should provide if corrections are to be made). Moreover, if the reporter believes that the information is collected as a matter of routine and that it is not studied carefully, he will become careless in his reporting.

As a result of the human factor, two systems of control may develop—the one designed by the "specialists" for the top level and the informal one used by all levels. A case relating to the control of inventory at a supply depot overseas in World War II illustrates this point. Stock records were kept by a separate department on prescribed cards. Posting to these records was from shipping and receiving documents. In theory, the depot commander should have contacted his stock records officer to find how many of a certain item were on hand. In practice, posting was not kept up to date, pilferage in the theater of operations was widespread (the thief did not fill out a shipping form), and nomenclature and marking on packages caused faulty records. A system that worked nicely for the continental United States did not provide accurate information overseas. As a result, an informal system was superimposed on the approved system. In effect, two systems were in operation—the theoretically sound system, almost totally ignored, and the practical system, poor in design, but the one that was used.

Reports that have come to be unrealistic are often continued as "window-dressing" for superiors. In one instance, a report of total space occupied by supplies in the above depot continued to overstate the space in use because all other depots were using "padded" percentages. These reports would show that 100 per cent of the space was in use when, in fact, a storage specialist would have known that such a high figure was improbable because of the need for working room, and because it was evident that part of some stacks could not be filled completely without hiding other supplies from view.

In setting standards, care must be taken to prevent the subordinates from feeling that standards will be changed merely because they are consistently met. Once a person accepts a standard and feels that it is reasonable, it is difficult to increase the required level without convincing him of the need for the change. Change of any kind is a disturbing factor to most people.

Even if the change is proper and necessary, the results might be the opposite from that expected because of the psychological reaction of those affected.

In one case, the son of the owner of a small business, who had received a formal business education in college and had become convinced of the desirability of a strong control system, returned to help his father run the business. The firm employed a number of "old timers" who had been allowed a great deal of freedom in their actions. The son noticed this when he observed that the workers often arrived late for work. His father had used no time clock. The son's first suggestion for improvement was the installation of a time clock. The result was an increase in the control problem.

A paradox develops in the operations of control systems that involve people. A fundamental element of control is the ability to measure actual performance. Accuracy of measurement is a prerequisite of automatic control systems using mechanical and electrical devices. However, a successful executive must be aware of the entire operation, the unmeasured, the nonmeasurable, as well as the measurable. Learned *et al.*, state: "But when they [executives] seek to measure the unmeasurable, when they require personal beliefs to be justified in quantitative terms, when they compel the lower ranks to spend their time in getting measurable results rather than in meeting actual operating problems, then control has become self-defeating."

A broad understanding of control will indicate that where human beings are involved, the technical design of the system is not the entire problem. A manager will do well to keep the human factor in mind.

Automation

The discussion of control should aid in understanding what is meant by *automation*. Unfortunately, this term means different things to different people. It is necessary to discuss several alternative definitions. The term was first used in the Ford Motor Company to mean advanced methods of materials handling that would substitute machines for labor in the solution of the problem of the movement of materials. In current usage, however, automation has three more complicated meanings, reflecting new developments in management.

1. First, automation refers to an integrated view of manufacturing operations. In this sense it describes continuous production, with separate processes so closely related that all parts fit into an electrically or mechanically connected series. This type of automation involves the handling of materials from one operation to another by mechanical means with little need for human effort. The idea goes farther than mere mechanization or more complicated materials handling equipment. It emphasizes the relationships of machines with each other.

Mass production, with the introduction of conveyorized assembly lines, in auto manufacturing, was a first step in this direction. Continuous processing in the oil refinery, however, is a more exact illustration. On the first assembly lines, manufacture was a collection of simple manual operations along a conveyor. Emphasis was on breaking the job into small parts; then human effort related them to the finished product. In the 1920's, when the oil industry changed from batch manufacture to continuous manufacture, it decreased the human attention needed in the intermediate steps—pipes were arranged so that the worker was used primarily at the beginning and the end of the process. The design of the system of pipes set the pattern of processing without human handling.

Increased mechanization often increases automatic continuous production, but not necessarily. If the introduction of the machine expands the human attention to its adjustments, it may make production less automatic. The steel industry uses large amounts of mechanical equipment, but is less continuous than automobile manufacture or oil refining.

2. The second meaning of automation is the increased use of automatic control devices using the closed loop feedback principle. Many who use the term insist that if the self-correcting function is not present, there is no automation. Automatic control involves the use of some mechanical or electrical sensing device which checks the operations of the machine and its output against a predetermined criterion, and translates this information to devices that adjust the input to effect desired output. This second development eliminates human checking and adjustment.

Automatic control substitutes instruments (servomechanisms, and so forth) for simple mental and physical actions. Increased automation may permit the reduction of the volume of capital goods. If automatic controls increase the capacity of a given amount of capital equipment, there may be no need for new machines to process the increased volume. A good example of the substitution of automatic control instruments for large amounts of other capital equipment is in railroading. Many double track lines have been reduced to single track using centralized traffic controls, while maintaining the same number of trains in operation over the single line.

Automatic controls are substitutes for human controls in many industries, but costs determine the speed with which automatic controls are introduced. However, in some industries current operations could not exist with dependence upon human controls. In handling radioactive material, the operation depends upon automatic controls because of the safety factor. In the operation of airplanes and missiles, automatic controls must be used because of space limitations and the need for quick action not within the capacity of a human being.

3. The third development included in the meaning of automation is that of the use of electronic computers. These "brains" posses characteristics that make them especially useful in business operations. They can store large amounts of information. They can make extremely rapid computa-

tions. They are available for work twenty-four hours a day. Their chief limitation is in the need for translating instructions from ordinary language into machine language and in system design. The computer must have exact and detailed instructions in quantitative form. Mathematical expression of relationships must exist before they can be put to work. For this reason, the speed by which computers can be employed in different jobs depends upon the speed by which relationships can be translated into measurable and quantitative data.

Computers have become important in two classes of operations. The first was in those fields in which complicated formulas required large amounts of human time for solution. The natural sciences and some branches of engineering made immediate use of the speed of computers. The second class includes those activities handling large masses of quantitative data, but in routine and simple manner. This class demands that the "memory" components of the computer be large, and that access to this information be rapid enough to suit its requirements. In some industries, automation is almost synonymous with electronic data processing. In banking, insurance companies, and the financial sections of other business firms, "office automation" means the substitution of electronic data processing for manual operations. In these firms, the data are used in managerial controls, but usually do not make use of closed loop feedback.

Computers have also stimulated the development of mathematical and statistical applications to new problems. Without computers little would be heard about "mathematical model building," "operations research," or "management science," for these are heavily dependent upon levels of computation that would prove uneconomical on the hand calculator. Automation is thus closely related to fundamental developments in management theory.

Automation requires a change in management practices. Since the control systems must be tailored to the situation, the manager must carefully plan the total operation. Automation places management in the position of machine designer. Flexibility of operations tends to be diminished (though some research workers are developing automation devices that may overcome this deficiency). Pressure is placed on the upper levels to improve their decision-making processes, since they work under a greater strain in planning, co-ordination, and control. Some authorities in management feel that this trend will decrease the need for middle management and increase the need for larger staffs at the top level.

Information and Communication

Since management involves the co-ordination of a group, it requires communications among its members. Control, however, is so closely related to communications that some writers do not attempt to distinguish between these functions.

Managerial consideration of communications problems is as old as management, but since World War II, managers have received help from mathematicians and engineers in solving these problems. The work of Claude Shannon of Bell Telephone Laboratories and Norbert Wiener of M.I.T. has formed the basis of a new scientific discipline known as *information or communication theory.* This theory suggests potentially useful generalizations for managerial control in the future.

Shannon and Weaver have distinguished three levels of communications problems: (A) The technical problem of how accurately symbols can be transmitted; (B) The semantics problem of how precisely the transmitted symbols can convey a desired meaning; (C) The effectiveness problem of how well the transmitted meaning affects conduct. The greatest development by these specialists outside management circles has been on Level A.

The most fundamental concept in information theory is the precise definition of information itself. Its definition in mathematical terms should not be confused with *meaning,* the critical problem on Level B; in other words, a message could be pure nonsense but have high information. Information may be contained in a message, but by no means is synonymous with message. In fact, *the more probable a message is, the less information it gives.*

Information is a measure of one's freedom of choice when one selects a message. If there is no freedom of choice, there is no information. For example, if "Q" is always followed by "u" in a language, there is no freedom of choice for the second letter, and the information provided by "u" is nil. The possibility of measuring information precisely has made feasible the modern digital electronic computer.

Information theory promises great things in the design of equipment to handle information. In this book, however, we are most interested in using several of its ideas for analyzing communication basic to control. A simple illustration of a communication system will indicate a universal framework of information for such areas as managerial control. Figure 11-3 demonstrates the transmission of information. A *message* (one from a large number

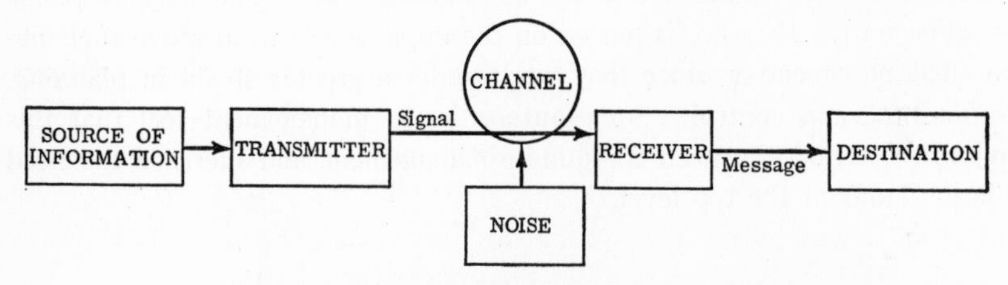

FIGURE 11-3 A Simple Communication System

of possible messages) is selected by the *information source,* changed into a *signal* by the transmitter, sent over a channel, changed back into the message by a *receiver.* Although the terms indicate engineering applications, the framework can be used for any type of communication. Wiener has studied the flow within the human body through nerves connecting the brain with the hands. In the typical process of talking, the framework would be from the brain as information source, the voice as the transmitter, sound pressure as the signal, the air as the channel, another's ear as the receiver.

The message that is transmitted and the message that is received may be entirely different as a result of *noise* (any distortion of a signal). Examples of *noise* are "snow" in television, static in radio, "jamming of the channel" by other people talking at the same time, and so forth. Combatting noise is a major problem in communication. Redundancy helps. "I love you" might be received as "I hate you," but "I love you, darling" has less chance of being distorted.

In management terms, short reports are a virtue but restatement is necessary to some extent in order to increase the chance that the message will be received with minimum distortion. Filters are used to reduce noise; but a filter tends to reduce the range within which the message can be received. A broker's ticker tape is expected to show such a message as "Ethyl 55¼," but we would suspect distortion if "Ethyl pregnant" was received.

Any further illustration of the technical aspects of this new field of human inquiry is beyond the scope of this book. It is mentioned briefly here for several reasons. First, cybernetics (the name means "steersman") is making interesting progress in interrelating all fields of study which deal with communications, information, and control. Secondly, managerial functions in the future may be described in the rigorous terminology of cybernetics. Thirdly, some of the generalizations reached in this other area have common sense meaning in managerial application. Fourthly, much of the new "hardware" used by the manager is built on principles developed in this area, and therefore the co-ordination of the human manager with his electronic helpers will depend upon a better understanding by managers of the language used by the designers of these helpers.

Summary

Control is based upon (1) a predetermined goal, (2) the measuring of actual performance, (3) the comparison of the goal with the performance, and (4) the correction of current activity. This general concept has many applications, some of which will be seen in the following chapters. Certain generalizations of control are helpful to a manager in maintaining a good control system. Furthermore, a manager will profit from understanding control as viewed by different specialists, including the human relations enthusiast, the electrical engineer, and the information theorist.

Bibliographical Note

Special applications of control will be discussed in later chapters with pertinent bibliographical notes appearing at the end of such chapters. However, control as a basic managerial function has been developed in a general manner by Newman, Koontz and O'Donnell, and McFarland in the management books referred to in a previous bibliographical note.

In recent years control has become a separate discipline of study as a result of the pioneering work of Norbert Wiener in *Cybernetics* (1948) and Claude E. Shannon and Warren Weaver in *The Mathematical Theory of Communications* (1949). This work has been followed by the publication of several special journals relating to automatic controls and a number of books in electrical engineering. Some of this literature has been translated into less technical language in such publications as Norbert Wiener's *The Human Use of Human Beings* (1954) and a collection of reprinted articles entitled *Automatic Control* (1955) in *Scientific American.*

Several books on automation discuss control as it relates to manufacturing and management. John Diebold's *Automation: The Advent of the Automatic Factory* (1952) was the first book opening the way for many such books in the 1950's. James R. Bright's *Automation and Management* (1958) provides not only a report on his empirical research on the subject but also an introduction to the other work in the field.

Production control has long been a field of study with considerable literature. Franklin G. Moore's *Production Control* (1951), C. A. Koepke's *Plant Production Control* (1949) and William Voris' *Production Control* (1956) are texts on this subject.

Questions and Problems

1. Give several examples of different types of predetermined criteria which may be used in a control system.
2. Many types of actions cannot be measured with precision. How can a control system be devised in such cases?
3. Give several examples of the use of strategic points in a control system.
4. Give an example of the use of a "closed loop" system of feedback.
5. Give an example of an "open loop" system of feedback.
6. Do the following make use of feedback?
   (a) an electric toaster
   (b) an oven in the kitchen on which one can set dials for turning on and off
   (c) an automatic gasoline pump at a service station
   (d) a speed warning buzzer on an automobile
7. Describe some of the symptoms that would indicate a faulty control system.
8. Why has the improvement in control become so critical in modern industry?
9. In the study by economists of business fluctuations, discretionary measures are often compared with automatic stabilizers as means of solving periodic unemployment. Is the theory of control useful in such discussions?
10. A college student often wishes to control the use of his time in his various activities. Using the four essentials of a control system, devise a control chart or other device by which he may improve this control.
11. What are the reasons behind the trend to centralize control in a business or government organization in the hands of a "controller"?
12. Explain the relationship between the exception principle and the idea of strategic point control.
13. Can a human being maintain more flexibility in control than can an electrical or mechanical device?

14. What are the human factors which cause a child to resist the control of his parents?

15. In what industries would you expect automation to become most important? Least important?

16. How can electronic computers help in the improvement of control?

17. One common application of the concepts of control is in production. What elements of a production process do you think would need special attention as to control?

18. In governmental agencies the control of the types of report forms and other printed information blanks has become a major problem. A special agency is charged with "forms control." Can you explain the need for such control? What actions would you take to gain better control over forms?

12

Extracts and Cases in Control

THE subject of control has been treated by industrial managers in many specialized compartments—production control, inventory control, quality control, budgetary control, cost control, forms control, and so forth. From the preceding chapter it is evident that control involves concepts applicable in all these uses. This chapter will provide an opportunity to reflect on both general principles of control as well as some special applications. In the first extract, Norbert Wiener shows that communications and control are fundamental to human activity, requiring an entire discipline which he calls cybernetics. In the second, Arnold Tustin explains the "feedback" concept in greater detail.

After Franklin Moore's extract summarizing production control, there is a discussion by James Bright of automation and its potential impact on management. The accelerated process of mechanizing and controlling promises many changes in management in the years to come. Bright's extract outlines the means by which industry is accomplishing automation, and points to the implications of these changes.

Each of the cases illustrates actual systems by which control has been accomplished in a firm. The M & Q case explains a simple procedure used by a small business to minimize clerical work. The Becker Laundry case describes the operations of a service type of firm; its purpose is to provide case material for setting up a simple production control system. The Delta Stores case discusses a system of controlling stock shortages in merchandizing. The student will find that these cases will give him the "feel" for the nature of control problems that no amount of text material can provide.

Extracts

Extract A

The Human Use of Human Beings (Norbert Wiener)

In giving the definition of Cybernetics in the original book, I classed communication and control together. Why did I do this? When I communicate with another person, I impart a message to him, and when he communicates back with me he returns a related message which contains information primarily accessible to him and not to me. When I control the actions of another person, I communicate a message to him, and although this message is in the imperative mood, the technique of communication does not differ from that of a message of fact. Furthermore, if my control is to be effective I must take cognizance of any messages from him which may indicate that the order is understood and has been obeyed.

It is the thesis of this book that society can only be understood through a study of the messages and the communication facilities which belong to it; and that in the future development of these messages and communication facilities, messages between man and machines, between machines and man, and between machine and machine, are destined to play an ever increasing part.

When I give an order to a machine, the situation is not essentially different from that which arises when I give an order to a person. . . .

The commands through which we exercise our control over our environment are a kind of information which we impart to it. Like any form of information, these commands are subject to disorganization in transit. They generally come through in less coherent fashion and certainly not more coherently than they were sent. In control and communication we are always fighting nature's tendency to degrade the organized and to destroy the meaningful; the tendency, as Gibbs has shown us, for entropy to increase. . . .

Messages are themselves a form of pattern and organization. Indeed, it is possible to treat sets of messages as having an entropy like sets of states of the external world. Just as entropy is a measure of disorganization, the information carried by a set of messages is a measure of organization. In fact, it is possible to interpret the information carried by a message as essentially the negative of its entropy, and the negative logarithm of its probability. That is, the more probable the message, the less information it gives. Clichés, for example, are less illuminating than great poems. . . .

I have said that man and the animal have a kinaesthetic sense, by which they keep a record of the position and tensions of their muscles. For any machine subject to a varied external environment to act effectively it is necessary that information concerning the results of its own action be furnished to it as part of the information on which it must continue to act. For example, if we are running an elevator, it is not enough to open the outside door because the orders we have given should make the elevator be at that door at the time we open it. It is important that the release for opening the door be dependent on the fact that the elevator is actually at the door; otherwise something might have detained it, and the passenger might step into the empty shaft. This control of a machine on the basis of its *actual* performance rather than its *expected* performance is known as *feedback,* and involves sensory members which are actuated by motor members and perform the function of *tell-tales* or *monitors*—that is, of elements which indicate a performance. It is the function of these mechanisms to control the mechanical tendency toward disorganization; in other words, to produce a temporary and local reversal of the normal direction of entropy. . . .[1]

Extract B

Feedback (Arnold Tustin)

The common pattern that underlies all these and many other varied phenomena . . . is the existence of feedback, or—to express the same thing rather more generally—interdependence.

We should not be able to live at all, still less to design complex control systems, if we did not recognize that there are regularities in the relationship between events—what we call "cause and effect." When the room is warmer, the thermometer on the wall reads higher. We do not expect to make the room warmer by pushing up the mercury in the thermometer. But now consider the case when the instrument on the wall is not a simple thermometer but a thermostat, contrived so that as its reading goes above a chosen setting, the fuel supply to the furnace is progressively reduced, and, conversely, as its reading falls below that setting, the fuel flow is increased. This is an example of a familiar control system. Not only does the reading of the thermometer depend on the warmth of the room, but the warmth of the room also depends on the reading of the thermometer. The two quantities are interdependent. Each is a cause, and each an effect, of the other. In such cases we have a closed chain or sequence—what engineers call a "closed loop." . . .

Feedback control, unlike open-sequence control, can never work without *some* error, for the error is depended upon to bring about the correction. The objective is to make the error as small as possible. . . .

Any quantity may be subjected to control if three conditions are met.

[1] Norbert Wiener, *The Human Use of Human Beings* (New York: Houghton Mifflin Company, 1954), pp. 16, 21, 24, 25.

First, the required changes must be controllable by some physical means, a regulating organ. Second, the controlled quantity must be measurable, or at least comparable with some standard; in other words, there must be a measuring device. Third, both regulation and measurement must be rapid enough for the job in hand. . . .

The time-delay often creates another problem: overcorrection of the error, which causes the system to oscillate about the required value instead of settling down. . . .

This oscillatory behavior, maintained by "self-excitation," is one of the principal limitations of feedback control. It is the chief enemy of the control-system designer, and the key to progress has been the finding of various simple means to prevent oscillation. Since oscillation is a very general phenomenon, it is worth while to look at the mechanism in detail, for what we learn about oscillation in man-made control systems may suggest means of inhibiting oscillations of other kinds—such as economic booms and slumps, or periodic swarms of locusts. . . .

To escape from the dilemma the designer can do several things. Firstly, he may minimize the time-lag by using electronic tubes or, at higher power levels, the new varieties of quick-response direct-current machines. By dividing the power amplification among a multiplicity of stages, these special generators have a smaller lag than conventional generators. The lag is by no means negligible, however.

Secondly, and this was a major advance in the development of control systems, the designer can use special elements that introduce a time-lead, anticipating the time-lag. Such devices, called phase-advancers, are often based on the properties of electric capacitors, because alternating current in a capacitor circuit leads the voltage applied to it.

Thirdly, the designer can introduce other feedbacks besides the main one, so designed as to reduce time-lag. Modern achievements in automatic control are based on the use of combinations of such devices to obtain both accuracy and stability. . . .

This situation is strikingly similar in principle (though immensely more complex) to the introduction of a predictor in the control of a gun, for all predictors are essentially analogues of the external situation. The function of mind is to predict, and to adjust behavior accordingly. It operates like an analogue computer fed by sensory clues.

It is not surprising, therefore, that man sees the external world in terms of cause and effect. The distinction is largely subjective. "Cause" is what might conceivably be manipulated. "Effect" is what might conceivably be purposed.[2]

[2] Arnold Tustin, "Feedback," *Automatic Control* (Copyright 1954 by Scientific American, Inc., by permission of Simon and Schuster, Inc.), pp. 11, 13, 14, 15, 17, 23.

EXTRACT C

Production Control (Franklin Moore)

The term "production control" as used in industry almost always refers to the internal operations of the company rather than to basic administrative choices of policy. There are countless variations in methods of controlling production but very few variations in fundamental functions regardless of the industry or the size of the factory. The nature of the industry and size of the company will affect the way production control is done, but the fundamental functions which have to be done are almost identical in all manufacturing plants. All factories, for example, get orders to produce a certain number of specified, completed units. Nearly all factories must determine the parts which will be required to make the products wanted. They must decide on the raw materials to be used and the operations which will have to be performed on them. Preliminary planning and preparation, to be sure that all necessary facilities for production will be available when needed, must be done in all companies. Work routing (the determination of the operations to be performed and their sequence) is done in all factories. All companies must make up and issue instructions to workers, and authority to produce must be released to the actual producing departments. Production must be directed, and materials must be transported through determined and controlled paths in all factories. Reports of what has been done are required. Comparisons should be made between planned and actual production. New plans and schedules must be made to cover new jobs and to replace plans and schedules not carried out. Variations between planned and actual production should be analyzed to determine the causes of the variations and measures taken to remove interferences, or unwanted variations from schedule will occur again and again. All these activities are sometimes referred to collectively as routing, scheduling, dispatching, progress control, and materials control. . . .

Production control functions play an important part in factory operation but they do not, by any means, constitute the only things done. Production control does not, for instance, cover personnel, direct supervision of the workers, design of the product, provision for machines and equipment, maintenance, power, accounting, and other activities. The production control department ordinarily works closely with the inspection, time study, and purchasing departments, and its relationship with the engineering department is very close in all companies. Indeed, engineering and production control functions are so closely related that the line of demarcation between the functions assigned to each is rarely drawn at exactly the same place. In small companies there may be no production control department, so the functions are divided between the engineering and the producing departments. In large companies having a production control department there is considerable variation in the way production control functions are distributed among the engineering, production control, and fabricating departments. . . .

The production control department serves as a funnel or channel through which information and authority pass to the factory.

The production control department is, however, more than a mere clearing house or forwarding agent for information and authority. Its functions are broader than this. Information is received in one form and passed on in another form. A process of translation and expansion is necessary. This the production control department does. It translates the orders for finished products into the numerous orders to do particular operations which the factory must have. Orders for finished units mean little to the producing departments. The producing departments perform individual operations, and their instructions must be to perform operations on specific materials, thereby making parts and, finally, finished products. It is the responsibility of the production control department to order the necessary operations performed and to see that these operations are coordinated and that finished products result. The orders to perform operations and to produce parts put the information into a form which can be understood by each factory department. . . .

The preparation for production would be incomplete . . . if it were confined to forms preparation alone, even though the preparation of these directives is the biggest part of the job. It is necessary to determine in advance the availability of all facilities and materials. Sometimes this checkup reveals that tools, jigs, fixtures, materials, and other items need to be procured. These items are provided by other departments, but the production control department does the checking and when necessary initiates action to secure the needed item. The production control department also follows up by checking with the department concerned from time to time to make certain that the item will be on hand when production starts.

In a few companies, the production control department does not have charge of the stock rooms. In those companies, the production control department must see that orders and parts lists reach the department responsible for the stock so that it can determine replenishment needs and originate replenishment orders. Production control may need to make sure that such replenishment orders have been made out so that production can proceed. In most companies, production control is itself responsible for the stock rooms and must watch stocks and anticipate demands. On purchased items this will mean frequent contacts with the purchasing department; on manufactured items it is production control's responsibility to see that things are done on time.

No matter what other responsibilities are, or are not, assigned to the production control department, the responsibility for checking with other departments concerned, to be sure that production can proceed, is almost always one of its duties. Failure to check and recheck constantly permits difficulties to arise. Many troubles which arise could be prevented by a good checking procedure. This responsibility for checking with other departments concerning their work can be the source of a certain amount of friction, yet if production delays are to be kept at a minimum it is necessary. A spirit of cooperation on both sides is essential or friction will result.[3]

EXTRACT D

Automation and Management (James Bright)

1. More production operations are being incorporated into an uninterrupted system of mechanization. This results from the mechanization of more tasks, from the compounding of several machine actions on one base, and from the intimate linking of machine work stations through transfer devices—in a word, *integration.*

2. Longer and more intricate sequences of machine action are being performed without manual assistance. Physically, longer sequences are created through centralized control stations ("control panels"). Chronologically, longer sequences result from the application of programming devices. Cams, gears, hydraulic, pneumatic, electrical, and electronic timing devices are the basis of most current programming systems. The application of the conveyor to in-process operations also is creating many programmed sequences. Punched cards, punched tape, magnetic tape, and similar media are in their infancy as program devices. However, it is evident that they will become the basis of extremely complex and precise automatic machine sequences.

3. Work feeding and work removal are being mechanized. In many cases the introduction and removal of work triggers machine action.

4. There is a shift from batch to continuous flow manufacturing. Continuous flow is being obtained by the mechanization of handling, usually with some form of conveyor or pipeline, but occasionally is based on automatic dispatch monorail or crane systems. It is this continuous, nonmanual movement of material that so frequently causes us to call the plant "automated," even though there is no significant difference in the production machinery. However, many batch operations are being performed automatically by application of program control.

5. To make continuous nonmanual operation practical in many cases it is necessary to measure characteristics of the material and to use this information to initiate certain machine responses. Thus, there is increasing use of sensing devices to identify and transmit information on weight, volume, dimensions, depth of holes, spatial location, tension, temperature, pressure, rate of flow, numbers of units, and various chemical characteristics (such as pH value).

6. Although sensing devices as initiating mechanisms are common and appear to be spreading rapidly, sensing devices as a means of providing self-correcting machine action are relatively rare in industry as a whole. This feedback control concept is, however, a highly active and expanding development in the process industries. It is being stimulated tremendously by demands of atomic energy work and development of new chemicals and their production processes.

[3] Franklin G. Moore, *Production Control* (New York: McGraw-Hill Book Co., Inc., 1951), pp. 7, 9, 85, 189–190.

7. There is growing emphasis on mechanizing secondary production functions such as scrap removal, inspection, counting, lubrication, and portions of tool control activity. Testing continues to be a target of automation where volume, reliability, and precision warrant it.

8. The richest mechanization trend (other than feedback control in the process industries) is, in my opinion, the growing effort to mechanize the assembly of parts. Historically, assembly has been highly mechanized in many packaging operations, but the assembly of parts into precise relationships has been, almost universally, a manual operation. This area now is slowly being attacked. . . .

9. Separation of the machine and its control point is growing. Remote control, in turn, encourages centralized control stations for larger and larger portions of the production system. These naturally encourage more and more interlocking of controls.

10. Mechanization is growing in activities chronologically at ends of the production line—product design at one and distribution activities at the other. The application of computers to engineering design and to inventory control, the use of palletizing machines to assemble loaded pallets, attempts at automatic order picking systems—all these reflect the spreading span of mechanization beyond the production floor. . . .

The automated line is a highly efficient producer of products for which it was designed and usually a very unsatisfactory producer of anything else. With automation, management cannot allow the easygoing, laissez-faire policy between the design of the product and the design of the production system that traditionally exists in most plants. Automation should be adopted only with the realization that it is a commitment to produce to a definite purpose: the size, shape, and construction of the product; the rate of production and the product mix must be determined; and the limitations of alterations must be understood by all phases of management.

Having achieved agreement on design objectives, extraordinary effort must be made to *anticipate* changes and to devise and build into the supermachine such flexibility devices or change-over procedures as will take care of inevitable changes with minimum difficulty. Full weight must also be given to the *probability* of changes.

Other critical factors that must be considered in anticipating change are (a) the types of materials used; (b) the technical processes employed; (c) the sources and character of supply of raw materials; and (d) character of demand. . . .

After the machine has been built and the break-in period has been mastered, management faces a somewhat different job from that in most plants today. There is more importance attached to *maintaining operating success*. The minimization of downtime is absolutely essential to a successful performance of an automated plant, for there is an extremely high price tag on each hour of downtime. Where maintenance could be tolerated as a minor problem and handled in an easygoing way in a conventional plant, it now becomes a vital matter. Management must establish a maintenance program and plan to deal with maintenance. . . .

The Need for Feedback

Management has a unique additional responsibility. If we regard the supermachine as the production tool, management is its control mechanism—the instrumentation for sensing the performance of the machine and its relationship to its tridimensional operating environment.

Management must provide the "feedback" from market to supermachine, from technological frontiers to the plant. Since time is everything, management must be as far ahead and as sensitive as possible in detecting the need for change.

Once management has collected data and identified trends, it must make a realistic and hard-boiled decision about scrapping or changing the supermachine. It may be very costly to continue on a wishful-thinking basis or an assumption that the future will take care of itself.

How can management do this sensing, balancing, data-relating, and interpreting job? The complexities of the relationships are so much greater and more significant under automation that all facets of the organization must be intimately conscious of what is happening in other parts of the business. So many factors are involved—sales, research, engineering, industrial relations, technological progress—that it would indeed require a crystal ball for any individual to anticipate the situation.

Under automation, therefore, it becomes the job of management to create superior teamwork. Automation is literally integration of the physical plant. Its counterpart for management is *integration of the organization.* The plant and its people may no longer be unrelated elements, each proceeding with little regard to the other's actions. An effective automation design team that knits together the requirements, plans, and adaptations of marketing, sales, product design, process design, purchasing, and manufacturing personnel to the total business goals is the first management step toward successful automation. The creation of an operating team to sense the need for change and plan the changes—*rapidly*—is the second.

This is a stiff challenge to management, but the rewards in productivity, capacity, quality, and compensation to all elements of the firm are worth it.[4]

Cases

Case A:

M & Q Florists' Suppliers

M & Q Florists' Suppliers was organized in 1932 by two brothers as a specialized distributor of florist supplies (other than fresh flowers). Personal

[4] James R. Bright, *Automation and Management* (Boston: Division of Research, Harvard Business School, 1958), pp. 222–223, 226, 234.

contact with customers was developed in the territory of Kentucky, Tennessee, Alabama, and Mississippi during the period 1932 to 1939. Previously, the brothers had gained experience from working with their mother who owned a retail florist shop.

From 1939 to 1942, the brothers found it desirable to expand their contacts through direct mail advertising. Personal contacts were continued during this period, but greater and greater use was made of mail. During World War II, one of the brothers served in the supply functions of the army while the older brother kept the organization together and actively planned for a postwar expansion program. During the war years, the older brother had concentrated on securing a source of supply of the various items of stock.

In 1946, the brothers completed a new warehouse in time for the Christmas sales of that year. The warehouse, constructed to the specifications supplied by the brothers, was rented so that all available capital could be placed in a large inventory of supplies. At the time of construction the warehouse appeared to be adequate; however, growth created pressures for the expansion of the physical plant.

The firm sold approximately 3,500 different items directly to retail florists entirely through the media of mailed catalogs and circulars. A catalog advertised the firm nationally as a "supermarket for florists' supplies." Low prices, a policy of cash or COD, and efficient methods of handling large quantities of merchandise were key to the brothers' concept of the business. They felt that they performed the function for retail florists similar to that of food supermarkets and mail order houses. Few competitors in the nation operate on the same basis. Chief competition came from one major competitor and from wholesale florists which offer supplies to retail florists in addition to fresh flowers. The latter operated at a larger markup and, therefore, at a price disadvantage with M & Q.

The catalog was published yearly, listing by stock numbers such items as ribbon, cards, wire and wire items, pottery, vases and baskets, wedding accessories, copper and brass items, artificial flowers, moss and mossed frames, and tools. Ribbon yielded the major portion of revenue. Although the management maintained a complete line of supplies, records showed that all profits came from 25 to 50 key items. Many items were stocked only to give complete service. Novelties were pushed from time to time as a market developed. Active accounts included approximately 10,000 customers. In addition to the annual catalog, the company distributed eight-page circulars stressing special occasions such as Easter, Mother's Day and weddings in June.

Sales were analyzed upon the basis of square inch space allocated in the catalog. In this manner facts were kept, analyzed, and interpreted concerning the profitability of each item advertised. The catalog contained complete descriptions—generally a picture or samples so that the retail florist could understand clearly what he was ordering. Since such detail was expensive, the brothers carefully studied items which would yield incremental returns sufficient to cover the cost of advertising.

Purchasing of the varied items required continued attention by the brothers. Many items came from foreign countries. They felt that M & Q's function was strictly in the merchandising field and not in manufacturing. Although it might have been possible to manufacture a number of the items sold, such action would have required amounts of capital, labor, and management attention that could better have been used in the marketing function. In addition, the owners felt that one never knows exactly what the costs are in a small manufacturing operation.

The firm employed a specialist in storekeeping and shipping. Other personnel included an office force of four persons and a warehouse force of 12 to 20 persons, depending upon the season of the year.

Primary means of outbound transportation were parcel post, railway express, and trucks. Most inbound merchandise was received by freight.

Inventory control in a business of this type is most important. M & Q had a system which involved the use of pairs of 5 x 8 cards (see Figures 12-1 and 12-2). The cards fitted into a multi-drawer filing cabinet. Card B was placed in the front with card A back to back with a B card of an alphabetically preceding item. The item illustrated in the figures was numbered 47 in the catalog with description—Rose bowl, 4 inches in dimension. Card A named the potential vendors with their quotations and dates of last quotations. Peculiar packing box information was recorded for each of the vendors. Card B gave the running inventory with dates of last physical inventory (taken twice a year) and quantity marked in red. Information on

B-47 Plain Crystal Rose Bowls 4"

No	VENDOR	ADDRESS		Unit	Date	Quote	Disc.	Net	Terms
1	Richard Worth Glass Co.	478 W 78 st. N.Y. N.Y.		12	6/60	1.40			
2	Robert Stores Corp.	Stirie, W. Va.		12	9/59	2.00			
3	R & X Glass Co.	E. Liverpool, Ohio		12	6/60	1.50			
4									
5									
6									
7									

No.	Box	Case	DIMENSIONS	DESCRIPTIONS	Colors	Unit	Box	Weight
#1		36	4"		Crystal	36		15 lbs
#2		36						
#3		36						

FIGURE 12-1 Inventory Card

Date	Unit	Stock	Date	Unit	Stock
5/31	Inv	33			
8/1	36	5			
9/11	36	12			
12/31	Inv	12			

Date	Vend	Unit	Cost	Pack	Frt.	Box No.	Box Cost	Real Cost	Profit	Sell Pr.
7/59		36	4.20	36	.35			4.55		6.37
1/60		36	4.50							6.37

Date	Inventory	Season	Total Sold
12/21	34	Fall '60	22 x 37

Shipping Weight		Competitive Prices		
Date	Other Firms	Packing	Price	Remarks
Fall	Decade	3 doz.	6.88	
Fall	Century	3 doz	7.54	

B-47 Plain Crystal Rose Bowls, 4"

FIGURE 12-2 Inventory Card

the cards included the cost of items, the current selling price of M & Q, competing prices and total quantity sold per season.

M & Q had four departments: Department A was the loose room; it handled small items which were packed after an order arrived. Department B handled the fragile items such as glassware and pottery. Department C processed the light and bulky items (wreaths, foliages, artificial flowers). Department D handled the heavy and miscellaneous items.

The policy of the company was to ship only in lots which were quoted in the catalog and which appeared as "unit" on the cards. Many items were kept in stock in a number of different colors. M & Q had found it desirable to maintain one card on each different item. Stock boys maintained a balanced stock of the proper colors. Order points were set on these items. Generally, a 20 day supply was kept on fast moving items. Some items, such as glass were produced by the manufacturer only after M & Q's order was received, and thus required a 60 to 90 day stock.

The owners felt that a good inventory control system was most important to their type of business. "We have learned to consider three important things in buying—price, quality, and service, and sometimes the last one can be the most important. We never make a dime on goods that vendors do not deliver, and there is no profit in sending our refund checks."

In an effort to cut the cost of paper work in the handling of the many orders, M & Q worked with a system using the customers' order as the control paper within the plant, sending the order back with the shipment as a packing list. Clipped to the order sent to the customer was a statement: "Dear Customer: We are returning your original order as an invoice. If for any reason you write to us about this shipment, be sure to return all papers. We have no copy."

When an order was received, a number was placed on the sheet in the upper right hand corner. The amount of money accompanying the order was marked with a red pencil. Any correction of prices was made in the right hand margin after the shipment was prepared. The only paper that originated in M & Q was an abbreviated invoice in triplicate. The original of this invoice went to the customer, the second copy was filed according to geographical location of the customer and the third copy was filed numerically. The information on the invoice was the date of the order, date shipped, how shipped, total pieces, order number, address of vendee, and the total of the bill.

As a result of this system, one of the owners stated, "We have to make almost any adjustment requested by the customer; we never have a total of just how much each customer spends with us during any given year. But up to now, we have figured that the elimination of paper work more than offsets the bad features."

One brother observed: "The one thing about our business that we are proud of is the fact that we have had to originate nearly all of our procedures, or adapt others to fit them. We have never had a pattern to go by—never a textbook that seemed to fit our problems. This has forced us to learn everything the hard way—and we are still working at it."

Case B:

Becker Laundry Company

The Becker Laundry Company operated a family laundry and dry cleaning business. It had grown from a meager beginning in 1914 to operations in 1960 which employed 75 persons who used 30 presses and serviced five branch stores and one delivery route.

The changing structure of the laundry business demanded close attention to routing and scheduling of orders. Increasing use of washing machines in the home, the development of wash-and-wear garments, and the advent of coin operated dry cleaning machines caused problems for the future more serious than the competitive efforts of other laundry firms. Becker's labor was chiefly women who received wages low enough to be affected by the continued changes in minimum wage laws.

The owners utilized advice from a trade association in attempting to improve their control of orders as they were received and processed in the plant. The system which had developed proved to be workable but needed continual study. The manager explained his dry cleaning operations as follows:

"When a customer brings in an order we record on a duplicate ticket his name, address, type of service desired, and the number of pieces in the order.

The order is then placed in a cloth bag and taken to the marking-in department. The information is transferred from the office ticket to a triplicate register ticket and each article is listed and priced. We use a pre-marked tag marking system consisting of a strip of five tickets plus a master stub. The master stub and the five tickets attached to it are all imprinted with the same number. Each article in the order is identified by having one of these tickets attached to it. The master stub plus any unused tickets are attached to the second copy of the triplicate register ticket.

"After marking-in, the garments are taken to the sorting department where the pockets are searched for any articles that might cause trouble in the cleaning process, such as matches, sharp objects, paper, lipsticks, etc. After they are searched, the garments are classified and sorted into different cleaning groups according to the type of fabric, color, and the degree of soil.

"They are then taken to the cleaning room in lots of one hundred pounds. In the cleaning room we have two dry cleaning washers which have a capacity of one hundred pounds each. In connection with these two washers we have a pressure filter, an extractor and a 100-pound drying tumbler. There is also a vacuum still for the purpose of distilling our solvent to rid it of all impurities that might accumulate during the cleaning process.

"Our dry cleaning cycle in the washer consists of a 15-minute 'run' on a 'batch' wash. A 'batch' wash is one in which the solvent is not changed. After this 'run' the washer is cut in to the pressure filter and the solvent in which the garments have been washing is pumped through the filtering system to remove the dirt and soil that have been removed from the garments and held in suspension by the soap and solvent. At the end of the filtering cycle which requires an additional 15 minutes, the garments are removed from the washer and placed in the extractor where by centrifugal force all but a trace of the cleaning solvent is removed. From the extractor, the garments are placed in the drying tumbler and the rest of the solvent is removed.

"The garments are taken from the cleaning room to the spotting department where they are looked over for spots and stains that have remained on them after being cleaned. Most spots that remain on the garments after dry cleaning are of the water soluble type and can be removed on the spotting board with a device using a mixture of steam, water and air.

"The garments are then taken to the repair department where they are checked for rips, tears, bad pockets, buttons, etc. It is in this department that the garments are sorted out as to which pressing unit they will go for finishing. The pressing department is broken down into the following units:

1. Children's garments and ladies wear except silks.
2. Men's coats and jackets.
3. Slacks, trousers, sport shirts, and sweaters.
4. Silk dresses and blouses, ties and scarfs.
5. Raincoats and topcoats.

The purpose in breaking the finishing operation down into different units is to try to keep all garments flowing through the plant at the same rate.

"After finishing, the garments are inspected and reassembled by the order using the pre-marked tag system."

The laundry operations were divided by the manager in the following manner:

"The customer's order when it is brought in is handled the same as a dry cleaning order—that is, by name and address. There are two types of laundry bundles. The small bundle, called a bachelor bundle, that usually consists of shirts, socks, underwear, and in some instances sheets and pillow cases. In this service each item is listed, marked, and priced by the piece. The other type service is the large bundle which is either rough-dryed or is an all-finish bundle. In the rough-dryed bundle the order is weighed in and priced by the pound. All flat articles, such as sheets, pillow cases, etc., are ironed and the wearing apparel and towels are tumbled dried and folded. In the all-finish bundle, each article is listed and marked and then the wear apparel is separated from the flat work for the purpose of pricing.

"The bachelor bundle is identified with a black ink mark while the all-finish bundle is identified with a clear ink containing a fluorescent dye which is only visible under an ultra violet light.

"After being marked-in, the articles are classified and sorted out as to their washing classification into chutes which lead directly to the washroom. The washing classifications differ in water temperature, type of soap used, and the speed at which the washers operate.

"Fabric classifications are broken down as follows: white flatwork, tumble work, shirts, sport shirts and socks, work clothes, and bedspreads and rugs.

"The articles are extracted after washing and moved to be ironed.

"The ironing and finishing departments are broken down into the following units:

1. All flatwork (six operators).
2. Handkerchiefs and socks (one operator).
3. Shirts (two 2-girl units).
4. Pants (two 1-girl units).
5. Sport shirts (2 girls who also shake out and count shirts and handle repair work).
6. Wearing apparel (two 1-girl units consisting of three presses each. Each unit has a girl that touches up on an ironing board).

"The four girls on the shirt units are on an incentive or piece-work wage, while all others work on a straight hourly wage.

"The final operation in the laundry is the check-out department. Here the different orders are reassembled by their laundry mark and wrapped."

Accurate scheduling of work and prevention of misplacing items obviously are essential in the modern laundry and dry cleaning business. The manager believes that the current system is workable but can be improved.

Case C:

Delta Stores[5]

The executives of Delta Stores, a chain of specialty stores in the South, were concerned with the problem of stock shortages (or shrinkage), which they considered to be a major factor contributing to the success or failure of the chain. They maintained this interest despite the fact that by national standards the chain's record appeared excellent—a figure of 0.7% compared with the national averages for department stores and specialty stores of 1.0% or higher. The organization of the company—the pattern of communications, the lines of authority, and the degree of centralization—was strongly influenced by the desire to keep shortages in line and to reduce them.

Store officials claimed that the nature of the Delta Stores' business was conducive to tight control over inventories. The stores sold higher priced merchandise, such as expensive dresses, furs, and cosmetics, along with some moderately priced lines. The average transaction was over $16.00, considerably higher than was usual for department or specialty stores. A given sales volume involved a smaller number of transactions and a smaller number of individual items in inventory. The management argued that under such conditions a tighter control was not only feasible but essential to profitable operations.

The stock shortage percentage varied from store to store. From time to time the ratio for a particular store would rise to 2.5% or higher, enough to turn profits into a loss. Company officials took a great interest in semiannual reports on shortages, especially in those stores showing unusually high ratios. These reports showed not only the over-all averages for each store, but also presented data by individual departments. For example, the sweater department of one store had maintained a high shrinkage for several years—higher than was usual for even this notoriously troublesome operation. In this case, the central management introduced an elaborate procedure for tracing precisely which particular sweaters were disappearing, but as yet the situation had not been brought under control. Normally, however, a store which showed a high shrinkage one year would be brought into line the next. To some extent this may have resulted from the fact that inventory errors unfavorable to the results in one period might be favorable to those in the next. But company officials felt that this automatic reversal of errors accounted for only a small part of the improvement in shortages. In other words, the reduction of shortages in an individual store resulted mainly from tighter control procedures.

The management believed that it was old-fashioned in its collection of de-

[5] This case was prepared by Professor W. W. Haynes for the University of California at Berkeley as a basis for class discussion. It is not designed to present either a correct or incorrect illustration of the handling of administrative problems.

tailed data on shortages store by store and department by department. Many other companies took the view that the cost of such control devices exceeded the benefits.

Table 12-1 illustrates the kind of information that was collected for departments in each store.

The Magnitude of the Stock Shortage Problem Nationally

Table 12-2 gives some idea of how shortages varied from store to store by presenting information on the range in stock shortage percentages. The term "common figures" in the exhibits refers to over-all representative figures or averages. The term "middle range" is synonymous with "interquartile range" and indicates how much better the record of the bottom of the first quarter of the companies was as compared with the top of the bottom quarter.

Table 12-2 reveals that stock shortages were higher as a per cent for larger stores. This appears to be a long-run phenomenon. The evidence on specialty stores is less complete, but indicates that the ratio of shortages to profits is larger in such stores than in department stores.

TABLE 12-1

EXTRACTS FROM A REPORT ON PHYSICAL INVENTORY VARIANCES, STORE X, JULY 11, 1958 *

Department Name	*Shrinkage Fall, 1957*	*Total Shrinkage Year Ending July 1958*	*Sales Year Ending July 1958*	*Percentage Variation*
Infants	$ 779.32	$1,322.91	$159,872.56	0.8
Children 3 to 6	801.11	1,291.47	211,322.59	0.6
Girls Wear	1,357.28	2,257.89	297,425.98	0.8
Toys	225.93	489.76	41,323.59	1.2
Gloves	1,683.76	3,190.20	283,679.81	1.1
Sweaters	5,922.45	9,321.33	521,489.22	1.8
Shoes	1,398.71	2,001.92	603,576.91	0.3

* The figures in this table have been disguised. The relative magnitudes are different from those actually experienced by this store.

Factors Contributing to Shortages

A survey made several decades ago indicated that there was a wide diversity of factors contributing to shortages. This survey is summarized in Table 12-3. Store officials varied considerably in their opinions as to the causes of shrinkage. They mentioned most frequently two factors: first, theft and pilferage, and second, the incorrect recording of markdowns. One interviewee objected vehemently to the emphasis placed by others on theft as an aspersion on the character of customers, but the general consensus was that theft was high on the list of causes.

TABLE 12-2

STOCK SHORTAGES, DEPARTMENT STORES
1953–1957

Total Net Sales	1953		1954		1955		1956		1957	
	Common Figures	*Middle Range*	*Common Figures*	*Middle Range*	*Common Figures*	*Middle Range*	*Common Figures*	*Middle Range*	*Common Figures*	*Middle Range*
$ 1,000,000– 2,000,000	0.9	0.73–1.11	1.0	0.53–1.26	1.15	0.60–1.39	0.9	0.66–1.20	0.9	0.67–1.06
2,000,000– 5,000,000	0.95	0.74–1.10	1.0	0.72–1.27	0.9	0.62–1.09	0.85	0.65–1.06	0.9	0.49–1.19
5,000,000–10,000,000	1.15	0.83–1.40	1.1	0.80–1.38	1.05	0.76–1.49	1.1	0.79–1.50	1.1	0.84–1.27
10,000,000–20,000,000	1.1	0.91–1.39	1.05	0.87–1.24	1.10	0.78–1.17	1.05	0.80–1.23	1.05	0.80–1.27
20,000,000–50,000,000	1.2	0.91–1.43	1.2	0.96–1.45	1.05	0.88–1.32	1.1	0.85–1.30	1.2	1.00–1.49
50,000,000 or more	1.55	1.23–1.71	1.4	1.22–1.53	1.25	1.09–1.45	1.3	1.20–1.51	1.4	1.20–1.68

STOCK SHORTAGES, SPECIALTY STORES

1953–1957

Total Net Sales	1953 Common Figures	1953 Middle Range	1954 Common Figures	1954 Middle Range	1955 Common Figures	1955 Middle Range	1956 Common Figures	1956 Middle Range	1957 Common Figures	1957 Middle Range
$5,000,000 or more	1.15	0.88–1.33	1.1	0.90–1.32	0.95	0.61–1.13	1.05	0.82–1.38	1.2	0.99–1.43

Source: Malcolm P. McNair, *Operating Results of Department Stores in 1953, 1954, 1955, 1956, 1957.*

TABLE 12-3

MAJOR CAUSES OF STOCK SHORTAGES IN DEPARTMENT STOCKS AS REVEALED IN A QUESTIONNAIRE INVESTIGATION

Cause	*No Times Mentioned*	*Weighted Rank* *
Theft and pilferage	21	59
Incorrect recording of mark-downs	11	55
Price changes	10	46
Careless inventory	10	24
Careless marking	9	23
Errors in checking merchandise	5	15
Bookkeeping mistakes	5	12
Overmeasurements, overweight, and losses due to sampling	3	6
Carelessness	1	5
Invoice discrepancies	1	4
Errors in figuring retail on invoices, mark-downs, and mark-ups	2	5
Retention of cash by salespeople	1	4
Discipline—lack of adherence to established procedures	1	4
Failure to record natural shrinkage or allowances	1	3
Decentralized marking, plus carelessness on part of department managers	1	3
Stock room errors	1	3
Samples not properly marked down	1	3
Incorrect handling of credits and refunds on merchandise returns	1	3
Customer adjustments	1	3
Group pricing	1	3
Unreported losses from damage and breakage	2	2
Loss in transit	1	2
Discrepancies on returns to vendors	1	2
Discrepancies on repair charges	1	1
Large, hectic sales events	1	1
Discounts	1	1
Careless auditing of invoices before payment	1	1

* The weighted rank is arrived at by assigning to a given reason the rank it was given by the informant and totaling these on the following basis: if ranked first, 5 points; second, 4; third, 3; fourth, 2; fifth, 1.

Source: Delbert J. Duncan, "The Control of Stock Shortages in Department Stores," *Harvard Business Review,* Winter 1938, p. 208.

Control Methods Used by Delta Stores

Several procedures by which Delta Stores hoped to control shortages have been mentioned. The collection of percentages by stores and departments helped focus attention on trouble spots. The detailed tracing of items in offending departments also provided information useful in control. In addition, bonuses paid store managers, buyers, and department heads depended partly on success in limiting shortages. The company did not use a formula in computing such bonuses, but made an over-all evaluation of the performance of the particular department or store official.

The management placed special emphasis on accuracy in the recording of receipts as a key factor in the control of shortages. A listing sheet was prepared on each package entering the store. One copy of this sheet was attached to the merchandise when it was unpacked. The other four copies were held for the buyers, each of whom was required to visit the receiving room to check receipts. Each buyer priced the goods intended for her department and signed the listing sheet. Her signature indicated that she was now responsible for the merchandise. She then had the task of seeing to it that the goods were transferred physically to her department without being sidetracked en route. In the meantime, copies of the signed listing sheet were used to charge the goods against her department and as the basis for the posting of accounts payable.

Great stress was also placed on the proper marking of goods which was done on the receiving floor before the goods were transferred to the departments. A marking manual was maintained indicating exactly how each type of merchandise was to be marked. All marking was done by machine; "blue pencil" marking was prohibited. All marking was required to be based on authorized documents. The buyer was supposed to double check the marking of goods destined for her department to make sure that the prices agreed with the prices she had entered on the listing sheets.

Similar controls governed the transfer of items from store to store, which in the case of Delta Stores was an extremely important problem. Some stores, called "satellites," received all merchandise by transfer from larger stores. Any errors in the recording of transfers would, of course, have a serious effect on stock shortages in both the shipping and receiving stores.

Care was also taken to assure proper recording of merchandise sold. The phrase "PDQ" was emphasized; that is, the accurate recording of Price, Department, and Quantity. Wrappers were expected to make a check of sales slips against the price tickets attached to each item, thus providing a check against error of the sales people. Sales personnel were carefully trained to copy price tickets accurately. Stress was placed on the firm attachment of price tickets to merchandise to prevent the transfer of tickets from low price to high price items. Employees were reminded that almost all of the paper work affected inventories.

Store officials considered cash refunds to be a potential source of shortages. As many people as possible were involved in the handling of refunds—the floor manager, the sales person, the wrap desk, and others. Care was taken that the refund was handed directly to the customer at the wrap desk. The standardization of procedures—for example, of the tickets attached to merchandise—was an important control in itself. One official expressed the view that control was a frame of mind; that system was conducive to control throughout the organization.

The maintenance of a neat and clear store also contributed to control over shortages. Company rules prohibited leaving clothes in fitting rooms. Policy also prohibited the stacking of goods in halls and stairways—though a trip through one of the stores revealed that this rule was not always followed. Furs were handled with extreme care. An inventory of furs was taken at the end of each day.

Control was maintained over the employees' entrance. When employees brought packages into the store these were taped and sealed. No package was permitted to leave the store with an employee without a proper seal. A store detective checked the employees out. Employee handbags were not permitted on the sales floors.

One official was concerned with the fact that the receiving room was not at the street level. This meant that the merchandise was transported by elevator before being checked by the receiving room, a factor that may have contributed to losses.

Organizational Considerations

The central management influenced store control in a number of ways, many of which have already been suggested. It issued an inventory manual with uniform procedures for all stores. It required that all stores use the same cutoff date for the taking of physical inventories. When the inventory was taken, a number of officials from the main office went out to the individual stores to observe and to make suggestions if particular items appeared to be out of control. These visits at inventory time lasted from two to four days. General company procedures, such as the uniform handling of receipts of merchandise, the marking of goods, and the maintenance of a neat store were imposed on the individual stores. Company officials considered uniformity of procedures to be of high importance, especially because of the large volume of transfers from store to store.

Head office officials doubted that these so-called centralized controls resulted in friction between central office officials and store managers. One executive pointed out that the store managers benefited from the special knowledge and experience of the experts in the main office. Another official, while agreeing in general with this view, recalled that he had been ordered out of one store tearoom by a manager who resented outside interference. Tearoom operations had at that time come up for special attention because of the losses the company was making in such departments. On the whole, however, the management denied that the influence of the central office was a kind of "dual command." They claimed that the store manager was boss over his domain and completely responsible for its operations.

Despite all of the attention that had been given control over stock shortages, the management remained dissatisfied with the existing percentages. They expressed the view that the improvement of controls should lead to a reduction in shrinkage to 0.5% or 0.4%. One official looked forward to even lower percentages.

13

Work Improvement and Work Measurement

WE have seen that a basic requirement for any control system is some concept of a standard. This chapter will discuss the technique by which one important type of standard—a time standard—is set. Before a standard can be determined, however, the conditions under which it is applicable must be studied. Work improvement precedes standardization and thus becomes the first subject of this chapter. The study of the methods used in performing an operation includes a broad range of subjects. If each worker uses a different method of doing the job, the time cannot be standardized because the job itself is not standardized. "A search for the best way," then, is the first step.

Work Improvement

Improvement of work is fundamentally a matter of attitude or philosophy. The key to this philosophy is an awareness of exactly what an operation involves and the details of what must be done. Once a person is shown the facts of each part of an operation, he often can develop ideas for its improvement through the use of common sense. However, a person can be trained to observe important details of an operation and to apply certain useful generalizations of work improvement.

Work improvement should appeal to everybody. Its goal is economy of effort. No matter in what type of activity a person is engaged, he usually is interested in maximizing output with a minimum of input. If he is convinced that increasing output is consistent with his structure of objectives, he will not lack motivation to improve his work.

The body of knowledge on work improvement is large and increasing rapidly. Although it is as old as civilized man, the first systematic attack in developing the philosophy is a product of the twentieth century. Frank Gilbreth, the original leader in the movement, called his approach motion study. Since his time, a number of other titles have been used to identify related areas of thought—methods analysis, work simplification, micromotion study, industrial engineering. All of these approaches are interrelated and should be studied together—in fact, work improvement is even broader than any of these. All of the physical aspects of operations can be considered as a part of the study—layout of the workplace (office and plant), materials handling, design of equipment, working conditions including lighting, color, air-conditioning, power, and so forth. Recently, the mental and psychological aspects of operations have been given considerable attention. The job can be improved physically while causing problems of monotony, fatigue, frustrations, and lack of challenge to the individual. Mechanization can reduce physical effort but may increase mental strains. Especially when automation increases the number of dials, control buttons and levers, the problems of human factors of equipment design become critical.

Taylor and Gilbreth took an engineering view of operations. Specialization and standardization were their key methods for increasing productivity. After analyzing an operation with close attention to each detail, they advised management to assume the responsibility for telling the workers exactly how, when, and what to do. This approach encouraged professionalization of the management function but decreased the challenge to individual workers. After the Hawthorne experiment at Western Electric, other specialists (sociologists and psychologists) began to give increased attention to other dimensions of work improvement.

Production managers have made greatest use of methods analysis. Too often, other managers have considered work improvement a specialized function that does not concern them. In fact, it is of such universal application that it is hard to find an area of human activity which cannot make use of the approach. Today, application in such areas as farming, surgery, kitchen planning, supermarket operations, rehabilitation of the handicapped, office routines, and others are common.

Motion Study

The theory underlying motion study is that if a manager studies each part of an operation in detail, he focuses attention on small potential areas of improvement, and can then modify the over-all operation by adding together these small improvements. In applying this theory, the specialist in work improvement develops a way of looking at any activity and questioning whether it can be improved. He never takes a present system as "the best way" until he looks at its various parts and questions each step. He is a perpetual disturbance, constantly challenging the *status quo*.

The type of questions generally asked as a starting point in motion study illustrates the way of thinking. Four general purpose questions are useful to anyone studying an operation:

1. *Can some element of the work be eliminated?* If there is any step which need not be done at all or any motion that is completely wasted, it should be eliminated. The idea is not profound BUT in practice it can help focus attention on requirements of the job. Elimination of unnecessary parts of an operation should obviously come before other considerations.
2. *Can some parts of the operation be combined?* If two parts of an operation can be done jointly, combining them will improve the operation. Hauling concrete and mixing it while in transit is a well-known illustration of this idea. Combination depends upon observing the necessary details of the operation before determining whether the parts can best be performed separately or jointly.
3. *Can the sequence be changed* so that the operation can be performed with less effort? In the simple process of dressing oneself, the sequence in which clothing is put on affects the total time of the process. In assembly operations, proper sequence can decrease effort. Anyone who has purchased disassembled furniture and failed to follow the enclosed instructions will be especially conscious of the consequences of improper sequence.
4. *Can the operation be simplified?* Many economies that evolve in manufacturing a product result in finding simpler ways of doing the job.

The reader should develop his own examples for the application of these four questions. He should not only memorize the questions but should make them a part of his thinking about all jobs. In using all of these questions, it is mandatory to describe in detail exactly what is being done. One cannot improve an operation which one does not visualize and analyze.

Just as an understanding of chemistry is based on the periodic table of elements, in motion study, understanding is increased by breaking the operations into elements. Gilbreth laid the foundation for his approach to motion study in the development of his seventeen *therbligs* (fundamental hand motions named by spelling Gilbreth backward). These therbligs, which are described in Table 13-1, force the observer to be conscious of small distinct parts of an operation. The reader should convince himself of this fact by studying the

TABLE 13-1

FUNDAMENTAL HAND MOTIONS [1]

1. *Search* refers to that part of the cycle during which the eyes or the hands are hunting or groping for the object. Search begins when the eyes or hands begin to hunt for the object and ends when the object has been found.
2. *Select* refers to the choice of one object from among several.
3. *Grasp* refers to taking hold of an object, closing the fingers around it preparatory to

[1] From Ralph Barnes, *Motion and Time Study* (New York: John Wiley & Sons, Inc., 4th edition, 1958), pp. 118–121.

TABLE 13-1 (Continued)

picking it up, holding it or manipulating. It begins when the hand or fingers first make contact with the object and ends when the hand has obtained control of it.

4. *Transport empty* refers to moving the empty hand in reaching for an object. It is assumed that the hand moves without resistance toward or away from the object; it begins when the hand begins to move without load or resistance and ends when the hand stops moving.

5. *Transport loaded* refers to moving an object from one place to another. It begins when the hand begins to move an object or encounter resistance and ends when the hand stops moving.

6. *Hold* refers to the retention of an object after it has been grasped, no movement of the object taking place. It begins when the movement of the object stops and ends with the start of the next therblig.

7. *Release load* refers to letting go of the object. Release load begins when the object starts to leave the hand and ends when the object has been completely separated from the hand or fingers.

8. *Position* consists of turning or locating an object in such a way that it will be properly oriented to fit into the location for which it is intended. It begins when the hand begins to turn or locate the object and ends when the object has been placed in the desired position or location.

9. *Pre-position* refers to locating an object in a predetermined place or locating it in the correct position for some subsequent motion. Pre-position is the same as position except that the object is located in the approximate position that it will be needed later.

10. *Inspect* consists of examining an object to determine whether or not it complies with standard size, shape, color, or other qualities previously determined. It begins when the eyes or other parts of the body begin to examine the object and ends when the examination has been completed.

11. *Assemble* consists of placing one object into or on another object with which it becomes an integral part. Assemble begins as the hand starts to move the part into its place in the assembly and ends when the hand has completed the assembly.

12. *Disassemble* consists of separating one object from another of which it is an integral part. It begins when the hand starts to remove one part from the assembly and ends when the hand has separated the part completely from the remainder of the assembly.

13. *Use* consists of manipulating a tool, device, or piece of apparatus for the purpose for which it was intended. Use begins when the hand starts to manipulate the tool or device and ends when the hand ceases the application.

14. *Unavoidable delay* refers to a delay beyond the control of the operator. Unavoidable delay begins when the hand stops its activity and ends when activity is resumed.

15. *Avoidable delay* refers to any delay of the operator for which he is responsible and over which he has control. It begins when the prescribed sequence of motions is interrupted and ends when the standard work method is resumed.

16. *Plan* refers to a mental reaction which precedes the physical movement, that is, deciding how to proceed with the job. Plan begins at the point where the operator begins to work out the next step of the operation and ends when the procedure to be followed has been determined.

17. *Rest for overcoming fatigue* is a fatigue or delay factor or allowance provided to permit the worker to recover from the fatigue incurred by his work. Rest begins when the operator stops working and ends when work is resumed.

table before reading further. Use the therbligs listed in Table 13-1, and analyze the simple operation of signing your name on a piece of paper. If the pen is in a pen holder on the desk, check the number of hand motions from the time of touching the writing instrument to the time the fingers leave the pen after putting it back into the holder. How many basic elements can you identify? Ralph Barnes, an expert in motion economy, found nine.

After identifying the detailed therbligs, it is necessary to consider certain generalizations which will help develop a better method. The principles of motion economy listed in Table 13-2 are the best known guides for this thinking. They should be studied carefully, not only so that the statements can be remembered, but also in order that the reasons supporting them can be understood.

TABLE 13-2

PRINCIPLES OF MOTION ECONOMY

I. *Use of the Human Body*

1. The two hands should begin as well as complete their therbligs at the same instant.
2. The two hands should not be idle at the same instant except during rest periods.
3. Motions of the arms should be in opposite and symmetrical directions, instead of in the same direction, and should be made simultaneously.
4. Hand motions should be confined to the lowest classification with which it is possible to perform the work satisfactorily. (Five classifications: 1. Finger motions; 2. Wrist motions; 3. Forearm motions; 4. Arm motions; 5. Body motions.)
5. Momentum should be employed to assist the worker wherever possible, and it should be reduced to a minimum if it must be overcome by muscular effort.
6. Continuous curved motions are preferable to straightline motions involving sudden and sharp changes in direction.
7. Ballistic movements are faster, easier, and more accurate than restricted or "controlled" movements.
8. Rhythm is essential to the smooth and automatic performance of an operation and the work should be arranged to permit easy and natural rhythm whenever possible.

II. *Arrangement of the Work Place*

9. Definite and fixed stations should be provided for all tools and materials.
10. Tools, materials, and controls should be located around the work place and as close in front of the worker as possible.
11. Gravity feed bins and containers should be used to deliver the material as close to the point of assembly or use as possible.
12. "Drop Deliveries" should be used wherever possible.
13. Materials and tools should be located to permit the best sequence of therbligs.
14. Provisions should be made for adequate conditions for seeing. Good illumination is the first requirement for satisfactory visual perception.
15. The height of the work place and the chair should preferably be so arranged that alternate sitting and standing at work are easily possible.
16. A chair of the type and height to permit good posture should be provided for every worker.

III. *Design for Tools and Equipment*

17. The hands should be relieved of all work that can be performed more advantageously by the feet or other parts of the body. (A human hand is a poor holding device.)
18. Two or more tools should be combined wherever possible.
19. Tools and materials should be pre-positioned wherever possible.
20. Where each finger performs some specific movement, such as in typewriting, the load should be distributed in accordance with the inherent capacities of the fingers.
21. Handles such as those used on cranks and large screwdrivers should be designed to permit as much of the surface of the hand to come in contact with the handle as possible. This is particularly true when considerable force is exerted in using the handle. For light assembly work the screwdriver handle should be so shaped that it is smaller at the bottom than at the top.

TABLE 13-2 (Continued)

22. Levers, crossbars, and hand wheels should be located in such positions that the operator can manipulate them with the least change in body position and with the greatest mechanical advantage.[2]

The reader should clarify his understanding of several key terms used in the motion economy principles. *Symmetrical* motions have corresponding size, shape, and relative position when viewed from the center. The numeral "8" and the letter "S" are symmetrical when divided by a horizontal line through the center. Symmetrical, *opposite* motions contribute to the balancing of members of the body. In walking we unconsciously advance the right arm when the right leg is in the rear position but often fail to use this same idea in other activities.

Ballistic in the motion economy sense is similar to its use in "ballistic missile." The movement is free, uncontrolled. More specifically, it means that a motion started by one set of muscles is not opposed by an antagonistic set. Continuous curved motions require less effort—one merely has to think about cutting grass with a lawn mower to illustrate the excess energy used if a square design is used instead of a circle. *Rhythm* is a term understood from its musical usage and generally is applicable in motion study.

Three basic ideas underlie a number of the specific principles of motion economy. *Momentum* can be an aid once an item is in motion, but it can cause problems if it is necessary to stop and start movement. *Gravity* is a basic law of nature, beneficial to a worker if he discovers how to use it to his advantage instead of having to fight it. The *definite* location for tools, materials, persons, and work in process is particularly important in planning the workplace. Each of us who has spent time looking for anything can appreciate the practical idea of keeping each thing in its place.

Process Analysis

In deciding whether to study an operation in the detail described in the preceding section, the methods analyst needs techniques which group activities in larger classes and which help him determine whether some technique other than motion study is required. If the job can be mechanized, an investment decision is involved. If the activity is not repetitive or costly, it may not be worth going into the details of motion study. The study of any procedure, system, or manufacturing operation can be summarized graphically by a variety of process charts. Symbols are used to picture an operation.

In process charting, actions are first classified into five groups using the following symbols:

[2] Adapted from Ralph M. Barnes, *Motion and Time Study* (New York: John Wiley and Sons, Inc., 4th edition, 1958), pp. 214–301.

○ Operation ....occurs when something is intentionally changed. It may involve physical or chemical characteristics, assembly or disassembly, processing information.

⇨ Transportation ....occurs when something is moved from one work center to another. It does not include those movements necessary for a part of the operation itself.

□ Inspection ....occurs when something is identified, verified for quality or quantity.

D Delay ....occurs when conditions do not permit any immediate further action. It may be intentional or unintentional.

△ Storage ....occurs when something is held, either for a short or extended period of time, and protected against unauthorized removal.

Symbols help in process analysis by classifying the steps in a task concisely and pictorially. They become a means by which the process before and after change can be compared easily and evaluated rigorously.

Process charts can be developed in various forms and for a number of different purposes. Several basic types will be illustrated in their simplified form so that the reader can visualize the means of applying this analytical device. The operations chart is a general purpose approach needing no printed forms. For example, assume the production of a widget made of three purchased parts to be assembled into a simple mechanism. Figure 13-1 depicts an operation process chart of the assembly. This process chart can

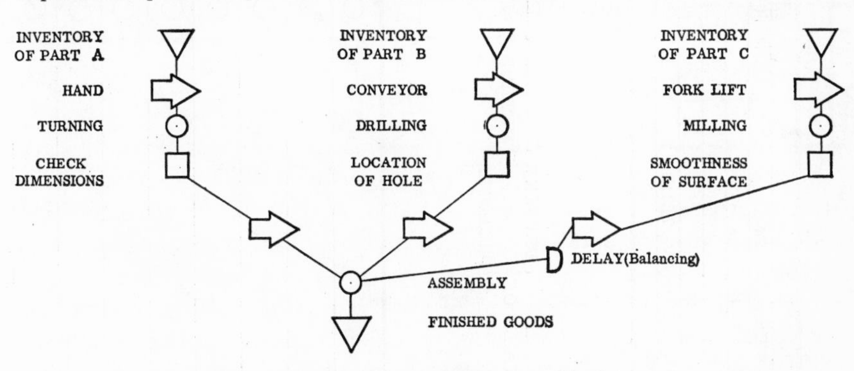

FIGURE 13-1 Operation Process Chart

be expanded into a process flow chart if it includes the time required for each operation and the distance parts are moved. The process flow chart makes use of a form with preprinted symbols. This form, illustrated in Figure 13-2, saves time if many operations are analyzed. The form is filled in by writing the details of the operation in the blank spaces, and by connecting the appropriate symbols with straight lines. In this way a profile type chart results.

FLOW PROCESS CHART

JOB

MAN OR MATERIAL
CHART BEGINS
CHART ENDS
CHARTED BY
DATE

SUMMARY

	PRESENT		PROPOSED		DIFFERENCE	
	No.	Time	No.	Time	No.	Time
OPERATIONS						
TRANSPORTATIONS						
INSPECTIONS						
DELAYS						
STORAGES						
DISTANCE TRAVELLED	Ft.		Ft.		Ft.	

DETAILS OF [PRESENT / PROPOSED] METHOD	OPERATION TRANSPORT INSPECTION DELAY STORAGE	DISTANCE BY FEET	TIME BY MINUTES
1.	○ ⇧ □ D ▽		
2.	○ ⇧ □ D ▽		
3.	○ ⇧ □ D ▽		
4.	○ ⇧ □ D ▽		
5.	○ ⇧ □ D ▽		
6.	○ ⇧ □ D ▽		
7.	○ ⇧ □ D ▽		
8.	○ ⇧ □ D ▽		
9.	○ ⇧ □ D ▽		

DETAILS OF [PRESENT / PROPOSED] METHOD	OPERATION TRANSPORT INSPECTION DELAY STORAGE	DISTANCE BY FEET	TIME IN MINUTES
1.	○ ⇧ □ D ▽		
2.	○ ⇧ □ D ▽		
3.	○ ⇧ □ D ▽		
4.	○ ⇧ □ D ▽		
5.	○ ⇧ □ D ▽		
6.	○ ⇧ □ D ▽		
7.	○ ⇧ □ D ▽		
8.	○ ⇧ □ D ▽		
9.	○ ⇧ □ D ▽		

At this point, improvement of the operation can begin by asking the four basic questions discussed earlier: Can anything be eliminated? Combined? Sequence changed? Simplified? If the layout of the plant is added to the above information, a flow diagram can be drawn showing the movement of parts by dashed lines on the layout.

An additional type of general purpose graphing device is the multiple activity chart. It charts the activity of two or more factors (e.g. a man and a machine) side by side using a time scale on the vertical axis. This chart is often called a simo chart since it compares activities which are occurring simultaneously. Two common types of multiple activity charts are illustrated in Figures 13-3 and 13-4. The reader should visualize other uses of this charting idea.

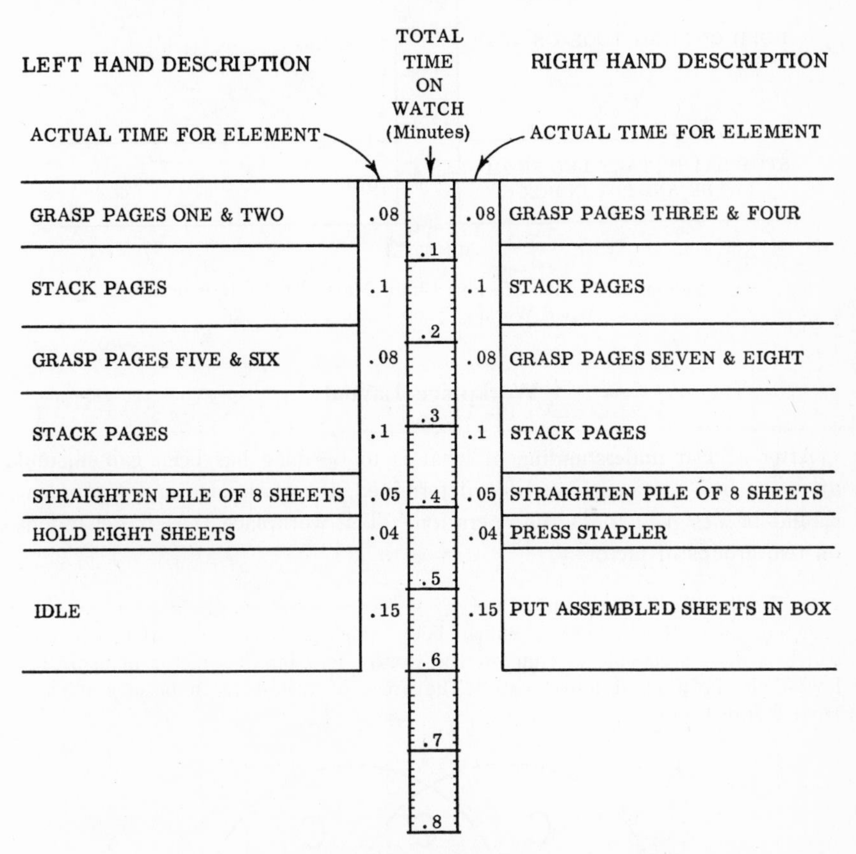

FIGURE 13-3 Left Hand, Right Hand Chart of Assembling Mimeographed Sheets

Detailed techniques of constructing the various types of process charts found in a number of handbooks on industrial engineering are simple and need not be dwelt on here. The attitude, the philosophy, and the concept of pictorially analyzing work, however, is necessary for all managers. Once the concept is understood, the manager can tailor the approach to fit his specific needs.

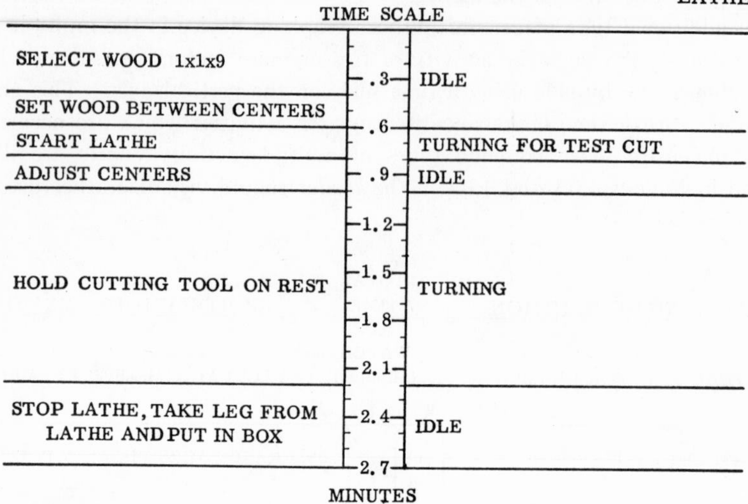

FIGURE 13-4 Man-Machine Chart, Making Table Legs in a Wood Working Shop Using a Lathe

Workplace Layout

After a clear understanding of what is to be done has been gained, and after the best motions have been determined, the workplace and equipment should be designed to fit the operation. The workplace thus is dependent on two groups of factors:

1. The details of the operation and
2. The characteristics of the human body which is to do the work. The area which is most accessible in front of the worker is a limiting factor in using the lowest classification of movements. The areas of easiest reach become obvious from Figure 13-5.

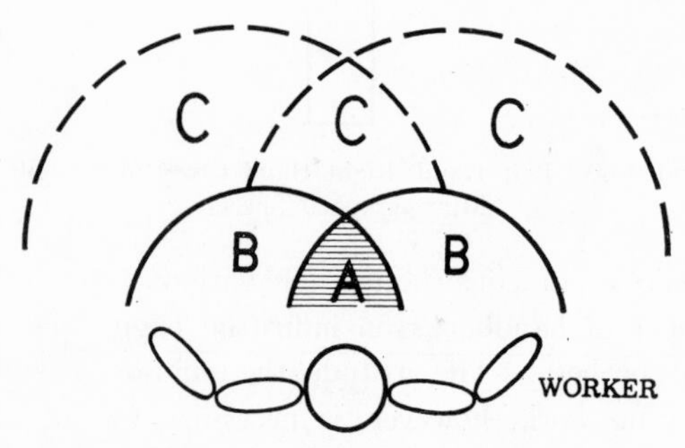

FIGURE 13-5 Work Place Areas

Area A is that portion of the workplace in which both hands of the worker can work jointly. In a small part of this area, both sets of fingers and wrists can handle the object without changing position. Area B is determined by the length of the two forearms. Area C is the maximum accessible area to arm movements without changing position of the body. An obvious conclusion is that the workplace should be arranged in a semicircle rather than in a rectangular pattern.

Reference to the principles of motion economy relating to the workplace will provide the reader with guides for workplace improvement. Tools and materials should be easily picked up, and be easily replaced in a fixed position. Gravity provides free power not only for feeding parts to the workplace, but also for delivery of the finished product. Jigs, fixtures, racks, and other simple devices will eliminate unproductive body movements.

A great deal of research has been done on the proper height of the work bench and the position of the worker. If he can be seated, he can remain comfortable and at ease. If he is right handed, the location of equipment and supplies should be located accordingly. The student who has used chair desks will be especially conscious of the proper design of the workplace and facilities. A right handed student need only be seated in a left hand chair desk to illustrate the frustration of improper workplace design.

Human Factors of Equipment Design

With the increasing complexity of manufacturing operations and controls, the workplace has sometimes been designed with principal emphasis on mechanical, electrical, and other nonorganic factors. This has led to development of machines and controls well-suited to the machine, but often difficult for the human to operate. The need is to design the machine to fit the man, not to adapt the man to fit the machine.

The limitations of mental and physical abilities have called for a special approach to the study of the workplace setting. Psychologists have been engaged in research to determine such things as the type of dials best suited to the vision of the human being, the nature of sound and human hearing, the effects of varied illumination, colored controls, and atmospheric conditions. *Human engineering* is a term used to identify this area of study, though the term is misleading. It is not the human who is being engineered, but the machine to fit the human. The constant is the human; the variable is the machine.

A human engineering specialist is concerned with the following human *attributes:*

1. *Anthropological characteristics,* such as relative height, weight and body size, perceptual capacities (including visual and auditory);

2. *Intellectual capabilities* of the human being who will probably operate the machine;
3. The *psychological aspects* of the man-machine system.

For example, only recently have automobile manufacturers been concerned with the height of the seat, the location of dials, reflection of shiny surfaces, and other factors to suit the driver. Bell Laboratories has studied the characteristics of the dial telephone. The question of whether to have an all numeral system or the numeral-alphabetic system seems simple enough, but becomes extremely important when designing an instrument to suit the typical user. For example, the confusion between the "o" in the alphabet and the "0" (zero) can become critical when long distance dialing is made available to the ultimate user.

Research in the man-machine relationships has produced interesting principles too numerous to discuss in detail in this book. Several observations will illustrate their nature.

The human body is so constructed that its best position for work is an erect one; that is, when standing or walking, a perpendicular line best describes the relationship of the leg, back, neck, and head. In a study of eight methods of carrying a load, the primitive method of using a yoke over the shoulders proved superior. The yoke method distributes the load over a large area, most capable of carrying the load while maintaining an erect posture. The armed forces give considerable training to service troops in lifting a load from the ground, showing that the back should be kept straight while a man stoops with his legs—the back is relatively weak compared with the muscles in the thighs. Chairs that support the back while it is erect are best. Anyone who has visited an orthopedic surgeon will remember that he advises a hard bed (supplemented often by a bed board) to keep the body straight while reclining.

Equipment should be provided so that proper posture of the human body will be encouraged. The equipment should allow the operator to stand or sit whenever he desires. The human body needs changes of position. Why is there a seventh inning stretch in a baseball game? On the other hand, why is attendance at a game with "standing room only" also tiring?

The secretarial typing chair is an example of equipment designed to suit human characteristics. Many studies supply information concerning the proper height, length, width of seats for given groups of people. The answer to the problem is not to use average dimensions of all people, but to adapt the equipment to fit the population which will use it. For example, in designing bombing planes, it was found that pilots were generally one inch taller than gunners. Equipment design should be tailored to such definite information.

Psychologists have suggested ways to improve industrial controls and equipment. Chapanis, Garner, and Morgan [3] summarize some of the information

[3] A. Chapanis, W. Garner, and C. Morgan, *Applied Experimental Psychology* (New York: John Wiley & Sons, Inc., 1949).

fundamental to improvement of equipment. Intensity, brightness, and glare of light affect production. Research in the use of color opens other areas of knowledge, valuable to the manager. Paint companies have done considerable work in "color dynamics" and "color conditioning."

Contributions in designing controls will illustrate the broad applicability of knowledge provided by experimental activities of psychologists. Some of this research performed at Wright-Patterson Field has improved dials in airplanes. Pilot errors were often the result of mistakes in equipment design:

1. Mistaking one control for another because of overcrowding or poor identification;
2. Making too many manual adjustments;
3. Forgetting something in a check-off procedure;
4. Knocking against a control crowded too closely to another;
5. Reaching errors, where the pilot must operate one control nearby, at the same time operating another too far away.

Common sense can simplify some tasks; if we want to make a lathe go clockwise, then the control should go clockwise. Increasing the distinguishability of controls by color coding, size coding, and shape coding improves accuracy. In one experiment, three clock-type dials with different numbers of tick marks were tested as they were read quickly by the pilot. The cleanest dial—the one with the fewest dial markings—proved to give the best results. There are many examples; but the important point for the reader is to comprehend the large amount of research information becoming available for use by the practicing manager.

Plant Layout

The improvement of work depends on studying not only the methods of the individual worker and his workplace, but also the relationships among work centers. Each center is an integral part of a larger unit—department and plant. A study of the flow of materials and parts into and out of a given work center necessarily involves the physical location of other work centers. *Plant layout* is the term used to refer to the arrangement of the physical facilities for the manufacture of a product. The manager must continually study relationships of the physical facilities if he is to develop the best layout to fit his needs. Numerous factors should be considered in this study: the nature of the product; the rate of production; the type of equipment used; the building design; the type of manufacture; the methods of material handling; the type of power used; and other physical requirements of the plant including lighting, heating and air conditioning, and so forth. The many details are beyond the scope of this book; the authors are primarily interested in the role of the manager and in some of the fundamental ideas that can serve as guides to his thinking.

A study of actual plant layouts is often disappointing, since many have not been planned in advance. In order to plan the optimum arrangement, the manager needs a means of visualizing the physical factors. A two dimensional drawing has been a basic tool for giving him a picture of the important physical factors. Planning layout is one of the first areas in which the manager has used the concept of simulation to precede a final decision. He may use three-dimensional models in addition to templates (two dimensional patterns of machines and space requirements) to plan on a small scale the actual physical arrangements. It is inexpensive to move templates or models in this planning stage, while it is expensive to move the actual machines and partitions.

The nature of the manufacturing process is a fundamental for deciding the physical pattern for men, machines, and space. In an oil refinery, the raw material literally flows through pipes with the "fractions" or components analytically separated in phases. In an assembly operation, parts are channelled to centers where the components are put together or synthesized into the final product. In machining operations, the nature of the cutting equipment makes the process an important determinant of the layout.

Classically, two plans for layout have been basic guides in a layout decision. *Process* (often called functional) layout is one in which the operational characteristics of the equipment determine the grouping of machines. *Product* (often called line) layout is one in which the product and its components are the determining factors for the physical location of equipment.

Process layout is particularly useful in manufacturing in job lots. The products to be produced often require different operations and sequences, and thus are scheduled into production in lots or batches having the same characteristics. The quantity of any given type of product is not great enough to arrange machines to suit any one product, for the next job lot would probably require a different arrangement. For this reason, similar machines and processes are grouped together in departments. For example, a machine shop is typically laid out on a process basis with all lathe work performed in one location, all milling work in another, heat treating in another, painting in another, and so on.

Process layout has its own unique advantages. Duplication of equipment is minimized and thus investment is lower. Greater flexibility is achieved since similar machines are grouped together. Because all of one type of process is placed together, supervision can be specialized for each process. In an arrangement by process, if one machine breaks down, another close by can continue to work. Also, *balancing* of production among the various processes is less critical, since any slack is more easily used when similar machines are together.

Product layout is particularly suitable for volume production of one basic product. It is the layout usually pictured as the American mass production type. Assembly of appliances, for example, is laid out according to product, with all toasters being assembled on one line, all electric razors on another, all space heaters on another, and so on. Product layout makes use of a flow concept, allowing materials to come in one end of a building and finished products to leave at the other. Special purpose machines can be placed at the proper spot for the production of a given product since the layout is not planned for many different types.

Product layout has its distinctive advantages, which tend to be disadvantages of process layout. Product layout minimizes the movement of materials and parts in production. Usually less inventory is needed, since materials flow along the line and do not wait for each process. Production time is less once the line has been set up. Space requirements are minimized in product layout. Once production is started, routing and scheduling of production is simpler because it is built partly in the line.

In practice, an actual layout takes on characteristics of product and process and often has elements of still other plans. Some large machines are built up in one location on the floor, with both raw materials and tools being carried to the construction area. This plan could be called a *construction type* layout since it is similar to the building of a house on a given lot. Another variation of layout concentrates on the *work area* for each worker. Materials and tools are temporarily moved to the area. The product is moved from work area to work area. This type of layout is used in repairing automobiles and in fabrication of bulky, nonstandardized products such as ocean liners.

The secret of tailoring the best layout to a given situation lies in keeping the basic plans in mind and in picking characteristics of any with special advantages. The production of large milling machines is an example of using ideas from different plans where they are needed. Product lines used for components feed into a construction area which is on tracks. The basic part of the machines that are standard for all types are produced in this line fashion, with the work area moving on the tracks. The unique attachments for each machine are produced in process departments and added to the basic machine at the proper time. Thus this layout for milling machines is planned with elements of product, process, and construction types of layout.

The combination of basic layout plans should depend on certain criteria of good layout. The following ideas are useful when making the layout decision:

1. Materials should be moved minimum distances with the least backtracking.
2. Flexibility should be provided so that temporary interruptions can be handled and new demands on production can be satisfied.
3. Plans for expansion should allocate space in advance for growth of key operations making a completely new layout seldom necessary.
4. Aisles should be planned with specific needs in mind. Space at entrances and exits to departments is critical, and should be adequate to avoid bottlenecks.
5. Storage areas should be planned.
6. The flow of personnel and material should be analyzed in detail.

Material flow is so fundamental to a good layout that a flow diagram superimposed on a layout can be useful in the analysis. Such a flow diagram (illustrated in Figure 13-6) indicates graphically where additional attention is needed in planning. The basic data for constructing the flow diagram consist of a detailed listing of operations including the nature of the operation, where and by whom it is to be done, materials to be used, sequence of operations, and so forth. A process chart is valuable in the preliminary study for preparation of a flow diagram.

Plant layout uses an approach similar to that of laying out an office, home, or any other physical space. A layout decision necessarily depends upon whether the building is already built (and thus is taken as a given for the decision), or whether the building can be built to fit the needs of the layout. It is preferable from a layout viewpoint to build the building around the layout. From an economic viewpoint, an existing building or a standard-shaped building may be preferable. The best layout from an engineering point of view may require a long, narrow building or an expensive building with an unusual shape. Thus, selection of building style and type is directly related to the ultimate layout decision.

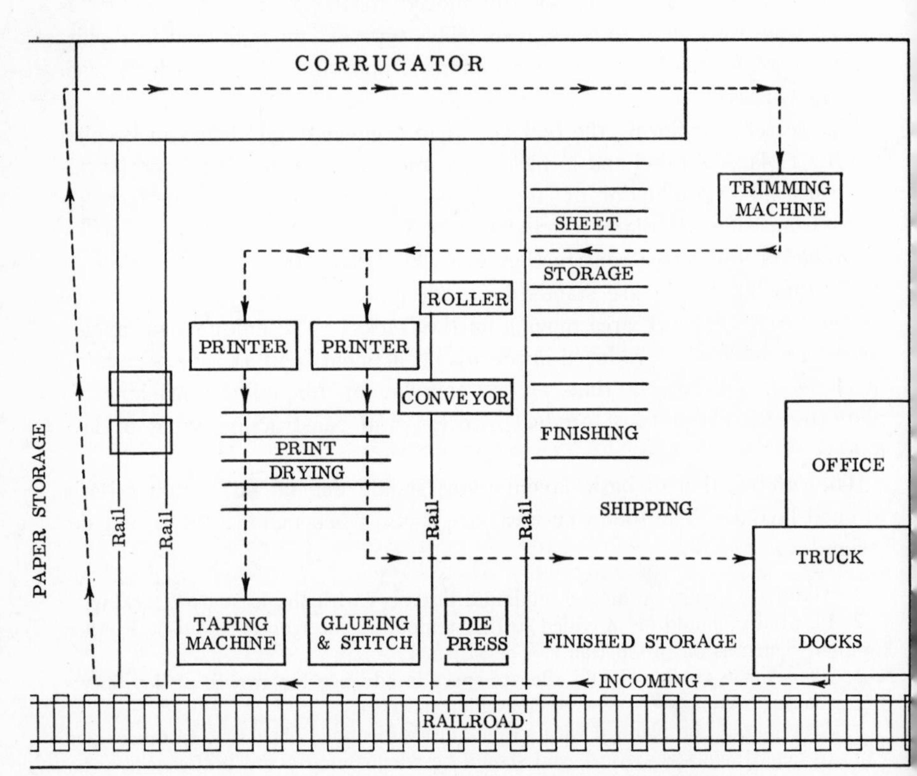

FIGURE 13-6 Planned Flow Diagram and Layout of Mengel Box Plant, Lexington, Kentucky

Materials Handling

If the man on the street was asked to come into a plant and make suggestions on work improvement, he probably would suggest adding a conveyor or some other mechanical method of materials handling. The "American way of production" is generally summed up in the mind of the layman as mechanization of handling materials within the plant. This book leaves the reader to visualize the "hardware" for materials handling, and instead concentrates on key concepts underlying the decisions of how to move materials and products through the plant.[4] The four questions discussed earlier in the chapter remain valuable in this aspect of work improvement. Since moving in itself does not improve the product, one should continually ask himself—"Is this move necessary?" If it is, only then is the question of how to handle the material pertinent.

Studies have shown that materials handling represents 10 to 90 per cent of total labor costs in plants. Mechanical devices are useful in the reduction of manual handling, but often simple ideas will reduce the need for complicated devices with their high maintenance costs. Flow is a basic concept. Air or water can be utilized, even those products which normally do not flow will move in water or air. Moving logs by water in a paper mill, moving grain by air (blowing) in filling storage elevators in a flour mill, and moving pulverized coal in water through pipes, illustrate the practical application of this concept. Gravity is a basic law for practical use. When materials are located in a high place, they can be economically moved to the lower levels by chutes, slides, or drops. Often some simple means can be devised using liquids and gravity to eliminate the need for complex devices that are interesting, but in fact, uneconomical.

In the study of a process chart, it may be evident that some other function can be performed simultaneously while moving. Storage of inventory in materials handling equipment has proved a useful idea. In automobile assembly, conveyors make it possible not only to deliver the parts at the point needed, but also to provide flexible storage for a variety of parts. Mixing, heating, curing, painting, and other processes can be performed at the same time that the product is being moved.

The use of the *unit load* concept will result in a safer, more economical, and faster flow than will the handling of many small parts. This concept states that the more pieces or pounds moved in a single handling operation, the lower the cost per unit, and the shorter the time required to move any given volume. It has been applied widely through the use of a pallet (a platform

[4] It may be useful to distinguish among several stages of material handling. *Traffic* refers to the movement of materials between plants; *transport* refers to the movement of materials between work centers; *transfer* refers to the movement of materials within the work station (e.g. transfer machines automatically shift products within a single integrated machine).

of wood or metal on which individual packages are stacked and strapped together) and a fork-lift truck (a hand or mechanical device that lifts pallets and moves materials). Warehousing has been revolutionized since World War II by the application of this idea, but new uses are continually being developed. Large metal boxes make garbage collection more sanitary and economical; truck-trailers are handled as units on railroads (piggy backing), eliminating loading and unloading; air cargo is expedited when entire sections of the fuselage can be loaded in one operation. Advantages of using the unit load idea include reduced packing costs, reduced space requirements, faster handling, reduced pilferage in transit, and reduced costs of handling.

Numerous mechanical devices are available to aid the movement of materials. The selection of the best type is an economic decision. Fixed path equipment, such as elevators, roller or belt conveyors, overhead conveyors, pipes, and gantry cranes may be preferable when there is large volume moving from a limited number of sources to a limited number of destinations. Varied path equipment, such as fork-lift trucks, small tractor-trailer trains, provide increased flexibility in handling. The separation of the power unit from the carrying unit has also made possible a higher rate of use of the expensive power source with varied hauling assignments.

Summary of the Discussion of Work Improvement

The improvement of work involves many dimensions. These have been discussed to point out the useful concepts and their relationships. Motion study (along with the more detailed techniques of micro-motion study) directs the observer to what may at first appear trivial details. The analysis of small parts of a job broken down into therbligs gives large cumulative savings. Process analysis carries the same line of thinking to larger segments of productive effort. Charting devices provide a simple and direct approach to an understanding of the relationships of individual operations, and offer a fine basis for considering the layout of the plant and materials handling.

Throughout this section, the mechanical aspects of production received the major attention, but even here human factors are important in the design of equipment and in training workers. Considering the technically most advanced methods as necessarily the best is dangerous when human factors and economic considerations are involved. Motivation must be taken into account. Much opposition to doing a job "the best way" results from a lack of clarity of objectives and poor communication.

Work Measurement

The improvement of work is a prerequisite for the measurement of work. If "a fair day's work" is to be determined, some assumptions must be made as to how the work will be done, the equipment to be used, and the conditions affecting the output. If "the best way" has been found by means of analytical study, it would be foolish for the management to permit its workers to use their old, inefficient techniques. Standardization of methods and equipment, therefore, logically follows from detailed study in work improvement and must precede the setting of time standards.

Purposes of Time Standards

Historically, time standards were desired for the purpose of determining a basis for incentive wage systems. It was often assumed that since time standards were necessary for incentive systems, incentive systems were a necessary factor for the use of time standards. This was unfortunate, for, when a plant tried an incentive system that caused troubles and was dropped, time standards suffered. In fact, much of the criticism of certain methods of setting time standards was actually criticism of their use in a given incentive system. Methods of setting standards enjoyed the same popularity and received the same criticism as incentive systems.

However, time standards are fundamental to the management of companies not using incentive wage systems. Time standards are essential also for planning and control of operations.

1. How can production scheduling be handled without knowing the time that each operation will take?
2. How can the output of one department or operation be balanced with the output of another department or operation without a knowledge of the time that it should take in each department or operation?
3. How can the accountant use standard costs in costing a process or product unless there is knowledge of the time required to perform the job?
4. In bidding on a job, how can the price be determined without estimating the time that it will take to do the job?

Methods of Setting Time Standards

Whenever a manager must determine how long an operation should take, he is involved with the problem of setting a time standard. The techniques available range from the simple to the relatively rigorous. The following methods have been used:

1. Arbitrary guess or intuition;
2. Past performance;
3. Stop watch time study (including compilation of standard data);
4. Pre-determined time systems (synthetic systems);
5. Work sampling.

The first two methods need little explanation. The first is developed as a matter of judgment in the mind of the manager. Rules of thumb in early times developed from previous arbitrary decisions. These were carried down as recognized standards without further proof.

The setting of standards by collecting data on the times that it has taken in the past to do the job can be made to appear very accurate. A mass of past data can be analyzed and manipulated, often by rigorous techniques, so that the resultant time standard seems satisfactory. The trouble with this approach is that it assumes past performance is good, and that future operations should be tied to past averages. Such reasoning does not attempt to study how long it *should* take. The addition of this normative element to the timing problem is essential, but causes the most serious criticisms. Abruzzi points out that it is necessary to distinguish between two types of processes in setting time standards—the estimation processes and the evaluation processes.[5] Estimation uses "scientific" tools and can be kept objective. Evaluation involves the use of judgment and thus cannot, by definition, be scientific or objective. Throughout the discussion of the methods of setting time standards, the reader will find it helpful to keep this distinction in mind. Much of the trouble in setting time standards flows from a confusion of evaluation with estimation.

Stop Watch Time Study

The foundations of scientific management were laid by F. W. Taylor in setting time standards. He developed the use of the stop watch as the measuring device. For a quarter of a century the stop watch was the symbol of a way of thinking. It continues to be of general use in many plants today; yet it is subject to criticism. Many users recognize its shortcomings and believe that it is not a "good" method—it is merely "the best there is!"

Numerous books cover the procedure of stop watch time study in detail for the purpose of training engineers to make time studies. Such details are unnecessary in the approach of this book, which does not attempt to tell *how to make a time study* but directs attention to *how a time study is made.* A manager must understand the meaning of the results of time study—time standards—but he need not have the skill to perform the routine tasks of the process. The understanding of what he has, when the engineer gives him a time standard set by stop watch time study, will enable him to utilize this valuable information. The manager must recognize what he does not have—an infallible "scientific" tool.

Stop watch time study includes:

1. The analysis of the time it takes to perform each part of a well-defined job by a given worker;
2. The appraisal of what a normal worker with a given amount of skill should accomplish, while working at a pace and with an effort that he can maintain without harmful effects; and
3. The estimation of all factors related to the job but not a direct part of it.

[5] Abruzzi, *Work, Workers, and Work Measurement* (New York: Columbia University Press, 1956).

Time study, therefore, involves a number of steps that intermix estimation and evaluation.

The most repetitive operations are the best ones for detailed study. Since the cost of making a study is significant, the decision of whether to make a stop watch time study of a given operation is the first step. After the jobs to be studied are selected, the specific workers to be studied on the jobs must be picked. Although theoretically it does not make any difference whether a fast, slow, or average worker is selected, the selection of an approximately normal worker has psychological advantages when viewed by other workers. Since they do not know the basic ideas of time study, they can only get an impression from what they see occurring in their department. If a fast worker is being studied by some outside man "from the front office," other workers can be expected to assume that the purpose is to "speed up" the process at the expense of the workers on the job.

Nothing is more important than securing the confidence of the production workers. If they are suspicious of the technique, there are many ways by which they can undercut the best planned time study. The worker being observed may intentionally work slower than he normally does in order to get a "loose" standard. In this way, his record will look well when future production is compared with standard. The time study man must detect any attempt by the worker to obtain such a loose standard. Some writers consider this process a "game" between workers and time study men.

After the preliminary planning for the study has been accomplished, and the clip board, stop watch, and observation sheet have been secured, the time study specialist must go on the floor and carefully observe the operation to be timed. At this stage, he must analyze the job in detail. He breaks the job into elements. These elements cannot be as short as the therbligs in motion study, because of the practical problem of observing the times with a stop watch. However, they must be short enough so that the details of the job can be timed accurately and identified for future analysis.

It is imperative that the manager understand why the job is broken into elements instead of timing complete operations. Over-all timing of jobs is not unique to the twentieth century, but time elements are.

1. The use of time elements improves the analytical approach. It enables the observer to determine the times for parts of the job and to watch for activity which is not an essential part.

2. If certain components of one job are common to other jobs, the time for the parts can be used in computing standards for other jobs. Formulas and tabular summaries developed from previous time studies can then be used as "standard data" in setting standards for similar operations.

3. If the elements are clearly defined and the times are given for each element, it becomes possible in the future to identify changes in the job and to make adjustments accordingly.

The assumption underlying the division of the operation into elements is that the elements are independent of each other and that they are additive.

In other words, it is assumed that the time for the total operation can be determined by adding the times for each of the elements—the whole is the sum of its parts. If a first element provides momentum which will decrease the time required for a second element, the assumption of independence is not satisfied.

Therefore, a critical step in making a time study is the careful breakdown of the operation into its elements. Other less important steps have received more attention in books on management, but what guides are there for determining what is a "good" element?

1. An element must be accurately defined. It must be a definite part of the operation with a precise start and a specific end. The breaking points (called timing points) must be defined so that they do not have any time length. In practice, an error develops here even when experienced time study men are used.

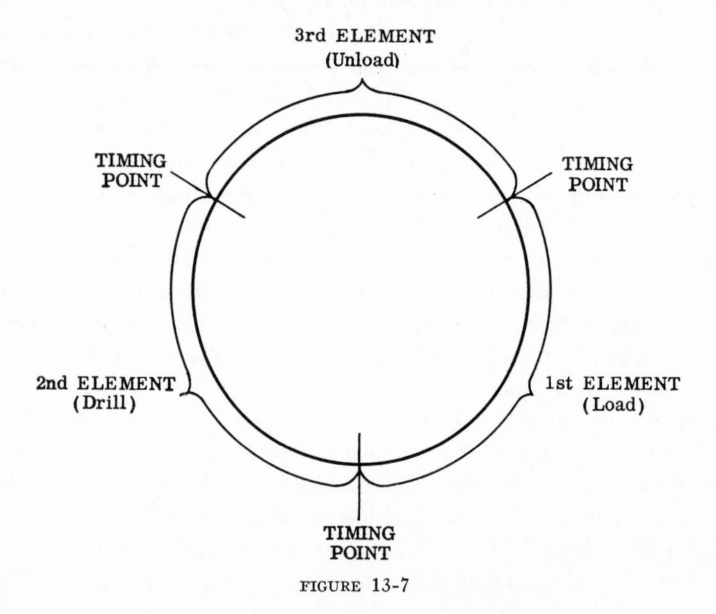

FIGURE 13-7

Figure 13-7 shows the relationship between timing points and elements. In the illustration there are three elements in this cycle of a simple repetitive operation: Load, Drill, Unload. Notice that the timing point has no time dimension because if it does, then a part of the total operation would not be included—that is, there would be a gap between the elements. On the other hand, there should be no overlap of elements. If there is overlap, the observer might call a part of the first element a part of the second. Obviously, if this should occur, the result would be variability in the observed times of the two elements. Variability in the readings for a single element indicates a decrease in reliability of the study and must be minimized.

2. Constant parts of the operation should be separated from variable parts.

3. Machine controlled times should be separated from worker controlled times. In this way, the observer can determine the elements that require special attention after the times are recorded.

4. All mutually dependent therbligs should be included in the same element, since the basic assumption of independence of elements is critical to the approach.

5. If some distinctive sound can be identified as a timing point, the distinction of elements in the actual observation can be improved.

After the elements have been distinguished, they are listed on an observation sheet such as the one shown in Figure 13-8. Each complete set of elements (called a cycle) is recorded in a column. The decision regarding the number of necessary cycles is a statistical one. The cycles merely constitute a sample from which an inference is to be made about the universe of operations of the type being time. The statistical formulas applicable are the same as those derived in a basic statistics course. An important assumption must be made if statistical techniques are to be used—that the variations in the times from one element to another are caused by chance or random factors.

ELEMENTS & TIMING POINTS (TP)	CYCLES										BASE TIME	RATING FACTOR	NORMAL TIME
	1	2	3	4	5	6	7	8	9	10			
1. Walk from area where full boxes are located to area where empties are	9	9	9	9	10	9	10				9.3	110	10.2
TP Grasp box 2. Take box to loading area	9	8	10	10	10	8	10				9.3	120	11.2
TP Open Flaps 3. Load Box	124	105	112	*	119	115	111				114.3	135	154.3
TP Release last bottle 4. Stamp, initial and place slip in box	12	12	11	A 25	10	10	12				11.2	130	14.6
TP Release packing slip 5. Close and tape flaps on box	12	14	12	14	15	16	15				14.0	115	16.1
TP Grasp box 6. Carry full box to shipping area TP Release full box	*	8	7	6	7	6	6				6.7	120	8.0 214.4
NOTES: A-Dropped stamp *-failure to obtain reading												ALLOWANCE FACTOR	1.10
												STANDARD TIME	235.8

Operation: Packing 20 oz. bottles in boxes

Operator's Name: Jo Gard
Date: December 16, 1959
Study by: H. K. Student
Approved: RWS

Time began Study: 4:00 p. m.
Time ended Study: 4:35 p. m.

SKETCH OF WORKPLACE

Empty Boxes
Packing List Blanks
Operator
Full Boxes
Tape Machine
Box
Stamp
Stamp pad
Bottles on conveyor

FIGURE 13-8 Observation Sheet for Stop Watch Time Study

In practice, this assumption for time study is only partially valid. Other causes for variations among cycle times for a given element include:

1. Recording errors on the part of the observer;
2. Possible overlapping of elements causing variations in the actual elements themselves;
3. Actions that are foreign to the element, but which occur at the time of observation.

These other causes for variation need not be detrimental if the observer is conscious of them and takes steps to handle them.

The actual recording of the observed times requires skill and practice. Suggestions on this phase are given in detail in any of the basic texts on time study. After these times have been recorded, several key steps in processing the data must be understood if the manager is to understand the meaning of the resulting time standard. It is convenient to name the times which result from each of three steps.

1. *Base time* is computed as the typical value representing the number of observed times; the calculation involves finding the best measure of central tendency of the sample data.
2. *Normal time* is base time adjusted by the rating of the observed worker against a subjective standard of proper speed, skill, effort, and working conditions.
3. *Standard time* is determined by adding allowances to normal time for certain types of actions not included in the operation, but indirectly related to it, such as maintenance, unavoidable delays, and personal time.

Base time is computed by some measure of central tendency of the individual observed times. The arithmetic mean, median, and mode may be used in this computation. The mean has been used more widely since it has certain mathematical advantages; however, since the extremely large and extremely small times have undue weight on the mean (by definition they are short or long and therefore are less important in finding the representative time), one useful modification is to take the mean of the middle values in an array. In any case, certain events may occur during the timing which are foreign to the operation and which should be omitted when computing the average. A note should be made for each of these foreign events explaining the reason for its being classified as irregular. If certain things occur periodically but not in each element (such as changing a tool), they can be considered as separate elements and timed accordingly, but adjusted for their lack of frequency. For example, if a change of tool occurs in each tenth cycle, the time for the change would be divided by 10 before adding to the other base times. Whatever is done with irregular factors, one should continually guard against using judgment to eliminate data without clearly considering the reasons for such eliminations.

Normal time = Base time multiplied by a rating factor. The step of rating the observed worker, sometimes called normalizing or levelling, is by far the most controversial step in setting a time standard with a stop watch.

The Society for Advancement of Management's Committee on the Rating of Time Studies (which has done much of the work on this step over a number of years) states: "Rating is that process during which the time study engineer compares the performance of the operator under observation with the observer's own concept of proper performance." It obviously is a matter of judgment and thus is open to attack. Many different solutions to the problem have been advanced. Some have resulted in entirely new approaches to setting time standards. Some have concentrated on means by which judgment can be guided and trained so that results would be consistent regardless of the individual engineer making the study.

The rating factor is usually stated as a percentage with 100 per cent representing normal. If the observer believes that the worker is slower than a "normal" person, the multiplying factor would be under 100 per cent, thereby shortening the base time. (Over 100 per cent would be used for a faster worker.) "Normal" to some writers relates only to speed, while effort, skill, and working conditions are considered by others. In any case, the real problem is to illustrate clearly what is meant by normal so that different observers will reach approximately consistent conclusions. One approach is to select representative jobs which can be duplicated, and use them as benchmarks for all activity. Motion picture films are useful in training time study engineers to agree on the concept of normal. "Normal" can take on policy aspects for a given company; such policy can be maintained by constant training and vigilance.

The reader may ask: Why not eliminate performance rating if it causes so much trouble? The answer is that as long as attempts are made to set a standard which is normative (involving what should be), the evaluation step must be included. We should not fool ourselves into thinking that judgment is not involved and that the results are "scientifically" determined. The answer is to seek better methods of rating or to develop new techniques eliminating the rating step. Constructive suggestions are needed in place of objections with no hint of how to improve the process.

Because there are factors to be considered but which are not included in the observation of the individual elements, *allowances* must be added to the normal time. If allowances were not clearly defined, they could be a catch-all making the previous precision meaningless.

The problem has been adequately solved through an understanding of what allowances should include, and by work sampling studies to determine the size of the allowances.[6] Maintenance should be considered at some point if the standard is to apply over a long period of time. Care should be taken, however, to prevent double counting allowances for maintenance and specific elements which have included maintenance in the base time.

Unavoidable delays should be recognized. For example, if the foreman

[6] See Chapter 26 for a discussion of work sampling.

interrupts the operator for purposes of supervision, this time is necessary and productive, but is not included in base time. Studies of the amount of personal time needed by a human being generally resulted in some agreement. Fatigue, however, is a complex physiological and psychological influence which has been studied, but which is difficult to handle as an allowance factor.

The fundamental principle to remember is that a standard should be set to allow for sustained action by the worker over a long period of time. Fatigue may be handled as a factor of base time, as an aspect of unavoidable delays (caused by fatigue), or as a separate allowance factor. Avoidance of double counting is the critical consideration.

Using Time Standards in Management

Ever since Taylor's fundamental work in time study, time standards have been used as a cornerstone of management. At the same time these standards have created many problems. A manager must keep in mind both the importance of standards and their limitations in order to avoid headaches from their use.

Taylor made broad claims of the scientific nature of time study. For the twenty years after his death in 1915, followers often used this new approach unwisely. "Efficiency experts" became a derogatory term by the 1930's. Even Gilbreth, before his death in 1924, criticized the extreme claims made for stop watch time study. Some lessons learned in the past are invaluable for the manager to remember when he uses a stop watch in setting time standards.

The time study engineer in plant organization is a specialist with functional authority who must work with line managers and directly with workers. When he enters a department to set a time standard, he is particularly vulnerable to hostility from the workers. He is not a part of the informal groups of the department, and often is considered an "outsider" who is threatening the current ways of operations. His first job in such a situation is to obtain the co-operation of the workers by explaining frankly what he is doing and why the standards can help workers as well as the company. He must become familiar with the operations quickly, but should understand that the workers who have performed the operations for a long time can give him helpful suggestions. If he takes the attitude that he has superior training and knowledge, he will cause friction and will undermine later applications of standards.

If a time standard is set hastily, the management will have difficulty instilling confidence not only in that standard, but also in the entire standards program. A "loose" standard is difficult to change once it has been adopted. A worker on a job having a "loose" standard becomes accustomed to the low requirements. If management tries to "tighten" the standard by making another time study, the worker will charge that a "speed up" is being attempted. There would be no reason for him to meet or exceed the standard if management takes this as evidence that the standard needs raising. For this reason, once a time standard is set for an operation, it should not be changed unless the operation has been significantly changed. With such a policy, management must determine what type of a change is significant. Typically, workers tend to make a number of small improvements in a job, none of which warrant a restudy. An accurate description of the job when it is timed, therefore, becomes especially important as the basis for determining when a job has changed enough to need a new standard. Comparison of the description at the time of the previous study with the description of the current operation will provide a means of showing workers the reason for the need of a new study.

Work improvement is the first step in studying an operation. After the work has been improved, the second step is to standardize "the best way" as the method that will be used. Thirdly, the time standard is set. A fourth step is essential, but often not emphasized sufficiently—training the worker and explaining the function of the time standard. Many of the problems in using time standards can be eliminated in this fourth step.

Setting standards by stop watch study is often expensive. Some companies find that one of the predetermined methods, or work sampling, can give them adequate standards at less cost. Others find that they can build a file of standards set by individual time studies, and develop *standard data* systems which make use of relationships of past time studies in their plant. In this manner, they can construct tables or develop formulas which enable the time study department to set standards on new jobs without actually using a stop watch again. In this procedure, the elemental times are found not by actual, new observations, but by using past observations of similar elements. The standard data procedure is similar to individual stop watch studies except that it uses tables and formulas instead of repeating the use of the stop watch each time.

Standard data systems are similar to synthetic sytems (such as MTM), but have one basic difference. The standard data are based on stop watch studies in the same company of actual operations, whereas synthetic systems, are based upon elemental times which have been obtained in a laboratory using motion pictures and other techniques of obtaining accurate times for short elements. Of course, these different methods of setting time standards can be used as checks against one another, in an attempt to reduce the error inherent in each method. The Necchi case in the following chapter is an example.

Evaluation of Stop Watch Time Study

It is clear that many sources of errors leave time study open to criticism. Time standards can be so poor that some believe that they should be completely disregarded; however, planning and control depend upon some concept of standard, and so time standards are necessary even if they are not perfect. In fact, it might be maintained that a poor standard is better than no standard at all. If this is true, the aim should be to improve the techniques of stop watch time study. Researchers and practicing industrial engineers do this continually. Another approach would be to develop entirely different techniques. Predetermined time measurements and work sampling are two other methods of setting standards; both are giving promising results. Methods-Time-Measurement (MTM), one type of predetermined time measurement, will receive attention in the next chapter. Work sampling will receive attention after a foundation of statistical inference is laid.

Some of the most disturbing evidence against stop watch time study comes from numerous research studies indicating the variations of results among time study observers. Some studies show approximately 10 per cent variation in standards set by the same individual, 25 to 35 per cent variation in standards set by different observers, and 15 per cent variation in standards set by observing different workers on the same job. Certainly, a manager should not ignore the amount of error that may be in his standards. In those cases in which standards are bases for wage systems, union leaders increasingly are reminding the managers that standards depend upon judgment and therefore should be a subject for collective bargaining.

A chief limitation of stop watch time study is the amount of judgment that remains in the process. In the preparation for making a time study, the observer must select the worker to be studied. The choice of elements depends upon judgment. Even in the calculation of base time from the individual observations, judgment must be employed in the choice of the proper measure of central tendency. Rating the speed and effort of the worker is completely a matter of judgment, although consistency of results can be improved by training observers to develop similar judgments of what is "normal." The factors to be included in the allowances necessarily involve judgment, as does the determination of the proper percentage to allow for personal time, unavoidable delays, and so forth.

Other fundamental criticisms of the time study technique have been advanced in recent years.

1. An assumption underlying the breaking of an operation into elements is that they are independent of one another, and that the sequence of the elements does not affect the readings. Experimental work indicates that this assumption is often unrealistic.

2. Another assumption of the time study engineer is that motion structures remain stable through time. In fact, a worker does find different and better motions that change the method which has been timed. If motion patterns change, then the time standard may need continual revision.

3. Time study uses a sample of an operation performed by one or two men as basis for inferring the operations of the total number of men performing that operation, and thus requires statistical verification of its reliability. In the past, the

time study engineer has determined the number of cycles to study by using rules of thumb or simple formulas. The reliability of the sample data from which the base time is computed depends upon the variation of the observed times. If the variation is small, greater confidence can be held in the results.

Summary

Work improvement and work measurement are two of the most important means of increasing the efficiency of operations. The improvement of work is not limited merely to the classic technique of motion study. In recent years, psychologists, medical research workers, sociologists, and others have provided the industrial engineer with new information promising progress in the future. The measurement of work was in transition during the decade of the 1950's. Stop watch time study remains the work horse in spite of its limitations.

Bibliographical Note

The writings of Taylor, Gilbreth and the other pioneers in scientific management are still some of the most valuable references on the subject of work improvement and work measurement. The best recent contributions are Ralph M. Barnes' *Motion and Time Study* (1958) and Marvin E. Mundel's *Motion and Time Study* (1950). *A Fair Day's Work* (1954) which reports much of the research findings of the Society for Advancement of Management is useful especially on the question of rating the worker in time study.

The reader may wish to study the details of several of the predetermined methods of setting time standards. One of these, MTM, is explained in *Methods-Time Measurement* (1948) by H. B. Maynard, C. J. Stegemerten, and J. L. Schwab. The work factor approach is summarized in H. B. Maynard's *Industrial Engineering Handbook*.

Some of the best critical discussion of time study can be found in William Gomberg's *A Trade Union Analysis of Time Study* (1955) and Adam Abruzzi's *Work, Workers, and Work Measurement* (1956). Recent developments in work sampling will receive attention in the bibliographical note to Chapter 25.

The details about the physical facilities in manufacturing operations often occupy a large amount of space in textbooks on industrial management. These details have been omitted in this book but can easily be found in the following volumes which specialize on key topics such as plant layout and materials handling: J. M. Apple's *Plant Layout and Materials Handling* (1950); W. G. Ireson's *Factory Planning and Plant Layout* (1952); *Plant Layout Planning and Practice* (1951) by R. Mallick and A. Gaudreau; John R. Immer's *Materials Handling* (1953), and *Modern Methods of Materials Handling* (1951) published by the Material Handling Institute.

Some of the most interesting recent research relating to the improvement of work has been done by psychologists. Much of the literature appears in journal articles and Air Force publications but the following two books provide an introduction: A. Chapanis, W. Garner, and C. Morgan, *Applied Experimental Psychology* (1949); and W. F. Floyd and A. T. Wilford (eds.), *Human Factors in Equipment Design* (1954).

Questions and Problems

1. What is the basic approach used in work improvement? What is the key way of thinking of the methods engineer?

2. Take a simple operation, such as making a telephone call, and break the operation into its fundamental hand motions. Distinguish carefully between each therblig.

3. What is the reason for breaking the operation into such small motions?

4. Explain the common sense behind the key terms of motion economy, such as, momentum, continuous and curved motions, ballistic, rhythm.

5. Why are symbols useful in process analysis?

6. Give some examples of balancing operations.

7. How does a left-hand-right-hand chart help attain balance?

8. Why is it important to consider human factors in designing equipment?

9. What are the chief advantages of process layout? Of product layout?

10. Give some examples of the unit load concept.

11. Is there a single "best way" to perform an operation? What factors would you consider in your evaluation of several alternative methods?

12. Why is it important to improve a job before setting a time standard for it?

13. Why are time standards usually important in an incentive wage system?

14. Is it possible to make work improvements without making a time study?

15. Why is time study generally preferred over past performance as a method of setting time standards?

16. What steps in time study involve the greatest amount of judgment?

17. Should all jobs be subject to time studies?

18. Is opposition by the individual worker to time study more likely than to work improvement?

19. How is it possible to determine what normal speed and skill is?

20. Why are unusually high or low times for a given element eliminated in determining base time?

21. Why is the determination of the number of cycles in time study a problem in statistical sampling?

22. Would you expect a time standard set by one time study engineer to be different from a time standard set by a second time study engineer?

23. In determining the number of time elements in an operation, would the use of a different number of elements cause variations in the final time schedule?

24. What are the basic reasons that time standards are fundamental to good control?

25. What is the difference between a therblig and an element of time study?

26. Considering the criticisms of stop watch time study, why has this method remained one of the essential techniques of the scientific manager?

27. Do you feel that time standards set by careful research in a laboratory are more useful than time standards set in the factory under operating conditions? What are the advantages of the laboratory approach? What are the advantages of the approach using actual working conditions?

28. Materials handling has received great attention since World War II. List the types of mechanical devices with which you are familiar.

29. Should a layout be determined before the type and shape of building is selected?

30. Are the types of lighting, the selections of colors for walls and equipment,

the methods of air conditioning, the use of music and elimination of noise, and other such considerations important in work improvement?

31. Does the location of a plant affect the questions considered in this chapter? How?

32. Do the flow of paper work and the location of offices affect the type of organization in a firm?

14

Extracts and Cases in Work Improvement and Work Measurement

SINCE the basis for "scientific management" was laid by Frederick W. Taylor and Frank Gilbreth, every student of management should understand their viewpoints and approaches. The first two extracts in this chapter are representative of their writings. The techniques of motion study and time study are at the heart of the methods preached by Taylor and Gilbreth and thus deserve the main emphasis. In recent years some writers have questioned the assumptions behind these techniques; the extracts from Adam Abruzzi and William Gomberg summarize the views of these critics.

The cases provide an opportunity to apply the principles of motion economy. The bolt and washer illustration has become a classic in orienting students to motion study. Each student can find many other practical applications in his daily experience. Washing dishes, checking out groceries at a supermarket, mopping a floor, dressing oneself, and many other routine activities can be improved upon by developing a consciousness of work improvement; one short example is included in this chapter.

Stop watch time study remains an important technique of the industrial manager, but other approaches have been developed as a result of its shortcomings. The Necchi case illustrates one of these newer techniques, Methods Time Measurement, and compares it with stop watch time study. The last case in this chapter indicates some of the problems of putting time standards into practice.

Extract A

Motion Study (Frank B. Gilbreth)

The motion study in this book is but the beginning of an era of motion study, that will eventually affect all of our methods of teaching trades. It will cut down production costs and increase the efficiency and wages of the workman.

There is a tremendous field, in all branches of all mechanical trades, for descriptions and illustrations in print of the best methods used by the best mechanics in working at their trade. We particularly request photographs showing such methods to the best advantage.

To be pre-eminently successful: (a) A mechanic must know his trade; (b) he must be quick motioned; and (c) he must use the fewest possible motions to accomplish the desired result.

It is a fact beyond dispute that the fastest bricklayers, and generally the best bricklayers, are those who use the fewest motions, and not those who are naturally the quickest motioned.

A bricklayer can do no better service for his craft than to devise methods for laying brick with fewer motions than are at present practiced by bricklayers.

It is a recognized fact among bricklayers, that they use one set of motions when they are trying to exceed the speed of a fellow workman, and another set when they are not especially rushed.

When a bricklayer shows an apprentice how to lay brick he invariably teaches the slow method. The result is, the apprentice learns to place the brick in the right place with the right amount of mortar under and against it, but the method used involves a great many more motions than are necessary.

The apprentice, after becoming an expert in this way, must then attempt to get out of the slow habits, due to unnecessary motions, and to learn to lay brick by a method that will enable him to complete his portion in the time that is allotted to journeymen. . . .

We have also found that the bricklayer picks up his stock with the least fatigue from a platform 2 ft. above the level on which he stands. The same is true of the height of the wall on which he lays the brick. We have consequently made the stock platform 2 ft. higher than the bricklayers' platform. We have arranged the lifting jacks to work on 8-in. notches, so that the stock platform and the top of the wall will be at the same level. This is the most convenient and comfortable arrangement for the bricklayer. It cuts down the distance for reaching for mortar, reaching for brick, conveying the brick from the staging to the wall, and conveying the mortar from the staging to the wall.

The bricklayer should always pick up those brick first that are on the side of the stock platform that is nearest the wall.

He should pick up the mortar from that part of the box that is nearest the wall, in order to reduce the conveying distance.

He should use the stock that is far away only when he has none near the wall.

Working up the mortar with the trowel should be dispensed with by having a tender on the stock platform with a water bucket and hoe to keep the mortar at the right consistency for the speediest bricklaying.

Even with a small number of masons, it pays to put a tender on the stock platform. He can not only temper up the mortar, but he can devote any spare time to piling up the brick on the inside of the stock platform with their faces up, so that the time of picking out the right brick can be reduced to almost nothing. . . .

In filling in the middle of a wall it is always quicker to lay those brick nearest the overhand side first and those nearest the inside face last. This order will allow the carrying of the brick from the stock platform to the wall with the most uniform speed, without a hitch or a change of direction of the motion.

Close watching of bricklayers will disclose the remarkable fact that years of constantly training the left hand to tell by feeling the top side from the bottom side of a brick, forms the habit of turning a brick over in the hand so as to have it right side up, even if it is being laid in the filling tiers. Few bricklayers realize that they do this, as it has become automatic with them to do it for the face tiers.

When seen to do this while laying on the filling tiers, they should receive a few reminders that they are not to do so, as it requires just so many more unnecessary motions and fatigues them for no purpose, making them require just so much more rest.

Teach them to make absolutely no motions and to have their hands travel no distance that does not give results.

In the selection of these methods as adopted here for the training of our young men, we have followed the best of the working methods of the men in our organization—which consist of bricklayers from many different nations, who have adapted themselves to the different conditions existing in various parts of the United States.[1]

Extract B

Time Study (Frederick W. Taylor)

The first impression is that this minute subdivision of the work into elements, neither of which takes more than five or six seconds to perform, is

[1] Frank B. Gilbreth, "Motion Study," from *The Writings of the Gilbreths* (Spriegel & Myers, Eds., Homewood, Ill., Richard D. Irwin, Inc., 1953), pp. 55, 63, 65.

little short of preposterous; yet if a rapid and thorough time study of the art of shoveling is to be made, this subdivision simplifies the work, and makes time study quicker and more thorough.

The reasons for this are twofold:

First. In the art of shoveling dirt, for instance, the study of 50 or 60 small elements, like those referred to above, will enable one to fix the exact time for many thousands of complete jobs of shoveling, constituting a very considerable proportion of the entire art.

Second. The study of single small elements is simpler, quicker, and more certain to be successful than that of a large number of elements combined. The greater the length of time involved in a single item of time study, the greater will be the likelihood of interruptions or accidents, which will render the results obtained by the observer questionable or even useless.

There is a considerable part of the work of most establishments that is not what may be called standard work, namely, that which is repeated many times. Such jobs as this can be divided for time study into groups, each of which contains several rudimentary elements. . . .

There is no class of work which cannot be profitably submitted to time study, by dividing it into its time elements, except such operations as take place in the head of the worker; and the writer has even seen a time study made of the speed of an average and first-class boy in solving problems in mathematics. Clerk work can well be submitted to time study, and a daily task assigned in work of this class which at first appears to be very miscellaneous in its character. . . .

The writer quotes as follows from his paper on "A Piece Rate System," written in 1895:

> Practically the greatest need felt in an establishment wishing to start a rate-fixing department is the lack of data as to the proper rate of speed at which work should be done. There are hundreds of operations which are common to most large establishments, yet each concern studies the speed problem for itself, and days of labor are wasted in what should be settled once for all, and recorded in a form which is available to all manufacturers.
>
> What is needed is a hand-book on the speed with which work can be done, similar to the elementary engineering handbooks. And the writer ventures to predict that such a book will before long be forthcoming. Such a book should describe the best method of making, recording, tabulating, and indexing time observations, since much time and effort are wasted by the adoption of inferior methods.[2]

Extract C

Work, Workers, and Work Measurement (Adam Abruzzi)

The Standardization Dogma. Like so many concepts in so many fields, the concepts of industrial engineering have been pushed much too far. In-

[2] Frederick W. Taylor. *Shop Management,* as reprinted in *Scientific Management* (New York: Harper & Bros., 1947), pp. 169, 176–177.

dustrial engineers thought they could standardize everything, presumably with the belief that if one dose of standardization was successful, two would be even more successful, and that complete standardization would result in an industrial Utopia. In the work measurement area alone this belief led to a multitude of what turn out to be arbitrary postulates; these include "one best way" concept, the standard data concept, the "normal" worker concept, the "abnormal" readings concept, the snap-back concept, and so many others.

It wasn't long before difficulties appeared. But this was attributed to defects in technique rather than in the basic dogma, which insists that there must be progressive responses to doses of standardization, with one hundred per cent results for one hundred per cent standardization. If there were problems, they simply had to be due to crude techniques.

This led to one of the most concentrated searches for refinement of technique known to man. In the work measurement area, computations were made to the *n*th decimal place, and measurement devices were developed capable of recording time values to infinitesimal fractions of a minute. Rating systems were invented that could presumably measure with fine discrimination. Standard data systems also were invented that could presumably give time values for everything, including mental processes, perhaps even for developing standard data systems.

But the difficulties grew. The basic dogma was inviolate so the difficulties were then laid to misapplication of technique. This led to a feverish search for recipes and prescriptions. In the work measurement area, detailed instructions were issued on how to hold stop-watches and pencils, and detailed instructions were issued on how to record data and make arithmetic computations. Rating films were developed in hopes of teaching everyone what a "normal" worker is by defining what a "normal" walker is.

But the difficulties still grew. The difficulties were now laid to workers. Workers just didn't seem to understand that one hundred per cent standardization, including, of course, one hundred percent control of their activities, was ideal and, hence, good for them. Workers simply had to be made to understand this, and this led to one of the most concentrated propaganda campaigns known to man.

Even the propaganda techniques followed the "one best way" approach and persuasion itself was to be imposed. Proof was by proclamation and proof was by pressure. The proclamations insisted that one hundred per cent standardization was good for workers, and if internal pressures didn't quickly turn the trick, industrial engineering firms were available to help push the process either as consultants or, what too often amounts to the same thing, as arbitrators. Then, too, there was always the device of appealing to cupidity—appealing to workers to give up their dignity at work in exchange for a concept in which their worth was to be measured in terms of production units.

But still there are difficulties, and the difficulties are spreading. Classical industrial engineers are now engaged in a mass assault on the real world on all three fronts. Proof by proclamation is the order of the day; proof is by refinement; proof is by prescription; proof is by propaganda.

But the real world refuses to become unreal. Difficulties will continue to spread as long as industrial engineers fail to recognize that there must always be a nonstandardized component of behavior and work; as long as they fail to recognize that this component is the distinguished component of work; as long as they fail to recognize that this is what makes work noble and men noble; as long as they fail to recognize that the field itself will never have nobility unless it enhances human nobility. . . .

Output-Incentive Plans. The trivialization of work has meant drudgery to workers because they could no longer consider their worth in terms of pride in craft, pride in creation, pride in unique accomplishment. The simplest measure of worth with trivial work is the measure of number. With trivial work one item is just like any other item; if work must be evaluated in terms of product, it must be evaluated in terms of number.

Having trivialized the worth of work, classical industrial engineers tried to trivialize the worth of workers in the same manner. If product worth could be measured in terms of production units, worker worth should be measured in terms of production units.

This is the reasoning underlying wage-incentive plans. This reasoning holds that human worth at the workplace can and should be measured by the number of units produced. It was reasoned that under the unit worth concept, workers would produce more units for more money and, since that would be the case, there would be no limit to production if pay were made proportional to output. . . .

The New Role of Workers. If in the industrial engineering revolution rationalization has succeeded in trivializing workers, the emerging revolution of automation will give workers a new stature. Trivial production tasks will be transferred to the machine—sufficient proof that these tasks are trivial. The industrial society, without the aid of those who keep rediscovering the problem, is solving the problem of drudgery by assigning to the machine the undistinguished skills responsible for drudgery.

A worker will become unproductive, to be sure, but only in the sense that he will no longer be evaluated directly in terms of production units. He will be external to the production activity, and he will be its master. This will require distinguished skills vastly greater than the skills required by the workers the machines replace. The status of human workers will be greatly enhanced, if only because they will have transferred to mechanical workers the privilege of doing trivial work of trivial worth. In the process human workers will also shed the concept that worker worth is trivial. They will have distinguished status because they will have distinguished skills. Output-incentive plans will vanish in the process since their only possible usefulness has been to attempt to reduce human beings to the level of machines; machines are already at the level of machines. . . .

With automation the need for labor production specifications in the classical sense will vanish along with their siblings, output-incentive plans. But there will remain a need for production specifications which will serve both management and labor. These specifications will be based on value parameters which are external to production activity. They will be attainable from the very beginning because those who design the production systems will give them the desired production properties. The specification-setting process will then become truly distinct from the estimation process.[3]

Extract D

A Trade Union Analysis of Time Study (William Gomberg)

It is thus interesting for the trade unionist to watch the ambivalence of management behavior. First management deplores the union's lack of interest in subjects like high productivity and its attendant techniques like accounting, time study, rate setting, and so forth. When the union is ready to discuss these subjects in collective bargaining, it is likely to be accused of invading management prerogatives.

The principal problem faced by trade unionists in coping with management techniques was first to have the fact recognized that the techniques of the industrial engineer belonged in the area of collective bargaining. In the course of developing this case an entire philosophy of trade union industrial engineering was developed. It does much to explain current labor movement attitudes toward time study specifically. . . .

The logical solution of the rate setting problem consists in this recognition of rate setting as essentially a bargaining arrangement that takes place in the factory when new products go into production. The function of the time study engineer is to keep this bargaining within rational bounds. However, the attempt to offer time study as a substitute for bargaining is questionable. It is an attempt to impose a task upon the technique which it is not equipped to handle. . . .

Attempts to develop machinery for the satisfactory development of production standards mutually acceptable to labor and management have led to two schools of thought. The first maintains that the initial setting of the production standard shall be a management function. Dissatisfied workers are permitted to register their dissatisfaction with any production standard through the normal grievance procedure. The second maintains that the setting of production standards should be a joint function of management and labor operating through joint administrative bodies.

The United Automobile Workers Union, C.I.O., indicates that it prefers

[3] Adam Abruzzi, *Work, Workers, and Work Measurement* (Morningside Heights, N. Y.: Columbia University Press, 1956), pp. 290–291, 292, 296, 297.

not to participate in the actual rate-setting function but always wants to be free to protest the rate that is actually set.

The U.A.W. has carried this policy to great lengths. Originally, the union was excluded from the setting of production standards because management insisted that this was its unilateral prerogative. Under the circumstances the union reserved the right to strike over production standards. For example, under the Ford agreement the impartial umpire arbitrating disputes under the agreement is explicitly excluded from the area of production standards. This was the pattern for industry. . . .

The chief claim made for worker participation in the setting of production standard is that it leads to a more peaceful and productive relationship than there would be without it. It is doubtful that its effect is a total release of the motivating drive which leads to maximum production. This matter of self-expression in industry has been somewhat overemphasized, perhaps to compensate for its having been completely overlooked previously. I have expressed my opinion on this subject earlier as follows:

> Actually, there is ground for suspecting that the great majority of those people who require this so-called self-expression outlet eventually wind up as local union leaders or members of the management hierarchy. Most of the others succeed in expressing themselves adequately in other leisure time pursuits.
>
> It is true, of course, that many workers have joined unions to overcome frustrations arising from being the victims of management's every whim and fancy. But once this right is established, the majority remain satisfied—so much so, it may be added, that there is often difficulty in securing adequate attendance at routine union meetings.[4]

Cases

Case A:

Improvement of Work—Case of the Bolt and Washers

Bolt and Washer Assembly. A manufacturing concern uses eight bolts, ⅜ inch by 1 inch fitted with three washers each, in the final assembly of one of its products (see Figure 14-1). Girls assembled the bolt and washers at work benches before the final assembly. Large quantities of these subassemblies were required.

Old Method of Assembly. The bolt and washer assembly was originally accomplished in the following manner. Containers with the bolts, lock washers, steel washers, and rubber washers were arranged on the top of the bench (in four boxes). The operator reached over to the container of bolts, picked up a bolt with her left hand, and brought it up to position in front of her. Then with the right hand she in turn picked up a lock washer from the con-

[4] William Gomberg, *A Trade Union Analysis of Time Study* (Englewood Cliffs, N. J.: Prentice-Hall, Inc., 1955), pp. 25, 249, 264, 271–272.

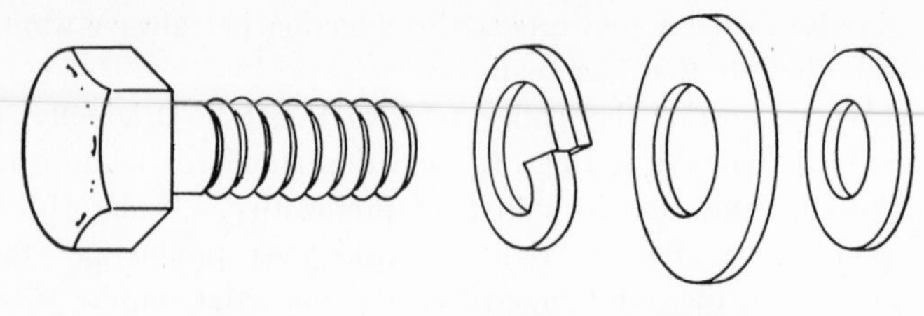

FIGURE 14-1 Bolt and Washer Assembly *

* The flat steel washer is larger in outside diameter than the rubber washer. The inside diameter of the rubber washer is made so that it fits snugly on the bolt (it will hold the metal washers on the bolt).

tainer on the bench and placed it on the bolt, then a flat steel washer, and then a rubber washer. This completed the assembly, and with the left hand the operator disposed of it in the container to her left.[5]

This operation was studied in great detail, with an application of principles of motion economy. New insights led to successive improvements in methods for this simple operation.

Case B:

Experimentation with Motion Study in the Home

One way to learn how to apply motion study principles is to find operations performed routinely many times in everyday life and practice the principles. Pick *one* of many activities such as washing dishes, setting the table, dressing, washing the car, mowing the grass, and so forth. Describe the present method in detail. Identify the different elemental motions involved. Check the principles of motion economy for guides. Develop the "best way" to perform the operations.

Lillian Gilbreth has been interested in such improvements in the operation of the house. Some of her comments are helpful in starting the reader in his own motion study experiment:

> What is to be studied? We choose always a problem that is of interest where improvements are needed and where it appears that a substantial saving could be made—the job some one hates, that takes a long time, that is monotonous. Dishwashing is perhaps the best example, as it embodies all three.
>
> The rules in industry concerning such a study require that the job chosen for study:
>
> 1. Shall have a great deal of hand work in it.
> 2. Must be performed many times:

[5] Ralph M. Barnes, *Motion and Time Study,* 4th edition (New York: John Wiley & Sons, Inc., 1958) pp. 194–195.

(a) by many people though only a few times by each (packing for summer vacations).

(b) many times though by only a few or perhaps only one person (bed making).

3. Shall have in it elements that appear in many other kinds of work (sorting—used in sorting clothes, dishes, papers). . . .

The next step, after the work has been selected and those who are to make the study and those to be studied decided upon, is to make a record of present practice. This means simply that one should make a detailed description of the work exactly as it is being done before the study is begun. This is necessary in order to have a starting point, something definite to discuss and study, and proof as to the method used. . . .

Another way of recording the method is by the pin or string plan. To make this, the observer follows the worker around with a ball of twine, measuring the distance traveled. She then makes a plan of the work place, placing pins at whatever points the worker has turned. She then measures the lengths of twine to scale and winds it around the pins to mark the path traveled.

A child may follow Mother around as she clears the table and gets the dishes ready for stacking, unwinding the ball of string as he goes. A sketch of the dining room and pantry is then made and her path traced by the string, pins being inserted, as suggested, at the turns.

As the method is changed, string of a different color may be used to measure the path. No one who has not made such a pin plan can know how interesting the process is. Nor can any one who has not seen one demonstrated realize how effective it can be. . . .[6]

Case C:

Necchi S. p. A. (B)

The Necchi company, originally a well-known cast-iron foundry, started manufacturing sewing machines in 1919. At that time, Italy imported 120,000 sewing machines, of which about 30 per cent came from Switzerland and 70 per cent from Germany. At first, production was run on a trial basis and did not exceed four or five units per day. In 1925, management was confident that they had acquired enough technical and marketing experience to launch a sewing machine under the Necchi name.

In 1938, sales of Necchi sewing machines, whose design had been constantly improved, had increased to 50,000 units per year. A new model with a special head for button-holing and fancy stitching introduced in 1936 had accounted for a large part of this success. This process of expansion interrupted by the war, continued even more markedly in the post-war years. In 1956, Necchi's production was up to 250,000 units, more than 50 per cent of total Italian production, and their sales were still increasing steadily with no indication of levelling off.

[6] *The Home-Maker and Her Job* by Lillian M. Gilbreth. Copyright, 1927, D. Appleton & Company. Reprinted by permission of the publishers Appleton-Century-Crofts, Inc.

This healthy state of business had been the result of several actions taken by management both in the technical and commercial fields. Necchi's foundry, for instance, which produced the component parts of the sewing machines, was highly rated among similar European shops. A high degree of mechanization in this as well as in other departments had brought about considerable savings in production costs. Moreover, a model of a new design had won world-wide recognition both among buyers and experts of industrial design.

The factory, located at Pavia, Italy, spread over an area of 147,881 square meters, 55 per cent of which was under cover. Several types of sewing machines, wooden cabinets, and foundry products such as pipe fittings, engine parts, and so forth, were turned out at this location. The total work force consisted of 4,500 employees divided as follows: 65% in the sewing machine division, 25% in the foundry and 10% in cabinet and furniture carpentry.

In October 1957, the head of the industrial engineering department requested Mr. Andreoli, a young engineer trained in motion and time methods by the MTM Association for Standards and Research in the United States, to make a survey of the company's current practices of methods study and time setting. The purpose of this survey was to make an appraisal of the situation and of the problems created by an extensive use of predetermined time standards such as MTM.

In 1951, Necchi management had introduced the MTM system (see Table 14-1) with a view toward achieving the following goals:

1. To develop and train supervisors to become highly methods conscious.
2. To establish work simplification by improving existing methods and analyzing motions elements.
3. To guide product design, to develop effective tool design, and to select effective equipment through forward planning of work methods.
4. To improve human relations in the plant by reducing the number of grievances on time standards and to overcome workers' resistance to changes in methods. It was recognized that when a man had worked on a given job for a period of time, he came to look at it as *his* job. He developed the feeling that he had vested interest in that job, which became stronger the longer he held it. As a result his inclination was to resist changes. With the MTM approach the manager hoped that it would be possible to carry out any corrections and simplification of methods during the creation and planning stages of a new job.

At that time, the existing methods department was given the responsibility of training people in the new technique. The engineers of the methods study department gathered all the books on the subject they could find and then started applying MTM to some shop operations. The outcome of these first experiments was far from satisfactory, due to the lack of theoretical knowledge and practical experience of the engineers.

At that time, four industrial engineers of Necchi were in the United States. The Necchi management sent them to Pittsburgh to attend a three weeks program held by the Methods Engineering Council. When these engineers came back to Italy, they started applying the MTM system anew in an experimental fashion for a few months. Only when it was clear that their engineers were able to master this new technique, Necchi management started planning general training programs. These training programs had the following objectives:

—to establish a common language throughout the plant,
—to sell MTM to the superintendent, foremen and workers,
—to develop methods men.

It was realized that for the new technique to be successful it would be essential to get production supervisors and foremen to co-operate with the engineers of the methods study department. The training program, therefore, started with a series of two-day courses for foremen and supervisors. The first day was devoted to the explanation of the element motions principles; the second day, the instructors illustrated with practical examples several of the benefits that could be derived from the application of the MTM system.

In accordance with the third objective set for the program, all the time study men took a much longer training course comprising 100 hours over a one and a half month period. In this course, the specific MTM technique was presented and discussed in detail. A company executive remarked that even if MTM did not result in any other gain, the methods consciousness it helped to develop in the time study department justified all the expense and efforts put into this program.

The application of the MTM technique to actual shop operations had purposely a slow start. The subgroup assembly department was first, for it offered a wide variety of manual operations which, in the opinion of the engineers, could be greatly improved by an analytical methods study. The great savings expected could be used as a strong argument to sell MTM to other department superintendents.

The methods engineers established a separate laboratory where a job could be studied and the best method developed, without any outside interference. After the workplace had been studied, the jigs and fixtures were set up, the best sequence of motions was determined, and a "lead-hand" was trained to perform the job according to the established MTM pattern. The "lead-hand" was expected to reach the MTM standard in two weeks. If not, the method was again analyzed and necessary changes made, until the man reached the standard. The time thus established became the basis for production planning, cost estimates, and incentive setting.

At this stage all the workers assigned to the operation that had been studied were trained in the laboratory to perform the job in the established time. As soon as they reached the production quota, the new method was introduced in the assembly department and a study of a new job was undertaken.

The results obtained by these first experiments were quite encouraging.

In one instance, the number of workers on a sub-assembly line was reduced from twelve to six, and in another, from 110 to 80. To overcome any possible unfavorable reaction from the workers, management made it clear that nobody would be laid off as a result of a method improvement. Since the company was undergoing a sizeable expansion, labor, released through the application of these methods analyses, could be used for increasing production or transferred to another department. It even became possible to create a number of new departments for production of parts, which had been supplied by outside producers.

In spite of these efforts, at the very beginning of its introduction, MTM caused some resistance from the workers. A union newspaper distributed among the workers maintained that MTM and the methods laboratory were new tricks devised by management to tighten piece rates.

To offset this reaction, the management made special efforts to stress the methodological aspects of MTM. They, therefore, decided not to use predetermined times for setting incentive rates. Instead, stop watch times were taken on the "lead-hand" at the conclusion of the laboratory training. The only change from the previous stop watch method for incentive rate setting was the adoption of the levelling technique and the elimination of the old rating system.

After a few months it became clear that the engineers of the methods department had won both supervisor and worker confidence. The number of grievances about time standards had dropped to an insignificant value. Being called for training in the methods laboratory was viewed by workers as a distinction and a recognition on part of management. Therefore, management decided to expand the activity of the methods department and to study all the operations in the main assembly lines and in the machine tool division.

To this end the methods and time department was given full responsibility over all the plant to improve existing work methods and to establish production rates. In carrying out this program, a great emphasis continued to be devoted to the educational aspects. The training course was enlarged to include such subjects as scientific management, methods study, time study, MTM, plant layout, materials handling, incentive wage plans, job evaluation, merit rating, statistical quality control, production planning and control, and elementary business economics. This educational program, which covered a three months period, was put under the direct supervision of a special assistant to the general manager.

Participation in this course was no longer limited to methods and time study men. Young foremen, equipment and machine designers, and customers' service engineers were selected to attend the program. The opportunity for attendance was offered also to some suppliers who worked closely with Necchi. The same assistant to the general manager started publishing a monthly company bulletin where recent problems solved by the methods department were illustrated.

About this time, early 1955, a change in the management of the engineering department caused the separation of the time study department from the methods department. The former group, because it was primarily concerned with rate setting and incentive payments, became a major department reporting to the cost control department. The methods department remained under the industrial engineering department and continued to be responsible for methods analyses and training.

An example which was used to illustrate the MTM technique was the assembly operation of the transmission group. This operation had been studied in the laboratory of the methods department in order to arrive at the best workplace layout. The methods engineers broke each operation down into elements, which they then further separated into basic MTM motions, which were classified and graded according to MTM tables and the corresponding times were recorded on standard sheets shown in Figure 14-2. An allowance was added to the MTM times to get the final time required.

After the job had been introduced into the shop for some time, and the workers had had sufficient training, a time study was taken (see Figure 14-3). Time study engineers divided the operation into the same elements as for the MTM study, and they took ten stop watch readings for each element. The average times were then levelled to the normal worker in terms of skill, working conditions and consistency. The engineers added a rest and fatigue allowance to the levelled times in order to arrive at a standard time, which then became the basis of the incentive system. As a final step, the time study department established the base rate for each job by means of a job evaluation rating.

Mr. Andreoli found that in the last years the extensive application of MTM and of time study had resulted in some discrepancies. Several operations analyzed with both methods had shown significant differences between the MTM time and the time arrived at through actual stop watch observations. The following operations illustrate this point:

Operation	*MTM Time*	*Stop Watch Time*
9660013 A	76	90
9660013 B	103	116
9660013 C	105	112
9660013 D	56	55
9660013 E	44	46
9660013 F	43	69

In order to find the reasons for these discrepancies, Mr. Andreoli met with Mr. Clavello, head of the methods department and with Mr. Lanati, head of the time study department.

Mr. Clavello maintained that these differences could be explained in two

NECCHI U.A.T. — METHOD STUDY SHEET — SYMBOL

OPERATION: Transmission Group Assembly — STUDY Nº: — CYCLE: — DATE: April 12, 1955 — SHEET Nº: 1

LEFT HAND	Wt.	LH	TMU	RH	Wt.	RIGHT HAND
1) LH picks up shaft d85508 from container, RH picks up spring 85561 and inserts spring on shaft. RH releases spring - RH & LH position shaft on jig - Press pedal to close chuck - Release LH & RH - RH picks up connection 85551 from container, LH picks up ring 8150 and positions ring on connection - LH releases ring.						
Reach for shaft in container		R40C *	16.8	R30C		Reach for spring in container
Grasp shaft in container		G 4A	7.3			
Move shaft to front		M40B	9.1	G 4B		Grasp spring in container
Hold			11.8	M24B		Move spring to container
Hold			5.6	G 2		Grasp
Hold			1.7	M 2C		Move spring to shaft
Hold			5.6	P1SE		Position Spring on shaft
Hold			3.3	M 4B		Thrust spring to shaft butt
Hold			1.7	RL 1		Release spring
Move shaft to jig		M10C	5.0	R 6C		Reach for shaft
		G 2	1.7	G 1A		Grasp shaft
			9.3	M14C		Move shaft to jig
Move shaft to stop		M2A	1.7	M 2A		Move shaft to stop
Release shaft		RL 1	1.7	RL 1		Release shaft
Reach for ring		R20C	12.0	R22C		Reach for connection
		Release	Pedal			
			9.1	G 4B		Grasp connection
Grasp ring		G 4C	12.9			
Move ring to front		M30B	13.2	M30B		Move connection to front
Eye focus on ring		EF	7.3			Hold
Grasp ring		G 2	5.8			Hold
Move ring to connection		M 2C	1.7			Hold
Position ring on connection		P1SE	5.6			Hold
Release ring		RL 1	1.7			Hold

* * * * * * * * * * * * * * * * * * * *

2) LH picks up cut washer 320070, positions it on groove - Releases - RH & LH move connection to stop on fixture to thrust cut washer on groove - Check fitting for ease of rotation.

(As with Element Nº 1, the motions for each hand are itemized and timed as shown above, but this detail is omitted for the sake of brevity of this Exhibit.)

Nº	ELEMENT DESCRIPTION	ELEMENT TIME TMU	CONVERTED 1/100 Min	ALLOWANCE %	TIME 1/100 Min	NUMBER PER CYCLE	TOTAL ELEMENT TIME 1/100Min
1	See above	148.8	8.8	20%	10.5	1	10.5
2	See above	128.8	7.8	20%	9.3	1	9.3
	Total of operations		3 - 8 (see sheet 2)				70.2
	* R49C Means "Reach, 40 centimeters, type C"				TOTAL FOR	CYCLE	90.0

FIGURE 14-2 (Front)

NECCHI U.A.T. — METHOD STUDY SHEET — SYMBOL

OPERATION: Transmission Group Assembly — STUDY Nº: — CYCLE: — DATE: April 12, 1955 — SHEET Nº: 2

LEFT HAND	Wt.	LH	TMU	RH	Wt.	RIGHT HAND

3) RH positions connection on shaft - LH picks up special blade - LH & RH push connection up to reference mark - LH puts down special blade - RH releases connection. (Detailed motion tabulation omitted for sake of brevity)

* * * * * * * * * * * * * * * * * * *

4) RH picks up screwdriver - RH & LH tighten setscrew 85567 on connection 85551 (Detailed motion tabulation omitted for sake of brevity)

* * * * * * * * * * * * * * * * * * *

5) LH picks up cut pin 300150 and inserts it on air operated hammer - RH operates hammer - LH picks up two-wing casting 85544 - RH releases hammer - Release foot pedal. (Detailed motion tabulation omitted for sake of brevity)

* * * * * * * * * * * * * * * * * * *

6) RH picks up spring 85547 and inserts it into hollow steel cylinder - LH inserts hollow steel cylinder into hole on barrel - LH releases - Reaches and picks up two-wing casting 85544 and positions it on shaft - Release. (Detailed motion tabulation omitted for sake of brevity)

* * * * * * * * * * * * * * * * * * *

7) LH picks up special pliers, RH picks up open side washer 084100 AT and positions it on special pliers - Release - LH, holding pliers, positions open side washer on shaft. (Detailed motion tabulation omitted for sake of brevity)

* * * * * * * * * * * * * * * * * * *

8) RH picks up nut 21339 - LH picks up headless bolt GAB - Screw nut on bolt, half way - RH starts bolt in threaded hole on barrel, Releases - LH picks up screwdriver, screws, releases - Press foot pedal to open jig - RH picks up assembled piece and puts it into tote pan. (Detailed motion tabulation omitted)

* * * * * * * * * * * * * * * * * * *

Nº	ELEMENT DESCRIPTION	ELEMENT TIME TMU	CONVERTED 1/100 Min.	ALLOWANCE %	TIME 1/100 Min.	NUMBER PER CYCLE	TOTAL ELEMENT TIME 1/100 Min
3	See above	142.0	8.5	15%	9.7	1	9.7
4	See above	99.6	6.0	15%	6.9	1	6.9
5	See above	154.5	9.3	15%	10.7	1	10.7
6	See above	156.0	9.4	20%	11.3	1	11.3
7	See above	179.2	10.7	20%	12.8	1	12.8
8	See above	260.1	15.7	20%	18.8	1	18.8

FIGURE 14-2 (Back)

NECCHI U.A.T.	TIME STUDY SHEET		DEPARTMENT ....WORK STATION........	SYMBOL
PART NAME: Transmission Sub-Assembly		Raw Material d 85508	MACHINE TOOL..............NUMBER........	INDEX
OPERATION DESCRIPTION: Group Assembly			JIGS & FIXTURES........................	1
			TOOLS..................................	
DATE 8/25/55	STUDY Nº 55/1306	SUPERCEDES Nº	WORKER: STANDING... MALE ... SITTING X. FEMALE X	GAGES..................................	OPERATION Nº 10
			LUBRICATION............................	

PHASE Nº	DESCRIPTION	WORKING CONDITIONS				LEVELED AVERAGES		
		Rpm	SPEED	FEED	DEPTH OF CUT	MACHINE IDLE	MACHINE TIME	MACHINE UNATTENDED
	The sub-assembly is made up of the following parts: d 85508 - 85545 - 320070 - 035150GAB - 300150 - 85544 - 8150 - 85551 - 85561 - 85562 - 21339 - 084100AT - 85547.							
1	RH takes finished piece from jig (completed in previous cycle) and puts it into totepan - RH picks up spring 85561, LH picks up shaft d 85508					5.51		
2	Insert spring on shaft - Set group on jig.					4.97		
3	RH picks up connection 85551, LHpicks up ring 8150 - Mount ring on connection.					7.45		
4	LH picks up cut washer 320070 - Thrust cut washer on groove of connection 85551. Check ring-connection fit for ease of rotation.					9.83		
5	LH picks up special blade - Mount connection 85551 on shaft d 85508.					12.74		
6	LH puts down blade - RH picks up screwdriver and tightens set screw 85562 on connection 85551.					11.23		
7	LH picks up cut-pin 300150, inserts it on air operated hammer - At the same time press pedal to move jig under hammer - Operate hammer to insert cut-pin into hole on barrel of d 85508 - Press pedal to move jig back to position.					9.55		
8	LH picks up two-wing casting 85544 - Mount it on ground butt of shaft d 85508, hub facing out.					7.78		
9	RH picks up open side washer 084100AT - LH picks up special pliers - Mount washer on groove of shaft d 85508 to hold two-wing casting.					17.17		
10	Check for ease of rotation					5.40		
11	RH picks up spring 85547 - LH picks up hollow steel cylinder 85545 - Insert spring into hole on cylinder - Assemble cylinder on barrel and fit two-wing casting on cylinder butt.					13.28		
12	LH picks up headless bolt 035150 GAB - RH picks up nut 21339 - Screw nut on bolt - Start bolt into threaded hole on barrel					16.84		
13	RH grasps air operated screwdriver and tightens headless bolt.					3.02		
Ev/1	Unscrew setscrew 85562 - pick up another screw and tighten it on connection. (Phase 6) (20% of the times)					0.86		
Ev/2	Disassemble open side washer 084100AT, if tne two wing casting 85544 is not free to rotate - Try another washer. (Phases 8 & 9) (5% of tne times)					1.35		
						126.88		
	FATIGUE ALLOWANCE ......6%........					7.61		
	Total carried from other sheets					-		

APPROVED: Time Study man	U.A.T.	Foreman	Allowed Set-up Time	Job Class	Piece Rate	Wage System	Average Set-up Time	Cycle Time	Average Time	Pieces Per Hour	Worker's Utilization	TOTAL	TOTAL	TOTAL
.....	.....	.....	....	1	3.36	......	....	1.17	1.46	51	100%	134.49		

FIGURE 14-3 (Front)

ways. First, the worker was actually following the method described by the methods department, but the time study man had a concept of normal worker which was different from the normal of the MTM system. When levelling stop watch readings, the time study engineer referred to an ideal pace somewhat slower than that of the "MTM worker." Therefore his subjective evaluation of the levelling factor was higher than it actually should have been. Secondly, Mr. Clavello said that the time study man was levelling

SHEET No. 1..

OPERATION No. 10...

DESCRIPTION (elements):
1. Set finished piece away - Pick up a new shaft and spring
2. Insert spring on shaft - Set group on jig
3. Pick up connection and ring and assemble ring on connection
4. Pick up cut-washer Thrust cut-washer on groove - Check
5. With special blade mount connection on shaft
6. Tighten Set-screw on connection
7. With air operated hammer, insert cut pin on barrel
8. Assemble 2-casting on butt
9. Wing ground of shaft
10. With special pliers, mount open-sided washer on shaft - Check for ease of rotation
11. Assemble spring and steel cylinder on barrel
12. Screw nut on headless bolt - start bolt on barrel
13. Tighten headless bolt
14. EV/1
15. EV/2

TIME STUDY SHEET

CYCLE NUMBER	1 Inc.	1 Acc.	2 Inc.	2 Acc.	3 Inc.	3 Acc.	4 Inc.	4 Acc.	5 Inc.	5 Acc.	6 Inc.	6 Acc.	7 Inc.	7 Acc.	8 Inc.	8 Acc.	9 Inc.	9 Acc.	10 Inc.	10 Acc.	11 Inc.	11 Acc.	12 Inc.	12 Acc.	13 Inc.	13 Acc.	14 Inc.	14 Acc.	15 Inc.	15 Acc.	REMARKS
1	4	4	6	10	6	16	8	24	8	32	13	45	7	52	8	60	16	76	4	80	17	97	30	127	3	130		20%		5%	
2	4	4	5	9	7	16	11	27	(34)	61	11	72	12	84	6	90	15	105	5	110	15	125	10	135	3	138		15			
3	5	5	5	10	6	16	6	22	7	29	5	34	8	42	8	50	12	62	4	66	9	75	12	87	3	90					
4	4	4	4	8	6	14	9	23	9	32	13	45	10	55	10	65	18	83	5	88	8	96	14	110	3	113					
5	6	6	4	10	7	17	8	25	7	32	10	42	9	51	5	56	15	71	5	76	9	85	15	100	2	102				25	
6	6	6	4	10	10	20	13	33	18	51	10	61	7	68	7	75	10	85	5	90	10	100	10	110	3	113					
7	4	4	5	9	7	16	9	25	7	32	10	42	8	50	8	58	20	78	7	85	13	98	11	109	2	111					
8	5	5	4	9	8	17	8	25	9	34	10	44	7	51	8	59	18	77	6	83	14	97	12	109	3	112					
9	7	7	4	11	6	17	10	27	11	36	11	47	11	58	5	63	19	82	5	87	16	103	20	123	3	126		17			
10	6	6	5	11	6	17	9	26	10	36	11	47	9	56	7	63	17	80	4	84	12	96	21	117	3	120					
TOTAL	51		46		69		91		118		104		88		72		159		50		123		155		28		32		25		JOB CLASS
AVERAGE OBSERVED TIMES	5.1		4.6		6.9		9.1		11.8		10.4		8.8		7.2		15.9		5.0		12.3		15.5		2.8		0.8		1.25		
LEVEL. SKILL / EFFORT	C2 / C1		C2 / C1		C2 / C1		C2 / C1		C2 / C1		C2 / C1		C2 / C1		C2 / C1		C2 / C1		C2 / C1		C2 / C1		C2 / C1		C2 / C1		C2 / C1		C2 / C1		up to 139 Class (1)
LEVELING FACTOR	1.08		1.08		1.08		1.08		1.08		1.08		1.08		1.08		1.08		1.08		1.08		1.08		1.08		1.08		1.08		from 140 to 161 Class 2
LEVELED TIME	5.51		4.97		7.45		9.83		12.74		11.23		9.55		7.78		17.17		5.40		13.28		16.74		3.02		0.86		1.35		from 162 to 183 Class 3
FATIGUE ALLOWANCE																															from 184 to 205 Class 4
AVERAGE TIMES																															from 206 to 227 Class 5

LEVELING FACTORS

SKILL		EFFORT	
+0.15	A 1	+0.13	A 1
+0.13	A 2	+0.12	A 2
+0.11	B 1	+0.10	B 1
+0.08	B 2	+0.08	B 2
+0.06	C 1	+0.05	(C 1)
+0.03	(C 2)	+0.02	C 2
0.00	D	0.00	D
-0.05	E 1	-0.04	E 1
-0.10	E 2	-0.08	E 2
-0.16	F 1	-0.12	F 1
-0.22	F 2	-0.17	F 2
CONDITIONS		CONSISTENCY	
+0.06	A	+0.04	A
+0.04	B	+0.03	B
+0.02	C	+0.01	C
0.00	D	0.00	D
-0.03	E	-0.02	E
-0.07	F	-0.04	F

PREPARATION TIME	AVERAGE TIMES
Informing the foreman	
Asking for instructions	
Getting tools from toolroom	
Setting up jigs and fixtures	
Getting machine ready	
Cleaning up work place	
Allowance %	
Total	

WORKER'S NAME .BIANCHI........

	JOB EVALUATION FACTORS		GRADE	POINTS
1	Education	14	1	14
2	Experience	22	1	22
3	Initiative	14	1	14
4	Physical requirements	10	2	20
5	Mental & Visual requirements	5	2	10
6	Responsibility for tools and equipment	5	1	5
7	Responsibility for materials and products	5	1	5
8	Responsibility for safety of others	5	1	5
9	Responsibility for work of others	5	1	5
10	Working conditions	10	2	20
11	Safety	5	2	10
	TOTAL POINTS			130
	JOB CLASS			1
	ALLOWED CLASS			

FIGURE 14-3 (Back)

the worker's performance correctly, but the worker was not following the method established by the methods department. It was very difficult, he added, to discover which was the right cause because for one thing the workers had many subtle ways to "make a job look longer than it actually was."

Mr. Lanati's side of the argument was that the present situation was the result of poor communication between the two departments, namely the methods department and the time study department. He said that the MTM times should have been communicated to his time study men by the people in the methods department. This practice would have eliminated loose standards. At present, when it was clear that the workers could beat a given standard, the time study man would make a few small changes in the work method. These changes would enable him to make a new time study and set up "a more realistic standard." Often times these changes were decided by the time study men, and were not communicated to the methods department.

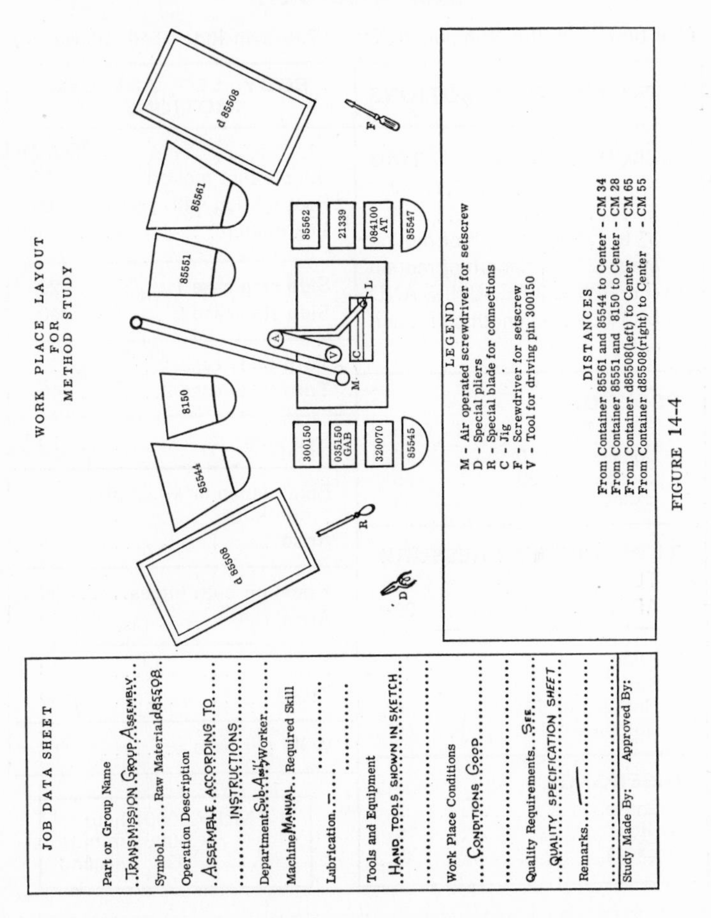

FIGURE 14-4

From this discussion Mr. Andreoli got the impression that these problems could be solved by combining both departments. He meant to present his proposal to the industrial engineering department manager and to suggest that times standards be set only by applying MTM which, he felt, would eliminate any subjective evaluation of the worker's performance.[7]

[7] Copyright 1958 by Institut pour l'Etude des Methodes de Direction de l'Entreprise, (IMEDE Lausanne, Switzerland).

TABLE 14-1

EXPLANATION OF MTM

METHODS-TIME MEASUREMENT APPLICATION DATA

SIMPLIFIED DATA

(All times on this Simplified Data Table include 15% allowance)

HAND AND ARM MOTIONS			
REACH or MOVE			**TMU**
1″			2
2″			4
3″ to 12″			4 + length of motion
over 12″			3 + length of motion
(For TYPE 2 REACHES AND MOVES use length of motion only)			
POSITION			
Fit	Symmetrical	Other	
Loose	10	15	
Close	20	25	
Exact	50	55	
TURN—APPLY PRESSURE			
TURN			6
APPLY PRESSURE			20
GRASP			
Simple			2
Regrasp or Transfer			6
Complex			10
DISENGAGE			
Loose			5
Close			10
Exact			30

BODY, LEG, AND EYE MOTIONS	TMU
Simple foot motion	10
Foot motion with pressure	20
Leg motion	10
Side step case 1	20
Side step case 2	40
Turn body case 1	20
Turn body case 2	45
Eye time	10
Bend, stoop or kneel on one knee	35
Arise	35
Kneel on both knees	80
Arise	90
Sit	40
Stand	50
Walk per pace	17

1 TMU = .00001 hour
= .0006 minute
= .036 second

TABLE I—REACH—R

Distance Moved Inches	Time TMU A	Time TMU B	Time TMU C or D	Time TMU E	Hand In Motion A	Hand In Motion B
¾ or less	2.0	2.0	2.0	2.0	1.6	1.6
1	2.5	2.5	3.6	2.4	2.3	2.3
2	4.0	4.0	5.9	3.8	3.5	2.7
3	5.3	5.3	7.3	5.3	4.5	3.6
4	6.1	6.4	8.4	6.8	4.9	4.3
5	6.5	7.8	9.4	7.4	5.3	5.0
6	7.0	8.6	10.1	8.0	5.7	5.7
7	7.4	9.3	10.8	8.7	6.1	6.5
8	7.9	10.1	11.5	9.3	6.5	7.2
9	8.3	10.8	12.2	9.9	6.9	7.9
10	8.7	11.5	12.9	10.5	7.3	8.6
12	9.6	12.9	14.2	11.8	8.1	10.1
14	10.5	14.4	15.6	13.0	8.9	11.5
16	11.4	15.8	17.0	14.2	9.7	12.9
18	12.3	17.2	18.4	15.5	10.5	14.4
20	13.1	18.6	19.8	16.7	11.3	15.8
22	14.0	20.1	21.2	18.0	12.1	17.3
24	14.9	21.5	22.5	19.2	12.9	18.8
26	15.8	22.9	23.9	20.4	13.7	20.2
28	16.7	24.4	25.3	21.7	14.5	21.7
30	17.5	25.8	26.7	22.9	15.3	23.2

CASE AND DESCRIPTION
A Reach to object in fixed location, or to object in other hand or on which other hand rests.
B Reach to single object in location which may vary slightly from cycle to cycle.
C Reach to object jumbled with other objects in a group so that search and select occur.
D Reach to a very small object or where accurate grasp is required.
E Reach to indefinite location to get hand in position for body balance or next motion or out of way.

TABLE II—MOVE—M

Distance Moved Inches	Time TMU A	Time TMU B	Time TMU C	Hand in Motion B
¾ or less	2.0	2.0	2.0	1.7
1	2.5	2.9	3.4	2.3
2	3.6	4.6	5.2	2.9
3	4.9	5.7	6.7	3.6
4	6.1	6.9	8.0	4.3
5	7.3	8.0	9.2	5.0
6	8.1	8.9	10.3	5.7
7	8.9	9.7	11.1	6.5
8	9.7	10.6	11.8	7.2
9	10.5	11.5	12.7	7.9
10	11.3	12.2	13.5	8.6
12	12.9	13.4	15.2	10.0
14	14.4	14.6	16.9	11.4
16	16.0	15.8	18.7	12.8
18	17.6	17.0	20.4	14.2
20	19.2	18.2	22.1	15.6
22	20.8	19.4	23.8	17.0
24	22.4	20.6	25.5	18.4
26	24.0	21.8	27.3	19.8
28	25.5	23.1	29.0	21.2
30	27.1	24.3	30.7	22.7

Wt. Allowance: Wt. (lb.) Up to	Factor	Constant TMU
2.5	0	0
7.5	1.06	2.2
12.5	1.11	3.9
17.5	1.17	5.6
22.5	1.22	7.4
27.5	1.28	9.1
32.5	1.33	10.8
37.5	1.39	12.5
42.5	1.44	14.3
47.5	1.50	16.0

CASE AND DESCRIPTION
A Move object to other hand or against stop.
B Move object to approximate or indefinite location.
C Move object to exact location.

TABLE III—TURN AND APPLY PRESSURE—T AND AP

Weight	30°	45°	60°	75°	90°	105°	120°	135°	150°	165°	180°
	Time TMU for Degrees Turned										
Small— 0 to 2 Pounds	2.8	3.5	4.1	4.8	5.4	6.1	6.8	7.4	8.1	8.7	9.4
Medium—2.1 to 10 Pounds	4.4	5.5	6.5	7.5	8.5	9.6	10.6	11.6	12.7	13.7	14.8
Large— 10.1 to 35 Pounds	8.4	10.5	12.3	14.4	16.2	18.3	20.4	22.2	24.3	26.1	28.2

APPLY PRESSURE CASE 1—16.2 TMU. APPLY PRESSURE CASE 2—10.6 TMU

TABLE IV—GRASP—G

Case	Time TMU	DESCRIPTION
1A	2.0	**Pick Up Grasp**—Small, medium or large object by itself, easily grasped.
1B	3.5	Very small object or object lying close against a flat surface.
1C1	7.3	Interference with grasp on bottom and one side of nearly cylindrical object. Diameter larger than ½″.
1C2	8.7	Interference with grasp on bottom and one side of nearly cylindrical object. Diameter ¼″ to ½″.
1C3	10.8	Interference with grasp on bottom and one side of nearly cylindrical object. Diameter less than ¼″.
2	5.6	**Regrasp.**
3	5.6	**Transfer Grasp.**
4A	7.3	Object jumbled with other objects so search and select occur. Larger than 1″ x 1″ x 1″.
4B	9.1	Object jumbled with other objects so search and select occur. ¼″ x ¼″ x ⅛″ to 1″ x 1″ x 1″.
4C	12.9	Object jumbled with other objects so search and select occur. Smaller than ¼″ x ¼″ x ⅛″.
5	0	Contact, sliding or hook grasp.

TABLE V—POSITION*—P

CLASS OF FIT		Symmetry	Easy To Handle	Difficult To Handle
1—Loose	No pressure required	S	5.6	11.2
		SS	9.1	14.7
		NS	10.4	16.0
2—Close	Light pressure required	S	16.2	21.8
		SS	19.7	25.3
		NS	21.0	26.6
3—Exact	Heavy pressure required.	S	43.0	48.6
		SS	46.5	52.1
		NS	47.8	53.4

*Distance moved to engage—1″ or less.

TABLE 14-1 (Continued)

TABLE VI—RELEASE—RL

Case	Time TMU	DESCRIPTION
1	2.0	Normal release performed by opening fingers as independent motion.
2	0	Contact Release.

TABLE VII—DISENGAGE—D

CLASS OF FIT	Easy to Handle	Difficult to Handle
1—Loose—Very slight effort, blends with subsequent move.	4.0	5.7
2—Close — Normal effort, slight recoil.	7.5	11.8
3—Tight — Considerable effort, hand recoils markedly.	22.9	34.7

TABLE VIII—EYE TRAVEL TIME AND EYE FOCUS—ET AND EF

Eye Travel Time $= 15.2 \times \frac{T}{D}$ **TMU,** with a maximum value of 20 TMU.

where T = the distance between points from and to which the eye travels.
D = the perpendicular distance from the eye to the line of travel T.

Eye Focus Time = 7.3 TMU.

TABLE IX—BODY, LEG AND FOOT MOTIONS

DESCRIPTION	SYMBOL	DISTANCE	TIME TMU
Foot Motion—Hinged at Ankle.	FM	Up to 4″	8.5
With heavy pressure.	FMP		19.1
Leg or Foreleg Motion.	LM —	Up to 6″	7.1
		Each add'l. inch	1.2
Sidestep—Case 1—Complete when leading leg contacts floor.	SS-C1	Less than 12″	Use REACH or MOVE Time
		12″	17.0
		Each add'l. inch	.6
Case 2—Lagging leg must contact floor before next motion can be made.	SS-C2	12″	34.1
		Each add'l. inch	1.1
Bend, Stoop, or Kneel on One Knee.	B,S,KOK		29.0
Arise.	AB,AS,AKOK		31.9
Kneel on Floor—Both Knees.	KBK		69.4
Arise.	AKBK		76.7
Sit.	SIT		34.7
Stand from Sitting Position.	STD		43.4
Turn Body 45 to 90 degrees— Case 1—Complete when leading leg contacts floor.	TBC1		18.6
Case 2—Lagging leg must contact floor before next motion can be made.	TBC2		37.2
Walk.	W-FT.	Per Foot	5.3
Walk.	W-P	Per Pace	15.0

TABLE X—SIMULTANEOUS MOTIONS

MOTION	CASE	REACH				MOVE						GRASP					POSITION						DISENGAGE	
		A,E	B	C,D		A,Bm		B		C		G1A G2 G5	G1B G1C		G4		P1S		P1SS P2S		P1NS P2SS P2NS		D1E D1D	D2	
				W*	O	W*	O	W*	O	W*	O		W*	O	W*	O	E**	D	E**	D	E**	D		E**	D
REACH	A,E	□	□	□	□	□	□	□	□	⊠	⊠	□	□	□	□	□	□	□	□	⊠	⊠	⊠	□	□	□
	B		□	□	⊠	□	□	□	⊠	⊠	■	□	□	⊠	⊠	■	⊠	⊠	⊠	■	■	■	□	□	⊠
	C,D			□	⊠	⊠	■	⊠	■	■	■	□	⊠	■	■	■	■	■	■	■	■	■	⊠	■	■
MOVE	A,Bm					□	□	□	□	□	□	□	□	□	□	□	□	□	□	⊠	⊠	⊠	□	□	□
	B							□	□	□	□	□	□	⊠	⊠	■	⊠	⊠	⊠	■	■	■	□	□	⊠
	C									⊠	■	□	⊠	■	■	■	■	■	■	■	■	■	⊠	■	■
GRASP	G1A, G2, G3											□	□	□	□	□	□	□	□	■	■	■	□	■	■
	G1B, G1C												■	■	⊠	■	■	■	■	■	■	■	■	■	■
	G4														■	■	■	■	■	■	■	■	■	■	■
POSITION	P1S																⊠	■	■	■	■	■	■	■	■
	P1SS, P2S																		■	■	■	■	■	■	■
	P1NS, P2SS, P2NS																				■	■	■	■	■
DISENGAGE	D1E, D1D																						□	□	□
	D2																							□	□

□ EASY to perform simultaneously.

⊠ Can be performed simultaneously with PRACTICE

■ DIFFICULT to perform simultaneously even after long practice. Allow both times.

MOTIONS NOT INCLUDED IN ABOVE TABLE

TURN—Normally EASY with all motions except when TURN is controlled or with DISENGAGE.
APPLY PRESSURE—May be EASY, PRACTICE, OR DIFFICULT. Each case must be analyzed.
POSITION—Class 3—Always DIFFICULT.
DISENGAGE—Class 3—Normally DIFFICULT.
RELEASE—Always EASY.
DISENGAGE—Any class may be DIFFICULT if care must be exercised to avoid injury or damage to object.

*W=Within the area of normal vision.
O=Outside the area of normal vision.
**E=EASY to handle.
D=DIFFICULT to handle.

Methods-Time Measurement—MTM—is a system originally established by Messrs. Maynard, Stegemerten and Schwab [8] for developing work methods and obtaining work standards. These authors say that MTM is a procedure which analyzes any manual operation and breaks it into the basic motions required to perform it, and which assigns to each basic motion a predetermined time standard which is a function of the nature of the motion and the conditions under which it is made. MTM consists of a concise catalogue of work motions with a table of time values for each. This catalogue divides all work motions into the following basic groups:

1. Reach
2. Move
3. Grasp
4. Turn
5. Position
6. Disengage
7. Release
8. Apply pressure
9. Body, leg, eye, and foot motions

Each of these basic motions is further divided into a number of classes and cases, and a table of time values furnishes a value for each class and case.

The procedure for using MTM can be summarized in two major steps. First, all motions required to perform the operation must be analyzed, classified, measured, and recorded. Secondly, the corresponding MTM time values are selected from the tables, applied to the analysis and totaled. A more elaborate outline of the MTM procedure includes the following steps:

—analyze every motion used in the operations
—identify then classify each motion used
—record each motion identified
—establish distances, adjust for "assisting motions"
—determine which motions are "limited"
—select time values from MTM tables
—total time for all motions in the operation
—add to total time allowances for fatigue, personnel, etc.

The proponents of MTM claim that the key to successful results with MTM is sound and thorough training, and that a period of guided application will shorten the time required by a trainee to reach an acceptable level of proficiency in analyzing operations. This training is conducted by special consulting firms that are members of the MTM Association for Standards and Research.

These firms maintain that MTM has many uses, among which is an improved procedure for handling these four industrial problems:

1. *Selection of Efficient Methods in the Planning Stages*

The MTM procedure has simplified the investigation of alternative methods for performing an operation before production is started. It provides a very accurate guide for developing and selecting the most practical and efficient method and allows for training of the operators in the proper procedure at the outset.

2. *Simplified Methods Training for Operators and Supervisors*

Detailed MTM motion analyses help operators to learn new operations more

[8] See H. B. Maynard, G. J. Stegemerten & J. L. Schwab, *Methods-Time Measurement*, (New York: McGraw-Hill Book Co., Inc., 1948).

rapidly. These analyses go a long way toward preventing operators from developing inefficient habit patterns which later must be corrected. It has been found that when a new operation is explained in terms of MTM motions and times, the operators acquire a better understanding of the nature and requirements of the job.

Supervisors trained in the use of MTM realize more fully the effect of good methods on costs. Ineffective motion sequences are easily detected by an MTM trained observer; he sees them almost automatically and plans for their elimination.

3. *Establishing Accurate Production Standards*

MTM makes it possible to establish accurate time standards for manual operations without the use of a stop watch. This eliminates the pressure imposed on workers who become nervous when being clocked. One of the most significant advantages of MTM is its speed in setting production and wage incentive standards. Often standards can be set with MTM in from 25%–50% of the time required to set standards by conventional time study methods.

4. *Securing Acceptance by Labor*

Acceptance of MTM by several labor groups has been an outstanding feature. It is felt that the following factors contribute to this acceptance:

—published data which has been independently checked and substantiated by research groups
—simplicity of application
—elimination or reduction of the use of a stop watch
—elimination of performance rating
—objectivity compared with the relatively subjective approach of stop watch studies.

Case D:

Central States Steel Company

A Method of Setting Performance Standards for Production Workers. The Central States Steel Company has had a well-developed industrial engineering program in effect for many years. This program has three objectives: (a) the study and improvement of production methods; (b) the setting of standards for worker performance; and (c) the exercise of cost control. In conjunction with the union which represents the company's production workers, the industrial engineering department has developed a procedure for establishing performance standards which is described in the following paragraphs.

Fundamentally, this procedure is a means of giving practical expression to the basic principle that "the employee is entitled to a fair day's pay in return for which the company is entitled to a fair day's work, and any performance above that 100 per cent standard is to be compensated in direct proportion, i.e. a performance of 125% of standard will be compensated at 125% of base pay." As a starting point, the industrial engineering department evaluated each job or occupation in the plant and then classified it into one of the more than thirty job classes. This established the base hourly rate for each job or occupation. Union agreement was obtained for each such job classification.

The 100 per cent standard, or the performance measure for a fair day's work for any job, is comprised of four factors: (a) work time, during which the individual actually exerts physical, mental, or visual effort; (b) attention time, during which the individual must be fully attentive to the machine, process, or operation; (c) a proper allowance for rest and personal needs; and (d) idle time, during which, by reason of the inherent nature of the job, the individual can perform no work or is not required to be attentive, and hence may relax; to this portion of a cycle time a 5 per cent allowance is added for personal needs. Factor (d), idle time, may range from zero to a substantial portion of an operation cycle. Those jobs in which there is no process, equipment, or other operating limitation, and thus no idle time, are termed unrestricted jobs. For unrestricted jobs, the standards are set at a level which will permit a sustained performance opportunity for an average or normal worker of 135 per cent, i.e., 35 per cent above the standard for a fair day's work measurement. For restricted jobs, the same 135 per cent performance opportunity is provided, but is applied only to that part of the job cycle which is comprised of factors (a) and (b); *viz.*, work time plus attention time.

To determine a performance standard, the Industrial Engineering Department has adopted a time study practice which can best be explained by giving an actual example. The operation, an unrestricted job, was packaging stacks of tin sheets for shipment. These sheets are used principally for the manufacture of tin cans and must reach the customer without damage in transit. Thus rugged and fully protective packaging must be provided.

As the tin sheets come out of the tinning process, whether by the hot-dip or electrolytic method, they are automatically piled on wooden pallets. These pallets serve as the bottom of the ultimate package and are equipped with five-inch runners so that fork lift trucks can handle the stacks. Tin sheets are produced in a wide range of sizes and gauges, and in several thicknesses of coating. The package unit is known in the trade as a "bundle," which, depending upon the size and gauge of the tin plate, varies somewhat in weight and over-all dimensions. The dimensions of a typical bundle are 25 inches wide, 29 inches long, and 15 inches high.

A bundle or stack of sheets on its pallet is transported from the tinning line by fork-lift truck and placed on the floor of the adjacent packaging area. The actual packaging operation is shown in some detail in Table 14-2, but essentially it involves forming a heavy pre-cut fibre carton around the stack of sheets, placing protective steel angles at each corner, and tightly wiring the angles to the bundle to form the completed package.

TABLE 14-2

PERFORMANCE STANDARD

Operation: packaging tin sheets
Unit: base box or bundle
Supplies: fibre protection pads
paper liners
fibre corner pads
steel angles
fibre covers
strapping wires—pre-cut to required length

TABLE 14-2 (*Continued*)

Portable hand tools: leather mallet
wire cutters
Griplock machine (for tighting or cinching wires around bundle)

Job class: No. 4 with a base rate of $1.55 per hour.

SUMMARY OF BASIC ELEMENTS

Description of Operation	*Standard Minutes Per Bundle*
1. Select and deliver to bundle one fibre protection pad and one full paper liner.	.468
2. Open, position, and fold paper liner over bundle.	.645
3. Select and deliver to bundle two horizontal wires.	.179
4. Form loop in horizontal wires and place around bundle.	.519
5. Select and deliver to bundle four corner angles and four corner fibre pads.	.365
6. Place corner angles and fibre pads under wires on bundle; tighten wires with Griplock machine.	2.166
7. Select and deliver to bundle four vertical wires.	.370
8. Thread four vertical wires through and parallel to runners of platform.	.873
9. Select and deliver to bundle one stenciled cardboard cover.	.154
10. Fold cover and place over bundle, pull wires up over top of bundle, and tighten wires by hand.	1.078
11. Select and deliver to bundle four top angles and four bottom angles.	.427
12. Place top and bottom angles under wires on bundle and complete wiring.	3.529
13. Obtain a supply of wires, fibre pads, and so forth, sufficient for one turn (shift).	.453
Total Standard Minutes	11.226
Total Standard Hours	.187

The process of setting the performance standard for packaging tin plate began with a series of detailed time studies made upon six different workers to observe various methods used, to improve methods including work place arrangement, and to determine the standard method. After physical changes had been made in the work place arrangement, and after the workers had learned the standard method, sixteen detailed time studies, each running from two to three hours, were taken of a number of different workers at various times during the day, and by two different time-study engineers. Finally, a detailed time study was made on one worker for an entire eight-hour shift to observe what, if any, outside interference might normally occur, such as delays in lift truck service, interruptions in work flow, or failure to have packaging supplies available.

During the first exploratory series of detailed time studies the elemental operations and their proper sequence were determined. There actually were sixty-two separate elemental operations involved in the complete packaging cycle. These elements formed the basis for the second series of time studies, including the eight-hour study. The time study engineers used the continuous method of stop-watch reading, and as each elemental time was recorded the elemental operation as performed was pace rated or speed rated. Later on, allowance for rest and personal needs was determined individually for each elemental operation. The actual time-study sheet had columns in which to record for each element the running time taken from the stop watch, the elapsed time, and the pace rating. When all of the detailed time studies were completed, the performance standard was calculated in the following series of steps:

(a) elapsed times were obtained for each element in every times cycle in each individual time study;

(b) each elapsed elemental time was converted to normal time by applying the pace rating, e.g., an elapsed elemental time of 1.2 minutes which had been performed at a pace of 125 per cent would have a normal elemental time of 1.5 minutes;

(c) the average of normal times was computed for each element; times which were substantially high or low were excluded from the averages only if they could be regarded as abnormalities resulting from some entirely irregular or foreign occurrence;

(d) the averaged normal elemental times taken from all of the individual time studies were averaged element by element, and to these times were added the predetermined allowances for rest and personal needs to derive the standard time for each element;

(e) natural groupings of small elements were made to establish basic elements; the sixty-two elemental operations were grouped into thirteen basic elements comprising from one to ten small elements; only the thirteen basic elements are shown in Table 14-2;

(f) the total of the thirteen basic elemental times gave the standard time for the operation;

(g) standard time in minutes was converted into standard hours to derive the final performance standard of .187 hours per bundle as shown in Table 14-2.

All pertinent information concerning the standard was assembled in an "Incentive Application Form" according to regular practice. Before the standard could be introduced, this form had to have the signed approval of the following executives: foreman of the department, general superintendent of the plant, vice president of operations, director of industrial relations, chief industrial engineer, and comptroller.

Prior to the establishment of the standard, the sixty or more workers on the packaging operation had been turning out about eighteen bundles per day per worker. When all of the work-place improvements had been completed over the entire packaging area and all of the workers had learned the new method, the usual rate review meetings of line supervisors and grievancemen were held. Since these meetings brought out no facts indicating lack of fairness in the rates, the standard was introduced. Daily production, however, rose only to an average of about twenty-two bundles per day per worker. It continued to fluctuate about this production rate for several months, as shown by the table (Table 14-3), despite the fact that the standard called

TABLE 14-3

PACKAGING PERFORMANCE—BUNDLES PER MAN DAY

Month	*Average Bundles Per Man Day*
January	18.0
February	18.0
March	20.0
April	19.0
May	20.0
June	19.5
July	20.0
August	20.0
September	25.0

N.B. Incentive plan introduced on June 12.

for 42.8 bundles as a fair day's performance and the expected normal performance on an incentive basis was 58 bundles per man day. Moreover, the workers had not filed a grievance regarding the standard although the union contract included a provision that grievance action could be initiated any time between 30 and 60 days after a rate installation. The tin mill was operating at capacity and the backlog of orders assured full scale operation for an indefinite period ahead. In fact, the company had decided to double the capacity as soon as all plans could be completed.[9]

[9] Paul E. Holden and Frank K. Shallenberger, *Selected Case Problems in Industrial Management* (Englewood Cliffs, N. J.: Prentice-Hall, Inc., © 1953), pp. 186–191.

15

Economic Analysis in Business Decisions

In the last few decades there has been a growing interest in economic analysis in business decisions. In a sense managers have always been economists, for they have been concerned with optimizing their objectives with the scarce means at their disposal. However, many management decisions have fallen far short of what might have been achieved with a more careful application of economic concepts.

Originally economics did not aim at business application. Economists have been concerned primarily with social issues: tax policy, tariff policy, price control, and the impact of monopoly. A great deal of economic theory appears at first to be too abstract and too dependent on simplifying assumptions to be of much business use. Nevertheless, just as some of the most abstract theory in the natural sciences has proved to be of the most practical significance, so the indifference curves, the propensities and elasticities of the economists may supplant many of the rules of thumb that managers have long accepted as the essence of practicality. This chapter will concentrate on economic concepts that have already proved themselves in clarifying business problems.

There is a close relationship between the growing use of economic analysis in business and the expansion of quantitative and mathematical approaches. The business economists and the operations research workers have the same objective—a more systematic and logical approach to decision-making. Therefore, it is no surprise that they have developed similar methods and similar conclusions. This chapter and those that follow emphasize these new analytical tools, not so much because they are in wide use today (in fact only few firms use them systematically), but because they promise to be important for the management of tomorrow.

Basic Cost Concepts

Orientation to the future

The first principle is that economics (and business decisions if they are aimed at reaching optimum positions) is concerned with the *future* rather than the *past.* The original cost of an asset, for example, may have little to do with the present value of that asset, and may be of little significance today in making a decision affecting operations in the future.

This view is not a new one. The expressions "let bygones be bygone" and "don't cry over spilt milk" are ancient recognitions of the fallacy of permitting the past to blind us in achieving better decisions in the future. To take an extreme case, if a firm spent $100,000 last month for a machine that proves to be useless (to the firm or to anyone else) this month, the best thing to do is forget the mistake and attempt to do better in the future. The past should influence present decisions in two ways only: first, we learn from our past failures and successes to make better decisions; and secondly, income taxes in the future will depend on past payments made for assets. The point to remember, however, is that decisions should try to get the most out of future outlays, not to cover up past mistakes. Only those costs not yet incurred are important to a business decision.

The definition of costs and profits

The second basic idea in business economics is that the definition of the terms *cost* and *profits* must be adapted to the particular problem at hand. What may be a cost for one decision may not be for another. This implies that accounting cost data must be adjusted to fit the particular decision.

Clearly this way of looking at costs and profits involves judgment on the part of the economist or decision-maker. The disadvantage is that one observer may reach a different conclusion from another, whereas in the usual financial accounting practice, the amount of personal judgment is limited by a series of conventions accepted by the accounting profession. However, allowance for judgment is not a disadvantage if the problem is one concerning an uncertain future for which exact measurements are not possible. Judgment can be improved by good analysis.

What is the meaning of *cost* according to the business economist? Cost is a sacrifice; in measuring costs, we are attempting to measure the extent of the sacrifices involved in particular decisions. Business decisions are based on measuring the benefits to be derived from those decisions against the sacrifices (costs) incurred. If benefits outweigh sacrifices, the decision is favorable; if not, the company should decide against the proposal or should seek a better alternative.

The $100,000 machine mentioned earlier, illustrates the point under discussion. If that machine is worthless today, no real future sacrifice is made by abandoning it; the fact that $100,000 was paid for it last month involves no sacrifice today because the mistake has already been made, and the loss incurred. On the other hand, if a company has paid $1.00 for a machine which today proves to be extremely valuable, the sacrifice in selling the machine may be quite large. Again, the tax considerations complicate such decisions, since the tax collector is interested in what such assets originally cost. However, at this stage it is best to avoid tax considerations and focus on fundamentals; once the basic ideas are understood, adjustments can be made for taxes.

If the concept of *cost* is entirely concerned with sacrifies, what meaning can be attached to the term *profits?* In this volume, the concern does not lie with the problem of recording profits which is one of the central interests of accounting. The recording of income—that is the issuance of profit and loss statements which tell whether the income of some past period has been high or low—is a different matter from making decisions which will optimize profits in the future. Therefore, this chapter is not concerned with profits in the sense used in accounting. It is concerned with the profitability of decisions affecting the future. To maximize profits, the principle is to make those decisions which will bring in the largest benefits (revenues) in relation to sacrifices (costs). This same principle applies to any company, whether it is already making large profits or losing money in the accounting sense.

The profitability of operating at a loss

How is it possible for operations at a loss to be profitable? The apparent paradox is easily cleared up. Two sets of concepts of cost and of profit-and-loss are confused: the economist's concepts and the accountant's concepts. The accountant may find that a department is operating at a loss, after deducting those items he recognizes as costs from the departmental revenues. The economist may find, however, that certain of these "costs" do not involve sacrifices and, as far as the future profitability of the department is concerned, do not require inclusion. Since these distinctions may at first be confusing to the reader, a simple illustration will clarify the issues.

A company has five departments, one of them devoted to producing toy rockets for children. The machinery in this department is highly specialized, suited only to producing such rockets. The department is showing a loss. The revenues are $60,000 per year; the costs charged against the department are $70,000, indicating a loss of $10,000. It appears that the department should be closed, but a fuller analysis may raise doubts about such a conclusion. A breakdown of costs reveals the following:

Direct materials	$20,000
Direct labor	20,000
Departmental overhead (including depreciation on the machinery)	20,000
General administrative expenses (a part of the over-all company expenses that have been allocated to this department)	10,000
	$70,000

The figures are simple for purposes of illustration. The question is whether all of these costs are true economic costs which should be taken into account in deciding whether to abandon the department. There is little question about direct materials: they involve an actual cash outlay to suppliers, and thus do mean a sacrifice; these costs could be avoided by closing the department. The same is probably true for direct labor: if the employees can be laid off, the sacrifice in cash wages can be avoided. The central issue pertains to the overhead and administrative costs. A large part of the departmental overhead may consist of depreciation on this specialized machinery. However, if this machinery is useless to any other kind of production or to any other company, no sacrifice is involved in its continued use, and thus the depreciation should be disallowed as an expense. In other words, the cost of such machinery is "sunk" or "unavoidable"; these costs will run on whether the department operates or not; they are irrelevant to the decision.

Similar reasoning can apply to a large proportion of the administrative expenses. These expenses may include the salaries of the president and other top officials and will continue even if the department is abandoned. The same may be true of depreciation on the buildings. Other expenses may decline with abandonment of the department, but not by the full amount charged against the department. When the costs that involve a sacrifice are added, we may find that they add to only, let us say, $53,000. In other words, there are $53,000 of expenses which could be avoided if the department were closed. However, since this would mean a loss of $60,000 in revenue, the company would be better off keeping the department. It will be more profitable to operate the department as long as revenues cover costs, after elimination of the so-called costs that do not fall into the economist's definition of that term.

The analysis in this section can be summarized in a simple rule: a company should continue an operation as long as the revenues cover the variable (incremental) costs and make some contribution to fixed costs. This introduces some new terms which will be defined in the following sections.

Before leaving this illustration, however, it should be pointed out that the department under consideration should be transferred to more profitable operations if they are available. The assumption made above is that no such opportunities are available; if they were, the measurement of sacrifices (costs) would require an adjustment. This introduces the important concept of opportunity costs (sometimes known as alternative costs) which also will be the subject of a later section.

The distinction between fixed and variable costs

Businessmen, accountants, and economists have long recognized the distinction between fixed and variable costs. Fixed costs are those costs which run on as a total regardless of the level of output. An example would be depreciation on machinery, usually charged off by the accountants whether production is high or low. From one point of view these are not actually costs, since they continue whether or not the machines are in use. Variable costs are those costs which increase in proportion to output; the larger the volume of production, the greater total these costs become.

The concepts of fixed and variable costs are "short run" concepts. That is, they apply in the short run when it is possible to vary some inputs used in production (such as materials and usually direct labor), but not others (such as the size of the plant and the amount of machinery). In the long run, it is possible to vary all inputs, so that there is no distinction between fixed and variable costs. This section is concerned with short run decisions—whether to increase or decrease the volume of output with given facilities.

To make certain that these concepts are understood, it is desirable to point out that fixed costs *per unit* decline as output increases; the costs are spread over a larger number of units of output. Businessmen refer to this fact by speaking of "spreading the overhead." Variable costs do not change in the same way with changes in output. In fact, in many industries variable costs may be fairly constant *per unit;* in other words, as a total they increase in almost exact proportion to output. In traditional economic analysis, average variable costs have been assumed to fall at first (due to certain efficiencies permitted by specialization at greater outputs), and then to rise (because of diminishing returns as more variable inputs are combined with the fixed inputs). These considerations result in the typical cost curves that appear in economics textbooks. Figure 15-1 illustrates such a curve.

The diagram shows a continual decline in average fixed costs as output increases. The average variable cost curve, on the other hand, is U-shaped, falling at first and then rising. The average total cost curve is simply a sum of the other two curves—it also has a U-shape.

Statistical studies of cost curves in manufacturing have raised doubts about whether unit costs always fall and rise as illustrated in the traditional textbook diagrams. There is no question about the fixed costs; by definition these must decline as shown. The question is whether in some industries variable costs may not be fairly constant per unit—up to full capacity whatever that point may be. However, this is not the moment to review the controversy over the measurement of such cost curves. The point here is that

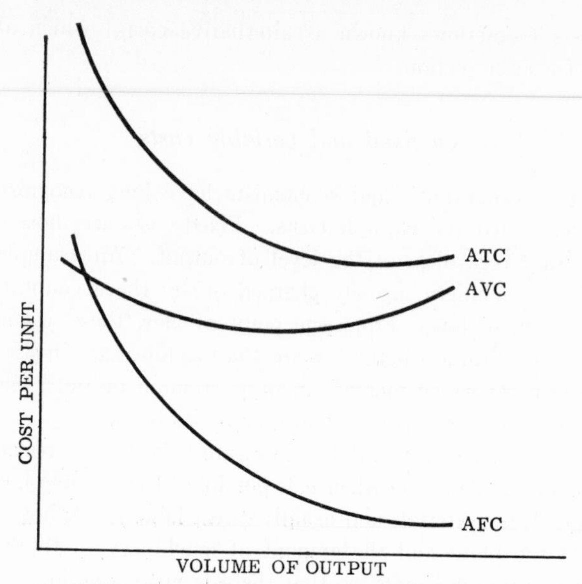

FIGURE 15-1 The Relation of Average Costs and Output

in some businesses it may be appropriate to assume constant average variable costs up to capacity (though even here questions of overtime and extra shifts must be faced). In the drawing of breakeven charts this assumption is usually made.

Breakeven charts

Once the distinction between fixed costs and variable costs is clear, the construction of breakeven charts is a relatively simple matter. Breakeven charts differ from the cost diagram just discussed in that they show both cost and revenue; they differ also in that they show the total costs for the whole output, not unit costs. Figure 15-2 illustrates a typical breakeven chart.

The chart indicates that fixed costs do not change as a total with changes in output. Variable costs are shown to rise in proportion to output. By showing such costs rising along a straight line, it is assumed that average variable costs remain the same at different levels of output. It would not be difficult to draw a chart consistent with a U-shaped cost curve, but this is not usually done in business practice.

The typical breakeven chart assumes that the price of the product is given, so that the total revenue curve becomes a straight line sloping diagonally upward to the right. The breakeven point itself is the point at which the total revenue covers both the fixed and variable costs. To the left of this point, the revenue falls short of total costs; to the right, there remains a profit above total costs. The breakeven point itself is not as important as

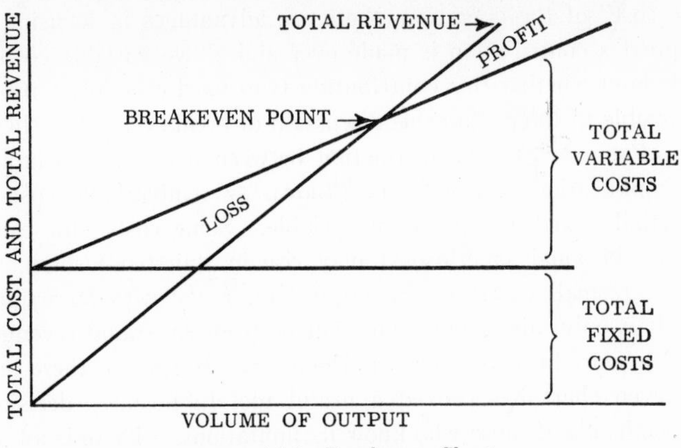

FIGURE 15-2 Breakeven Chart

the name of this type of graph might indicate. The important factor is the estimate of the profits or losses possible at high or low levels of output. The diagram indicates what most businessmen consider one of the determinants of profits: the expansion of sales and output to get full use of fixed facilities.

A redrawing of the breakeven chart will make it more consistent with this discussion. Instead of drawing in the fixed costs first and then adding the variable costs to the fixed costs, the opposite procedure can be followed. This form of the chart is shown in Figure 15-3.

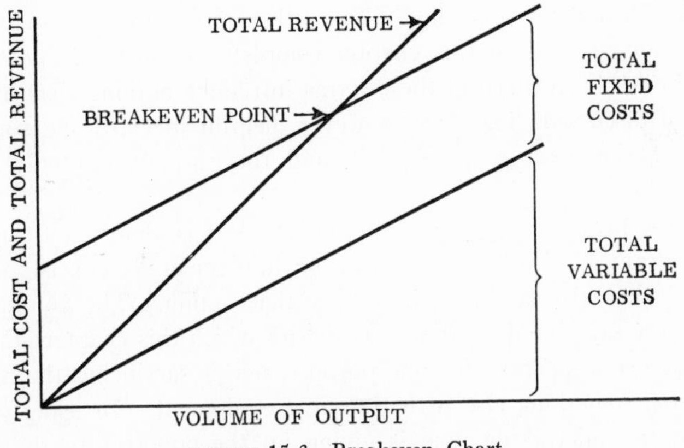

FIGURE 15-3 Breakeven Chart

The advantage of this form is that it shows at each level of output the *contribution of total revenue to fixed costs and profits.* The vertical distance between the total revenue line and the variable cost line shows the extent to which the company is succeeding in meeting its variable expenses and contributing to overhead and profits. Since, as has already been explained, there is some doubt that fixed costs (sunk costs) should be included in the "true economic cost" of the operation, there are advantages in focusing attention on how great a contribution is made over and above variable costs, without worrying about whether this contribution is to fixed costs or to profits.

It is possible to complicate this discussion of breakeven charts in a number of ways. For example, the distinction between fixed and variable costs is an oversimplification. Some costs (known as semivariable costs) are no doubt partially fixed and partially variable. Some costs (for example the salaries of additional supervisors) may rise in stairstep fashion, remaining constant over small variations in output, but rising with large increases in output. It is only fair to point out that both expenses and revenues can be influenced by variables not shown on the chart. In spite of these limitations, the breakeven chart has proved a useful tool in business decisions, especially in the hands of those who know its limitations. There is an advantage in a device that cuts through complications to get at fundamental relationships; there is also the danger that such a simplification may direct attention to only part of the problem, to the exclusion of other equally important considerations.

Opportunity costs

The reader may feel that enough cost concepts have been introduced and that any further variations will complicate the subject beyond comprehension. However, a large number of other terms are used both in business practice and in the theoretical literature. Two other terms are necessary to make the discussion of costs in this chapter complete—*opportunity costs* and *incremental costs*. In a sense, these terms introduce nothing that has not already been discussed. They are, however, helpful in clarifying some points that need to be made more explicit, and they are undoubtedly useful in decision-making.

The concept opportunity cost (alternative cost) is almost self-explanatory. The cost of any kind of action or decision fundamentally consists of the opportunities that are sacrificed in taking that action. The concept simply returns to the sacrifice definition of cost with which this chapter started. In deciding to use a machine for one purpose, one is sacrificing the alternative of producing something else with the same equipment. In using one's cash to finance an undertaking, one is giving up the opportunity to invest the money in stocks and bonds. Each possibility must be compared with alternative opportunities.

To return to the illustration of the $100,000 machine that appeared earlier in the chapter, the reason that the machine may involve no expense in the future is that its use involves no sacrifice—it is perfectly useless for any other purpose. The opportunity cost is zero and in this case, this is the true measure of the sacrifice involved in its application. On the other hand, the machine costing $1.00 in the past, may be expensive in the sense that if it is used for one purpose it cannot be used for another; valuable alternative uses are sacrificed.

Recognition of the opportunity cost concept may draw attention to certain costs not reflected in the accounts. Such costs are sometimes known as *implicit* or *imputed* costs, since they do not explicity appear in the profit-and-loss statement. For example, if one sets up a corner grocery store as a sole proprietorship, he should recognize that he has given up the opportunity to earn an income elsewhere; this is one of the costs of his grocery business, even though it is not explicitly included as a cost in his accounts. Similarly, the interest or profits he could earn by investing the money tied up in the grocery business in bonds or other assets are really costs, even though they are not deductible for income tax purposes.

This point can be stated in a simple rule: If an alternative opportunity is sacrificed there is a cost; if there is no sacrifice, there is no cost. In the next chapter, applications of such thinking should clear away any confusion remaining in the reader's mind.

Incremental cost

The next concept, that of incremental cost, is closely related to the economist's *marginal cost*. Marginal cost may be defined as the addition to total cost resulting from producing *one more unit*. Incremental cost may be defined as the addition to total cost resulting from a particular decision. Both are concerned with changes in total cost. The term incremental cost is more widely used in business for reasons that are clear. First of all, businesses are concerned with more than increasing or decreasing the level of output. For example, in purchasing a new labor-saving machine, what is wanted is a measurement of the prospective savings in cost (reduction in total cost) resulting from that machine. Secondly, even if the issue is one of increasing or decreasing output, businessmen normally think in terms of increases or decreases of a substantial percentage rather than by a single unit. The incremental cost concept is a more flexible tool, though in some respects a cruder one than marginal costs.

The types of business problems to which the incremental cost concept is applicable are without number. A few illustrations will suffice to indicate the wide applicability of the concept.

1. A firm with idle facilities might investigate the possibility that a special order at below the usual price could cover the incremental costs and make a contribution to overhead and profit. In evaluating such a proposal, the management should make certain that the additional revenue from such a sale is itself entirely incremental and does not damage the regular sales of the company. Again, such business should not be taken if there are more profitable ways of using the facilities.
2. A firm considering a reduction in price should compare the incremental cost

of the additional output it will sell with the additional revenue, taking into account that some revenue will be lost through the reduction in price itself.

3. A passenger airline with idle space on many of its planes might consider whether some cargo shipped in that idle space would bring in added revenue which would more than cover the incremental costs involved. In such a case, the incremental costs should be low because the planes will fly anyway and there will be few added costs in including the cargo.

4. A company facing the decision to make or buy, that is, to manufacture a part itself or buy on the outside, should compare the incremental cost of manufacture (rather than the full cost) with the outside price. Other considerations would enter into such a decision, of course, such as supplier dependability, and company know-how, but the relevant cost concept is the incremental one.

5. A utility attempting to sell off-peak services (it being a serious problem in most utilities that consumption of such services is not steady, leaving considerable idle capacity) should investigate whether special rates or other attractions to off-peak use will bring in revenues which will more than cover incremental costs.

These illustrations should make the reader aware of the wide applicability of the concept. The term is used frequently in large business, and while it is less known in small business, it is much more widely applied than businessmen realize. Perhaps the illustrations selected are unfortunate in that they imply that incremental reasoning necessarily leads to low prices. There is, in fact, nothing inconsistent between incremental reasoning and charging "what the traffic will bear." This point will be developed later when demand considerations are taken up.

Before leaving the subject of incremental costs, a discussion of overhead (or burden) is in order. Accountants have long been faced with the problem of the allocation of overhead costs over the various departments and products of a company. The usual solution is to allocate such costs on some preselected basis, such as direct labor costs, direct labor hours, machine time, or floor space. While such allocations may be desirable for accounting purposes, they may be misleading in making decisions. For example, if the question is one of replacing one machine with another that uses less labor time, there may be a temptation to apply the overhead allocation percentage to the savings in labor cost. Let us suppose that the savings in direct labor amount to $10,000 per year and that overhead is allocated at 75 per cent of direct labor costs. It would be wrong to assume that there will be a $7,500 saving in overhead. The only way to ascertain the actual saving in overhead is to examine the various items of expense that are included, and to estimate how these will be affected by the decision. In the case just illustrated, it could well be that there will be no actual savings in overhead—the incremental saving consists entirely in a saving in labor cost with no change in overhead. The example helps support the claim made earlier in the chapter that cost concepts must be adapted to the particular use. "Tailor-made" costs must be substituted for arbitrary cost allocations, useful in some cases but not in others.

A Review of Cost Concepts

The discussion in this chapter has introduced a wide variety of cost concepts. Writers on business economics have drawn up tables, pairing each concept with its opposite. Table 15-1 presents such a table incorporating the concepts discussed in this chapter. Many other pairs could be introduced into the table, but this would carry the discussion beyond the scope of this volume.

TABLE 15-1

VARIOUS COST CONCEPTS IMPORTANT IN BUSINESS DECISIONS

Concept	*Its Antithesis*	*Purpose of the Distinction*
Implicit costs	Explicit costs	To assure full recognition of opportunity costs whether or not explicitly recognized in the accounts.
Variable costs	Fixed costs	To separate those costs that vary with output from those that do not.
Incremental costs	Sunk costs	To separate those costs affected by the decision from those which run on as before.
Direct costs	Overhead costs	To separate those costs which can be directly attributed to particular products from those which pertain to broader administrative units.

It may be a useful exercise for the reader to attempt to determine the situations in which each distinction will be helpful. A review of the illustrations earlier in this chapter should be helpful in bringing out the relevance of each pair of concepts.

Demand

There is much more to managerial economics than the analysis of costs. Demand or market considerations are a major influence on business decisions. In fact, there are many decisions for which economic analysis indicates that demand should be the primary influence.

Elasticity of demand

The usual starting point in the discussion of demand is the concept of *elasticity.* Elasticity should be defined broadly at first, for it is an idea that can be applied to many types of relationships, not merely to demand. As the name implies, an elasticity concept measures the responsiveness of one variable to changes in another. Suppose that A is the independent variable (the cause) and B the dependent variable (the effect). We may wish to measure the degree to which B responds to changes in A. It is often convenient to compare percentage changes in B with percentage changes in A, for a ratio between these percentages is an abstract number that can be compared with similar figures for other variables. This is precisely what a measure of elasticity does—it compares the percentage change in one variable to the percentage change in another. The concept of elasticity has been applied to many economic relationships, such as the relation of costs to output, the effectiveness of advertising, and the response of demand to changes in income.

The best known of the elasticity measures is the elasticity of demand, more precisely known as the price elasticity of demand. It measures the responsiveness of the quantity demanded to price change. A high elasticity (one greater than 1.0) indicates that the quantity purchased varies more as a per cent than the changes in price that bring about the quantity change. A low elasticity (less than 1.0) indicates a low response to price change. The formulas for computing elasticity may be found in any elementary economics textbook.

Pricing

Estimates of demand elasticities are a major consideration in pricing, whether those estimates are made statistically or are based on a subjective evaluation of past experience. In fact, one outstanding writer on managerial economics states that cost is often unimportant and demand is *the* influence to take into account.[1] In discussing the problem of pricing in a firm producing many products, this writer argues that cost should set the lower limit for price, but should not be a determinant of price. Indeed, the determinants should be the competitive situation and demand elasticity. When cost *is* a consideration, it is the incremental or marginal cost that deserves attention.

The following hypothetical illusion will clarify the importance of demand elasticities. Suppose a firm produces five products. One of these, Product A, is not covering all of its costs. Another, Product B, is returning a nice profit. It would be desirable to expand the output of B at the expense of A, but in the short run this is impossible because the facilities are specialized. An investigation of the elasticity of demand for A indicates that nothing can be done about price—the demand is highly elastic for increases in price, and inelastic for decreases. However, if the revenue from Product A is sufficient to cover all of the variable costs plus some contribution to overhead and profits, it may be best to leave things alone for the short run (that is, until it becomes necessary to replace plant or equipment). Thus, demand is the primary influence on the price of Product A. The situation for Product B

[1] Joel Dean, *Managerial Economics* (Englewood Cliffs, N. J.: Prentice-Hall, Inc., 1951), p. 471.

is different. An investigation shows that the demand for Product B is inelastic—there are no close substitutes produced by competitors. In this case, the firm may profit by raising its price. But note that such an increase in price is based on an evaluation of demand and not on cost.

In such a short space the subject of pricing cannot be developed in full detail. Nevertheless, we have tried to show that demand and cost considerations may both be important in pricing, but their relative importance varies from one situation to another. If we have done nothing else, we hope that we have raised doubts in the mind of the reader about the simple notion that all there is to pricing is the adding up of costs with a margin for profit.

Forecasting

Since decision-making is oriented to the future, it is dependent upon forecasts of future demand. In many firms, these forecasts are made in a haphazard way—the firm may not be large enough to afford more elaborate procedures. Many managers rely on business publications containing forecasts—and this is often the only thing that can be done in view of the high expense of making one's own forecasts.

In any case, it will profit the businessman to learn about economic forecasting. Even if he intends to rely primarily on outside forecasts, he must evaluate them and this requires a basic knowledge of what is involved. Forecasting is still an undeveloped science subject to considerable error. A study of forecasting will at least warn the manager of the limitations of the published forecasts and also help him form his own judgments.

The only type of forecast to be discussed here is the short-range forecast. This forecasts for the coming year but no longer. The best known approach to such forecasting is the use of a Gross National Product model. This might well be called a Keynesian model, for it is heavily influenced by the macroeconomic theory of J. M. Keynes, the British economist who has been the greatest influence on modern economics. The Gross National Product model is based on the simple notion that total demand (total expenditure) for the country as a whole governs economic activity. In forecasting, then, the problem is one of estimating this total demand.

The procedure is to break the Gross National Product down into its main components, for these are the components of total demand. In 1960 these components were at the following levels: [2]

Consumer Purchases		$321 billions
Durable consumer goods	$ 44 billions	
Nondurable consumer goods	151	
Services	126	

[2] Data from the U. S. Department of Commerce (published in the *Survey of Current Business*).

Private Investment Expenditures		79
Residential construction	21	
Nonresidential construction	19	
Purchases of durable equipment	28	
Accumulation of inventories	11	
Net Foreign Investment (the difference between exports and imports)		1
Government Expenditures		98
Federal government spending	52	
State and local government spending	46	
Total Gross National Product		$500 billions

In forecasting, each of these components requires separate attention. There are various sources of information that may be useful. For example, the budget of the Federal Government, along with Presidential addresses on the budget, will give some clues regarding the level of Federal spending. It is also desirable to look at Congressional attitudes toward the budget, for it is not usually the case that the President will receive exactly what he wants. Furthermore, one may look at possible changes in conditions which might cause revision in the thinking of the President and Congress. On estimating private investment, useful surveys of business plans for long term investments (plant and equipment) are made by the Department of Commerce and the Securities and Exchange Commission. It might be dangerous to assume that these plans will always conform to the actual investment expenditure, but they do give useful suggestions of how business is thinking. Inventory investment is much trickier, because the rate at which firms accumulate inventories can change sharply from one period to the next. In forecasting consumption, there is the problem that one of the major influences on consumption is income (or the Gross National Product) itself, the very figure one is trying to forecast. This may seem to involve circular reasoning, but there is nothing illogical about trying to forecast a total which requires the forecasting of parts dependent on that total. Simultaneous equations can break through this problem of circularity very neatly, but it is not necessary to resort to econometrics to handle it.

One section of a chapter cannot tell the reader how to meet all of the difficulties of forecasting these components. In fact, professional forecasters would admit that they are still struggling with them. If the reader will devote some thought to the simple ideas developed here, he will be able to make more sense out of the discussions of forecasting found in such publications as *Fortune, Business Week, Wall Street Journal, United States News and World Report,* and other periodicals containing forecasts. By knowing the conjectural nature of some of the materials in these forecasts, he will be aware of the uncertainty that must always surround them.

There are other methods of forecasting and there are difficult problems of relating the national economic forecasts to forecasts for the individual firm. In some industries there is a fairly neat relationship between the Gross National Product and the demand for the product of individual firms. However, this is not always the case. Many firms find it more profitable to use their internal organization in making up forecasts. One way of doing this is to require that the individual salesmen forecast sales in their districts; then after a review by top management or forecasting specialists, consolidate their estimates. In the future, there will undoubtedly be a refinement of statistical methods applicable to forecasting both national aggregates and the sales of individual firms. Forecasting is in the process of development. The progressive manager will want to watch this development.

Conclusions

The best way to summarize this chapter is to enumerate its most important principles. A full understanding of these principles, along with practice in their application to actual business situations, will benefit anyone who plans to take part in business decisions. Four important principles will be reviewed here:

I. The Incremental Principle—*A decision is sound if it increases revenue more than costs, or if it reduces costs more than revenue.* This will seem too obvious to deserve much emphasis, but this chapter has shown that its application is not obvious at all, and that using full cost or average cost as the basis for decision is an easy error to make.

II. The Principle of Time Perspective—*A decision should take into account both the short run and long run effects on revenues and costs, giving appropriate weight to the most relevant time periods.* In using incremental reasoning, there is a danger of placing too much weight on the immediate consequences of the decision, with too little attention to the repercussions in the longer run.

III. The Opportunity Cost Principle—*Decision-making involves a careful measurement of the sacrifices required by the various alternatives.* This again will seem obvious in this abrupt form. Yet the sophisticated application of the opportunity cost concept is one requiring a great deal of thought and experience.

Up to the present point, there is one feature of time that has been ignored. Revenues and costs in the future are less valuable than money flows at the present. To compare these cash flows over time, it is necessary to apply the principle of discounting, the fourth main principle.

IV. The Discounting Principle—*If a decision affects costs and revenues at future dates, it is necessary to discount these costs and revenues to present values before a valid comparison of alternatives is possible.* This principle will be a central concept in the chapter on investment decisions.

Bibliographical Note

A pioneer volume in relating the economic view of costs to the needs of business is J. M. Clark's *Studies in the Economics of Overhead Costs* (1923). Progress in the development of managerial economics culminated in Joel Dean's *Managerial Economics* (1951), a volume that rests heavily on the work of others but which is outstanding in emphasizing the practical implications of economic theory. Even today there is no other volume that is so successful in translating abstract analysis in terms that have immediate meaning in business practice.

The textbook by Milton H. Spencer and Louis Siegelman, *Managerial Economics* (1959) is especially strong in reviewing empirical studies of cost and demand functions. J. Howard's *Marketing Management* (1957) reflects the growing attention to economic analysis in marketing. M. Colberg, W. C. Bradford, R. M. Alt *Business Economics* (revised edition, 1957) has cases along with the text material. Only by considerable practice in applying economic concepts in actual case situations does one attain a realistic grasp of business economics. J. Johnston's *Statistical Cost Analysis* (1960) presents an over-all survey of statistical studies of costs up to the present. For references to more specialized sub-topics the reader is referred to the bibliographies in Spencer and Siegelman.

Most textbooks on business cycles contain chapters on economic forecasting. John P. Lewis's *Business Conditions Analysis* (1959) is outstanding in its treatment of forecasting. V. L. Bassie's *Economic Forecasting* (1958) is a detailed treatment of the subject, with many provocative viewpoints.

Two recent studies of actual pricing practices are A. D. H. Kaplan, J. B. Dirlam, and R. F. Lanzillotti, *Pricing in Big Business* (1958) and W. W. Haynes, *Pricing Decisions in Small Business* (1961). Jules Backman has edited a collection of readings entitled *Price Practices and Price Policies* (1953).

Questions and Problems

1. If a business has bought an asset for $20,000, does it make sense for it to refuse to sell it for anything less "because this would involve a loss"? Discuss. Would your answer be the same if adjustments for depreciation and taxes had been made?
2. The following argument is commonly heard: "If a business refuses ever to price below cost, it is certain not to lose money."
3. If pricing is aimed at profits in the future and if accounting measures past or historical events, has accounting anything to contribute to pricing?
4. Evaluate: "The allocation of overhead cost is irrelevant to business decisions and should be ignored."
5. What is the opportunity cost of using a building in manufacturing that has been completely written off on the books and thus involves no depreciation expense?
6. Firm X is a multi-product concern. One department is constantly losing money, failing to cover total costs. Under what circumstances should the department be abandoned?
7. Are variable costs and opportunity costs the same? Give illustrations.
8. Are variable costs and incremental costs the same? Give illustrations.
9. In an interview a business man stated: "Fixed costs must come first. You

must first make certain that you cover fixed costs and then do what you can about variable costs." Comment.

10. Draw breakeven charts to show the following:

(a) a situation in which the price of the product increases;

(b) a situation in which materials costs rise, but other costs and prices remain the same;

(c) a situation in which a labor-saving machine is introduced and the break-even point is raised;

(d) a situation in which a labor-saving machine is introduced and the break-even point is lowered.

11. Are the labor-saving machines in the previous question (a) both desirable? (b) neither desirable? (c) one desirable but the other undesirable?

12. A company has the following cost situation:

Fixed costs $300,000
Variable costs $4.00 per unit
Stairstep costs, rising by $40,000 for every 100,000 units increase in output
Price of the output—$6.00

(a) Find the breakeven point.

(b) Find the profit at sales of 250,000 units.

13. In the previous problem assume that overtime must be paid labor beyond outputs of 200,000 units. This overtime will increase variable costs by 20 per cent per unit for all units over 200,000. Draw the breakeven chart.

14. Discuss the difficulties of drawing a breakeven chart for a multi-product firm. What solution might meet some of these difficulties?

15. According to the law of diminishing returns, what should a breakeven chart look like?

16. If a firm must lower price to raise volume, how does this affect the appearance of his breakeven chart? Draw one to fit this situation.

17. Evaluate: "Pricing on the basis of incremental costs means low prices and cannot be profitable."

18. Give an illustration of a situation in which estimates of incremental costs would help in a decision to make or buy.

19. Give an illustration of a situation in which estimates of opportunity costs would help in a decision to make or buy.

20. A store sells a variety of products. The management believes some of them have elastic demands because the consumers buy these items frequently and compare prices. Others have inelastic demands because the customers do not make such comparisons. What are the implications for price policy?

21. A manufacturer produces five lines. Two produce a high unit contribution to overhead and profits; two others produce only a fraction of this unit contribution to overhead and profits; the fifth makes no contribution at all. Discuss the implications for management.

16

Extracts and Cases Involving Managerial Economics

As stated in the last chapter, economists have not traditionally concerned themselves with detailed business decisions. Rather, they have been concerned with social questions and public policy—and with satisfying our curiosity about why the economy performs as it does. Occasionally, however, some economists have taken a closer look at the individual businessman and his problem of choice, and even have been willing to prescibe rules leading to profitable decisions. More recently, a more specialized branch of economics, known as "business economics" or "managerial economics" has developed. The following extracts are taken from works of both the general economists and the business economists.

The cases that follow the extracts provide an opportunity to apply economic analysis to some actual business situations.

Extracts

Extract A

Principles of Economics (Alfred Marshall)

Supplementary [fixed] cost must generally be covered by the selling price to some considerable extent in the short run. And they must be completely covered by it in the long run. . . . Supplementary costs are of many different kinds; and some of them differ only in degree from prime [variable] costs. For instance, if an engineering firm is in doubt whether to accept an order at a rather low price for a certain locomotive, the absolute prime costs include the value of the raw material and the wages of the artisans and labourers employed on the locomotive. But there is no clear rule as to the salaried staff: for, if work is slack, they will probably have some time on their hands; and their salaries will therefore commonly be classed among general or supplementary costs. The line of division is however often blurred over. For instance, foremen and other trusted artisans are seldom dismissed merely because of a temporary scarcity of work; and therefore an occasional order may be taken to fill up idle time, even though its price does not cover their salaries and wages.[1]

Extract B

Studies in the Economics of Overhead Costs (J. M. Clark)

Should we, or should we not, count "overhead costs" in deciding whether a given thing is worth producing? There is no universal answer: no formula by which all cases can be settled in advance. However, in a general way the rule is: whenever a policy is being considered which will involve "overhead expenditures" that could otherwise be avoided, they are part of the cost of that policy; likewise, when we are comparing two policies, each of which involves its own overhead, each should have its own overhead charged against it; but whenever we are choosing between two policies under both of which the same overhead outlay will have to be met, that overhead outlay is not a part of the cost specifically traceable to either policy.[2]

Extract C

Managerial Economics (Joel Dean)

To an accountant, net income is essentially a historical record of the past. To an economist, net income is essentially a speculation about the future. . . .

In general, the kind of profit measurement needed for most business decisions comes closer to the ideal of the economist than to the practice of the accountant. . . .

Records of historical outlays, based upon . . . rigid classifications and formal proportionalities need to be drastically reworked for decisions about the future. Classification should depend upon the nature of the rival programs being considered, and therefore change from problem to problem. . . .

The word "cost" has many meanings in many different settings. The kind of cost concept to be used in a particular situation depends upon the business

[1] Alfred Marshall, *Principles of Economics,* 8th edition (London: The Macmillan Co., 1920), pp. 360–361.

[2] J. Maurice Clark, *Studies in the Economics of Overhead Costs* (Chicago: University of Chicago Press, 1923), p. 21.

decision to be made. There is a widespread and unfortunate notion that financial accounting costs are universally practical for all kinds of business decisions because they are "actual" in the sense of being routinely recorded somewhere. . . .

The popularity of the cost-plus method [of pricing] does not necessarily mean that it is the best available method. In most situations it is not, for several reasons:

1. It ignores demand. It fails to take account of the buyer's needs and willingness to pay, which govern the sales volume obtainable at each of a series of prices. What people will pay for a product bears no necessary relation to what it costs any particular manufacturer to make it.
2. It fails to reflect competition adequately. The effect of a price upon rivals' reactions and the effect upon the birth of potential competition are omitted from this simple formula.
3. It overplays the precision of allocated costs. The costs of individual products cannot be determined exactly in multiple-product firms where common costs are important and are arbitrarily allocated to products. Equally defensible bases for apportionment yield significantly different product costs. Hence the figures on full costs used in the formula are generally less factual than their role in pricing warrants.
4. It is based upon a concept of cost that is frequently not relevant for the pricing decision. For many decisions, incremental costs rather than full costs should be controlling. Moreover, it is not current costs, and certainly not past costs, that are needed to price future output, but rather forecasts of future costs. Opportunity costs, i.e., alternative uses of facilities, are important, but they are not usually reflected in accounting systems.[3]

Cases

Case A:

Zorach Printing Company (B)

The Zorach Company was engaged in the job printing business in a large Mid-western city, facing competition from several dozen firms. Its business was fairly small, averaging around $250,000 per year. The firm was not particularly profitable—in fact, the tendency was for the small profits of one year to be offset by small losses in the next. Some of the directors of the firm felt that there was a danger that the losses might become substantially larger.

The firm usually operated below capacity, though at times the work piled up and employees were paid overtime. Because of the unsteady flow of orders, frequently the company did not have enough work for its 35 employees. The management felt that this was characteristic of the job order

[3] Joel Dean, *Managerial Economics* (Englewood Cliffs, N. J.: Prentice-Hall, Inc., 1951), pp. 13, 25, 251, 257, 450–451.

business. To lay off employees in those weeks when work was slack involved the risk of loss of the highly skilled work force.

The firm had to compete with other firms for its business. Some of its customers were relatively faithful, but others were extremely conscious of price and quality. The firm had an excellent reputation on quality, but had lost some customers in recent years because of prices that were allegedly high. The usual practice in making price estimates was to estimate the full cost of the product, including materials, direct labor, and an overhead allocation percentage, and then add to this a per cent mark-up for profits. This had long been accepted as sound business.

Material costs amounted to around 35 per cent of total costs. Cost of direct labor was also about 35 per cent, leaving about 30 per cent to cover depreciation, executive salaries, sales commissions, power, heat, and miscellaneous expenses.

A new director of the firm was concerned with its inability to make profits and with the danger of missing debt payments. The director was familiar with such business economics concepts as breakeven charts, incremental costs and opportunity costs, but was at first uncertain as to their relevance in this firm. He first tried to construct a breakeven chart based on his general knowledge of the behavior of materials costs, labor costs, and overhead. He was aware that the firm was operating close to the breakeven point, but he was also interested in estimating the behavior of costs away from the point, and the relation between the probable incremental cost of added business and the revenue that could be gained from that business.

On the basis of his analysis of costs, the new director raised questions about the pricing policies of the company.

Case B:

Zorach Printing Company (C)

The Zorach Printing Company had only two salesmen on its payroll. These salesmen were given a guarantee plus expenses. One salesman consistently made commissions that more than covered the guarantee, but the other, being relatively new in the business, had not in the six months of his employment earned his guarantee. He was selling at a rate of approximately $2,500 per month, which at the commission rate of 10 per cent would not cover his annual guarantee of $4,000.

The Vice-President of the company felt that the new salesman was not proving himself and that he should be dismissed. The new director argued to the contrary, that this salesman should be retained even if he failed to earn his guarantee. The director suggested that an additional salesman be hired.

Since most of the sales were made within the city, the transportation and similar sales expenses were small, never amounting to more than $1,000 or $2,000 for the entire concern. Because of his effort to develop some out-of-city business, the new salesman was absorbing a high proportion of these expenses. For a number of months, the issue of what to do about this salesman was studied but not resolved.

Case C:

The Harmon Corporation (A)

The Harmon Corporation was a small firm, tightly held by a few stockholders, most of whom were related. The company manufactured wooden parts which were shipped to larger concerns in various parts of the United States. The profits of the company had justified substantial dividends and, in addition, had made possible the building up of large liquid assets. The seven directors of the company were interested in investing part of these funds in other profitable ventures. They discussed several alternatives. One was to establish a branch to produce parts similar to the ones now manufactured, but located in another part of the country. A second was to invest in the expansion of a highly profitable advertising business that two of the directors were managing. A third, the one which received the most serious attention, especially from the president and the secretary of the company (both of whom were on the board), was to establish a subsidiary corporation to own and operate a bowling alley in the same town as the parts plant.

A manufacturer of pin-setting equipment and bowling lanes assisted the directors in making estimates of costs and revenues on the bowling alley. The investment in the building and land would come to $100,000, of which $85,000 could be borrowed at 6 per cent from an insurance company. The bowling lanes would cost $88,000; the manufacturer would accept a down payment of $22,000, the remainder to be paid off in five years. The interest on the $66,000 balance would also be 6 per cent. The total investment of funds by the Harmon Corporation would be $50,000. Of this total, $15,000 would provide a payment on the land and building, $22,000 the payment on the bowling lanes, and the remaining $13,000 would serve as working capital. The pin-setting equipment would be leased from the manufacturer on a royalty basis—the rental depending on the volume of business.

The estimates of the volume of business were an average of 752 lines a day for 300 days during the year. The average price would come to 42 cents per line—or even as high as 45 cents; the directors decided to use the conservative figure. Additional income would come from shoe rentals, the sale of balls, bags and shoes, and from other activities.

Table 16-1 is a statement of projected income and expense on the bowling alley. Before it was possible to compare alternative opportunities for investment, it was necessary to make a thorough analysis of expected bowling lane profits. An outside acquaintance of one of the directors suggested that a breakeven chart might be useful in this analysis.

TABLE 16-1

HARMON CORPORATION

PROJECTED INCOME AND EXPENSE STATEMENT ON BOWLING ALLEY FOR THE FIRST YEAR OF OPERATION

Lines per day—752 300 days	Per year—225,600
Income	
16 lanes × 47 lines per day per lane @ 42¢	$ 94,752.00
Shoe rental	6,750.00
Sales—balls, bags, shoes	2,000.00
Cigarettes, ball cleaning, snack bar—net	3,000.00
Gross Income	$106,502.00
Expense	
Salaries	$ 20,000.00
Rental of pin-setting equipment 225,600 @ 10¢	22,560.00
Service costs, pins, supplies	5,857.00
Depreciation on building—40 yr. on $100,000 = 2500	2,500.00
Depreciation on lanes—10 yr. on $80,000 = 8,000	8,000.00
Utilities	4,500.00
Advertising and promotion	1,200.00
Insurance (fire, etc.) on $188,000	1,500.00
Taxes—ad valorem	3,800.00
Federal, state and local licenses	1,000.00
Social security taxes	600.00
Overhead absorbed from Harmon Corp.	10,000.00
Total Expenses	$ 81,257.00
Net Income	$ 25,045.00

N.B. Interest expenses not included above.

Case D:

Harmon Corporation (B)

The directors of the Harmon Corporation discovered upon further investigation that the pin-setting equipment rental charges varied with the volume of business. The royalty would be 10 cents per line for the first 160,000 lines; 8 cents for the next 80,000 lines; and 6 cents for all lines above 240,000 per year. Adjustments in the breakeven chart were made accordingly.

It was also discovered that the investment in the building and land was not entirely a "sunk" cost. If the bowling alley venture were not to work out, the building would be suitable as a grocery store. Thus, there was a question of what level of fixed costs at zero level operations should be shown on the breakeven chart.

Case E:

Harmon Corporation (C)

One of the directors estimated the profits that would be earned if the $50,000 were invested in the advertising business rather than in a bowling alley. His estimate came to $23,731 per year. The interest expenses would be approximately the same as those on the bowling alley, since an equivalent amount of money would be borrowed. This director put up several arguments for investing in the advertising alternative. One was that he and another director had gained considerable experience and skill in advertising over the years. Another was that the profitability of the advertising business was more certain. The plan was to buy out an already existing business on which the profits would be known. Furthermore, almost anyone could go into the bowling alley business—competition from new entrants might cut into profits.

On the other hand, this particular bowling alley might have a semi-monopoly position in its location. The town had a population of 15,000—not large enough to support two alleys. There was no town within 30 or 40 miles large enough to support a bowling alley.

Part of the uncertainty about investment in the bowling business arose from a disagreement among the directors about closing on Sunday. Two directors were strongly opposed to Sunday operations on religious grounds, and all estimates were made on this basis. Sunday would probably be one of the most active days if the alley were open. The directors favoring the advertising alternative, while agreeing to the Sunday closing policy, argued that this was just another reason for rejecting the bowling alley opportunity. They also predicted that the pressure to open on Sunday would become strong in the future, especially if the profits fell below estimates, and that this might lead to conflict among the directors.

Thus the alternatives up for consideration were:

1. A bowling alley closed on Sunday;
2. A bowling alley open on Sunday;
3. Expansion of the advertising business;
4. Establishment of a new branch for the production of wooden parts. (No estimates were made on this alternative.)

17

Investment Decisions

FEW decisions are as important to a firm as its decisions on the purchase of capital equipment. Some decisions are easily reversed; but investment decisions have a long run impact that may affect the profitability of the firm for years or decades. It is surprising, therefore, that many firms use haphazard procedures in selecting investments. However, larger firms are inaugurating a more systematic treatment. In the last few decades, there has been considerable development of the fundamental theory of investment decisions, and of methods by which business can apply this theory to their own problems. In recent years, an interest in mathematical approaches has developed. The firm must economize in the refinement of its decision-making processes; it would be wasteful to spend more on evaluation of alternatives than the prospective savings. But with the improved training of managers and with the growing availability of electronic computers, more attention will be given to systematic approaches to decisions on the purchase of new equipment.

A firm faces three kinds of investment decisions. One pertains to the replacement of capital equipment as it wears out or becomes obsolete. Another pertains to capital equipment required for expansion. A third arises from innovation—the displacement of old technology by new, involving, for example, investment in labor-saving or capital-saving equipment. The same general principles may be used in either case. Most of the illustrations in this chapter and the next will relate to machinery and equipment, but a similar analysis applies to buildings and other types of capital investment.

The Investment Demand Schedule

Making investment decisions is choosing among the many investment opportunities open to the firm. Clearly the firm will wish to avoid unprofitable investments, but even among the profitable possibilities, there is a problem of choice. A limited quantity of funds is available. There are added capital costs in acquiring additional funds, the possibility of weakening the capital structure of the firm, or dilution of the control of the present owners. Thus the funds must be rationed among the investment opportunities. This rationing is called *capital budgeting*. The problem is one of selecting those investments which will contribute the most to the profitability of the firm. Measuring this contribution to profitability is the central concern of this chapter.

The objective of capital budgeting is to rank the various investment opportunities according to the prospective earnings they will yield. These prospective earnings may be expressed as a percentage return on the original investment, usually called "rate of return," "internal rate of return," or "marginal efficiency of capital." Since earnings are in the future and involve considerable uncertainty, prospective yields must be estimated. Personal judgment in making such estimates may be so great that doubt is cast on the usefulness of refined mathematical approaches to the problem. On the other hand, there is a growing interest in a systematic treatment of uncertainty itself.

After the investment opportunities have been evaluated, they may be ranked according to the magnitude of the rates of return. Some investments may promise a return of 30 per cent, others 20 per cent, and so on down to negative returns. If these are plotted on a graph, the result looks like the well-known demand curve of economics—in fact this *is* a demand curve. It expresses the quantity of investment to be undertaken at various costs of capital. If the cost of capital is low (which might be true if the company has a great deal of cash on hand with few outside opportunities to apply that cash), a larger volume of internal investment is justified. If the cost of capital is high (the company being short of funds and the cost of obtaining funds on the outside being high), there must be a restriction on the volume of investment. Such an investment demand schedule is shown in Figure 17-1.

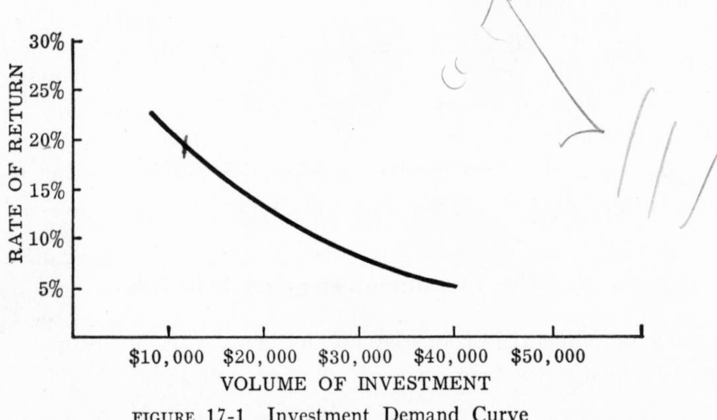

FIGURE 17-1 Investment Demand Curve

According to Figure 17-1, if the cost of capital is 20 per cent, the firm should invest around $15,000 in new capital equipment; if the cost of capital is only 5 per cent, investment should be $40,000. The advantage of ranking investments from those with high prospective returns to those with low returns is that the firm will thus give the highest priority to those alternatives which offer the highest profits.

Organization for Capital Budgeting

Organizational channels should permit a comparison of investment opportunities throughout the company. In a small company this offers no great difficulty; the top management of such a company should be able to evaluate the available investment opportunities. Employees should be constantly watching for new prospects for profitable investment. In some companies, suggestion systems have produced many useful ideas not recognized by higher levels of management. Management should continually examine the possibility of investment in new lines, in diversification of the product, or in developing entirely new products.

In larger companies channels must exist through which proposals of various departments and plants may flow. Most of the proposals should be screened by plant managers, divisional heads, and budgetary committees before reaching the board of directors. With the growing interest in decentralization in management, many companies prefer to delegate investment decisions to the lower levels of management. Most companies permit plant managers to spend sums below a certain amount—for example, $50,000—without referring such decisions to higher headquarters. Other companies delegate the entire problem of investment to the divisions or plants. While this may mean that some parts of the company are using funds on less profitable investments than others, the advantages of decentralization in stimulating initiative and in improving morale may more than compensate for any discrepancies in profits. The systematic treatment of some management problems may have to yield to the human needs of the enterprise.

There is no simple formula for prescribing the organization involved in capital budgeting. Each company should give thought to the organizational channels that will best fit its needs.

Nonquantitative Investment Criteria

Most of this chapter will describe quantitative approaches to the evaluation of investment prospects. But it would be misleading to state that most companies make use of such quantitative procedures. Quite the reverse is the case—most companies reach a rough conclusion that an investment is or is not needed.

The trend is toward more systematic quantitative treatment of investment decisions, but there are limits to this development. The problem of uncertainty may be so overwhelming as to preclude any significant quantitative treatment. The human aspects of the problem—investment problems are related to questions of morale, prestige, power, and "empire building"—call for criteria of choice not easily measured. Furthermore, some investments may be so clearly important to the future of the companies concerned that no quantitative treatment is necessary.

One method of handling investment decisions qualitatively is to rank them according to their urgency. Some projects are needed at once; others are more easily postponed. Some investments may be of great strategic importance to the future of the company. The trouble with such nonquantitative approaches is that they open the way to pressures within the organization and to disputes about what is urgent and what is not. Some projects that are postponable may nevertheless be highly profitable. For example, if the company were considering a move into a new product line, which is easily postponable, investments in less profitable existing lines may appear to be more urgent.

It is easy to criticize nonquantitative approaches to management decisions. But the persistance of such approaches may indicate that there is more to be said for them than is realized at first. The question of when it becomes profitable to substitute mathematical models for subjective analysis is itself one involving an investment decision. When does it become profitable to invest in a staff and in organizational procedures which will make possible the quantitative evaluation of investment proposals? The difficulty of giving a quantitative answer to this question should raise doubts in the minds of the extreme enthusiasts for mathematical model building.

Quantitative Approaches

There is not a single quantitative approach that is applied universally to investment problems. Instead there is a wide variety of possibilities, from the simple to the extremely complex. Considerable theoretical precision in measuring the profitability of new investment is possible, but this chapter will stop short of the detailed refinements. Although this approach will sacrifice some theoretical accuracy, sufficient material is presented to meet most management problems.

The quantitative approaches reviewed here are as follows:

1. Payback period
2. First year performance
3. Present value
4. Discounted rate of return
5. Payback reciprocal

Each of these methods is applied in practice, some more extensively than others. The payback (or payout) approach is perhaps most common but is being replaced by more sophisticated models.

1. Payback period

There are two steps in the payback approach:

1. Computation of how long it will take the investment to pay for itself, that is, computation of the payback period.
2. Comparison of this payback period with some predetermined standard period in which the investment should pay for itself. If the equipment will pay for itself in less time than the predetermined period, the investment is considered profitable; if not, the investment will be abandoned.

The computation of the payback period can be summarized in a simple formula:

$$P = C/R$$

in which P represents the payback period, C the original cost of the investment (sometimes called the supply price), and R the annual return in dollars expected from the investment. Each of these terms is self explanatory, except R, which calls for some comment. R might represent the savings in direct labor cost resulting from introducing the new machine—this would be the case of a labor-saving investment. It might be the expected profits above variable costs of investment in a new department. In any case, R is measured after added variable expenses have been deducted from the expected added revenue or the expected savings in cost. In other words, R is an incremental concept, involving the incremental type of reasoning developed in the preceding chapters. Depreciation on the new equipment is not deducted from the added revenue or savings in computing R, since the formula attempts to determine how long it takes to recover capital rather than the profit on the investment above depreciation.

A simple illustration may help clarify the approach. Assume that a company is considering investment in a new machine. The facts about the machine are as follows:

Cost (supply price)	$10,000
Expected life	5 years
Annual savings in direct labor costs	$4,000
Payback criterion	3 years

The payback period in this case is 2½ years ($10,000 divided by the annual savings of $4,000). Since this is less than the required payback period of 3 years, the investment has satisfied the requirements.

Computation of the payback period is complicated by the corporate income tax. For a company in the 52 per cent tax bracket, over half of the added profits will go to the government. This does not mean that the payback period will be twice that shown here—depreciation is deductible for tax purposes, so that only the return above depreciation will be taxed. The more ambitious students may wish to compute the payback period for the illustration presented above taking taxes into account; trial and error or simple algebra will assist in reaching the answer.

Whether or not taxes are taken into account, the payback approach is a crude determinant of investment decisions. Suppose, for example, that the above $10,000 machine is a special purpose machine likely to become obsolete in 5 years. Now consider another $10,000 machine, but this time a general purpose machine that may not become obsolete and will not wear out for 15 years. If both machines will produce an annual saving of $4,000 per year, both are equally acceptable according to the payback criterion. Yet, the second of these machines is more clearly profitable, since it will produce revenues for many more years. In this way the payback period can be quite misleading on the profitability of alternative investments.

2. *First year performance*

Another relatively simple way to evaluate a purchase of equipment is to compare the cost of operation before and after acquisition of the equipment. If the equipment is for additional production, the issue is whether it will produce enough added revenue to cover all of the added variable costs (mainly direct labor and materials), and in addition cover depreciation on the new equipment plus a profit sufficient to justify assuming the risks involved. Using this method, depreciation is charged against the new machine, say, by the straight line method.

Suppose that a new wing to a factory is under consideration. The following information is supplied:

Cost (supply price) of the new wing	$150,000
Cost (supply price) of added machinery	80,000
Expected life of the new wing	30 years
Expected life of the added machinery	8 years
Expected additional sales revenue after transportation and selling expenses	$110,000/year
Expected additional variable costs (direct labor, materials, power)	75,000/year

If one subtracts from the additional revenue of $110,000 the incremental variable costs of $75,000 and the straight line depreciation of $15,000 ($10,000 on the equipment and $5,000 on the building) he is left with an incremental profit for the first year of $20,000. Whether this is sufficient to justify the investment depends on an evaluation of the uncertainty concerning revenues and costs and also on alternative opportunities for investment. If 6 per cent interest is charged on the new investment, most of the profit is absorbed. A 20 per cent interest, which might be charged if the investment is extremely risky or if it competes against highly profitable alternatives, would leave the project with a loss for the first year. But, the sum of money tied up in the investment will decline year by year; the first year figure may be unduly conservative on prospective profits.

Several limitations of this approach are apparent. Only the first year is taken into account. A prediction for later years may indicate a rise or fall in revenues (and also a change in costs), so that the profits of $20,000 would not apply to the whole life of the addition. Also, this method, like the payback approach, makes no effort to discount for the fact that most of the revenues will be in the future. Future dollars are not worth as much as present dollars. The first year performance approach assumes implicitly that the profits for the first year will carry on for the full life of the investment, and also that future dollars are equal to present dollars. Despite these limitations, this approach may elucidate the profitability of many investment prospects, leaving borderline cases for greater refinement in analysis.

The above illustration was one of a new addition to production capacity. If the question is one of replacement of already existing equipment, the procedure is approximately the same. However, several points must be kept in mind. Instead of added revenues, the new machine may produce savings in variable costs as compared with the old machine (though it is also possible that the new process will add to revenues by increasing capacity or by improving quality). The depreciation on the old machine can be ignored since it is a "sunk" cost. The salvage value of the old machine should be taken into account; one procedure would be to subtract such salvage value from the cost (supply price) of the new machine.

The following is an illustration of a replacement problem:

Original cost of old machine	$10,000
Book value after depreciation of old machine	4,000
Cost (supply price) of new machine	15,000
Variable costs using old machine	30,000/year
Variable costs using new machine	25,000/year
Estimated life of new machine	6 years
Salvage value of old machine at present time	$ 1,000
Estimated salvage value of new machine six years from now	Zero

The $5,000 of savings in variable costs will more than cover the depreciation on the new machine, which on a straight line basis is $2,500 (or slightly less if the salvage value of the old machine is deducted from the cost of the new machine). The original cost of the old machine and the book value of the old machine are irrelevant to the decision, for they do not refer to the future. If 10 per cent interest is charged against the $14,000 additional investment, the decision would be to replace the machine. This procedure fails to deal with years past the first one.

3. *Present value*

A more sophisticated and more accurate method for evaluating investment prospects is to compute the "present value" of the new equipment. The process of estimating present values is known as *capitalization,* and is the basic idea behind all valuation, whether it concerns real property, stocks and bonds, or any type of equipment.

The fundamental idea behind capitalization is that the value of any asset depends upon its future return. A house has value because it will produce services in the future (or rental income). A share of stock has value because it is expected to yield dividends (or capital gains) in the future. If an investment is not expected to produce any benefits in the future—either monetary or psychic returns—it is valueless today.

Two kinds of information are required to compute the capitalized value of an asset:

(1) The expected future returns, year by year. These will include the expected salvage value of the asset at the end of its life of service.

(2) The rate of discount to be applied to those future returns to arrive at their present value. This rate of discount should be higher for risky assets than for ones involving relative certainty. The rate of discount should be higher the higher the cost of capital or the higher the expected rate of return on alternative investment opportunities.

A well-known formula for capitalization should be learned by all students of business. The formula is:

$$V = \frac{R_1}{(1+i)} + \frac{R_2}{(1+i)^2} + \frac{R_3}{(1+i)^3} + \frac{R_4}{(1+i)^4} + \dots + \frac{R_n}{(1+i)^n} + \frac{S}{(1+i)^n}$$

in which:

V = Present (or capitalized) value of the asset
$R_1, R_2, \dots, R_n$ = Expected dollar returns in each year of the life of the asset
S = Salvage value of the asset in year n
i = Interest rate appropriate for discounting the future returns on this type of asset

No student should use a deficiency in mathematical training as an excuse for not learning this formula and understanding its full meaning. The algebra involved is simple, and the formula should appeal to common sense. The applications of mathematics in the management of the future will go far beyond the level of algebra required here. It should be obvious that the higher the R's (the expected returns), the higher the value of the asset. The higher the discount rate applied, the lower the present value. Returns in distant years are discounted more heavily than those in early years. An asset producing no return for twenty years is less valuable today than one producing the same return next year, since the money received next year can be reinvested in other profitable ventures. Also the uncertainty is greater the more distant the expected returns.

A simple example will illustrate the application of this method:

Cost (supply price) of the machine	$2,000
Expected return (above variable costs) in the first year	1,650
Expected return (above variable costs) in the second year	1,210
Salvage value at the end of the second year	242
Interest rate	10 per cent

The solution is as follows:

$$V = \frac{\$1,650}{(1.10)} + \frac{\$1,210}{(1.10)^2} + \frac{\$242}{(1.10)^2} = \$1,500 + \$1,000 + \$200 = \$2,700$$

Since the present value of the machinery is greater than its supply price, the investment is a sound one.[1] It is not necessary to take depreciation into account in this method. It might be said that, since the approach is concerned with recovery of capital, it automatically takes care of depreciation. If the future returns (including the salvage value) are not high enough to cover depreciation and the interest on the money tied up in the investment, the present value will turn out to be less than the supply price.

One brief comment is in order. The formula presented above implicitly assumes that the whole return each year comes at the end of that year. In actual fact, the company will be making a return on the machinery throughout the whole period. The error involved is usually small. There are formulas accounting for a continual flow of benefits from the investment, but these involve calculus and will be omitted here.

It is surprising that wider use is not made of the present value method. It is not particularly laborious (with the assistance of discount tables). It does consider the whole life of the asset, and it does discount future earnings. Thus, it is both theoretically sound and computationally manageable. Many feel that the additional refinement compared with the cruder methods already discussed is not justified, in view of the errors of estimates for future years. But whether the method is actually applied with precision in each investment decision, there can be no doubt of the importance of the concept of capitalization itself.

4. *Discounted rate of return*

Estimating the discounted rate of return on an asset is related to computing its present value. The rate of return (or marginal efficiency of capital)

[1] This assumes that the interest rate reflects the full opportunity costs; that is, the profits that can be earned on alternative investments.

has the important advantage over present value of being expressed as a percentage. Thus it can easily be compared with percentage returns on other investment opportunities in the investment demand schedule which was discussed earlier. How is it computed?

Two items of information are needed. The first is the same information required in computing the present value—the expected returns (including salvage value) spread over the life of the asset. The other is the cost (supply price) of the asset itself. The formula is similar to that for the present value:

$$C = \frac{R_1}{(1+r)} + \frac{R_2}{(1+r)^2} + \frac{R_3}{(1+r)^3} + \ldots + \frac{R_n}{(1+r)^n} + \frac{S}{(1+r)^n}$$

The difference is that now the unknown, instead of being V (the present value) is r (the rate of return). What we are trying to find is the rate of return which, when applied to the future dollar returns, will discount those returns to be equal to C (the cost or supply price of the asset). The greater the expected future returns, the greater will be r (the rate of return). The cheaper the asset, the greater the rate of return. This is common sense stated in symbols.

A simple illustration is presented to show how the formula is applied:

Cost (supply price of the machine)	$4,000
Expected return (above variable costs) in the first year	2,400
Expected return (above variable costs) in the second year	1,440
Expected return (above variable costs) in the third year	1,400
Salvage value at the end of the third year	328

Substituting this information in the formula results in:

$$\$4{,}000 = \frac{\$2{,}400}{(1+r)} + \frac{\$1{,}440}{(1+r)^2} + \frac{\$1{,}400 + \$328}{(1+r)^3}$$

By trial and error, that is, by substituting successive values for r to arrive at sums of the right hand side of the equation closer and closer to $4,000, the reader will find that the value of r is 20 per cent. A direct mathematical solution is cumbersome, especially if a large number of years is involved, although an electronic computer could handle this problem easily.

The question now is whether the 20 per cent return is high enough to justify the investment. As was explained earlier in the chapter, this depends upon the cost of capital, which involves both the availability of funds at various rates and the alternative investment opportunities. If the rate of interest (including consideration of risk and uncertainty) on this type of investment is 10 per cent, the investment is a worthwhile undertaking. It may help to point out that whenever the present value of an asset exceeds its supply price ($V > C$), the rate of return will exceed the rate of interest ($r > i$).

5. *Payback reciprocal*

In recent years, some attention has been devoted to the payback reciprocal as a means of evaluating investment prospects. The payback reciprocal is a rough estimate of the rate of return. If the payback period is four years, the payback reciprocal is one-fourth or 25 per cent. It can be shown mathematically that this will give a close estimate of the rate of return discussed in the preceding section, if the actual life of the investment is much longer than the payback period and if the returns are expected to be the same year after year. If, however, the R's vary from year to year, or if the salvage value of the asset is a significant consideration, or if the asset has an expected life not much different from the payback period, this approach will involve considerable error.

The formula for the payback reciprocal is:

$$r = \frac{R}{C}$$

The r here is only an estimate of the true rate of return discussed in the preceding section.

Economic Life of an Asset

This discussion of investment decisions has assumed that the life of the asset under consideration is given. However, most machines do not suddenly expire, they gradually accumulate deficiencies as compared with new, more modern equipment. New equipment may save on variable costs; it may also increase revenues by producing better services or a better quality product.

The methods so far discussed do indicate when a machine should be replaced. In general terms, if a new machine will produce savings or additional revenues that will, when discounted, determine a present value for the new machine warranting its purchase, the old machine should be replaced by the new. In other words, if the rate of return on the new machine (which arises from its savings in variable costs or from added revenues) exceeds the rate of interest, the investment is a sound one. Nevertheless, in these approaches (the present value approach and the rate of return approach) there still remains the question of how long a period in the future should be considered. If the life of the machine is estimated at three years instead of five, the present value and the rate of return will be affected. Therefore, it is necessary to estimate the probable life of the equipment in advance.

The rule for determining the length of life is a simple one, though its actual application involves estimating uncertain costs and revenues. A machine should be abandoned or sold when it produces an excess of revenue over variable costs which is equal to the interest on the salvage value of the machine, plus the loss in salvage value arising if it is retained. If the excess of revenue over costs exceeds this amount, the machine should be retained. In terms of an equation, the rule is as follows:

$$R(T) = iS(T) + S'(T)$$

in which:

$R(T)$ = Return in dollars of revenues over variable costs in period T
i = Interest rate
$S(T)$ = Salvage value in period T
$S'(T)$ = Loss in salvage value during period T

The problem is to solve for T, the time at which the return on the machine is just equal to the interest on the salvage value plus the loss in salvage value.[2]

A simple illustration should clarify what is involved in the above equation. Assume a machine with the following characteristics:

1. An excess of revenue over costs in the first year of $900, which diminishes because of the growing inefficiency of the machine by $200 per year.
2. A salvage value at the end of the first year of $1,500; at the end of the second year of $1,000; at the end of the third of $700; the fourth, $500; the fifth, $350; and the sixth, $200.
3. An interest rate of 20 per cent.

By trial and error, it is easy to determine that the machine should be sold at the beginning of the third year. In the third year, the machine will produce $500 of revenue over costs; the interest on the salvage value at the beginning of that year will be $200; and the loss in salvage value is expected to be $300 for the coming year. More refined methods (involving calculus) would indicate that the machine should actually be sold sometime during the third year; by considering only values for discrete intervals an error is involved which in most cases is not too serious.

More advanced treatments of equipment investment decisions consider the fact that the firm may be examining not the purchase of one new machine, but a chain of machines, each replacing the preceding one. The mathematics involved in this refinement is too advanced for this volume.

Conclusions

To what extent is there a justification for the quantitative treatment of investment decisions? This chapter does not give a clear answer to that question; the answer will be determined by the managers of the future. It is safe to conclude that some of the haphazard methods used at present, especially in small firms, must frequently lead to a misapplication of investment funds. But in many operations, the important element is probably the im-

[2] For a fuller discussion see Edward H. Bowman and Robert B. Fetter, *Analysis for Production Management* (Homewood, Illinois: Richard D. Irwin, 1957), pp. 315–316.

agination and initiative in developing new products, new selling techniques, and new production methods. A firm using the most advanced mathematical tools in a routine way, without such imagination and initiative, may fail in the competition with newer products and methods. In those industries in which there is a continual tendency toward obsolescence of old techniques, the quantitative approach may be extremely limited. The exact timing of obsolescence is not easily determined in advance, except in those industries in which technological change comes steadily—for example, in the improvement of electricity generation plants.

Whether or not the formulas in this chapter are applied in a mechanical way, there can be little doubt that the theory involved in the quantitative approaches is valuable to decision-makers. The value of any new equipment depends upon its future service. Evaluating this future performance involves discounting at appropriate rates of interest, thus taking risks and opportunity costs into account. Without some recognition of these fundamental considerations, it is difficult to see how sound investment decisions can be made.

Bibliographical Note

The economic theory involved in investment decisions can be traced back to the late nineteenth and early twentieth centuries. But treatment as a separate subject in its own right, with emphasis on practical applications, is relatively recent. Friedrich and Vera Lutz, *The Theory of Investment of the Firm* (1951) is a technical, abstract work requiring some background in calculus. Joel Dean, *Capital Budgeting* (1951) is another influential volume, the essence of which is included in his *Managerial Economics.*

R. Eisner, *Determinants of Capital Expenditure,* and Meyer and Kuh, *The Investment Decision* (1957) are outstanding empirical studies based on the investment performance of actual firms. Martin Solomon, Jr., *Investment Decisions in Small Business* (1961) emphasizes some special difficulties of small firms in applying the refined theories that have been developed and suggests advantages of simpler alternative methods.

George Terborgh has written about the MAPI approach to investment decisions in his *Dynamic Equipment Policy* (1949) and more simply in his *Business Investment Policy* (1958). The outstanding selection of readings on the subject is Ezra Solomon (ed.), *The Management of Corporate Capital* (1959).

Questions and Problems

1. A firm is considering an investment in labor-saving equipment which will cost $110,000. The following information is supplied:

   Annual savings in labor costs $50,000
   Overhead allocation at 90% of direct labor cost
   Expected life of the equipment—4 years
   Length of life used in computing straight line depreciation—4 years

Expected salvage value at the end of 4 years—$10,000

(a) Compute the payback period ignoring taxes.

(b) Compute the payback period assuming corporate taxes at 50% of profits.

(c) Compute the payback reciprocal for (b).

(d) Compute the per cent return based on first year performance ignoring taxes.

(e) Compute the per cent return based on first year performance assuming corporate taxes at 50%.

(f) Compute the present value assuming a cost of capital of 20%, ignoring taxes.

(g) Compute the present value assuming a cost of capital of 20% and assuming taxes at 50%.

(h) Estimate the discounted rate of return ignoring taxes. Do this by trial and error. First try 10%. Then raise or lower to approach the correct answer.

(i) Estimate the discounted rate of return taking taxes into account.

2. Can you think of a situation when one of the investment criteria would be favorable to the investment but others would be unfavorable?

3. Which investment criteria are easiest to apply? Should management be influenced by ease of computation?

4. Would your answer to (3) be the same if there were high uncertainty about the expected savings?

5. A recent work on investment decisions argues that many businesses should stress the search for investment alternatives rather than devote too much effort to computations on the few alternatives that come to their attention. Discuss.

6. A company official proposed this policy: "Each year purchase plant equipment in an amount equal to the depreciation charge." Evaluate.

7. Mr. X is considering purchase of a $2,500 automobile. He expects it to provide travel services worth $1,000 each year. He expects to obtain $500 worth of satisfaction in the first year from just having a new car and showing it off to his friends. He expects to travel 10,000 miles per year in the car. He estimates his variable costs at $400 the first year, with an additional amount equal to $150 times the square root of the age in years. (This would cover gasoline, oil, inspections, tires, batteries, and other repairs. He is uncertain about the exact years into which these would fall.) He expects the value of the car each year to be two-thirds of the value in the previous year. He believes he can earn 10% on any funds he has available. How long should he expect to use the car? What is its present value? (N.B. This problem is difficult and needs careful thought.)

18

Extracts and Cases on Investment Decisions

THE following extracts not only review the principles involved in investment decision discussed in the previous chapter, they also should clarify and elaborate those principles. The cases present an opportunity to apply those principles to concrete situations.

Extracts

Extract A

Managerial Economics (Joel Dean)

The crucial estimate in analyzing demand for capital is the productivity (i.e., rate of return) of the proposed capital expenditure. Since capital productivity is the key factor in sound budgeting of internal investments, the care and precision with which it is estimated are likely to make the difference between good investment decisions and bad ones.

General principles for estimating capital productivity are summarized [here]. . . .

1. Recognition of the source of productivity of capital is essential to correct estimation of capital earnings. . . . The most important direct sources are cost savings and sales expansion. Cost savings are the source for investments in replacement and modernization of equipment. Added sales volume (or more profitable volume) is the source for investments that involve new products or expansion of capacity to produce old ones. . . .

2. Earnings must be estimated on an individual project basis. It is the prospective profitability of *individual units* of *added* capital investment that is the key to their appraisal in allocating capital funds. Return on old, sunk investments has only historical interest and no relevance to decisions on new investments. . . .

3. It is *future* profit on additional investment that is relevant. Thus, profit projections must be based on estimates of future prices, future costs, and so forth. The record of the past is useful only as a guide to estimates of the future.

4. Capital productivity estimates usually should involve comparison of future costs and profits with the *appropriate alternative*. . . .

5. Capital productivity should be measured by earnings over the whole life of the asset. . . . Estimates of economic life are always inexact, but they are essential for measuring capital wastage costs. . . . Payout period . . . is a misleading measure of capital productivity. . . .

6. Discounting the stream of earnings to take account of the diminishing value of distant earnings is an integral part of the theory of capital value. . . . When the economic life of assets is short or fairly uniform, when earnings estimates are necessarily rough, and when uncertainty rises steeply in the distant future, this refinement is not worth its complexity cost.

On the other hand, discounting has practical importance when there are distinctive time patterns of the income streams of different assets, and when the rate of discount (logically the firm's cost of capital) is high, e.g., 15 to 20 per cent.

7. The amount of investment to be used for comparison with earnings should be the average capital tied up in the asset over the period being considered . . . rather than the initial capital outlay.

8. Estimates of earnings (whether from cost savings or from added profits) should take account of the indirect effects of the proposed capital outlay upon the operation of existing facilities. . . .

9. In a self-adjusting competitive economy, there is a tendency for capital expenditures to destroy the economic opportunity that creates their profitability. Abnormal profits are indicators of the richest opportunities for more investment, and expenditures will flow in their direction until increasing costs or output tend to cause firms to overshoot the optimum outlay level. In the process, they destroy the abnormal profits. This risk of destroying should be examined in connection with each profitability estimate. . . .

10. For some kinds of investments it is impractical to estimate a rate of return. The benefits are so diffused and conjectural (e.g., research laboratories and employee club houses) that they defy quantification. Earnings of others are so high and so apparent (e.g., replacing a washed-out railroad bridge) that estimating a return is an academic exercise. Earnings on other projects are patently too low to warrant return estimates. Capital productivity should be measured only when there is a factual foundation for estimates and for projects of borderline productivity.[1]

Extract B

Analysis for Production Management (Edward H. Bowman and Robert B. Fetter)

A decision model for replacement of equipment should portray the basic economic problem in such terms that the parameters may be evaluated with generally available business data. At the very least, it must be economically feasible to secure the required data. Also, the model should be capable of modification to fit the requirements of as wide a range of situations as pos-

[1] Joel Dean, *Managerial Economics* (Englewood Cliffs, N. J.: Prentice-Hall, Inc., 1951), pp. 562–564.

sible. The model should portray, symbolically, the economic problem involved in selecting the best course of action given some alternatives regarding the acquisition of production equipment. The model should first aim at economic soundness and then be modified in order to

1. Allow for the use of data which it is economically feasible to secure, and
2. Be reasonably easy to use by those who have the responsibility for making such decisions.

This second condition does not mean that necessary economic soundness should be sacrificed merely for computational ease. Rather, it must be recognized that modern business machines can make relatively short work of what might formerly have been considered insurmountable computational difficulties. The basic criterion for the model should be that of both economic soundness and of understanding on the part of those who must use such decision models. . . .

The important point . . . is that the model is a means to a decision, and it is the decision that is important. Usefulness is the proper criterion for choosing a model, and if it isn't useful, the best advice is to get another model. The simplest effective model which can be designed to aid in making a given kind of decision should always be used. The best course of action is to design a model based on the given situation.[2]

Cases

Case A:

A Case in the Economic Life of an Automobile [3]

In 1960, John Doran, a university student, was considering selling his automobile. The car was over seven years old. The car was a six cylinder model of one of the Big Three brands and was, therefore, one of the least expensive American cars available at the time it was purchased—the purchase price had been around $1,800. The owner drove the car about 8,000 miles per year—about half of the miles in town and the other half driving longer distances to and from his home town to the location of the university. He estimated that his expenses annually were as follows:

Gasoline and oil	$220
Inspections and lubrication	40
Repairs (including tires, battery, etc., but averaging several years together)	120
Depreciation (charging the original $1,800 off on a straight line basis over 10 years)	180

[2] Edward H. Bowman and Robert B. Fetter, *Analysis for Production Management* (Homewood, Illinois: Richard D. Irwin, 1957), pp. 314, 331.

[3] While this case is hypothetical, it is based on observation. The reader will be able himself to evaluate its "realism."

Present depreciated book value	540
Value of the car on a trade-in on a new car priced at $2,300	300
Value of the car if sold to a used car dealer	160
Interest that could be earned on money if not invested in the car	5%
Loss in trade-in value or in used car lot value if the car were kept one more year	$30

The question was whether it would be economical to sell his automobile and use public transportation instead. Mr. Doran estimated that he saved $100 in local bus fares by using the car. He also estimated that he saved $250 in longer distance transportation costs. He felt that the car had a considerable convenience value in saving time waiting for buses and getting him to his exact destination—he estimated that this was worth at least $200 per year to him. He recognized that some students received some prestige or snob value from owning a car, but he felt that he was above such considerations—the car simply provided transportation and saving of time as far as he was concerned.

The reason he was considering selling the car was that the repair costs were beginning to mount. While repairs, including tires and batteries, had amounted to only an average of $120 per year for the past three years, the car was reaching an age at which some major repairs were imminent.

Case B:

A Case in Replacing an Automobile

The same student, John Doran, unexpectedly received an inheritance from a distant relative amounting to $1,000. This made possible an alternative he had not considered previously—the purchase of a new car or a newer used car. By trading in his old car he would be able to escape the uncertainty of having to pay for some major repairs in the near future. He found that he could buy a new model of one of the Big Three for $2,400 less a $300 trade-in on his old car. This would mean that he would have to borrow $1,100 to finance the car. One of his friends was anxious to sell a three-year old car (again a standard model of one of the Big Three) at a price of $1,200. The car had travelled 25,000 miles and was in excellent condition. John Doran had full confidence that the car had received good treatment during its lifetime.

John Doran expected to use a new car the same way he had used the old one—averaging about 8,000 miles per year. He felt that the gas, oil, lubrication, and inspection expenses would be about the same as before—perhaps slightly lower—but he expected that the repairs would be much less. The second-hand car he was considering had a new set of tires and a new battery.

In considering the problem he decided to make an estimate of the present value of each alternative as far as his own personal use was concerned. He did not expect to get any added satisfaction from the newness of the replacement—again he was interested only in transportation and convenience.

Case C:
The Mapi Formula

The Machinery and Allied Products Institute has pioneered in the development of formulas applicable to investment decisions. George Terborgh, the research director of the Institute published a volume in 1949 discussing the theory of equipment replacement.[4] In more recent years the formula has been refined and developed in a form more easily understood by the practical businessman.[5] It is only fair to state, however, that the theory behind the formula is complex and difficult, and even a matter of dispute among writers on investment. In a volume such as this, it would be well to avoid the refinements of this theory.

Terborgh and his associates emphasize several points which should receive attention from any managers faced with investment policy, among which are the following:

1. An investment formula should make some kind of projection of technological change, that is, of obsolescence. The MAPI formula builds such projections into its formula and its charts.
2. The formula should provide a means for comparing investment now with investment at some future time, thus taking possible deferment into account.
3. The formula should make automatic corrections for taxes paid out of earnings arising from the investment.
4. The formula should concern itself with loss in salvage value on the old equipment and capital consumption of the new equipment, which requires an estimate of the salvage value of the new equipment at the end of its service life.

Fortunately for the practitioner, the MAPI formula is available in a form which makes a computation of the "urgency rating" of an investment relatively easy. This "urgency rating" is a "rate of return" kind of figure, though one involving different assumptions from the rate of return discussed earlier in this book.

The best way to discuss the MAPI formula is to present an illustration from actual practice. This is a case from the MAPI files, modified somewhat to illustrate particular points. The problem is one of replacing gear shapers. The details are as follows: [6]

> The proposal suggests replacing eight No. 6 Fellows Gear Shapers with 4 new No. 36 Fellows Gear Shapers at an installed cost of $112,000. The present machines are between 35 and 42 years old. They represent a liability, for major breakdowns could occur at any time. Indeed their condition is such that major repairs will be necessary in the near future, estimated at

[4] George Terborgh, *Dynamic Equipment Policy* (New York: McGraw-Hill Book Co., Inc., 1949).

[5] George Terborgh, *Business Investment Policy: A MAPI Study and Manual* (Washington: Machinery & Allied Products Institute, 1958), pp. 168–171.

[6] *Ibid.*, pp. 168–171. This case, like the others in the manual, is offered as a useful, but not perfect, example of the analytical art.

$6,000 per machine. This figure includes a charge of $1,000 for down time attributable to the capital additions. Once they have been rebuilt, there is still no assurance that further capital additions will not be necessary thereafter. Accordingly the total rebuild cost of $48,000 is prorated over 5 years (approximately), with an annual charge of $10,000.

The requirements of the work presently being handled on the No. 6 gear shapers are such that little precision is necessary. If it were, the present equipment would be unable to handle the work because of its worn condition. Although the ability of the proposed equipment to produce to closer tolerance is of little value for the work now being processed on the old machines, it will increase high-precision capacity. With the new units, there will be 7 machines of this type in the department. This will make it possible to interchange work between the 7 machines whereas the present No. 6 machines are unable to handle some of the larger or more precise work. A value of $3,000 a year has been assigned to this greater flexibility.

A saving in direct labor will be realized from the ability of the new machines to produce approximately twice as fast as the old. This saving is estimated at $1,280 a year, plus fringe benefits of $155 or $1,435. In addition, their heavier and more rigid construction should produce greater cutter life. A total of $2,000 a year has been assigned to this factor.

It is estimated that approximately 300 man hours of maintenance labor will be spent on the rebuilt gear shapers in the coming year. To arrive at a more realistic figure for the cost of one hour of direct labor spent in repairing a machine, the analyst attempts to account for the expenses involved in equipping and maintaining the repair man as well as for the direct labor time. Accordingly, the figure of $10 an hour is used to reflect the full cost of the repair man. This is arrived at by establishing a burden rate for the Machine Repair Department in much the same way as such rates are calculated for a production department. . . . The cost of maintaining the old equipment is therefore put at $3,000 a year (300 man hours at $10), plus $500 for maintenance materials consumed. Maintenance on the proposed equipment is assumed to be negligible.

Down time can be expected on the rebuilt equipment arising from ordinary maintenance. Delays in production will be inevitable, and expense will arise from the resulting bottlenecks. The total annual cost of this down time is placed at $1,675. A saving of floor space of 250 square feet is anticipated, valued at $2.00 a foot for $500 annually. On the other hand, the new equipment is charged with $1,680 a year for additional taxes and insurance.

Stipulations

Project operating rate	2,000 hours
Service life	20 years
Terminal salvage ratio	20 per cent
Tax rate	50 per cent

The first step in the analysis is to fill in the appropriate spaces on the summary of analysis sheet (Figure 18-1). This sheet is one prepared by MAPI, but individual companies may develop their own to fit their individual needs. The sheet provides spaces for taking into account all of the direct and indirect advantages of the project. The total at the bottom of the sheet is the sum of all of these advantages.

PROJECT NO. 5 SHEET I

SUMMARY OF ANALYSIS
(SEE ACCOMPANYING WORK SHEETS FOR DETAIL)

I. REQUIRED INVESTMENT

1	INSTALLED COST OF PROJECT		$ 112,000	1
2	DISPOSAL VALUE OF ASSETS TO BE RETIRED BY PROJECT		$	2
3	CAPITAL ADDITIONS REQUIRED IN ABSENCE OF PROJECT		$ 48,000	3
4	INVESTMENT RELEASED OR AVOIDED BY PROJECT (2+3)		$ 48,000	4
5	NET INVESTMENT REQUIRED (1−4)		$ 64,000	5

II. NEXT-YEAR ADVANTAGE FROM PROJECT

A. OPERATING ADVANTAGE
(USE FIRST YEAR OF PROJECT OPERATION)*

		Increase	Decrease	
6	ASSUMED OPERATING RATE OF PROJECT (HOURS PER YEAR)		2,000	6
	EFFECT OF PROJECT ON REVENUE			
7	FROM CHANGE IN QUALITY OF PRODUCTS	$	$	7
8	FROM CHANGE IN VOLUME OF OUTPUT			8
9	TOTAL	$ A	$ B	9
	EFFECT OF PROJECT ON OPERATING COSTS			
10	DIRECT LABOR	$	$ 1,280	10
11	INDIRECT LABOR			11
12	FRINGE BENEFITS		155	12
13	MAINTENANCE		3,500	13
14	TOOLING		2,000	14
15	SUPPLIES			15
16	SCRAP AND REWORK			16
17	DOWN TIME		1,675	17
18	POWER			18
19	FLOOR SPACE		500	19
20	PROPERTY TAXES AND INSURANCE	1,680		20
21	SUBCONTRACTING			21
22	INVENTORY			22
23	SAFETY			23
24	FLEXIBILITY		3,000	24
25	OTHER			25
26	TOTAL	$ 1,680 A	$ 12,110 B	26
27	NET INCREASE IN REVENUE (9A−9B)		$	27
28	NET DECREASE IN OPERATING COST (26B−26A)		$ 10,430	28
29	NEXT-YEAR OPERATING ADVANTAGE (27+28)		$ 10,430	29

B. NON-OPERATING ADVANTAGE
(USE ONLY IF THERE IS AN ENTRY IN LINE 4)

30	NEXT-YEAR CAPITAL CONSUMPTION AVOIDED BY PROJECT:			30
	A DECLINE OF DISPOSAL VALUE DURING THE YEAR		$	
	B NEXT-YEAR ALLOCATION OF CAPITAL ADDITIONS		$ 10,000	
		TOTAL	$ 10,000	

C. TOTAL ADVANTAGE

31	TOTAL NEXT-YEAR ADVANTAGE FROM PROJECT (29+30)		$ 20,430	31

* For projects with a significant break-in period, use performance after break-in.

FIGURE 18-1

The next step is the computation of the MAPI urgency rating which, as has been stated, is in the nature of a rate of return, but not the same rate obtained by other methods. Figure 18-2 provides a form on which these computations may be made. At the top (line 32), the appropriate figure is the total advantage computed on Figure 18-1, corrected for taxes (if the tax rate is 50 per cent only half of the total advantage would appear here). The next task is to figure the MAPI chart allowance on the project, which in-

PROJECT NO. 5 SHEET 2

III. COMPUTATION OF MAPI URGENCY RATING

32 TOTAL NEXT-YEAR ADVANTAGE AFTER INCOME TAX (31 — TAX) $ 10,215

33 MAPI CHART ALLOWANCE FOR PROJECT (TOTAL OF COLUMN F, BELOW) $ 2,576 *

(ENTER DEPRECIABLE ASSETS ONLY)

Item or Group	Installed Cost of Item or Group A	Estimated Service Life (Years) B	Estimated Terminal Salvage (Percent of Cost) C	MAPI Chart Number D	Chart Percentage E	Chart Percentage × Cost (E × A) F
Gear Shapers	$112,000	20	20	1	2.3	$ 2,576
					TOTAL	$ 2,576

34 AMOUNT AVAILABLE FOR RETURN ON INVESTMENT (32—33) $ 7,639

35 MAPI URGENCY RATING (34 ÷ 5) · 100 % 12

* Since the chart allowance does not cover future capital additions to project assets, add an annual proration of such additions, if any, to the figure in Line 33.

FIGURE 18-2

volves the use of Figure 18-3. To use this chart, one must estimate the service life of the equipment and the terminal salvage value. For example, in this particular case the estimated service life is 20 years and the estimated terminal salvage is 20 per cent. By moving along the horizontal scale of the chart to 20 years and up to the curve representing salvage value of 20 per cent, we find that the MAPI chart per cent is 2.3. For our purposes, we might consider this to be a capital consumption allowance, though the theory involved is extremely complex, incorporating, for example, adjustments for

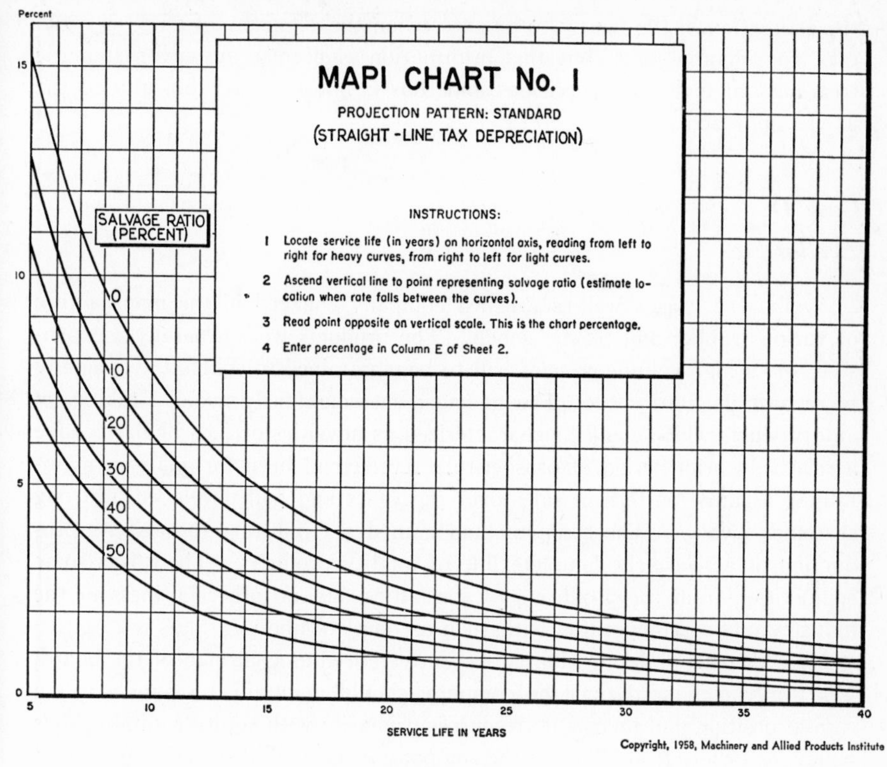

FIGURE 18-3

the fact that we have overstated the income tax in our computation of overall advantage.

By multiplying this capital consumption percentage of 2.3 per cent by our installed project cost (line 1 of Figure 18-1), we arrive at a dollar capital consumption figure. As shown on Figure 18-2, we deduct this from the after tax advantage, which will give us the amount available for the return on the investment. When we compute this as a per cent of the net investment (line 5 on Figure 18-1), we obtain the MAPI urgency rating, which is the figure we have been seeking.

How do we use this urgency rating? The procedure is to compare it with similar ratings on other investment opportunities, selecting those investments with the highest ratings. One should not, of course, select any investments with urgency ratings (rates of return) below the interest on debt and the cost of equity capital needed to finance the investment.

On first reading, the MAPI system may seem rather complex. But it should be clear that in practice it provides a relatively simple routine for computing rates of return as long as one does not bother about the theory underlying the routine. The use of the MAPI chart is easy and the remainder of the computations involve only simple arithmetic. It is true that the estimation of the figures to be entered on the summary of analysis could take considerable time, but this information is needed for any systematic treatment of investment decisions and thus is not a special difficulty of the MAPI approach.

Case D:

Avella, Inc.[7]

Avella, Inc. was a well-established company engaged in the manufacture of various rubber and plastic goods. The products were generally inexpensive, and a high volume of sales had to be maintained to enable the company to recover its fixed costs. The management consciously avoided taking on any products which could be characterized as novelties or fads likely to have a relatively brief period of prosperity. Avella had been fortunate in maintaining a stable pattern of sales over the years and had developed a strong customer loyalty. The company had gained a reputation through its production of a relatively complete line of quality products. There was some competition from the producers of specialties, but no other business in the industry offered competition with such a complete line.

Mr. Edgar A. Gordon, who had recently retired as chairman of the board, was firmly convinced that the company should maintain a strong working capital position and finance its resources primarily with equity capital. This policy, he believed, would place the company in a favorable position to exploit opportunities when they arose and would have the further advantage of providing protection during prolonged periods of general economic decline.

This policy was being carefully reviewed. Many of the officers and directors believed that a restrictive cash policy had checked the growth of the company and had resulted in the loss of many favorable opportunities for profitable investment. There was no desire, however, to make rapid changes. The position of the firm and its policies and procedures were being currently examined.

The company had maintained a minimum cash balance of approximately $1,500,000 at all times. Throughout the year, cash needs were carefully budgeted and potted on a broken-line graph as shown in Figure 18-4. Any cash flow in excess of what was required to finance current operations was invested in short-term government securities. This investment was adjusted up or down according to the seasonal needs for cash. Careful budgeting had resulted in stabilizing the cash balance at about the desired level.

During 19__, Avella, Inc., increased its working capital by $1,310,000.

[7] This case was prepared by Professor Carl L. Moore of Lehigh University as a basis for class discussion. This case is not designed to present illustrations of either correct or incorrect handling of administrative decisions.

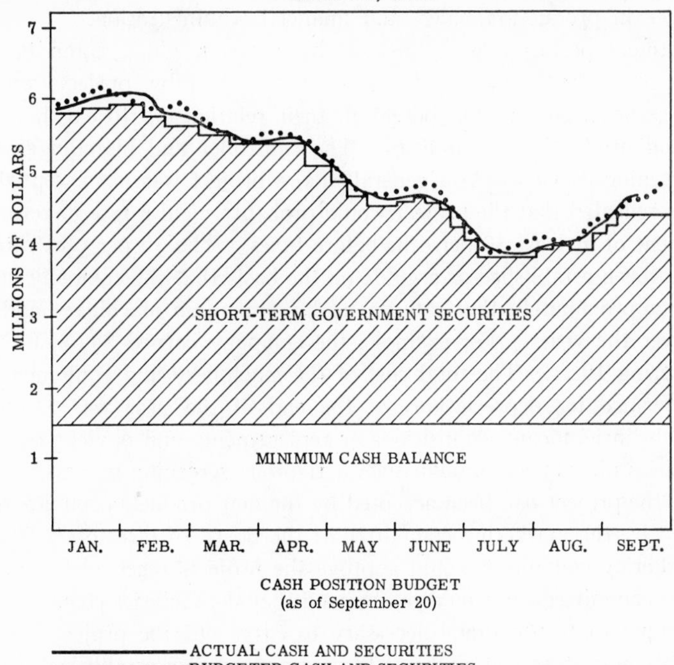

FIGURE 18-4

Source of Net Working Capital:	
Net income before depreciation charges of $1,302,994	$3,510,050
Uses of Net Working Capital:	
Dividend payments	$1,250,100
Fixed asset additions	949,950
Total	$2,200,050
Net Increase in Working Capital	$1,310,000

The statement of financial position at December 31, 19__ and the condensed operating statement for the year 19__, as given in Table 18-1, were considered by the controller to be typical. The gross cost of the plant and equipment at the end of the fiscal year was $24,362,130. After deducting the accumulated depreciation of $16,740,630, there was a remaining net book value of $7,621,500.

The controller of the company, Mr. Charles A. Penberthy, was in the process of reviewing the way in which business investment opportunities were evaluated to determine their economic feasibility. Mr. Penberthy was well acquainted with the various activities of the company through his long years of service in production, sales, and financial administration.

Investment proposals were initiated by a new products committee which worked closely with the director of research. Possible projects were carefully screened as to market potential, their relationship to existing product lines, and production possibilities. The controller and his staff assisted in this screening process. As a general rule, a project was not accepted unless analysis revealed that the project would probably yield a rate of return upon investment of at least 30 per cent before taxes. The 30 per cent rate of return had been established as a guide on the basis that the company had been earning approximately that rate on its investment in machinery and equipment over the years. For example, the company earned $4,686,073 before taxes during 19___. The total cost of the machinery and equipment (without allowance for depreciation) at the end of the year was $15,654,257. Relatively insignificant acquisitions or replacements and obvious cost saving possibilities did not go through such a rigorous screening process.

After the project had been accepted by the new products committee, it was reviewed by the marketing committee of the board of directors. Ordinarily the marketing committee would approve the projects received from the new products committee and would recommend that the facilities committee of the board appropriate the funds necessary to carry out the project. The new products committee, well aware of the company policy established while Mr. Gordon was chairman of the board, did not bother to submit projects which could not show a potential rate of return of at least 30 per cent.

The rate of return as computed by the company was the net dollar advantage before taxes divided by the average annual investment.

$$\frac{\text{Net Dollar Advantage Before Taxes}}{\text{Average Annual Investment}} = \text{Rate of Return}$$

Both the net additional revenue and the direct cost savings to be derived from the project were considered in arriving at the net dollar advantage before taxes. The net additional revenue was the gross revenue anticipated from the project as reduced by the cost of goods sold and estimated selling and administrative expenses. The cost of goods sold was computed in the conventional manner, including the cost of direct materials, direct labor, and manufacturing overhead. Manufacturing overhead, including depreciation, was applied to the products on a predetermined rate basis as a percentage of direct labor cost. An allowance of 17 per cent of the estimated gross revenue was deducted for selling and administrative expenses. This percentage had been established from past experience studies which showed that the selling and administrative expenses which should be identified with a product were approximately 17 per cent of sales. Finally, depreciation computed on a straight-line basis on the facility cost and on what was called the capital corollary was deducted to arrive at the net dollar advantage before taxes.

The capital corollary represented the allocated investment in floor space used. Mr. Penberthy maintained that each machine had to absorb a portion of the cost of space used. If the allocated plant costs such as depreciation, taxes, and insurance were not considered, the building expansion required to accommodate additional equipment would be unfairly charged against the last piece added, when in reality all additional pieces helped bring about the need for building expansion. The corollary investment was estimated to amount to 70 per cent of the cost of the equipment. Some time in the past a study was made over a period of time to determine the relationship between plant costs and investment. As a result of this study, it was found that the allocated plant costs would amount to about 70 per cent of the investment in equipment.

Net Dollar Advantages Before Taxes

1. Direct cost savings before depreciation		$
2. Increased revenue:		
Sales	$	
Cost of goods sold	———	
Gross profit	$	
17 per cent allowance for selling and administrative expenses	———	
Net revenue addition		———
3. Gross dollar advantage [(1) + (2)]		$
4. Less depreciation of facility cost and capital corollary		———
5. Net dollar advantage before taxes [(3) — (4)]		$

The total average annual investment was then computed. The cost of the equipment itself was divided in half to arrive at an average. The capital corollary cost amounting to 70 per cent of the equipment cost was similarily averaged. Furthermore, a provision was made for the increase in working capital which would be required to support the project.

A study had been made showing that approximately

9 per cent of the estimated gross revenue was held as accounts receivable,
21 per cent of the estimated cost of goods sold was invested in inventories, and
5 per cent of the estimated cost of goods sold was held as a minimum cash balance.

Accordingly, these percentages were applied to the expected gross revenue and cost of goods sold resulting from the project to arrive at the additional investment held in the form of working capital.

Investment

½ Facility estimated cost	$
½ Capital corollary	
Total working capital	————
Total Average Annual Investment	$

As an example, an evaluation of a proposal to manufacture a certain type of air mattress to be used in swimming pools is given in Table 18-2.

Projects which were accepted were subject to a postcompletion audit. If the results did not come close to expectations, a decision was reached as to whether or not an additional audit was to be made. In certain cases it was believed that if more time were allowed, the project would eventually meet the requirements. On the other hand, some projects might show that there was little opportunity for improvement and that additional audits would not be justified. An unsuccessful project might be liquidated, or it might be continued as a sort of necessary evil which had to be tolerated. For example, a project might be maintained, which did not justify itself, in order to round out the product line.

Mr. Penberthy and his staff were actively investigating the possibility of improving the method by which business investment proposals were evaluated. Both Mr. Penberthy and his staff had been reading current literature on the subject and had attended various conferences dealing with this topic.

TABLE 18-1

AVELLA, INC.

STATEMENT OF FINANCIAL POSITION
DECEMBER 31, 19__

Current Assets	
Cash	$ 1,707,269
U. S. Government Securities at cost including accrued interest	3,111,398
Accounts receivable	7,818,592
Inventories	8,616,133
Prepaid expenses	309,380
Total Current Assets	$21,562,772
Current Liabilities	
Accounts payable	$ [illegible],141,834
Accrued taxes, wages, and miscellaneous expenses	1,788,636
Estimated Federal income tax liability less U. S. Treasury notes of $1,080,000	183,301
Total Current Liabilities	$ 3,113,771
Net Working Capital	$18,449,001

TABLE 18-1 (*Continued*)

Other Assets	
Miscellaneous investments	590,417
Real estate, machinery, and equipment at cost less depreciation	8,420,152
Net Assets	$27,459,570
Capital	
Common stock	$ 7,413,480
Capital in excess of par value	2,527,242
Reinvested earnings	17,518,848
	$27,459,570

STATEMENT OF EARNINGS
FOR THE YEAR ENDED DECEMBER 31, 19__

Sales and Other Income	$48,654,260
Costs and Expenses	
Cost of products sold	$30,232,458
Selling, administrative and general expenses	13,735,720
Federal income tax, estimated	2,479,017
Total Costs and Expenses	$46,447,204
Net Earnings	$ 2,207,056

TABLE 18-2

AVELLA, INC.

ECONOMIC EVALUATION OF FACILITY ACQUISITION PROPOSAL
NET DOLLAR ADVANTAGES BEFORE TAXES

Increased revenue:		
Sales	$793,278	
Cost of goods sold	558,774	
Gross profit	$234,504	
17% allowance for selling and administrative expenses	134,857	
Net revenue increase		99,647
Gross dollar advantage		$ 99,647
Less depreciation of facility		
Cost and capital corollary		25,730
Net dollar advantage before taxes		$ 73,917

INVESTMENT

One-half facility estimated cost	$ 75,675
Capital Corollary	
One-half other fixed assets	52,973
Total working capital	216,677
Total average annual investment	$345,325

TABLE 18-2 (*Continued*)

$$\frac{\text{Net dollar advantage before taxes—\$73,917}}{\text{Total average annual investment—\$345,325}} = 21.4\% \text{ rate of return}$$

Explanatory Notes:		
Total facility cost	$151,350	
(Est. life of 10 years, no residual salvage value)		
Capital corollary (70% of $151,350)	$105,945	
Sales	$793,278	
Cost of goods sold	$558,774	
Selling and administrative expenses (17% of $793,278)		$134,857
Total Working Capital:		
Accounts receivable (9% of $793,278)	$ 71,395	
Inventories (21% of $558,774)	117,343	
Cash (5% of $558,774)	27,939	
Total Working Capital		216,677
Depreciation [10% of ($151,350 + $105,945)]		25,730

19

Use of Accounting in Planning and Control

ACCOUNTING has been a basic tool for management ever since the idea of double entry bookkeeping was introduced before Columbus discovered America. Modern education for business usually starts with the fundamentals of accounting because they are the most familiar approaches to recording, classifying, and presenting quantitative facts about the firm.

In the beginning the role of accounting was that of a *recorder* of contractual obligations, providing an historical review. Directly from this role, accounting took on a second function—*reporting* by consistent statements the status of the firm at points in time(in the balance sheet), and the measurement of revenue and expense over periods of time (in the income statement). With the development of the corporation and resulting absentee owners, the need was increased for objectivity and consistency. The *auditing* function became essential as different financial interests (stockholders, creditors) sought reliable information about the operations of the firm. Until recently, conventional accounting thus remained oriented to the financial requirements of the firm. These stressed the accurate and consistent statement of what had happened in the past. Rules of professional conduct *for these functions* have specifically prohibited the use of an accountant's name in conjunction "with an estimate of earnings contingent upon future transactions in a manner which may lead to the belief that the member vouches for the accuracy of the forecast."[1]

Even as early as the decade of the 1920's, a view of accounting began to include additional functions (see the extract by J. O. McKinsey). These,

[1] Rules of Professional Conduct (American Institute of Certified Public Accountants as revised, December 19, 1950).

under the heading of managerial accounting, provided tools for the diagnosis of critical problems requiring management attention. Accountants became more interested in aiding managers in *planning* and *controlling.* They began to look at the future in spite of the loss of precision resulting from uncertainty. Accountants participated in the development of standards and budgets dealing with what revenue and cost *should be*—not only with measuring what *had been.* Accounting became accounting *for* management in addition to accounting *of* management.

Distinctions between Financial Accounting and Managerial Accounting

In this chapter the functions of managerial accounting will be discussed; it is assumed that the reader is familiar with the conventional subjects taken up in a beginning year of accounting. A summary of a few characteristics of financial accounting, however, will provide a basis for showing important distinctions.

Financial accounting

Financial accounting evolved largely as needs arose and was unaffected by economics. The tests of accounting principles, theory, and conventions were utilitarian in satisfying the needs of reporting the stewardship of management and in providing information to interested groups external to the business unit. The measurement of profits and valuation of assets and equities were the ultimate interests of these groups. To provide this information, the accountant had to decide arbitrarily on some time period in which to split up the flow of revenue and costs into segments. Distinctions between such classifications as operating expense and capital expenditure depend upon these *time* classifications.

Financial accountants see themselves as neutral observers who report facts as they exist or have existed. They take an unbiased view without trying to affect the facts as they occur. The future is not yet a fact, and therefore the financial accountant feels that he cannot include the future in his reports. Of course, even the financial accountant cannot avoid some responsibility for his impact on operations, since his judgment has determined the manner in which the facts have been reported.

The financial accountant always attempts to report in a conservative manner—in a less rather than more favorable light. The value of his reports to those outside the firm is increased by this characteristic. Consistency of method of reporting from one year to the next is basic. There may be a number of ways to treat a certain matter, but once a given way is used, the next reports must use the same way (or provide warning of any change). Using original cost in all valuations may have its limitations for decisions, but the results are consistent and objectively determined.

The essence of financial accounting is in the double entry method of bookkeeping and in internal control. Each part of a whole must be accounted for. The whole is the sum of its parts and if one small part is omitted, time and effort must be expended to place it into its proper pigeonhole. The rigor of the accountant and his precision provide a sound and solid footing upon which one can proceed in analysis. The use of the dollar as a common denominator makes possible rough comparisons of like things at different dates or unlike things at a given date.

Managerial accounting

Since accountants report data to many different types of users, it is not surprising that some users have found that they would have preferred a different method of classification or additional information. Recently accountants have been striving to expand their services for the manager. The manager must look to the future; he must make relevant approximations and not worry with balancing to the last penny; he must have data tailored to his specific needs; he must include many factors as bases for a decision; consistency with the past is not of primary concern; he must analyze certain economic costs even though they are not included in the structure provided by the financial accountant.

The managerial accountant can provide this additional information with analysis which does not necessarily agree precisely with general accounts. The economist gives heavy weight to opportunity costs in making a decision; yet the financial accountant finds the recording of such costs outside the framework of his system. The managerial accountant can help by using conventional accounts and adding more information for specific purposes.

The managerial accountant must find a criterion by which he can compare alternatives. He must envisage what costs *should be,* what sales can *be expected,* and what *plan* of interrelating present action with future expectations is appropriate. In other words, he must have *standards,* he must *forecast,* and he must *budget.* All of this must be related to the organizational structure so that responsibility can be fixed for control of the different variables.

The view in this book is that accounting is a basic tool for management, and that it should not be considered only a mechanism of recording and reporting past data from a neutral position. Management should integrate the viewpoints of the accountant, the statistician, and the economist for better decision making and control.

The managerial accountant must recognize the limitations of conventional records and employ economic analysis in order to aid the manager in decision making. Some of the limitations of conventional accounting are:

1. Managerial decisions often require information regarding the *current value* of resources, whereas the use of the "cost principle" in conventional accounting results in measurement of *unamortized* cost of these resources.

2. Conventional accounts use the dollar as its common denominator, but do not recognize that the *purchasing power* of the dollar has been decreasing.

3. Figures are classified as needed for financial reports, and usually are *not separated* by function, activity, product line, class of customer, or other operational segment.

4. Fixed costs are allocated to units of production in some arbitrary manner so that an *average cost* can be determined. The manager needs information on an *incremental* basis and will often be confused by reports in which unit total costs are emphasized.

5. Since accounting techniques stress objectivity and detail, the interpreter of accounting reports often forgets that a great deal of *judgment* goes into the reporting and that assumptions are involved.

6. Conventional records and reports are concerned mainly with the *past,* whereas the manager must consider the future.

7. Cost to the financial accountant is measured and recorded orginally in cash or cash equivalent, whereas the manager should consider the broader economic concept of *opportunity costs.*

This chapter will not be concerned with the mechanics of recording and reporting financial data. Some of the techniques of *diagnosis* which make direct use of conventional reports will be summarized. Secondly, the role of accounting in decision-making and *planning* will be presented. Thirdly, the basic attitude necessary for the accountant to aid in the controlling process will be analyzed. In short, let us turn to the *interpretation* of accounting data, the relation of accounting to *budgeting,* and the role of *controllership* in modern management.

Appraisal of Past Actions

Accounting statements provide a wealth of material to help a manager understand the present state of his business and past events. Typically, the quantity of available information is staggering and can cause mental indigestion if the manager does not use proper techniques of financial statement analysis. Appraisal requires some knowledge of criteria by which one can judge a situation to be acceptable or latent with troubles.

An absolute quantity in a financial statement by itself may have limited meaning, while if compared with other quantities it will provide guide posts for decisions. Three approaches to comparisons are useful:

1. Comparing ratios of different absolute quantities from a company's statements for a given time with ratios of similar firms for the same time;
2. Comparing absolute quantities and/or ratios for the same firm over a number of past periods;
3. Comparing past relationships with some desired condition.

Ratio analysis

Ratio analysis stresses the relationships of classifications in financial statements. Roy A. Foulke of Dun and Bradstreet, Inc., has collected information over several decades on the ratios of a large number of firms in different lines of business activity and has published a useful manual[2] that includes these ratios. He recommends comparison of fourteen key ratios of a given firm with averages for similar firms and offers generalizations as warning signals (such as, funded debt should never be larger than net working capital).

Certain key ratios call attention to tendencies that might cause financial embarrassment. A manager must be able to look at financial statements and find danger signals. Is he carrying an excessive investment in fixed assets? Will his current debts cause him trouble when they come due? Are the interest charges on his long term liabilities too burdensome? Are inventories on hand too large relative to his volume of business, or is there evidence that part of the finished stock of goods cannot be sold under current price policies? Is he extending credit to customers who are not paying their debts quickly enough? Is too much cash being drained from the business through dividends that are too high? Financial ratios give the manager a clue in his search for answers to such questions.

A successful firm must meet its maturing obligations promptly. It is for this reason that the current ratio $\left(\frac{\text{Current Assets}}{\text{Current Liabilities}}\right)$ is one of the most widely used tools of financial analysis. Since assets often shrink in value and liabilities usually come due, there is an obvious need for some fund that can be available as a cushion. For a long time many have considered a 2:1 ratio to be satisfactory. However, the analysis is not quite so simple. For one thing, if cash is low and debts are maturing rapidly, the current ratio could appear satisfactory (because current assets include large accounts receivables and high inventory) and still the firm will face financial embarrassment. It is clear, then, that the types of the current assets and current liabilities are pertinent to the appraisal.

The current ratio of 3:1 might be too low during one season of the year and a 1½:1 adequate for another season. If a business man must carry large inventories up to Christmas and pay for the goods before he liquidates the inventories, he must obtain additional working funds. If the manager operates a public utility which can depend upon prompt payment for its services but has few short term obligations, he may be able to operate successfully with current assets only slightly larger than current liabilities. On the other hand, if the manager operates a furniture store which must carry a large assortment of items in stock and which may allow its customers plenty of time to pay for purchases, he may find that a 4:1 ratio is not good enough. If times are good and money is flowing into the business without much pressure, a low current ratio may be adequate; during a depression the same ratio could spell disaster.

In times of rapid expansion, the manager often underestimates his total

[2] Roy A. Foulke, *Behind the Scenes of Business* (Dun and Bradstreet, Inc., 1952), pp. 27–28.

capital needs. He may figure that a new wing will require a certain sum of money and that equipment will require an additional amount, but he may forget that increased sales and payrolls will demand a large increase in working funds. Under these conditions, unless he forecasts his additional needs the current ratio computed from his past experience will mislead him.

Some executives prefer to watch the absolute amount of working funds instead of the current ratio. They recognize that ratios can play tricks. The fact that the denominator of the current ratio changes with each new situation makes comparisons among ratios difficult. For example, take a firm with $200,000 in current assets and $100,000 in current liabilities—thus a current ratio of 2:1. The ratio can be improved in appearance without changing any factor other than paying off some of the debts with some of the cash. If $50,000 of debts are paid in this illustration, it would change the ratio to 3:1—this looks better, but what real difference is there? Actually, because of the reduced amount of cash, the firm might be in a poorer position to meet future obligations.

Among other useful ratios providing clues for a manager is the merchandise turnover $\left(\frac{\text{Cost of Goods Sold}}{\text{Average Inventory}}\right)$. It represents the number of times that the average inventory (beginning inventory plus ending inventory divided by 2) is being converted into cash or other assets. Notice that this ratio relates a quantity in the income statement to a quantity in the balance sheet. The higher this ratio is, the greater the number of times the company has been able to sell items carried in stock. Of course, the merchandise turnover is only as sensitive as the manner of computing average inventory makes it. If the average inventory is computed annually and the policy is to reduce the stock at times when a physical count is made (usually at the end of a year), the turnover can be misleading. Since the numerator of the ratio is the cost of goods sold and not sales, varying selling prices will not affect the ratio.

Two ratios measuring the rate of earnings may offer additional clues concerning the past condition of the business. The ratio of net income to sales $\left(\frac{\text{Net Income}}{\text{Net Sales}}\right)$ indicates the percentage of a sales dollar being earned by the company. Again, the ratio can be misinterpreted unless the analysis considers the factors behind the data. Does a low ratio mean that the firm is doing a poor job? In the case of food distribution, the ratio is very low (1 per cent to 3 per cent), but volume of sales may mean high absolute profits. In retail marketing of furniture, this ratio is higher (7 per cent to 10 per cent), but slow turnover might mean that this business is less profitable. The ratio has important implications when the manager is considering whether he will strive for low-margin-high-volume or high-margin-low-volume business. Sales and production policies are especially relevant to interpretation of these data obtained from the accounting department.

Another important ratio is the rate of return on equity $\left(\frac{\text{Net Income}}{\text{Equity}}\right)$. This ratio is significant in evaluating the success of the firm in achieving profits. In all financial discussions, this ratio is fundamental. Its chief limitation for decision-making purposes is that it provides a net figure and tells little about why it is not greater. The manager needs to follow the factors affecting net income back through costs, price, volume, and so forth, in order to analyze what changes need be made. Of course, if the firm tends to use large amounts of borrowed capital in place of owners' funds, the ratio will indicate a higher return than if equity is large with little borrowed money.

The numerator (net income) of the rate of return on equity ratio can be computed either before or after corporate income taxes are subtracted. If net income before taxes is used, the ratio will indicate the progress of earnings excluding the effect of taxes, a factor not directly under the control of the management. Typically, the denominator of the rate of return ratio includes the book value of the owners' equity; however, the market value of this equity may be used by those who wish to consider the current opportunities for investment.

There are many other ratios which can be computed from the financial statements. Some will add important new information; others may show the same information in a different form. No single ratio serves the purpose of telling everything about the firm—in fact, a number should be used jointly. Ratio analysis can be helpful to the manager in his search for possible areas needing his attention.

Comparative analysis over time

In addition to ratio analysis (sometimes called a static approach), the comparison of statements of a given firm over time (a dynamic approach) will yield trends in the development of a firm. Many annual reports of corporations today provide comparative balance sheets and income statements for the past three, five, or ten years. The analyst can make this information more meaningful by using several simple techniques.

First, he could compute ratios of each item on each side of the balance sheet to the totals. For example, cash might be stated as 5 per cent of total assets and accounts payable as 3 per cent of total liabilities and equity. The same type of ratios could be computed for the Income Statement using Net Sales as the basis; Cost of Goods might be 85 per cent of Net Sales. This simple first step, called *common size statements*, can provide a clue to a problem which otherwise might be overlooked.

The difficulty with common size statements is a lack of some criterion of a "proper" percentage. For this reason, it is helpful to compute similar ratios for different years. Again the analyst must beware of the problem of the changing denominators of ratios. If the ratio of Cost of Goods Sold to Net Sales is 85 per cent for one year and 88 per cent for the next, this increase might have been caused by a decrease in price at which sales were made, an increase of cost of raw materials greater than an increase in price, or any number of variations in the components of each of the two absolutes in each of the two years.

What then is the value of such computations? The greatest help is gained in the process of computing the derived facts, a process that forces the analyst to look at "the elephant from different perspectives." Again, if the process is used naïvely and mechanically, it can yield more misconceptions than useful interpretations.

Another step in considering comparative statements, which will satisfy some of the shortcomings of the above process, is the computation of increases and decreases in each item of the statements from one year to the next (computing an index of each year's absolute value relative to a base year). For example, there is a firm with Net Sales for 1959 of $10,000,000; for 1960 of $11,000,000; for 1961 of $12,000,000. If 1959 is used as the base of comparison (as the denominator of the ratio), 1960 will have an index of 110 and 1961, 120. Notice that the rate of increase, nevertheless, has declined from 10 per cent for 1960 relative to 1959 to 9 per cent for 1961 relative to 1960. Percentages and ratios can help show relationships, but they can also be tricky to interpret.

Source and application of funds

Among the types of accounting analysis most useful to a manager is the study of funds. It is often not clear from the balance sheet and the income statement where funds have gone and from where they came. The accountant can prepare a formal statement, the Statement of Source and Application of Funds. The method of developing this statement is covered in a course in accounting and will not be dwelt on here. The point of view, one highly useful to management, will be stressed.

The term "funds" has different meaning in different usages. In this context, it is broader than cash but not as broad as current assets. Generally, net working capital (current assets minus current liabilities) is the pertinent measure. Funds can be said to be any assets which can be freely used to acquire other assets and/or to pay obligations. Most of the information can be obtained from the comparison of balance sheets of two dates.

The analysis of the flow of funds helps answer such questions as: "Where did the company's profits go?" "What happened to the money secured from the sale of additional stock?" "Did the amount that was charged as depreciation (requiring no cash outlay) go for purchase of new equipment?"

Those accounts not included in current assets and current liabilities will reveal sources of funds or their application. The most important sources of funds are:

1. Proceeds from the sale of securities;
2. Proceeds for the sale of fixed assets;
3. Sale of investments in other companies;
4. Net income from operations.

The most important applications of funds are:

1. Payment of dividends;
2. Purchases of new fixed assets;
3. Payment of long term debts.

One special note is important in computing the sources of funds. In the computation of net profits, *depreciation* is recorded as an expense but is a noncash expense and does not require funds; therefore, it must be added back as a source of funds; strictly speaking, depreciation does not provide funds but represents that part of revenue generated by operations not appearing in the income statement as a part of net income. In other words, depreciation does not provide funds; it preserves them.

After a manager has studied the historical data provided by financial accounting, he is better able to plan for the future. After he checks where he obtained funds and where he applied them, he becomes anxious to estimate where he will obtain sufficient funds for the future and to what uses he can best place them. A case in the next chapter will illustrate how a company uses the point of view of sources and applications of funds in estimating future needs. Let us now turn to the contribution of accounting to planning.

Accounting Techniques for Planning

One of the tools available to a manager as he concentrates on future actions is a budget. Budgeting has become one of the means by which planning for the future can be brought out of the clouds of vision, hope, and nebulous generalizations and stated in definite quantitative terms. Although it is a primary interest of the chief accounting officer, it cannot be effective unless every part of the organization understands its role.

Budgeting

A business budget is a complete set of management plans expressed in quantitative terms by which objectives can be achieved for a definite period in the future. It will be seen that it serves as the predetermined criterion, found in Chapter 11 to be an essential of any control system. Moreover, if it is accepted by the operating department heads and not considered a gimmick of the accounting department, it can serve as a major tool of coordination. It must be built up by realistic estimates of operating supervisors at the bottom of the organization, but must be supported by the chief executive officer in his policy decisions. The form of the budget depends directly upon the particular organizational structure of the firm. It is a way of defining departmental objectives, relating them to company-wide objectives, and controlling performance.

A company budget is a composite of a number of budgets. A sales budget based upon a well worked out sales forecast often serves as a starting point in the process. A production budget may then be constructed which in turn necessitates a purchasing budget for raw materials. A capital budget must consider the long range building and equipment requirements which will make possible current operations consistent with the production budget. The financial budget provides plans for the necessary working capital and long term financing. All such subsidiary budgets must be constructed with consistent assumptions.

Responsibility for maintaining proper relationships among these budgets rests on the controller or some other staff executive. However, since budgeting should reflect the joint thinking of, and be made effective by, operating executives, a budget committee composed of representatives of all major departments actually makes the planning decisions. Budgeting depends upon the attitude of all management. The effects of specific parts of budgets limit the actions of each level of the organization. Human nature tends to rebel against "straight jackets." However, if a person has a fuller understanding of the need for budgets and of the way in which they are developed, he will be more willing to accept them as reasonable guides.

In the process of constructing a comprehensive budget, management must locate basic estimating factors (these were called critical or limiting factors when discussing decision making in general in Chapter 9). These factors serve as starting points in the building of a budget. It was mentioned previously that the sales forecast may be this starting point; however, under different situations other forecasts serve as basic estimating factors. During a wartime period, the personnel officer may find labor in such short supply that it requires him to consider his forecast of available labor as the limiting factor. In a new industry such as plastics, the supply of the required type of raw material may be the basic estimating factor, and the purchasing officer must make a forecast of the probable quantity that can be obtained.

One of the first questions which management must answer in constructing a budget is the period of time for which estimates shall be made. Two general factors provide the range of the length of the time period: first, it should be short enough to permit making fairly accurate predictions; and secondly, long enough to raise significant problems of policy, strategy, and procedure.

A number of specific factors affect the length of the budget period. The availability of factual information will increase the accuracy of prediction. The stability of the market faced by the firm will affect the forecast. In electric utilities, demand is stable and budgets can be made for five or ten years ahead; in automobile production, an annual forecast may need rapid revisions. The rate of technological progress may disturb the demand for competing and complementary goods on one hand, and the costs of production on the other. The budget period must be co-extensive with the accounting period so that comparisons between actual results and the budget figures can be made. Both of these should coincide with the natural cycles of activity of the business. If seasonal variations are pronounced, budgets should be short enough to avoid averaging out the meaningful factors. The length of the production cycle, credit extensions to customers, and lags in delivery are also important in determining the length of the budget period.

Flexible budgets

Since so many variables must be considered in budgeting, and since forecasting may be inaccurate, a manager might conclude that budgeting is a nice tool for the other fellow, but not for him. However, no matter how uncertain a manager's forecasts may be, he still will be better off attempting to look to the future than "playing by ear." Moreover, he will find additional budgeting concepts that will help him further.

The *flexible* budget will meet some of his criticisms. Up to this point, it has been assumed that one set of plans based upon definite quantities of a forecast will be made. This can be called a *fixed budget,* one that does not plan for changes. The *flexible budget* is set up to show expected costs of production at various levels of operations, as illustrated in Table 19-1. In effect, a flexible (sometimes called variable) budget is a collection of several budgets—one for each of several levels of operations. The necessary refinement in variable budgets is in the separation of costs into variable and fixed (discussed in Chapter 15). In fact, if a breakeven chart has been made, it may give a graphical picture of the over-all variable budget. Separating variable from fixed costs in each of the budgetary units will furnish useful information to lower management. For a firm with a number of departments, this separation of results is a sizable job, but one that is rewarding since it makes the budgetary process more useful to each department head. With a variable budget, the operating manager need not curse the forecaster of sales or claim that the budget is no longer useful because it was prepared for a different level of activity. He has the means of adjusting plans to reality. Many of the tools available for a flexible budget, such as equations which express the relationship of costs to levels of operations, offer additional help, but are outside the scope of this book.

TABLE 19-1

FLEXIBLE BUDGET

	Rate of Operations (000 omitted)			
	700 units of output	*800 units*	*900 units*	*1000 units*
Type of Costs				
Manufacturing Costs:				
Direct Labor	$ 350	$ 400	$ 448	$ 497
Raw materials	700	800	900	1,000
Burden	400	415	425	435
Selling Costs:				
Salesmen (on commission)	700	800	900	1,000
Advertising	200	200	200	200
Administrative Costs:				
Fixed	200	200	200	200
Variable	50	55	58	60
Total	$2,600	$2,870	$3,131	$3,392

Other budgeting approaches

The *moving budget* is another approach to help the manager who is ready to toss out budgeting because it requires precision in forcasting not possible in his firm. The moving budget consists of planning for a certain length of time in the future, let us say one year; however, at the end of each month, this budget is revised for the next twelve months, which means adding one more month to the plan than was included in the planning of the previous month. The planning thus moves ahead one month at a time, but always for a fixed period (12 months in this case). In effect, the moving budget is a series of budgets for a given period revised through time. Attention should be directed to the fact that a moving budget in our illustration is not a series of monthly budgets, but is an annual budget, periodically revised.

Budgeting makes possible still more definite estimates of the future, especially by the financial executive. A pro forma (estimated) income statement and balance sheet can be prepared to show the expected profits for the period and financial condition at the end of the period. In this manner, the premises resulting from the budgeting process can be stated quantitatively, and conclusions made. Even if the premises are not valid, the process will help the manager understand "what happened" when the results develop. He can then make better use of his past experience in planning for the future.

Budgeting is valuable if used only as a planning tool, but is doubly helpful if it forms the basis for better control. This is the reason that much of the thought on the subject appears under the heading budgetary control. Again it is seen that planning is possible without control, but control depends directly upon maintaining some basis of comparing planned action with actual performance. This leads us to consider the functions of a specialist who is concerned with the budget and with control—the controller.

Accounting Techniques for Control

Accounting techniques for control are now referred to as controllership. In the last thirty years, controllership has developed into a major staff function in many business firms. The Controllers Institute of America, with over 2,500 members, has attempted to define the functions of a controller in a concise manner:

> 1. To establish . . . and maintain . . . an integrated plan for the control of operations. . . . 2. To measure performance. . . . 3. To measure and report on . . . the effectiveness of . . . procedures. . . . 4. . . . to supervise all matters relating to taxes. 5. To interpret and report on the effect of external influences. . . . 6. To provide protection for assets of the business.

At first glance, these functions appear to be so broad that they include much of the function of management. Upon closer study, it is evident that this is another example of a functional specialist who advises the line executive. The controller does not make the final decisions, but serves as an important advisor. He is more than the chief accountant who records and reports historical facts; he is a statistician who collects, analyzes, presents, and interprets quantitative data; he considers economic concepts of the type presented in Chapter 15; he plans for the future and often is the budget officer; he must establish procedures consistent with the organizational structure.

Standard costs

As was discussed in Chapter 11, a control system of any type depends upon comparing actual performance with some predetermined criterion. Accounting as a control technique is no exception. Various types of cost accounting systems can be used to record actual performance. The problem then becomes what type of predetermined criterion is available for emphasizing the difference between what *should* occur and what *did* occur. Two criteria are in general use: standard costs and budgets.

A standard cost system produces predetermined costs which can be compared with actual costs. Standard costs include material requirements, labor operations performed, and the burden applicable. In setting up a standard material cost, management finds the standard quantity for the product and assumes a standard unit price for this material. It finds standard labor costs by using standard times for each operation (obtained by time study) and multiplying them by standard wage rates. Standard overhead rates can be determined by allocating overhead expenses at *normal* levels of production. In this way the expected costs can be itemized and then totaled to obtain the predetermined costs for the product.

After the standard costs are obtained, it is possible for the management to record the actual costs that are experienced and to compare these actual costs with the predetermined costs. Any differences can then be recorded in a *variance* column for each of the detailed costs (such as material cost variance, labor cost variance, burden variance). This information will then point to those factors which differ from what is expected. Management can seek explanations for the variances and consider appropriate action. This approach applies the exception principle; it brings to management's attention outcomes that are sharply different from expectations.

Budgets are plans for some future period. These plans are built up from basic estimating factors and are subject to errors in prediction. They tell us what we have decided should occur. Standard costs differ from budgets in a number of ways:

1. Standards should be set by some systematic technique (such as those discussed in Chapter 13), whereas budgets are more "subjective."
2. Standards refer to specific, detailed units of processes or products, whereas budgets relate to departments and general grouping of units.
3. Budgets are subject to revision more frequently than standards.

Both standards and budgets make possible a study of those operations which are out of line. They economize on managerial effort by pointing out those areas which probably do not need attention.

Responsibility accounting

The secret to providing accounting data for managerial use is in the selection of the proper classification of accounts. Most classifications in a conventional accounting system are designed to provide reports to stockholders, reports to regulatory commissions, and to satisfy the tax requirements of the Internal Revenue Service. These classifications provide an accounting *of* management and, of course, are necessary under the present institutional structure. The classifications needed in accounting *for* management are supplementary ones and provide information which can be used to make decisions.

Responsibility accounting is one aspect of accounting for control. It refers to a method by which costs are identified with persons who are capable of controlling them. Such classification necessarily must fit the organizational structure. Its essence is in segregating those costs which are *controllable* by a specific operating executive from those which are not within his control. This idea, if carried to all levels of management, will enable each manager to know what is expected of him and to spot more precisely the source of troubles.

In a previous chapter, it was seen that there are many different cost concepts important for different usages. The noncontrollable-controllable classification together with the setting of criteria of performance for each operating unit are the essential requirements for managerial accounting. In determining those costs which are controllable by a given manager, it is necessary to analyze each cost element separately. It is not enough to assume that all variable costs are controllable and all fixed are noncontrollable. It depends upon the authority of the person being considered. For example, direct labor may be classified from the viewpoint of top management as variable and controllable (if the worker can be hired or laid off depending upon volume of production), but may be noncontrollable, with respect to a given foreman if he does not have the authority to lay off without receiving approval from some other manager. General lighting is often considered as fixed from the viewpoint of the company as a whole, but may actually be partially within the control of a foreman who can turn off lights which are not in use.

A problem in classifying costs for purposes of responsibility accounting is that usually costs have already been classified for some other purpose, and there is a temptation to use other bases of classification, since the data are already available in that form. Product costs are often available for purposes of inventory valuation, pricing, and other uses. Costs of performing a given function may be available also. However, these costs may not be pertinent to the problem of controlling the performance of a given manager. The chief defect is in the tendency to allocate certain costs (burden) on some arbitrary basis in order to gain other objectives. If this allocation involves mixing noncontrollable costs with controllable for a given position, the operating manager may be placed either in a frustrating position of being held responsible for costs out of his control, or in a position for "passing the buck" and providing alibis. For this reason, accounting for control should involve a minimum of allocation of costs which cannot be changed by the manager in question.

If a standard or budget for controllable costs is set for each responsible person, both the individual person and management will then have a basis upon which performance can be evaluated. The greatest value derived from responsibility accounting is in the up-to-date information relating to *variances* from some criterion given to each responsible person for his own analysis. It permits operating personnel to correct their own mistakes before they are required to explain to a superior why a certain cost is too high. This emphasis will increase the acceptability of the system by those who can actually change the costs. Of course, responsibility accounting provides information needed to correct the situation if a subordinate does not measure up to the criterion that has been set.

Summary and Conclusions

Managerial accounting is a tool by which a manager is aided in planning and controlling operations. Analysis of past experience is a starting point, but must be supplemented by looking into the future. Budgeting and standards serve as essential tools upon which a control system is based. Recent developments in controllership, in responsibility accounting, and in accounting for decision making indicate that accounting is still in the process of development, especially in directions that will meet new needs in internal management.

Bibliographical Note

Managerial accounting is a recent development. After James O. McKinsey directed interest toward the use of accounting in management in his *Managerial Accounting* (1924), the approach did not appear in well-developed book form until William J. Vatter's *Managerial Accounting* (1950). In the last part of the 1950's several books appeared, including Harold Bierman's *Managerial Accounting* (1959) and Robert N. Anthony's *Management Accounting* (1960).

Accountants have done most of the writing on the use of accounting in management. However, one of the latest volumes on the uses of accounting in planning and control, *Accounting in Action* (1960) by Billy E. Goetz and Frederick R. Klein, is presented from the management point of view. An earlier book by Billy Goetz, *Management Planning and Control* (1949), offers a less comprehensive, but more advanced treatment, of some of the topics discussed in this chapter.

During the last two decades considerable research appeared in journal articles and monographs. William E. Thomas' *Readings in Cost Accounting, Budgeting and Control* (1955) is a valuable collection of some of the most important articles on the subject. Many articles on uses of accounting in management continue to appear in the three most important journals: *NAA Bulletin, Accounting Review,* and *Controllership.* Also, the National Association of Accountants publishes a series of Research Reports relating accounting to management.

The following books report research and cover specialized subjects: D. R. C. Halford, *Differential Costs and Management Decisions* (1959); A. Weyman Patrick, *The Theory and Technique of Cost Accounting in the Hosiery Industry* (1956); F. C. Laurence and E. N. Humphreys, *Managerial Costing* (1947); Eric A. Camman, *Basic Standard Costs* (1932); and J. W. Culliton, *Make or Buy* (1942).

Questions and Problems

1. Compare the functions of financial accounting with those of managerial accounting.

2. Using the financial data in Table 20-3, compute the following ratios for Ashland Oil & Refining Company for 1958 and explain what value they have to a manager:

(a) the current ratio
(b) ratio of net income to sales
(c) rate of return

3. Is it possible for an accountant to record opportunity costs?

4. How does the classification of costs into controllable and noncontrollable depend upon the organizational structure?

5. Is the exception principle valuable in responsibility accounting?

6. Will the construction of a variable budget help in the development of a break-even chart?

7. How do some cost systems make use of time standards?

8. Does the fact that a company pays its employees by piece rates affect the classification of costs into fixed and variable?

9. What is meant by a *pro forma* income statement? How would it be helpful to a manager?

10. Is it always desirable to allocate fixed costs to individual departments? Is this allocation misleading if the data are used for decision making?

11. What is the cost per mile of operating an automible? (After considering this question, see if William Vatter's analysis quoted in Chapter 20 is helpful.)

12. What value is there in the construction of common size statements? Use the financial data in Table 20-3 to construct a common size balance sheet and income statement.

13. How is a statement of source and application of funds useful?

14. How do budgets help in planning? In controlling?

15. Why do many companies have a functional specialist called the controller?

16. What is the danger of using book value of an asset in a decision concerning the asset's future use?

20

Extracts and Cases in Managerial Accounting

A PERSON with a good background in the mechanics of financial accounting still needs practice in applying the concepts of managerial accounting. This chapter includes cases to provide such practice. In addition, it quotes from two pioneering works in the use of accounting data for decision-making. The extract from McKinsey, written over twenty-five years ago, provides a clear statement of some timeless ideas. The extract from Vatter's article offers a simple illustration of cost analysis. The statement of a committee of the American Accounting Association in 1959 summarizes the place of managerial accounting.

Extracts

Extract A

Managerial Accounting (James O. McKinsey)

Financial statements are primarily expressions of business relationships. The abstract facts stated in the balance sheet or statement of income and expense may be interesting in themselves, but they will usually mean little until relationships are considered. The amount of inventories, of plant investment, or of current liabilities may be interesting in itself but of more importance are the turnover of inventories, the turnover on plant investment, and the ratio of current assets to current liabilities. Similarly, the amount of sales, expenses, or net income is more significant when judged in connection with turnovers, expense ratios, and the earnings on capital. These relationships can be best expressed by means of ratios. The most significant of these ratios are those showing the following:

1. The relation of borrowed capital to total capital
2. The relation of owned capital to total capital
3. The relation of each kind of assets to total assets
4. The relation of current assets to current liabilities
5. The relation of borrowed capital to the cost of capital
6. The relation of net profit to total capital
7. The relation of net profit to net worth
8. The relation of gross sales to gross profits
9. The relation of sales to net profits
10. The relation of sales to inventories
11. The relation of sales to accounts receivable
12. The relation of sales to fixed assets
13. The relation of sales to total assets
14. The relation of costs and expenses to sales
15. The relation of average inventory to cost of goods sold

The foregoing are intended to be suggestive only of the type of ratios which may be used in interpreting financial statistics. Obviously these ratios are of little significance if taken for one business at one time. After the ratio is obtained, there is no means of deciding whether it indicates a desirable or an undesirable condition. But if a firm knows from its own experience or the experience of other firms what the ratio should ordinarily be, it then has a standard by which to judge the ratios shown by its current reports. Much can be done by trade associations, public bodies, and private research to develop such ratios for the use of executives. Ratios thus developed and used serve as standards by which to judge the efficiency with which capital is used. . . .

Budgets as a Type of Operating Standards

If effective control is to be exercised over current operations, it is necessary to plan these operations and to set up standards of performance for the separate units of the organization. This results in the preparation of departmental and subdepartmental budgets. A budget is a statement of anticipated performance of one or more units of organization which has been approved by the executives, and in some cases by the board of directors. . . .

Budgets serve not only as standards by which to control current operations, they serve also as a means of co-ordinating the activities of the several departments. . . .

Since it is the purpose of budgetary control to assist in the correlation of the activities of all the departments, the budgetary program is as broad and comprehensive as the business itself. Since the budgetary program involves the activities of all the departments, it is not desirable to delegate its execution to any one department. To do so will lead almost inevitably to jealousy, misunderstandings, and friction. Rather an organization should be set up which (although including the executives of all the departments) has a head who is independent and superior to the departmental executives.

In harmony with this point of view, the president or general manager should have direct control of the budgetary program. He must of necessity delegate to other executives and employees many of the duties thus imposed on him. He should, however, have final decision, subject to the approval of the board of directors, on all program matters including cases of disagreements between departments. . . .

The budget committee, in addition to supervising the budgetary program, may render useful service as a co-ordinating board and as an advisory body to the general manager. Students of administration are coming more and more to realize the interdependence of business activities. No department can carry on its activities without influencing the activities of other departments, and in turn being affected by their activities. Each department is, therefore, interested in the activities of every other department. The budget committee, composed as it is of the heads of the different departments, affords an opportunity for these executives to discuss their mutual problems. Each can secure the reaction of all the others, can obtain both their criticism and advice. Moreover, the executives learn to know each other, and to understand each other's point of view. This promotes cordiality and co-operation, which are among the first essentials of effective administration. . . .

Although the majority of firms with budgetary control follow the plan of having the estimates prepared in the general office by the senior executives, it is becoming recognized that better results may be obtained if those responsible for carrying out the estimates are the ones responsible for originating them.[1]

Extract B

Tailor-Making Cost Data for Specific Uses (W. J. Vatter)

The methods of assembling and applying cost information to the solution of business problems depend upon the specific purpose or use to be made of the figures. Data which may have one meaning under one set of circumstances will have an entirely different meaning under other conditions. Let me illustrate this by a very simple and common case, the family car. The data are those which could have come from your personal records—if you are accountant enough to keep such records, which I am not! The questions I shall ask are those which have actually been asked in recent months by my own family. I am fairly sure that these same questions have arisen in your own case. The data are as follows:

[1] James O. McKinsey, *Managerial Accounting* (Chicago, Ill.: The University of Chicago Press, 1924), pp. 27–30, 108–109, 112, 117.

Annual Cost of Operating the Family Car

Fuel (720 gallons at 29 cents)	$208.80
Lubricating oil and additives	30.00
Chassis Lubrications	16.50
Inspections and maintenance	35.00
Washing and polishing	28.50
Licenses, city and state	26.50
Garage rent (less portion applicable to storing furniture, etc.)	126.06
Public liability & property damage insurance (net after dividend)	67.80
Depreciation $2,500 − $900 ÷ 4 =	400.00
Personal property taxes (Valuation $200)	8.00
Total	$947.16
Per mile, for 10,800 miles, 8.77 cents	

These figures presumably answer the question of how much it costs to drive a car per year. However, the only reason for wanting to know that, is to be able to make a better decision with regard to some proposed action. The question of whether one can "afford" a car is too vague and meaningless to warrant much discussion here. I can assure you (from my own experience in selling cars) that the reasons for automobile ownership are far removed from any question of economy or cost, in the great majority of cases.

Suppose the car is now in service and the question is raised to whether it should be used in preference to other transportation for a business trip of, say, 1,000 miles. Looking at the items in the cost schedule, it appears that the cost of fuel, lubrication, and perhaps some of inspection and maintenance, are relevant to the decision. These are costs that would be increased if we drove the car the extra distance, whereas washing and polishing, licenses, garage rent, insurance, depreciation, and property taxes would be irrelevant to the decision because they would be the same in total, whether or not the proposed trip is made. If (as some folks do) we trade cars often enough so that we do not purchase tires, it could well be argued that nothing should be shown for this item, since it is covered by depreciation. But, if we do not trade often enough to be able to overlook tire replacements, these should be about one-fourth cent per mile. Thus we have a per mile estimate of roughly three cents a mile as out of pocket cost to be considered in this situation. However, there probably should be something added to cover the extra *collision* risk (which presumably we are carrying without an insurance contract) and there may be other items, such as extra meals, bridgetolls, overnight lodging, etc., to take into account. Evidently what it costs to drive a car depends upon what you intend doing with it.

Some of you may say, "That's easy—it is the variable costs that are important anyway. Fixed costs are the ones to ignore!" Do not be too sure about that, either. If the question is asked as to whether or not the family should operate two cars instead of one, so that the use of the car by one person does not leave the rest marooned, the answer is to be found in a quite different way.

The variable costs, those which increase in total with the number of miles driven, are, in this case, quite irrelevant, unless the two cars in question have very different operating characteristics. These will be the same for either car for any given number of miles. If the total mileage for two cars is more than for one, then the variable costs are relevant, but only for the additional mileage. The fixed costs are really the important ones for this question. To acquire a second car will double the washing and polishing, the licenses, garage rent, insurance, depreciation, and perhaps more than double the personal property taxes. Worse yet, there should also be added the investment aspect of the transaction. Whether or not interest is a cost, it must certainly be taken into account when a decision involves tying up funds for such a purpose. Small wonder that the second car is often a smaller and less expensive vehicle. My own is a jalopy in the strict sense of that term!

All of this may raise another question—whether it is really wise to own a car in the first place. There are other means of transport—livery, taxicab, and car rental services would insist that at least there is something to be said for their side of the case. How could we use the figures given to establish an answer to this kind of a question?

If we should give up automobile ownership, the costs shown in the schedule would be saved, except for the item of depreciation. This is ordinarily computed on the difference between original cost and ultimate trade-in value at the end of the intended service-life. In this case, the figures are a new cost of $2,500 three years ago, an expected trade-in at the end of four years at $900. The difference of $1,600 is spread over four years. Will this $400 per year be saved by disposing of the car? The car in question actually has a present market value of $800. If it is used for another year, it will bring only $600. The relevant depreciation for this purpose is only $200 for the next year, regardless of the other figures. But we should also include interest on the $800 present market value. If we had no car, the money could be put to work. What it would earn is what we lose by keeping the car.

There are perhaps other cost items that should be included. What about the dry-cleaning bills arising from walking three blocks in the rain to get the car from a parking space, while taxicabs roll past the door of the theater? Or how about the suit that was ruined changing a tire just after leaving a friend's home at 12:30? Indeed, there are costs that do make a difference and there are computations other than the ones shown in the schedule. My illustration may seem biased against car ownership, but that is because I have not mentioned other, perhaps more important, factors than those included in the costs. My wife and I have two cars and I am sure we could not get along without both of them. She will not let me use hers, and I am too lazy to walk, even to the drugstore!

The question of whether or not one can really afford to operate a car may have strange implications. One member of our faculty (not an accountant nor in the business school) once asked what could be done about the very high cost of operating his car, which he figured at some 16 cents per mile. The reply given him (by one who was something of a practical joker) was, "You don't drive the car enough for it to be efficient—hire a boy to drive it around the block for several hours each Saturday. That will get your cost down." I am sorry to report that the professor was stopped from his endeavor only by a vigorous persuasion on the part of a more kindly colleague! [2]

Extract C

Report of Committee on Managerial Accounting

Management accounting is the application of appropriate techniques and concepts in processing the historical and projected economic data of an entity to assist management in establishing a plan for reasonable economic objectives and in the making of rational decisions with a view toward achieving these objectives. . . .

Alternative decisions relating to such matters as whether to make or buy, pricing, advertising programs, research programs, capital additions, methods of financing, and similar planning problems rest fundamentally upon the economics of each alternative under consideration. The economics of each alternative are measured largely through accounting data. Significantly, such decisions are based primarily on estimates of an accounting nature as opposed to historical accounting data.

Such functions as capital budgeting, short-run and long-run pricing, optimization of product mix, efficient utilization of assets, production scheduling, and the like provide examples of the essential nature of situations and operational activities where accounting-based data are essential to efficiency. . . .

Development of the concept of responsibility accounting represents an important milestone in the use of accounting-based data for control. In order to control business operations it is important that a very definite and particular approach to account classification be followed with a minimum of allocation and with a close tailoring of the system to the organizational structure of the firm—the assigned authority and responsibility throughout the firm. Since control is achieved through people and not through things, accounting-based data must be reported primarily in terms of the responsibilities of people for internal control purposes.

[2] W. J. Vatter, "Tailor-Making Cost Data for Specific Uses," *N.A.C.A. Bulletin,* 1954 Conference Proceedings, as reprinted in W. E. Thomas (ed.) *Readings in Cost Accounting Budgeting and Control* (Cincinnati: South-Western Publishing Co., 1955), pp. 316–318.

To be most useful to management, accounting information must be tailored to the needs of those who make decisions at the various levels of responsibility. In order to accomplish best this tailoring process, psychological and personnel problems must be recognized. Thus management accounting assumes significance with respect to human relations. Accounting information does not itself effect the proper business decision. It finds usefulness only to the extent that there is communication to responsible individuals in such a way as to motivate these individuals to appropriate action. Thus its usefulness is largely dependent upon adequate oral and written communication and a proper attitude of receptiveness on the part of management.[3]

Cases

Case A:

The Q & Z Motor Transport Company

The Q & Z Motor Transport Company, a Class I highway carrier of freight, connects three large midwestern cities, A, D, and E. The company was incorporated on Jan. 1, 1948.

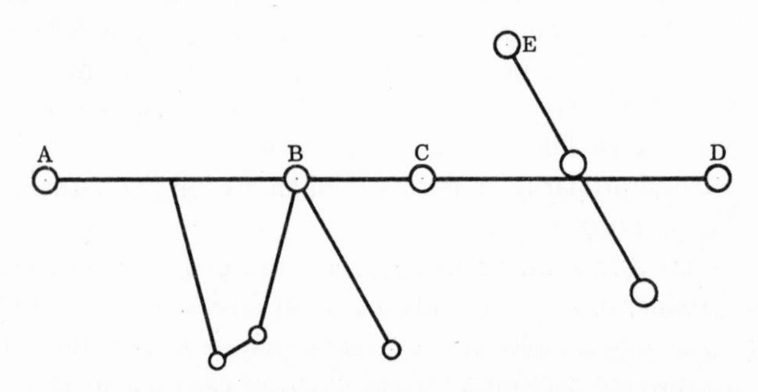

FIGURE 20-1 Map of Major Routes Covered by Q & Z Transport Company

The business was developed from a one truck operation in 1934 to a scale of approximately $400,000 gross revenue per year. The Federal Motor Carriers Act was passed in 1935 soon after the start of business and brought with it more stringent regulation. Certain routes in the present system were obtained under the "grandfather rights" of the above law. These rights gave the companies existing at the time of the passage of the law the right to operate over their existing routes. In 1938, the founder obtained a radial certificate from the Interstate Commerce Commission which permitted it to

[3] "Report of Committee on Management Accounting," *Accounting Review,* April, 1959 (American Accounting Association), pp. 210–212.

act as a contract carrier of agricultural products between its home state and any of 19 other states. Twenty-five per cent of the gross income of the company resulted from hauling agricultural products; tobacco was, by far, the most important of the agricultural products. Since 1938, the system has been expanded by purchase of operating rights from other companies. This expansion was in keeping with the general practice in the trucking industry of securing as many rights as possible in order to enlarge the area of operation. A number of the lines which were added were "feeder" runs, many of which today are operated at a loss due to the small amount of freight traffic flowing in and out of the smaller towns.

The company is regulated by both the Interstate Commerce Commission and the Division of Motor Transport in the state in which it does most of its business. It holds Certificates of Convenience and Necessity on a number of potentially profitable routes. The main route between cities A and D is most valuable since both cities are important industrial centers. The management, nevertheless, has great difficulty on all routes in operating at capacity loads in both directions. The experience has been that trucks starting from cities A and D are approximately 100 per cent loaded. One of the directors believes that the most important problem is to cultivate originating freight for proper balance.

The company has secured contracts for special business. One was a contract to move prefabricated houses for a government project. In addition to maintaining the regular routes pictured in the accompanying sketch, and hauling tobacco, the company is agent for one of the national household moving lines. Household goods can be carried into most of the 48 states under the rights of this national organization. An executive feels that the rates on this type of trucking are high enough to pay 16 per cent of the receipts to the national organization, to return with an empty van, and still to make a profit on the operation. One moving van is owned for purposes of such operations.

Since its incorporation, the company has had operating losses. A uniform system of accounting prescribed by the Interestate Commerce Commission provides a basis for the various reports of the company. Cost information is at a minimum; however, through the work of a trade association, it is possible to compare certain important balance sheet and profit and loss items with those of similar companies.

In January, 1948, the company operated seven terminals, but the number has been decreased to four, one each at cities A, B, D, E. The general policy of the present management has been to consolidate operations and to eliminate unprofitable routes. The present four terminals are in leased facilities.

Rates charged by the company for common carrier operations are approved by the ICC. Applications can be made for special commodity rates and rates on the moving of agricultural products. Leaf tobacco is exempt from this regulation.

Expenses of the company for a recent year were:

Labor (Drivers and Dock workers)	$104,000
Transportation Expense (other than labor)	79,000
Terminal and Traffic	75,000
Office Expense	37,000
Maintenance	25,000
Insurance	22,000
Taxes and Licenses	18,000
Depreciation	14,000
Rents	9,000
Other Expenses	20,000
	$403,000

Rolling Equipment Owned:

Type	*Number*
Tractors	12
Trailers–Freight Van	38
Flat	8
Moving Van	1
1½ ton Trucks	3

Employees:

Type	*Number*
Office Workers	12
Truck Drivers	22
Platform Workers	7
Maintenance	2

The management feels that although the company has never made a profit since incorporation, a profit is possible. Shortage of cash is a pressing problem. Reduction of claims against the company, prompt processing of the claims, and better service to the clients will improve the gross revenue. Operation at more efficient levels, economizing on office force, purchase of new equipment, and stress on scheduling and greater tons moved per driver will reduce costs.

Management Personnel of Q & Z Transport Co.

Position	*Duty*
President (the founder)	General Direction and Control
Vice President	Claims Agent
Secretary-Treasurer	Bookkeeper and Office Manager
Corporation Counsel	Legal Adviser
Supervisor	Terminal Manager at A
Supervisor	Terminal Manager at D
Dispatcher (part-time)	Dispatcher at B

The office manager is keenly interested in analyzing costs of each part of the business in order to aid in making decisions on whether to eliminate a feeder route and the fee to charge in contract hauling. Although he has the information for ICC reports, he is wondering what other classifications of costs would be helpful and how he should analyze them.

Case B:

Ashland Oil & Refining Company (C)

The executives of the Ashland Oil & Refining Company determine the sources and applications of funds for the past, but stress also the same approach in estimating working capital for the future. The estimated working capital (see Table 20-1) summarizes the major prospective sources and applications of funds for the next year. This schedule is supported by a detailed cash forecast (not illustrated), a summary of detailed capital expenditures, and a detailed forecast of changes in inventory over the next year. Changes in inventory, of course, reflect changes in production and sales and provide management with specific information concerning the amount of excessive inventories in prospect if additional sales are not secured.

Management analyzes each of the rows of the working capital statement. The company believes this analysis is useful in decision-making.

Case C:

Ashland Oil & Refining Company (D)

The functions of a controller have developed rapidly in recent years. Some functions are recognized generally in industry, but each company tailors the position to fit its needs. The person actually serving in the position also helps delineate his own scope of operations as William J. Vatter observes: "The controller contributes something to management, else he does not belong on the team. In making this contribution, he can and does affect top management's concept of his task; but he may do much to broaden and deepen managers' views of their own problems, and by this means create their conception of his task through his own efforts."[4]

In the Ashland Oil & Refining Company, the functions of the controller can best be outlined in terms of his relationships:

1. Internally with other executives and with his own subordinates; and
2. Externally with persons and agencies outside the company.

The student will find it helpful to relate the organizational concepts of line, staff, and functional authority with each of these relationships.

[4] William J. Vatter, "Accounting Education for Controllership," Paper presented to meeting of American Accounting Association, Sept., 1949.

TABLE 20-1

ASHLAND OIL & REFINING COMPANY AND SUBSIDIARIES
ESTIMATED WORKING CAPITAL AT END OF QUARTERLY PERIODS
JULY 1, 1959 TO SEPTEMBER 30, 1960

	Quarter Ending				*Total Year Ending*	*Quarter Ending*
	9-30-59	*12-31-59*	*3-31-60*	*6-30-60*	*6-30-60*	*9-30-60*
Working capital at beginning of period	$45,959,000	$47,103,000	$49,327,000	$47,783,000	$45,959,000	$48,798,000
Net profit after income tax	2,800,000	3,290,000	3,290,000	3,000,000	12,380,000	3,000,000
Provision for depreciation, depletion, and amortization	3,975,000	4,100,000	4,125,000	4,125,000	16,325,000	4,135,000
Provision for surrendered leases	80,000	70,000	70,000	70,000	290,000	70,000
Amounts borrowed (+) or repaid (—) under revolving notes	2,000,000	4,000,000			6,000,000	—1,000,000
	$54,814,000	$58,563,000	$56,812,000	$54,978,000	$80,954,000	$55,003,000
Capital expenditures	$ 4,953,000	$ 6,332,000	$ 6,589,000	$ 3,756,000	$21,630,000	$ 2,924,000
Loans to jobbers, producers, and others	573,000	508,000	544,000	479,000	2,104,000	514,000
Dividends	1,898,000	1,896,000	1,896,000	1,895,000	7,585,000	1,893,000
Preferred stock and debt retirement—net	287,000	500,000		50,000	837,000	278,000
	$ 7,711,000	$ 9,236,000	$ 9,029,000	$ 6,180,000	$32,156,000	$ 5,609,000
Working capital at end of period	$47,103,000	$49,327,000	$47,783,000	$48,798,000	$48,798,000	$49,394,000

The company grew rapidly through mergers. In 1947, just prior to this growth, the position of controller was established. It was filled by a person who had worked for the company for 14 years in accounting and who had held the position of Assistant to the President immediately preceding the creation of this new position. Soon after, the company merged with Allied Oil Company (which was approximately of equal size at the time of the merger), and the chief accountant of Allied was made Auditor of Ashland Oil, reporting directly to the president (i.e., auditor functions were made independent of controller functions).

The controller serves as chief of a department with over 150 personnel. Most of these serve in general financial accounting, detailed cost studies, payroll (cash payments are made by the Treasurer of the company), and tax reports. Two types of reports are prepared monthly—

1. Income statements and balance sheets for the information of the Board of Directors and
2. A detailed operating report (over 200 pages) which records costs of each department.

These reports are made available on the 20th of the month following the subject month of operations by using electric accounting machines.

Internal Relationships

Communication from the controller to the chief executive officer is direct. Written reports form the basis for daily telephone conversations. Few staff meetings are held; communications are usually oral (mostly by telephone) and between two executives at a time. Monthly, a letter from the controller to the chief executive and the Board informs, explains, and interprets reports.

From time to time, the controller and the chief executive analyze potential mergers. Often in preliminary negotiations, the controller has served as the financial advisor on factors affecting decisions to merge. At times the controller works on special projects that require an understanding of the financial situation. For example, in one case he spent a week with an independent oil producer who had received large advances of funds and who had gotten into financial difficulty. The controller, with the co-operation of the producer, worked out a program by which the producer could weather the financial storm, stay in business, and pay back the money owed the company.

Little of the controller's time is spent with subordinates of the accounting department, since the chief accountant (who reports to the controller) supervises the department. Only on questions concerning exceptions to general instructions does the chief accountant consult with the controller.

The controller spends some of his time in committee work with other executives, especially the Treasurer and Director of Purchases. He is a member of the budget committee and is a principal executive interested in the printing of the annual report. Most of the controller's contacts with other executives is on an informal basis, interpreting cost reports. Each department head receives monthly cost information for his own department. If there is some question, the line executive contacts directly an accountant who specializes on costs of his department. Use of the cost reports is made chiefly in these informal contacts. The controller helps in this interpretation. There is little feeling that the controller is making use of the large amount of information in his hands to undermine line executives. They feel that he is an advisor to all levels.

External Relationships

The controller and the certified public accountants maintain communications throughout the year. Since the outside accounting firm must certify the annual statements, they provide advice on key accounting issues arising during the year.

Since the company has grown rapidly, the need for new capital has forced the management to stress the acceptability of the company in investment circles. In a period of eight years, seven prospectuses were prepared in this continuing search for additional funds. The controller is legally one of the executives held responsible for the accuracy of statements in prospectuses. Releases of financial data to investment analysts add to the variety of reports prepared by the controller.

The management is conscious of good relations with stockholders. The controller often finds a visiting stockholder on his calendar for the day.

Underwriters of various issues of new stock and bonds make contact with internal management through the controller. As outside specialists in new financing, the underwriters must work closely with the controller in keeping the company in a desirable position in the securities market. At times in which mergers are being considered, underwriters must be kept advised as to the desires and needs of the parties concerned.

Increasingly, governmental agencies have required lengthy reports from corporations. Since the controller is the one legally charged with compliance, he must keep up with the regulations of the Securities and Exchange Commission. The importance of tax considerations and the need for rulings from the Internal Revenue Service have added important responsibilities to the controller. A special section of the department gives its full attention to tax matters. Regulations by state governments add other duties to those of the controller.

Controllership has increasingly become a professional activity with a professional society to maintain standards. The controller maintains contact with other controllers both through the society and individually. On matters which affect other oil companies, the controller checks for advice and joint analysis. Annual reports are exchanged with a large number of firms. The increasing use of electronic equipment requires that the controller keep in touch with electronic manufacturers so that the best procedures can be placed in operation.

In Ashland Oil, relations with the general public are partly assumed by the controller. He is one of the executives who is familiar with all branches of operations from the production of crude oil, through refining and transportation, to the retail marketing of products. Tours of the plants and offices are often arranged through the controller in co-operation with the Personnel Director.

Like all executives, the controller faces the problem of a scarcity of time in which to perform his functions. He must determine which duties he can best delegate, which techniques of communications he can use in his relationships with others, and how to train subordinates for their immediate job and for future advancement.

Case D:

Ashland Oil & Refining Company (E)

In recent years, most companies have included balance sheets and income statements in their annual reports. The management of Ashland Oil & Refining Company supplements the financial statements with charts and interpretative comments so that the reader of the annual report can gain additional understanding of the condition of the business. Many of the ratios and common size statements do not appear in the annual report; however, the information in Tables 20-2 and 20-3 provide absolute quantities with which the reader can analyze the data.

If you were a stockholder in the company, you might be interested in interpreting the data in the financial statements so that you could understand the condition of the company. The key to this process is to ask yourself basic questions such as, "Is the company earning satisfactorily?" "Does the company have sufficient funds?" and so forth, and then to compute relationships which indicate answers to the questions.

TABLE 20-2

ASHLAND OIL & REFINING COMPANY

1954–1958 FIVE YEAR COMPARISON

Consolidated Balance Sheet Assets — At September 30	*1958*	*1957*	*1956*	*1955*	*1954*
Current assets:					
Cash & U. S. Government Securities	$ 15,527,868	$ 14,123,821	$ 13,644,393	$ 15,942,059	$ 11,304,062
Accounts receivable	27,004,468	26,750,259	26,860,347	22,366,466	19,251,067
Inventories	44,617,290	45,146,450	41,237,097	37,450,280	39,827,273
Prepaid taxes, insurance and misc.	2,389,353	1,850,419	1,597,742	804,350	848,020
Total current assets	89,538,979	87,870,949	83,339,579	76,563,155	71,230,422
Investments and other assets	11,177,724	11,552,799	10,403,139	7,890,560	7,426,497
Property account—net	87,743,156	86,680,199	81,053,001	70,132,006	73,014,850
Deferred charges	183,656	223,960	217,574	234,532	251,491
Total Assets	$188,643,515	$186,327,907	$175,013,293	$154,820,253	$151,923,260
Liabilities					
Current liabilities	$ 34,000,189	$ 38,858,705	$ 37,211,853	$ 27,042,262	$ 25,543,808
Long-term debt	38,840,000	29,935,000	27,721,000	29,717,000	31,697,000
Capital Stock:					
Preferred	33,631,050	34,406,240	36,024,490	31,085,850	32,788,420
Common	5,734,582	5,728,559	5,553,038	5,433,532	5,426,507
Surplus	80,437,694	77,399,403	68,502,912	61,541,609	56,467,525
Total Liabilities	$188,643,515	$186,327,907	$175,013,293	$154,820,253	$151,923,260

TABLE 20-3

ASHLAND OIL & REFINING COMPANY

1954–1958 FIVE YEAR COMPARISON

Consolidated Operating Statement Fiscal Year Ended September 30	*1958*	*1957*	*1956*	*1955*	*1954*
Net sales	$280,124,973	$320,248,921	$279,949,629	$245,881,349	$227,947,516
Cost and expenses	216,321,003	243,511,244	212,241,007	189,238,735	181,364,723
Gross income	63,803,970	76,737,677	67,708,622	56,642,614	46,582,793
Selling, administrative, and general expense	30,686,348	29,464,072	26,378,784	22,884,638	20,828,393
Operating income before depletion, depreciation, and amortization	33,117,622	47,273,605	41,329,838	33,757,976	25,754,400
Depletion, depreciation, and amortization	14,992,225	15,496,188	14,576,560	13,743,573	13,753,041
Operating income	18,125,397	31,777,417	26,753,278	20,014,403	12,001,359
Interest, dividends, and other income	1,416,531	1,756,187	1,441,339	800,233	1,751,519
	19,541,928	33,533,604	28,194,617	20,814,636	13,752,878
Other deductions	1,159,666	994,327	890,675	958,604	1,024,802
Income before taxes on income	18,382,262	32,539,277	27,303,942	19,856,032	12,728,076
Income taxes—estimated	8,050,000	16,320,000	13,800,000	9,750,000	6,100,000
Net Income	$ 10,332,262	$ 16,219,277	$ 13,503,942	$ 10,106,032	$ 6,628,076
Earned per share of common stock after providing for preferred stock dividends	$ 1.51	$ 2.52	$ 2.13	$ 1.56	$ .92

21

Schematic Analysis in Decision Making

As the managerial process has increased in complexity, a need has grown for devices to clarify the significant relationships and emphasize the most important elements. To meet this need, management has developed pictorial and simple numerical methods as aids in decision making. The expression *schematic analysis* will be used to cover these methods. This chapter will discuss some of the most widely known applications of these pictorial and numerical methods.

Diagrams, graphs, and scales are often an essential first step in the analysis of the large volumes of data generated by specialized departments. Charting devices developed for one phase of management have proved to have wide potential use in other departments. Therefore, it is important that the reader understand the fundamentals of the charting or scaling device, so that he can think through possible applications in areas other than those illustrated.

This book has already presented many illustrations of schematic presentation. The use of organization charts in plotting the flow of authority in a firm has been shown. The study of work improvement made considerable use of process charts. The discussion of plant layout emphasized flow diagrams. The strengths and weaknesses of breakeven charts in portraying cost-revenue relationships have been discussed.

Everyone has heard the expression "get all the facts before making a decision." Like most such rules, this is only a partial truth. First of all, it is impossible to obtain *all* the facts. Secondly, we must concentrate on the *pertinent, relevant* facts. Too great a volume of information may lead to "factual indigestion." It is necessary to organize the facts in ways that will help us understand their meaning. This is where schematic techniques fit in—they help us focus on the relevant facts and they suggest some of their implications.

This chapter will deal with the following kinds of schematic analysis, in this order:

1. Charts involving time,
2. Drawings and designs representing physical characteristics,
3. Sketches and plans used in systems design,
4. Diagrams showing physical flow,
5. Schemes of human relationships,
6. Graphs of frequency distributions and probabilities,
7. Analogues of mental processes,
8. Graphs of functional relationships,
9. Profiles, check lists, and evaluation scales.

Charts Involving Time

The simplest and most widely applied graphs in business are those plotting changes over time. On such graphs, time is usually plotted on the horizontal scale. Any recent business magazine or newspaper will present illustrations of line charts showing fluctuations in sales, production, or prices over time. When large volumes of data are presented in tables, it is difficult to discern the important trends and relationships. Graphical treatment often points up the important developments, or at least suggests hypotheses worthy of further consideration. Figure 21-1 presents the simplest kind of line chart, showing a single variable plotted on an arithmetic scale. Usually such a chart covers events in the past, but sometimes projections are extrapolated into the future (illustrated by the broken line). Such extrapolations are risky and should be based on more than a simple extension of past trends; they require an analysis of the underlying factors that might contribute to an acceleration or deceleration of such trends.

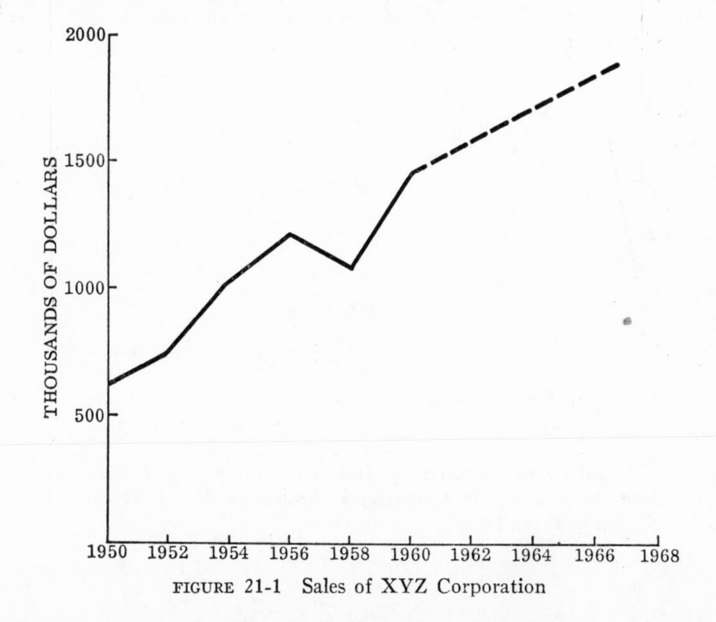

FIGURE 21-1 Sales of XYZ Corporation

The arithmetic scale (used in Figure 21-1) is adequate for showing absolute amounts of change. Frequently the lines will represent ratios or index numbers instead of data expressed in the original units of measure; price indexes and indexes of industrial production are well-known illustrations. But more specialized scales make possible types of comparison that are difficult on arithmetic scales. For example, semi-logarithmic paper helps in the comparison of rates of change over time; it also helps compare one series with another that is much larger. Figure 21-2 compares the rate of growth of one company with the growth of a large industrial segment. It shows quite forcefully that the net profits of one company increased at a much faster rate between 1944 and 1948 than did those of the major companies. This fact would not show up nearly so clearly on a table.

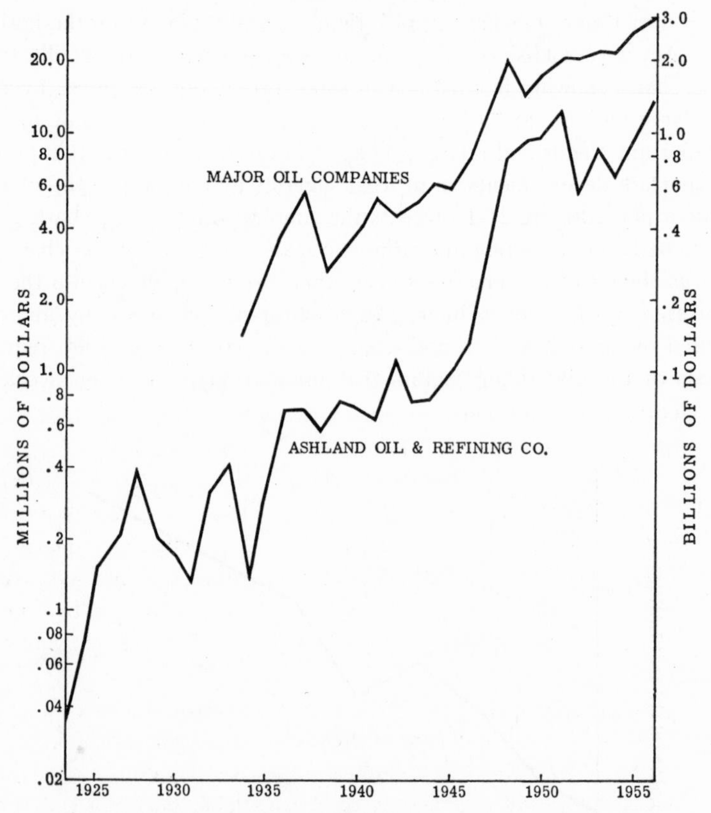

FIGURE 21-2 Semi-logarithmic Chart Showing Rate of Growth of a Company's Profits Compared with the Industry *

* Used by permission from Joseph L. Massie, *Blazer and Ashland Oil—A Study in Management* (Lexington, Ky.: University of Kentucky Press, 1960).

Gantt Charts

One of the most fundamental charts in the internal management of a manufacturing firm is the Gantt chart. It, like the line charts already discussed, emphasizes time, but in a special way that is useful for scheduling and decision making. These charts were developed by H. L. Gantt, one of the leaders of the "scientific management" movement during World War I. They have undergone many refinements and have been adapted to a wide variety of uses.

The best known application of the Gantt chart is in production control. This variation is known as the "progress chart," since it portrays planned production and actual performance over time. A special variety is the "machine-record" chart on which each machine is listed vertically on the left side of the chart, with horizontal bars representing the progress of output on each. A "man" chart differs merely in including each man in the left column instead of each machine. Similarly, charts can be drawn to represent progress on *operations,* or in the production of *parts* in preparation for assembly, or in showing the status of the *ordering and receipts* of purchased parts. Variations on the Gantt chart are thus suited to the planning and control of a number of key factors in production.

The principles of construction and use of Gantt charts will be discussed more fully. In a sense, the charts convert measurements in terms of tons or cubic feet or dollars into time units. Thus, a horizontal unit of space (let us say a quarter of an inch) may represent one day; but it also can represent the production capacity of a machine for that one day. Let us say that a particular machine produces a standard quantity of 1,200 units per day. The horizontal distance of one quarter inch will then represent 1,200 units. If we wish to represent a plan to produce 12,000 units in the near future, this can be shown by a bar drawn through ten quarter inch spaces, indicating that it will take ten days to produce this planned quantity. We can also plot actual performance (progress) in the same space by another type of bar. We thus achieve a simple comparison between plans and performance.

Figure 21-3 presents an illustration of a simple Gantt chart. An angle (⌈) opening to the right indicates when work is to begin and an angle (⌉) opening to the left indicates the planned time of completion. A light line represents the percentage of work actually completed during a time period, while a heavy line represents the cumulative actual production for a number of periods. Numerals in the upper left corner of a cell indicate the planned production, while numerals in the upper right represent actual production for that period. In this manner, the Gantt chart shows planned production and actual production, both in particular time periods and cumulatively over a number of units of time. The result is a quick survey plus precise details, all relative to a fixed scale of time.

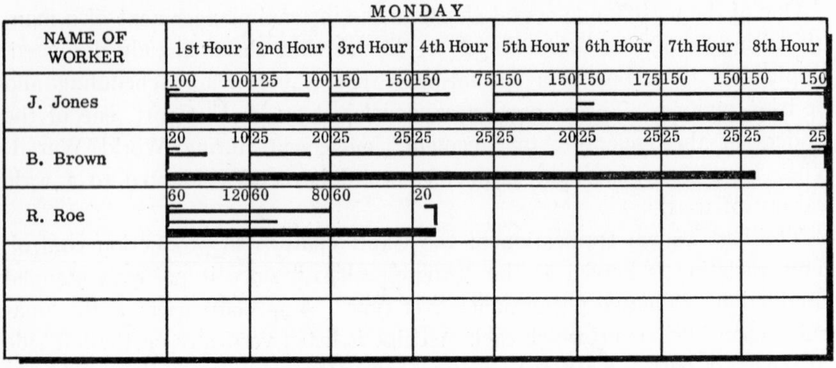

MONDAY

NAME OF WORKER	1st Hour	2nd Hour	3rd Hour	4th Hour	5th Hour	6th Hour	7th Hour	8th Hour
J. Jones	100 100	125 100	150 150	150 75	150 150	150 175	150 150	150 150
B. Brown	20 10	25 20	25 25	25 25	25 20	25 25	25 25	25 25
R. Roe	60 120	60 80	60	20				

FIGURE 21-3 Section of a Man Record (Gantt) Chart

Drawings and Designs Representing Physical Characteristics

Everyone is familiar with the large class of schemes which describe the physical characteristics of land, buildings, and products. All types of geographical *maps* fall into this classification. *Plant layouts* are scaled drawings of the physical characteristics of the building and of the location of equipment. Blueprints and shop drawings are fundamental schemes for understanding the physical characteristics of products; a few of their fundamentals will be discussed.

Shop drawings [1]

Too often a new manager who has received no engineering education is unfamiliar with the techniques of reading blueprints. He tends to avoid any attempt to interpret shop drawings because he feels that it is "engineering." He fails to realize that he does not have to be able to *draw* blueprints in order to *read* them. The purpose of this section is to indicate to the uninitiated reader that blueprint reading is not difficult; prints merely use conventions which, at first, are unfamiliar. Of course, the reader will not be an expert in reading blueprints after studying the following few pages, but we believe that he can learn enough so that he will be able to teach himself the details when it appears desirable on the job.

Blueprints are media of communication. In a manufacturing operation, they provide the facts about the product. Together with a list of specifications ("specs") they provide fundamental information for the staff and line

[1] If the reader has had a course in mechanical drawing, he may wish to omit this section.

departments. These facts are determined by the engineering department and drawn by its drafting section. The language used by engineers in these blueprints has been standardized to the extent that it can be understood throughout the world. Many managers have no need to be draftsmen, but most must be able to understand the language originating in the engineering department.

Shop drawings are two-dimensional representations of three-dimensional objects. Learning to visualize three dimensions from the flat blueprint is, therefore, one of the essentials of reading blueprints. Engineering drawings are prepared to scale. In the quest for precision, the draftsman has developed a number of techniques for accurately showing shape and dimensions. Furthermore, the draftsman uses numerous conventions to represent on paper exactly the characteristics of the three-dimensional object. To read blueprints, one must remember these conventions just as he must understand the conventional signs on the familiar road map in order to travel over unknown territory. Actually reading blueprints is the only way to gain competence in understanding the language; however, three fundamentals will provide the starting point—(1) visualization, (2) reading dimensions, and (3) remembering the conventions.

1. Shop drawings do not show the third dimension directly as the picture drawing (Figure 21-4a) does. Usually, the shop drawing gives three conventionalized views of the object as it would appear if seen from different directions: top view, front view, and side view illustrated in Figure 21-4b.[2] These views, not usually named on the blueprint, are identified by their relative location to each other. The view at the top of the drawing would represent the appearance of the object if you look down on it; the front view (the one directly under the top view) is the appearance if you held the object up and looked straight at it; the side view (unless noted to the contrary) is the appearance if you leaned around to the right side of the object and looked at it from the right side. Any surface of the object can be used as the front view but, once it is determined, then the top and side views become definite.

The key to blueprint reading is to look at these three views and obtain a three-dimensional mental picture. Before reading further, close this book and hold it up so that you are looking at the front cover. In Figure 21-4b that view is the front view. Look down on the top of the book and then lean around to get the side (right) view. To check yourself on your visualization, see if you can understand that the numbers in each corner of the views identify the same corners of the book, but from three two-dimensional views. Why are corners 4, 6, and 7 numbered in only one view? Why is corner 2 numbered in all views? The trick is to look at the three views

[2] For the sake of simplicity, the drawing in Figure 21-4b does not give a complete description of this book. For example, in the top view, the curve in the binding is squared off in the drawing; and in the side view, lines are omitted which would indicate the projection of the front and back covers.

at once and mentally fold the top view back over the front view and fold the side view back around the front view. Once you are able to do this quickly and habitually, you have the visualization phase of blueprint reading.

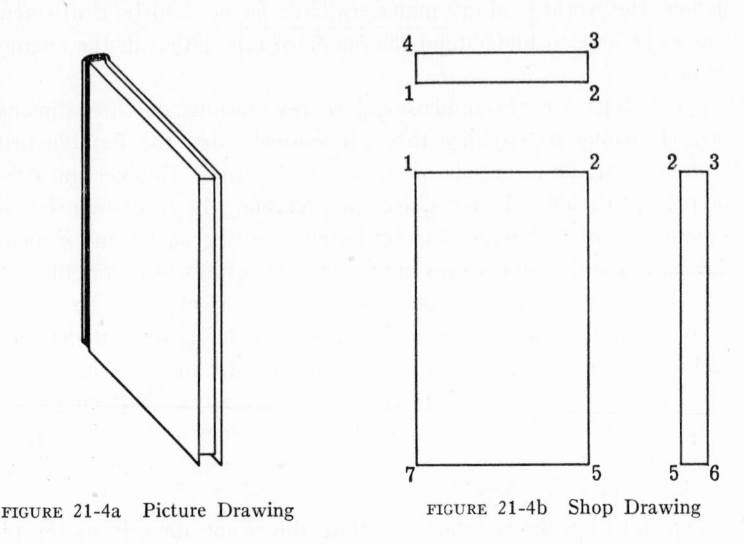

FIGURE 21-4a Picture Drawing FIGURE 21-4b Shop Drawing

2. Dimensions are written in inches and fractions of inches. They are placed on the blueprint near the center of the line which represents the *edge* of a straight surface. Often dimension arrows are used to indicate the exact edge intended. Since blueprints must have many numbers and lines, dimensions are not repeated on more than one view even though the edge can be seen from other views. (Note: Dimensions are usually found in a view which does not show the full surface; dimensions are placed on edges.) A hole is located by its center; the size of a hole is given by its radius (R) or its diameter (D). Rounded corners are measured by the radius (e.g., ¼ R).

Figure 21-5 is a drawing illustrating a few of the common conventions. Conventions need only be memorized and held in mind as one develops a mental picture of the object.

3. The conventions needed to read Figure 21-5 are: (1) Edges which are invisible from a given view are represented by dotted lines. (2) Edges which are visible from a given view are represented by solid lines. (If an invisible edge lies directly behind a visible edge, the solid line is used.) (3) Holes are located by giving the distance from the center of the hole to the edges. (4) Lines used to show dimensions are lighter than lines representing edges. (5) If a surface is to be machined (e.g., on a shaper or milling machine), the edge of that surface is identified by a finish mark—*f*.

Blueprint reading, of course, involves many more conventions, dimensions, and more difficult shapes. Threads, circular shapes, gears, and other characteristics will be encountered. All of the complications, however, are merely

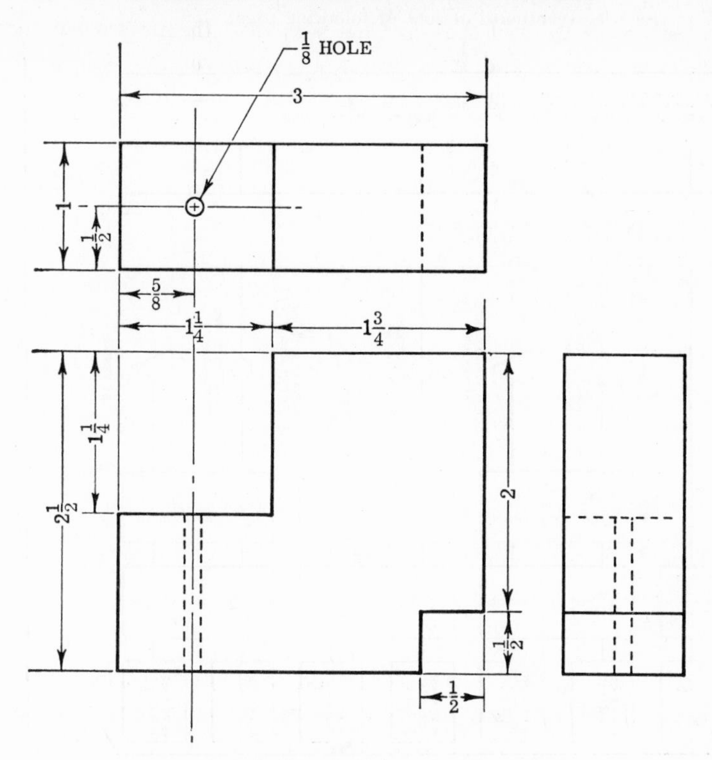

FIGURE 21-5 Shop Drawing of a Step Block

an extension of this simple description. A manager in a manufacturing firm, whether his specialty be in law, accounting, marketing, finance, or some other operational field, will find that this type of scheme will help him understand operations and their relationships to his job.

Sketches and Plans Used in Systems Design

The manager continually plans systems. Procedures and routines are established to provide consistent and co-ordinated actions which are repetitive and which, therefore, (in line with the exception principle) should be handled at lower levels of the organization. Sketches of procedures can show the functions to be performed by different sections. They also can indicate the number of copies and distribution of forms to those departments which need the information.

The purchasing procedure of a state university is illustrated in Figure 21-6.[3] This chart can be used both for the analysis and design of the purchasing system, and for presenting the flow of paperwork to a new employee.

[3] A. P. Nestor, "Your Purchasing Procedure," *College and University Business,* Vol. 28, No. 2 (February 1960), pp. 29–32.

(continued at foot of following page)

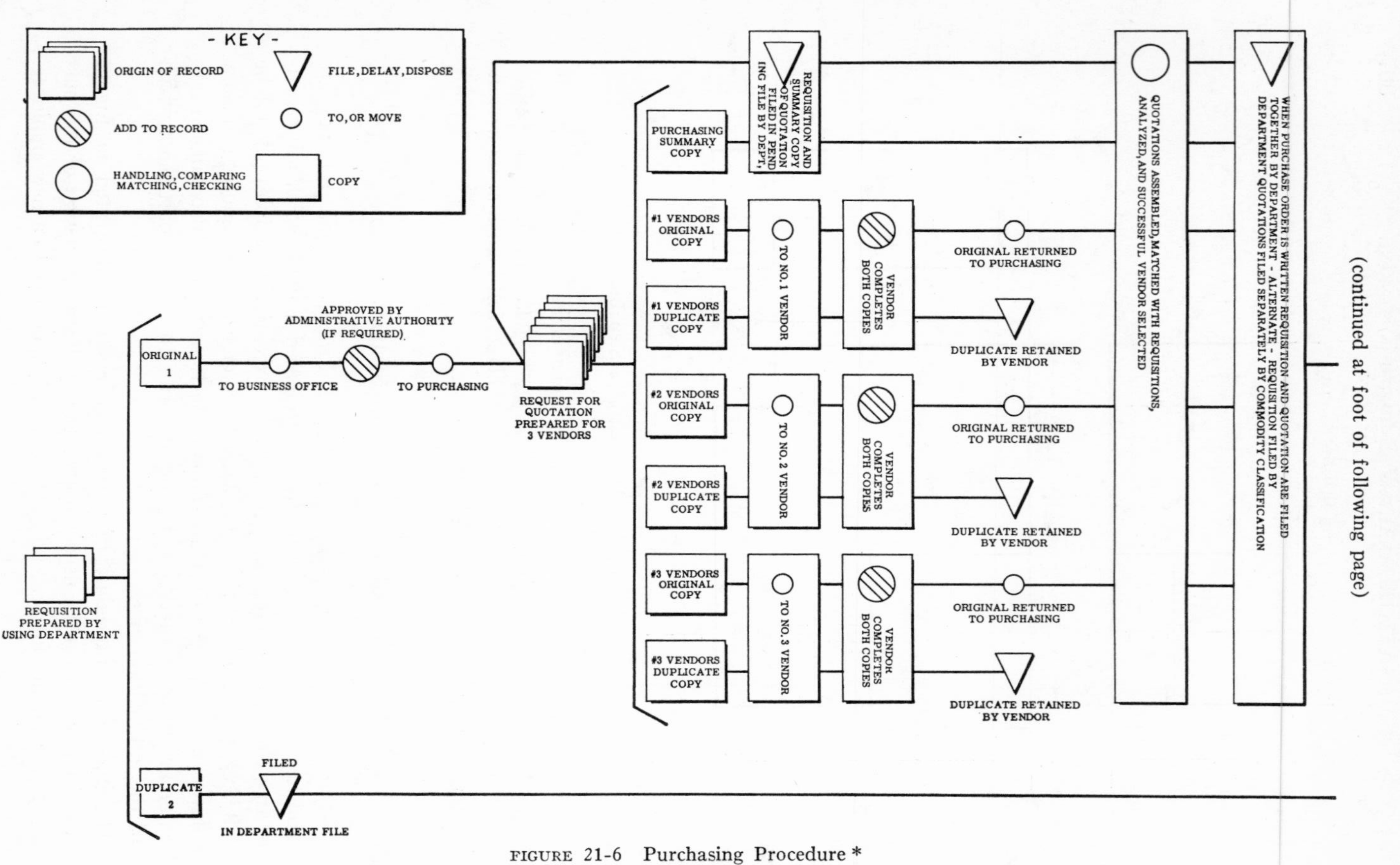

FIGURE 21-6 Purchasing Procedure *

* A. P. Nestor, "Your Purchasing Procedure," *College and University Business*, Vol. 28, No. 2, February 1960, pp. 29–32.

(continued from preceding page)

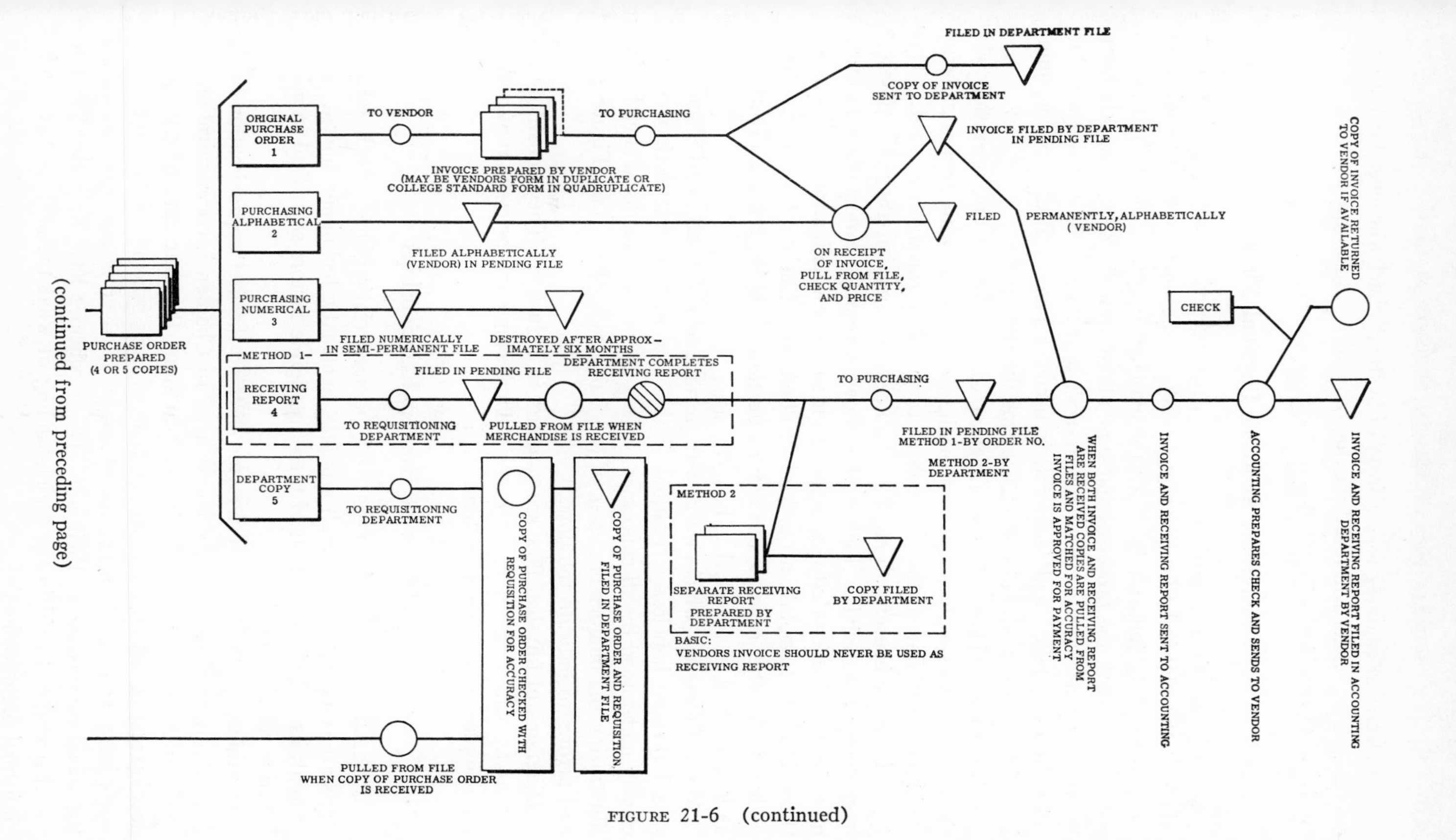

FIGURE 21-6 (continued)

The electrical engineer uses a form of systems chart whenever he analyzes circuits. The reader will recall the diagrams of wiring on the back of a home electrical device such as a radio.

Diagrams Showing Physical Flow

One of the primary media by which a manager visualizes operations as a whole is the physical flow diagram. The specific charts used depend upon the nature of the industry in which the manager operates. Usually a person not familiar with the processes and symbols of an industry can quickly learn to comprehend a flow chart of the over-all operations. As the diagram becomes more detailed and technical, it becomes more difficult for the uninitiated to understand, but more useful for the specialist.

In an earlier chapter, a flow diagram of the Mengel box operation was shown. It was simply a diagram of the plant layout with arrows showing the direction of flow of the materials as they moved through the plant. This type of scheme is useful to anyone who needs information about the physical movement of materials. Figure 21-7 shows a composite flow diagram of an oil refinery. Notice that it is possible for someone who knows nothing about the operations to obtain a quick orientation to operations by studying such a chart. Another example of the use of a flow chart is shown in Figure 21-8 as it is applied in the steel industry.

Many industries which work with forms, reports, and legal documents would become hopelessly confused if the flow of the paperwork were not clearly understood by all concerned. This flow of documents is sketched by illustrating the number of copies of a document as blocks (see Figure 21-6) and arrows to indicate the flow.

Diagrams of physical flow are common in industry. They constitute one means by which the manager keeps from becoming hopelessly confused by the complexity of modern systems.

Schemes of Human Relationships

Management essentially deals with human relationships. Such relationships are complex even in small groups. Schematic techniques offer a means of analysis and simplification of these intangible factors so critical in administrative relationships.

Organization charts are devices for showing the first approximation of the flow of authority through the hierarchy. In Chapter 5, communication networks of small groups were sketched to show the different patterns which develop among individual persons. Both of these schemes of human relationships have wide applicability for managers in their attempt to comprehend the social dimensions of their job. Other schemes have been developed by social scientists to aid in the understanding of what the authors have called "informal organization."

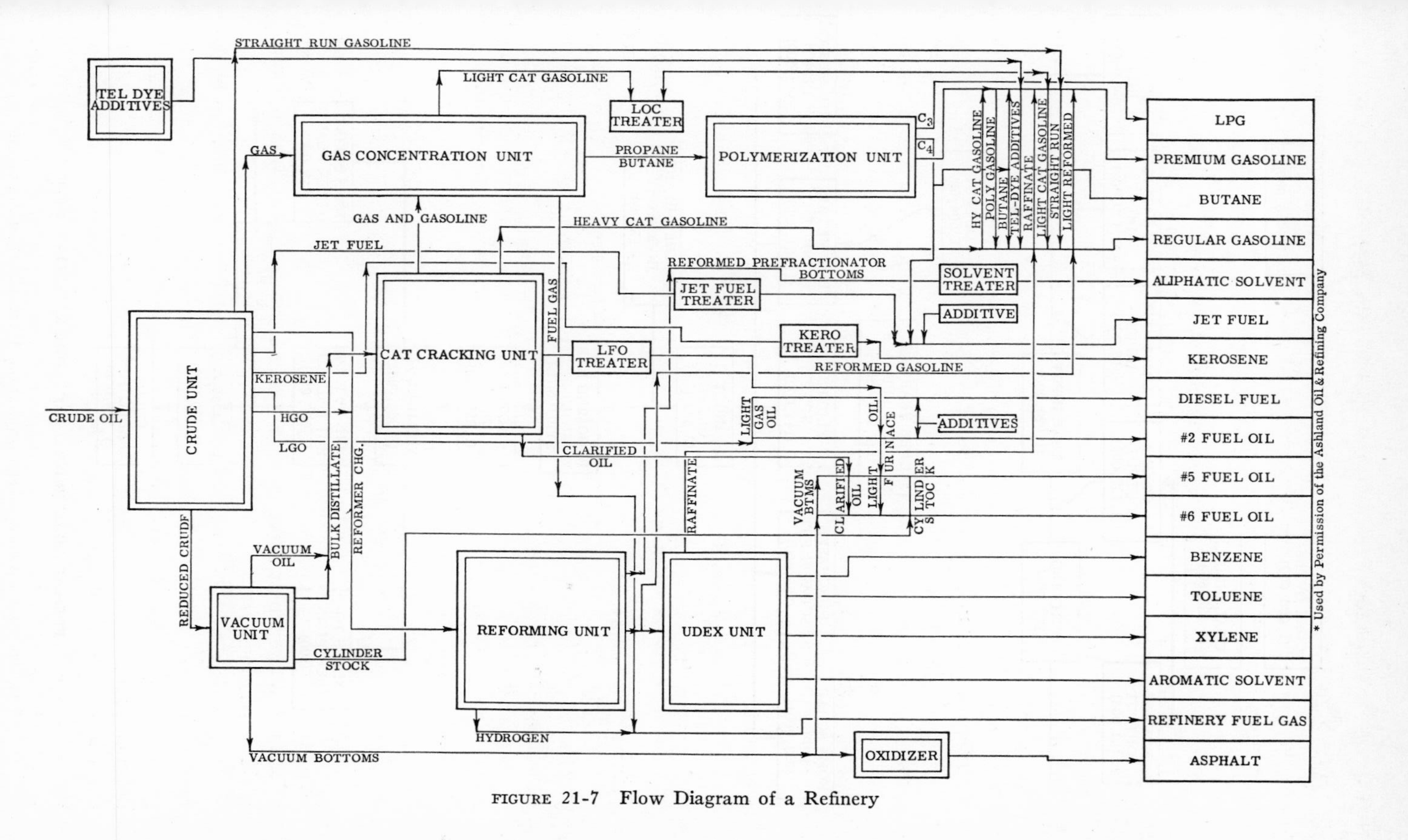

FIGURE 21-7 Flow Diagram of a Refinery

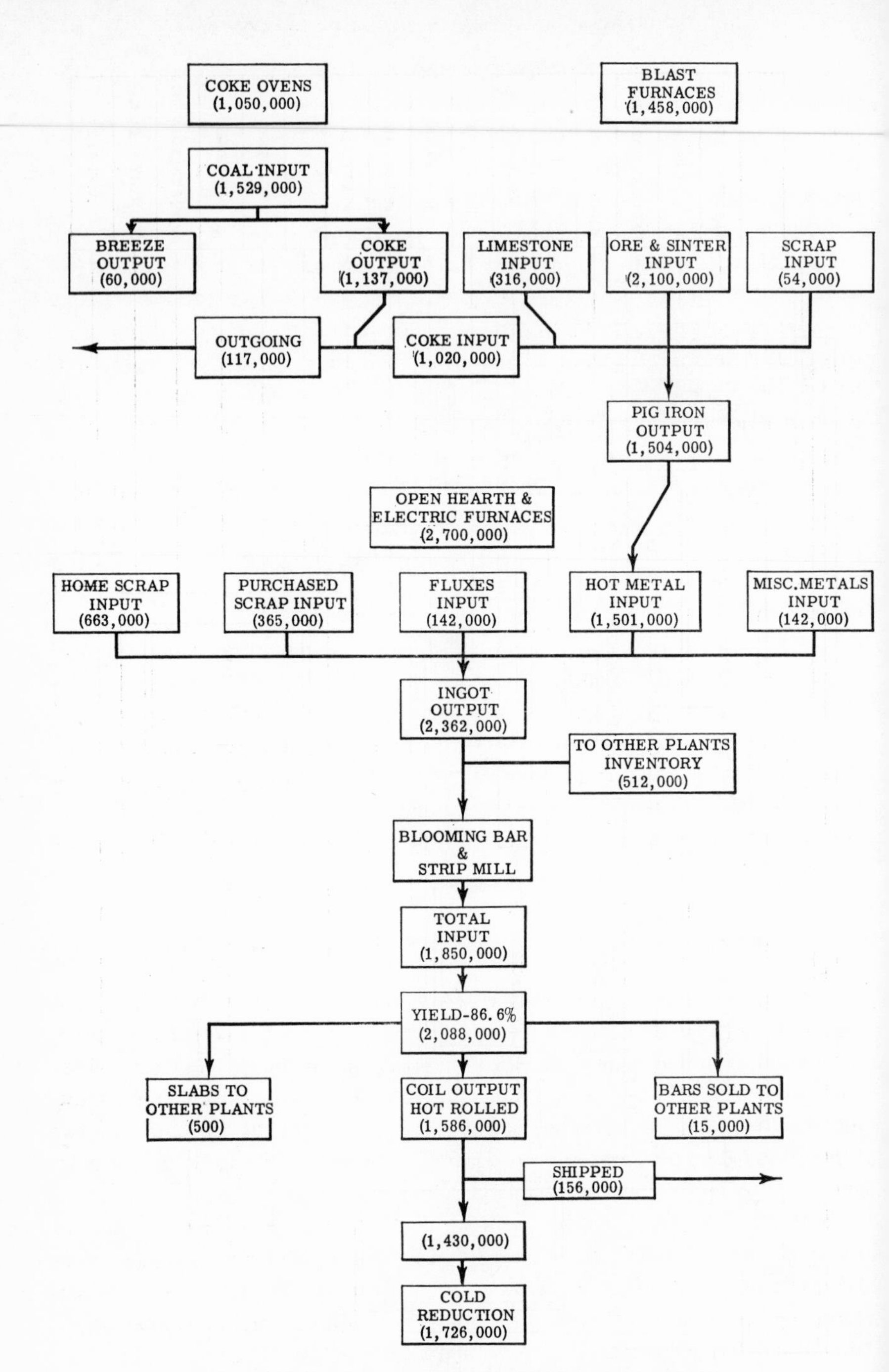

FIGURE 21-8 Armco Steel Corporation, Flow Chart of Input and Output, Middletown Works, 1959

Sociometric tests and the schematic device called sociograms were first developed by J. L. Moreno several decades ago to measure the factor of interpersonal feelings. In the next chapter, an extract from Moreno introduces the symbols that he used and several examples of the structures of social relationships one can sketch with his approach.

Although the first uses of sociograms were in studying social unrest and co-operation in school groups, they have become another tool available for work relationships in business enterprises. The basic data for constructing a sociogram come from answers, by the individuals in a group, to questions specifically designed to show spontaneous choice and feeling. For example, let us assume an office in which sixteen girls are working as secretaries. Each girl can be asked to choose the first three girls with whom they would like to work closely. Answers are organized into classes, namely, attraction (like), repulsion (dislike), and indifference (neutral). Other questions could be asked regarding choices of a leader yielding patterns of dominance, or regarding choices of those with whom personal problems can best be discussed, yielding patterns of trust, and so forth. Facts collected in this manner can then be charted. With this visual means, the researcher can identify different types of patterns—"star" (a person receiving the greatest number of choices), "isolate" (one receiving no choices), "triangle" (A is chosen by B, B by C, and C by A which is the beginning of a clique or subgroup).

The sociogram helps identify certain facts important for a manager to understand. Its use in social research has pointed out important human relationships. It has helped determine the number and size of cliques, the general morale and cohesiveness of work groups, those who may need counseling guidance, and potential supervisors.

Graphs of Frequency Distributions and Probabilities

Nothing is less meaningful than a large number of raw statistics which have not been grouped in some manner. Grouping data into frequency tables is a common technique of organizing them to help interpretation. These tables, with a column showing the limits or midpoints of classes and a column showing the number of frequencies within the classes, provide the basis for two types of graphs—polygons and histograms. Figure 21-9 shows a simple polygon; Figure 21-10 shows the same data in a histogram.

Both the frequency polygon and the histogram are general purpose schematic techniques which can be used for analyzing many types of data. Some typical uses are: showing the number of accidents in the plant, the wage pattern, the age of accounts receivable, the size of sales orders, and other operational and financial data.

Often it is desirable to visualize the total number of frequencies over a given value or under a given value. In this case, we organize all values in classes above (or below) the value of interest into a cumulative frequency table. We then can make a chart of these cumulative frequencies, known as an *ogive.*

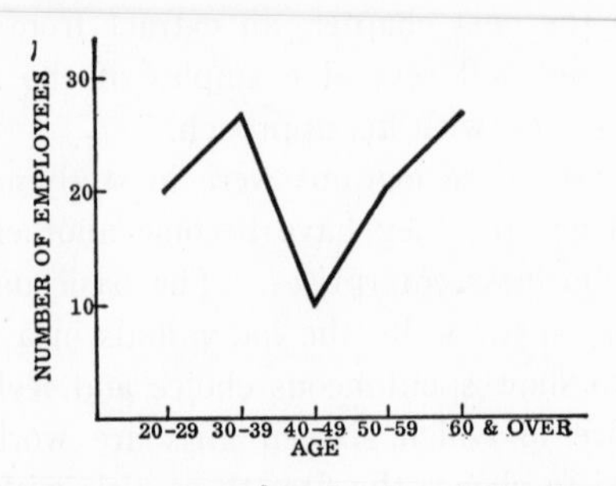

FIGURE 21-9 Age Distribution of Employees

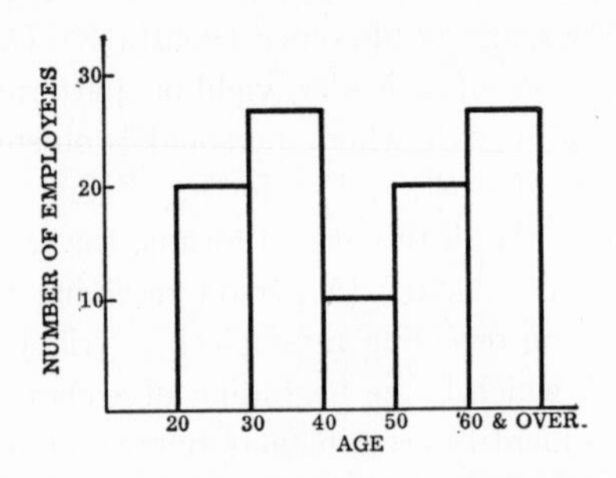

FIGURE 21-10 Age Distribution of Employees

In addition to the description of a mass of data, the frequency polygon helps clarify the analysis of cases of uncertainty. The more explicit a manager can be concerning the "probabilities" of the occurrence of an event, the better basis he will have for his decisions. He may gain an idea regarding the probabilities through past experience, as insurance companies do when determining the probability that a man age 40 will die in the next year; or, he may determine logically what he believes to be the pattern of expected events from the inherent characteristics of the situation, as one may do when determining the probabilities of tossing heads twice in succession if there is an equal chance of tossing a head on any single toss. Figure 21-11 is a graph showing a probability distribution of the date on which accounts receivable will be paid.

Analogues of Mental Processes

The recent emphasis on decision-making has increased the use of sketches for describing and analyzing mental processes. In Chapter 9 we made use of a conceptual framework of such abstract ideas as policies, strategies, and so forth. Schemes are increasingly used to reduce abstract thought to some visual pattern.

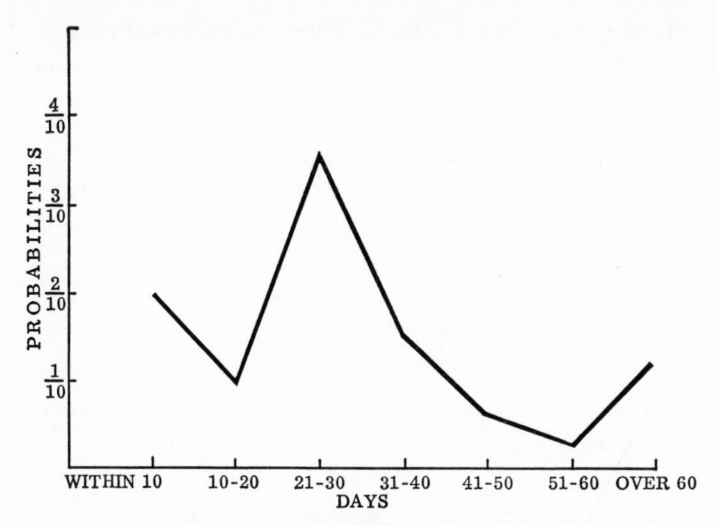

FIGURE 21-11 Estimated Probabilities of Payments on Accounts Receivable

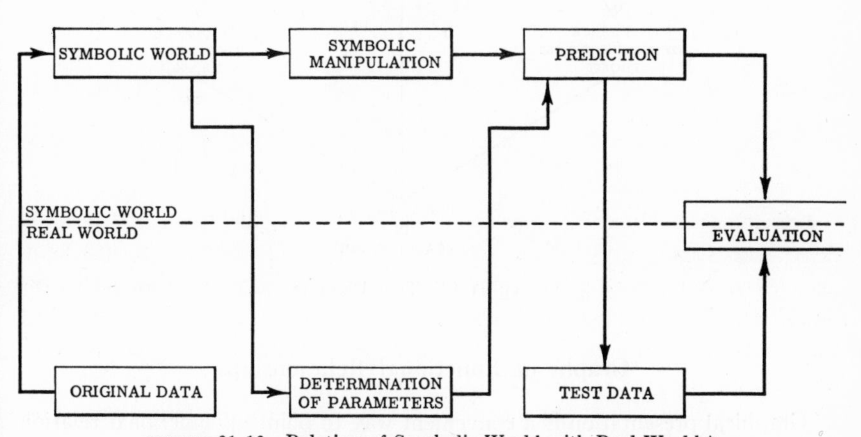

FIGURE 21-12 Relation of Symbolic World with Real World *

* Irwin D. F. Bross, *Design for Decision* (New York: The Macmillan Company, 1953), p. 174.

Bross presents the place of the symbolic approach in a diagram (Figure 21-12). He uses a schematic approach to clarify how schematic (symbolic) techniques are used to explain the "real world." He stresses the necessity of crossing back and forth between the real world and the symbolic world. The symbolic world develops a rigorous framework of thought; however, unless facts from the real world continually flow into the symbolic world, the symbolic world might drift away from providing practical answers to real problems.

We may wish to visualize all of the logical possibilities of a given situation before making a decision. One analogue with many uses is called a tree diagram. Figure 21-13 illustrates the construction of a tree of the logical possibilities of a $40,000 investment in a branch store. In this illustration, uncertainty is pictured in a simplified form—three possibilities with the chances of each path noted on each line with additional possibilities branching out. This type of diagram helps a person organize his approach to problems. In complex problems there may be many levels of branches and thus numerous paths from the trunk (original decision) to the branches at the top of the tree (possible consequences).

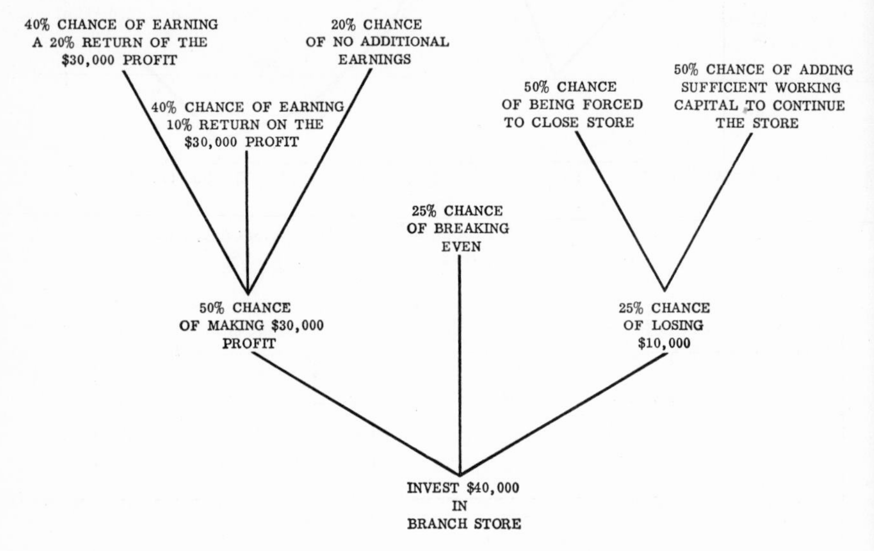

FIGURE 21-13 Tree Diagram

Graphs of Functional Relationships

Graphical presentation is a convenient way to point up functional relationships among variables. Two variables can be graphed easily—one on the vertical and one on the horizontal scale. Examples of such charts are numerous and include scatter diagrams, demand and supply curves, graphs of cutting speeds of metals, and so forth. The breakeven chart illustrated earlier shows the functional relationship of costs and revenue to rates of operations.

Anyone with a background in mathematics will remember that he can form two-dimensional graphs by assuming different values of x and y, plotting the x values on the horizontal scale and the y values on the vertical scale. Three dimensions are more difficult to plot and four or more variables will require mathematical equations in the description of the relationships.

Figure 21-14 is an example of one of the many uses of graphs of functional relationships. It shows the relationship of the scale of operations to costs and revenue. The economist uses such charts to illustrate the effects on costs of varying the rate of operation of a fixed plant and varying the scale of operations. In Figure 21-14 the economies of large diameter pipe lines appear evident as one compares the 10″ line with the 30″ line. Any given size line can carry varying amounts of oil (by adding pumping stations); thus the cost per barrel for transportation for any given size pipe is shown by one of the U-shaped curves. Even if exact data cannot be obtained from actual operations for all rates of production and sizes of equipment, the general pattern helps the manager to see the conditions he faces. He can collect cost data at some points and empirically test his estimations of the shapes of the curves.

Profiles, Check Lists, and Scales as Aids to Evaluation

There are many additional types of approaches to organizing facts for decision making. This section will illustrate some of the most common uses of tables and numerical scales. Most are general purpose and available for use in many types of problems other than those illustrated.

Point systems of evaluation

The use of point systems is widespread in personnel management. Many merit rating systems and job evaluation systems make use of this simple procedure for systematizing evaluation. The key to the point system approach is to assume a total number of possible points which each of a number of factors can receive. In this first step, one can build in the weighting of each factor depending upon its relative importance. For example, if there are five factors to be considered and each is of equal importance, the points allocated to each would be $\frac{1}{5}$ of the total.

Point systems can be used in any type of problem even though the facts are qualitative. For example, in the location of a plant, the manager considers numerous factors including labor costs, transportation, location of raw materials, tax structure of the state and local government, cultural attractions for employees, and so forth. If the point system is to be used, the qualitative factors must be quantified by assuming a certain number of points for each factor. This process is helpful in specifying exactly the relative weight given to each factor. Its principal shortcoming is that it often leads its user to feel that he has "objectively" made the decision when, in fact, different users can arrive at different answers. The fact that the answers are numerical does not make them less subjective—the numbers are merely useful assumptions.

The next chapter includes an example of the use of a point system in the over-all evaluation of the management of companies. Table 21-1 illustrates a typical structure for the point system in job evaluation.

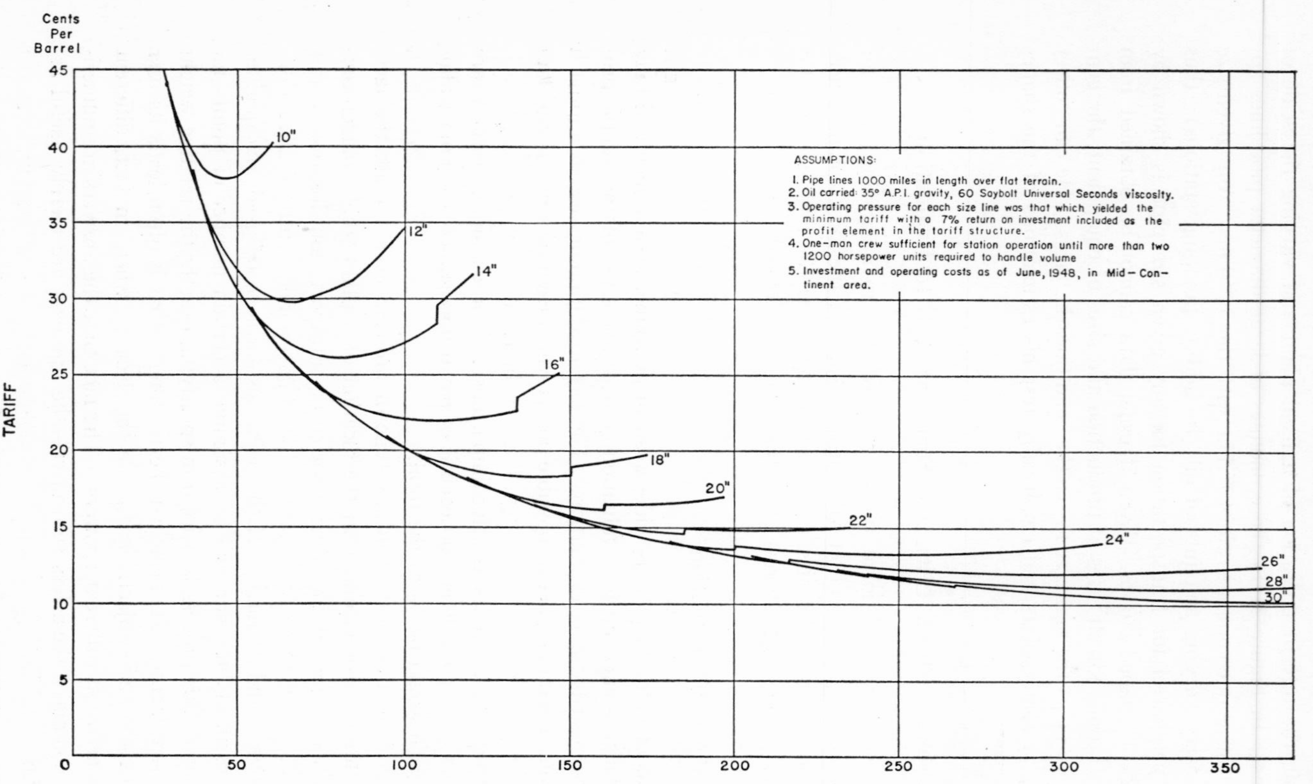

FIGURE 21-14 Unit Costs (Plus 7% Net Profit) for Different Size Pipe Lines, 1948 *

* As reprinted in John G. McLean and Robert Wm. Haigh, *The Growth of Integrated Oil Companies* (Boston: Division of Research, Harvard Business School, 1954), p. 185.

TABLE 21-1

POINT SYSTEM FOR JOB EVALUATION

Point Allowances for Job Characteristics and Conditions

	Maximum Points	*Points Allowed for Job Titled—Service Man, Shipping Room*
Education	100	50
Experience	100	75
Aptitude (Accuracy, Dexterity)	125	70
Physical Demand (Fatigue)	50	40
Mental Demand (Concentration, Speed)	100	70
Responsibility for Equipment	50	45
Responsibility for Product	50	5
Responsibility for Safety of Others	50	40
Working Conditions (Hazards, Heat, Dirt, Noise)	25	10
Total	650	405

Profiles for comparing characteristics

The psychologist has long used the profile type of scheme to present the results of his study on the characteristics of individuals and groups. Often he uses standardized tests to measure aptitude, interest, personality, and other characteristics important to the manager of personnel. The profile chart makes it possible to compare visually the results for a given individual or group with a standard previously determined by widespread use of the same battery of tests in other groups having common characteristics.

The reader who has taken a series of psychological tests in an educational placement program or who has been to a "vocational guidance" center to help decide on a suitable occupation, probably has been given his results in the form of a profile chart. In the next chapter we shall see one application of this schematic device in reporting the attitude of employees to management.

Check lists and organized notes

Everyone runs into the type of situation calling for a decision based upon a number of factors. We try to develop a system to help us remember and not overlook important aspects of the subject. The simplest and most generally used system is a check list. If we wish to make sure that we send Christmas cards to all of our important friends, we can systematically develop a list and check them off as we write the cards. If a manager is faced with a promotion decision, he may list the candidates and list the desirable characteristics in making a decision. If a company is planning to build a new plant, it may make a list of the important factors to consider and then check possible locations against this list.

One form of check list classifies the strong points and weak points of different alternatives. Many textbooks place considerable weight on encouraging the student to memorize lists of advantages and disadvantages of given courses of action. Such lists may be useful as a first step for understanding the nature of the factors important to the decision. However, the check list should be used only to start deeper thinking on the subject; it should not degenerate into a mechanical process which, in fact, eliminates thinking. Lists of advantages and disadvantages merely state certain points without showing their relative importance. Out of twelve factors included in a list, one factor may be critical and the others relatively unimportant. The tendency in using check lists may be to weigh factors equally, when their actual importance differs greatly.

Schematic Analysis in General

Schematic analysis offers some systematic pattern for an interpretation of many factors important to business decisions. This chapter has introduced a few examples of the varied types of approaches to give the reader a start in developing his own techniques.

The tools in this chapter are general in purpose. In some types of problems they are the best available at present. In other types they are merely the first step in a process of formally solving problems. The more rigorous (and often more expensive) quantitative methods currently being developed partially remedy the following limitations of the analysis discussed in this chapter: (1) Different answers to a problem can be found by different managers with no way of determining "the best." (2) Schemes need to be made more definite and detailed if electronic and mechanical devices are to be utilized. (3) Schemes are low powered tools relative to mathematics as a means of abstractly handling relationships and arriving at entirely new theories.

Both formal models and informal schemes are extremely valuable to the manager. His choice of the proper tool of analysis can be a very important decision.

Bibliographical Note

Information on schematic techniques is scattered in books in such areas as statistics, engineering, mechanical drawing, motion and time study, mathematics, art, psychology, and sociology. The following references cite those books that describe techniques most useful to a manager. E. H. Bowman and R. B. Fetter summarize some useful schemes in one chapter in their *Analysis for Production Management* (1957).

The Gantt chart became a basic scheme for simplifying the details of scheduling production after its introduction by Henry L. Gantt in *Organizing for Work* in

1919. Many interesting adaptations of the Gantt chart are given in Wallace Clark's *The Gantt Chart* (1938). Commercial variations of the Gantt chart include the Produc-trol board supplied by the Wassell Organization and Schedugraphs sold by Sperry Rand.

The reading of shop drawings is developed in an elementary manner in *Drawing, Sketching, and Blueprint Reading* (1954) by S. L. Coover; in *Basic Mechanical Drawing* (1959) by H. E. Welch; and in *A Primer of Blueprint Reading* (1955) by Thomas Diamond.

Schemes of human relationships are used widely in books dealing with organization charts, sociology, and social psychology. The sociogram has become one of the best known schemes since the pioneering work of J. L. Moreno's *Who Shall Survive?* (1934).

Schemes illustrating mental processes are appearing more frequently in books. Some interesting examples of such schemes can be found in J. G. March and H. A. Simon, *Organizations* (1958) and I. D. J. Bross, *Design for Decision* (1953).

Questions and Problems

1. Using the verbal description in the Delta Stores case (see Chapter 12) devise a schematic presentation that will help you visualize the system used to control stock shortages.
2. Using the verbal description of the flow of work in the Becker Laundry case, chart the path of clothes through the plant, starting with receipt from the customer to delivery back to him.
3. Make a sociogram showing the human relationships in your current management class.
4. Make a Gantt chart showing the planned and actual use of your time for the next week.
5. Collect examples of various types of schematic presentations that you notice in current newspapers and magazines.
6. Review the subjects discussed in this book up to this point, looking for examples of the various types of schematic presentations used.
7. Why do many charts use special scales to present data? Semi-logarithmic paper?
8. In what courses have you made use of charts with time on one axis?
9. What are the advantages of the point system for job evaluation illustrated in Table 21-1?
10. Devise a point system which would help you evaluate the different job opportunities as they are offered when you are graduated.

22

Extracts and Cases on Schematic Analysis in Decision Making

SCHEMES for analyzing and presenting ideas are continually being developed for specialized uses. Many schemes already used can be adapted to new applications in entirely different areas of management. The chapter will begin with the best known charting device in management, the Gantt chart, an excellent illustration of a versatile tool applicable to many kinds of problems.

In recent years, the study of systems and procedures has increased in importance. This study concentrates on visualizing all components of a system and their relationships to each other. Our second extract discusses the place of charting in systems work.

Schemes often form the basis of a new area of research. The extract by J. L. Moreno provides an introduction to the study of human relationships through the medium of the sociogram. Recent research on management has attempted to make use of charts in the understanding of problems of internal organization.

Jackson Martindell, the author of the next extract, uses scaling techniques in the evaluation of company management. He attempts to place numerical values on the factors important to over-all success. The reader will want to form his own opinions on the usefulness of this approach.

The extract by David Moore and Richard Renck illustrates profiles as schematic techniques in attitude surveys. Profiles have many uses in presenting information about people.

The cases in this chapter illustrate the wide use of schematic devices. The first presents a use of charts in the management of the armed forces.

The second shows two forms used in rating the quality of performance of an individual (usually called merit rating). The third illustrates charting in making a plant layout. The student will wish to refer to the discussion in Chapter 13 on work improvement when he prepares this third case. The fourth case presents a comprehensive review of subjects previously discussed, and shows how several types of schematic analysis give the manager a means of visualizing his production problem. In addition, this case illustrates the complexity of production control.

Extract A

Progress Charts (H. L. Gantt)

This is an actual Ordinance Department chart (see Figure 22-1), entered up to the end of December, 1917, the names of the items being replaced by letters. It was used to illustrate the methods employed and to instruct people in the work.

The distance between the current date and the end of the heavy or cumulative line indicates whether the deliveries of any article are ahead or behind the schedule and how much. It is thus seen that the short lines indicate instantly the articles which need attention. . . .

This chart is shown only as a sample and represents a principle. Each item on such a chart as the above may have been purchased from a dozen different suppliers, in which case the man responsible for procuring such articles had the schedule and progress of each contract charted in a manner similar to that on Chart A. Chart B is such a chart. The lines on Chart A represented a summary of all the lines on the corresponding detail charts.

Similar charts were used during the war to show the schedules and progress in building ships, shipyards, and flying boats—and are now being used for the same purpose in connection with the manufacture of many kinds of machinery. The great advantage of this type of chart, known as the straight line chart, is that it enables us to make a large number of comparisons at once.

From the illustrations given, the following principles upon which this chart system is founded are easily comprehended:

First: The fact that all activities can be measured by the amount of time needed to perform them.

Second: The space representing the time unit on the chart can be made to represent the amount of activity which should have taken place in that time.

Bearing in mind these two principles, the whole system is readily intelligible and affords a means of charting all kinds of activities, the common measure being time.[1]

[1] From *Organizing for Work* by H. L. Gantt, copyright, 1910, by Harcourt, Brace & World, Inc., pp. 81–83; renewed, 1947, by Margaret Gantt Taber. Reprinted by permission of the publishers.

Entered to December 31st 1917.

ARTICLES	1917 TOTAL ORDERED	January	February	March	April	May	June	July	August	September	October	November	December
A	664,632	10M	11M 21M	32M	43M	16M 59M	37M 96M	22M 118M	20M Z 138M	52M 190M	157M 347M	257M 604M	39M 643M
B	142,004	618 Z	2618 3M	3618 7M	3M 10M	4M 14M	4M 18M	11M 29M	11M 40M	21M 61M	22M 83M	26M 109M	23M 132M
C	156,670				18 Z	Z	16	2M Z 2M	2M 4M	7M 11M	22M 33M	34M Z 67M	101M
D	4,000	250 Z	Z 500	750	1000 252	1252 0	Z 1252 0	Z 1252 0	Z 1252 873	Z 2125 625	2750	3375	4000

A. Progress Chart

CONTRACTOR	ORDER NUMBER	1917 AMOUNT ORDERED	January	February	March	April	May	June	July	August	September	October	November	December
Total	A	664,632	10M	11M 21M	32M	43M	16M 59M	37M 96M	22M 118M	20M Z 138M	52M 190M	157M 347M	257M 604M	39M 648M
1	6228	57,000	9500	19M	29M	38M	48M	Z 57M						
2	6254	8,120					4060	4060 Z 8120			1504 3 Z 3008	4510	Z 6014	Z 7518 2
3	6562	22,000						2200 Z	Z 4400	Z 6600	8800	11M	Z 13M	Z 16M
4	EE24	25,000									5M Z	10M 15M	25M	3000
5	6505	81,000						22M	18M 40M	Z 58M		5M Z		
6	EE45	100,000										38M	37M 75M	25M 100M
7	EE59	225,000									25M Z	100M Z 125M	225M	
8	6292	131,512											105M Z	10M Z 115M
9	6298	5,000		1250	2500	3750	5000							
10	6391	10,000					3323	6646	Z 9969		522	1044	1566	Z 2088 2

B. Order Chart.

A—At the left of the chart is a list of articles to be procured. The amounts for which orders have been placed are shown in the column headed "Amount ordered." The dates between which deliveries are to be made are shown by angles. The amount to be delivered each month is shown by a figure at the left side of the space assigned to that month. The figure at the right of each time space shows the total amount to be delivered up to that date.

If the amount due in any month is all received, a light line is drawn clear across the space representing that month. If only half the amount due is received, this line goes only half way across. In general, the length of the light line or the number of lines indicates the amount delivered during that month.

The heavy line shows cumulatively the amount delivered up to the date of the last entry. It will be noted that, if this line is drawn to the scale of the periods through which it passes, the distance from the end of the line to the current date will represent the amount of time deliveries are behind or ahead of the schedule. It is thus seen that the short cumulative lines are the ones which require attention, as they represent items that are farthest behind schedule. Z represents no deliveries.

B—The top line on this chart is a summary of the individual orders and is represented on chart A by line A.

FIGURE 22-1 Gantt Progress and Order Charts

Extract B

Systems Charting (R. W. Pomeroy)

Graphic presentation is to the systems profession what a numbers system is to the field of mathematics—a language of abbreviation enabling the understanding of complex phenomena in relatively short periods of time.

Charting is by no means the sole province of the systems function. It is an integral part of the activity of almost all professional techniques, a heavily relied-upon device for simplification and presentation in hundreds of different contexts. But outside the field of pure science, few areas rely so much on the use of graphic presentation as does the systems profession. . . .

The survey phase of the systems job is the original investigation into present procedures. At this time, the study is concerned with how the job is now being done. The information the analyst needs must be correct and thorough. The collection of the thousands of detailed facts that will be put together to form so complete a picture is neither difficult nor esoteric. It is done by asking questions of everyone concerned with the job being studied and writing down the answers. But, when this is done, the interviewer sets aside his lay techniques and becomes a systems analyst. He now makes use of the flow chart, a simple device that will transform the vast jumble of disconnected details he has assembled into a single, simple roadmap that defines complete clerical procedure.

The mapmaking process is analogous to the working of a jigsaw puzzle. Each detail is pulled from the pile in turn and made part of the over-all picture. On completion of the picture, the elemental segments have been arranged to form a compact area of complete comprehension. It is important to realize that it is this comprehension that the analyst gains. The chart itself is the desired end product by which the analyst has *learned* the procedure.

A very important part of this learning is that in seeing *how* the job is done, we come to understand a great deal of the *why*. Training takes over from there. We sense—usually see on the chart, though occasionally we refer admiringly to a man who can "smell" or "feel"—areas of potential improvement. What has been a simple investigation now begins to take on direction; it begins to point out the areas of greatest potential for improvement.

These two phases, comprehension of present procedures and indication of the best paths for future action, constitute the greatest value of the flow charting method. Flow charts could be destroyed at this point and would still have made their major contribution. Beyond this point, flow charts, although of great usefulness, are of diminishing importance.

A by-product use of flow charts in the survey phase is in sparking employee interest in the systems job and in helping to dispel the fear of changes to come.[2]

EXTRACT C

Sociograms (J. L. Moreno)

Wherever two or more people are functioning as a social group that group not only consists of those individuals, but, more important perhaps, if that is possible, than the individuals themselves and without which their functioning as a social group could not be expressed, are the relations which maintain between them. It is these intangible, imponderable and invisible aspects of the situation which enable the mathematical sum of a certain number of individuals to function as a social group. . . .

An instrument to measure the amount of organization shown by social groups is called *sociometric test*. The sociometric test requires an individual to choose his associates for any group of which he is or might become a member. He is expected to make his choices without restraint and whether the individuals chosen are members of the present group or outsiders. . . .

The findings . . . are presented in Tables, in Frequency Histograms, and particularly through the means of a process to visualize the position of each individual within his group as well as the interrelations of all other individuals as these are affected by attractions and repulsions, the sociogram . . . [which use symbols like the following]

○ A circle represents a girl.
△ A triangle represents a boy.
◎ A double circle or double triangle signifies that the respective individual is a member of a different group from the chartered one.
—— A line drawn from one individual to another individual represents the emotional reaction of the one individual to the other.
In one-color charts each line represents an attraction.
In multi-colored charts each different color represents a different emotional reaction:
A red line represents attraction;
A dotted line represents indifference;
A black line represents repulsion.
——➤ An arrowed line indicates one-sided reaction.
—+— A crossed line represents two-sided reactions.[3]

[2] Richard W. Pomeroy, "Systems Charting," in *Systems and Procedures: A Handbook for Business and Industry,* ed. Victor Lazzaro (Englewood Cliffs, N.J.: Prentice-Hall, Inc., © 1959), pp. 63–64.

[3] J. L. Moreno, M.D., *Who Shall Survive?* (Washington, D.C.: Nervous Mental Disease Publishing Company, 1934), pp. xi, 11, 26, 30, 114–116.

[Figure 22-2 illustrates the use of these symbols.]

Two sub-groups are centralized each about two dominating individuals who have no attractive forces uniting them.

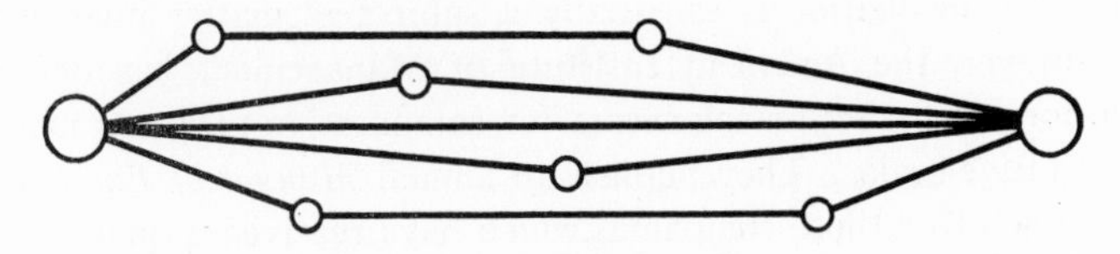

A group in which two dominating individuals are strongly united both directly and indirectly through other individuals.

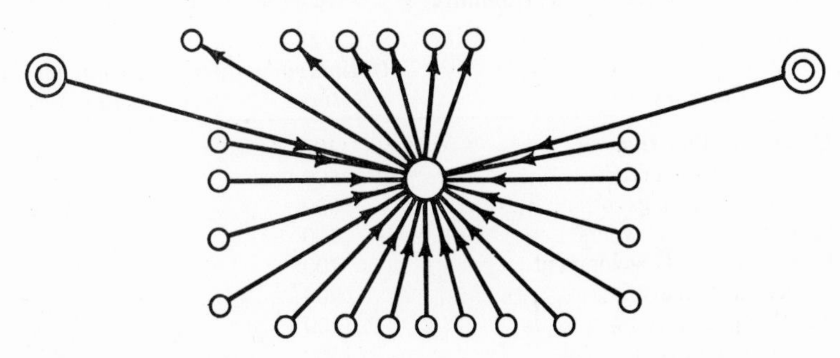

Attractions and repulsions take the form of a pair: in *a* mutual attraction (red pair); *b,* mutual rejection (black pair); *c,* mutual indifferences; *d,* attraction vs. rejection; *e,* attraction vs. indifference.

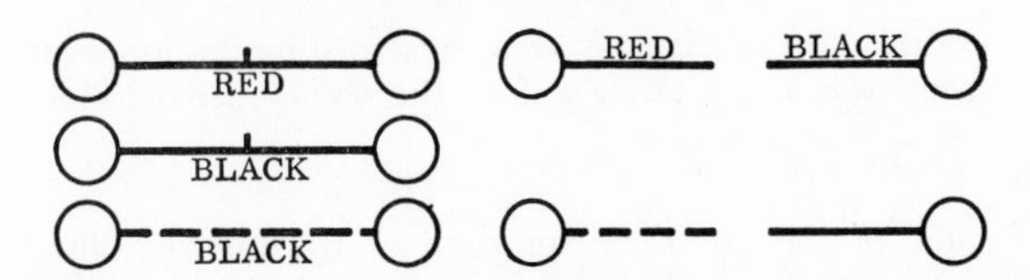

Subject rejects six and is rejected by fifteen individuals within his own group; is rejected further by two individuals outside of his own group. The result is an isolated and rejected individual.

FIGURE 22-2 Examples of Sociograms *

* *Ibid.*

EXTRACT D

Scaling Techniques for Appraising Over-all Company Performance (American Institute of Management)

[The evaluation of over-all performance of a company is desirable for use by investors, management specialists, a company's own personnel, and economists. A company's success can be measured to some degree by net profits over a period of time, growth relative to other companies in the industry, morale of its employees, and other techniques such as "management audits." The process of evaluation is essentially a subjective matter involving judgment. However, the American Institute of Management has developed a technique for appraising managements for comparative purposes making use of a quantitative scale. They publish an annual *Manual of Excellent Managements* which lists those companies which have received a quantitative rating of over 7,500. These points are determined by using the following basic scale and weights [4] after a study of the management using public information plus answers to a lengthy questionnaire:]

Category	*Optimum Rating*	*Minimum for Excellence*
Economic Function	400	300
Corporation Structure	500	375
Health of Earnings	600	450
Service to Stockowners	700	525
Research and Development	700	525
Directorate Analysis	900	675
Fiscal Policies	1100	825
Production Efficiency	1300	975
Sales Vigor	1400	1050
Executive Evaluation	2400	1800
Total	10,000	7,500

This point system of evaluation has been developed by the American Institute of Management as a comparative guide; the values derived should not be regarded as statistical measures.

A sample of some of the questions for each of the ten classifications will give a clearer picture of the process used by the Auditors:

Economic Function—25 a. In what ways have the company and its products contributed to the economic welfare of its community, the nation and the world? 25 b. What plans exist for further contributions of this kind? 26. In the opinion of management, what are the most significant differences

[4] See Jackson Martindell, *The Scientific Appraisal of Management* (New York: Harper & Bros., 1950).

between the company and the rest of the industry, as regards the topics covered in this category?

Corporate Structure—27. Is there an organization chart of top management? If so, please attach a copy. Please also supply copies of any charts which show channels of communication as opposed to organization. . . . 48. What are the normal channels for official communication between junior executives in different departments? To what extent are they side-stepped unofficially? . . .

Health of Earnings—51. What proportion of annual net income has been retained in the business in each of the past fifteen years? . . . 56. Has the company ever omitted preferred dividends or defaulted on its bond? . . .

Service to Stockowners—69. Who are the company's ten largest stockowners? What per cent of the stock does each own? 70. If there is a majority stockowner group, to what extent does this group exercise active control over the company's management? 71. Have any large stockowners disposed of their holdings during the past ten years? Are the reasons known? What were they? . . .

Research and Development—97 a. Does the company have a centralized research department? What research activities is it assigned? 97 b. What research activities are conducted by other departments? 97 c. Please provide an organization chart for all research groups. . . . 99 a. When was the research department established? 99 b. Where is it located? 99 c. What are its major current projects or areas of research? . . .

Directorate Analysis—130 a. What material is provided directors in advance of meetings? Please supply examples. 130 b. How far in advance of each meeting do directors receive this material? . . . 135. What has been the record of attendance of each director at full meetings for the past two years? His attendance at committee meetings? 136. To what extent do outside directors participate in non-board committees or other non-board activities? . . . 144. Is any plan for compulsory retirement in effect? What is it? If there is none, is any contemplated? . . .

Fiscal Policies—148. Was initial financing through public or private funds? . . . 151. Has the company ever passed through a financial reorganization? If so, please give full details. . . . 154. Does the company prepare a capital budget? A sales budget? An operating budget? Please describe each, its preparation and use. . . . 165. To what extent are plant and equipment depreciated? What method is used? How have depreciation funds been used? . . . 179. Are manufacturing statements projected as against estimated sales? . . .

Production Efficiency—182. What has been the plant investment per production employee for each of the past ten years? The investment on machinery? . . . 186. What plans exist for additional plant facilities? . . . 197. To what extent can the company maintain profit margins in periods of declining sales? . . . 204. To what extent is production control decentralized? What is management thinking on this point? . . . 211 a. What has been the general reaction of employees to technological changes? To other changes? 211 b. What methods have been used to prepare the way for changes? . . . 221. What incentive system exists? How does it work? . . . 233. Is there a job evaluation program at the lower levels of employment? Please describe it. . . .

Sales Vigor—244 a. Are the company's sales efforts broken down into geographic or product lines? Which? 244 b. What considerations induced the company's sales management to select this breakdown? . . . 247. Does the company own or control any of its distributor organizations? 248 a. How many customers are there? 248 b. How many dealers? 248 c. How many distributors? 248 d. What is the annual turnover of dealerships and distributorships? . . . 256 a. Are market forecasts made? How detailed? How often? How far ahead? 256 b. Are they formally compared with actual results? . . . 262. What are the operational relationships between sales, production and other departments, especially the sales department's participation in production scheduling? . . . 268 a. What are the company's pricing philosophy and methods? 268 b. To what extent does it control retail prices? 268 c. Do price changes usually precede or follow those made by competitors? . . . 273 a. What is the link between advertising, sales and production policies? 273 b. How does each influence the others? . . .

Executive Evaluation—284. What major changes have occurred in executive personnel in the past ten years? Why did each occur? 285. What is the company's formal policy with regard to promotion including that of executive and departmental officers? . . . 287. What college recruitment program exists? Please describe and summarize its results. . . . 295. Does the company insure any of its executives? Which ones? . . . 299. How many hours a week, on the average, has the president devoted to business in the past month? Each vice president? . . . 301. In the opinion of management, what aspects of its individual executives, executive staff as a whole, and its organization are most distinctive? [5]

Extract E

Profile of Scores of Professional Employees (David G. Moore and Richard Renck)

[Attitude] surveys make use of a standardized attitude questionnaire developed by the Industrial Relations Center and known as the *Employee Inventory*. The *Inventory* consists of seventy-eight statements covering most aspects of work, to which employees may either "agree," "disagree," or re-

[5] *Manual of Excellent Managements 1957* (New York: American Institute of Management, 1957), pp. 7, 254–265.

main "undecided." Scores are calculated in terms of percentage favorable response. Results are plotted on profile charts which automatically compare the group survey with a cross-section of American employees [See Figure 22-3]. For each category of the *Inventory* the obtained score of the group is shown in the body of the profile chart and its corresponding percentile value in the black band at the top and bottom of the chart. This permits

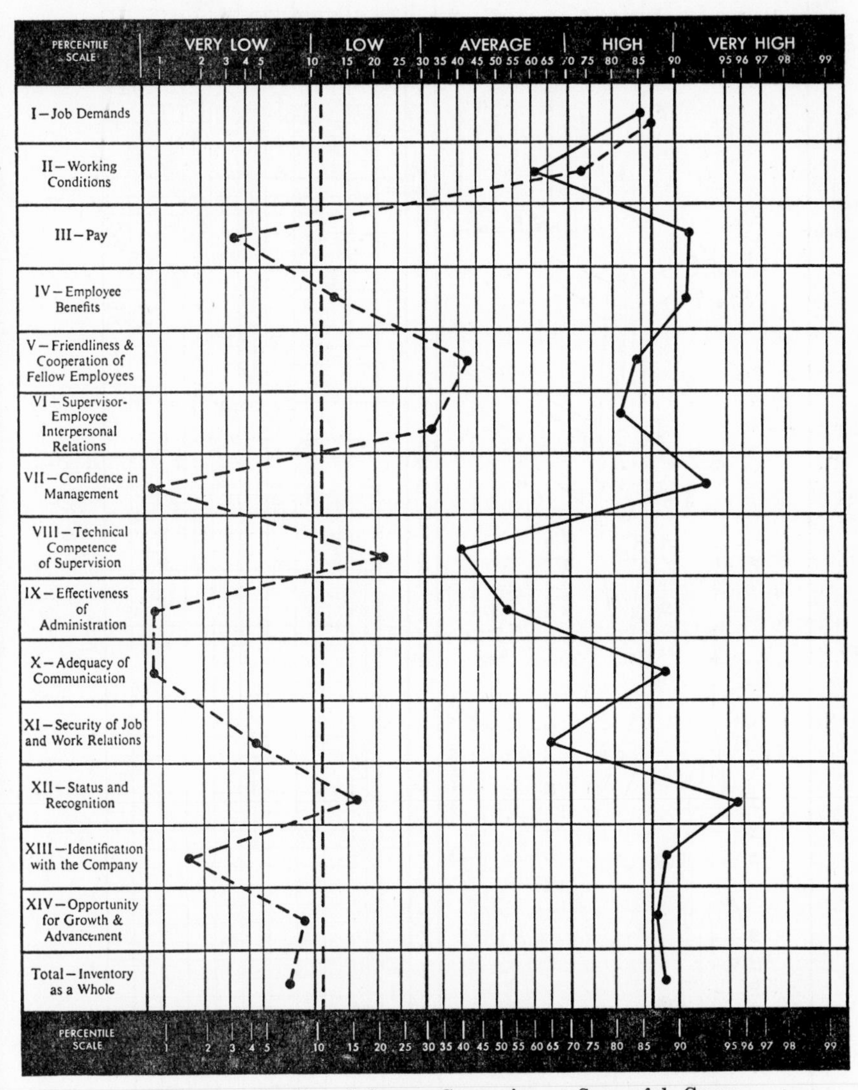

FIGURE 22-3 Profile of Scores Comparing a Successful Group ($N = 17$) with an Unsuccessful Group of Natural Scientists ($N = 14$) *

* David G. Moore and Richard Renck, "The Professional Employee in Industry," *Journal of Business,* January 1955.

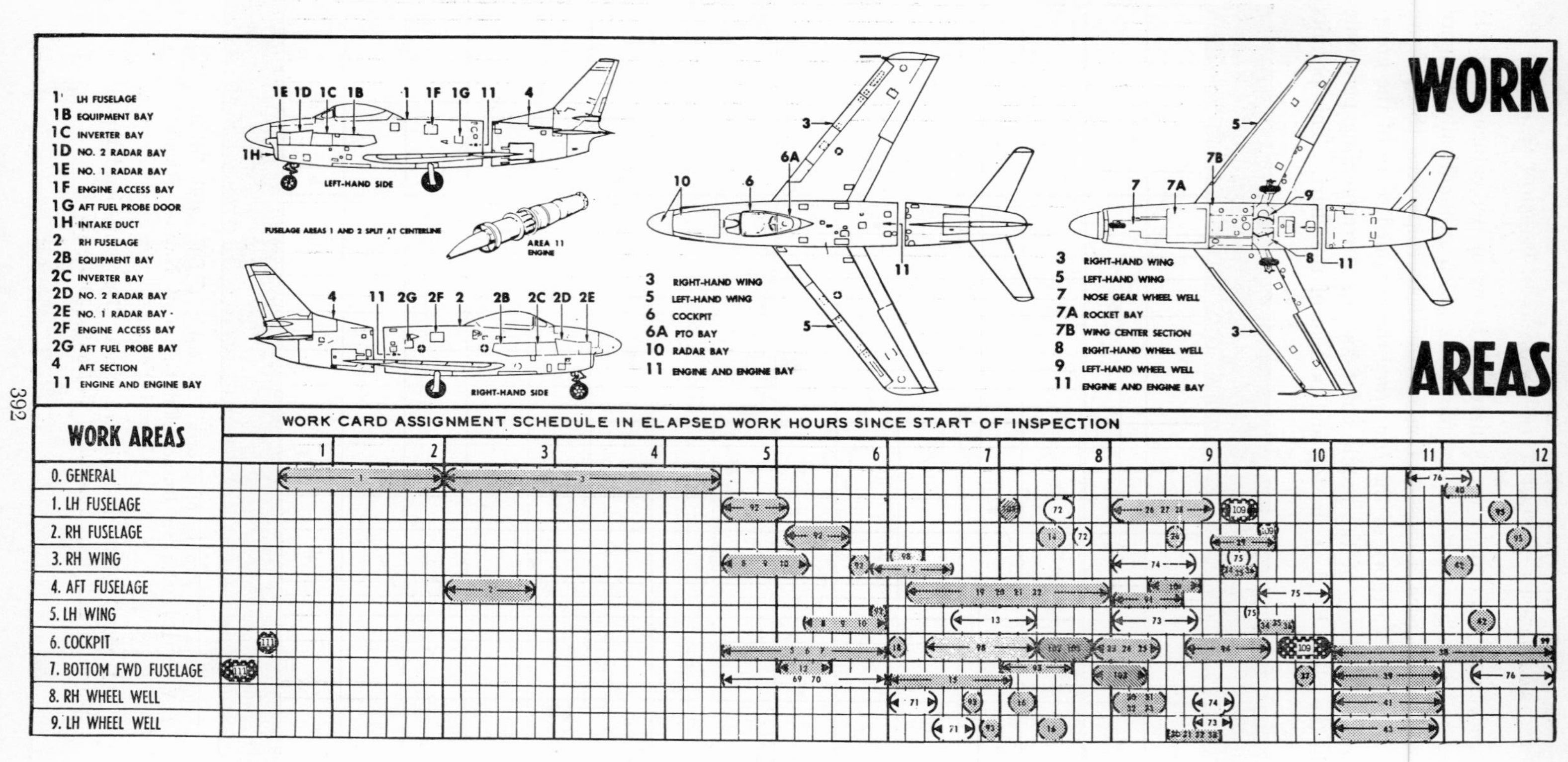
WORK AREAS
1 LH FUSELAGE
1B EQUIPMENT BAY
1C INVERTER BAY
1D NO. 2 RADAR BAY
1E NO. 1 RADAR BAY
1F ENGINE ACCESS BAY
1G AFT FUEL PROBE DOOR
1H INTAKE DUCT
2 RH FUSELAGE
2B EQUIPMENT BAY
2C INVERTER BAY
2D NO. 2 RADAR BAY
2E NO. 1 RADAR BAY
2F ENGINE ACCESS BAY
2G AFT FUEL PROBE BAY
4 AFT SECTION
11 ENGINE AND ENGINE BAY
LEFT-HAND SIDE
RIGHT-HAND SIDE
FUSELAGE AREAS 1 AND 2 SPLIT AT CENTERLINE
AREA 11 ENGINE
3 RIGHT-HAND WING
5 LEFT-HAND WING
6 COCKPIT
6A PTO BAY
10 RADAR BAY
11 ENGINE AND ENGINE BAY
3 RIGHT-HAND WING
5 LEFT-HAND WING
7 NOSE GEAR WHEEL WELL
7A ROCKET BAY
7B WING CENTER SECTION
8 RIGHT-HAND WHEEL WELL
9 LEFT-HAND WHEEL WELL
11 ENGINE AND ENGINE BAY
WORK AREAS
WORK CARD ASSIGNMENT SCHEDULE IN ELAPSED WORK HOURS SINCE START OF INSPECTION
1 2 3 4 5 6 7 8 9 10 11 12
0. GENERAL
1. LH FUSELAGE
2. RH FUSELAGE
3. RH WING
4. AFT FUSELAGE
5. LH WING
6. COCKPIT
7. BOTTOM FWD FUSELAGE
8. RH WHEEL WELL
9. LH WHEEL WELL

FIGURE 22-4

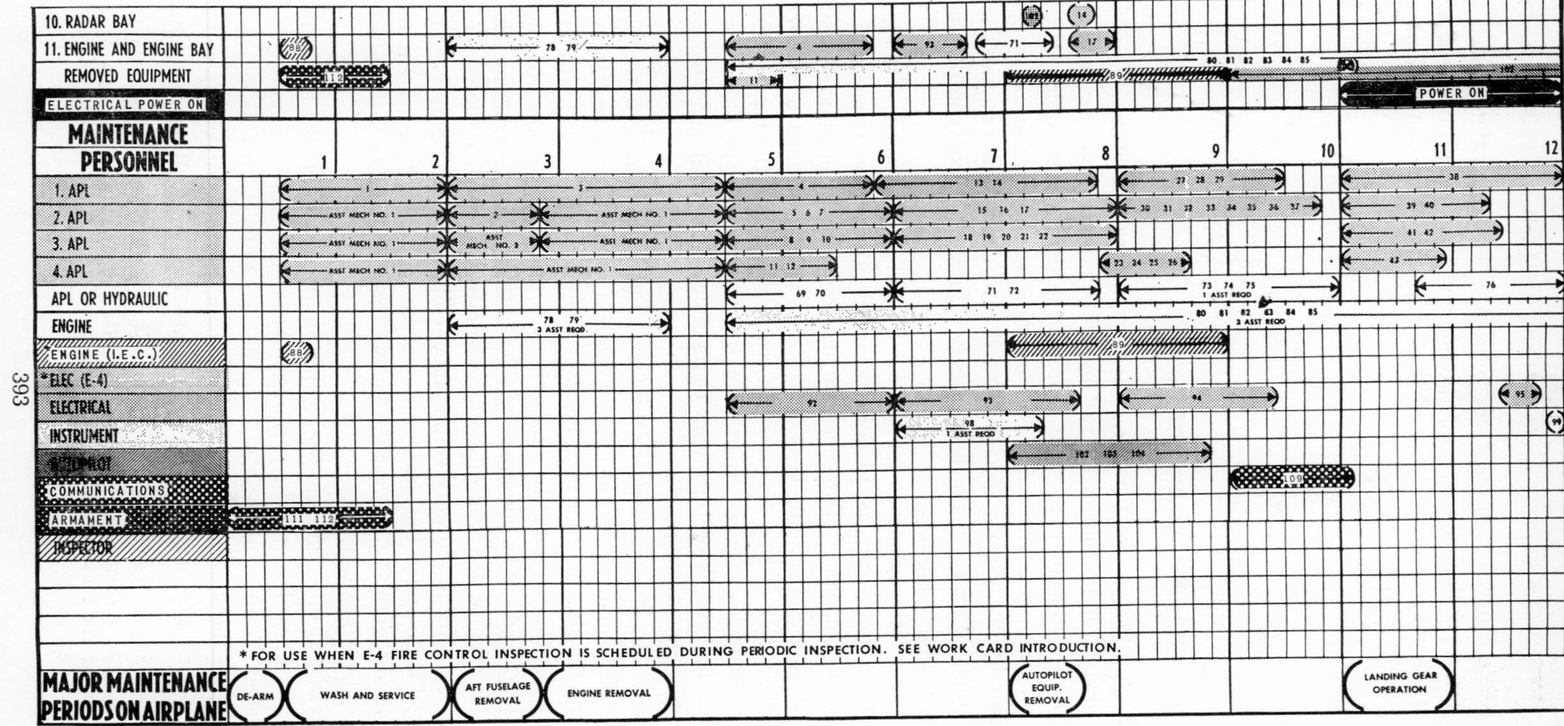

FIGURE 22-4 (continued)

immediate conversion of obtained scores into percentile values just as in any standard psychological test. Interpretation of the profile is based on analysis of the general scoring tendency of the group and on the fluctuations around this general scoring tendency.[6]

Cases

Case A:

Periodic Inspection of Aircraft

Many activities are repetitious and require careful attention to details. The periodic inspection of aircraft by the Air Force is an example of such activities. Inspections must be thorough, using a system which will insure that all details are checked. Planning for these inspections is made more complex by the various specialists needed to check different parts and by limitations of space in the work areas. Moreover, each type of plane requires a unique routine.

The inspection sequence for the F-86D and F-86L is one of the simpler procedures, yet it involves planning for about 37 work hours and 139 sets of working instructions. Two schematic devices are fundamental to the inspection function: (1) Gantt type charts showing the planned *work areas* for each of the 139 groups of inspection requirements and the types of Maintenance Personnel required to perform the different sets of inspection steps, and (2) Periodic Inspection Work Cards showing in detail each step required in each of the 139 sets.

Figure 22-4 illustrates part (the first 12 working hours) of the planning chart. The first part of the chart includes a schematic representation of the airplane showing the code classifications of work areas. The lower left hand part of the Gantt type chart shows the code of the type of maintenance personnel required. The upper part of the Gantt type chart shows the scheduled time for each of the sets of work assignments in each of the work areas. (Numbers refer to the work card number—illustrated in Figure 22-5.) Figure 22-5a illustrates the work card for the 26th set of inspection requirements and Figure 22-5b shows the back of the card showing the detailed parts of the plane involved.

A reader of this chart and work card can determine that the lubrication referred to on card 26 will be performed during the 9th work hour by one of the general airplane maintenance personnel (APL). This work should be finished on the 9th work hour since a communications specialist will be on the left-hand side of the fuselage using card 109 on the 10th work hour. If

[6] Reprinted from David G. Moore and Richard Renck, "The Professional Employee in Industry," *The Journal of Business,* Vol. XXVIII, No. 1, January 1955, pp. 58, 64, by permission of The University of Chicago Press.

CARD NO.	WORK AREA(S)	TYPE MECH RQR	MECH NO.	CARD TIME	SKED STARTING TIME	PUBLICATION NUMBER AND DATE
26	1, 2	Aircraft	4	15		WC 1F-86D-6-PE 8 April 1960

MAN MIN	WORK AREA	WORK UNIT CODE FOR DISCREPANCY: SYS	SUB-SYS AND COMP	PERIODIC / DOCK — INSPECTION REQUIREMENTS — ELECTRICAL POWER [X] OFF [ ] ON
15	1C,2			1. Lubricate per requirements as indicated on back side of card using table of lubricant chart for reference.
	2C, 2F	49		a. Brake cylinder and mechanism 6 places each side.
		13		b. Nose gear lowering and door mechanism 7 places.
		41		c. Heat exchanger door 6 places.
		13		d. Horizontal stabilizer bobweight bungee 2 places.
		11		e. Step mechanism 5 places.

TABLE OF LUBRICANTS

IDENTIFICATION SPECIFICATION LETTERS		TYPE OF LUBRICANT
OGP	MIL-L-7870	OIL, GENERAL-PURPOSE LUBRICATING
OAI	MIL-L-6085	CIL, AIRCRAFT INSTRUMENT, LOW VOLATILITY LUBRICATING

F-86D-6-0-106

CARD NO.	WORK AREA(S)	TYPE MECH RQR	MECH NO.	CARD TIME	SKED STARTING TIME	PUBLICATION NUMBER AND DATE
26	1, 2	Aircraft	4	15		WC 1F-86D-6-PE 8 April 1960

FIGURE 22-5a Work Card for Aircraft (Front) *

* Used by permission of the United States Air Force.

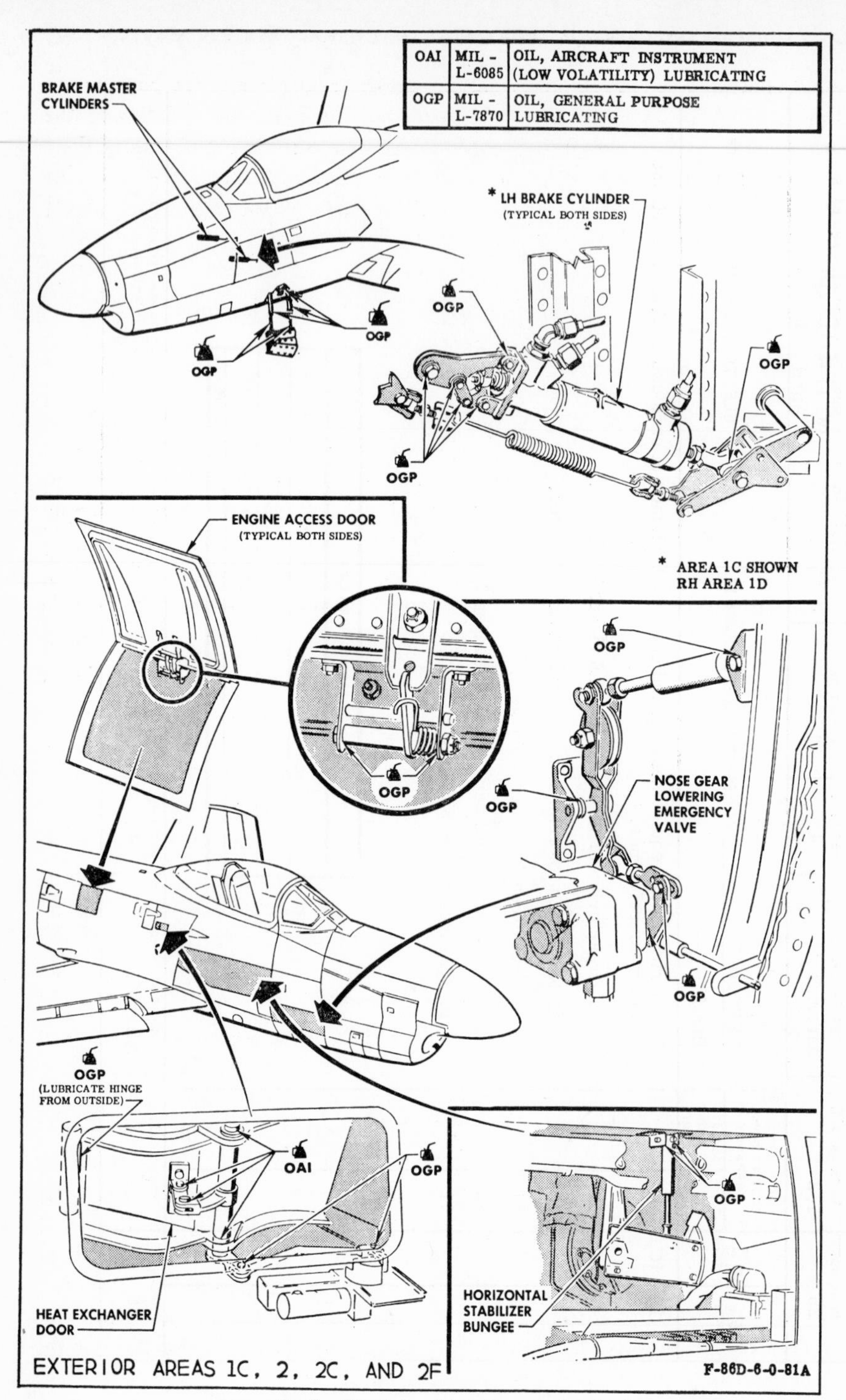

FIGURE 22-5b Work Card for Aircraft (Back) *

* Used by permission of the United States Air Force.

additional work is needed, involving this set of requirements, the last part of the 10th hour is available since the space will be free (top chart) and the 4th general airplane maintenance (APL) person will have the time. With this group of schematic aids, the reader can determine the tightness of the schedule, the utilization of personnel, and the exact nature of a set of inspection requirements.

Case B:
Merit Rating Schemes

The problem of determining the quality of performance of persons is one of the most important and frustrating questions facing managers. Pay rates, promotions, special privileges, and many other things can depend upon the decision. Some criteria are objectively measurable, such as seniority, quantity accomplished, and so forth. Merit rating systems attempt to quantify other important factors while striving for objectivity. Various scaling techniques can be used on the merit rating form. Two such forms are presented in Figure 22-6 and Figure 22-7. Management is continually attempting to improve reports and to understand the process actually used in filling out the blanks.

Case C:
Plant Layout of The R-T Printing Company

The R-T Company is a job order printing company in a medium-sized city. For a number of years the printing plant has been located in a basement and on the third floor of a leased building in the business district.

The type of work done by this company can be exemplified by the following procedure on a typical small town telephone directory. (Numerals in parentheses indicate the machine or workplace involved in the old layout illustrated in Figure 22-8).

First Step: *The Composing Room*—Order comes from office; job is taken to the composing room where the type is to be set. The Compositor goes to the proper type case (1) [7] and set the type, or, he goes to the magazine rack (5), gets the proper magazine, places it into the linotype machine (4). He then assembles the type in proper order at the flattopped type cases (2). If any cutting or mitering must be done, the saw (7) or miterer (9) will be used. A proof is then made on the proof press (11) and is sent to the office where it is read and corrected. On return to the composing room any corrections are made, and the type is prepared to be placed on the press at the lock-up (8). The type is then ready to print.

[7] Numbers in parentheses identify the equipment used (See Figure 22-8).

STUDENT'S NAME ______________________ Quarter ______________________

Instructor ______________________ Course ______________ No. Students ________

Unless otherwise indicated, it will be assumed that these ratings are based primarily on PERFORMANCE IN THIS CLASS. Please indicate the basis of your ratings by checking one of the following: (1)____Know student by name only, through written work handed in.
(2)____Recognize student in class, but have no idea of his activities outside.
(3)____Know something of the student's activities outside this class.

To rate the student, put a check mark (✓) in the appropriate box. The relative positions of the check marks within the boxes need not be considered. The idea is simply to assign the student to either the highest or lowest quartile or the middle 50 per cent of the general student population with respect to the quality being rated. If you feel that you have no basis for a judgment regarding any specific quality, please leave that rating blank.

1. Performance in this course: thoroughness and competence of the work (ordinarily will agree with course grade) — A B C D F
2. Intelligence: ability to think and learn, grasp of ideas, alertness, resourcefulness — Highest 25% ... Lowest 25%
3. Industry: regularity and perseverance of application, thoroughness, determination — Highest 25% ... Lowest 25%
4. Initiative: evidence of imagination, independence, intuition, capacity for self-starting — Highest 25% ... Lowest 25%
5. Impression upon others (especially upon you): evidence of group adjustment; honesty and sincerity, tact, good taste in dress, speech, and action — Highest 25% ... Lowest 25%
6. Written English: grammar, rhetoric, logic — Highest 25% ... Lowest 25%
7. Spoken English: fluency, clarity, force — Highest 25% ... Lowest 25%

OUTSTANDING CHARACTERISTICS. Note any strong impressions you have of the student, such as: more precise ratings of above qualities, specific accomplishments (musical ability, languages, etc), special backgrounds (travel, engineering, business experience), particular weaknesses (excessive shyness, overaggressiveness, physical disabilities).

Suggestions for improvement:

If you would be willing to recommend the student strongly for any of the following classes of work, please so indicate with a check mark (✓):
Executive or supervisory (dealing with associates)______________________
Executive (policy-making)______________________
Research and analytical (investigation and planning)______________________
Sales and promotional (persuading outsiders)______________________
Teaching (interest in students and ideas, expository ability)______________________
Routine administration (system, records, day-to-day responsibility)______________________

Use the back of this sheet for any additional comments you wish to make concerning the student.

FIGURE 22-6 Student Rating Form

I. IDENTIFICATION DATA

1. LAST NAME—FIRST NAME—MIDDLE INITIAL	2. GRADE	3. PERMANENT AF GRADE	4. AFSN
5. AERONAUTICAL RATING	6. PAFSC	7. PERIOD OF REPORT FROM	TO
8. ORGANIZATION	9. PERIOD OF SUPERVISION	10. REASON FOR REPORT	

II. DUTIES

III. PERFORMANCE FACTORS (Compare this officer ONLY with officers of the same grade)

1. JOB KNOWLEDGE					
NOT ☐ OBSERVED	SERIOUS GAPS IN HIS KNOWLEDGE OF FUNDAMENTALS OF HIS JOB.	HAS A SATISFACTORY KNOWLEDGE OF ROUTINE PHASES OF HIS JOB.	IS WELL INFORMED ON MOST PHASES OF HIS JOB.	HAS EXCELLENT KNOWLEDGE OF ALL PHASES OF HIS JOB.	HAS EXCEPTIONAL UNDERSTANDING OF HIS JOB. EXTREMELY WELL INFORMED ON ALL PHASES.
2. COOPERATION					
NOT ☐ OBSERVED	INCLINED TO CREATE FRICTION. DOES NOT GET ALONG WELL WITH OTHERS.	SOMETIMES INDIFFERENT TO OTHERS. COOPERATES TO A FAIR DEGREE.	GETS ALONG WELL WITH MOST PEOPLE.	WORKS IN HARMONY WITH OTHERS. A VERY GOOD TEAM WORKER.	EXTREMELY SUCCESSFUL IN WORKING WITH OTHERS. ACTIVELY PROMOTES HARMONY.
3. JUDGMENT					
NOT ☐ OBSERVED	HIS DECISIONS OR RECOMMENDATIONS ARE WRONG MORE OFTEN THAN RIGHT.	IS PRONE TO NEGLECT OR MISINTERPRET FACTS. COMMITS OCCASIONAL ERRORS IN JUDGMENT	JUDGMENT IS USUALLY SOUND AND REASONABLE.	HIS JUDGMENT CONSISTENTLY RESULTS FROM SOUND EVALUATION OF ALL THE FACTORS INVOLVED.	OUTSTANDINGLY SOUND AND LOGICAL THINKER WITH AN EXCEPTIONAL GRASP OF THE SITUATION INVOLVED.
4. MANAGEMENT QUALITIES					
NOT ☐ OBSERVED	INEFFECTIVE IN THE CONSERVATION OF MATERIEL OR ECONOMICAL USE OF MAN POWER.	UTILIZES MEN, MONEY, AND MATERIALS IN A BARELY SATISFACTORY MANNER.	CONSERVES MEN, MONEY, AND MATERIALS BY IMPLEMENTING AND MAINTAINING ROUTINE MANAGEMENT PROCEDURES.	IS EFFECTIVE IN ACCOMPLISHING SAVINGS IN MEN, MONEY, AND MATERIALS BY DEVELOPING IMPROVED MANAGEMENT PROCEDURES.	EXCEPTIONALLY EFFECTIVE IN THE UTILIZATION OF MEN, MONEY, AND MATERIALS.
5. LEADERSHIP					
NOT ☐ OBSERVED	FAILS TO COMMAND. UNABLE TO EXERT CONTROL.	MANAGES IN SOME INSTANCES TO OBTAIN EFFECTIVE COOPERATION.	DEVELOPS ADEQUATE COOPERATION AND TEAMWORK UNDER NORMAL CIRCUMSTANCES.	COMMANDS RESPECT OF HIS SUBORDINATES. IS EFFECTIVE EVEN UNDER DIFFICULT CIRCUMSTANCES.	OUTSTANDING SKILL IN DIRECTING OTHERS. INSPIRES CONFIDENCE EVEN UNDER VERY DIFFICULT CIRCUMSTANCES.
6. COMMUNICATION FACILITY					
NOT ☐ OBSERVED	UNABLE TO EXPRESS THOUGHTS CLEARLY. LACKS ORGANIZATION.	EXPRESSES THOUGHTS SATISFACTORILY ON ROUTINE MATTERS.	ORGANIZES AND EXPRESSES THOUGHTS CLEARLY AND CONCISELY ON ROUTINE MATTERS.	EXCELLENT COMMAND OF WRITTEN AND ORAL EXPRESSION. CONSISTENTLY ABLE TO EXPRESS IDEAS CLEARLY.	OUTSTANDING ABILITY TO COMMUNICATE IDEAS TO OTHERS THROUGH WRITTEN AND ORAL EXPRESSION.
7. PROMOTION POTENTIAL					
NOT ☐ OBSERVED	DEFINITELY LIMITED. PRESENT JOB IS TAXING HIS CAPABILITIES.	PRESENT GRADE IS COMMENSURATE WITH ABILITY.	HAS THE CAPACITY FOR FURTHER GROWTH AT NORMAL RATE.	VERY PROMISING PROMOTIONAL MATERIAL. CAPABLE OF INCREASED RESPONSIBILITY AND ADVANCEMENT.	ONE OF THE FEW EXCEPTIONAL OFFICERS. SHOULD BE CONSIDERED FOR MORE RAPID PROMOTION THAN HIS CONTEMPORARIES.

8. ADDITIONAL FACTORS

FACTORS	INADEQUATE	SATISFACTORY	COMPETENT AND EFFICIENT	EXCELLENT	OUTSTANDING
a.					
b.					
c.					

AF FORM SEP 58 77 JUN 58 EDITION OF THIS FORM MAY BE USED.

USAF OFFICER EFFECTIVENESS REPORT

FIGURE 22-7

Second Step: *The Bindery*—The stockman goes to the proper stock shelf (S), moves the paper to the cutter (31), and cuts it to the proper size. The stock is then sent to the pressroom.

Third Step: *The Pressroom*—The type, stock, and ink (23) are placed on the proper press; the job is printed. The type is returned to the composing room.

Fourth Step: *The Bindery*—All pages, covers, and inserts are brought to the bindery. They are folded (38), gathered at the bindery tables (28), stitched (35), and trimmed at the cutter (31). The job is taken to the wrapping table (39); it is then sent to the customer.

R-T recently lost the lease on its present space and thus must find a new location. Due to other financial commitments, the company cannot build a new building to fit its requirements precisely; however, they have been able to find space on one floor that will fit their needs. The new location has 5,000 square feet, approximately square. It has one entrance having double doors.

The management is planning its new layout and asks you to submit a solution. The function of each of the pieces of equipment is stated in Table 22-1. The shape and dimension of each piece (approximately to scale) are shown in Figure 22-8 showing the old layout.

TABLE 22-1

FUNCTION OF EQUIPMENT OF R-T PRINTING COMPANY

Number	*Name*	*Size (feet)*	*Function*
1.	Type Cases	2½ x 6	Storing of metal type.
2.	Type Cases	2½ x 6	Storing of metal type, and flat working top.
3.	Dead Storage	3 x 6	Cuts, plates, and so forth.
4.	Linotype Machines	5 x 5	Molds hot lead into lines of type.
5.	Magazine Rack	3 x 6	Holds all molds for Linotype Machines.
6.	Lino Dump	3 x 7	Bin for rough lead for Linotypes.
7.	Saws	2½ x 2½	Trim, cut, and so forth, lines of type.
8.	Lock-up	3 x 7	Type is here placed into the frames that are put into the presses for printing.
9.	Miterer	2 x 4	Cuts borders of the type so they will fit together smoothly.
10.	Mat Maker and Sterocaster	2 x 4	Makes molds for lead impressions to print pictures, illustrations, and so forth.
11.	Proof Press	2 x 4	After type has been set, one impression is made to see that everything is correct.
12.	Machinist Workbench	3 x 4	Tools are kept here for repairing the machines.
13.	Printing Press (Sm)	5½ x 5	Prints
14.	Printing Press (Sm)	4 x 5	Prints
15.	Printing Press (Sm)	4 x 7	Prints
16.	Printing Press (Sm)	4½ x 7	Prints
17.	Printing Press (Sm)	5 x 5½	Prints

TABLE 22-1 (*Continued*)

Number	*Name*	*Size (feet)*	*Function*
18.*	Printing Press (Sm	4 x 4	Prints
19.	Printing Press (Sm)	5½ x 5	Prints
20.	Printing Press (Lg)	4 x 11	Prints
21.	Printing Press (Lg)	6 x 13	Prints
22.	Stock Tables	2½ x 13	Pressman gets paper, called stock, ready to go onto press.
23.	Ink Cabinets	2 x 4	Storage place for printing inks.
24.	Supplies Cabinet	1 x 2	Keeps miscellaneous printing supplies.
25.	Wash Basins	———	A pressman, since he always handles paper, must keep his hands clean. He will wash them up to 35 or 40 times a day.
26.*	Sm Hand Elevator	———	For sending small jobs and other things up to above floors.
27.*	Lg Mechanical Elevator	———	Bringing down stock, and so forth.
28.	Bindery Tables	4 x 8	Gathering, hand folding, inserting, and so forth.
29.	Rest Rooms		
30.	Perforator	6 x 6	Perforates.
31.	Cutter	8 x 8	Cuts stock into desired size for printing.
32.	Cutter Work Table	3 x 5	Stack and arrange stock before and after cutting.
33.	Ruling Machine	6 x 18	Makes lines on paper (similar to lines on notebook paper).
34.	Supplies Cabinet	3 x 3	Keeps miscellaneous supplies.
35.	Stitchers	3 x 3	Puts wires through books and magazines to bind them.
36.	Punch	3 x 4	Punches holes.
37.	Padding Table	5 x 8	For gluing pads of paper.
38.	Folder	8 x 11	Folds paper.
39.	Wrapping Table	3 x 7	Wrapping finished jobs.
S.	Stock Shelves	3 x 5	Holds stock.
	New Equipment To Be Used in New Building, in Addition to the Above.		
1.	Slug Caster	3 x 5	Casts blank lead fillers to fill in between type.
2.	Printing Press (Sm)	4 x 5	Prints
3.	Printing Press (Lg)	7 x 15	Prints

* Not to be used in new building. (Sm) and (Lg) mean Small and Large.

Case D:

The Drexel Furniture Company [8]

The Drexel Furniture Company and its wholly owned subsidiaries manufacture a complete line of wooden furniture, but the company's national reputation was established on its dining and bedroom furniture. The firm

[8] This case was prepared by Professor John E. Dykstra for use at University of North Carolina.

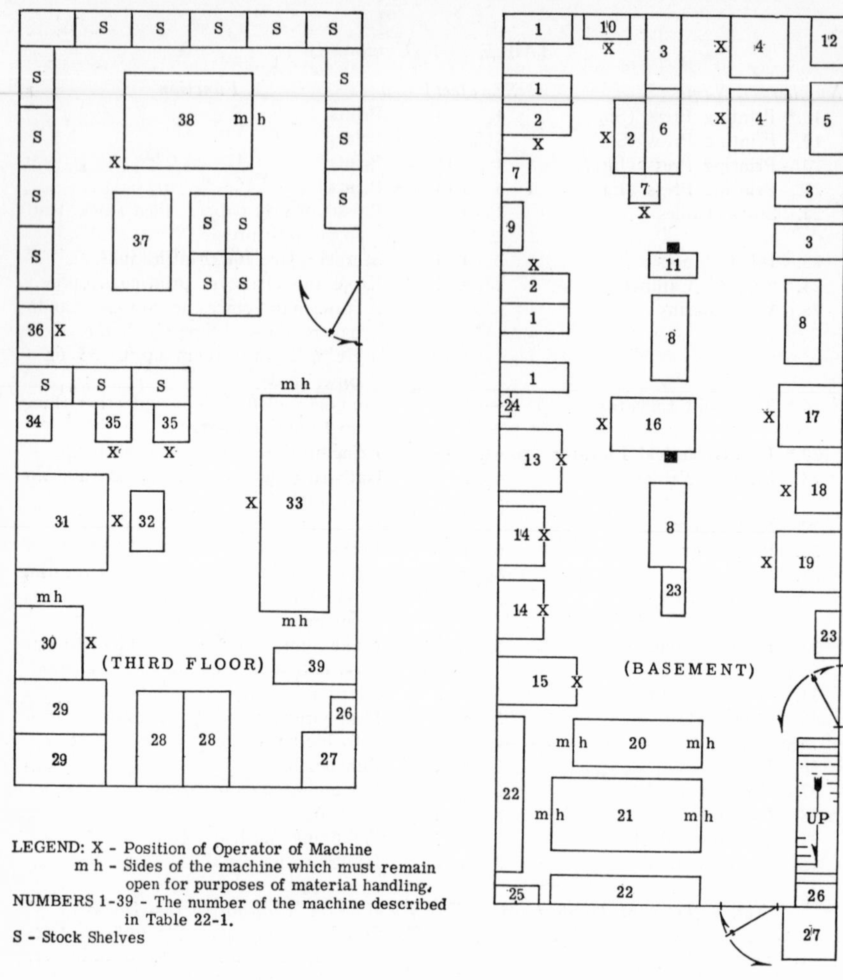

FIGURE 22-8 The R. T. Printing Company

has six plants in Drexel, Morganton, and Marion, North Carolina, devoted primarily to the production of a diversified line of dining and bedroom suites. The company is one of the largest in its field, doing about thirty million dollars worth of business annually.

In common with most furniture manufacturers, the Drexel Furniture Company used a simple line organization for many years, with each plant autonomous under a plant manager. Indeed, this is largely true at the present time. The vice-president in charge of manufacturing has a staff but individual plant managers do not. In recent years, the company established a cost system and a centralized planning department in the home office at Drexel, North Carolina.

The main function of the central planning department was to prepare master cutting schedules for each plant which were designed to co-ordinate production with sales. Since no time standards were available, plant loadings were computed on an empirical formula based on the dollar sales value of the furniture to be manufactured. After the plant manager received his cutting orders from the home office, he did all the detailed production planning and control work with the help of his foremen. This system was used in all Drexel plants except one.

A few years ago, the company bought out a small competitor to increase capacity. The firm was not particularly successful and required extensive managerial reorganization to weld it into the Drexel family. In an effort to increase the efficiency of this plant, known as No. 6, the new manager agreed to experiment with centralized production planning. A staff department under his supervision was responsible for planning and follow-up. Production control continued to be a line responsibility.

Although the planning department had the backing of the vice-president of manufacturing and the plant manager, it was not accepted with any enthusiasm by the foremen. They had grown up in the autonomy of pure line organization and had qualified for their jobs from long experience rather than from formal education. To them, planning was an essential part of their jobs which they felt quite competent to perform. As a result, members of the new department encountered considerable passive resistance, but this was anticipated. They felt that patience, tact, and an informal educational program would solve the problem. They were careful not to over-step the lines of responsibility and authority and made it clear that they "knew their place."

The planning department made a significant gain when it won the reluctant permission of the foremen to make time studies in the plant, on the condition that the information was to be used for planning purposes only. Several members of the new department were graduate industrial engineers. They made extensive time studies on all machine operations from which standard data were developed for computing set-up and running time for any job which might be assigned to any machine in the factory. With this information, accurate machine loadings were practical, not only for existing styles, but also for new designs as they were developed. The standard time data were also useful to predetermine manufacturing costs and to evaluate alternate manufacturing methods.

Production Planning—Preparatory Work

The production planning system developed for Plant No. 6 is detailed below, using a typical piece, a Mr. & Mrs. Dresser, item No. 6 in the 2650 line bedroom suite, as an illustration.

When the design for this dresser was first conceived, a simple drawing, showing the elevation and plan, was made by the designer for approval by both sales and manufacturing. No construction details were shown on the drawing which was little more than an artistic sketch to show what the designer had in mind (see Figure 22-9).

After the design was tentatively approved, a full-scale working drawing was prepared, showing all construction details and dimensions. Next, a cost was estimated and a price determined and the results were resubmitted to sales and production for final approval. After the decision to add the Mr. & Mrs. Dresser to the line was made, the working drawing was turned over to the production planning department in Plant No. 6.

As soon as the production planning department received the working drawing, the preparatory work for planning was done in the following manner.

1. The "bill out" clerk prepared a "bill sheet" (Figure 22-10) from the working drawing. The "bill sheet" is essentially a bill of materials, exclusive of hardware, listing all 44 structural parts required for one complete dresser. In addition, finish dimensions, material thickness, species of wood, rough dimensions (to allow for machining waste), number of pieces, construction details, and the total rough board feet required for each part were taken off the drawing and listed.

2. The completed bill sheet was given to the departmental drafting clerk for detailing manufacturing instructions for machine operators. He initiated a route sheet on an Ozalid master for each structural part listed on the bill sheet (see Figure 22-11). First, he filled out the top section of the route sheet. The top line identified the part; the second line gave the rough machine department information; and the third, the finish machine data. Next, he made sketches of the construction details shown on the bill sheet, in the "Notes" column of the route sheet.

3. Next, the route sheets were given to the route clerk, who had considerable manufacturing "know-how," for developing manufacturing procedures for each part. Since woodworking machinery is general purpose, usually there are a variety of ways by which a particular part can be manufactured. It was the route clerk's responsibility to recommend the most economical sequence of operations for the production of each part. Generally, he followed past practices on similar parts made for other styles. On new work, he recommended the routing which standard time data calculations proved to be best, in terms of cost and total production time required. He consulted with, and got the approval of, the plant manager and foremen on all routings. Line supervisors had final authority in deciding on the routing of all parts, and route sheets were always subject to their opinions and desires.

After routes were decided upon and approved, the route clerk listed the operation number and description, in the proper sequence, in the columns provided on each route sheet. Then, he computed the set-up time and machine running time per 100 pieces for each machine listed, using standard time data. The results were entered in the columns provided, to the right of the operation description on the route sheets.

After the route clerk completed all 44 route sheets for the Mr. & Mrs. Dresser, he prepared a summary sheet (Figure 22-12) which showed the total standard time (set-up plus running time per 100 dressers) for each different machine required to manufacture the complete dresser. This sheet was developed to facilitate machine loading calculations.

4. A rough machine check list was prepared next on an Ozalid master (see Figure 22-13). This list was made from the rough machine column on the bill sheet and checked against the second line of each route sheet. There must be a route sheet for each part and all dimensions must be in agreement on the several forms.

5. A finish machine parts control sheet was also prepared in the same manner as the rough machine check list (see Figure 22-14). Finish machine dimensions were taken off the bill sheet and checked against the third line of the individual route sheets. In addition, the finish machine routing was laid out in reverse order and from right to left by machine operation number, in the operations columns on the form. Where individual parts were to be joined together in the finish machine department as a sub-assembly, as in the case of parts 13, 14, and 15 (base frame front, end and back rails) the routings were tied together with an X. Subsequent operations thereafter were to be performed on the sub-assembly as a unit.

6. The complete set of Ozalid masters was checked and filed for use when a cutting order calling for a 2650 suite appeared on a master cutting schedule. This entire procedure was repeated for each item in the suite: mirrors, chest, three sizes of beds, night stand, and the like. A suite may contain as many as seventeen or more individual pieces and a complete set of forms must be prepared in advance of manufacture for each piece of furniture.

Production Planning Procedure—Company-Wide

The central production planning department in the executive offices at Drexel, North Carolina was responsible for master planning and scheduling for all Drexel plants. In carrying out this function, the department prepared cutting orders and fitted them into proposed cutting schedules.

A cutting order (Figure 22-15) was made out to meet sales requirements for each piece of furniture in the suite. Economic manufacturing lot sizes were also taken into consideration in determining quantities. A separate cutting order was issued for each individual suite requiring manufacture to meet customer needs.

Next, the individual cutting orders were fitted into a master cutting schedule to distribute the work to the several plants in accordance with delivery requirements and availability of production capacity, as shown in Figure 22-16. Although a particular suite would normally be assigned to the same plant each time it was manufactured, it might be necessary to shift it to another to meet scheduled delivery. Both firm and proposed cutting orders for three months or more in advance were included on the proposed cutting schedule.

Copies of the master schedule were distributed to all plant managers and to Plant 6 in Production Planning. Cutting orders were issued to the individual plants as they were confirmed for manufacture by the production manager. At Plant No. 6, cutting orders were sent to the planning department while in other plants, they went directly to the plant manager.

Production Planning Procedure—Plant No. 6

1. When Plant No. 6 Production Planning received a cutting order, it was turned over to the Ozalid machine operator. She pulled the complete set of masters for each piece of furniture on the cutting order from the route file and duplicated them. The Ozalid copies and the cutting order were sent upstairs to a planning department clerk for posting.

2. The quantity indicated on the cutting order was entered in the top left box (Articles Wanted) on each route sheet (Figure 22-11). Next, the number of rough pieces required, including an allowance for normal waste and spoilage, was computed for the number of articles wanted and posted in the Rough Pieces box on each route sheet. The number of finish parts required to assemble the ordered quantity was also entered. For example, this was simply the number of dressers ordered, multiplied by the number of pieces of the particular part required per dresser.

3. Next, the planning department clerk computed the standard time for the desired number of pieces for each operation on every route sheet and posted the figures in the columns to the right of the time standards for set-up and running time per 100 pieces previously recorded.

4. Then, she extended the total time standard for the entire cut on the time standards summary (Figure 22-12) by machines.

5. The rough pieces required were summarized next from the individual route sheets to the Amount column on the Rough Machine check list (Figure 22-13). This, too, was done for each piece of furniture on the cutting order.

6. Finally, she summarized the finish pieces needed in the same manner on the Finish Machine parts control sheets (Figure 22-14). The extended forms were sent to the head of the planning department for machine loading.

7. The total standard time for the entire cutting order was figured by machines from the individual piece standards summary sheets (Figure 22-12) to determine the machine loadings. This was simply a matter of multiplying the standard running time per 100 dressers by the number required to fill the cutting order and adding in the standard set-up time. This was done for each piece of furniture on the cutting order and a grand total found. The results were plotted on a Gantt chart (Figure 22-17) for each machine in the plant, which gave a visual picture of the work ahead.

At the top of the chart, the cabinet room schedule was plotted from the information at the bottom of the cutting order (Figure 22-15) in accordance with the sequence indicated on the cutting schedule (Figure 22-16). This indicated when work had to be available from the finish machine room in order to permit assembly on time. Notice that cutting order number 6050 was scheduled to start in the cabinet room on December 19 and was to be completed on January 6.

The computed machine loadings were plotted for each machine center, by cutting order, along the lines labeled "Machine Load," showing the amount of work ahead of each machine in the plant. Loadings were computed to the nearest full day's work and colors were used to distinguish individual cutting orders on the chart, since several were normally in process simultaneously. (Three are shown on Figure 22-17 and cross hatching is used to permit duplication.)

The cutting orders were planned by machine center and plotted in the sequence indicated for the cabinet room at the top of the chart as closely as machine availability would permit. Every effort was made to plan the work to meet the desired delivery dates. It must be remembered that a cutting order was for a complete suite, not simply a single piece such as a dresser, and that the machine loadings were for the entire order.

8. Immediately prior to the scheduled date to put the cutting order into production, the head of the planning department conferred with the plant manager, on the production problems which were most likely to require his attention. They went over the Gantt charts together, and the head of planning suggested dispatching sequences which he felt would put the least strain on the plant. He gave all the route sheets, rough machine check lists, and finish machine parts control sheets for the entire cutting order (totaling perhaps 700 individual pieces of paper) to the plant manager at the conclusion of the discussion. This completed the planning part of the work done by the production planning department for Plant No. 6.

Production Control Procedure

1. Actual dispatching of work to the plant was done by the plant manager, who decided which pieces of furniture on the cutting order to put into production first, bearing in mind machine availability and the total production time required. In general, those pieces with the longest production time were started first. Machine availability was determined by personal experience and consultation with foremen. Route sheets for the furniture selected were given to the rough machine foreman together with the rough machine check lists. The finish machine parts control lists were sent to the finish machine parts control clerk.

2. The rough machine foreman selected route sheets for individual parts, which were to be cut out of the same species and thickness of wood, but of different lengths, from the batch at his disposal. He, too, bore in mind production time requirements of individual parts and started the more complicated ones into production first so that they would have time to arrive at the cabinet room along with those which could be made faster, but would be processed later.

3. The selected route sheets were given to the cut-off saw operator, so that he could set stops for the different rough lengths required. After he was set up, he gave the route sheets to the rip saw operators. Usually, each rip saw operator worked with one route sheet and kept a piece count so that he could notify the cut-off saw operator when to stop cutting that particular length.

Since wood is nonhomogeneous and subject to many defects (such as knots, rot, and wind shakes), it was essential to give the cut-off saw operator a variety of lengths from which to choose. He could cut each board to best advantage and eliminate unusable portions with the latitude of sizes provided.

As the boards were cut to rough length, they were fed automatically into a true surface planer, then to a thickness planer, and delivered to the rip saw operators by belt conveyor. As previously noted, each rip saw operator normally specialized on one cut length at a time. Each board was ripped, again eliminating minor wood defects, and stacked on a hand truck. The operator kept count of the rough pieces produced and signalled the cut-off saw operator to stop cutting his size when he got the count required on the route sheet.

4. After the required number of pieces had been cut for a particular part, the rip saw operator put the route sheet (enclosed in a plastic envelope) on top of the truck load and trucked it to wherever he could find a space for it on the factory floor. As individual route sheets were completed, the foreman was notified and more were dispatched to the cut-off saw operator and the process was repeated.

5. The work was assigned to the next operation on the route sheet (either gluing or planing) at the discretion of the foreman in charge. When an operator finished a load in accordance with route sheet instructions, he moved it to any convenient spot he could find and reported to the foreman for his next assignment. Occasionally, an operator thought he had completed the work on a part when, in fact, another truck load had been overlooked. Unless the foreman had an opportunity to make an immediate count, he was likely to assign the man another job without realizing that some of the work was lagging behind. When this happened, extra machine set-ups became necessary and work had to be expedited to catch up with the normal flow.

6. Machine operators kept a record of the time spent by cutting order number and entered this information on a report. This time was cumulated daily by the machine center and sent to the production planning department office. This actual manufacturing time was deducted from the total standard time computed for the cutting order (Figure 22-12) and the difference indicated the amount of work still ahead to complete it. The reported production time was also plotted on the Gantt chart to the nearest half day, in the proper color by machines along the "Work Reported" line. (See Figure 22-17 which shows the actual production per day through December 13.) In addition, the cumulative "Work Completed" line was extended. This line summarized the work completed by cutting order. The difference between the machine load line and the work completed line provided a visual check on the progress of the cutting order through the plant, by comparing the standard time planned with the actual time run. The difference between the lines indicated the amount of work still to be done by cutting order.

For example, for machines 8 and 9 (tenon machine and panel sizer) a half day's production was reported as completed on December 13 on cutting order 6050 for the 2650 suite. The order was calculated to require 9 production days, starting at noon on December 4 and ending at noon on December 17. Actually a full day's work was done on this order prior to December 2 (shown on a previous Gantt chart), a half day was completed on December

2, and by December 13 a cumulative total of 8½ days was completed. This total was shown on the "Work Completed" line, which, when compared with the "Machine Load" line, showed that a half day's work was still ahead of machines 8 and 9, but that the order was well ahead of schedule at the close of December 13. If any lags were noted, the plant manager was notified so that he could expedite the work. Note that this follow-up was on the basis of the entire cutting order and not on particular pieces of furniture.

7. As parts for a particular piece of furniture were completed in the rough machine room, the quantities were reported on the rough machine check list, which provided an individual parts follow-up. By consulting this list, the foreman could follow the progress of work through his department and be sure that all the parts required had been fabricated in the correct quantities. Since he knew that proper quantities were produced at the cut-off saw, and if the same amount did not come through as finished, it followed that some loads had been overlooked. When this happened, he had to search among the trucks of parts on the factory floor until "lost" loads were found. Then, he made sure that they were put into production with a minimum of delay.

8. As parts were completed in the rough machine room, they were trucked by the final rough machine operator to any convenient location he could find in or near the finish machine room. The route sheet was left on top of the load in every case.

9. The finish machine foreman followed the same general procedure as outlined for the rough machine room. They knew what cuttings and pieces of furniture were in process from the parts control sheets. They assigned work to the operators on the basis of parts and machine availability. In so far as possible, they put those parts with the longest series of operations into production first. It was necessary to hunt for truck loads to be sure that the desired parts had been completed by the rough machine department before attempting to assign work to finish machine operators.

10. As operations were completed on each part, the control clerk entered the date finished above the operation number on the parts control sheet. If only part of the pieces called for were finished, this was noted on the control sheet and also on a Parts Control Report, which was made in duplicate. The original was given to the foreman so that the balance could be found and put into production. If any lags in the flow of work through the finish machine room were discovered by the control clerk, they were also entered on the Parts Control Report. The duplicate copy was retained at the desk of the parts control clerk to provide a follow-up on the foreman and to prevent alibis that they had no knowledge of the delays. In the event that work reported as requiring attention failed to come through properly, the plant manager was notified. Work completed was reported daily to production planning for computing the work ahead and for posting on the Gantt charts, just as was done in the rough machine follow-up.

11. As parts were completed in the finish machine room, the parts control clerk recorded the total production in the extreme right hand column of the finish machine parts control sheet (Figure 22-14). This quantity had to agree with the amount scheduled for delivery to the cabinet room. Usually, shortages were a matter of "lost" loads rather than defective work. When discrepancies were found, the foreman had to check for lagging loads and see that they were finished up. The delivery date to the cabinet room was noted on the parts control sheet by the clerk. Obviously, it was essential that some of all parts for a given piece of furniture be available to the cabinet room, if assembly was to be accomplished. Again, assembly should not start so soon that the finish machine room could not make complete delivery on the entire quantity or extra set-ups would become necessary which would cut efficiency and raise costs.

12. Cabinet room production was recorded by cutting order, as in the case of the machine departments, and reported daily to production planning for work ahead calculation and Gantt chart plotting. As before, lags were called to the attention of the plant manager for corrective action.

13. Once the assembled furniture left the cabinet room, it went through the finishing operations in an automatic, direct line flow. When each piece was finished, it was given a final inspection and cased for shipment. Production was reported back to planning by cutting order number just as in all previous departments.

14. The general procedure described above continued until all the furniture on the cutting order was put into production by the plant manager. He was kept informed of the progress of the cutting order by Production Planning through their Gantt charts, as previously noted. Planning could not tell him about any individual piece of furniture, or part thereof, but only about the progress of the entire cutting order, in terms of the total computed standard time versus the reported actual production time. Detailed information was available to him from his own memory, from foremen and from check list sheets.

Results

Drexel Furniture Company experienced a marked improvement in production efficiency and costs since the inauguration of this system of centralized staff planning and decentralized line control. Indeed, it planned to introduce the system in its other plants as plant managers agreed to it and as the necessary standards information could be accumulated.

While the members of the planning department itself were not satisfied with the system, which they recognized was far from ideal, they felt that real progress had been made to get the system accepted by line supervision. They hoped to extend and improve staff assistance in the area of production control.

While the system yielded very good results, it was not without faults. Some of the major ones, listed by management, were the following. Foremen sometimes altered routings as shown on route sheets, in spite of earlier agreement that they represented the best procedure. Usually, this was done to balance machine loadings or because "lost" parts required expediting without interfering with equally urgent work on a particular machine. Although this practice solved immediate production problems, it adversely affected costs. Furthermore, it disturbed future machine loadings and tended to make more routing alterations necessary. Again, routings were disregarded as a matter of expediency to keep machines running with the minimum of lost time. That is, if work ahead of one machine was low, it was not uncommon to transfer jobs scheduled for another machine to it, to provide work for an operator. There was so much work-in-process inventory that the foremen found it difficult to keep control of the work ahead. When the scheduled work for a given machine was not immediately available, foremen would re-route something else rather than keep a man and machine waiting while they found the right load.

While a large amount of work-in-process was inevitable because of the wide variety of pieces in suites, the situation was aggravated because foremen tended to allow more processing time than was necessary. Frequently, work was started early to provide a safety factor in case of machine breakdown. However, failure of a single part to reach the cabinet room on time would shut down the rest of the plant.

In-process inventories tended to be excessive for yet another reason. Rough machine room foremen were prone to judge departmental efficiency on the basis of the total number of board feet cut per day. Frequently, therefore, they issued route sheets in sufficient quantity to cut a whole load of lumber of a given specie and thickness, particularly if it happened to be five quarter or thicker. This saved lost time in changing kiln trucks at the cut-off saw but it resulted in cutting stock as much as 30 days in advance of need. This extra cutting had to be done at the expense of other work that was required to meet the production schedule.

To meet these undesirable conditions, the planning department was considering the installation of a control clerk in the rough machine room. A parts control form (Figure 22-18) was being considered to provide better control over the flow of work through the department. Since the majority of parts produced followed common routes through the rough machine room, the operations were listed across the top of the form in proper sequence from left to right. Any operations not required for any given piece were crossed out. For example, the dresser top, Part 1 (see Figure 22-11) did not go through the last three operations, plane, rip and mould.

With the help of this form, it was felt that a clerk could follow the progress of work, on the 2650-6 dresser for example, and with a parts control report to foremen, could keep the flow of work moving along according to schedule.

Essentially, this was merely putting the same type of control system in the rough machine room as was used in the finish machine department. While the plant manager had approved this proposal, the planning department anticipated some resistance and resentment from the rough machine foremen.

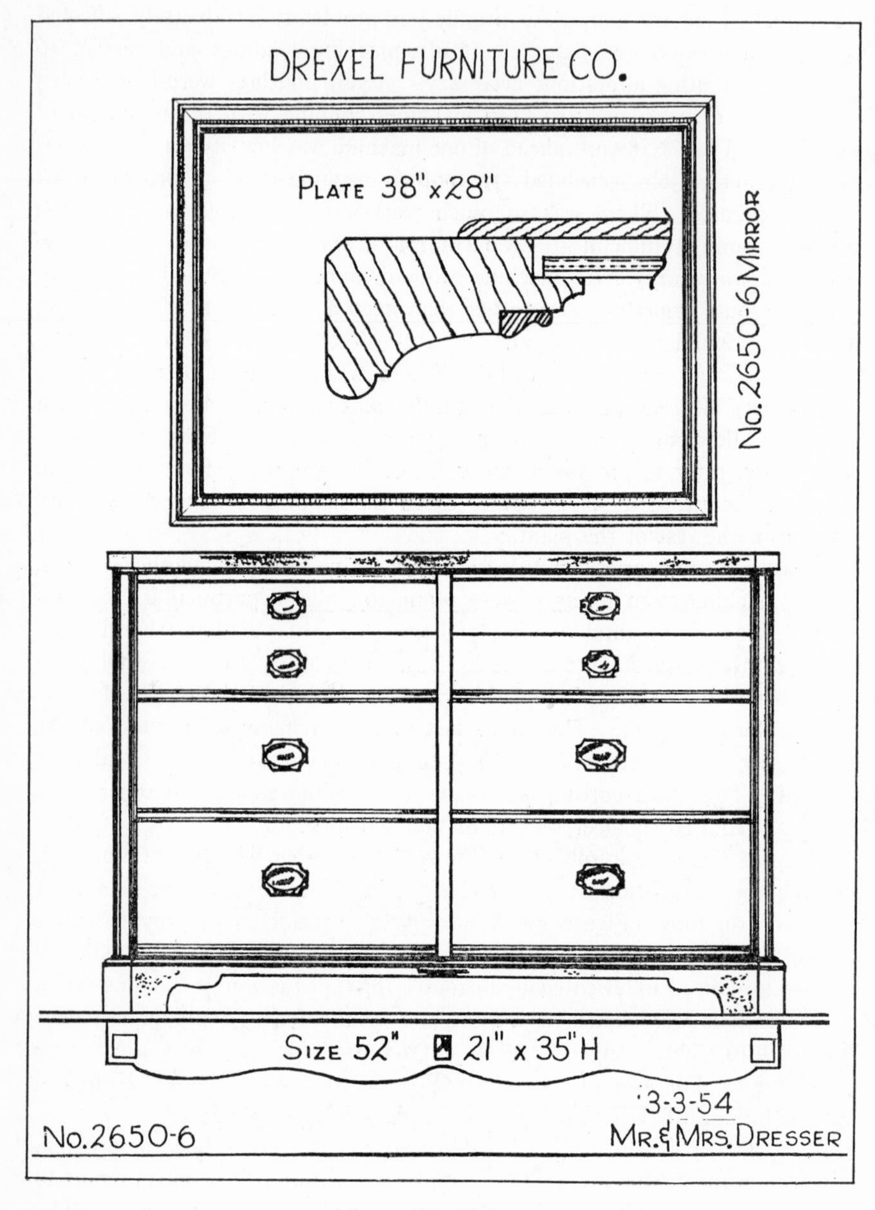

FIGURE 22-9

PLANT NO. 6 DREXEL FURNITURE COMPANY Page 1 of 2

BILL SHEET OF ONE Mr. & Mrs. Dresser SUITE NO. 2560-6 FINISH 52X21X35 DATE FORM NO. 2201-A

Part No.	No. Part per Article	Part Name	Finish Size Length	Finish Size Width	Finish Size Thick	Finish Size B.S.	Material Thick	Material Kind	Rough Size Length	Rough Size Width	Rough Size Thick	Rough Pcs. per Article	Special Notes	Net Rough Footage per Article
1	1	Top	52	21	1 1/16		5/4	Pop.	53	22	15/16	1	5 Ply A.F.C. & Gum	10.121
3	2	Front Post	29	1 3/4	1 3/4		8/4	Gum	30	2	2	2	Groove 1/4 x 1/2 Deep - 1/4 Face	1.667
4	2	Back Post	29	1 3/4	1 1/4		6/4	Gum	30	2	1 1/2	2	Groove 1/4 x 1/2 Deep - 1/4 Face	1.272
9	2	End Panels	29 1/4	16 1/2	3/16		1/8	R.C.	17 3/4	30 1/2	1/8	2	3 Ply A.F.C. & Gum	7.720
11	4	End Panel Rail	16 9/16	1 1/2	9/16	15 9/16	4/4	Pop.	17 5/8	1 3/4	1	4		.856
13	1	Base Frame Front Rail	52 3/4	4 1/16	13/16		4/4	Gum	53 3/4	4 5/16	1	1	Bond, Assemble & Shape Net 52 1/2 x 21 1/4	1.610
15	1	Base Frame Br. Rail	47 3/4	1 3/4	13/16	46 3/4	4/4	Pop.	48 3/4	2	1	1	Tenon 1/4 x 1/2 Long in Center	.677
14	2	Base Frame End Rail	17 5/16	3	13/16		4/4	Gum	18 3/8	3 1/4	1	2		.830
16	3	Dust Bot. Munts	16 9/16	3 1/2	3/4	15 9/16	4/4	Pop.	17 5/8	3 3/4	1	3	Tenons 1/4 x 1/2 Long in Center	1.377
17	1	Center Pilaster	28 1/2	1 3/4	1	27 1/2	5/4	Gum	29 1/2	2	1 1/4	1		.495
19	2	Top & Bot. Parting Rail	49 1/4	3 7/16	3/4	47 3/4	4/4	Gum	50 1/4	3 11/16	1	2		2.574
19-1	4	Parting Rail	24 9/16	3 7/16	3/4	23 3/8	4/4	Gum	25 5/8	3 11/16	1	4		2.612
21	4	Dust Bot. Bk. Rail	50	1 7/16	3/4	48 3/4	4/4	Pop.	51	1 11/16	1	3		1.791
24	4	Dust. Bot. End Rail	16 9/16	2 1/2	3/4	15 9/16	4/4	Pop.	17 5/8	2 3/4	1	4	Tenons 1/2 x 1/2 Long in Center	1.348
24-1	2	Bot. Dust Bot. End Rail	16 9/16	2	3/4	15 9/16	4/4	Pop.	17 5/8	2 1/4	1	2	Tenons 1/4 x 1/2 Long in Center	.550
25	6	Dust Bottoms	21 7/8	16 1/2	1/6			R.C.					3 Ply Gum	15.042
27	4	Caster Blocks	2	2	3		5/4	Gum	15	15	1 1/4	3/9	Glue 3 pcs. 1 1/16	.642
28	2	Front Base Rail	23 9/16	4 1/8	1 1/4		4/4	Pop.	25 5/8	18 1/2	3/4	15/16	5 Ply Mfg. Swirl & Gum	1.900
28.1	2	Corner Base Rail	2 3/16	4 1/8	1 1/4				14 1/2	13 1/2	1 1/8	1/6	5 Ply Mfg. Swirl & Gum	.284
28-2	1	Base Center Block	1	1	1 1/4								5 Ply Mfg. & Gum Use waste from Part #29	
29	2	End Base Rails	19 5/8	4 1/8	1 1/4		5/4	Pop.	20 5/8	13 1/2	1 1/8	2/3	5 Ply Mfg. Swirl & Gum	1.613
30	2	Back Base Rail	12 7/8	4 1/8	13/16		4/4	Pop.	13 3/4	4 3/8	1	1		.570
31	2	End Panel Moulds	15 9/16	7/32	7/32		4/4	Gum	16 5/8	3 1/2	1	1	Mould 7/32 x 9/16 & Split	.058
31-1	2	Pin Tray Runners	16 7/16	1/2	1/4		5/8	Syc.	17 1/2	3/4	5/8	2		.182
32	1/10	Drawer Front Block A	25 3/4	18 1/2	9		4/4	Pop.	25 3/4	18 1/2	3/4	12/10	5 Ply Swirl & Gum U-Cut	3.912
	2	Dr. Front A	23 5/16	8 3/16	13/16			Veneer	26	9 1/4		2		
32-1	1/10	Dr. Front Block B	25 3/8	18 1/2	9 3/4		4/4	13 Pop.	25 3/8	18 1/2	3/4	13/10	5 Ply Mfg. Swirl & Gum B-L B-R	4.238
	2	Dr. Front B	23 5/16	8 7/16	13/16			Veneer	26	9 1/2		2		

FIGURE 22-10

DREXEL FURNITURE COMPANY

ROUTE SHEET:

WANTED			CLASS 8	JOB NO.	PART NO.
ARTICLES	ARTICLE NAME & NUMBER 2650-6 MR. & MRS. DRESSER	PART NAME 5 PLY A.F.C. & GUM TOP			1
ROUGH PCS.	MATERIAL: KIND POPLAR, THICK 5/4	ROUGH LENGTH 53	ROUGH WIDTH 22	ROUGH PLANE 15/16	ROUGH pcs/art. 1	ROUGH FT. PER ARTICLE 10.121
FINISH PARTS	PARTS PER: ROUGH PIECE 1, ARTICLE 1	FINISH LENGTH 52	FINISH WIDTH 21	FINISH THICK 1 1/16	B. S.	ROUGH FT. PER PART 10.121

Machine or Motion	Oper. No.	DESCRIPTION OF OPERATION	S.U.	RUN
1	1	CUT	1.0	68.2
2	2	PLANE	—	—
3	3	RIP	2.0	138.0
5	4	SIZE	3.0	40.7
37	5	GLUE	1.0	29.8
2	6	PLANE	2.0	11.8
9	7	5 PLY	—	60.7
9	8	SIZE	5.0	18.8
9	9	TRIM	5.0	9.6
32	10	MARK	—	22.2
11	11	BANDSAW	5.0	44.4
12	12	SHAPE	10.0	81.4
24	13	SAND	—	36.6
	14			
	15			
61	16	CUT DOWN		173.0
67	17	GLUE SIZE		62.4
62	18	S.S. 2 ENDS		241.2
62	19	S.S. FRONT		253.0
	20	POLISH		173.0
	21			
	22			

NOTES

21″ · 1 1/16″ · 21″ · 52″

FIGURE 22-11

DREXEL FURNITURE COMPANY

TIME STANDARDS SUMMARY

SUITE NO. 2650 ITEM NO. 6 - Mr. & Mrs. Dresser

Machine	Operation	Set-Up	Run/100	Run/	Total Standard Time
Cut-off	1	40	859.3		
Planer	2	26	118		
Rip Saw	3	80	1694.5		
Moulder	4	320	513		
Size Saw	5	48	523		
Tenon Machine Panel Sizer	8 & 9	307	321		
Variety Saw	10	100	278		
Band Saw	11	75	687		
Shaper	12	235	4351		
Router	15	200	493		
Boring Machine	16 & 18	144	595		
Mortice	19	42	103		
Lathe	20	-	-		
Dovetail	23	135	559		
Drum Sand	24	5	733		
Jointer	25	10	60		
Bell Rail	29	9	58		
Electronic Core Machine	37	16	273		
Cold Press	39	-	339		

FIGURE 22-12

ROUGH MACHINE - CHECK OFF LIST

SUITE NO. 2650-6 MR & MRS DRESSER 1 of 2 JOB NO.

AMOUNT	PART NO.	PCS. PER CASE	PART NAME	LENGTH	WIDTH	THICK		TOTAL
	1	1	TOP	53	22	15/16		
	3	2	FRONT POST	30	2	2		
	4	2	BACK POST	30	2	1 1/2		
	9	2	END PANELS	17 3/4	30 1/2	1/8		
	11	4	END PANEL RAIL	17 5/8	1 3/4	1		
	13	1	BASE FRAME FRONT RAIL	53 3/4	4 5/16	1		
	15	1	BASE FRAME BK. RAIL	48 3/4	2	1		
	14	2	BASE FRAME END RAIL	18 3/8	3 1/4	1		
	16	3	DUST BOT. MUNTS	17 5/8	3 3/4	1		
	17	1	CENTER PILASTER	29 1/2	2	1 1/4		
	19	2	TOP & BOT. PARTING RAIL	50 1/4	3 11/16	1		
	19-1	4	PARTING RAIL	25 5/8	3 11/16	1		
	21	4	DUST BOT. BK. RAIL	51	1 11/16	1		
	24	4	DUST BOT. END RAIL	17 5/8	2 3/4	1		
	24-1	2	BOT. DUST BOT. END RAIL	17 5/8	2 1/4	1		
	25	6	DUST BOTTOMS	21 7/8	16 1/2	1/16		
	27	4	CASTER BLOCKS	15	15	1 1/4		
	28	2	FRONT BASE RAIL	25 5/8	18 1/2	3/4		
	28-1	2	CORNER BASE RAIL	14 1/2	13 1/2	1 1/8		
	28-2	1	BASE CENTER BLOCK	1	1	1 1/4		
	29	2	END BASE RAIL	20 5/8	13 1/2	1 1/8		
	30	2	BACK BASE RAIL	18 3/4	4 3/8	1		
	31	2	END PANEL MOULDS	16 5/8	3 1/2	1		
	31-1	2	PIN TRAY RUNNERS	17 1/2	3/4	5/8		
	32	2	DRAWER FRONT A	23 5/16	8 3/16	13/16		
	32-1	2	DRAWER FRONT B	23 5/16	8 7/16	13/16		

FIGURE 22-13

DREXEL FURNITURE COMPANY
PARTS CONTROL SHEET

QUANTITY REQUIRED ______
PLANT Table Rock #6
DATE ______
DEPARTMENT FINISH MACHINE
SHEET NO 1 OF 2
ARTICLE M&M DRESSER
SUITE NO. 2650-6
ORDER NO. ______

PART NO.	PART NAME	DIMENSIONS Lg.	Wd.	Thk.	B.S.	Quant. per Art.	No. Days in Process	Ripsaw and/or Size	Mould and/or Plane	OPERATIONS 18	17	16	15	14	13	12	11	10	9	8	7	6	5	4	3	2	1	SCHED. DEL. Date	Pc's.	DELIVER Date	Pc's.
1	Top	52	21	1 1/16		1															39	9	9	32	11	12	24				
32	Dr. Front A	23 5/16	8 3/16	13/16		2								BLOCK 39	25	32	11	39	25	8	10	25	12	12	12	23	18				
32-1	Dr. Front B	23 5/16	8 7/16	13/16		2								39		25	32	11	39	25	8	10	25	12	12	23	18				
32-2	Dr. Front C	23 5/16	9 3/16	13/16		2								39		25	32	11	39	25	8	10	25	12	12	23	18				
28	Front Base Rail	23 9/16	4 1/8	1 1/4		2								39	25	32	11	39	25	8	10	24	12	32	11	12	18				
28-1	Corner Base Rail	2 3/16	4 1/8	1 1/4		2														39	9	10	24	12	10	10	12				
28-2	Base Center	1	1	1 1/4		1																		10	24	10	12				
29	End Base Rail	19 5/8	4 1/8	1 1/4		2												39	9	9	10	24	12	12	32	11	18				
3	Front Post	29	1 3/4	1 3/4		2																Rm 4	9	19	19	24	12				
4	Back Post	29	1 3/4	1 1/4		2																Rm 4	9	19	19	24	12				
17	Center Pilaster	27 1/2	1 3/4	1		1																		Rm 4	9	24	10				
19	Top & Bot. Post Rail	49 1/4	3 7/16	3/4	47 3/4	2														Rm 4	8	32	11	12	18	18	24				
19-1	Parting Rail	24 9/16	3 7/16	3/4	23 3/8	4																Rm 4	8	32	11	12	24				
21	Dust Bot. Bk. Rail	50	1 7/16	3/4	48 3/4	3																				Rm 4	8				
22	Top Back Rail	50	2	3/4	48 3/4	1																			Rm 4	8	18				
30	Back Base Rail	12 7/8	4 1/8	13/16		2																Rm 4	9	12	32	11	18				
11	End Panel Rail	16 9/16	1 1/2	9/16	15 9/16	4																				Rm 4	8				
13	Base Frame Front Rail	52 3/4	4 1/16	13/16		1												Rm 4	9	18	18* (crossed out)	24	32	11	12	15	18				
14	" " End Rail	17 5/16	3	13/16		2												Rm 4	9	18	* (crossed out)										
15	" " Back Rail	47 3/4	1 3/4	13/16	46 3/4	1													Rm 4	8	* (crossed out)										
24	D. Bot. End Rail	16 9/16	2 1/2	3/4	15 9/16	4																			Rm 4	8	8				
24-1	Bot. D. Bot. End Rail	16 9/16	2	3/4	15 9/16	2																			Rm 4	8	8				
16		16 9/16	3 1/2	3/4	15 9/16	3																				Rm 4	8				
51	Pin Tray	6 1/8	5 1/2	1		2																	9	Rm 4	10	* (crossed out)	24				
51-1	" " End	5 9/16	1 1/16	3/16		4																	Rm 4	24	10	* (crossed out)					
31		15 9/16	7/32	7/32		2																			Rm 4	10	10				
31-1	Pin Tray Runner	16 7/16	1/2	1/4		2																			Rm 4	10	24				

FIGURE 22-14

CUTTING ORDER

TABLE ROCK PLANT NO. 6
(Plant)

No. 6050
Date November 20, 1957

JOB. NO.	ITEM NO.	DESCRIPTION	QUANTITY	REMARKS
2650	1	Full Size Bed	175	
2650	2	3/4 Bed	100	
2650	3	Twin Bed	250	
2650	4	Vanity	100	
2650	5	Bench	100	
2650	5	Vanity Mirror	100	
2650	6	Mr. & Mrs. D	250	
2650	6	Mirror	300	
2650	7	Chest	150	
2650	7	Mirror	100	
2650	8	Night Stand	255	
2650	9	Dresser	100	Superwood No. 5521,
2460	6	Dresser	175	Sirocco Parkwood Top,
		Top Only	1	Sir Francis Drake Hotel, San Francisco

AVERAGE PRODUCTION 9 DAYS

EST. START DATE 11/25/57

EST. OUT DATE 12/12/57

EST. SHIP DATE 1/18/58

Authorized By: Frank C. Patten, Jr.
Production Control

FIGURE 22-15

Date November 12, 1957

Page 2

PRODUCTION PLANNING MEMO NO. 277 TO ALL CONCERNED.

SUBJECT: Proposed Cutting Schedule

TABLE ROCK PLANT NO. 6

SUITE NUMBER	C.O. NUMBER	DAYS PROD.	KILN DATE	CONFIRMED C.O. REQUIRED	START CABINET ROOM	SHIPPING DATE	REMARKS
7100-6 2nd Cut	6044	13				11/7	45%
107-6 1st Cut	6045	13			10/31	11/26	17%
7050	6046	14	9/15	10/27	11/12	12/15	
Singer Desk	6047	4			11/25	12/30	100%
131	6049	6		11/2	12/12	1/9	
2650 & 2460-6	6050	9	10/18	11/5	12/19	1/18	
Singer Desk	6053	8	11/7	11/26	1/9	1/26	100%
Government Contract	P	10	11/19	12/8	2/19	2/10	
MARION PLANT NO. 2							

FIGURE 22-16

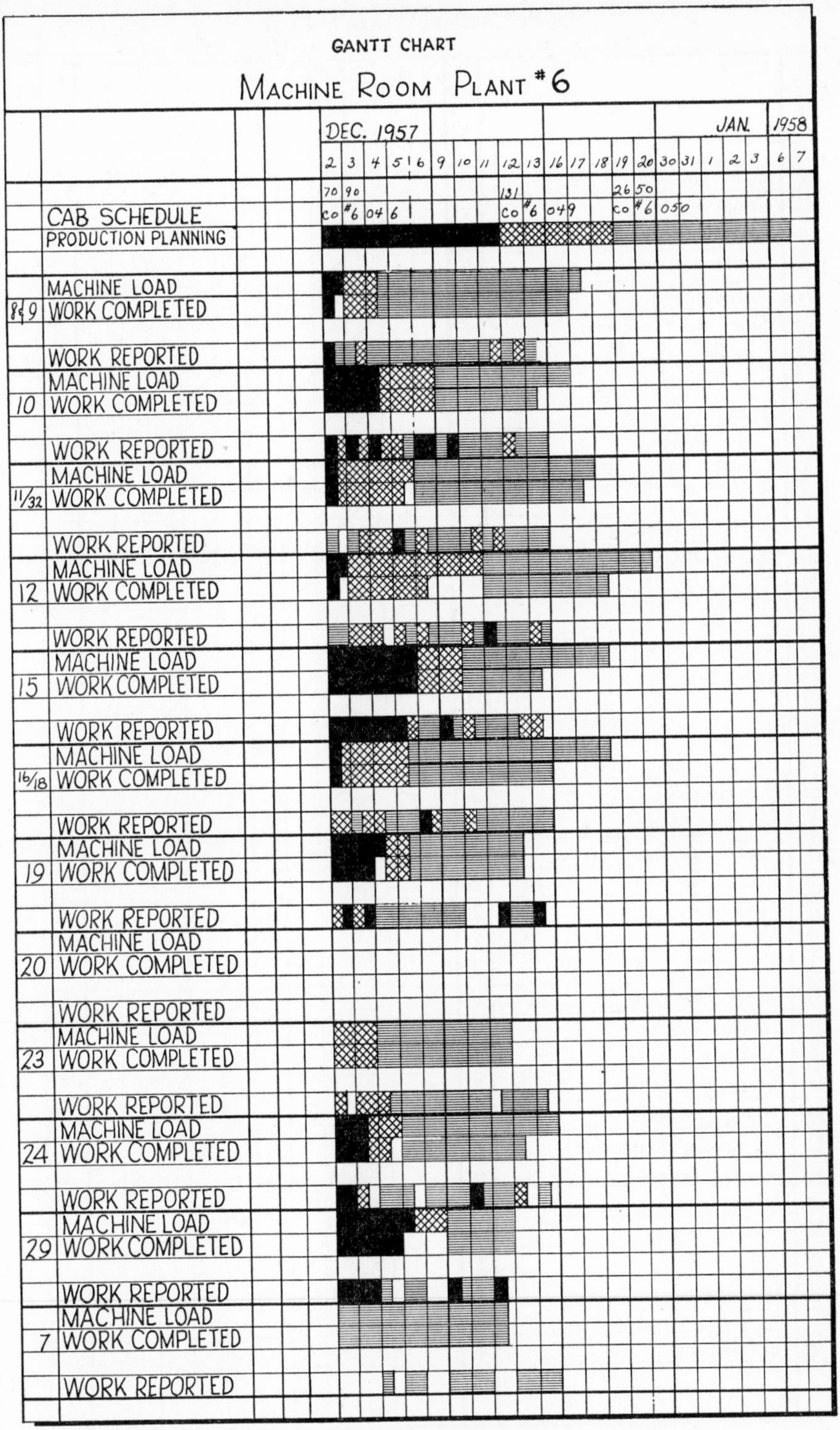

GANTT CHART

MACHINE ROOM PLANT #6

DEC. 1957 — JAN. 1958

2 3 4 5 6 9 10 11 12 13 16 17 18 19 20 30 31 1 2 3 6 7

70 90 131 26 50

CO #6 04 6 CO #6 049 CO #6 050

CAB SCHEDULE
PRODUCTION PLANNING

8 & 9 MACHINE LOAD
WORK COMPLETED
WORK REPORTED

10 MACHINE LOAD
WORK COMPLETED
WORK REPORTED

11/32 MACHINE LOAD
WORK COMPLETED
WORK REPORTED

12 MACHINE LOAD
WORK COMPLETED
WORK REPORTED

15 MACHINE LOAD
WORK COMPLETED
WORK REPORTED

16/18 MACHINE LOAD
WORK COMPLETED
WORK REPORTED

19 MACHINE LOAD
WORK COMPLETED
WORK REPORTED

20 MACHINE LOAD
WORK COMPLETED
WORK REPORTED

23 MACHINE LOAD
WORK COMPLETED
WORK REPORTED

24 MACHINE LOAD
WORK COMPLETED
WORK REPORTED

29 MACHINE LOAD
WORK COMPLETED
WORK REPORTED

7 MACHINE LOAD
WORK COMPLETED
WORK REPORTED

FIGURE 22-17 Gantt Chart

	ROUGH MACHINE - CHECK OFF LIST													SUITE NO. 2650	
	2650-6 Mr & Mrs Dresser			Sheet No. 1 Of 1										JOB NO.	
PART NO.	PART NAME	PCS. PER CASE	AMOUNT	DATE	RIP	JOINT	SIZE	GLUE	PLANE	GLUE VEN.	PLANE	RIP	MOULD		DELIVERED
1	Top	1													
3	Front Post	2													
4	Back Post	2													
9	End Panels	2													
11	End Panel Rail	4													
13	Base Frame Front Rail	1													
15	Base Frame Back Rail	1													
14	Base Frame End Rail	2													
16	Dust. Bot. Munts	3													
17	Center Pilaster	1													
19	Top & Bot. Parting Rail	2													
19-1	Parting Rail	4													
21	Dust Bot. Bk. Rail	4													
24	Dust Bot. End Rail	4													
24-1	Bot. Dust Bot. End Rail	2													
25	Dust Bottoms	6				Machine R									
27	Caster Blocks	4													
28	Front Base Rail	2													
28-1	Corner Base Rail	2													
28-2	Base Center Block	1													
29	End Base Rail	2													
30	Back Base Rail	2													
31	End Panel Moulds	2													
31-1	Pin Tray Runners	2													
32	Drawer Front A	2													
32-1	Drawer Front B	2													
32-2	Drawer Front C	2													
33	Drawer Sides -A-	4													
33-1	Drawer Sides -B-	4													
33-2	Drawer Sides -C-	4													
34	Drawer Backs -A-	2													
34-1	Drawer Backs- B-	2													
34-2	Drawer Backs -C-	2													
35	Top Drawer Partitions	2													
36	Drawer Bottoms	6				Machine R									
37	Drawer Guides	6													
38	Drawer Runners	6													
39	Drawer Tilts	2													
47	Back Panel	1				Machine R									
51	Pin Tray	2													
51-1	Pin Tray Ends	4													

FIGURE 22-18

23

Mathematical Approaches to Business Decisions

THE dictum that "science is measurement" may be inadequate as a definition of what science actually is. However, it does point up the desire of most fields of study to arrive at generalizations expressible in quantitative form. There are two interrelated ways of achieving such a quantitative form for one's ideas. One is to express these ideas —generalizations, hypotheses, theories, models, or whatever one wishes to call them—in mathematical form. If, for example, one observes that there are approximately four times as many dogs' legs as there are dogs, one may wish to express this in the form of an equation, such as:

$$L = 4D$$

If one tries hard enough he should be able to reduce most generalizations to some such form, though the generalizations of greatest interest are likely to be rather complex.

Statistics is a second approach to the quantitative treatment of relationships among variables. Statistics is concerned with relating one's theories or generalizations to observed fact. In recent years, statisticians have developed rigorous methods for determining the extent to which generalizations are supported or refuted by the data at hand. Statistics and the mathematical expression of theories go hand in hand. It is quite possible to check an ordinary verbal statement statistically: if one claims that there are more dog tails than dogs, it is not necessary to work up an equation before a statistical check is possible. But expression of the theory in mathematical form is more convenient for the statistician, since this will tell him exactly which variables he is to measure, and precisely what is the quantitative relationship that he is to verify.

To be sure, it is possible to express a theory in mathematical form without any statistical support whatever. The absence of statistical backing is not necessarily a reflection on the adequacy of the hypothesis. Some of the most important parts of what we call "knowledge" have not as yet been subjected to statistical test, and to take a know-nothing attitude toward such knowledge would indeed be retrogressive.

It is not surprising that management has traditionally remained a non-quantitative branch of knowledge, depending little upon mathematical forms of expression or statistical test. However, in recent years there has been a growing tendency to use mathematics and statistics in dealing with management problems. Some managers are skeptical of the applicability of such techniques to their nebulous functions, but others welcome these new developments as signs of a growing maturity in the study of management.

The emphasis on quantitative treatment of management problems goes under a number of names: Operations Research, Management Science, or Mathematical Model-Building. This chapter will present an introduction to these subjects, leaving most of the statistical issues for Chapters 25 and 26.

Before the reader becomes alarmed and protests that his mathematical training is inadequate, a note of reassurance is in order. This chapter is on mathematical model building, but it is nonmathematical in character. No mathematics beyond high school algebra is required. All that is necessary is that the reader be willing to accept the substitution of symbols for words and to look closely at some simple equations. This chapter will not train the reader to be an Operations Research expert, for this does require a mathematical training (and a great deal more material than can be presented in one chapter). But this chapter and the three that follow will attempt to clarify what these quantitative approaches mean, and to motivate the reader to move on to higher levels of competence in this area by further study.

The Advantages of Mathematical Approaches

The expression of one's ideas in mathematical form has advantages that should be apparent to the most skeptical reader. If one states that X is related to Y, it is certainly economical of space to express that statement in mathematical form:

$$X = f(Y)$$

This equation can be translated into words: X is a function of Y, which is just another way of saying that the terms are related. Such a statement is vague; it may be that X increases as Y increases or the reverse; or the relationship may be more complex. It is desirable to be more precise by introducing into the equation coefficients which will say precisely what the relationship is. For example, if one hypothesizes that the size of staffs grows geometrically with the size of the enterprise, he could express this as follows:

$$S = 0.02X^2$$

in which:

S represents the number of staff employees and

X represents the total number of employees

Such an equation has the advantage of precision. It says exactly what statement is being made about the relationship between these variables. Another advantage is that one is likely to ask himself, when he substitutes symbols for ordinary language, exactly what the symbols mean. In the above illustration, the expression "size of the enterprise" may appear to be clear at first, but a closer look reveals that it is in fact extremely ambiguous. Does size refer to the physical dimensions of the plant, to the volume of sales, to the payroll, or to the number of employees? The mathematician gets frustrated if he has to use symbols that are not clearly defined. Already the contact of management with mathematics has introduced desirable precision.

The reader should be warned that the above equation is for illustrative purposes and that, in fact, it does not make sense if X (the number of employees) is increased beyond 50 (in which case the predicted number of staff employees becomes larger than the total number of employees of all kinds). But sometimes an equation that becomes ridiculous beyond certain values makes good sense within limits—the equation may give a "good fit" within a certain range.

Another advantage of mathematical treatment is its capacity to handle a large number of variables. In the past, the manager has been able to argue for the superiority of his judgment over models on the grounds that his judgment could take a larger number of factors into account. Now that mathematical methods can incorporate large numbers of variables in a systematic way, this particular argument for "judgment" becomes less tenable. Furthermore, the mathematical expression of these complex relationships makes it easier to check against the facts to see whether the relationship actually does exist, for mathematical models can be expressed in forms amenable to statistical test. The manager is capable of "feeling" that there are relationships which, in fact, do not exist, and ignoring others that may be important.

Furthermore, mathematical models force us to state clearly (even to ourselves) what our goal is and what assumptions have been made. The human mind tends to use fuzzy notions concerning objectives. Even a simple model in mathematical symbols will improve our thought processes—regardless of whether we can manipulate the symbols mathematically for a solution. On the other hand, no amount of high powered computation will serve a useful purpose unless the initial statement of the objective is carefully thought out by one who understands the subject matter being studied. In other words, the initial statement of the problem should be handled by a specialist in the subject area, not by a mathematician who does not know the manner in which the results will be used. An extract in the next chapter will provide an interesting illustration of confusion in setting objectives.

The development of the electronic computer has been a major stimulus to the use of mathematical approaches. Systems of equations which would have taken years of computation by pencil and paper methods, and months with the aid of the desk calculator, can now be solved in hours. Thus, problems, which formerly were left to the intuitive judgment of managers because of the heavy cost of more systematic solution, may now be attacked mathematically at relatively small expense. This is not to say that all computer solutions are economical; there is evidence that some computers have not paid for themselves. An electronic computer is an expensive piece of equipment and will not pay for itself unless it does significant problems under the supervision of competent personnel.

Managerial judgment will continue to take a nonmathematical bent for decisions that involve human relations, questions of ultimate values, and other (so far) nonquantifiable considerations. The claims of some operation research workers that they are ready to consider the whole enterprise, including its organizational aspects, appear to be pretentious, or at least extremely premature. This field of endeavor, like most others, has produced its enthusiasts who at times overstate their case.

Linear programming

Linear programming, with its successes in solving certain kinds of management problems, is a good starting point to illustrate the uses of mathematical analysis. Linear programming is a means of making decisions—or at least in indicating optimum solutions—based on the consideration of certain quantifiable variables. The method became known in the 1950's, especially under the influence of Tjalling Koopmans, George Dantzig, and other applied mathematicians.

Linear programming has the following characteristics:

1. It is concerned with attainment of an *optimum* position in relation to some objective. Usually the aim is to *minimize* costs or to *maximize* profits—but the minimization or maximization could apply to other objectives.
2. It involves the selection among *alternatives* or the appropriate combination of alternatives.
3. It takes into account certain *constraints* or *limits* within which the decision is is to be reached. For example, if the problem is to decide what quantities of several products should be scheduled for production, the capacities of the various departments would be taken into account.
4. It not only requires that the variables be quantifiable, it also rests on the assumption that the relations among the variables are *linear*.

If the assumption of linearity is not relevant, it may be necessary to apply more complicated mathematical programming procedures. Frequently the assumption of linearity is close enough to reality to justify overlooking the small error it may introduce.

A well-known illustration should clarify what is involved—it is the problem of attaining an adequate diet at minimum cost. Certain constraints are established: the diet must include quantities of each vitamin and sufficient calories—these magnitudes are established at the outset. Various foods are available, each with different combinations of vitamins and calories. One food item may be rich in Vitamin B_1, but low in calories and in the other vitamins; another low in Vitamin B_1, high in the other vitamins, but low in calories; and so on. The price of each food item is given. Thus we have the following conditions:

1. An objective—the minimization of costs.
2. Constraints—the attainment of the necessary daily requirements of vitamins and calories.
3. Linear relations between quantities of food and vitamin and calorie content. It is reasonable to suppose that if one increases the quantity of beans in the diet, the amount of vitamins and calories contributed by the beans will go up in proportion.
4. Prices of the various foods. Here again the linear assumption seems reasonable —twice as many beans will cost twice as much (assuming no quantity discounts).

There is no reason why the solution of this problem could not be obtained by trial and error—in fact earlier writers did work on the problem in that way. But trial and error becomes laborious, especially if many different vitamins and foods are under consideration. An advantage of linear programming is the saving of time in reaching a solution; and with the use of an electronic computer this saving becomes greater. The fact that linear programming informs us when the best solution is reached is also an advantage. In addition, several specialized short-cut methods, such as the distribution (or transportation) method, have been developed to diminish the computation time.

A series of illustrations should bring out the essentials of the method. These illustrations are simpler than the kinds of decisions made by linear programming; the aim here is to establish the point of view without becoming too involved in detailed computations.

A Simple Banking Illustration. The first illustration is so simple it falls outside the usual framework of linear programming. However, it does involve linear functions and the objective of minimizing costs. Its solution requires nothing beyond the simplest high school algebra. Suppose that a family is considering maintaining a checking account in a bank. The bank offers two plans: the first requires no minimum balance, but ten cents is charged for each check written; the second plan requires a \$200 minimum balance but makes no charge for checks. The problem is to make a choice between the two alternatives.

The problem is so simple that the reader may reach the solution almost intuitively. Nevertheless, one may proceed by mathematical and diagrammatic methods. The first step is to set up equations relating total cost to the number of checks on each method. The following symbols are used:

$C =$ Total cost per month

$x =$ Number of checks written per month

The equation for the first plan becomes

$C = .10x$

For the second plan, the equation is based on the sacrifice of interest or dividends involved in maintaining the minimum balance. Assuming that the family will invest in bonds returning 6 per cent if it does not maintain the minimum balance of $200, this means that this plan involves a sacrifice of $12.00 per year or $1.00 per month. (Note that the opportunity cost idea introduced in Chapter 15 is applied.) The cost equation is simple, the total cost being independent of the number of checks:

$$C = \$1.00$$

We might then determine the point at which these two costs are equal (a kind of breakeven point). We set the right-hand sides of the two equations equal to each other and solve for x. The answer is 10 checks per month. This means that the total cost will be the same on either plan if an average of ten checks is written each month. If the average number of checks is greater than 10, the second plan is preferable; if less than 10, the first plan will reduce costs. Figure 23-1 is a diagrammatical summary of the problem.

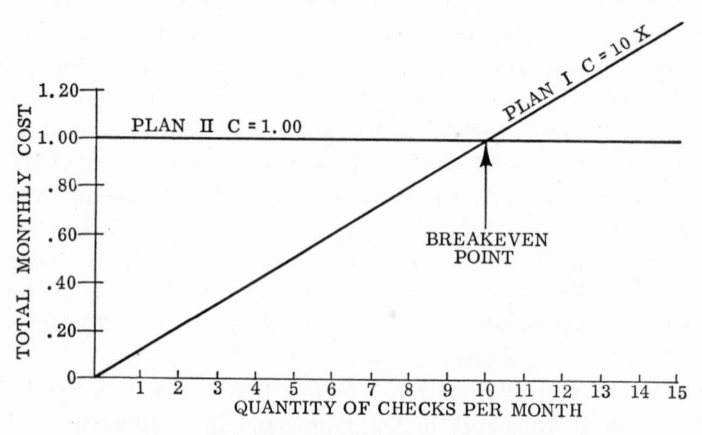

FIGURE 23-1 Total Cost of Two Alternative Check Plans

A Simple Output Decision. The next illustration is closer to the more usual linear programming problem, but it will be kept simple enough to diagram. The number of variables will be below that encountered in a realistic business situation.

The Hofmeier Manufacturing Company turns out two products for which there is an unlimited demand; it can sell any quantity it likes at the given market price. The first product is birdcages and the second rattraps. The plant has limited capacity in its four departments—the wire parts manufacturing department, the wooden parts manufacturing department, the birdcage assembly department, and the rattrap assembly department. The objective is to maximize profits. This requires a decision on the quantities of each product.

The wire parts manufacturing department turns out parts for both products. It could produce parts for 100,000 birdcages per year if it were not required to produce rattraps. It could produce parts for 300,000 rattraps and no birdcages. Thus the capacity of the department can be expressed in this form (letting x represent the quantity of birdcages and y the quantity of rattraps):

$$100{,}000 = x + \frac{y}{3} \quad \text{(capacity of wire products department)}$$

This equation indicates that the reduction of the output of birdcages will permit the addition of three times as many rattraps.

In the wooden parts department, however, it takes as much capacity for the rattraps as for the birdcages. The equation is:

$$150{,}000 = x + y \text{ (capacity of wooden parts department)}$$

The assembly departments are specialized; no rattraps are assembled in the birdcage assembly department and vice versa. This provides two more equations:

$$90{,}000 = x \text{ (capacity of birdcage assembly department)}$$

$$120{,}000 = y \text{ (capacity of rattrap assembly department)}$$

All of these capacity limits can be shown on a single diagram. The horizontal axis represents the quantity of birdcages and the vertical axis the quantity of rattraps. The first step is to plot the wire products capacity—a straight line sloping downward to the right, showing combinations of the two products that are possible within the capacity limits. At one extreme there is the possibility of 100,000 birdcages and no rattraps; at the other, 300,000 rattraps and no birdcages. All other combinations fall on the straight line connecting these two extremes—for example, 50,000 birdcages and 150,000 rattraps. (The reader might wish to test whether other combinations will fall on this line.) A similar line is drawn for the wooden products department with extremes at 150,000 birdcages (and no traps) and 150,000 rattraps (and no cages). The capacity of the birdcage assembly department is represented by a vertical line at 90,000—the department can handle 90,000 cages and any number from zero to infinity of traps (since no effort on traps in that department is required at all). Similarly, the capacity of the other assembly department is shown by a horizontal line at 120,000 traps. It should be apparent that these capacities act as constraints, so that in Figure 23-2 the company cannot operate beyond the heavy lines shown. The area within these lines represents the *technical* possibilities, and thus is called the *feasibility space.* To the right or above these lines involves going beyond the capacity of one department or another.

Which point on these heavy lines will be most profitable? This question involves more than technical factors, and to answer it, economic information is needed—some identification of the relative profits provided by the two products. Let us assume that the birdcages sell at $10.00. The variable costs are $7.00. The fixed costs will be ignored, since these will run on regardless of the decision. Thus each birdcage sold contributes $3.00 to overhead and profits. The rattraps sell at $5.00 (they are chrome plated and automatic). They involve variable costs (incremental costs) of $2.50, and thus make a contribution to profits of $2.50 apiece.

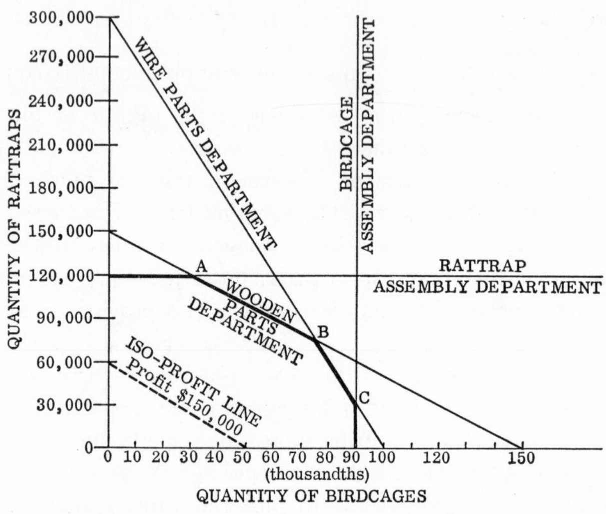

FIGURE 23-2 Linear Programming: Graphic Solution

The most profitable position will be at one of the corners of the heavy line in Figure 23-2—there are three such corners, A, B, and C. The proof of this point will be left to the mathematicians, but the reader should grasp it intuitively. If birdcages were extremely profitable but traps only slightly so, it would be sensible to produce the largest number of the former (90,000), and then use any slack capacity to produce as much of the latter as possible. This would bring us to corner C. If the traps were much more profitable than the cages, the decision should be to produce at corner A (120,000 traps and 30,000 cages). But a profit of $3.00 on the cages and $2.50 on traps leave us in doubt. The way to solve the problem graphically is to draw a series of iso-profit lines on the graph. (An iso-profit line shows all the combinations of the two products that will result in the same total profit.) Take for example, a profit of $150,000. This could be achieved by selling 50,000 cages or 60,000 traps, or any combination on the broken line shown on Figure 23-2. A large number of iso-profit lines could be drawn parallel to the one shown, each based on a profit of $3.00 and $2.50. They are not shown because they add too many lines to our simple chart. The iso-profit line that is drawn is *not* the most profitable one, since it requires only a fraction of the available capacity. The reader will recognize that the highest iso-profit line that can be reached with this capacity will pass through corner B. The most profitable corner is the one that barely touches the highest attainable iso-profit line. Thus, the most profitable combination is 75,000 birdcages and 75,000 rattraps.

This combination results in a contribution to overhead and profit of $412,500. If it had been decided, by hunch, to produce the combination at corner A, the contribution to overhead and profit would have been only $340,000. Provided that the assumptions fit the conditions, linear programming (or its equivalent) can add $72,500 to the profits.

Methods actually used and kinds of problems handled

The graphic technique just demonstrated cannot handle the kinds of problems business is likely to encounter. If the number of products in our illustration had been three instead of two, it would have been necessary to use the third dimension. To go further and teach the methods actually used raises difficulties beyond the scope of this book. Two basic approaches are used in linear programming. One, the simplex method, is based on a branch of mathematics unfamiliar to many readers—matrix algebra. The other approach, which includes the distribution method, saves time, but involves tedious routine. Since the emphasis of this book is on concepts rather than techniques, there is not much to be gained from a detailed description of the steps taken in working through a linear programming problem.

The aim here is to provide a knowledge of the kinds of problems amenable to linear programming, along with an awareness of the assumptions and limitations of the method. A manager does not have to be a linear programming expert to recognize the kinds of situations in which the method might be appropriate, and he may have even better knowledge than the expert about what the method cannot do.

In this connection, it will be useful to outline some of the problems that have been solved by linear programming:

1. Minimization of transportation costs. If a company has a number of plants scattered around the country and a number of sales outlets, it may wish to determine which plants should supply which outlets. This is not as simple a problem as it might at first seem. It is not merely a matter of selecting the lowest transportation costs for Outlet 1, for this may mean that Outlet 4 must use higher cost routes than would have been the case if Outlet 1 had not entered the picture. The optimum solution will involve a simultaneous consideration of all the plants and outlets, and all the transportation channels. The problem might be complicated by differences in production costs at the different plants and by the possibility of excess capacity. Linear programming can deal with those complications—provided that the linear assumption is appropriate.

2. Determination of product mix. Our rattrap and birdcage illustration was of this character. In actual practice, the most important application has been in refining oil—oil can be converted into many different products and determination of the most profitable combinations is extremely important.

3. Blending. Again this application is especially important in the oil industry—

in determining the most economical combinations of gasoline to provide a given blend. There are other possible blending problems amenable to this treatment. For example, some coals have coking qualities and others do not (or do in lesser degrees). The coking coals are more expensive. It is possible to mix the more expensive and less expensive coals to provide a blend to meet requirements at minimum costs.

4. Scheduling production. If a plant has a number of general purpose machines to be used in producing a variety of products, some patterns of machine use will be more economical of time than others. It may take longer to turn out a particular product on one machine than on another. The product may not be produced on the faster machine—if its capacity is limited, if idle time exists on the slower machine, or if alternative products can make more profitable use of the faster machine.

This list of applications is by no means complete; in fact new uses are continually being found. The illustrations should, however, be sufficient to indicate the kinds of problems amenable to this kind of solution. The reader should be able to identify a linear programming type of situation even though it does not fall among the illustrations discussed here.

Other mathematical models

Linear programming is the best known mathematical technique in business decisions, but it is only one of many approaches that can be applied. At the present time, there is a rapid proliferation of mathematical models—systems of equations attempting to portray one or another aspect of management. Some models are the product of theoreticians who are not interested in immediate application; others are developed in a form that can be immediately useful to management.

The earliest and most convincing of the models dealt with purely technological matters—with relations among certain physical forces, as in astronomy, physics and engineering. When economic considerations are introduced, the analysis becomes more complex and uncertain; thus it is no surprise that mathematical solutions for economic problems came somewhat later. Even then it was necessary to assume a simple economic objective—such as minimization of cost or maximization of profit—for mathematical tools are not suited (at the present stage of development) to the choice of goals. The use of mathematical models in the area of human relations and organization is still in its infancy and is rather controversial. As has been suggested, mathematical techniques become most cumbersome when related to objectives and values. While some research workers are concerned with a more systematic treatment of values, they are entering an area that has long troubled the philosophers; it seems unlikely that they will be able to solve this problem in the near future.

Thus, there is a hierarchy of management problems, ranging from those most suited to quantitative treatment (on the technical side), to those in which quantification is most difficult (on the human and value side). Several illustrations should clarify what is involved in mathematical model building in these areas.

Taylor's Metal Cutting Experiments. Some operations research workers say that the subject was invented in 1940 or 1941 in connection with anti-submarine warfare. No subject is born overnight, however, and it should not be surprising to find that earlier workers were using methods not much different from modern operations research or management science. A good illustration is F. W. Taylor's work on the art of cutting metals.[1] Taylor not only built a mathematical model, he also used a "team approach" (another characteristic of operations research), relying on several research workers with different backgrounds. He conducted thousands of experiments on a variety of metals with different cutting tools, and concluded with a mathematical formulation of the solution. It is difficult to see in what respects Taylor's work is different from modern operations research. His model was relatively simple and he did not have access to an electronic computer, but his point of view was the same. No doubt Taylor himself was applying on a large scale, and more systematically, methods already in use.

Taylor's objective was the determination of the appropriate cutting speed of machine tools. He considered twelve variables:

a. Quality of the metal to be cut (hardness, and so forth)
b. Diameter of the work
c. Depth of the cut
d. Thickness of the shaving
e. Elasticity of the work and the tool
f. Shape of the cutting edge of the tool
g. Chemical composition of the steel used in the tool
h. The cooling medium
i. Duration of the cut
j. Pressure of the shaving upon the tool
k. Changes of speed and feed possible on the lathe
l. The pulling and feeding power of the lathe at various speeds

Taylor's method of experimentation was to hold all but one of these variables constant and then experiment with various combinations of the variable under different cutting speeds. The relationship of cutting speeds to thickness of the shaving was plotted on a graph. Then Taylor fitted a mathematical expression to the plotted points to represent the "law" of the effect of the thickness of the shaving upon the cutting speed.

Not only did Taylor express these relationships in a series of formulas, he and his co-worker, Carl Barth, developed special slide rules embodying these formulas and enabling employees to determine the correct speed without any difficult computations.

[1] Taylor's findings were published in the paper, "On the Art of Cutting Metals," published in the American Society of Mechanical Engineers, *Transactions,* Vol. 28 (1907).

Economic lot size models

Most readers will accept the idea that mathematical equations can be fitted to technological relationships such as those studied by Taylor.[2] However, when it comes to determining the most economical decision—for example, deciding which of a number of alternatives will minimize cost—doubts will arise. As early as 1915, formulas for the determination of economic lot sizes appeared. These were mathematical models, worthy of comparison with modern operations research models. The early models are still useful in developing insights into the problem of deciding what size lot to manufacture.

It might at first seem that the larger the lot size, the better. When each new lot is started, there are setup costs involved. The larger the lot, the smaller the unit setup costs, for they will be spread over a larger volume. Figure 23-3 illustrates this fact. The curve showing this relationship between lot size and per unit preparation (setup) costs is a special type of curve called a rectangular hyperbola (provided that the setup costs are entirely fixed for different size lots). Another class of costs increase as the lot size increases, and are known as carrying costs. They arise from the fact that the larger the number produced at one time, the larger the size of the inventory to be stored. As the inventory increases in size, there will be an increase in the following carrying costs:

a. Interest costs—more money will be tied up in larger inventories
b. Rental on storage space
c. Property taxes and insurance
d. Obsolescence—the larger inventories increase the risk that these will become obsolete before they are used up or sold
e. Deterioration—certain items tend to deteriorate in storage, and the larger the inventory, the longer the period of storage, and thus the greater the deterioration.

As shown in Figure 23-3, we usually assume that carrying costs rise in proportion to the size of the lot—we go further and assume that the relationship is linear. Setup costs per unit decline as described by a rectangular hyperbola.

Thus, two opposing sets of costs are evident. There will be a point where the total of the two will reach a minimum (point M in Figure 23-3) and this is the economic lot size. This minimum will be at the size at which the unit setup cost curve intersects the unit carrying cost line, under the conditions specified; if the costs behave in a more complicated way the relationship will be more complex.

It is easy to demonstrate mathematically that under these conditions a

[2] It would be wrong to state that economic considerations were absent from Taylor's study, though he did not explicitly include dollars and cents considerations in his models.

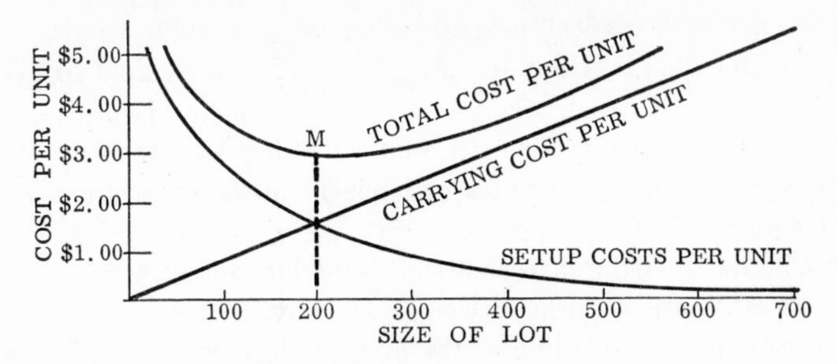

FIGURE 23-3 Economic Lot Size Model

simple formula will provide the answer on the economic lot size.[3] This formula is:

$$Q = \sqrt{\frac{2RS}{I}} \text{ in which:}$$

Q = Economic lot size.
R = Annual use of the item in units per year.
S = Setup cost each time a new lot is started.
I = Carrying cost per unit per year.

This general type of economic lot size formulation is also applicable in determining the size of batches to purchase. The reader should be warned, however, that special considerations enter into particular problems, calling for adjustment in the model. For example, if discounts for large lots are offered by the supplier, these discounts may come in discontinuous jumps, complicating the mathematical treatment. As Bowman and Fetter warn, the "important job is to build a model to fit the problem, not to memorize one that has already been built."[4]

A human relations model

The next illustration goes beyond technological and simple economic considerations and attempts to apply mathematical symbols to human behavior itself. Some readers will be irritated by this attempt, and perhaps they are right, but it is well to approach this question with an open mind. Two remarks are in order at the outset. First, it is possible to use mathematical formulations even when measurement is not possible, for a mathematical model may point up relationships even when these cannot be quantified. Secondly, it may be possible in the future to attach quantities to considerations that now appear qualitative in character. As Herbert Simon has stated,

[3] A clear presentation of this proof and of the whole lot size problem appears in Edward H. Bowman and Robert B. Fetter, *Analysis For Production Management* (Homewood, Ill.: Richard Irwin, 1957), pp. 241–248.

[4] *Ibid.*, p. 248.

qualitative, nonmathematical generalizations that contain words like "increase," "greater than," "tends to" are a challenge to the applied mathematician. He says that "such terms betray the linguistic disguise and reveal that underneath the words lie mathematical objects—quantities, orderings, sets—and hence the possibility of a restatement of the proposition in mathematical language." [5]

Simon has constructed a mathematical model incorporating parts of a well-known nonmathematical work by George Homans, *The Human Group.* Simon believes that a substitution of the mathematical for the verbal formulation leads to a clarification of what is being said. The model considers a group of employees whose behavior is characterized by four variables:

$I(t)$—the intensity of *interaction* among the members at points in time.

$F(t)$—the level of *friendliness* among the members.

$A(t)$—the amount of *activity* carried on by the members within the group.

$E(t)$—the amount of *activity* imposed on the group by the external *environment.*

The model is concerned with the interaction among these variables over time (which accounts for the "t's"). Simon, on the basis of Homans' work, postulates three sets of relations.

1. $I(t) = a_1F(t) + a_2A(t)$

This states that the intensity of interaction increases with the level of friendliness and the amount of activity within the group.

2. $$\frac{dF(t)}{dt} = b[I(t) - \beta F(t)]$$

This expresses the view that the rate of increase in friendliness depends upon the extent that interaction exceeds that "appropriate" to the existing level of friendliness. "That is, if a group of persons with little friendliness are induced to interact a great deal, the friendliness will grow; while, if a group with a great deal of friendliness interact seldom, the friendliness will weaken." [6]

3. $$\frac{dA(t)}{dt} = c_1[F(t) - yA(t)] + c_2[E(t) - A(t)]$$

This states that the amount of activity within the group increases if the actual level of friendliness is higher than that "appropriate" to the existing amount of activity and also if the amount of activity imposed by the external environment exceeds the existing amount of activity.

The small "d's" will be familiar to those with a background in calculus. For others, it is enough to translate them as rates of increase over time. Simon admits that these three equations represent only part of Homans' system. He also admits that the linear relations in the equations are an oversimplification; while he corrects this in a later section of his discussion,

[5] Reprinted with permission from Herbert A. Simon, *Models of Man: Social and Rational* (New York: John Wiley & Sons, 1957), p. 99.

[6] Simon, *Ibid.,* p. 101.

the authors will omit his more complex nonlinear treatment. Thus only a part of Simon's analysis is covered here.

It is possible to derive a number of conclusions from these postulates. If E, the task imposed on the group externally, is increased, there will follow an increase in group activity, the amount of friendliness, and the amount of interaction. If, on the other hand, E drops toward zero, activity, friendliness, and interaction all decline. In other words, too low a requirement of activity—too low a task—will lead to social disintegration. Another conclusion is that if there is a strong feedback from friendliness to interaction to friendliness, high morale will result. But in breaking up tasks so that there is little relationship among them (a low a_2), morale will be low.

Simon does not insist that this model is correct, though it is consistent with some of the empirical studies cited by Homans. What this mathematical formulation does accomplish is the precise statement of propositions which in ordinary language remain ambiguous. Once the postulates are determined, one can use mathematical methods to derive the inevitable consequences; mathematics serves as an exact system of logic; in ordinary language it is easy to be careless or obscure about one's logic. Furthermore, Simon was able to derive some propositions not discussed by Homans, by following up mathematically the implications of the model.

This type of model raises at least two serious questions:

1. Will it be possible at some later date to measure the variables, so that the symbols can be replaced by actual numbers? Psychologists and sociologists are developing measuring instruments which may be able to deal with such concepts as friendliness and interaction. The future will tell how successful these attempts turn out to be.
2. Is it possible to test such models in a systematic way to determine their validity? As yet, the social sciences have lagged in empirical testing of hypotheses, but there is evidence of a growing interest in verification.

Conclusions

The authors picture an imaginary "typical" reader. He approaches a chapter like this one with strong doubts. He knows that managers have not run their businesses in the past by mathematical rules, and he doubts that they ever will. He is irritated by some of the grandiose claims of the operations research experts. He has heard rumors of failures—of systems that have been abandoned and computers that did not pay off. He thinks it unlikely that he will ever have to know anything about these methods.

Yet, if he is willing to maintain an open mind, his curiosity will be aroused. This linear programming method does have its place after all—though one wonders whether a small firm has much to gain from it. If this chapter has been successful, this skeptic will then begin to wonder when or where these methods might work. He can see the applicability of mathematical models in dealing with certain technical problems—engineers have been doing this sort of thing for years. And then he will recognize that we are on the threshold of the use of mathematical models with possibilities of dramatic advances.

If the "typical" reader combines his skepticism with a bit of the spirit of adventure, he will be intrigued. He may wish to read more about "management science," and "operations research," and "models." The authors hope he will start following the discussion of these subjects in the journals and the business magazines. And in some cases, we hope, the reader will be so aroused about the possibilities of these approaches that he will decide to take more mathematics and plunge head-on into the study of quantitative methods in business decisions. For, although the authors are no mathematicians, they are convinced that the management of the future will be much more concerned than at present with these methods.

Bibliographical Note

A book that promises to become a classic in the mathematical treatment of business and economic behavior is John von Neumann and Oscar Morgenstern, *Theory of Games and Economic Behavior* (1944). Several books on game theory, based on this fundamental contribution, but requiring less rigor in mathematics, are: John D. Williams, *The Compleat Stategyst* (1954) and J. C. McKinsey, *Introduction to the Theory of Games* (1953). An outstanding contribution, with emphasis on the treatment of uncertainty, is R. Duncan Luce and Howard Raiffa, *Games and Decisions: Introduction and Critical Survey* (1957). The relevance of the theory of games to management is still controversial; the remainder of this bibliography is concerned with subjects that have proven their worth in business.

Operations research covers a variety of topics; outstanding works include: C. W. Churchman, R. L. Ackoff, and E. L. Arnoff, *Introduction to Operations Research* (1957); E. H. Bowman and R. B. Fetter, *Analysis for Production Management* (1957); and M. Sasieni, A. Yaspan and L. Friedman, *Operations Research: Methods and Problems* (1959). Valuable collections of articles emphasize actual applications to industrial problems. They include J. F. McCloskey and F. N. Trefethen (eds.) *Operations Research for Management,* Vol. I (1954); J. F. McCloskey and J. M. Coppinger (eds.) *Operations Research for Management,* Vol. II (1956); and E. H. Bowman and R. B. Fetter (eds.) *Analyses of Industrial Operations* (1959).

The leading works on linear programming and related subjects are: A. Charnes, W. W. Cooper, and A. Henderson, *An Introduction to Linear Programming* (1953); and Tjalling Koopmans (ed.) *Activity Analysis of Production and Allocation* (1951). A treatment requiring less mathematics but offering more economic interpretation is R. Dorfman, P. Samuelson, and R. Solow, *Linear Programming and Economic Analysis* (1958). J. G. Kemeny, J. L. Snell, and G. L. Thompson, *Introduction to Finite Mathematics* (1957) is an excellent treatment of matrix algebra, symbolic logic, linear programming, and other subjects important in modern management science. C. C. Holt, F. Modigliani, J. F. Muth, and H. A. Simon, *Planning Production, Inventories and Work Force* (1960) presents another mathematical approach to optimum decisions in manufacturing.

Questions and Problems

1. Which do you think is more suited to mathematical treatment: decisions about the extent and character of the advertising program or about the control of inventories? Discuss.

2. In general, would you expect mathematical approaches to be more advanced in the marketing or in the production areas of management? Discuss.

3. List as many kinds of managerial decisions as possible that might be suitable for linear programming.

4. The economic lot size model presented in the chapter is an oversimplification as related to actual problems in industry. Explain why this is the case. What elements must be added to the model to make it more realistic?

5. What are the criteria by which one could decide whether a problem is suited to treatment by linear programming?

6. It has been suggested that job evaluation is a phase of management that should be treated mathematically. Discuss.

7. A well-known topic in linear programming is called the transportation problem. Suppose a company has three factories, F_1, F_2, and F_3, and three warehouses, W_1, W_2, W_3. The factories supply these warehouses, which are located at varying distances from the factories. Because of these varying distances, the transportation costs from factories to warehouses vary from a low of $4.00 to a high of $8.00 per unit. The company wishes to minimize transportation costs. The costs from the factories to the warehouses may be presented in the form of a matrix.

	W_1	W_2	W_3	Factory Capacities
F_1	$5.00	$6.00	$7.00	100
F_2	$6.00	$8.00	$6.00	120
F_3	$7.00	$4.00	$5.00	150
Warehouse requirements	150	120	100	

N.B. The ambitious student may wish to consult a book on linear programming to learn about the transportation (distribution) method, which is a systematic way of solving this and more complicated problems.

In each cell of the matrix is entered the cost from a particular factory to a particular warehouse—the figure of $5.00 in the first cell is the cost from F_1 to W_1. Each factory has a limited capacity, as shown in the right-hand column. F_1 has a capacity of 100 units per time period; F_2 a capacity of 120 units; and F_3 a capacity of 150 units. Each warehouse requires certain quantities to be delivered, as shown in the bottom row. W_1 requires delivery of 150 units; W_2, 120 units; and W_3, 100 units.

(a) The objective is to assign factory capacities to warehouse requirements in order to minimize costs. It costs only $5.00 to ship from F_1 to W_1. Can there be any doubt that this is part of the optimum solution?

(b) Assign the factory capacities to the warehouses in any way that you like so that all factory capacity is used and warehouse requirements are satisfied. Why might there be questions whether this is an optimum allocation?

(c) Compute the total cost of the allocation that you have made.

(d) By trial and error reallocate the transportation routes to determine whether the costs can be reduced.

(e) Would this trial and error approach be suited to a larger matrix, with many factories and warehouses? Discuss.

8. In the rattrap and birdcage illustration in the chapter, assume that the profit is $1.00 on the traps and $3.00 on the cages. Find the optimum combination.

24

Extracts and Cases on Mathematical Approaches

THIS chapter's aim is to encourage reflection on the role of mathematics in business decisions. Since it is not assumed that the reader is a trained mathematician, a full mathematical treatment is not given, and some subjects are left in a state of suspension. The authors believe that this treatment will indicate what quantitative models have done, can do, might do in the future, even though it does not tell the reader specifically how to do it. It is our hope that the reader will continue to reflect critically on the strength and weaknesses, the relevance or irrelevance, of these techniques.

Extracts

EXTRACT A

Introduction to Operations Research (West Churchman, Russell L. Ackoff, and E. Leonard Arnoff)

During World War II, military management called on scientists in large numbers to assist in solving strategic and tactical problems. Many of these problems were . . . executive-type problems. Scientists from different disciplines were organized into teams which were addressed initially to optimizing the use of resources. These were the first "O.R. teams."

An objective of O.R., as it emerged . . . is to provide managers of the organization with a scientific basis for solving problems involving the interaction of components of the organization in the best interest of the organization as a whole. A decision which is best for the organization as a whole is called an optimum decision; one which is best relative to the functions of one or more parts of the organization is called a suboptimum decision. The problem of establishing criteria for an optimum decision is itself a very complex and technical one. . . .

O.R. tries to find the best decisions relative to as large a portion of a total organization as is possible. For example, in attempting to solve a maintenance problem in a factory, O.R. tries to consider the effect of alternative maintenance policies on the production department as a whole. If possible it also tries to consider how this effect on the production department in turn affects other departments and the business as a whole. . . . O.R. attempts to consider the interactions or chain of effects as far out as these effects are significant. In particular practical applications, however, the scope of O.R. is usually restricted either because access to higher and higher levels of organization is closed off or because of the limitations of time, money, or resources. . . . There is always a difference between what one tries to do and what one actually does. O.R. is here defined in terms of its important goal: an overall understanding of optimal solutions to executive-type problems in organizations. . . .

Because O.R. has emerged out of other sciences it borrows from them quite heavily. This same pattern has been followed in the "birth" of each scientific discipline. It is always difficult to distinguish a new field from those out of which it arises because of the overlap of problems, methods, and concepts. In time the differentiation becomes more complete and practitioners are no longer plagued with the question: "How does this differ from such and such a field?" The rapid growth of O.R. under its own name testifies to an increasing recognition of its uniqueness. But the differentiation is far from complete.

The overlap of methods, techniques, and tools between O.R. and other fields is largely due to the way in which O.R. was initially and is still carried on. It is research performed by teams of scientists whose individual members have been drawn from different scientific and engineering disciplines. One might find, for example, a mathematician, physicist, psychologist, and economist working together on a problem of optimizing capital expansion.[1]

Extract B

Scientific Programming in Business and Industry (Andrew Vazsonyi)

The most difficult problem, when applying mathematical techniques to business situations, is to establish the mathematical model. For this reason, a thorough understanding of the concept of mathematical models, how to develop them and how to test them, is most necessary. Unfortunately, it

[1] C. West Churchman, Russell L. Ackoff, and E. Leonard Arnoff, *Introduction to Operations Research* (New York: John Wiley & Sons, 1957), pp. 6–9.

is very difficult to explain what a mathematical model is, what it does, and how one should go about setting one up. . . . It might be useful at this stage to say a few words about the advantages of using mathematical models. The following list should help:

(a) The mathematical model makes it possible to describe and comprehend the facts of the situation better than any verbal description can hope to do.

(b) The mathematical model uncovers relations between the various aspects of the problem which are not apparent in the verbal description.

(c) The mathematical model indicates what data should be collected to deal with the problem quantitatively.

(d) The mathematical model establishes measures of effectiveness.

(e) The mathematical model explains situations that have been left unexplained in the past by giving cause and effect relationships.

(f) The mathematical model makes it possible to deal with the problem in its entirety and allows a consideration of all the major variables of the problem simultaneously.

(g) A mathematical model is capable of being enlarged step by step to a more comprehensive model to include factors that are neglected in verbal descriptions.

(h) The mathematical model makes it possible to use mathematical techniques that otherwise appear to have no applicability to the problem.

(i) A mathematical model frequently leads to a solution that can be adequately described and justified on the basis of verbal descriptions.

(j) It is often the case that the factors entering into the problem are so many that only elaborate data processing procedures can yield significant answers. In such a case, a mathematical model forms an immediate bridge to the use of large-scale electronic data processors.[2]

EXTRACT C

Design for Decision (Irwin D. J. Bross)

Models are vitally important in scientific work and, in my opinion, in any intellectual endeavor. An understanding of the nature and role of a model is prerequisite to clear thinking.

In ordinary language the word "model" is used in various ways. It covers such diverse subjects as the dolls with which little girls play and also the photogenic "dolls" who occupy the attention of mature men. I shall be concerned here with model in the sense of replica (as in a model airplane). . . .

Abstract Models

In the scientific world physical models are occasionally used for instructional purposes. In a planetarium you will generally find a model—little spheres which revolve on wire arms around a big sphere—which presents a picture of the astronomer's conception of the solar system. This sort of

[2] Andrew Vazsonyi, *Scientific Programming in Business and Industry* (New York: John Wiley & Sons, 1958), p. 18.

model is often used to demonstrate a phenomenon such as an eclipse. A rather similar physical model is sometimes employed to explain the atom to the general public. The solar model and the atom model illustrate one striking and sometimes confusing characteristic of models; two very diverse phenomena can sometimes be represented by similar models. . . .

All of us are accustomed to using verbal models in our thinking processes and we do it intuitively. Verbal models have played an important role in science, especially in the preliminary exploration of a topic and presentation of results. Verbal models are subject to a variety of difficulties, some of which I have discussed earlier, and most scientific fields have advanced (or are trying to advance) to the next stage—symbolic models of a mathematical nature. Astronomy was one of the first subjects to make this transition to the symbolic model. It should be noted that *until* this stage was reached there was really no reason to prefer a model with the sun as a center to a model with the earth as a center.

Symbolic Models

In a symbolic model, the balls and wire arms of the physical model of the solar system are replaced by mathematical concepts. Geometrical points are substituted for the balls. The next problem is to replace the wire arms which hold the balls in place. Now the wire arms have fixed lengths, and these lengths can be stated numerically. If all of the little balls revolve in the same plane, only one additional number is needed to locate the geometrical point. This number would be the angle between the wire arm and a stationary arm which would serve as a reference point.

Hence two numbers—the radius (length of arm) and an angle—will fix the location of the geometrical point just as effectively as the wire arm fixes the location of the little sphere in the physical model. Actually the astronomer's model is much more complicated than the symbolic model which I have described, but the general principle of construction is the same. . . .

Even though great care is lavished on the construction of the physical model the predictions which would come out of it would depend on friction, vibration, and other characteristics of the *model.* Hence the prediction would be rendered inaccurate by the entrance of attributes other than the ones which were deliberately built into the model to simulate the solar system.

In a *mathematical* model, on the other hand, the material of the model itself—in this case the symbolic language—does not ordinarily contribute such extraneous and undesirable attributes. If we want friction in the mathematical model we can put it in symbolically, but otherwise this friction will not appear in the model and hence cannot disturb our predictions. In the physical model the process of abstraction tends to introduce new and irrelevant details, while in the mathematical model the process of abstraction does not.

In this sense, therefore, a mathematical model is simple whereas a physical model is complex. It may strike you as curious that I should say that Einstein is working with an extremely simple model in his theory of relativity, while a schoolboy is working with an extremely complex model when be builds an airplane. If you think it over carefully, however, you may see the justice of the statement. . . .

The model itself should be regarded as arbitrary; it represents an act of creation like a painting or a symphony. The model can be anything its creator desires it to be. In practice, of course, it is generally stimulated (and therefore affected) by data from the real world. . . . Artistic creations also use sensory data. Even in abstract canvasses there is some influence from the original data (sensory experience). If the modern artist paints the portrait of a woman, it may not look like a human being to me. But presumably the dabs of paint have some relationship to the woman, though it may require an expert to understand this relationship. Similarly, a physicist's mathematical model of the atom may be far removed from any material substance; again only an expert can appreciate it.

In many cases the symbolic representation used in the model is chosen because it was successfully used in previous models, because it seems plausible to the creator, or because it is convenient. However, some very useful models are based on assumptions which are not evident from common sense or—as in the quantum model—are actually repugnant to common sense.[3]

EXTRACT D

Choice of Objectives in Operations Research (Charles Hitch)

The validity and therefore the usefulness of operations research depend upon the skill with which projects are designed and particularly upon the shrewdness with which criteria ("payoffs," "objectives functions") are selected. . . .

Calculating quantitative solutions using the wrong criteria is equivalent to answering the wrong questions. Unless operations research develops methods of evaluating criteria and choosing good ones, its quantitative methods may prove worse than useless to its clients in its new applications in government and industry. . . .

Occasionally an obviously appropriate one-dimensional objectives function permits a neat, simple, and completely persuasive solution to be presented —even in military applications. But criteria which appear plausible or

[3] Irwin D. J. Bross, *Design For Decision* (New York: The Macmillan Company, 1953), pp. 161, 163–164, 165, 167, 174–175.

even obvious at first glance are quite likely to turn out to be traps for the unwary. Let me take an example from Morse and Kimball with which most operations researchers are familiar. . . .

The data revealed that, over a wide range, the number of merchant vessels sunk in a U-boat attack on a convoy was proportional to the number of U-boats in the attacking pack and inversely proportional to the number of destroyer escorts, but independent of the size of the convoy. They also revealed that the number of U-boats sunk per attack was directly proportional both to the number of attacking U-boats and the number of defending escorts. The objectives function was taken (plausibly) to be the "exchange rate" or ratio of enemy losses (measured in U-boats) to our losses (measured in merchant ships).

I quote the conclusion: "The important facts to be deduced from the set of equations seem to be: (1) the number of ships lost per attack is independent of the size of the convoy, and (2) the exchange rate seems to be proportional to the square of the number of escort vessels per convoy. This squared effect comes about due to the fact that the number of merchant vessels lost is reduced, and at the same time the number of U-boats lost per attack is increased, when the escorts are increased, the effect coming in twice in the exchange rate. The effect of pack size cancels out in the exchange rate. From any point of view, therefore, the case for large convoys is a persuasive one.

"When the figures quoted here were presented to the appropriate authorities, action was taken to increase the average size of convoys, thereby also increasing the average number of escort vessels per convoy. As often occurs in cases of this sort, the eventual gain was much greater than that predicted by the above reasoning, because by increasing convoy and escort size the exchange rate (U/B sunk)/(M/V sunk) was increased to a point where it became unprofitable for the Germans to attack North Atlantic convoys, and the U-boats went elsewhere. This defeat in the North Atlantic contributed to the turning point in the 'Battle of the Atlantic.' "

This happy outcome depended on the intuition and good sense of the participants rather than upon a sophisticated choice of criterion. The criterion actually chosen can be criticized from many points of view. For example, while enemy losses and our losses would clearly both be important elements in the ideal objectives function, there is no reason (and none is suggested by our authors) why one should be divided by the other. What is far more important in this case is the complete neglect of another dimension of the objectives function which appears to an outsider to be as important as those considered—viz., the reduced operating efficiency of ships in large convoys, and hence the inverse relation between the size of convoy and the capacity of any given number of merchant ships to transport men and material across the Atlantic. It is not true that the case for large convoys is a persuasive one "from any point of view." Collecting large convoys takes time. The arrival of large convoys swamps port facilities, which means longer turnaround times. Because the speed of a convoy cannot exceed that of the slowest ship, there will be an inverse average relation between its size and speed. It might well be worth a few additional sinkings to insure the delivery in time of the forces required for the Normandy invasion. The complete omission of this objectives dimension is curious because it is so admirably adapted to analysis by quanitative methods. Presumably the explanation is that a quantitative analysis had already been made of the effect of convoy size on the carrying capacity of the merchant fleet, and the commander was therefore able to weigh, if only in some intuitive manner, the gain and the cost of marginal increments in convoy size.

That something was wrong with their plausible criterion should have been immediately evident to the authors: it proves far, far too much. It shows that it would be desirable to increase the size of convoys without limit—until the whole merchant fleet and all the destroyers are assembled in a single convoy. The authors, it is true, warn that the equation cannot be expected to be valid for "very small" and "very large" values—but this is a conventional warning against extrapolating functions far beyond the range of the data from which they are derived. The important point is that, long before the whole Atlantic fleet becomes a single convoy, the significant reductions in losses will have been achieved and the reduction in the efficiency of utilization of shipping will have become unacceptable.

It will always be necessary to use judgment and good sense in applying the results of operations research, but we must try to find criteria which place a less overwhelming burden on these qualities.

There is, parenthetically, one other moral I wish to draw from this example before leaving it. The authors conclude, we have seen, that the results of their recommended action were even more successful than their equations had predicted, because the U-boat fleet was withdrawn and sent elsewhere on other missions. This is really a case of taking one's sub-optimization criterion too seriously. By that criterion results were better than predicted, but if we look at a higher level criterion—say, effect on probability of winning the war—it is certain that Allied operations elsewhere were adversely affected by the diversion of the U-boat fleet. Moreover, presuming that the Germans made a rational decision, their U-boats, or the resources going into them, made a more significant contribution to German prospects of victory in the war elsewhere—after enlargement of the convoys—than they could have made by continuing to operate in the North Atlantic. In terms of the higher criterion, the effect on the probability of winning the war of taking the recommended action was less than one would infer from the calculation of results in the North Atlantic, which was based on the assumption that enemy U-boat tactics and deployment would remain unchanged. For when we change our operations, different tactics and deployment become optimal for the enemy. By adopting them he can, in general, reduce his loss, as he did on this occasion.[4]

Extract E

The Organization Man (William H. Whyte, Jr.)

[Scientism] is the promise that with the same techniques that have worked in the physical sciences we can eventually create an exact science of man. In one form or another, it has had a long and dismal record of achievement; even its proponents readily admit that the bugs are appalling. But this has not shaken the faith in scientism, for it is essentially a utopian rather than a technical idea. . . .

E. B. Weiss, perhaps the best-known consultant in the merchandising field, explained to readers that it isn't simply that such advances as electronic calculators and automatic factories are going to make for more efficiency. A whole new science, he says, is abuilding, and with the confusion between control of the physical and control of the mental which is characteristic of believers in scientism, he proclaims that "The Second Industrial Revolution will substitute the machine for the common, and for some fairly uncommon, functions of the human *mind*." It is not his contention, he says in qualification, "that the robot will replace *all* human endeavor." But almost all. After initial successes, such as cutting out the personal element in retail selling, making inventory-taking automatic, the machine will advance into hitherto sacrosanct areas, and with what seems unwonted relish, he cites a scientist's prophecy that in time the machine will replace man in the realm of reasoning and logical deduction. "*Next Week:* No. 2 in this series—How Cybernetic Principles Are Being and Will Be Applied in Factory, Office, and Warehouse."

The field of public relations is particularly susceptible. Here, for example, the *Public Relations Journal* editorializes on the subject:

"Now, whether he knows it or not, every practicing public-relations man is an engineer too—a *social engineer.* He develops new relationships and operations in society, designs new organizations and institutions, sets up and lubricates the human machinery for getting things done. The challenge of social engineering in our time is like the challenge of technical engineering fifty years ago. If the first half of the twentieth century was the era of the technical engineers, the second half may well be the era of the social engineers."

Dip into personnel journals, advertising trade journals, and you will find

[4] Charles Hitch, "Sub-Optimization in Operations Problems," *Journal of the Operations Research Society of America* (May, 1953), pp. 87, 90–92.

the same refrain. A lot of it is sheer malarkey, of course, but I think most of it is evidence of a genuine longing to be related to a faith.[5]

Cases

Case A:

Analysis for Production Management (Edward H. Bowman and Robert B. Fetter)

A manufacturer who had one plant and several warehouses was interested in the optimum size territory to serve directly from the warehouse connected physically to his plant. The advantages of direct delivery from the plant warehouse is that the intermediate step of bulk delivery from plant to branch warehouse is eliminated. Delivery was made from the various warehouses to retail stores. The question was how far out from the plant its delivery trucks should serve.

An equation of incremental analysis was used for this problem. It was an expression of distribution cost (IC) and savings (IG) per piece for the marginal truck load of goods added to the delivery radius. [Note: IC represents incremental cost; IG incremental gain.] That is, the unit of measure added was one truck load at a particular section of the perimeter. Many, many such truck loads are contained in the total area served by the plant warehouse. As the number of pieces in a truck load which may be delivered within one working day will differ with the distance out the truck must go, the equation must be in terms of cost per piece. IC has this dimension. The objective was to minimize the cost per piece. The incremental cost expression developed was as follows:

$$IC = \frac{2T_m \times P_d + T_f + D_h \times \text{hrs./day}}{\text{pcs./hr.}\ (\text{hrs./day} - 2 \times P_d \times \text{hrs./mi.} - D_f)}$$

where

T_m = truck operating cost per mile,
P_d = plant to perimeter delivery distance (a round trip once per day),
T_f = truck fixed cost per day,
D_h = driver cost per hour,
hrs./day = total duty hours per day,
pcs./hr. = number of pieces that could be delivered per hour,
hrs./mi. = hours per mile for the truck,
D_f = driver fixed time per day, such as check in and check out, coffee time, etc.

It can be seen that this incremental cost, the cost of a delivered truck load (only one per day) at the edge of the territory expressed in dollars/

[5] William H. Whyte, Jr., *The Organization Man* (New York: Simon and Schuster, Inc., 1956), pp. 23–26.

piece, is an increasing function of the variable to be manipulated by management, P_d, the distance to the perimeter of the plant warehouse territory (i.e., how large should the territory be?). As this distance (area) was increased, the incremental cost/piece increased. This was for two reasons. The numerator, which is cost per day, increases with P_d, i.e., $2T_m \times P_d$. The denominator, which represents the number of pieces which can be delivered from the truck (and per day), decreases with an increase in P_d, i.e., $-2P_d \times$ hrs./mi.

The incremental gain expression was as follows:

$$IG = \frac{S_l + B_e + 2S_oD_p + S_f + 2S_d \cdot \text{hrs./mi.} \cdot D_p + I_w}{P_s} + \frac{2T_mD_b + T_f + D_h \cdot \text{hrs./day}}{\text{pcs./hr.}\ (\text{hrs./day} - 2D_b \cdot \text{hrs./mi.} - D_f)}$$

where the additional notation is

S_l = semi (trailer truck) load and unload costs,
B_e = branch expense per semi,
S_o = semi operating cost per mile,
D_p = miles from plant to branch,
S_f = semi fixed costs per day (an amortization type charge),
S_d = semi driver cost per hour,
I_w = inventory cost per semi,
P_s = pieces per semi,
D_b = miles from branch to delivery.

The expression for incremental gain represents the cost of making the same delivery from a branch warehouse, including the intermediate step of shipment to that warehouse. Therefore it is shown in two steps. It is considered as the incremental gain because a delivery made from the plant does not have to be made from the branch, and as the plant territory is increased, incurring the incremental costs, the deliveries from the branches are saved, providing the incremental gains. This increase (conceptually) in the plant territory is continued as long as the incremental costs are less than the incremental gains, or until IC = IG, the equation of condition.[6]

Case B:

The Zion Truck Rental Company

The Zion Truck Rental Company was in the business of renting trucks and automobiles to the general public. The company excluded college students from its car rental clientele because of an impression that wear-and-tear was too high for that category of customers. This case, however, is concerned

[6] Edward H. Bowman and Robert B. Fetter, *Analysis for Production Management* (Homewood, Illinois: Richard Irwin, 1957), pp. 281–283.

with trucks, not automobiles. In particular, the problem is one of the replacement of trucks.

The company maintained a fleet of thirty trucks of different models, makes, and sizes. The replacement policy of the company was simple: replacement at 100,000 miles. The actual practice did not reflect this policy. All but two of the trucks were replaced before the 100,000 mile limit was reached. In some cases, the company found that the trucks were not of the right size to meet customer needs and replaced them with larger trucks. In other cases, maintenance costs reached a level that seemed to call for replacement.

A young research worker won co-operation from the company in examining its records. He was interested in determining whether the systematic application of a mathematical equipment replacement model would reduce company costs. The company had at one time kept records on fuel consumption, but had not found them useful and had destroyed them. Company officials argued, however, that fuel costs had little relation to age. It was true, they stated, that fuel costs would go up for a while, but after a tune-up they would fall again. It was the time since the tune-up, rather than age, that determined fuel costs.

The other considerations that might be fitted into a mathematical model were the rate of obsolescence (new trucks presumably being more productive than old ones because of technological improvements), the decline in the trade-in value of the trucks as they became older, and maintenance costs. The research worker decided to start with maintenance costs. The company turned maintenance records over to him. In the main, these were receipts for repairs performed at a local garage. The receipts indicated the particular vehicle that had undergone repair. They did not cover all parts replacements, however, since the company did some of its own parts replacement work. Unfortunately there were no adequate records on these replacements.

The research worker then set about to analyze the maintenance cost records systematically. His aim was to determine whether there was a clear-cut change in maintenance costs as age (measured either in years or miles) increased. He plotted quarterly maintenance costs on a scatter diagram, with the mileage of the vehicle on the horizontal axis and maintenance cost on the vertical axis. The dots did not fall into a recognizable pattern. There were some low maintenance costs at 60,000 to 80,000 miles as well as at 5,000 to 10,000 miles. There were some high costs between 40,000 to 60,000 miles but many more low costs. Furthermore, the research worker recognized that his sample was biased. Some vehicles were traded in at 50,000 or 60,000 miles—they might have shown high maintenance costs if they were retained, but there were no data to indicate whether or not this was true. The researcher was also disturbed by the fact that there were a number of different kinds of trucks in the group and that probably it was improper to show them all on the same graph. But graphs for single trucks, or even for three or four, showed such erratic patterns that they obscured any relationship.

The issue became one of deciding whether to continue with the analysis. A related question was whether a systematic mathematical treatment of maintenance costs, and of the other variables, such as fuel costs and obsolescence, would lead to a more profitable company policy. He was open to suggestions as to what types of simple models, if any, could be built which would help the management in its equipment replacement decisions.

Case C:

Economic Equipment Policies: An Evaluation (Vernon L. Smith)

Consider a firm engaged in a process of production requiring units of a particular class of industrial equipment, such as trucks, metal working machines, chemical reactors, pumping equipment, and so forth. Suppose, for the sake of reducing the problem to its most essential elements, that the equipment employed by the firm is all of the same make, model and vintage.

Also, for the present, let the common assumption be entertained, that output and therefore the stock of machines is held constant. An economic replacement policy for the firm is defined as one that optimally spaces the purchases and retirements of the firm's stock of equipment. This is determined by finding that period of equipment service that maximizes the present value of the net earnings profile of the present and all future equipment in the chain of renewals extending as far into the future as the firm's profit horizon. If that horizon is taken to be infinite, then mathematically the problem is to maximize

$$v = \sum_{k=\theta}^{\infty} e^{-\rho kL} \left\{ \int_0^L Q(kL,t) e^{-\rho t}\, dt - p + S(L) e^{-\rho L} \right\} \tag{1.1}$$

with respect to L, where v is the present value of the net earnings profile per unit of equipment, ρ is the continuous rate of interest, L is the period of equipment service in, say, years, p is the initial cost per unit of the equipment under consideration, and $S(L)$ is its market resale value after L years of service.

The function $Q(kL,t)$ represents the earnings or quasi-rent of a unit of equipment net only of its operating costs, as a function of its age t and the point in calendar time, kL, when the equipment was purchased new. It is technological—or more accurately, structural—change, affecting the performance of successive new models of equipment, that causes equipment earnings to depend upon the calendar time that has elapsed up to the point at which the kth replacement is made.

A graph of $Q(kL,t)$ is shown in Figure 24-1 for the special case in which Q is linear in kL and t, i.e., where

$$Q(kL,t) = A + \alpha kL - \beta t; \qquad k = 0,1,2,.. \tag{1.2}$$

and the origin is the point in calendar time at which the present equipment was placed in service. The term $A + \alpha kL$ is the obsolescence function as

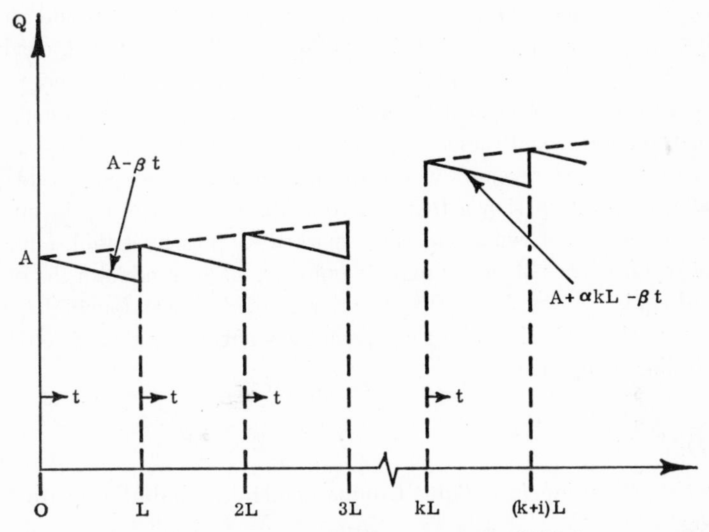

FIGURE 24-1 Graph of Quasi-rent Profile $Q(kL,t)$

measured by the effect of structural change on the initial earnings of the new equipment that becomes available each year. It is assumed that structural change does not alter the (in this case linear) shape of the earnings profile, but increases the *initial* intercept rate of earnings of new equipment at the rate of α dollars/year/year. After an asset has been in service L years, it will have accumulated an obsolescence of αL dollars/year relative to the newest model then available.[7]

If $R(kL,t)$ is the gross revenue rate and $E(kL,t)$ the operating expense rate of the equipment, then the quasi-rent function can be written as

$$Q(kL,t) = R(kL,t) - E(kL,t) \tag{1.3}$$

In general, one will expect $R(kL,t)$ to be a nondecreasing function of kL, and a nonincreasing function of t, while $E(kL,t)$ will be a nonincreasing function of kL, and a nondecreasing function of t. As a rule, revenue will be expected to fall and expenses to rise with age, while revenue will rise and expenses fall with technological advance. . . .

[It] seems fair to assert that the results of this inquiry tend to show that trucking firms, and perhaps business firms generally, are not likely to follow replacement policies that deviate seriously from optimal policies. This is

[7] The term $\alpha + \beta$ is what George Terborgh (*Dynamic Equipment Policy* [New York: McGraw-Hill Book Co., Inc., 1949]) calls the inferiority gradient or the total rate at which an existing installation develops inferiority relative to the most recently available model. In the present treatment the inferiority gradient has been divided into an obsolescence component α and a deterioration component β.

especially true when we measure the deviation in terms of the relative cost of alternative policies. This conclusion need not apply to all types of equipment nor to all industries since it is certainly possible for the various parameters of the replacement problem to assume values which would yield a sensitive profit optimum. But it does not appear likely that such conditions will occur often, simply because the only components of cost and revenue that enter into the replacement decision are those which vary with equipment age and technology, and these components are normally small in comparison with those costs and revenues which are independent of age and technology.

Finally, it has been shown that, whereas equipment theory may not be a business decision tool which can effect marked savings by establishing more rational replacement policies, it may be quite useful as a guide to the optimal choice of equipment type. In the example studied, it was found that under certain conditions diesel trucking equipment can effect considerable economies over gasoline equipment.[8]

Case D:

Production Planning in a Paint Company (Holt, Modigliani, Muth and Simon)

At an early stage in our research program a large company gave us the opportunity to work on live decision problems by providing us access to the operations of one of its divisions. The cooperation of this company is responsible in no small part for the results we have obtained.

Background. The effort to carry sufficient inventory of each product at warehouses and retail stores had built up total inventories that seemed excessively large. Nevertheless, demand runs on individual products resulted in stockouts, lost sales, and extreme demands on factory production during the peak sales season. One technique for coping with this situation was use of several types of priority orders on the factory, in addition to normal replenishment orders. There was some interest in the company in the possibility of ameliorating the situation by centralizing information on stocks and sales at all levels, with the probable exception of information from independent retailers. That such a policy might pay off was indicated by the fact that an informal and partial system of this sort was said to have worked quite well.

The company was also interested in stabilizing production throughout the year. It appeared that employees tended to reduce their efforts in the off season in an attempt to spread out the work. A policy of smooth production would possibly remove fear of seasonal layoffs and improve efficiency. It

[8] Vernon L. Smith, "Economic Equipment Policies: An Evaluation," *Management Science,* October 1957, republished in Edward H. Bowman and Robert B. Fetter, eds., *Analyses of Industrial Operations* (Homewood, Illinois: Richard D. Irwin, 1959), pp. 444–462.

might also reduce the premium costs associated with overtime payments during the peak season. However, stabilized production would lead to higher inventory costs because of wide seasonal fluctuations in sales.

The factory management wanted to schedule economical production runs of each product without excessively large inventories at the factory warehouse. The factory problem was further complicated by emergency orders from the warehouses, which required prompt filling to keep customers satisfied and to minimize lost sales.

Research on Quantitative Decision Analysis: The research team undertook to study the factory decisions, the warehouse decisions, and factory-warehouse joint decisions. We studied the structure of the decision problems including goals, costs, relationships, forecasts, and the decisions to be made. When those were expressed in mathematical form we faced some unsolved analytical problems that called for research. Our objective was to obtain simple mathematical decision rules that could be easily used to make decisions that would be the best or close to the best in terms of management's objectives.

Simulation Test of Rules for Aggregate Production and Work Force: Initially we made an analysis of the aggregate decisions at the factory. We formulated a mathematical model that took into account the costs of the regular payroll, overtime, finished goods inventory at the factory warehouse, back orders, hiring, and layoffs. By solving the mathematical problem we obtained simple decision rules (or formulas) that indicated for any planning period the production and size of the work force that would yield the lowest costs, taking into account the current inventory position, the number of employees and the forecasts of future demands on the factory. . . .

The production and work force decisions that the paint company had made over a six-year period were analyzed in detail. With this knowledge of the decision problems that had confronted the paint factory, the decision rules were applied, after the fact, to simulate what would have occurred if the new rules had been used during this period.

To calculate this hypothetical performance, there was needed for each planning period a set of forecasts of future orders (in order to calculate the corresponding employment and production decisions for that point in time). Since no explicit forecasts had been recorded by the company, we could not operate with the same forecast information that had been available to the factory management when their decisions were made. As a substitute, two different sets of forecasts were computed which, in terms of accuracy, would probably bracket the forecasts that had been available to the company. The first set of forecasts are the data on actual orders. Such a *perfect forecast* depends of course on hindsight, and hence could not actually be used in planning for the future. However, the perfect forecast establishes the upper limit to the improvement that could be obtained by a good decision rule. The second set of forecasts was simply a moving average of past orders.

The total of orders for the coming year was forecasted to be equal to the orders that had been received in the year just past. This *moving average forecast* was then converted to a monthly basis by applying a known seasonal adjustment. We now had a basis for a three-way comparison of decision performance: (1) the actual performance of the factory, (2) the performance of the optimal decision rule with perfect forecasts, and (3) the performance of the optimal decision rule with moving average forecasts which set a lower limit to that forecasting accuracy likely to be attained in practice.

The extreme variability of the orders received by the paint factory is shown in Figure 24-2. Depressed business conditions are clearly reflected in the first year. The effects of inventory speculation by distributors and dealers is shown in the later high orders and rapid decline of orders thereafter, coincident with eased tensions. Hence, the time covered by this study includes a period of extreme order fluctuations as well as a period of more moderate fluctuations. The severity of the fluctuations gives some assurance that the decision rules will be subjected to a severe test. Although it is not quickly to be seen, there is a significant seasonal pattern in orders.

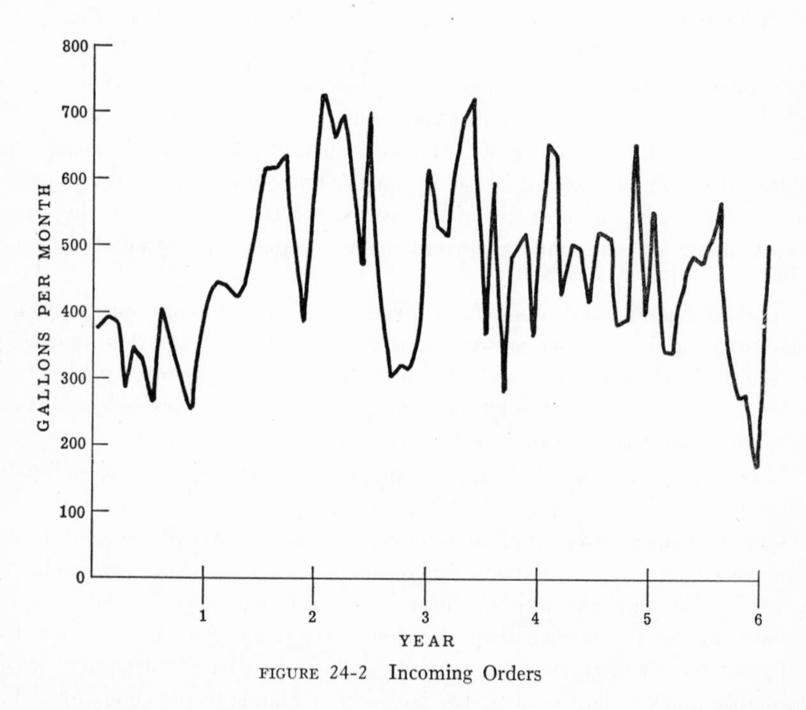

FIGURE 24-2 Incoming Orders

Figure 24-3 shows that the actual production fluctuations of the factory were considerably sharper on a month-to-month basis than those called for by the decision rule with either moving average or perfect forecasts. With a perfect forecast the decision rule avoids almost completely sharp month-to-month fluctuations in production, but responds to fluctuations of orders that persist over several months.

The decisions scheduling the size of the work force are shown in Figure 24-4. Again, the decision rule proposes smoother changes and avoids sharp month to month fluctuations in work force. The fluctuations in work force with the perfect forecast, while substantial in size, are actually occasioned by the severity of order fluctuations and the desire to avoid costly accumulations of inventory and back orders. The additional work force fluctuations that are observed under the moving average forecast are attributable to forecast errors. For example, an erroneous forecast of high sales yields the decision rule to build up the work force. The combination of low sales and large work force causes an accumulation of inventories which, in turn, necessitates a reduction in the work force to reduce inventory to the optimal level. The differences shown in Figure 24-4 between work force fluctuations under the perfect forecast and under the moving average forecast, using the same decision rule in both cases, illustrate the importance of accurate forecasts to the stability of employment.

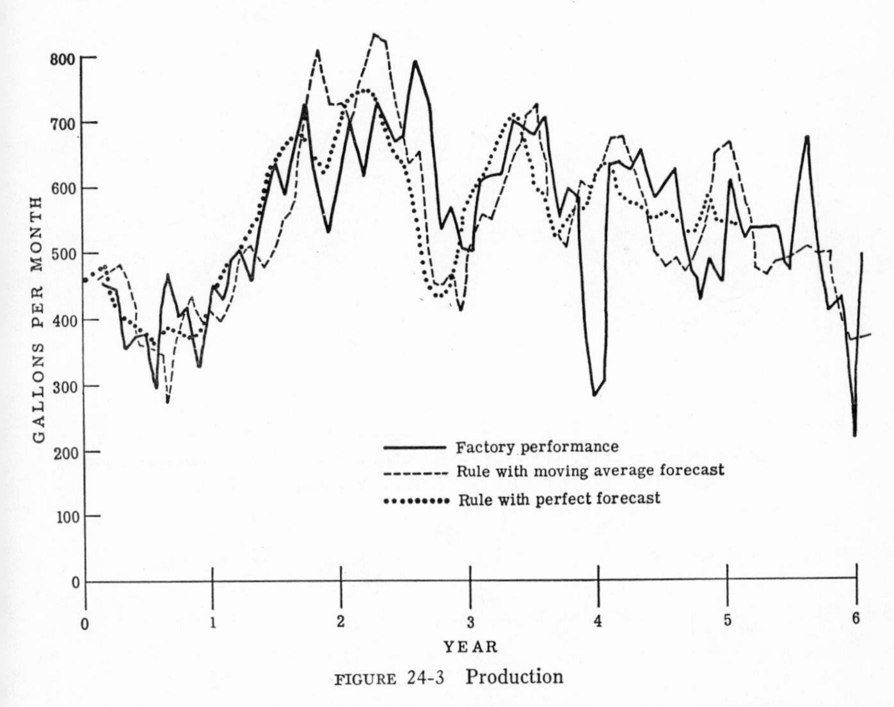

FIGURE 24-3 Production

The perfect forecast foresaw the increased orders and increased the size of the work force sharply in the second year. Using the moving average forecasts, the decision rule increased the work force about six months later. While the factory actually started its employment buildup as early as the decision rule did, using perfect forecasts, its rate of buildup was considerably slower; consequently, its peak of employment occurred at the time when, as it happened, orders declined sharply. The decision rule using the moving average forecast worked tolerably well even under such severe circumstances as the outbreak of war.

Overtime hours are plotted in Figure 24-5 to compare performance between the factory and the decision rule. The inadequacies of the moving average forecast appear clearly in the second year, when the sudden increase in orders, which was not foreseen by the backward-looking forecast, led to a large amount of overtime.

Performance in the control of inventory is shown in Figures 24-6 and 24-7. These show separately the two components of net inventory: actual physical inventory and back orders. The decision rule operating with the perfect forecast displays in Figure 24-6 the ability to hold inventories quite close to the level that gives the lowest cost of inventory-holding and back orders. Deviations from this optimal level do occur, but they are not of large amplitude.

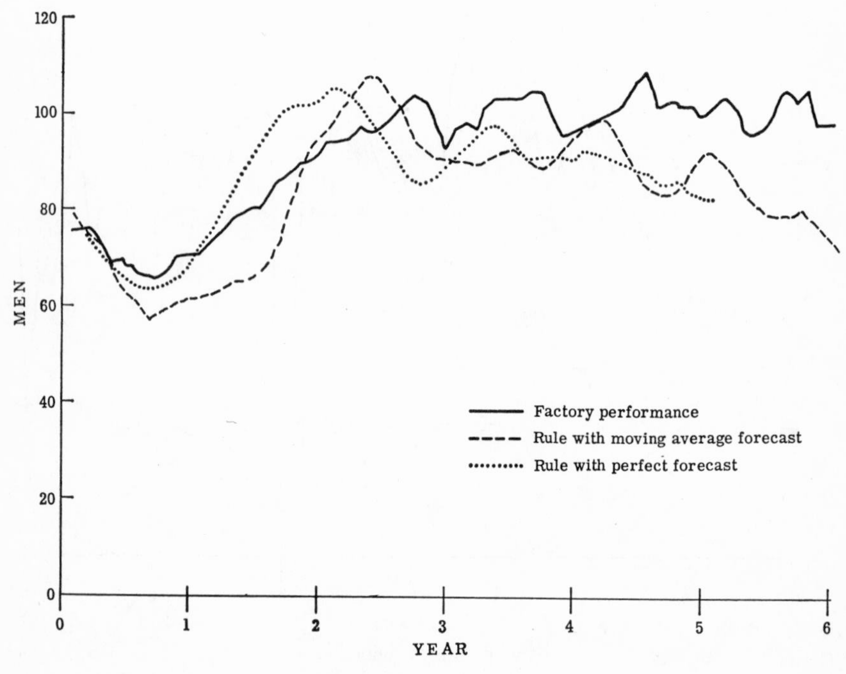

FIGURE 24-4 Work Force

In contrast, the decision rule operating with the moving average forecast allowed inventories to fall substantially during the sudden increase in sales, and later, when orders declined, inventory rose sharply. However, inventory recovered from its low point much earlier under the decision rule than the factory actually did. When orders declined sharply in the winter, the decision rule using the moving average forecast was able to bring down the resulting excess inventories about as quickly as the factory did in fact.

The penalty that accompanies low inventory appears clearly in the plot of back orders in Figure 24-7. With the moving average forecast, back orders rose sharply during the period of demand, but these back orders were soon liquidated. For the actual factory performance, back orders did not return to their normal level until much later. When high orders are speculative, as was the case during this period, it is difficult to judge how much weight should be attached to the poor service to customers evidenced by large back orders. The decision rule treated these back orders seriously and responded accordingly.

Cost Comparisons. One way to judge decision-making performance is to apply the criteria that serve as the basis for the decisions. To the extent

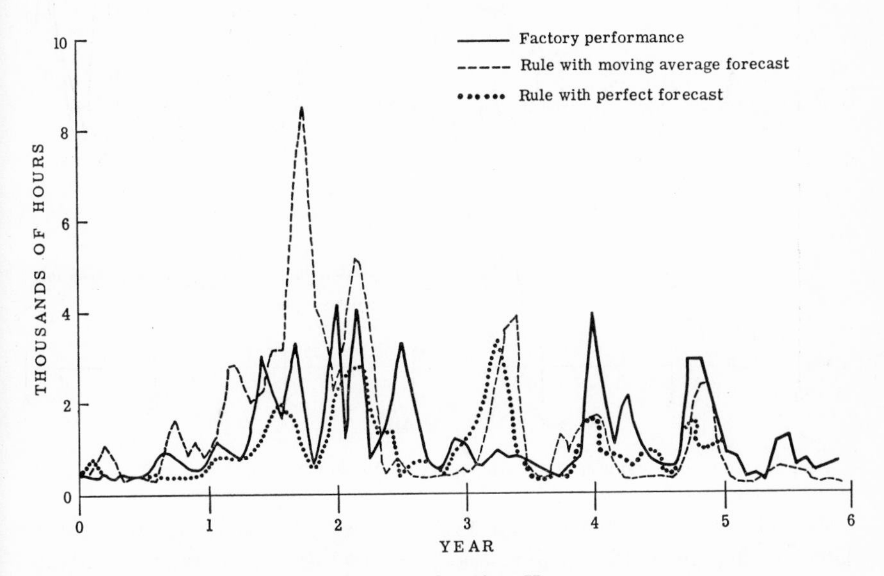

FIGURE 24-5 Overtime Hours

that minimizing the costs (that appear in the cost function) was the goal of the factory management, the comparison between the costs of the factory and of the decision rule calculated on this basis is significant. However, the production executives were concerned during this six-year period with other goals besides minimizing the particular costs that were included in the statistical decision analysis. Pursuit of the other goals would undoubtedly raise these costs. Hence, performance comparisons based exclusively on the types of costs that are included in the cost function do not tell the whole story.

Because reconstructing a history of factory operations for six years is itself a substantial research job—involving in this case the allocation of costs between paint and other products, the indirect calculation of certain information that had never been recorded, and the estimation of non-accounting costs—the figures that were obtained must be presented with a certain tentativeness. The estimates of what the costs would have been *if* things had been done differently are particularly subject to limitations in accuracy. In spite of their limitations, the cost differences to be presented are, in our opinion, significant. To evaluate the cost performance of the decision rules, we used, so far as possible, the exact (non-quadratic) cost structure estimated directly from the factory accounting and other data.

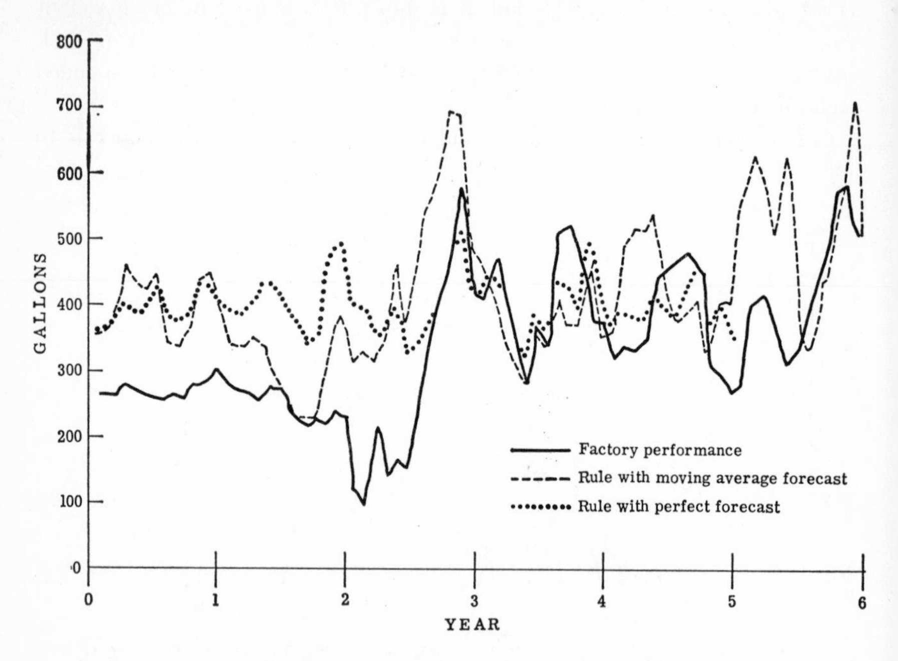

FIGURE 24-6 Inventory at End of Month

Payroll, overtime, inventory, back order, hiring, and layoff were calculated for five years, the longest period for which cost figures were available for a complete three-way comparison. The decision rule, operating with the modest forecasting ability of the moving average, gave a cost saving compared to the factory performance of 29 per cent on the average.

The decision rule with perfect forecasts had lower costs than with moving average forecasts, by ten per cent on the average. Since the same decision rule is used with both sets of forecasts, this difference in cost performance is entirely attributable to improved forecasting. How much of this saving could have been achieved by substituting more refined forecasting methods for the moving average, we do not know. Obviously, perfect forecasts are unattainable. However, the data suggest that the expenditure of some thousands of dollars for improved forecasts would more than pay for itself in decreased production costs even for this small factory.

It is worth noting that the cost saving attributable to use of the decision rule is greater than the additional cost saving that would be secured by the complete elimination of forecast errors. Perhaps forecasting future orders accurately isn't as important as has commonly been thought by production people. Judging by this particular factory and period, making good use of crude forecasts is more important than forecasting perfectly.

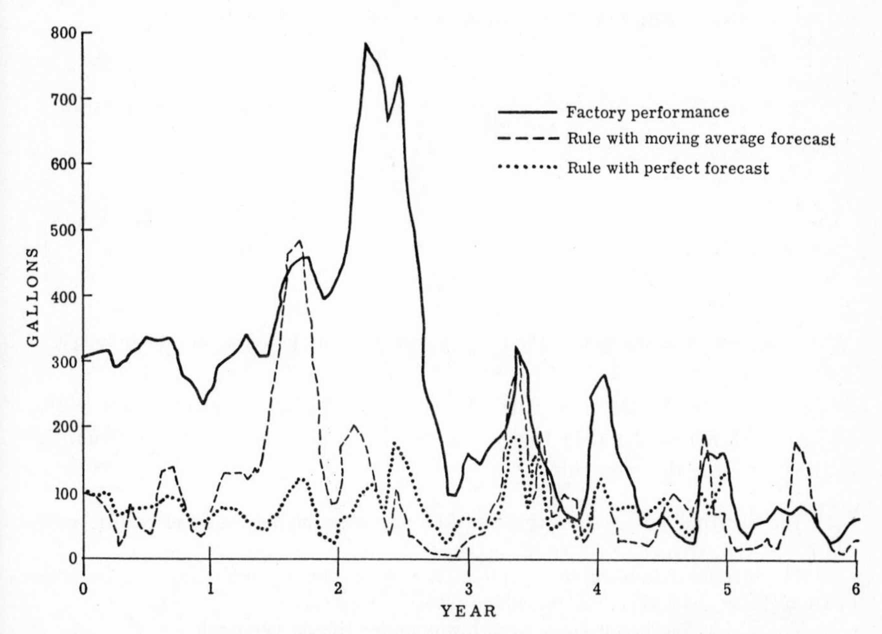

FIGURE 24-7 Backlog of Unfilled Orders at End of Month

Scheduling production and employment in a period of recession and war is difficult, because of large and unpredictable fluctuations in orders. It is understandable that savings through improved decision techniques should be large. The period also poses obstacles to estimating an appropriate penalty cost for back orders.

Cost comparisons for periods that exclude the second year should be more representative of normal times. If we drop out the second year and compare the perfect forecast cost performance with that of the moving average for the remaining four years, we find that the imperfect forecasting raises costs five per cent on the average, compared to ten per cent when the second year is included.

The plot of actual factory inventory in Figure 24-6 shows that the factory in its control of inventories acted *as if* the cost of back orders relative to the cost of holding inventories had increased during the six-year period. The cost structure that we estimated is more nearly in line with the implicit back order and inventory costs of the later three-year period. Consequently, cost comparisons from the later period may be more significant than cost comparisons covering the whole six years.

To compare the cost performances of the factory, and the decision rule with moving average forecasts when sales follow a fairly normal pattern of fluctuations, we chose the final three-year period. As shown in Table 24-1

TABLE 24-1

COMPANY AND DECISION RULE COST COMPARISONS *

Costs for Final 3-year Period	*Company Performance*	*Decision Rule, Moving Average Forecast*
Regular payroll	643.1	588.3
Overtime	42.0	48.6
Inventory	139.8	152.6
Back orders	166.9	126.0
Hiring and layoffs	8.2	6.1
Total Cost	1000.0	921.6

* The costs were scaled so that the total cost of company performance equals 1000.0.

the costs under the decision rule with moving average forecasts were eight per cent below the actual factory costs for the three-year period. Economies achieved by the decision rule:

1. The overtime costs under the decision rule were higher, but the regular payroll costs were enough lower to make a net saving;
2. The inventory holding costs were higher under the decision rule, but the back order penalty costs were low enough to make a net saving;
3. The hiring and layoff costs were lower under the decision rule.

It appears that the cost savings during this period of normal paint sales were attained by the decision rule through a combination of several different kinds of cost savings, and not through some simple improvement that might be hit upon through casual analysis.

It may be objected that our estimates of the factory cost structure might be in error, so that the factory performance is being judged by an erroneous criterion. Such errors are possible, but it should be remembered that the decision rule is designed to minimize a given cost function. If the cost estimates were changed, the costing of factory performance would be different, but also a new decision rule would be calculated—of which the decision behavior would be different. Consequently if in the cost structure changes were made that would reduce the estimated cost of the factory performance, the estimate would then have to be compared with the cost performance of a decision rule changed to be optimal under the new cost function.

The cost savings of eight per cent by the use of the decision rule and an additional five per cent saving from improved forecasts are, in the opinion of the authors, reasonable estimates, but it should be kept in mind that the size of the first of these figures depends as much on the original judgmental decisions as on the decision rules.

We believe that these comparisons between the actual decision performance of the factory and the hypothetical performance of the decision rule justify the following conclusion: *If the decision rule were to be applied using practically obtainable forecasts, it would perform significantly better than the judgmental methods that have been used by the factory.* Furthermore, this improved performance probably could be obtained with a smaller expenditure of executive time and effort than that which previously went into the decisions.

Factory Test. When further research produced decision rules for allocating the aggregate production to individual products . . . the company management decided to institute an operating test of the new decision methods. A sample of products was chosen that constituted roughly ten per cent of the sales volume of the factory. The aggregate production of these products was controlled by a decision rule as if they constituted the entire output of the factory. This production was scheduled over the products in a way that kept back orders to the minimum consistent with keeping total inventory low. Six months of operations on this basis showed that fluctuations in aggregate production were reduced, and both back orders and inventory levels were reduced.

These encouraging results led to a decision to increase the number of products controlled by the decision rules so that 25 per cent of the total sales volume was involved in the test. A special effort was made to include slow-moving products whose sales tended to be erratic. Again the operating test proved successful. Ultimately the new decision system was adopted for all the products that were produced to stock. This accounted for roughly three-fourths of the factory's production. Management was pleased with the results, and the decision rules have been guides in production planning for several years.

During this period, monthly production of nearly a thousand products has been scheduled by a clerk using a desk computer. Sixteen hours of clerical work are required each month to prepare product sales forecasts for the following month. Sixteen hours are required to bring the product inventory positions up-to-date. Twenty-six hours are required to apply the decision rules for making decisions on aggregate production, aggregate work force, and production of individual products. Once a year twenty-four hours are required to calculate new seasonal patterns for each of the products. This works out to about 3.8 minutes monthly of clerical time to schedule a month's production of a product. Additional time is required to expedite production and assign production to machines.

These figures show that even a small operation can apply these methods —the factory in this case employed roughly a hundred people. On the basis of the results achieved in the factory test, the company assigned regular company personnel to investigate extending the decision system to include the warehouses, and to study the possibilities of using an electronic computer in operating the system centrally.

Warehouse Simulation Study. A tentative warehouse inventory control system was given a 30-day simulation test on a sample of eight important products. The results were encouraging. In addition to showing that the proposed system would function in principle, it suggested that inventories could be reduced by 40 per cent and customer service improved at the same time. When these results were presented to management, it was decided that a larger sample of products and warehouses spanning a longer period of time should be analyzed as the basis for a final evaluation and decision.

A five-man study group representing the departments of the company that were directly affected was appointed. The primary responsibility of the study group was to select a fairly large sample which could be thoroughly analyzed to compare what actually did happen with what would have happened under the proposed system. To obtain a representative sample seven warehouses at varying distances from the factory and with different sales volumes were chosen. A record was obtained for each warehouse, on a weekly basis, of every product received at the factory and every product shipped. This information, for a period of 52 weeks, was punched into 200,000 cards. (An electronic computer was required to handle the simulation problem because of its size.)

Comparisons between the simulated system and the actual performance were to be based on three factors: inventory levels, number of stock-outs, and shipping costs. The data were collected for the actual operations of the warehouses, and generated for the proposed system by starting the simulated system with a given inventory and allowing the proposed inventory control system to operate the warehouses through the remainder of the test period. The test provided a weekly record of actual and simulated inventory balances; the volume, frequency, and duration of actual and simulated stock-outs; the cost of actual and simulated shipments; and the composition and kind of simulated shipments. In the test the proposed system compared with the existing one as follows:

1. Average inventories were reduced by 50 per cent, at the same sales volume.
2. It was estimated that sales would have increased by five per cent because inventories, although lower, were in better balance and fewer stock-outs occurred.
3. Freight costs were reduced by five per cent because the proposed system called for large, regular shipments, and fewer emergency shipments, and reduced interwarehouse transfers of inventory.

In addition to the results of the simulation tests, visits to the warehouses indicated that management personnel were devoting too much time to clerical functions. Maintaining inventory and sales records was purely a clerical task, but frequent turnover of personnel imposed on the manager the burden of training replacements, and maintaining close supervision. The accuracy and value of the records was directly dependent upon the amount of time the manager devoted to this task.

Ultimately, the recommendation was made to the board of directors that the company institute the proposed system and install an electronic computer. The recommendation stated that the proposed system had the following advantages which could not be evaluated quantitatively:

1. The manufacturing and distributing activities would be co-ordinated both as to current decisions and future plans.
2. Clear-cut routines would be established for decisions on most products, so that more time and flexibility will be left to management to handle exceptional cases.
3. Inventory would be distributed among the factories and warehouses so as to be of best advantage to the company as a whole.
4. Through the exception method, management would be provided with more information in fewer reports.
5. The tendency to ever increasing clerical cost would be avoided, particularly where turnover and training expenses are high.
6. Although data processing would be centralized, the responsibility and authority for the successful operation of each factory and warehouse would remain as it is—decentralized.

The board of directors approved the recommendation and preparations currently are under way for introducing the new decision system.

Much of the improvement in the system is expected to result from the fact that the information flows would be speeded up by the centralization of sales information. Where formerly a factory might be acting on information that lagged behind warehouse sales by as much as six to eight weeks, this lag would be reduced to a few days, a week at the most.

When the new system is fully extended to roughly half a dozen factories each supplying a set of distribution warehouses, annual net savings are conservatively estimated to be more than two times the estimated cost of $700,000 for staff, and rental and installation of a large electronic computer to implement the system.[9]

[9] Charles C. Holt, Franco Modigliani, John F. Muth, and Herbert A. Simon, *Planning Production, Inventories, and Work Force* (Englewood Cliffs, N. J.: Prentice-Hall, Inc., 1960), pp. 15–28. The system is being designed and installed by the Electronic Planning Department in cooperation with the Paint Division.

25

Probability and Statistics in Management Decisions

UNCERTAINTY is a pervasive feature of management. Today managers must make decisions governing future operations without complete knowledge about the nature of future conditions or the efficacy of various alternatives.

Two opposite reactions to uncertainty are possible. One is to conclude that the future is so unpredictable that no refined analysis is justified; the manager with this viewpoint will resort to a rule of thumb or another short cut. The other is to deal systematically with the uncertainty itself, with careful evaluations of probabilities and applications of statistics wherever possible. Usually it is economical to take some intermediate position between complete reliance on "hunches" and minute analysis of every element of uncertainty.

This chapter is concerned with the treatment of probabilities. Managers who are familiar with methods for dealing with probabilities should be more capable of making sound decisions, whether or not they carry out the analysis in detail. Probability theory and statistical analysis involve a *point of view* that is certainly useful in itself. Since this chapter is an introduction to the subject, its aim will be to explain this point of view rather than to develop trained statisticians in one or two easy lessons.

Probablity As a Point of View

Degrees of uncertainty

Uncertainty varies in degree from one kind of decision to another. A few illustrations should make this clear. The illustrations are ranked in order from relatively high uncertainty to relatively low.

(1) Let us consider the case (an actual problem observed in a recent study of decisions) of a dry cleaning establishment considering setting up a new branch. This firm has heretofore operated entirely from its central plant. Now it is contemplating renting space for a branch for receiving and delivering clothes to be cleaned—the actual cleaning will still be done in the central plant.

The uncertainty in this case is high for several reasons. While the company has access to population estimates for the area surrounding the new shopping center where the branch would be located, it does not know what proportion of that population actually uses the shopping center. Nor is it clear into what income brackets these families fall, or how frequently they use cleaning facilities. There is uncertainty about the effect of branches of other cleaning firms in other shopping centers and the importance of door-to-door delivery service. In short, the greatest uncertainty relates to the potential demand for the branch's services—the company can make fairly accurate estimates of costs based on its past experience.

If this company had established other branches in the past, it might have a sounder basis for probability analysis; or if it had access to the experience of other firms, the uncertainty would be less severe. The question is whether under these circumstances one can do better than apply a hunch or a rule of thumb. The management can take action to *reduce* the risks involved in investing in the branch. It may be desirable to maintain high flexibility in costs—for example, to lease space on a short term contract rather than to buy a building.

There are ways of reducing the uncertainty about demand. For example, it is possible that a market survey would provide a more exact estimate of potential demand. Then the problem would be to weigh the costs of the survey, which might involve door-to-door canvassing of the neighborhood or a sample survey, against the reduction of uncertainty that would result.

This illustration is by no means at the absolute extreme of uncertainty. After all, the service being sold, cleaning, is one with which this firm and others have had experience. If the product were a new one, never before tested in the market, the uncertainty would be even greater.

(2) A problem involving less uncertainty, and one thus more amenable to probability analysis, is the well-known question of scrap allowances. A company, which produces on order and which does not maintain an inventory of finished goods because each order is different, is faced with the problem of scheduling extra units to allow for scrap in the process of production. If the particular order under consideration is enough like former orders, information about the proportion of scrap on these earlier orders will help in the evaluation of the current problem. If too few extra units are scheduled, there may not be enough good units to fill the order—there may be heavy expenses in setting up production of added units. If too many extra units are produced, there will be waste of materials, labor, and machine time

spent on unneeded production. Information on past orders will clarify the probability that, let us say, five per cent extra units, or ten per cent, and so on, will be needed. Later in this chapter there will be a discussion of how these probabilities would be treated in arriving at an economical decision. The point here is to recognize that this is the kind of problem in which probability analysis makes sense. It is reasonable to believe that those managers who keep records on past experience and use this experience in establishing probabilities on future orders are more likely to make sound decisions on scrap allowances.

(3) Another case in which the systematic evaluation of probabilities is applicable is the problem of determining the size of inventories. Too small an inventory will result in the loss of sales or too many setups. Too large an inventory will involve unnecessary carrying costs, that is, storage costs, interest costs, risks of obsolescence, and so on. Past experience may provide a basis for establishing the probabilities that additional units will be needed. Such probabilities can then be used in determining the appropriate inventory size, as later sections of this chapter will explain.

(4) Quality control is an area in which statistical analysis has been applied for several decades. Inspection of each individual item of output, to determine whether it meets specifications or not, may be too expensive. Fortunately, it is possible to take samples from the total output which will provide enough information about the total output to tell us the extent to which standards are being met. This is another application of probability analysis. The samples do not state exactly what the charactertistics of the total output are, but they do provide highly accurate estimates of those characteristics along with measures of how much error is likely. Statistical quality control is so important that it will receive special attention later in this chapter.

(5) The case of insurance is the earliest application of statistical analysis to personal and business problems. Insurance is a method for converting uncertainty into certainty by the pooling of risks. The owner of a house, for example, faces the possibility of the loss of that house by fire, but he is highly uncertain about the chances that the loss will occur. Insurance companies can convert the high degree of uncertainty about individual losses into a high degree of certainty about pooled losses.

Insurance rests upon the *law of large numbers,* a fundamental principle in the theory of probability. This law states that certain mass phenomena have a tendency toward regularity in behavior. There will be a high degree of uncertainty about drawing the ace of spades from a deck of cards on the first try. But out of 5,200 trials from complete decks, there is a high degree of certainty that between 95 and 105 aces of spades will be drawn. The number of houses that will burn down may be estimated fairly accurately in the mass, even though we cannot know exactly which houses these will be.

Similarly, past experience will provide reasonably accurate estimates of the numbers of deaths that will take place in each age category.

Only when the law of large numbers is applicable, is a sound insurance program possible. The principle may not apply to earthquakes, for example, unless one considers a long period of time. When regularity in mass phenomena occurs it is possible to transfer risks. An individual or a business can pay premiums to an insurance company in return for a promise to pay for fire losses. If a firm owned a large number of buildings—let us say 5,000—it might find it possible to use *self-insurance;* the predictability of fire losses each year might be stable enough that the company could absorb these losses as expenses without fear of a great financial blow in a single year. Normally, however, it is only when the uncertain losses of a large number of firms or individuals are pooled that the required degree of stability is achieved.

Insurance thus results in a reduction of uncertainty. In place of incurring a high degree of uncertainty about the occurrence of a particular event, the insured now pays a definite premium. The insurance company reduces the uncertainty by pooling the risks and applying the law of large numbers. This can be condensed into a definition of insurance as "a social device whereby the uncertain risks of individuals may be combined in a group and thus made more certain, small contributions by the individuals providing a fund out of which those who suffer losses may be reimbursed."[1]

(6) In many decisions there is so little uncertainty about some of the considerations that it can be ignored. For example, if a company produces one type of product over and over again, it can make estimates of cost for that product with a high degree of certainty. The problem is to select the appropriate cost concept—for example, the estimate of opportunity costs or incremental costs that is best suited to the decision at hand. Statistics will be of no assistance in selecting the correct measures of cost; once the measure is found, the uncertainty is likely to be so small that no evaluation of possible errors will pay for the effort involved.

Six kinds of situations, ranging from high uncertainty to low, have been presented. At the extremes, when uncertainty is so high it defies systematic treatment or so low it reduces the contribution of statistical analysis, management may be wise in not becoming too involved in the refinements of probability theory. Between these extremes, however, in those cases in which there is uncertainty and in which past experience or samples from present experience can help build up probability schedules, systematic treatment is frequently justified. In these cases, management must weigh the costs against the benefits to be derived from more thorough analysis of the problem.

[1] Robert Riegel and Jerome S. Miller, *Insurance Principles and Practices,* 4th edition (Englewood Cliffs, N. J.: Prentice-Hall, Inc., 1959), p. 26.

The personal element: likes and dislikes for risk

It is necessary to dispose of a complication that is difficult to handle—the fact that not all people have the same degree of aversion to uncertainty. Some people will go to considerable trouble to avoid risks. Such people will not only avoid a "fair" bet—for example, they will refuse to pay $1.00 for a one-hundredth chance to win $100. They will even avoid such risks when the odds are in their favor, as would be the case if the above bet cost only $.50. The reference is not to the aversion to gambling on moral grounds, but to the dislike of risk itself. Other individuals will be willing to pay $1.50 or even more to gain the chance to win the $100, and will do so even when there is no pleasure in the process of gambling itself.

If there are such differences in the taste for risk, how is it possible to give advice on decisions involving uncertainty? A decision that will seem too risky to one manager might appear to be an exciting challenge to another. One way of dealing with this problem is to measure the individual's willingness to take risks. Economists, psychologists, and statisticians have shown that this kind of measurement is possible in theory, even though it can involve difficulties in practice.

At our present state of knowledge, however, it is appropriate to cut through these individual differences in attitudes toward risk. For example, it involves little error to assume that the individual manager will treat a 50 per cent chance of winning $1,000 and 50 per cent chance of losing that amount as having no net gain. It is also reasonable to assume that most managers will not take a risk unless there is a potential premium involved. Most managers would reject the 50/50 risk mentioned above because it offers no such premium. The greater the uncertainty, and the larger the sums of money involved, the greater the risk premium required. A small firm, for example, might well reject a risk involving a 50 per cent chance of making $150,000 or a 50 per cent chance of losing $100,000 since the latter event would involve financial bankruptcy.

There is a steady flow of decisions in most firms. If the managers select those which offer greater chances of gain than of loss, they will be contributing to the over-all profitability of the concern over time. Some of the risks will fail. However, if there has been a correct evaluation of probabilities, a larger number will win, and by the law of large numbers, the taking of risks will contribute to profits. In addition, most companies are owned or managed by a number of individuals. Whose propensity for or aversion to risk should be taken into account? The separation of ownership and management in the large corporation makes it difficult to determine whose likes or dislikes for risk need be considered.

The rest of this discussion will ignore individual differences in the aversion to risk. For small sole proprietorships, these differences are important;

for larger concerns, it is enough to estimate the extent to which evaluation of uncertainty will contribute to profits over time, without worrying about individual differences of this kind.

An inventory problem

In developing this discussion of probabilities, it is best to start with the simplest illustrations. In the area of inventory decisions, the case of deciding how many Christmas trees a seller should stock in preparation for the coming season, is a classic for teaching purposes.[2] The uncertainty concerns demand—the seller does not know how many trees he will sell this year. The following assumptions are made:

1. No additional trees can be ordered after the selling season has started.
2. Unsold trees will involve a total loss.
3. The cost of each tree to the seller is $1.00 and his mark-up is $1.00.
4. The seller's estimates of sales are as follows:

100 per cent chance he will sell 1,000 trees or more
75 " " " " " " 1,300 " " "
50 " " " " " " 1,500 " " "
25 " " " " " " 1,800 " " "
0 " " " " " " 2,400 " " "

How many trees should the seller stock? The reader should try to work out the answer by common sense methods. He should recognize that if he stocks too few trees, he loses the profit of $1.00 per tree; if he stocks too many, he must junk trees costing him $1.00 each. It is reasonable that he should keep stocking trees up to the point at which the probability of having too many trees is equal to the probability of having too few. This is the point of 50 per cent probability, at which 1,500 trees are stocked.

Suppose the margin of profit is higher. In this case, the seller should take more of a risk, for now the reward for having trees on hand is potentially greater per tree than the penalty for having too many. If, for example, the markup were $3.00 per tree, it would be desirable to stock 1,800 trees. It is true that at this level, the chances of having too many trees (75 per cent) are three times as great as those of having too few (25 per cent)—but this is proportionate to the relative rewards and penalties.

The reader should have an intuitive feel for the following equation. In this kind of inventory situation, the seller should continue to stock additional units of X up to the point at which this equation holds:

$$p(x) = \frac{c}{m + c} \quad [3]$$

$$IG = IL$$

[2] This illustration is developed in E. H. Bowman and R. B. Fetter, *Analysis for Production Management* (Homewood, Ill.: Richard D. Irwin, 1957), pp. 285–287.

[3] The seller should stock inventory up to the point where incremental gain (IG) equals incremental loss (IL).

Incremental gain is the profit per tree times the probability of selling x trees, or

$$IG = m \cdot p(x)$$

where m = markup per tree (in dollars)
$p(x)$ = probability of selling x trees

Incremental loss is the cost of each tree times the probability that x trees will not be sold, or

$$IL = c \cdot [1 - p(x)]$$

where c = cost of each tree
$1 - p(x)$ = probability that x trees will not be sold

Hence:

$$IG = IL$$
$$m \cdot p(x) = c\,[1 - p(x)]$$
$$m \cdot p(x) = c - c \cdot p(x)$$
$$m \cdot p(x) + c \cdot p(x) = c$$
$$p(x)\,[m + c] = c$$
$$p(x) = \frac{c}{m + c}$$

The symbols have the following meanings:

$p(x)$ — The cumulative probability that this quantity or more will be sold
c — The loss per unit on quantities not sold
m — The markup per unit

The question that should be bothering the reader is where the probability schedule on the Christmas trees came from. This is the point at which the real difficulties arise. Past experience may help the seller formulate his probabilities, but the past is often a misleading guide to the future. If past sales have been erratic, fluctuating from year to year, there is a statistical problem of developing a table of probabilities from this record that goes beyond the scope of this volume. The seller may prefer to base his estimates on forecasts of selling conditions this year, but again he is faced with the problem of translating these forecasts into probability schedules.

It is desirable to point out that most inventory problems do not involve as great uncertainty as this Christmas tree problem. On most items, the company will have some fairly continuous experience, either on the item itself or on items closely comparable, so that probabilities can be established more firmly than in the illustration above. A more usual problem is that of min-max inventory control, in which the company uses the stocked item continuously but wishes to determine how much it should stock.

Min-max inventory control

A more typical situation than that just described is one in which there is continuous (or approximately continuous) usage of the inventory over time, with uncertainty about how much to keep on hand to meet the needs and to minimize costs. As before, the cost of keeping too small an inventory is the loss of sales that will result from running out of stock from time to time. The cost of too large inventories consists of storage costs, interest on the money tied up, and perhaps the risk of obsolescence incurred because unnecessarily large inventories are carried. The lot size (economic lot sizes are discussed elsewhere) will help determine the amount of inventory on hand at any particular moment, since it will indicate the quantity added to the inventory.

Two quantities must be determined in min-max inventory control: the reorder point and the order quantity. If there were no uncertainty, the pattern of the balance on hand might resemble that shown in Figure 25-1.

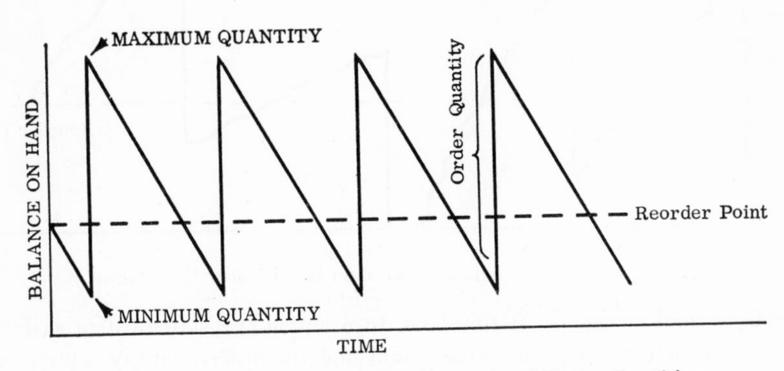

FIGURE 25-1 Fluctuations in Balance on Hand Under Conditions of Certainty

In this case, when the quantity on hand falls to the reorder point, an order is processed for the order quantity. Since there is no uncertainty, this order quantity will arrive just as the inventory falls to the minimum quantity. Thus inventory rises to the maximum—the maximum consisting of the minimum plus the order quantity. As usage continues, the inventory will again fall toward the reorder point.

This is not the situation in the usual inventory problem involving uncertainty. In the first place, it would not be necessary to maintain a minimum quantity (or safety reserve) at all if there were complete certainty—the new order would arrive exactly on time, just as the inventory falls to zero. In the usual situation, there are two kinds of uncertainty: uncertainty about the rate of usage itself and uncertainty about the amount of time it will take to deliver the new order. Usage of the inventory will speed up as the demand for the company's products increases and slow down in periods of decline in sales. The times it takes to deliver an order will depend upon the supplier and on the transportation medium—these are subject to uncertainty. If the part stored in inventory is one manufactured by the company itself, there will be some uncertainty about the length of time it will take to process the order; there may be bottlenecks in production, breakdowns of machines, and so on.

Thus it is clear that min-max inventory control involves uncertainty; the theory of probability is applicable. Instead of the pattern of inventory rising and falling as in Figure 25-1, it will look more like that in Figure 25-2.

At times the inventory will fall below the minimum, possibly even down to zero, because of rapid usage or delays in delivery of new orders. At times the inventory will exceed the intended maximum, because of slower usage after the order was sent, or because of rapid delivery.

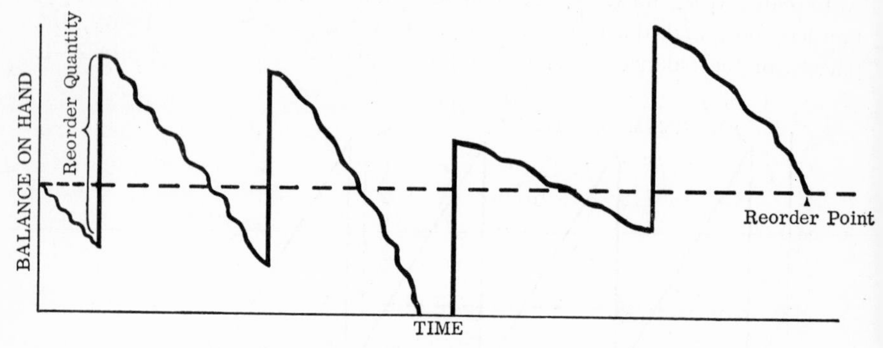

FIGURE 25-2 Fluctuations in Balance on Hand Under Uncertainty

It is beyond the scope of this book to examine the statistical procedures involved in determining the reorder point and the order quantity under conditions of uncertainty. The theory is complicated and the computations cumbersome. The point here is that the problem of inventory control is largely one of uncertainty, and its solution does involve some thinking about probabilities. It is not clear that refined statistical procedures for computing the optimum solution are always (or even usually) justified, for these procedures involve considerable expense. It is clear, however, that recognition of the probabilistic nature of the problem will lead to better judgments about inventories. The objective here is again to investigate a point of view that is relevant to a class of business decisions. The reader who seeks greater refinement may wish to refer to the books listed in the bibliography at the end of this chapter.

Scrap allowances

One additional illustration may clarify the relevance of probability theory in certain types of decisions. The decision on scrap allowances is common in business; it involves uncertainty. The managers cannot assume that every unit of product is perfect; there will be some defects. If a particular order is for a special item not kept in stock, there arises the problem of deciding how many extra units (in addition to the size of the order) to produce to cover these defects. If past experience indicated that there were always five per cent defects, there would be no uncertainty, and five per cent extra units would be produced. Past experience is not so kind; it will show fluctuations in the proportion of scrap, and thus will lead to uncertainty about how many defects will occur this time.

In this situation, there is a reward for producing more and more units: the greater probability that it will be unnecessary to produce a second lot because of insufficient allowance for scrap in the first lot. There is also a penalty: the risk that too much is spent on unnecessary extra units which will be discarded. The solution is to keep on increasing the scrap allowance until the rewards (the incremental gain) no longer exceed the penalties (the incremental loss). Just where is that balance between rewards and penalties? If setup costs are large but the variable costs of output small, it is clear that the scrap allowance should be large to reduce the chance that the second large setup costs will be incurred. However, if setup costs are small, it is no longer profitable to produce so many extra units and take on such a large risk of producing too many unnecessary units.

Some Generalizations

Since the objective of this chapter is to develop a point of view about probabilities, it is now desirable to bring out the common features of the illustrations presented so far. In each case there has been a question of how far management should go in a particular direction: how large an inventory it should build up; how many extra units to produce as a scrap allowance. In each case there have been rewards in increasing the relevant quantities of inventory or scrap allowance—rewards for not being caught short. These are called incremental gains. But as we move in this direction, these rewards become smaller—it becomes less and less probable that the extra units will be needed. At the same time there are penalties—the costs of unnecessary extra units. As the number of units is increased, the penalties become larger and larger, and the probability that we have gone too far becomes greater. Finally a point is reached at which the added gains no longer exceed the added penalties.

It is possible to express this idea in terms similar to those in the earlier discussion of business economics. There is a unit *incremental gain* in adding more units; but there is also a unit *incremental loss*. As we increase the size of inventory or the scrap allowance from nothing to very small quantities, the incremental gain is large and the likelihood of loss small. But as we increase the quantities we get closer to the point at which the incremental gain equals the incremental loss; when this point is reached, it is time to stop, because beyond, the added losses exceed the added gains.

There is no need to restrict ourselves to inventories and scrap allowances. The principle discussed here is quite general. There are many kinds of activities involving potential gains and losses but also requiring an evaluation of uncertainty. The football team on the thirty yard line with only one down to go, but with three yards to go for a first down, may face the decision of trying for a field goal. The potential reward is three points, but the probabilities of actually making the kick may be small. If the team's experience indicates greater skill in running deep in the opponent's territory than in kicking, the chances of making a first down may be greater. As the distance to the goal line decreases, the probability of a successful field goal increases; the team may be more favorable to taking this chance, unless they are so close to the goal line that the chances of a touchdown become too inviting. It is obvious that a football team is concerned with probabilities of this sort. It may be that the uncertainty is so great and time so short that the evaluation of probabilities will be haphazard; but even the inexperienced spectator feels that he is qualified to judge how well the team has analyzed the situation.

The general rule for all situations of this sort is to strive for the decision that will bring the probabilities of success or failure in line with the magnitudes of the rewards and penalties. Past experience may be the best guide to the estimating of probabilities, but experience can be a deceptive guide. Judgment is required in determining whether a careful evaluation of probabilities is justified and, if so, what technical procedures should be applied.

Sampling and Statistical Quality Control

This chapter has introduced probabilistic reasoning in general terms, with illustrations of types of situations in which such reasoning may be appropriate. The discussion has been nontechnical. To provide a deeper insight into what statistical methods are accomplishing in management, it is desirable to become more technical. Proofs and formulas will be avoided; no distinctions will be made among various types of distributions. The presentation will remain nonmathematical, but will be more specific about how statistical methods, and particularly sampling theory, is being applied to some important problems. The reader should be prepared for rather tight and specific reasoning about particular applications. Even the nonstatistician in management should have a fairly detailed knowledge of what is being done with such methods.

Sampling is the best known branch of statistics in management. Its chief application, one that has been used successfully in business for several decades, is statistical quality control. Frequently, information from samples will provide reliable material about the characteristics of a larger universe from which these samples are taken. To be sure, there are some cases in which sampling will not do an adequate job. For example, in the production of parachutes 100 per cent inspection is necessary. There are cases at the other extreme in which sampling is the only feasible approach to quality control. Such would be the case when inspection requires the destruction of the object being inspected. In the intermediate range between these extremes lies the majority of cases, in which samples provide means of cutting inspection costs; at the same time they provide adequate information about the production process to permit control. Here, as elsewhere, there is an economic problem of determining how far the inspection process should be carried.

Sampling

Sampling enables us to draw inferences (or make generalizations) about a mass of items, based upon the careful study of a smaller number of items drawn from the mass. The whole mass is called the universe (or population) and the smaller number of items a sample.

We frequently come into contact with sampling in our daily lives. If we purchase a sack of potatoes, only a few potatoes can be seen; however, we draw an inference about the whole mass (or universe) by only inspecting a few. If these few look good, it might be assumed that the whole sack of potatoes is good.

Another example should prove helpful. Suppose that we are manufacturing twelve-inch rulers. If we had a measuring device that was accurate enough, it would be found that none of these rulers is exactly twelve inches long, although each may be close to it. One ruler perhaps is 12.007 inches, while another may be 11.999 inches, but none is precisely twelve inches. If the length of the ruler is close to twelve inches, we can say that this variation is due to chance. If the ruler were sixteen inches long, however, we would say that chance was not responsible, but that some outside force (such as an incompetent machine operator) caused it.

Let us suppose that we have a stack of 5,000 rulers, and want to find the average length of all 5,000. We could pick up one and measure it. If it is 12.005 inches long, we could assume that the average length of all rulers is 12.005 inches, but intuition says that this conclusion would not be reliable. If we drew a sample of thirty and computed the average, more confidence could be attached to the outcome; but there would remain a risk that we are wrong. In fact, a risk would be involved with *any* size sample, unless all 5,000 rulers are individually measured and the average computed. In general, it can be stated that:

> For a given population the smaller the sample size, the less confidence can be placed in its findings, and the reliability of a sample increases as the sample size increases.

This is nothing new, because everyone knows that a sample of 100 is more reliable than a sample of 10, if they both come from the same population; however, as the sample size increases, the reliability does not increase in proportion to the increase in sample size. In other words, a sample of 1,000 is not 10 times as reliable as a sample of 100. For many purposes, four or five may prove reliable enough. This is a question of economics as well as statistics. How much more expense is involved in order to obtain a larger sample in relation to the increase in valuable information gained? This is another problem of incremental cost versus incremental gain. Generally speaking, the absolute size of the sample determines the reliability and *not* the percentage of the universe included in the sample.

Measures of central tendency and dispersion

Measures of central tendency give the average. There are many types of averages, but only one will be considered—the arithmetic mean, henceforth referred to as the mean or $\overline{X}$. For instance, if three rulers were 12.007, 11.999, and 11.997 inches long, the mean ($\overline{X}$) would be 12.001 (12.007 plus 11.999 plus 11.997 divided by 3).

Measures of dispersion state how closely the individual items cluster around the mean or some other average. One measure of dispersion is the range, the difference between the largest and smallest items in a sample. In the previous example, the range would have been 12.007 minus 11.997 or .010 inches. Another measure of dispersion is the standard deviation.[4] The standard deviation is more sophisticated, but involves more calculation. It has been found that for samples of less than 10 from a normal population, the range is usually an adequate measure of dispersion. Because of its simplicity and its reliability when used with small samples, quality control makes much use of it.

The normal distribution

Another concept, the normal distribution, can be graphically shown as a bell shaped curve (see Figure 25-3). This normal distribution describes a population of items that is symmetrically distributed on both sides of the mean. Also, items that are nearly equal to the mean occur most frequently. In the normal distribution, 68.26 per cent of the items are found to be between plus one and minus one standard deviation; 95.44 per cent between plus two and minus two standard deviations; and 99.73 per cent between plus three and minus three standard deviations. In reality, items that are normally distributed are probably rare, but many universes are so close, that for all practical purposes, they can be considered normal.

If all possible samples of size n are taken from a population, and the mean of each sample is computed, these means form a distribution of means. If a universe is normally distributed, the distribution of all possible sample means, regardless of sample size, will be normal. If the universe is *not* normally distributed, the distribution of all possible sample means becomes more

[4] The standard deviation is obtained by finding the difference between each item and the mean, squaring each difference, adding the squared differences, dividing by the number of items and taking the square root. The term *standard deviation* is often symbolized by the Greek letter sigma (σ). In the example of the rulers, the standard deviation was .0043 inches.

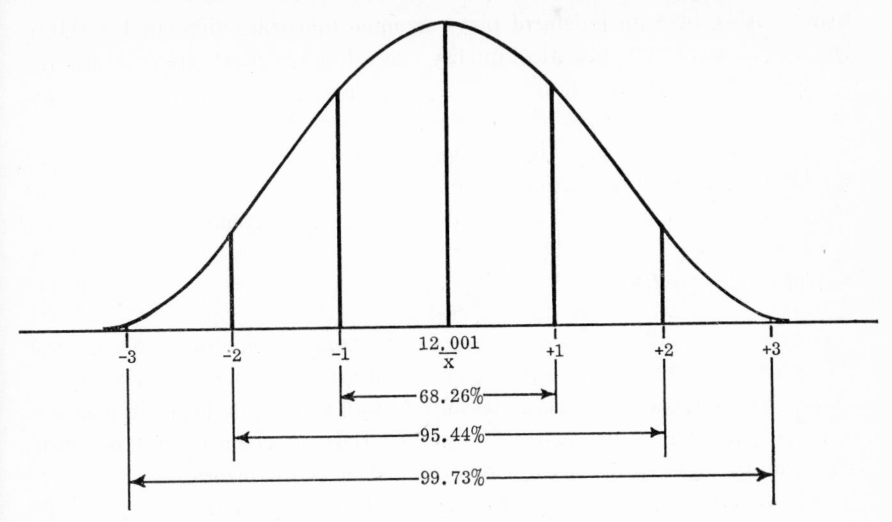

FIGURE 25-3 Normal Curve

normal as the sample size increases. If the distribution of sample means is normally distributed, the same generalizations apply to the means as applied to the normal distribution of individual items. It can be predicted how much sample means will vary from the true mean of the population. The section below, dealing with control charts, assumes that the population is nearly normal. In this case, small samples could be used, with assurance that, in the long run, the means of the samples will distribute themselves in a normal pattern (see Figure 25-3).

Statistical quality control

Quality control assures that quality standards are being met. Quality control is not new; manufacturers have always tried to meet specifications. Statistical quality control, on the other hand, is new, partly because the field of statistics itself is relatively young, and partly because it has taken time for widespread acceptance.

Statistical Quality Control is concerned primarily with control charts and acceptance sampling. Both of these aim at assuring that certain standards are met. Control charts are used *during* production to determine whether production quality is being maintained. Acceptance sampling is used to determine whether or not a particular lot or batch of items meets the desired specifications.

Prior to statistical quality control, some manufacturers would inspect each item for quality. This is called 100 per cent inspection or screening. Besides being costly in terms of man-hours, the effectiveness of 100 per cent inspection is impaired by human fatigue. Even though an inspector examines each item, some defectives are still missed because the job is monotonous and tiring. Also, because judgment plays an important role, different inspectors grade differently. In statistical quality control, a few items are carefully inspected; this diminishes fatigue error. In some cases, sampling is not applicable and 100 per cent inspection is necessary; the cost of letting a defective slip through might be too great. Possibly any kind of sampling would cost too much in relation to the consequences of letting defectives pass. This is again a question of incremental gain versus incremental loss.

Variation in quality

No two manufactured parts are exactly the same. Sometimes only minute differences are present; just the same, there are differences. Variations in quality of production may occur because of tool wear, differences in machine operators, differences in quality of raw materials, or chance. For our purposes, all of these variations will be classified in two categories:

(a) Those variations due to *chance* (random variation),

(b) Those variations not due to chance.

In the latter case, the reason for variation of quality of production is called the *assignable cause.* If variations in the quality of output are due to chance, they obey statistical laws, and the amount of variation can be predicted. In this case, the conditions that cause this variation are said to be *under control.* On the other hand, if the variation in quality of output is not due to chance (and this can be detected), the conditions that cause variation in quality are said to be *out of control,* and the variation is due to an assignable cause.

Control charts

In order to illustrate the concept of statistical quality control, control charts will first be discussed. In many cases, the most useful control charts deal with the mean and the range. Suppose, again, that we are manufacturing twelve-inch rulers. From past production figures, we calculate the mean length of rulers and call it $\overline{\overline{X}}$ or the estimated mean of the universe. Since this will be a large sample, say 100 or more rulers, it is generally a reliable estimate of the mean of the universe.

Further, suppose that samples of five rulers are taken at regular intervals and that for each sample, the mean length ($\overline{X}$) and the range are computed. Since no two rulers are exactly the same length, there will be variations in the different $\overline{X}$'s that are obtained. If these variations are due to chance (random variations), the sample means will be distributed in a statistical pattern; an example is found in Figure 25-4. Now let us remember that this is *a distribution of sample means* and not of individual items. The means of the samples will tend to cluster around the mean of the universe. On the control chart shown in Figure 25-5, $\overline{\overline{X}}$ will be the central line. In this control chart, the number of the sample (i.e., 1st, 2nd, and so forth) is along the

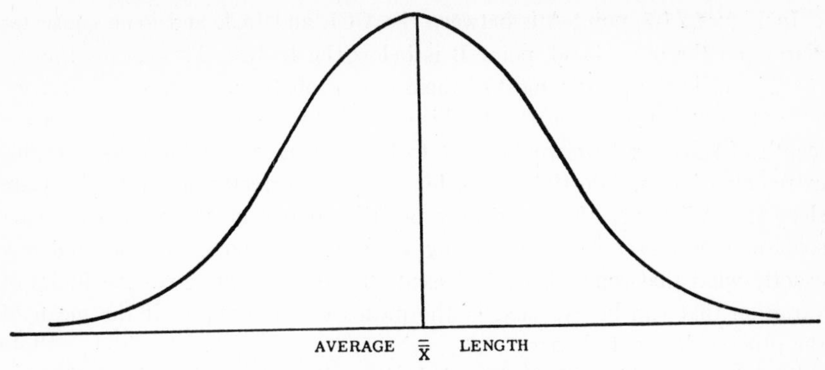

FIGURE 25-4 Distribution of Sample Means

horizontal axis; the means of the samples are plotted according to the vertical dimension.

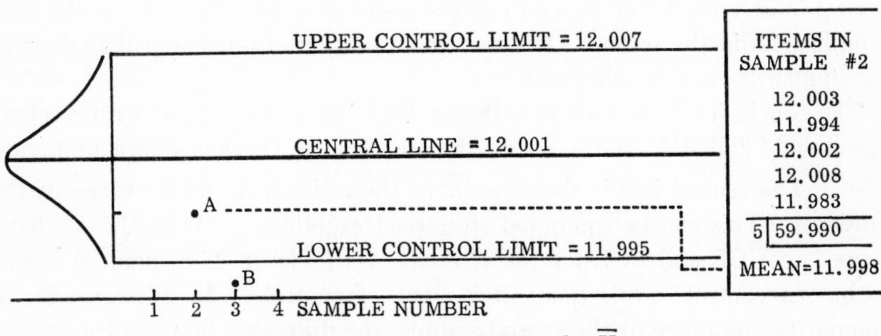

FIGURE 25-5 Control Chart for $\overline{X}$

The purpose of this chart for $\overline{X}$'s will be to tell us if the mean of the universe (or the average length of rulers produced) changes or gets "out of control." We know that if the average length of rulers produced does not change, the means of the samples will cluster around the central line.

Now we need an upper control limit (UCL) and a lower control limit (LCL) to tell us when the average length has changed.[5] To illustrate this, assume that $\overline{\overline{X}}$ is 12.001 inches. We now take a sample of five rulers from the production line and the average length of these five rulers happens to be 11.998. The question now is whether or not this is too much variation in length to be considered due to chance. The UCL and LCL attempt to answer this question, though we can never *prove* that the variation is not due to chance. If the point falls above the UCL or below the LCL we assume that this much variation in sample means from their mean is not due to chance; an investigation is made to find an assignable cause (the process is considered out of control).

[5] Practically any textbook dealing with statistical quality control describes methods of computing UCL and LCL; see Grant, Peach, Bowman and Fetter, or Duncan.

In Figure 25-5, point A is between the UCL and LCL and is no cause for alarm; on the other hand, point B is below the LCL.[6] This means that of the 5 items in the sample, most of them were probably small in order to average out to such a small mean. In this case, there is too much variation in the length of rulers and we would want to look for an assignable cause for this extreme variation. Possibly a machine is set incorrectly or the workers are sleeping. Whatever the cause may be, the control chart has warned that something has *probably* gone wrong somewhere, although it does not say exactly what that something is. Essentially, the $\overline{X}$ chart gives the limits of variation that can be expected in the means of our samples if the mean of the process does not change.

The $\overline{X}$ chart alone is not enough because it says nothing about the dispersion of the process; for example, if a sample of three rulers is drawn, and their lengths are: 11.001, 12.001, and 13.001—the mean is 12.001 inches. If the lengths had been 11.999, 12.001, and 12.003 the mean would have again been 12.001 inches, but we can observe there is more dispersion in the first sample than in the second. Changes in dispersion also can signal that quality standards are not being met.

The conclusion is that along with the $\overline{X}$ chart, we must have a range chart (commonly called R chart). An example of an R chart is shown in Figure 25-6. The central line is shown as $\overline{R}$ or the estimated average range of the universe. This can be computed from past experience. As in the $\overline{X}$ chart, there is a UCL and LCL for the R chart.[7] In Figure 25-6, point A seems to be "in control" while point B is "out of control." In other words, in computing the range of the second sample, the difference between the largest and smallest items in the sample was too large to be considered due to chance.

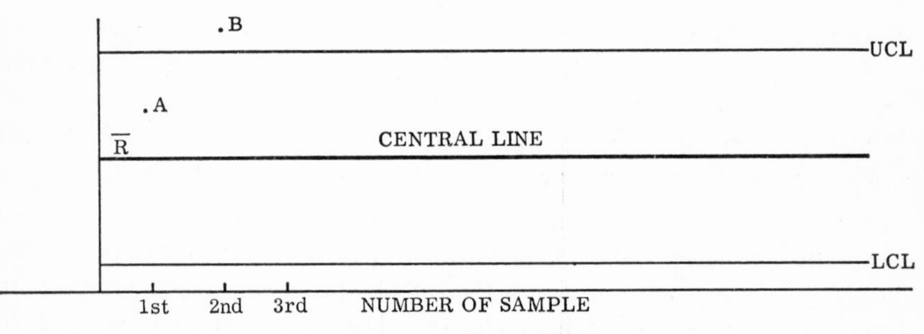

FIGURE 25-6 Range Chart

The R chart gives the limits of the range that can be expected if the dispersion of the universe does not change.

[6] In actual practice, no decisions will be made until after about 25 samples have been taken.

[7] For samples of less than 7, zero is used as the lower control limit.

The exception principle again

Both the $\overline{X}$ and R charts make use of the exception principle that was discussed in Chapter 3. The charts are simple enough to be plotted by clerks, and only when control limits are exceeded is the service of the supervisor required. The routinization of quality control procedures frees the supervisor for other, more challenging tasks.

Control charts in action

Now that the $\overline{X}$ and R charts have been discussed, let us look at a few of them in operation and try to interpret their meaning.

Acceptance sampling

We now turn from control charts to acceptance sampling. Let us assume that instead of being the manufacturer of 12 inch rulers, we are now a purchaser.[8] We want to be sure that the rulers we buy are approximately 12 inches in length. Suppose that the manufacturer has shipped a lot of 5,000 rulers to us. Each one could be measured individually, but this might be too expensive. Sampling might save us from such a costly task. Many different methods of sampling could be used; two of these methods will be briefly discussed, single and sequential sampling.

Single Sampling Plans. This method, as the name implies, requires that one sample be taken from the lot, and acceptability be determined. This is a statistically sound method, and although it may seem unfair to the manufacturer, it really is not, *if done properly.*

Suppose a decision has been made that we do not want rulers longer than 12.005 inches or shorter than 11.995 inches. In order to derive the plan, three things must be found:

(a) The upper acceptance limit for $\overline{X}$
(b) The lower acceptance limit for $\overline{X}$
(c) The number of items in the sample

A single sampling plan that might be appropriate is: [9]

(a) Upper acceptance limit 12.003
(b) Lower acceptance limit 11.997
(c) Number in sample 57

[8] Although our example involves a purchaser of goods, the concept of acceptance sampling is just as applicable to manufacturers.

[9] Method of computation can be found in A. J. Duncan, *Quality Control and Industrial Statistics* (Homewood, Ill.: Richard D. Irwin, 1959), p. 246.

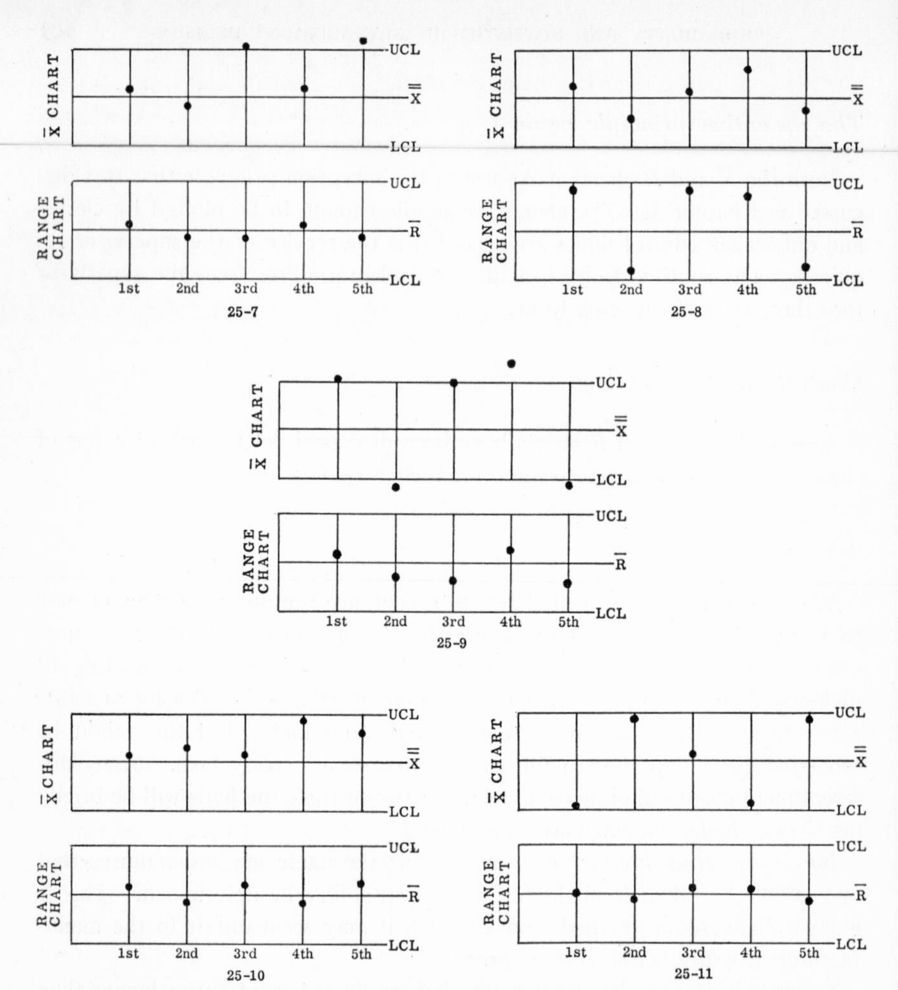

FIGURES 25-7 through 25-11. In Figure 25-7 it can be seen that the means of samples number 3 and 5 are out of control. There is a possibility that the mean of the universe is shifting upward. Notice that there is a trend in that direction. The range seems to be acting randomly. In Figure 25-8 none of the points is out of control but there is cause for concern. There is much variation in the ranges but very little variation in the means. Variation within samples is much greater than variation among samples. This may be a prelude to trouble. Causes of this are improper sampling procedures, machine trouble, etc. At any rate trouble is brewing. In Figure 25-9 all points in the $\bar{X}$ chart are out of control. This could mean that the quality striven for cannot be achieved or that improper production methods are being used. The ranges are not out of control, so the former possibility is more likely. In Figure 25-10 no points on the $\bar{X}$ chart are out of control, but since they all are above the presumed mean (central line) of the universe, the actual mean of the universe has evidently shifted upward. This is similar to Figure 25-7, and since the ranges are acting in a random manner, the conclusion is further substantiated. In Figure 25-11 we can see that there is great variation among sample means but very little variation within the samples. This indicates the strong possibility that similar items are used in each sample, i.e., they are definitely related to each other, rather than being related to the universe mean. Maybe improper sampling methods are being used. Maybe different workers are using methods or measuring devices which are inaccurate. Again, no points are out of control, but much information is gained from our control charts.

Now what must be done is to select 57 rulers at random and compute the mean; if the mean falls between 11.997 and 12.003, we accept the lot—if not, we reject it or inspect the entire lot.

Sequential Sampling Plans. In sequential sampling plans, a sample is drawn and the mean computed as before. The difference is that there are now three alternative courses of action: (1) accept, (2) reject, or (3) take another sample. The lot can be accepted or rejected as before, but if the mean is in the fringe area between acceptable and nonacceptable, another sample can be drawn. This method is no more reliable than single sampling; however, it can be less expensive, because over-all less sampling will be performed.

Variables and attributes

So far the discussion has dealt with the mean and the range. These are commonly called variables. There are other methods of quality control pertaining to what are called attributes. The common attribute is the percentage defective. In attribute sampling, the only concern is whether or not an item is defective. Had we been worried about cracked rulers instead of the length, attribute plans would have been used. Sometimes there is a choice between attributes and variables. Ruler lengths could have been set up as attributes by saying that ruler lengths shorter than 11.995 or longer than 12.005 are defective. Attributes can be used for control charts and acceptance sampling, but usually variables plans require a smaller sample for the same degree of reliability. On the other hand, there is more computation when using variables. The choice is again an economic one. An attribute plan can always be substituted for a variables plan. The cost of each plan will most likely be the determining factor as to which to use.

Economics and Quality Control

Tolerances

Tolerances are permissible technical deviations from standards set by management; tolerance limits delineate the maximum and/or minimum acceptable variation from the "perfect" model of the product. For example, if a customer desired rulers that did not vary from 12 inches by more than ¼ inch, management would set 11.75 and 12.25 as its tolerance limits. These tolerance limits are not to be confused with control limits. Control limits are determined by the machine's capabilities rather than by management. For example, if a machine can produce products with great precision, control limits would be narrow; that is, control limits would fall close to the mean of the process. If, however, the machine is not capable of precise production, control limits would be wider.

The relationship between tolerance limits and control limits is an important one. These relationships can be classified into three general cases:

1. Tight tolerance limits and loose control limits
2. Loose tolerance limits and tight control limits
3. All other cases

In the first two cases, it might not be economical to use control charts at all.

In the first case, management desires more precision than the machine is capable of producing. For instance, management wants rulers produced that will not vary from 12 inches by more than .001 inch. After examining the machine's capabilities, it is found that (say) 60 per cent of the machine's output varies by more than this. If this is the best that the machine can do, and tolerances cannot be revised, we will not be able to produce the rulers. In this case, it is clear that control charts would not be used, since there would be no production to control.

The second case is the opposite extreme. Management desires rulers produced that do not vary from 12 inches by more than .25 inches. The machine generally produces rulers that vary by about .020 inches. In fact, it has never produced a ruler that varied from 12 inches by more than .1 inch. In this case, if control limits were determined by routine methods, we would try to keep production "too perfect."

This case is illustrated in Figure 25-12. The mean of the third sample

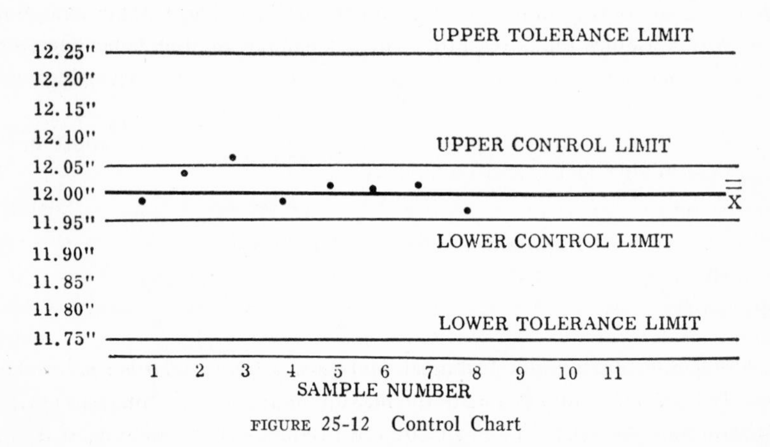

FIGURE 25-12 Control Chart

exceeded the upper control limit. This means that production would probably be halted and an assignable cause sought. But there is no need for such tight control on output, since we are still far from exceeding the tolerance limits. In this case, a control chart may not be needed at all, and maintaining one could be a waste of money. If there is a chance of exceeding the tolerance limits, the control limits could be modified by widening them.

In all other cases, routine methods of calculation would most likely be employed and there would be a need for control charts.

Control limits

Consider a point out of control on a control chart. Chance may have caused this condition and not an assignable cause. In other words, assume that the mean of the universe did not shift or change. Nevertheless, a sample with a large mean was selected at random. Control limits may be set by routine methods so that this will occur only about 3 times in 1000 samples if no assignable causes are at work. Control limits could have been set out so far from the central line that there is never a point out of control, but let us look at the consequences. If the mean of the universe shifts upward, the sample mean will more probably fall within our control limits, and we are less likely to catch the shift. On the other hand, if the control limits are set closer to the mean, we would be more likely to catch a shift, but would be looking for trouble when none existed more often than 3 times in 1,000. The importance of catching a shift of the mean of the universe must be weighed against the extra cost involved in looking for trouble when none exists. Theoretically, the UCL and LCL should be set at the points where the incremental gain and the incremental cost are equal. In practice, this is difficult, if not impossible, to calculate precisely, but the concept should be used; when setting control limits, at least a rough approximation at equating incremental cost and incremental gain should be attempted. Modified methods of determining control limits are an attempt at this. Any further discussion of the intricacies of statistical quality control would take us beyond the scope of this volume.

Other Applications of Sampling

In the future, sampling methods will be more widely known in business. This will be true even outside of the area of quality control. In fact, the movement is already well under way. Market research, for example, is a subject heavily dependent upon the collection and evaluation of sample data. If one wishes to predict the effect of a new selling technique, management may try it out on a sample from the total population. Accountants are beginning to apply systematic sampling theory to the collection of certain kinds of information for which formerly 100 per cent coverage was obtained. A more thorough analysis of a sample of bad debts may turn up some important considerations overlooked in the total allowance for bad debts. Sampling is being applied to the estimation of inventory amounts, to auditing, the aging of receivables, and the confirmation of accounts receivable.

The reader may find it profitable to reflect on the various phases of management in which sampling theory may prove useful in the future: in production control, in the collection of cost data, in estimating costs on new orders, in the evaluation of the reasons for returned merchandise or complaints, in determining the potential market for a new branch store, and so on. Apparently the manager of the future will find it necessary to know at least enough statistics to be able to communicate with statisticians, even if he is not a statistician himself.

Bibliographical Note

One of the most fundamental works relating probability theory to decision making is Robert Schlaifer's *Probability and Statistics for Business Decisions* (1959). A more elementary introduction to the subject, and to models in general, is found in Irwin Bross, *Design for Decision* (1953).

There are specialized volumes dealing with specific applications of statistics in business. Among the outstanding works on statistical quality control are Eugene L. Grant's *Statistical Quality Control* (2nd ed., 1952) and A. J. Duncan's *Quality Control and Industrial Statistics* (rev.ed., 1959). The pioneer in this field was Walter A. Shewhart of Bell Telephone Laboratories, who published his volume, *The Economic Control of Quality of Manufactured Product,* in 1931. The applications of statistics in work sampling appear in Ralph M. Barnes, *Work Sampling* (2nd ed., 1957) and Bertrand Hansen, *Work Sampling for Modern Management* (1960).

Other applications appear in the works on operations research cited in Chapter 23, such as Churchman, Ackoff and Arnoff; and Bowman and Fetter. The reader may wish to follow current developments in the two leading journals: *Management Science* and *Operations Research.*

Questions and Problems

1. When is insurance feasible in dealing with risk and uncertainty? Explain.
2. When is self-insurance appropriate? Explain.
3. Discuss applications of incremental reasoning in:
   a. Determination of scrap allowances
   b. Determination of the size of inventories
   c. Quality control
4. Is it reasonable for a manager to assign probabilities to outcomes that are highly uncertain? Discuss.
5. Discuss the use of probabilistic reasoning in the following decisions:
   a. A decision to fly rather than drive to a conference
   b. A decision to cease drilling for oil in a particular location
   c. A decision to buy storm windows
6. Can you think of problems other than quality control for which control charts might be suitable?
7. Draw control charts for processes that are (a) in control and (b) out of control.
8. How does acceptance sampling differ from sampling to control a process?
9. What economies are made possible by sequential sampling?
10. Compare the procedure for controlling attributes with that for controlling variables.
11. Department *A*'s quality control procedure consists of measuring the diameter

of every twentieth item. The control chart has control limits of 1.5 inches and 1.8 inches. A part is discovered with a diameter of 1.9 inches.

a. Is the process out of control?

b. What action is required?

c. Should all previously produced parts be examined?

12. Discuss the statement: "We cannot use statistical quality control because we cannot afford the risk of sending a defective item to a customer."

13. A company produces light bulbs. To determine whether or not a bulb is defective, it is connected and burned continuously until it burns out. A meter records the length of life. Compare this quality control problem with that in the manufacture of automobile tires.

26

Extracts and Cases on the Uses of Statistics in Management

THIS chapter provides an opportunity to evaluate the relevance of statistical methods in business. The only way to learn statistics itself is to take formal work in the subject. This book can only provide an introduction to the methods involved. What is attempted in this chapter is the stimulation of thought about where statistics fits into business practice and about its prospects in future management.

This chapter contains two kinds of materials that should help the reader formulate opinions on the relevance of statistics. There are a series of extracts from the works of well-known writers who have considered this problem. These are followed by several cases, permitting the reader himself to develop his own thought.

The chapter starts with a general statement on the statistical approach by one of the best known of the world's statisticians. This is followed by extracts emphasizing specific applications in business. The chapter concludes with two actual case situations, one involving statistical quality control, the other work sampling.

Extracts

Extract A

The Statistical Approach (M. G. Kendall)

I should like you . . . to see my subject as I see it myself, not as the pedestrian science of handling numerical data, not even as a comparatively new branch of scientific method, but as the matrix of quantitive knowledge of nearly every kind, as the principal instrument yet devised by man for bringing within his grasp the terrifying complexity of things and relations-between-things, and as a powerful illuminant of the process of rational thought itself . . . To give an idea of the extraordinary range of my subject as it now exists I take some examples more or less at random from the work of the past twenty-five years. In agriculture the whole theory and practice of plant breeding and of field trials has been revolutionised. In industry the spread of statistical methods of quality control has been as rapid as it has been successful. In meteorology the statistician is at last getting to grips with the enigmatic behaviour of the weather. In nuclear physics the statistical approach is now a basic part of the subject. To take more particular instances, statistical methods are used in the study of epidemics, telephone traffic, industrial accidents, the standardisation of drugs, the measurement of human abilities, the migration of insects, the efficiency of examiners, the building-times of pre-fabricated houses, the distribution of blood-groups, factory production costs, flutter in aircraft structure, and in fact in almost every branch of science and industry. The statistician does not indeed stop there. He is extending his interests into domains which have not hitherto been considered as possible fields for the application of numerical methods. . . .

Like mathematics, [statistics] is a scientific method, and a method which is scientific is *ipso facto* capable of general application. The mere ubiquity of the statistical approach, then, striking as it may be, is not its most important feature. What marks it out for special attention is that it deals, not with individuals, but with aggregates. Statistics is the science of collectives and group properties. The statistician is interested in the individual only as the member of the group. It is from this basic fact that his strength and his weakness both arise. His strength because most, if not all, natural laws are group properties; his weakness because he sometimes throws into a group individuals which are not homogeneous and misses something in his summarisations. His common sense usually saves him. That is why all good statisticians lay such emphasis on the importance of common sense. But we should in fairness admit that he is in danger of failing to see the trees for the wood. It is inevitable that he should be so, for one cannot watch the aggregate and at the same time keep every item of it in focus.

In general, the laws obeyed by collectives are determined empirically and a large part of statistical technique is concerned with the setting up of a calculus of collective phenomena to handle observations in the aggregate. But there are also laws of a peculiar kind in mass action which permit of the prediction of the behaviour of an aggregate when it is quite impossible to frame laws concerning the individual. We are permitted, in a sense, to derive law from the actual absence of law. In fact, under certain conditions, the more numerous the perturbative influences at work on the individual, the more definite the law obeyed by the aggregate. We may go further still. There are certain aggregates, called random or stochastic, the members of which not only do not conform to law in the older sense of nineteenth-century determinism but are actually *conceived* of as not conforming to any such law. We say that they happen by chance. And yet we can derive quite definite laws which are obeyed by aggregates of such individuals and we can say without paradox that chance is subject to law.[1]

Extract B

Statistical Analysis for Management (E. H. Bowman and R. B. Fetter)

Modern statistical methods find wide application in production management. Variation in the output of a process, whether it be quality, quantity, or cost which is the measured characteristic of output, is the rule rather than the exception. Knowledge concerning the expected variation is essential if control is to be instituted over a process. Decisions as to whether a process is giving the desired output can only be made if the manager knows what to expect of a process and can decide precisely when a process is not meeting these expectations. The statistical control concept provides for this kind of decision.

In many cases, inferences must be drawn about the output of some process based on less than complete information. When this is necessary, formal sampling plans provide the manager with good decision rules. The economic criteria which establish the necessity for the use of sampling plans should be known and understood by management.

Industrial experimentation is seeing wider and wider use in industry today as the means whereby useful information may be gathered economically and with greatest efficiency. Decisions should always be based on the best and most complete information which it is feasible to get. Modern statistical techniques aim at the efficient gathering and utilization of information. . . .

Broadly speaking, the objective of control in production is to get assurance that operations occur according to plans. This implies that in order to control a process, one must predict the behavior of the process. Through past experience, one is able at least to determine the limits within which any given characteristic has varied. By assuming that the same set of causal factors will continue to operate in the future, it is usually possible to make a prediction of the expected behavior of the process. Then, of course, if a change occurs in the cause system which produced the past variation, this fact should be quickly apparent through a change in the variation of current output. . . .

[1] M. G. Kendall, "The Statistical Approach," in *Readings in Market Research* (London: British Market Research Bureau Limited, 1956), pp. 1–4. The article was published originally in the May, 1950 issue of *Economica.*

A production process consists of a series of inputs designed to produce some given output. Typical classes of inputs are men, equipment, materials, etc. Variations in these input factors occur, over time, as do variations in the relationships of the inputs to each other. These variations in the input factors constitute a cause system which produces some variation in the uniformity of output. Assuming that the variation within, and between, input factors is stable, then the variation in output will be stable, and therefore predictable. The introduction of some change in the input variation or of some previously absent cause of variation should quickly be made known by some change in the output variation. The objective of *statistical control* is to set up a formal control system whereby such changes in the chance cause system operating in a given situation may be made known and action taken accordingly.

For example, the variation in the cost of producing some item may be discovered by an analysis of past performance. Through application of the technique of statistical control, the expected value and limits of variation of this cost with a stable chance cause system may be discovered, and thus a mechanism established for identifying assignable causes of variation in cost. Furthermore, the technique aims at improving the cost performance by the following:

1. Directing attention at both mean cost and variation in cost
2. Discovering causes for good, as well as poor, cost performance

The statistical control technique may be used in the control of machine breakdowns in order to discover the presence of assignable causes, as well as to gauge the effectiveness and economic worth of a preventive maintenance program. It may be used in the analysis and control of production rates, accidents, personnel turnover, and, in fact, in most situations where control is desired over some process which may be typified by some measurable characteristic.[2]

EXTRACT C

Work Sampling (Ralph M. Barnes)

Work sampling has two main uses. (1) Work sampling may be used to measure activities and delays—for example, to determine the percentage of the day that a man is working and the percentage of the day that he is idle. (2) Work sampling, under certain circumstances, may be used to measure manual tasks—that is, to establish a time standard for an operation. . . .

Work sampling employs a random sampling theory similar to that used in quality control. The method consists of selecting samples at random

[2] Edward H. Bowman and Robert B. Fetter, *Analysis for Production Management* (Homewood, Ill.: Richard D. Irwin, Inc., 1957), pp. 145, 148, 149–150.

from a large group, and when a sufficient number of samples have been selected, a prediction is made for the whole group.

The determination of the percentage of the working day that the operator or machine is working or idle is based upon the theory that the percentage *number* of observations recording the man or machine as idle is a reliable measure of the percentage *time* that the operation is in the delay state, if sufficient observations are taken.

Briefly, the work sampling procedure in its simplest form consists of making observations at random intervals of one or more operators or machines and noting whether they are working or idle. If the operator is working, he is given a tally mark under "working"; if he is idle he is given a tally mark under "idle." The percentage of the day that the worker is idle is the ratio of the number of "idle" tally marks to the total number of "idle" and "working" tally marks. . . .

Many operations or activities which are impractical or costly to measure by time study can readily be measured by work sampling. . . .

Time study permits a finer breakdown of activities and delays than is possible with work sampling. Work sampling cannot provide as much detailed information as one can get from time study.[3]

EXTRACT D

Developments in Statistical Sampling for Accountants (Lawrence L. Vance)

An outstanding case in which statistical estimation was used to establish an inventory figure for regular accounting purposes is the Minneapolis-Honeywell Case. The case concerns the work in process inventory of one division of the company. This inventory contains about 40,000 lots located in several departments. The lots differ considerably both physically and in cost. Less than 2% of the lots cost over $1,200 each, but this 2% accounted for 30 per cent of the total cost of the inventory. In order to satisfy themselves of the validity of the statistical method and to gain experience in its application, the people involved ran experiments for three years before using the method as a substitute for a 100% count. The first experiment consisted of taking a random sample of about 500 out of 5,000 items in one department. The sample was taken from lot tags used in the regular physical inventory of the department. Since the sample was 10% of the population the inventory cost of the sample items was multiplied by 10 to get the estimate of the total cost of the inventory of the department. This total came within $\frac{1}{10}$ of 1% of the physical count. The experiment was repeated the next year with another satisfactory result. At this point the plan was

[3] Ralph M. Barnes, *Work Sampling* (New York: John Wiley & Sons, Inc., 1956), pp. 3, 5, 6–7.

revised to take into account the fact that the inventory could be divided into high value and low value lots, i.e., stratified. High value lots were defined as those costing $500.00 and over. The plan then provided for counting the high value lots 100%, and for a sample of about 10% of the low value lots. When this was applied in a third experiment the sample consisted of 4,200 items out of a total of 40,000 items. The estimate this time was within $^8\!/_{10}$ of 1% of the physical count figure. Both these percentages represent a high degree of precision and so were considered satisfactory. The experiments had been done on the basis of documents from the physical inventories, and it remained to be seen if they could be successfully applied in the shop. Problems common to all physical inventory taking were involved: how to identify lots and segregate them for counting, for example. In addition, high and low value lots had to be distinguished and means of drawing a random sample of the low value lots had to be devised and applied on the floor of the working areas. A test of the procedures devised for these possibilities proved successful and authorization was given for applying the method to an actual inventory determination. Instructions were prepared, forms designed, personnel selected and trained, and the whole process scheduled. The physical inventory as usually taken on a complete basis required five working days. The statistical plan called for the whole job to be done in one continuous 16-hour period. When it was carried out it was completed in many departments in 8 hours, and was completed in all at the end of the planned 16 hours. . . .

Another area of application of statistical estimates as a substitute for full accounting calculation is the settlement of inter-company receivables and payables. This has been accomplished by some of the air carriers, who have thousands of inter-line revenue allocations to make each month. The case I will describe is the one first adopted by TWA, United, and Northwest airlines, and which has now been incorporated in the Revenue Accounting Manual of the International Air Transport Association for use by any airlines that wish to join with others in using the statistical method. The problem of interline revenue settlements is a substantial one and is growing larger. For example, United Air Lines picks up over 100,000 coupons per month from tickets sold by other airlines. Furthermore, there are more than 60 possible fares for a trip from Chicago to New York, to take a single case. The cost of pricing a monthly bill from United to TWA involving 20,000 coupons valued at $600,000 is $1,500.00. In discussing the possibility of solving the rising clerical cost of this operation by statistical sampling it was decided that the sample should provide an estimate within ±1% of error for a cumulative six-month period. It was also decided that this precision was to be achieved on a confidence level of 95%. In other words, a 5% risk of being wrong was taken. A stratified sample of the coupons is taken, the strata being first class, coach, military, and others. The sample is selected by taking a number from 1 to 10 at random and picking the coupons that have this number as the last digit in the ticket number. In the cast of small lots, if this digit does not occur frequently enough, the next higher one is used, and so on. Then the tickets selected for the sample are priced in the usual way. This total is then multiplied by the ratio of the sample size to the total lot size and this estimate of the total amount due on the whole batch of tickets is billed to the airline that sold the tickets. The tickets are sent to the other airline so it can check the computations made. But no one checks the tickets that are not included in the sample. A representative of United estimates that in a year's billing of $7,000,000, the error will be plus or minus $3,400. In United's case the yearly cost of billing one carrier on the old basis is $15,000, so the saving is substantial.[4]

Extract E

Decisions Under Uncertainty: Drilling Decisions by Oil and Gas Operators (C. Jackson Grayson, Jr.)

I do not intend to infer that . . . informal decision making necessarily leads to "wrong" decisions. The danger in such decision making—by mental processes alone—is its susceptibility to error. The human mind, although a wonderful creation, simply cannot efficiently handle very complex and uncertain problems by itself. Oil operators, for example, have to collect, sift, and weigh available geological data, make assumptions about a number of variables, form predictions for a range of possible outcomes, think of a number of possible alternative courses of action, consider personal or company objectives, and choose a course of action. In the process the possibility of overlooking some factors or making errors in calculation is obviously great. And errors, in the expensive oil business, can be very costly (ruin), or, at a minimum, can lead to inconsistent action and a decreased opportunity to achieve some desired goal.

Granted then that the drilling decision is a difficult decision problem, is there anything better than just intuitive decision making? I think so. . . .

. . . [A] decision maker may find it useful to construct a "Payoff Table" when faced with a drilling decision. Such a table is merely a convenient form for systematically arranging and relating all the elements in any decision:

1. A statement of possible *acts* available to the decision maker.
2. A statement of the possible *events.*
3. Assignment of the *probabilities* of occurrence of each event.
4. Assignment of the *consequences* of each act-event.
5. Selection of one of the acts by means of some *criterion.*

[4] Lawrence L. Vance, "A Review of Developments in Statistical Sampling for Accountants," *The Accounting Review* (January 1960), pp. 20–21 and 24–25.

PAYOFF TABLE

		Possible Acts		
Possible Events	*Probability of Event Occurring*	*Don't Drill*	*Drill with 100% Interest*	*Farm-Out Keep ⅛ . . . Override*
Dry Hole	.70	$0	−$ 50,000	$0
100,000 bbls.	.20	$0	$ 50,000	$12,500
500,000 bbls.	.10	$0	$450,000	$62,500
Expected Monetary Value		$0	$ 20,000	$ 8,750

A statement of the (1) possible acts and (2) possible events is not so difficult. As acts, operators can "don't drill," "drill with 100% interest," "farm out, keep ⅛ override," etc. Events can be thought of as either a "dry hole" or a range of reserve sizes, such as "100,000 barrels," "500,000 barrels," etc.

The most difficult tasks are (3) assignment of probabilities, (4) assignment of consequences, and (5) selection of an appropriate decision criterion to choose a course of action.

First, as to the assignment of probabilities, I suggest . . . that the geologist make such assignments in the form of numerical "personal probabilities." Geologists are presently engaging in a similar process when they talk about possible events in terms of "good," "fair," "poor," "gut cinch," "Grade A," etc. All of these are, in a sense, personal probability estimates. All that is proposed in a formal decision system is that the geologist go one step further. He can, through use of a hypothetical betting system, crystallize the same probability "judgment" and express it in the form of numbers. Why numbers?

One reason is that numbers offer a more *precise* way of conveying meaning to others. Words and shadings in tone are inexact and capable of being misinterpreted. For example, how good is "good"? How fair is "fair"? Also, numbers make it possible to *combine,* in a convenient and accurate fashion, the geologist's judgment about the chances of success with the other factors entering into the decision.

The next step in the decision process is to assign consequences to possible act-events. This is a difficult step—much more difficult, in fact, than most people presume. First, there is the problem mentioned earlier of accounting for the time value of dollars to be received in the future. And second, there is the question as to whether consequences can be accurately represented by dollars. The usual assumption made by most businessmen is that a "dollar is a dollar" and that it means the same to all men. But this is not true.

Consider the example of a well that will cost $50,000 to drill. What does the potential loss of $50,000 mean to different persons? Certainly, not the same thing. For, to a man with only $50,000 in the bank, it means potential financial ruin! To a major oil company with millions in annual expenditures, it means very little.

The gain of $50,000 is extremely important to an operator on the brink of bankruptcy; it is of minor significance to an operator with $1 million in the bank. It is clear, therefore, that gains and losses of dollars have different "subjective values" for different operators, depending on their bank accounts at the time of the decision, and their personal preference for taking risks. And the employment of dollars to measure consequences, while useful for many decisions, is not always adequate.

It is suggested, . . . that operators assign a subjective or "utility," value to potential dollar consequences. To do this, it is necessary for the operator to construct a "utility function" for himself or for his firm.

During this research I experimented with the construction of such utility functions for individual independent operators. The technique would require too much space to describe in this introduction, but essentially I presented the operator with many possible hypothetical alternatives, one after another, and from his responses derived a function that reflected his individual subjective value assignments to potential monetary consequences—both gains and losses.

With such a function, it is then possible for an individual operator, or a firm, to convert dollar consequences of act-events into units of measurement that reflect what the dollars mean to him, or his firm, individually. And these units of measurement, we arbitrarily call *utiles*.

The operator now has assigned *utiles* to the consequences of all possible act-events, and he has assigned *probabilities* of occurrence to each possible event. The next step is to weight the utiles by the probabilities, calculate the "weighted average consequence" of each act, and select that act that has the largest weighted average consequence. If dollars are used to measure consequences, this is known as choosing the act with the greatest "expected monetary value," and if utiles are used, then the selection is made of the act with the greatest "expected utility value."

This illustration is simple, but it points out the systematic manner in which the elements of a decision can be individually analyzed and how these elements can then be put together in a logical fashion. There is no trick to it. It is only a formal way of following through what most good decision makers do implicitly. . . .

. . . [A] decision maker is often faced with the following basic choice: (1) make a final decision on the basis of presently available information, or (2) obtain more information (seismic, drill stem test, etc.), *at a cost,* before making his final decision. The additional information may aid him in making the final decision, but is it worth the cost of obtaining it? . . .

[Most] operating men will probably object to the use of these decision aids as being too complex, strange, and just plain unworkable. . . .

In answer to some of the probable objections, first let me point out that any idea that is different from what an individual knows today is bound to be strange at first, because it *is* new. It may require some study and thought, but so does any worthwhile innovation.

Second, operators will undoubtedly object to the assignment of numbers to uncertainties. "All of those figures represent assumptions . . . and you could make some other assumptions . . . and get different figures." Exactly! Any operator—in fact, anyone—who has to take action is *forced* to make such assumptions. Whether he does it consciously or not, *he has to make assumptions and predictions about the future.* Otherwise, there would be *no* basis for his action, no rationality. Action would be pure stimulus and response, with no reason intervening. All that these decision aids propose is that the decision maker make these assumptions more explicit in an effort to reduce the probabilities of error and inconsistent action. And, if there is any quarrel at all, it should not be with the fact that assumptions lie back of the figures, but with the *method* used to capture these assumptions.

Third, note that these aids are designed to *aid, not replace,* the decision maker. They are designed to enlarge and make more efficient the use of judgment, not to remove it. Formal analysis is not the opposite of judgment. Rather, it is a method whereby the *skilled judgments of individuals are drawn upon and combined to reach a decision.* Formal analysis catches, so to speak, the years of experience and intuitive power of each individual in the decision chain, and focuses them on the decision at hand. This is probably the hardest point for people to understand, for once they see numbers, they react. They feel that numbers imply "outside" interference, and that formal analysis implies rejection of "personal judgment and experience." This is not so.[5]

Cases

Case A:

Ontario Tire Company Limited [6]

Statistical quality control

After presenting a paper to the American Society of Quality Control, Mr. Glen Russell, Quality Control Engineer of the Ontario Tire Company Limited

[5] C. Jackson Grayson, Jr., *Decisions Under Uncertainty: Drilling Decisions by Oil and Gas Operators* (Boston: Harvard University, Division of Research, 1960), pp. 19–24.

wondered what he could do to improve the control of the thickness of the rubber in the inner tubes manufactured in the Ontario Tire plant.

The Ontario Tire Company Limited manufactured tires and tubes for use on automobiles, trucks, and farm implements which it sold throughout Canada. In the manufacture of inner tubes, rubber was extruded (from a machine called a tuber) in a continuous tube after which it was cut into specified lengths. A hole was punched in each length, a valve inserted and vulcanized in place, and finally the ends of the length of rubber butt-welded to form a completed inner tube. The tube was then inflated, placed in a mold, and cured by the application of heat.

The thickness of the rubber in the finished tube depended solely on the thickness at the time of extrusion which could be controlled accurately by the operator. A different die was inserted in the tuber for each size of tube made.

After being extruded, the rubber tube travelled on conveyors and hand trucks to the various operations that were performed on it. The total time from extrusion to final inspection varied from 8–24 hours, depending on the time that elapsed while the tubes were waiting at a work station.

Usually the volume of tubes sold by the company was sufficient to warrant three shifts. They worked 7 a.m. to 3 p.m.; 3 p.m. to 11 p.m. and 11 p.m. to 7 a.m.

An excerpt from Mr. Russell's paper on Quality Control is reprinted below:

Tube Weight Control

By controlling tube weights, one indirectly controls tube wall gauge. Tube weight and gauge are dependent upon and controlled by the tube extrusion process. Our tubes are extruded in a continuous circular form then precut to a specified length before splicing. Production operators are supplied with weight and gauge specifications for all sizes of tubes. The objectives of weight control are: (1) to produce as many tubes as possible within the weight tolerances specified (2) to avoid excess useage of tube stock and keep costs to a minimum.

Before 1947 tube weight sampling and checking was done by the preparation production operators. Records showed almost all tubes within tolerances. Yet stock records continuously showed an excess useage of tube stock over standard.

This prompted an investigation by the Quality Control Department, and in 1947 an inspector was assigned to sampling and weighing of a small percentage of all sizes of tubes produced.

An analysis of this data showed that the tube weight picture was not as rosy as it seemed, but was running according to distribution A shown in Figure 26-1. The average weight of all tubes was found to be 2.0% over standard. Individual tube weights ranged all the way from 8% below standard to 12% above standard for a total spread of 20%. Specified tolerances at this time were quite rigid at −2% to +3% for a total of 5%. As a result approximately 50% of all tubes were above the maximum tolerance.

Further investigation showed that the cause of this overweight was a shrinkage of the tubes upon cooling after extrusion. During the next year this shrinkage was determined exactly for all sizes of tubes and allowances were made for it in processing specifications. This corrected the overweight condition as shown in Figure 26-1, distribution B. The result was reduction in excess tube stock useage of $10,000 annually.

We next went to work on tube weight variation. Charts were posted daily showing tube weight results of each tuber operator. A thorough analysis was made of the variables causing weight variation such as, tuber set-up, raw scrap work-off, blending stock, weight checking done by tuber operators. By May 1950, variation had shown a good improvement and for this particular month we were able to run to an 8% spread in one popular size tube. Also theoretical control limits worked out to an 8% spread. It was at this point that we decided that the specific tolerances (−3% to + 2%) were too tight. The Specifications group were then asked to set more realistic tolerances. The outcome of this was the decision to specify only a lower tolerance and this would be considered as a Minimum Acceptance Limit. This was set at 8% below the present standard and was known to be satisfactory as far as tube service was concerned.

The purpose in setting only a minimum tolerance provided an incentive to the tube department to reduce tube weight spread. By reducing spread they could lower their average weights and reduce tube stock useage accordingly.

By June of 1951, overall tube weight spread was reduced to 8%. This enabled us to run according to distribution D in Figure 26-1. With the reduction in spread to 8%, we were able to reduce average tube weights by 4%. This resulted in a further reduction in tube stock useage amounting to $20,000 annually.

In this case, our improved quality control resulted in reduced tube weight variation, a larger percentage within tolerances, plus the added benefit of better control of stock useage.

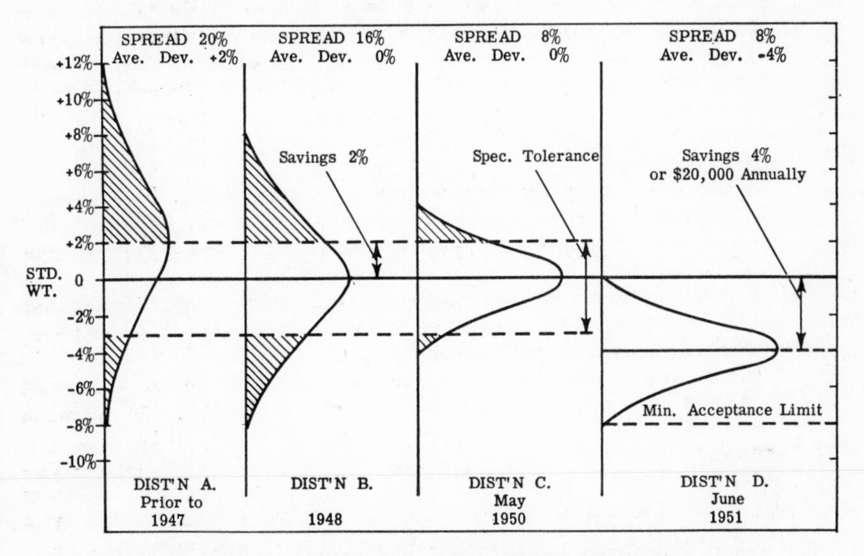

FIGURE 26-1 Improvement in Tube Weight Distributions

The inspection system established in 1951 to obtain the results outlined in the paper was continued during subsequent years. The system involved having the chief inspector check the weight of finished tubes frequently throughout the day and record the weight on a printed form (see Table 26-1). About 3:30 p.m. each day this form was pinned on a bulletin board to enable the tube operators to learn how closely they were adhering to specifications. The next day, at approximately the same time, the form was removed and sent to the Quality Control department and the new one pinned on the board. The chief inspector who looked after all this, Mr. G. Galbraith, attempted to weigh about 100 tubes each day, some from each of the three shifts. His hours were from 8 a.m. to 5 p.m.

TABLE 26-1

ONTARIO TIRE COMPANY LIMITED

Quality Control Report for Finished Tube Weights for June 26, 1958

Size	*Min. (lbs.)*	*Max. (lbs.)*	*Operator*	*Sample Weights (lbs.)*
Heavy Duty				
Size 1	7.06	7.66	D	7.26, 7.09, 7.21
				7.22, 7.32, 7.10
				7.31, 7.28, 7.12
				7.24, 7.46
Size 2	10.61	11.52		Nil
Size 3	8.27	8.97	D	8.64, 8.56, 8.54
				8.62, 8.64, 8.56
				8.52, 8.60, 8.71
				8.70
Size 4	5.97	6.48	G	6.45, 6.40, 6.35
Passenger				
Size 5	2.37	2.57	D	2.54, 2.57
				2.50, 2.54, 2.48, 2.54
				2.46, 2.50, 2.52, 2.45
				2.54, 2.53, 2.50, 2.50
				2.56, 2.50
Size 6	2.37	2.57	G	2.56, 2.54, 2.55, 2.66
				2.54, 2.54, 2.32, 2.54
				2.54, 2.28
			D	2.66, 2.68
Size 7	2.49	2.70	D	2.66, 2.67, 2.68, 2.60
				2.66, 2.64, 2.66, 2.64
				2.65, 2.61, 2.62, 2.58
				2.56, 2.60, 2.62, 2.66
				2.70, 2.58, 2.69, 2.70
				2.64, 2.60, 2.60, 2.64
				2.60, 2.68, 2.68, 2.68
				2.62, 2.66, 2.70
Size 8	1.96	2.13	D	2.12, 2.08, 2.12, 2.10
				2.11, 2.12, 2.10, 2.12
				2.11

The weight scales were located close to the conveyor that carried the finished tubes to the final inspection. As often as he could during the day, Mr.

Galbraith took a completed tube off the conveyor without regard to size, weighed it, and recorded the weight in the proper column of his chart. If the weight was over or under the limits for that size of tube, he drew it to the attention of the operator.

In addition to checking the tube weights, Mr. Galbraith also checked the width and gauge of tire tread rubber, examined it for defects, checked on the packing of the tubes in boxes, checked width and gauge of sidewall rubber, and spot-checked the inspectors who examined all of the finished tubes for defects. Any tubes that had been rejected Mr. Galbraith inspected personally. He occasionally checked the timers on the curing molds and if they were in error he would draw it to the foreman's attention.

If trouble arose with a part of a process in his sphere of activity, Mr. Galbraith worked with the men until the problem was solved. Any tubes that were returned by customers were examined by him in an effort to determine the reason they were defective.

Because of the variety of Mr. Galbraith's work, he found it difficult to weigh tube samples according to any set pattern. He had therefore adopted the habit of taking a tube off the conveyor and weighing it whenever he happened to be near the scales. Consequently, there were days when he was able to weigh only a few tubes, in which case the results obtained were usually added in with the following day's results. Mr. Galbraith felt that if he weighed approximately 100 tubes each day he was able to determine if the process was under control.

TABLE 26-2

ONTARIO TIRE COMPANY LIMITED

Production Report for June 26, 1958

Size	*No. of Tubes Produced*
Heavy Duty	
Size 1	200
Size 2	90
Size 3	150
Size 4	220
Passenger	
Size 5	1700
Size 6	500
Size 7	1200
Size 8	300

If, when he weighed a tube, he found it under the minimum, he then examined it closely. If he found thin spots, he scrapped the tube. If he could find no thin spots, he let it pass. If he found a tube that was over the maximum weight he did nothing more than record it on the Quality Report, as with all other tubes he weighed. However, if he found several that were over-weight, he drew it to the attention of the operator.

As each tube was stamped with the initial of the tuber operator, Mr. Galbraith was able to note which of the three operators had run any particular tube.

There was a weigh scale located adjacent to the tuber which permitted the operator to check the weight of the material he was extruding shortly after it left the tuber. Usually the operators did not consider it necessary for them to check the weight.

As raw rubber cost approximately 28¢ per pound, Mr. Russell felt that substantial savings could result from rigid control of the amount used in each tube while still maintaining the company's standards of quality.

Case B:

Northern Metal Products Ltd.[7]

In the Fall of 1955, an Industrial Engineer with Northern Metal Products Ltd. conducted a study using work sampling techniques. Following this study, in February 1956, the Plant Industrial Engineer, Mr. R. Moodie, was faced with the decision of whether to pursue the matter further or not.

The Company. Northern Metal Products Ltd. was located in a large Ontario city and made a wide variety of Metal Products which it sold to other manufacturers and to wholesale outlets. The company employed a total of 3,000 men, most of whom were paid according to some kind of bonus or incentive scheme.

Most of the individual processes required the men to work in groups or crews. Through the years the method of performing work changed and new machines were introduced, but the crew sizes were not always changed accordingly. In one case, a group of workers had originally had many duties to perform in the operation of a machine, but in time the machine had been improved to the point where a large percentage of the worker time was idle while the men waited for the machine to complete a cycle. In such cases, the company felt justified in getting the workers to perform additional tasks in their idle time, so that the size of the work crew might be reduced by transferring some of the men to other work.

While the information required to determine which jobs feil into this category could readily be acquired from an extensive new time study of all jobs in a problem area, such a study would require a team of engineers much larger than was on staff at Northern Metal Products Ltd. Mr. Moodie felt, however, that work sampling might produce results with satisfactory accuracy at a fraction of the cost of a complete time study.

The Work Sampling Study. Mr. Moodie believed that the main use of work sampling was to determine the percentage of time that a man or machine was idle and the percentage of time when occupied. He also thought that the time that the man was occupied could be broken down into the times he spent on various tasks, and that from this, in certain instances, an incentive rate could be set. However, at this stage he was concerned only with determining the accuracy of work sampling techniques when applied to work load studies—that is, assessing the percentage of a man's time that was being used productively.

In an effort to establish the usefulness of work sampling in the Northern Metal Products Ltd. plant, it was decided to undertake a pilot survey using work sampling methods.

One of the Industrial Engineers, Mr. R. Campbell, was asked to conduct the study, and at Mr. Moodie's suggestion, selected the Continuous Coating Department as the best current test location. Because this was a new department where operating methods and crewing were still in a state of flux, it offered an excellent opportunity for comparing work sampling results against an accurate conventional time study.

The Continuous Coating Department coated light gauge strip steel with another protective metal. The steel arrived at the department in coils about three feet in diameter which were hoisted by crane onto a mandrel. The entry end laborer and stocker welder threaded the strip of steel through a set of rollers. It was then fed through an acid bath to clean it, heated and passed through a tank of the molten metal that was to become the coating.

After another cleaning, the coated steel strip was either coiled or cut into rectangular pieces and piled. Each piece was stencilled with the company or customer name and identity information about the product. When the end of the coil at the entry end was reached, the stocker welder welded the start of a new coil on the tail of the old and the process continued.

Once started, the operation was continuous except for miscellaneous delays, break-downs and so forth. While the machine was operating properly, some of the workers had little to do but remain at attention for a repetition of the cycle and to watch the material and the process for faulty operation. But when the machine was out of adjustment or broken down, the workers were usually all busy trying to get it running again. Mr. Campbell decided that if a man was tending a machine, i.e., watching it while it worked, he was considered to be working.

Mr. Campbell selected twelve occupations in the department as the ones he wished to study. For his sample to be statistically correct, he felt that he should observe the workers on a random-time basis. However, because of the hazards inherent in material handling, and high speed plant activity, safety regulations could prevent the observer from occupying a specific location at a particular time. Since the validity of a day's study would be questionable if an observer missed one or more prescribed observations, he took samples on a random-number basis instead.

To do this, he assigned numbers to each of twelve occupations. On the first day of the study he selected, at random, one of the two tables of random numbers (see Table 26-3). Next, without looking, he pointed his pencil at a number in the table. This was then the number of the job he was to observe first.

He then proceeded to a pre-determined point from which to observe that job and waited until the sweep second hand of his watch reached a quarter minute point. At that instant he observed the worker and recorded whether he was working or idle, without regard to whether or not he could be working. The precaution of taking an observation only at a quarter minute point was included to help prevent any bias resulting from an observer's personal prejudices. An observer could affect study results by speeding up or slowing down his pace when approaching a worker, thus observing him according to those influences.

Mr. Campbell then referred to the table of random numbers again, and returning to the number selected previously, moved either left, right, up, or down one space, noted the number in that space, and moved to the observation point of the job with that number. If the number was greater than 12, he ignored it and used the next number to it. He repeated this procedure all day, but always moving in the same direction in the table of random numbers. The next day he selected a new table, a new starting point in it, and a new direction of movement within the table. Once again he made as many observations during the day as time would permit.

If a number came up more than once in succession, only one observation was made, but it was recorded as many times as its number came up.

If a man who was often sent on messages was absent from his work station, inquiries were made of the foremen as to his whereabouts. In cases of uncertainty, the benefit of the doubt was allowed the worker.

Mr. Campbell and another observer sampled the twelve occupations for ten days, a total of 160 study hours. Analysis of the results required 60 hours, making a total of 220 hours. Mr. Campbell felt that to achieve the same results by time study, 960 study hours, plus 480 analysis hours, totalling 1,440 hours would have been required.

During the two weeks of work sampling, time studies of two of the jobs were taken. Results of the work sampling are shown in Table 26-4 and of the time study in Table 26-5.

TABLE 26-3

NORTHERN METAL PRODUCTS LIMITED

Random Numbers 1–15

10	5	12	2	8	11	11	11	7	6	14	13	6	4	1	13	4	2	7	15	3	8	4	2	6	14	5
8	5	7	1	3	1	12	8	9	8	9	13	7	7	13	13	11	11	1	14	6	15	2	10	13	11	7
12	2	9	11	4	4	14	9	14	4	5	12	2	11	7	13	9	9	15	10	13	14	8	15	14	14	2
11	3	8	5	4	2	6	6	4	13	8	13	12	4	10	7	1	2	14	3	8	13	5	5	11	14	3
9	5	9	2	11	3	14	9	7	7	14	8	6	12	8	3	6	5	14	7	1	9	4	2	5	9	3
12	13	7	14	12	7	7	8	5	8	12	8	15	12	3	12	6	3	4	1	5	12	4	6	15	4	2
15	7	3	10	8	5	15	8	10	3	4	10	15	12	4	11	12	14	4	15	14	10	2	4	8	15	15
4	6	15	15	3	8	15	7	8	1	10	6	13	13	4	15	10	6	10	3	2	5	5	15	9	13	9
11	6	6	15	4	15	2	7	1	15	11	9	11	8	5	1	5	14	13	13	9	1	8	14	9	7	14
9	2	7	15	3	14	15	13	15	11	12	1	3	6	10	10	15	11	12	1	1	11	6	15	12	13	8
1	11	1	14	6	13	10	14	6	10	13	1	3	15	8	13	8	1	5	5	10	11	11	9	5	5	9
6	9	15	10	8	9	5	1	14	10	5	2	6	2	14	5	2	1	15	9	6	3	10	2	10	14	14
6	2	14	3	1	12	3	15	9	6	10	3	10	13	6	4	7	15	5	10	7	6	7	8	1	13	11
12	5	14	7	5	10	10	15	4	10	7	11	5	6	5	7	1	7	2	5	15	13	14	14	11	1	13
10	3	4	1	14	5	1	5	8	2	15	6	2	8	7	4	1	5	3	3	4	13	7	14	11	7	8
5	6	4	15	2	1	9	6	14	1	12	2	14	13	11	8	11	15	10	11	12	15	14	15	1	1	4
15	14	10	3	9	11	3	12	3	14	10	9	5	9	1	3	9	10	4	14	11	6	5	5	4	5	3
8	11	13	13	1	11	10	5	6	10	2	13	11	4	1	3	7	5	11	7	14	7	13	12	15	7	11
2	1	12	1	10	3	4	5	3	13	3	7	3	12	7	8	11	11	15	2	7	3	4	6	1	9	8
7	1	5	5	6	6	14	3	6	6	7	10	1	2	8	15	10	14	1	4	5	3	5	15	12	15	13
1	15	15	9	7	13	12	3	14	15	7	13	11	14	15	8	8	7	13	9	5	11	7	9	5	3	10
1	7	5	10	15	13	1	8	2	8	1	7	14	6	3	13	2	1	7	1	15	11	1	12	7	14	6
11	5	2	5	4	15	11	2	7	2	2	6	7	8	4	8	5	3	13	12	1	15	15	15	6	2	6
9	15	3	3	12	6	12	11	10	7	10	15	10	4	6	7	4	7	14	11	8	4	13	2	7	10	15
7	10	10	11	11	7	8	8	9	11	10	11	1	7	4	15	5	2	12	9	8	14	1	15	13	14	12
11	5	4	14	14	3	8	1	3	3	14	1	15	8	5	2	4	15	10	11	5	5	9	5	13	3	1
10	11	11	7	7	14	3	3	6	7	9	3	4	5	9	8	5	12	2	8	10	7	8	12	2	15	10
8	14	15	2	5	5	12	14	2	4	8	6	13	8	14	2	5	7	1	3	11	12	12	4	15	10	6
2	7	1	4	5	13	9	14	11	12	7	13	12	12	8	10	2	9	11	4	1	8	3	4	15	3	2
5	1	13	9	15	9	10	13	11	8	10	14	5	12	3	8	3	8	5	4	4	4	5	4	9	9	12
4	3	7	1	1	5	6	5	12	10	6	7	10	12	11	12	5	9	2	11	2	11	5	6	4	13	7
5	7	13	12	8	7	4	15	10	5	10	10	5	8	14	11	13	7	14	12	3	9	1	12	11	11	10
14	9	14	11	8	2	9	14	11	13	12	3	13	13	3	9	7	3	10	8	12	15	12	6	12	3	5
14	2	12	9	5	15	8	8	9	1	4	8	7	7	2	12	6	15	15	3	7	10	7	8	11	11	3
4	15	10	11	10	5	10	11	3	7	1	14	11	6	11	15	6	6	15	4	5	10	13	8	6	15	12

TABLE 26-3 (continued)

NORTHERN METAL PRODUCTS LIMITED

Random Numbers 1–15

8	10	9	11	10	8	5	12	2	8	10	15	8	3	10	7	9	3	12	8	4	8	5	3	7	1	15
3	4	5	3	8	10	2	7	1	3	11	5	10	14	6	4	8	7	15	4	6	7	4	7	13	12	1
14	6	5	1	11	8	3	9	11	4	1	11	11	14	10	12	7	6	4	7	4	15	5	9	14	11	8
12	11	6	8	14	12	5	8	5	4	4	12	8	13	14	8	10	13	13	8	5	2	4	2	12	9	8
9	5	10	3	4	11	13	9	2	11	2	14	9	5	3	10	6	14	12	5	9	8	5	15	10	11	5
4	13	4	13	10	9	7	7	14	12	3	6	6	15	6	5	10	7	5	8	14	2	5	12	2	8	10
13	7	6	1	5	12	6	3	10	8	12	14	9	14	3	13	12	10	10	12	8	10	2	7	1	3	11
13	5	12	15	5	15	6	15	15	3	7	7	8	8	6	1	4	3	5	12	3	8	3	9	11	4	1
8	4	7	14	6	4	2	6	15	4	5	15	8	11	14	7	1	8	13	12	11	12	5	8	5	4	4
10	14	10	2	4	11	11	7	15	3	8	15	7	7	2	14	13	14	7	8	14	11	13	9	2	11	2
14	11	5	5	7	9	9	1	14	6	15	2	7	9	7	9	13	6	11	13	3	9	7	7	14	12	3
15	8	6	11	8	1	2	15	10	13	14	15	13	14	10	5	12	7	4	7	2	12	6	3	10	8	12
3	3	10	11	10	6	5	14	3	8	13	10	14	4	9	8	13	2	7	6	11	15	6	15	15	3	7
5	11	3	11	9	6	3	14	7	1	9	5	1	7	3	14	8	12	11	1	13	4	2	6	15	4	5
1	5	11	14	14	12	14	4	1	5	12	3	15	5	6	12	8	6	4	13	13	11	11	7	15	3	8
3	11	6	12	13	10	6	4	15	14	10	10	15	10	2	4	10	15	12	7	13	9	9	1	14	6	15
4	15	15	7	13	5	14	10	3	2	5	1	5	8	11	10	6	15	12	10	7	1	2	15	10	13	14
13	7	8	5	11	15	11	13	13	9	1	9	6	1	11	11	9	13	12	8	3	6	5	14	3	8	13
4	5	7	3	2	8	1	12	1	1	11	3	12	15	12	12	1	11	13	3	12	6	3	14	7	1	9
10	14	14	1	7	2	1	5	5	10	11	10	5	6	10	13	1	3	8	4	11	12	14	4	1	5	12
6	3	5	2	10	7	15	15	9	6	3	4	5	14	11	5	2	3	6	4	15	10	6	4	15	14	10
2	5	3	2	4	1	7	5	10	7	6	14	3	9	9	10	3	6	15	5	1	5	14	10	3	2	5
3	2	14	11	13	1	5	2	5	15	13	12	3	4	3	7	11	10	2	10	10	15	11	13	13	9	1
4	2	9	7	5	11	15	3	3	4	13	1	8	8	2	15	6	5	11	8	13	8	1	12	1	1	11
13	8	8	5	9	9	10	10	11	12	15	11	2	6	1	12	2	2	2	14	5	2	1	5	5	10	11
4	14	1	3	3	7	5	4	14	11	6	12	4	8	14	10	9	14	2	6	4	7	15	15	9	6	3
7	1	9	12	14	11	11	11	7	14	7	8	3	4	10	2	13	5	13	5	7	1	7	5	10	7	6
11	13	9	8	10	10	14	15	2	7	3	8	5	13	13	3	7	11	6	7	4	1	5	2	5	15	13
7	13	1	3	14	8	7	1	4	5	14	3	2	7	6	7	10	3	8	11	8	11	15	3	3	4	13
10	12	6	12	14	2	1	13	9	5	5	12	4	8	15	7	13	1	13	1	3	9	10	10	11	12	15
15	1	9	14	5	5	3	7	1	15	13	9	2	3	8	1	7	11	9	1	3	7	5	4	14	11	6
11	10	9	11	15	4	7	13	12	1	9	10	2	1	2	2	6	14	4	7	8	11	11	11	7	14	7
11	1	11	8	6	5	9	14	11	8	5	6	11	15	7	10	15	7	12	8	15	10	14	15	2	7	9
13	1	14	2	4	4	2	12	9	8	7	4	8	11	11	10	11	10	2	15	8	8	7	1	4	5	8
6	3	15	11	13	5	15	10	11	5	2	9	1	10	3	14	1	1	6	3	13	2	1	13	9	5	7

TABLE 26-4

NORTHERN METAL PRODUCTS LIMITED

WORK SAMPLING RESULTS

Day	Work and Attention Observations	Idle Observations	Total Observations
Occupation No. 1—Stocker-Welder			
1	58	35	93
2	42	24	66
3	54	32	86
4	27	23	50
5	56	29	85
6	30	24	54
7	72	42	114
8	35	32	67
9	48	32	80
10	52	27	79
Occupation No. 2—Entry End Laborer			
1	23	34	57
2	41	31	72
3	28	42	70
4	20	27	47
5	22	31	53
6	28	21	49
7	27	25	52
8	17	29	46
9	24	27	51
10	19	31	50
Occupation No. 3—Entry End Crane Operator			
1	21	62	83
2	16	53	69
3	20	52	72
4	22	64	86
5	21	57	78
6	21	60	81
7	20	57	77
8	15	48	63
9	16	50	66
10	21	66	87
Occupation No. 10—Reject Laborer			
1	17	51	68
2	22	51	73
3	18	64	82
4	19	62	81
5	17	53	70
6	20	60	80
7	16	49	65
8	18	54	72
9	18	49	67
10	15	48	63

TABLE 26-4 (continued)

NORTHERN METAL PRODUCTS LIMITED

WORK SAMPLING RESULTS

Day	Work and Attention Observations	Idle Observations	Total Observations
Occupation No. 11—Stenciller			
1	25	56	81
2	20	45	65
3	24	54	78
4	25	55	80
5	26	59	85
6	27	55	82
7	21	52	73
8	25	59	84
9	28	55	83
10	18	44	62
Occupation No. 12—Coating Section Laborer			
1	37	23	60
2	46	26	72
3	44	24	68
4	43	26	69
5	40	22	62
6	42	16	58
7	40	24	64
8	37	29	66
9	51	19	70
10	48	35	83
Occupation No. 7—Lead Hand Shipper			
1	67	36	103
2	72	44	116
3	51	36	87
4	63	30	93
5	77	34	111
6	64	33	97
7	78	32	110
8	69	32	101
9	60	35	95
10	84	38	122
Occupation No. 8—Weigher			
1	62	33	95
2	83	45	128
3	76	41	117
4	90	44	134
5	63	29	92
6	75	35	110
7	82	40	122
8	67	31	98
9	69	32	101
10	74	39	113

TABLE 26-4 (continued)

WORK SAMPLING RESULTS

NORTHERN METAL PRODUCTS LIMITED

Day	*Work and Attention Observations*	*Idle Observations*	*Total Observations*
Occupation No. 9—Piler			
1	82	35	117
2	81	17	98
3	96	27	123
4	97	24	121
5	96	22	118
6	72	18	90
7	80	15	95
8	82	22	104
9	81	8	89
10	70	17	87
Occupation No. 4—Tractor Operator			
1	24	34	58
2	29	33	62
3	41	39	80
4	33	44	77
5	30	35	65
6	28	32	60
7	33	39	72
8	35	43	78
9	23	31	54
10	31	39	70
Occupation No. 5—Ass't Line Operator			
1	33	21	54
2	38	29	67
3	38	20	58
4	46	31	77
5	50	31	81
6	39	25	64
7	44	28	72
8	37	26	63
9	49	29	78
10	41	32	73
Occupation No. 6—Exit End Crane Operator			
1	53	74	127
2	38	54	92
3	43	55	98
4	47	66	113
5	44	57	101
6	51	67	118
7	34	50	84
8	38	52	90
9	43	65	108
10	39	55	94

TABLE 26-5

NORTHERN METAL PRODUCTS LIMITED

TIME STUDY RESULTS

Day	*% Work and Attention*	*% Idle*
Occupation No. 1—Stock-Welder		
1	54	46
2	52	48
3	59	41
4	—	—
5	—	—
6	—	—
7	52	48
8	54	46
9	53	47
10	61	39
Occupation No. 7—Lead Hand Shipper		
1	68	32
2	71	29
3	—	—
4	—	—
5	—	—
6	73	27
7	68	32
8	54	46
9	—	—
10	67	33

27

Management in the Present and Future

OUR tour through the subject of management is at an end. As stated at the beginning, our objective has been more than a mere description of different activities of managers; our attention has been directed to the fundamentals underlying a variety of managerial activities. We have emphasized a point of view and have often left an elaboration of details for later study. This last chapter cannot summarize these fundamentals, but it can emphasize the relationships among the subjects that have been discussed, so that the reader will not close this volume with the impression that the subjects he has studied are bits and pieces with little connection.

This chapter also will point out probable trends in the future; management is changing rapidly. We are not as interested in past and current practices as in fundamentals which will be valid in the future.

Management—A Study of Interrelationship

One way we have already demonstrated the interrelations among the chapters is to include cases in later chapters that call for the application of concepts introduced earlier. For example, cases involving phases of production control appear at various points in the volume, becoming more complex as additional types of analysis are added to the tool kit. Production control, as its name implies, involves the fundamentals of control discussed at one point. Since production control must operate through an organization, the early chapters on organization are relevant to a full comprehension of what it involves. To illustrate, one of the major issues that a company faces in setting up a production control organization is that of centralization versus decentralization. How much of the authority over scheduling should be concentrated in a central production control department? Many companies have concluded that much of the detailed scheduling can best be delegated to those close to the workplaces, but the expansion of automatic data processing may exert a pressure toward greater centralization.

To continue the discussion of production control and how it involves an integration of the analysis in various chapters, it is clear that graphs and other schematic devices are normally an essential part of scheduling and dispatching. Some of these charting methods are modern elaborations of Gantt charts, but continued ingenuity can be expected in developing new ways of reducing the complexity of the real productive processes to simplifying models of various sorts. Production control also requires economic analysis, as is clear in the determination of economic lot sizes—a problem which is amenable to mathematical treatment. There is a close relationship between production control and accounting, as indicated by the fact that a significant proportion of the work of some public accounting firms is concerned with production control. In the case of inventory control, which is an essential part of production control, the maintenance of perpetual inventory records is an activity of great importance to the accountant. Perpetual inventories are useful in determining reordering times; they are also important in the maintenance of the financial accounts.

The most important recent developments in production control are those in the mathematical and statistical directions. Production control involves the feedback concept, and like other feedback problems, is suitable material for mathematical model building. Probability theory is clearly relevant, for the heart of the scheduling problem is uncertainty about the orders that will be produced in the future. Some big firms are claiming large savings from the application of statistical decision theory to the determination of production runs. One illustration would be the determination, from the pattern of sales at the beginning of a season, of what the probabilities of sales might be later in the season—a determination that might cut down the losses from the production of unneeded inventory.

Some firms are beginning to apply linear programming to their production control problems, particularly to the problem of scheduling different lines of product on limited numbers of machines. Another quantitative technique, computer simulation, is being applied to problems of inventory control. One way of avoiding serious errors in building up inventories is to simulate demand and production conditions on an electronic computer to determine the costs of various decisions under conditions of uncertainty.

Perhaps we have said enough about production control to justify the conclusion that every chapter in the book makes some contribution to the understanding of that subject. Our approach has been to discuss the underlying lines of analysis that contribute to all phases of management—we believe that specialized chapters on production control would fail to emphasize the basic ideas that run throughout the realm of management. The same reason accounts for the absence of chapters often found in management books—chapters on personnel management, materials handling, plant layout, office management, research and development, financial controls, purchasing, and marketing.

As has been suggested in the preface and throughout the preceding discussion, the subject of management can be broken down into different operating phases. The traditional approach has been to devote chapters to particular kinds of applications—for example, to plant layout or to office management. This book was subdivided into basic areas of analysis that cut across the operating fields: organization, motivation, control, and so on.

Management in the Future

We have seen that the study of management is relatively young. Much refinement is possible and probable. Immature ideas are being restudied. Recently, there have been many changes and new developments. The next decade promises to bring an acceleration in the rate of introduction of new ideas. Throughout this book we have encouraged the reader to study skeptically the ideas currently held.

The *fundamentals* discussed in this book will form the basis for the development of management in the future. We have given little attention to elaborate description of *past practices* because they will undoubtedly change by the time many readers find themselves in managerial positions.

A number of factors evident at present point out the probable nature of the changes in management to be expected. First of all, *technology* is providing equipment that will not only improve production techniques but also communication and decision-making processes. Automation, with its continuous production, feedback, and electronic computers, will have a great impact on managerial functions. Secondly, the increased application of *mathematical approaches* promises to provide means for improving decisions. The advantages and limitations of the mathematical models will be the subject of much discussion in the near future. Thirdly, the *social* and *cultural* position of the manager will place greater demands upon his decisions. The increased size of organizations, attention to the dignity of the individual, social pressures toward conformity, increased leisure, and accelerated activities will require changes in a manager's way of thinking. Fourthly, the type of *people* becoming available for use in management will make it possible to do many things which heretofore have been merely hopes. The larger number of highly educated personnel will enable management to develop different approaches to its problems. More and more people will be challenged to use their unique mental powers and leave to the machines the routine and programmed activities.

Recently there has been much planning for education for management in the next two or three decades. The central thought of much of this planning has been, not to train a manager for action in the 1950's with a study of the practices of this decade, but to offer him a point of departure in his own thinking that will enable him to create new and better managerial approaches in the 1960's and 1970's.

Several writers have attempted to predict the character of management in the future. Leavitt and Whisler [1] feel that planning and creative work will be moved upward in the organization to the level of top management. Decisions will be reached with the help of a number of specialists at the top in a group in place of a single chief executive. Middle management will be divided more distinctly into two types—those who will become a part of top management and those who will be downgraded into routine executors. The distinction between the top management and the routine operators will become clearer—like that now existing between the worker and first line supervisor. These observers see a tendency to recentralize many functions in top management, with less "participation" of the middle managers.

Peter Drucker, another forecaster of developments in management, emphasizes different trends. He foresees a general upgrading of labor, semi-skilled workers becoming skilled, and skilled becoming professional employees. Unlike Leavitt and Whisler, he predicts a de-emphasis of specialization and a greater stress on managers who see the business as a whole. He sees a need for general education for managers. He would not agree with Leavitt and Whisler that the trend toward decentralization will be reversed; instead he believes there will be a growing scope for federal decentralization.

Thus, the exact nature of future developments is uncertain and a matter for conjecture and speculation. This is indeed another argument for the training of managers in flexibility—a stress on thinking processes rather than on specific techniques. If this book has contributed to the kinds of skills that will foster the flexibility and imagination required in the management of the future, it will have achieved its purpose.

[1] Harold J. Leavitt and Thomas L. Whisler, "Management in the 1980's," *Harvard Business Review,* November–December 1958, pp. 41–48.

Index

E

F

G

J

K

L

M

N

O

P

Q

R

S